2.50

POE'S COTTAGE AT FORDHAM

From the etching by Charles F. W. Mielatz

AMERICAN LITERATURE

A STUDY OF THE MEN AND THE BOOKS
THAT IN THE EARLIER AND LATER TIMES
REFLECT THE AMERICAN SPIRIT

BY

WILLIAM J. LONG

"As a strong bird on pinions free,
Joyous, the amplest spaces heavenward cleaving,
Such be the thought I'd think of thee, America!"

GINN AND COMPANY

BOSTON · NEW YORK · CHICAGO · LONDON
ATLANTA · DALLAS · COLUMBUS · SAN FRANCISCO

𝕿𝖍𝖊 𝕬𝖙𝖍𝖊𝖓𝖆𝖚𝖒 𝕻𝖗𝖊𝖘𝖘
GINN AND COMPANY · PRO-
PRIETORS · BOSTON · U.S.A.

TO

FRANCES

MY LITTLE DAUGHTER OF THE

REVOLUTION

PREFACE

The aim of this book is to present an accurate and interesting record of American literature from the Colonial to the present age, and to keep the record in harmony with the history and spirit of the American people.

The author has tried to make the work national in its scope and to emphasize the men and the books that reflect the national traditions. As literature in general tends to humanize and harmonize men by revealing their common characteristics, so every national literature unites a people by upholding the ideals which the whole nation reveres and follows. Any book therefore which tends, as Lowell once said, to make you and me strangers to each other or to any part of our common country can hardly be considered as a true part of American letters. For there are no Mason-and-Dixon lines, no political or geographical divisions in the national consciousness. Bradford and Byrd, Cooper and Simms, Longfellow and Lanier, Hawthorne and Bret Harte are here studied side by side in their respective periods, not as representative of North or South or East or West, but as so many different reflections of the same life and the same spirit.

Though our Colonial and Revolutionary writers are but little known to modern readers, considerable attention has here been given them, and for three reasons : because they are well worth knowing for their own sakes ; because American literature did not begin with Irving or Franklin, as is often assumed ; and because our present literature and history have no vital significance if dissociated from the past. For two hundred years our countrymen toiled obscurely and heroically in a great wilderness that was then called "the fag ends of the earth." Animated by a great love of liberty, and determined to secure it forever to their descendants, they sought first to create free states, and then to establish a free nation on democratic foundations. No greater work was ever undertaken by human hearts and hands; no single achievement of the ancient or the modern world was ever characterized by finer wisdom or courage or devotion. The men and women who did this work were splendidly loyal to high principles; "they steered by stars the elder shipmen knew"; and so deeply did they implant their moral and political ideals in the American mind that the man or the book that now departs from them is known, almost instinctively, to be untrue to his own country and people.

To know these men and women is to have the pride and the strength of noble ancestry; it is to have also a deeper love and veneration for America; and the only way to know them, the founders of our nation and pioneers of our precious liberty, is through their own writings, which furnish the human and intensely personal background of their history. This knowledge of our country, of the noble lives that were lived here, of the brave deeds that were wrought and the high ideals that were followed before our day, — this vital connection with the living and triumphant Past which comes from literature is the foundation of all true patriotism.

The general plan of this work is like that which the author followed, and which proved effective, in an earlier history of English literature. It divides our literary history into a few great periods, continuous in their development, yet having each its distinct and significant characteristics. Colonial literature, for example, is regarded as an expression of the fundamental moral and spiritual ideals of America, and Revolutionary literature as a reflection of the practical and political genius of the

nation. The study of each period includes : a historical outline of important events and of significant social and political
conditions ; a general survey of the literature of the period, its
dominant tendencies, and its relation to literary movements in
England and on the Continent ; a detailed treatment of every
major writer, including a biography, an analysis of his chief
works, and a critical appreciation of his place and influence in
our national literature ; a consideration of the minor writers
and of the notable miscellaneous works of the period ; and at
the end a general summary, with selections recommended for
reading, bibliography, texts, suggestive questions, and other
helps to teachers and students.

In the matter of proportions, it should be clearly understood
that the amount of space given to an author is not in itself
an indication of the relative amount of time which the student
should give to that author's works. A trustworthy history of
our literature will not fail to record and to appreciate the important work of Freneau, for instance, or of Charles Brockden
Brown ; but very little time can be given to the reading of such
authors, for the simple reason that their works are not available.
In dealing with our early literature, very little of which is now
accessible, a textbook must in some degree supply the place of
a library, and the text has here been expanded with a view to
presenting a faithful record of Mather and Edwards, of Hamilton and Jefferson, and of many others who in the early days
exercised a profound influence on American life or letters. It
is hoped that, by reading and freely discussing the text of the
Colonial and Revolutionary periods, teachers and students may
form a clear and just conception of the beginnings of our literature before taking up the study of Irving, Bryant, and other
familiar writers of the nineteenth century.

Among these later writers also the amount of space which
each receives is no sure indication of the present value of his

work or of the amount of time which one may profitably spend in his company. For authors are much like other folks; some are to be known as familiar friends, and it is enough for certain others if we know about them. It is often assumed that, because a text devotes five pages to one poet and ten to another, the latter must be regarded as more important than the former; but the assumption is without foundation, since there must enter into the history of an author many considerations besides the literary merit of his work. Poe and Whitman may serve us as excellent examples. In comparison with Longfellow, who has an unfailing charm for young people, comparatively few works of Poe or Whitman will be read; but that is no reason why either poet should be slighted in a just history of our literature. One must not forget that Longfellow is our loved household poet; that it is a simple matter to do justice and render generous tribute to his work, since his place is secure and his merit well recognized. Poe and Whitman, on the other hand, are the most debatable figures in our literature, and whatever critical estimate one may make of either will almost certainly be challenged. It has seemed desirable, therefore, to give such authors ample treatment in order that the student may understand not only the spirit of their work but something also of the critical controversy which has so long raged around them.

To those who may use this book in the classroom the author ventures to state frankly his own conviction that the study of literature is not a matter of intellectual achievement, but rather of discovery and appreciation and delight, — discovery of the abiding interests of humanity, appreciation of the ideals that are as old and as new as the sunrise, and delight in truth and beauty as seen from another's viewpoint and colored by his genius or experience. One might emphasize the fact that literature is not history or science or criticism or college English, or anything else but its own lovely self. Literature is the winsome reflection of life, which is the most interesting thing in the world ; and the study of such a subject should never be made a task but a joy. It might be advisable, therefore, to forget for the nonce our laboratory methods and to begin and end our study of American literature with the liberal reading of good books, with the joyous appreciation of the prose and poetry that reflect the brave American experiment in human living. " The interests that grow out of a meeting like this," said Emerson, " should bind us with new strength to the old, eternal duties."

WILLIAM J. LONG

STAMFORD, CONNECTICUT

CONTENTS

PAGE

GENERAL REFERENCES xviii

CHAPTER I. THE COLONIAL PERIOD I

Introduction — the Spirit of our First Writings. Beginnings of American Literature. Why the Colonists wrote Few Books. Why study Colonial Records?
Colonial Annalists and Historians. Bradford. Winthrop. Some Old Love Letters. Sewall. Byrd. Various Chronicles of Colonial Days. Satire and Criticism. Histories. Indian Narratives.
Colonial Poetry. The *Bay Psalm Book*. Characteristics of Early Poetry. Anne Bradstreet. Wigglesworth. Godfrey.
Theological Writers. Cotton Mather. Edwards.
Summary of Colonial History and Literature. Selections for Reading. Bibliography. Questions. Subjects for Essays.

CHAPTER II. THE PERIOD OF THE REVOLUTION . 86

Historical Outline. Social Development. The Stamp Act and what followed. The Revolution. The Constitution.
Literature of the Revolution. General Tendencies. Revolutionary Poetry. Revolutionary Prose. Citizen Literature.
Transition from Colony to Nation. Benjamin Franklin.
Orators and Statesmen of the Revolution. Typical Speeches. Otis. Patrick Henry. Revolutionary Statesmen. Washington. Permanent Political Parties. Hamilton. Jefferson.
The Poetry of the Revolution. Songs and Ballads. The Hartford Wits. Barlow. Dwight. Trumbull. Beginning of Romantic Poetry. Freneau. Miscellaneous Verse.
Various Prose Works. Thomas Paine. John Woolman. Beginning of American Fiction. Charles Brockden Brown.
Summary of the Period. Selections for Reading. Bibliography. Questions. Topics for Research and for Essays.

xi

CHAPTER III. THE FIRST NATIONAL OR CREATIVE
PERIOD 169

The Background of History. National Unity. Expansion. Democ-
racy. Industrial Development.
Literature of the Period. General Characteristics. Poets and Prose
Writers. Irving. Bryant. Cooper. Poe. Simms.
Minor Fiction. Catherine Sedgwick. Susanna Rowson. Melville.
Dana. Kennedy.
Minor Poetry. The Knickerbocker School. Willis. Drake. Halleck.
The Orators. Clay. Calhoun. Everett. Webster. The Historians.
Miscellaneous Works. Juveniles.
Summary of the Period. Selections for Reading. Bibliography.
Questions. Subjects for Research.

CHAPTER IV. THE SECOND NATIONAL OR CREATIVE
PERIOD 270

History of the Period. General Outlines. The Age of Agitation.
The War.
Literary and Social Movements. National and Sectional Literature.
Mental Unrest. Communistic Societies. Brook Farm. Transcendental-
ism. General Characteristics of the Major Literature.
The Greater Poets and Essayists. Longfellow. Whittier. Emerson.
Lowell. Holmes. Lanier. Whitman.
Minor Poetry. Lyrics of War and Peace. Southern Singers. Timrod.
Hayne. Ryan. Singers East and West. Taylor. Stoddard. Joaquin
Miller. Various other Poets.
Novelists and Story-tellers. Hawthorne. John Esten Cooke. Harriet
Beecher Stowe. Bret Harte. Typical Story-tellers.
Miscellaneous Prose Writers. Thoreau. The Historians. Motley.
Parkman.
Summary of the Period. Selections for Reading. Bibliography.
Questions. Topics for Research and for Essays.

CHAPTER V. SOME TENDENCIES IN OUR RECENT
LITERATURE 447

Impossibility of a History of the Present Age. Reminiscent Writ-
ings. Hale. Curtis. Higginson. Mitchell. Discovery of American
Literature.
The Poetry of the Present. The New Folk Songs. Stedman. Aldrich.
"America Singing."
Our Recent Fiction. Romance and Realism. Representative Real-
ists. Howells. Modified Types of Realism and Romance. The Modern
Novel. Mark Twain. Joel Chandler Harris. Conclusion.

PAGE

CHAPTER VI. BOOKS AND WRITERS OF THE PRES-
ENT DAY 472

The flood of books: outstanding characteristics. Present-Day Authors and Readers. Old Writers and New. Limitations of Our Study.

Present-Day Fiction. A Typical American Novel: *Vandemark's Folly*. Novels of Society. Booth Tarkington. Edith Wharton. The Romance of History. S. Weir Mitchell. Mary Johnston. Winston Churchill. American Types. Influence of *David Harum*. Irving Bacheller. Joseph Lincoln. James Lane Allen. John Fox, Jr. Owen Wister. Gertrude Atherton. Mary Austin. J. Willard Schultz. The Social Novel. Definition. Frank Norris. Later Attempts. The Novel of Adventure. Popularity of the Type. Romance of the North. Jack London and His Followers. Stewart Edward White. Romance of the West. Zane Grey. Typical Yarns.

The Short Story. Qualifications. The Many Short-Story Writers. " O. Henry."

Present Day Poetry. Sara Teasdale. Edwin Arlington Robinson. Vachel Lindsay. The Classical School. Edith M. Thomas. George Edward Woodberry. Katharine Lee Bates. Poets of the Great War. Outdoor Poets. Robert Frost. Clinton Scollard. Free Verse. Divergent Opinions. Amy Lowell. Carl Sandburg.

The Modern Stage. Three Varieties of Present-Day Drama. The Little Theatre. Typical Plays. Josephine Preston Peabody. David Belasco. Augustus Thomas. Eugene O'Neill. Percy Mackaye. William Vaughn Moody. Booth Tarkington. Edward Knoblauch.

Conclusion: a short cut through present-day literature.

INDEX 503

FULL-PAGE ILLUSTRATIONS

PAGE

POE'S COTTAGE AT FORDHAM . . . . Frontispiece
From the etching by Charles F. W. Mielatz

TITLE-PAGE OF THE "*DAY OF DOOM*" 50
By Michael Wigglesworth, 1715. Courtesy of the Lenox Library

BENJAMIN FRANKLIN 106
From the portrait by Duplessis

THE TORY'S DAY OF JUDGMENT 136
*An illustration from John Trumbull's "M'Fingal," New York, 1795.
Courtesy of the Lenox Library*

THE EDICT OF WILLIAM THE TESTY 186
*Knickerbocker's "History of New York." From the painting by
Boughton; property of the Metropolitan Museum of Art*

RIP VAN WINKLE 192
A portrait of Joseph Jefferson as Rip Van Winkle, by Marion Swinton

**STATUE OF WILLIAM CULLEN BRYANT, NEW YORK PUBLIC
LIBRARY** 202

WASHINGTON IRVING AND HIS LITERARY FRIENDS AT SUNNYSIDE 250

ABRAHAM LINCOLN 270
Pen etching by R. M. Chandler. From a photograph made in 1864

HENRY WADSWORTH LONGFELLOW 284
From an engraving after the portrait by Lawrence

THE PARISH PRIEST 292
*From "Evangeline," edition of 1882. Engraved by F. O. C. Darley.
Courtesy of Houghton Mifflin Company*

RALPH WALDO EMERSON 318
*From an unfinished portrait by Furness. Courtesy of the Pennsyl-
vania Academy of the Fine Arts, Philadelphia*

THE LIBRARY OF CONGRESS, WASHINGTON, D.C. 448

LIST OF ILLUSTRATIONS

PAGE

The Settlement of Jamestown. *From a print in the Congressional Library,
Washington* 8
Governor Bradford's House. *From a print owned by the Lenox Library* . 11
A Portion of the Bradford MS. "History of Plimoth Plantation" . . . 13
Old Fort, Plymouth. *From an old engraving* 15
John Winthrop. *From the Van Dyke portrait* 19
Samuel Sewall. *From an old engraving* 27
William Byrd. *From the portrait at "Brandon," Virginia* 33
Westover, Virginia — Home of the Byrds 38
John Eliot. *From a portrait in the possession of the family of the late
William Whiting* 43
Title-page of "*The Bay Psalm Book.*" *The first English book printed in
America. Courtesy of the Lenox Library* 44
Illustration from the *Doctrina Christiana*, printed in Mexico City by Juan
Pablos in 1544. *The first book printed in America that contained
cuts to illustrate the text* 45
Title-page of the "*New England Primer*," *First Edition, 1727. Courtesy
of the Lenox Library* 52
Cotton Mather. *From the Peter Pelham portrait. Courtesy of the American
Antiquarian Society, Worcester, Mass.* 57
Harvard College in 1726. *From a print by Paul Revere* 60
Title-page of the "*Magnalia Christi Americana.*" *London, 1702* . . . 65
Jonathan Edwards. *From a portrait that was owned by the late Eugene
Edwards* 71
Benjamin Franklin. *From a print by Ritchie, after the drawing by C. H.
Cochin, 1777* 99
Title-page from "*Poor Richard's Almanac.*" *From the third impression
of 1733* 105
Franklin's Printing Press 110
Patrick Henry. *From the portrait by Thomas Sully* 113
George Washington. *From the Athenæum portrait by Gilbert Stuart* . . 115
Alexander Hamilton. *From the Trumbull portrait. Courtesy of the New
York Public Library* 118
Early View of King's College (Columbia). *From an old engraving* . . . 119

Thomas Jefferson. *From the painting by Gilbert Stuart, Walker Art Building, Bowdoin College* 123
Street Front of the University of Virginia (1819–1826), designed by Thomas Jefferson 126
Monticello, Jefferson's Home 127
Independence Hall, Philadelphia 131
Joel Barlow. *From the portrait by Robert Fulton* 134
Timothy Dwight. *From the portrait by Trumbull* 135
Yale College in 1820. *From an old engraving* 136
Early View of Princeton College, N. J. *After a wood engraving by A. Anderson Hall* 139
Philip Freneau. *From an engraving by Halpin* 142
First Page of "*The Crisis*," by Tom Paine. *Courtesy of the Pennsylvania Historical Society, Philadelphia* 150
Charles Brockden Brown. *After the miniature by William Dunlap, 1806. Courtesy of the Lenox Library* 155
The Franklin Bicentennial Medal. *Designed by Louis and Augustus Saint-Gaudens to commemorate the two hundredth anniversary of Franklin's birth, and presented to the French Government by the United States* . . 168
Emigration to Western Country. *After a drawing by Darley* 171
Early view of Chicago. *From an old print* 176
Street Scene in Modern Chicago 177
Washington Irving 179
New Amsterdam, 1664. *From a copper plate by Augustyn Heermanns* . . 185
Henry Hudson entering New York Bay. *After painting by Edward Moran. Courtesy of the Honorable Theodore Sutro* 188
Sunnyside, Irving's Home on the Hudson 193
William Cullen Bryant. *From a photograph by Sarony, New York* . . . 196
James Fenimore Cooper. *From the portrait by C. L. Elliott* 207
Otsego Lake, Cooperstown, N.Y. 217
Edgar Allan Poe. *From a daguerreotype. Courtesy of Brown University Library* 226
Fitz-Greene Halleck 253
Daniel Webster. *From a painting owned by Mr. George A. Plimpton* . . 257
J. J. Audubon. *After the miniature by F. Cruikshank* 259
The Front Hall, Longfellow's Home, Cambridge 288
Kitchen and Hearth in Whittier's House at Haverhill 303
John Greenleaf Whittier 308
The Old Manse, Concord 323
Emerson's Study 325
James Russell Lowell 338
Lowell Home, Cambridge 342
Oliver Wendell Holmes 352

PAGE

Great Pine on Wendell Farm, Pittsfield 354
Sidney Lanier 359
Walt Whitman. *After the portrait by J. W. Alexander, in the Metropolitan Museum of Art* 370
Bayard Taylor 385
Nathaniel Hawthorne 391
The Wayside, Concord 395
The Great Stone Face 399
Harriet Beecher Stowe 410
Thoreau's Hut and Furniture on the Shore of Walden Pond 422
Francis Parkman. *From a daguerreotype* 431
Eugene Field 451
James Whitcomb Riley 452
Thomas Bailey Aldrich 454
Samuel Clemens (Mark Twain). *From a photograph taken in 1897* . . . 464

GENERAL REFERENCES

The authorities and references named in this book are arranged in two main divisions. In this first list are general works in literature and history that will be useful throughout the entire course of study. This will be supplemented at the end of each chapter by a special bibliography of works dealing with the period under consideration. There are four of these special bibliographies, which include also the most available texts and the best selections for reading.

American Literature. There is no complete or authoritative history of the subject. One of the best general surveys is Richardson, American Literature, 1607–1885, 2 vols., or Students' edition, 1 vol. (Putnam, 1888). This is a critical work and contains no biographical material. Two other general histories, each containing a small amount of biography interspersed with critical appreciation, are Trent, American Literature, in Literatures of the World series (Appleton, 1903), and Wendell, A Literary History of America, in the Library of Literary History (Scribner, 1900). There are also nearly a score of textbooks dealing with the same subject. Pleasant for supplementary reading is Mitchell, American Lands and Letters, 2 vols. (Scribner). A brief but excellent outline is given in White, Sketch of the Philosophy of American Literature (Ginn and Company).

Periods and Types of Literature. The only complete and scholarly work dealing with any period of our literary history is Tyler, History of American [Colonial] Literature, 2 vols., and Literary History of the Revolution, 2 vols. (Putnam).

Critical Appreciations. Brownell, American Prose Masters; Burton, Literary Leaders of America; Vincent, American Literary Masters; Vedder, American Writers of To-day.

Poetry. Stedman, Poets of America; Onderdonk, History of American Verse; Collins, Poetry and Poets of America; Otis, American Verse, 1625–1807.

Fiction. Erskine, Leading American Novelists; Perry, A Study of Prose Fiction; Smith, The American Short Story; Canby, The Short Story in English; Matthews, The Short Story: Specimens illustrating its Development; Baldwin, American Short Stories; Howells, Criticism in Fiction; James, The Art of Fiction; Loshe, The Early American Novel.

History, Humor, etc. Jameson, History of Historical Writing in America; Payne, Leading American Essayists; Haweis, American Humorists; Payne, American Literary Criticism; Sears, History of Oratory; Fulton and Trueblood, British and American Eloquence (lives of twenty-two orators, with selections); Seilhamer, History of the American Theatre, 1749–1797, 3 vols.; Roden, Later American Plays, 1831–1900; Smyth, The Philadelphia Magazines and their Contributors; Hudson, Journalism in the United States; Thomas, History of Printing in America (1810).

Literary Essays. One of the most significant features of our later literature is the number of books of literary essays and reminiscences, such as Lowell's My Study Windows, and Among my Books, Howells's Literary Friends and Acquaintance, Trowbridge's My Own Story, Woodberry's Makers of Literature, Higginson's Cheerful Yesterdays, and many others. These will be referred to in the special bibliographies.

Sectional Works. National Studies in American Letters, edited by Woodberry, is a series of volumes each dealing with a group of authors: Higginson, Old Cambridge; Swift, Brook Farm; Addison, The Clergy in American Letters; Nicholson, The Hoosiers; etc. (Macmillan). Baskerville, Southern Writers, 2 vols.; Holliday, History of Southern Literature; Moses, Literature of the South; Lawton, The New England Poets; Venable, Beginnings of Literary Culture in the Ohio Valley.

Biography. Several series of extended biographies are available, the most complete being the American Men of Letters (Houghton). A few of our leading authors are found also in English Men of Letters, in Great Writers series, and in the brief Beacon Biographies. The best of these works will be referred to in the special bibliographies. Biographical collections are Adams, Dictionary of American Authors (Houghton, 1897); Appleton's Cyclopedia of American Biography, 6 vols. (Appleton, 1886–1889); Allibone, Dictionary of English Literature and British and American Authors, 6 vols. (Lippincott, 1858–1891); Mary Howes, American Bookmen (Dodd, 1898); Fields, Biographical Notes and Personal Sketches (Houghton, 1881); Tuckerman, Personal Recollections of Notable People, 2 vols. (Dodd, 1895).

Bibliography and Chronology. A very useful book of reference is Whitcomb, Chronological Outlines of American Literature (Macmillan, 1906). Wegelin, Early American Poetry, 2 vols., Early American Fiction, Early American Plays; Foley, American Authors, 1795–1895 (privately printed, 1906). For a list of historical romances see the second volume of Baker, History in Fiction, 2 vols. (1907), or Nield, Guide to the Best Historical Novels and Tales (1902). The best guide to periodicals is Poole's Index to Magazine Literature.

Books of Selections. *General:* A single volume covering the entire field of American prose and poetry is Readings in American Literature, edited by Miss MacAlarney and Miss Calhoun (announced, 1913, Ginn and Company); Stedman and Hutchinson, Library of American Literature, 11 vols. (Webster, 1888–1890); Duyckinck, Cyclopedia of American Literature, 2 vols. (revised 1875, Scribner); Bronson, American Poems, 1625–1892 (University of Chicago Press, 1912); Lounsbury, American Poems (Yale University Press, 1912); Stedman, An American Anthology, 1787–1900 (Houghton, 1900); Carpenter, American Prose (Macmillan, 1898); Harding, Select Orations Illustrating American Political History, 1761–1895 (Macmillan); Johnson, American Orations, 3 vols. (Putnam); Kettell, Specimens of American Poetry, 3 vols. (1829); Griswold, Poets and Poetry of America (1842), Prose Writers of America (1847), Female Poets of America (1848).

Colonial and Revolutionary: Trent and Wells, Colonial Prose and Poetry, 3 vols. (Crowell); Cairns, Selections from Early American Writers (Macmillan).

National Period: Page, Chief American Poets (Houghton); Sladen, Younger American Poets, 1830–1890 (Crowell); Knowles, Golden Treasury of American Songs and Lyrics (Page); Crandall, Representative American Sonnets (Houghton).

War and Patriotism: Eggleston, American War Ballads and Lyrics, 2 vols. (Putnam); Moore, Songs and Ballads of the American Revolution (1856); Sargent, Loyalist Poetry of the Revolution (1857); Moore, Songs of the Soldiers, 3 vols. (Putnam, 1864); Brown, Bugle Echoes, Northern and Southern songs of the Civil War (White, 1886); Matthews, Poems of American Patriotism (Scribner); Nellie Wallingford, American History by American Poets, 2 vols. (Duffield); Stevenson, Poems of American History (Houghton); Scollard, Ballads of American Bravery (Silver).

Sectional: Trent, Southern Writers: Selections in Prose and Verse (Macmillan); Mims and Payne, Southern Prose and Poetry (Scribner); Louise Manly, Southern Literature (Johnson).

Miscellaneous: The Humbler Poets: Newspaper and Periodical Verse, first series, 1870–1885, edited by Thompson; second series, 1885–1910, edited by Wallace and Rice (McClurg); Lomax, Cowboy Songs and Other Frontier Ballads (Sturgis); Barton, Old Plantation Hymns (Boston, 1899).

On the Study of Literature. Woodberry, Appreciation of Literature; Harrison, The Choice of Books; Stedman, The Nature and Elements of Poetry; Caffin, Appreciation of the Drama; Perry, Study of Prose Fiction; Gayley and Scott, Introduction to the Methods and Materials of Literary Criticism. A useful little book for students and teachers preparing for college-entrance English is Trent, Hanson and Brewster, An Introduction to the English Classics (1911, Ginn and Company).

Texts and Helps. Before beginning the study of literature the teacher or student should write for the latest catalogue of such publications as the Standard English Classics (Ginn and Company), Riverside Literature Series (Houghton), Maynard's English Classics (Merrill), Pocket Classics (Macmillan), Lake Classics (Scott), Everyman's Library (Dutton), etc. Almost every educational house now publishes an inexpensive series of texts devoted to the best works of English and American authors. Many of them are well edited and arranged with special reference to class use. In studying the major writers these handy little volumes will be found much more satisfactory than the cumbersome anthologies. (References to the various school series will be made in " Selections for Reading " at the end of each chapter. Standard texts of complete works will be listed in the special bibliographies.)

American History. *Textbooks :* For ready reference the student should have at hand a concise, reliable text, such as Montgomery, Student's American History; Muzzey, American History; Channing, Student's History of the United States; Elson, History of the United States; etc. For more extended reading the following are recommended:

General : The American Nation, edited by Hart, 27 vols. (Harper), is the most complete history of our country. American History Series, 6 vols.: Colonial Era, by Fisher; French War and the Revolution, by Sloane, etc. (Scribner). Epochs of American History, 3 vols.: The Colonies, by Thwaite; Formation of the Union, by Hart; Division and Reunion, by Wilson (Longmans). Narrative and Critical History of the United States, edited by Winsor, 8 vols. (Houghton); McMaster, History of the People of the United States, 1784–1860, 8 vols. (Appleton). An especially valuable reference work for the student of our early literature is American History told by Contemporaries, edited by Hart; 4 vols. (Macmillan).

Social : Low, The American People, a Study in National Psychology, 2 vols. (Houghton, 1909, 1911).

Political : Stanwood, History of the Presidency to 1896, a revised edition of the same author's History of Presidential Elections (Houghton); Johnston, American Political History, 2 vols. (Putnam); Gordy, History of Political Parties in the United States, 2 vols. (Holt), covers the period from 1787 to 1828.

Biography : Lives of important historical characters in the American Statesmen series (Houghton); other biographical series are the Makers of America (Dodd), Great Commanders (Appleton), and the so-called True Biographies (Lippincott). Individual biographies, collections, and autobiographies will be listed in the special bibliography at the end of each chapter.

Bibliography : Channing, Hart and Turner, Guide to the Study and Reading of American History (revised 1912, Ginn and Company); Andrews, Gambrill and Tall, Bibliography of History (Longmans).

AMERICAN LITERATURE

CHAPTER I

THE COLONIAL PERIOD (1607-1765)

I. INTRODUCTION — THE SPIRIT OF OUR FIRST LITERATURE

"The which I shall endevor to manefest in a plaine stile, with singuler regard unto yᵉ simple trueth in all things."

Bradford, *Of Plimoth Plantation*

The Coming of the Ships. Long ago, so the legend runs, a little ship without a name came sailing into the harbor of our **The Ship** ancestors. The deck was covered with gold and **of Fancy** jewels, with swords and battle-axes and coats of mail ; and in the midst of these warlike things was a baby sleeping. No man ever sailed that ship ; she came of herself, bringing the child whose name was Scyld.

So appeared among men the hero and father of the race of heroes. Many years did he rule them, leading them to victory in war and to prosperity in peace, but always reminding them that he must some day return to the deep whence he came. Then Scyld being mortal died, and lo ! the same mysterious ship appeared silently in the harbor. With sad hearts they carried the hero aboard and laid him by the mast, a ring of weapons around him, a hoard of jewels on his breast, and a great golden banner streaming to the wind over his head. Then the sails filled, the helm answered an unseen hand, and the ship put out to sea.

Such is the old story, found in shining fragments, like a broken mirror, among the earliest records of the English race.

Centuries later, and bringing leaders of a mighty nation, another little ship came sailing into another harbor. There were **The Ship** children aboard this ship also, and in the wild scene **of Oak** of ocean and forest and winter sky they seemed as sadly out of place as the little Scyld, asleep among the swords and battle-axes. But these little ones were not alone ; mothers held them close, and near at hand stood the fathers, — brave, resolute men, who loved freedom as their old Saxon ancestors loved it, and who were determined to have it at any cost. No friendly eyes watched the coming of this little ship ; no friendly voices hailed her from the shore. As the record says :

"They had now no friends to welcome them, nor inns to entertaine or refresh their weatherbeaten bodys, no houses much less townes to repaire to, to seeke for succoure. . . . And for the season, it was winter, and they that know the winters of that countrie know them to be sharp and violent, and subject to cruel and fierce stormes. Besides what could they see but a hideous and desolate wilderness, full of wild beasts and wild men ? And what multitudes there might be of them they knew not. Neither could they, as it were, go up to the top of Pisgah to view from this wilderness a more goodly countrie to feed their hopes ; for which way soever they turned their eyes (save upward to the heavens) they could have little solace or content in respecte of any outward objects. For summer being done, all things stand upon them with a weatherbeaten face ; and the whole countrie, full of woods and thickets, represented a wild and savage view."

Those who have ever sailed into a northern harbor in mid-winter will understand the "weatherbeaten face" that looked sternly upon the strangers. Yet they went ashore, men, women and little children ; and their first act was to kneel and give thanks to God, who had brought them over the winter sea to offer the freedom of His great wilderness.

The bitter winter dragged slowly along, and every day death came out of the woods and beckoned them to follow, some by hunger, some by disease, some by wasting loneliness that knew no remedy. Soon half their number were sleeping in "God's Acre" under the pines ; but not one of the little company faltered or turned back from the work to which he had set his hand. When spring came the " weatherbeaten face " looked more kindly. They planted corn ; laid out a town, with its streets, dwellings, church and schoolhouse ; elected their own leader, and called a town meeting " to frame just and equal laws for themselves and their descendants." Then the ship sailed away, and left them alone to build a nation in the wilderness.

Such is the story of the second little ship, sailing with the Pilgrim Fathers on one of the world's momentous voyages. It is recorded with noble simplicity in the earliest authentic history of the American people.[1]

Beginnings of American Literature. These two ships, one built of seasoned oak, the other of pure fancy, may serve to suggest the contrast between our earliest literature and that of England, or Greece, or any other nation. These older literatures begin, as children's stories do, with the free play of imagination, with legends of gods and heroes, of magic and dragons and fairy ships. Generations of unlettered men repeat and enlarge these stories, until some great poet appears and weaves the scattered threads of legend into an epic, like *Beowulf* or the *Odyssey*, which becomes a standard of heroism. So do most national literatures begin, and they still appeal powerfully to the imagination in two ways : they recall the recent wonder of our own childhood, and they suggest the far-off childhood of the race of men to which we belong.

Our American literature has a very different story to tell. Its poverty is that it has no past, no golden age of dreams and magic. It must begin all over again, like Robinson Crusoe on his island, not with fancy but with fact, not as a child but as a man full-grown. For our ancestors were writing a new page in the world's history. Isolated as they seemed, shut in by sea and wilderness and forgotten by the nations, they had the most compelling of all motives, a call from God ; and deep in their souls

---

[1] Bradford, *Of Plimoth Plantation.* The quotation is abridged from chap. ix, and the spelling is slightly modernized.

was the unalterable purpose to found a new society based upon the Puritan ideals of democracy and righteousness. Hence in their literature there are no myths or legends, no heroes or dragons or fairy ships, but careful historical records written, as Bradford says, "in a plain style, with singular regard unto the simple truth in all things."

We shall better appreciate the spirit of Colonial literature if we compare Bradford's story with that of Captain John Smith, who sojourned here for a time, but whose work belongs to England rather than to America. Both men were born in the most splendid period of English letters; but while Smith writes as an Elizabethan, showing on every page the romantic enthusiasm and exaggeration of the age, Bradford avoids all ornaments of style and regards exaggeration as unworthy of himself or his subject. "Heaven and earth," writes Smith, "never agreed better to frame a place for a man's habitation." And then, as if the work of heaven and earth were not enough, he bedecks the same with flowers of his own imagination, like a true Elizabethan. Moreover, he has always a double motive: to glorify his own adventures, and to induce emigrants to settle the colony in which he has an interest; and knowing that greed of gain is a powerful motive, he speaks artfully of the pearls found in the mussels, and of the "rocks interlaced with veins of glittering spangles."

Bradford holds steadily to a single motive; he is beginning a new nation of freemen, and only the truth will serve for a foundation. What he writes, therefore, is as rugged as the coast where the *Mayflower* found her anchorage. One might say, in explanation, that Smith landed in Virginia in the glory of the Southern spring, while Bradford's eyes rested first on the bleak New England coast in midwinter; but the difference between the two men is radical and fundamental. Looking upon the same object and describing it, one will entertain us, and the other tell us the truth. Thus, Bradford makes fishing for cod a part of the day's work, done to support the colony; Smith revels in the æsthetic pleasure and financial profit of angling, and so tickles at once our sporting instinct and our cupidity :

And is it not pretty sport, to pull up two pence, six pence, twelve pence, as fast as you can hale and veare a line? . . . And what sport doth yeelde a more pleasing content, and less hurt or charge, than angling with a hooke, and crossing the sweet ayre from ile to ile over the silent streames of a calm sea? [1]

Again, both writers were in frequent contact with the Indians ; but Smith alone uses his imagination to embroider the handiwork
Smith's Indians of God. He pictures the savages as gigantic, impressive creatures, " the calves of their legs being three-quarters of a yard aboute." Instead of greasy chiefs, overworked squaws, and the general squalor of an Indian camp, he gives us emperors, queens, courtiers ; and to show that love is love and hearts are hearts the world over, he records the romantic story of the " princess " Pocahontas, " the numparell of Virginia," " the emperour's dearest and well-beloved daughter." [2]

"At last they brought him [Smith] to Werowocomoco, where was Powhattan their Emperour. Here more than two hundred grim Courtiers stood wondering at him, as he had beene a monster ; till Powhattan and his train had put themselves in their greatest braveries. Before a fire, upon a seat like a bedstead, he sat covered with a great robe made of Rawocun skins, and all the tayles hanging by. . . . At [Smith's] entrance before the King, all the people gave a great shout. The Queene of Appamatuck was appointed to bring him water to wash his hands, and another brought him a bunch of feathers instead of a towel, to dry them. Having feasted him after their best barbarous manner, a long consultation was held ; but the conclusion was, two great stones were brought before Powhattan. Then as many as could laid hands upon him, dragged him to the stones and thereon laid his head. And being ready with their clubs to beate out his braines, Pocahontas the King's dearest daughter, when no intreaty could prevaile, got his head in her armes, and laid her owne upon his to save him from death : whereat the Emperour was contented he should live." [3]

---

[1] From *A Description of New England* (1616).

[2] Later, Smith forgets his romance and tells us that the " emperor " left his daughter a prisoner for six months, because he was unwilling to return a few muskets which he had stolen, as the price of her ransom.

[3] From Smith, *General History of Virginia* (1623). This doubtful story is not mentioned in his earlier record, *A True Relation* (1608). Some historians accept the story as true. See Fiske, *Old Virginia and Her Neighbors*, I, 103-112.

Bradford's record of the Indians is altogether different. He
tells us simply of an alarm at dawn, of a large band of savages
Bradford's   who yelled fiendishly while they discharged their
Indians   arrows, but who fled into the woods at the charge
of a few determined men, — men who had said their prayers and
who could not be stampeded by any brave yelling. He shows
us how Samoset came with open palm, in sign of peace ; how
they fed him and sent him back for the chief of the tribe ; and
how they made a fair treaty, giving the exact obligations of both
parties. He takes us through 'the terrible Pequot uprising, but
without drum or trumpet or any of the sham heroism which fills
our minds and newspapers whenever the bugles blow for war.
He shows the war just as it was, a dirty and unpardonable business, brought on, as usual, by greed and evil passion, and utterly
lacking in the glory which imaginative historians have woven
into it. He takes us among the wretched wigwams, where scores
of savages are dying of smallpox and neglect. In a few tense
lines he draws an appalling picture of this loathsome disease ;
and then :

" The condition of this people was so lamentable, and they fell down so
generally of this disease, as they were not able to help one another ; no, not
to make a fire, nor to fetch a little water to drinke, nor any to bury the
dead ; but would strive as long as they could, and when they could procure
no other means to make a fire, they would burn the wooden trayes and
dishes, and their very bowes and arrowes. And some would crawle out on
all fours to gett a little water, and sometimes die by the way, and not be
able to gett in againe. But those of the English house, though at first they
were afraid of the infection, yet seeing their woeful condition and hearing
their pitiful cries, had compassion on them, and dayly fetched them wood
and water, and made them fires ; gott them victuals whilst they lived, and
buried them when they died. . . . And this mercie which they shewed them
was kindly taken, and thankfully acknowledged of all the Indians that knew
or heard of the same." [1]

Here, in the plain facts, is something better than war or
romance to stir the heart of a young Galahad. Occasionally the
record grows grimly humorous, as when some pious people in

---

[1] From Bradford, *Of Plimoth Plantation*, record of year 1635.

England got rid of their "crackbrained" minister by sending him over to edify the Colonists ; or tense with restrained emotion, as in the Pilgrim's departure from home ; or exquisitely tender, as in the account of Brewster's noble life and service ; but there is no attempt at effect, no conscious appeal to the imagination. Our interest is held partly by the plain humanity of the story, and partly by the absolute sincerity, which shines steadily, like a subdued light, behind every page of Bradford's writing. In a plain style, with an eye single to the truth in all things, — the spirit of America is reflected in that first paragraph of our first national record.

Why the Colonists wrote Few Books. The writing of any people divides itself into two classes, known as primitive or Folklore folklore literature and the literature of culture. The Literature first consists of the songs and legends — mostly of great age, and by unknown authors — associated with the early history of the race ; the second of the poems, dramas, essays and novels produced by the two forces of nationality and civilization. For the former, popular myths and traditions are essential ; but before these can appear, generations of men must live and die in a land ; the mighty deeds of the pioneers must be told over and over again, growing the while like snowballs rolled by children, until by the play of imagination the deed and the doer become symbols of an heroic age. Moreover, men learn to love their native rivers and hills, not for their natural beauty, but largely for their historic and romantic associations, — golden memories, which link the past to the present and make us all one family, children of the one loved mother. So it was in Greece and Rome, so in every nation that cherishes an epic of its golden age of childhood. But our American ancestors, beginning life and literature in a new land, a place not a country, without traditions or legendary heroes like Arthur and Achilles, could not possibly have produced a folklore. Such literature is never "created" ; it grows from generation to generation.

The greater literature of culture was also denied the Colonists. To produce such a literature peace, leisure, an ideal rather than Literature a practical view of life, and a strong, centralized of Culture government are all essential. Such blessings were far removed from the pioneers. They were compassed by perils and hardships; their hands were busy subduing the wilderness, their minds occupied with problems of free government and religious toleration. Here, for instance, is a handful of people landing in Virginia. They have left behind all that men com-

monly hold dear; they face a wilderness full of difficulties and appalling dangers. In a surprisingly short time they solve the problem of making the wilderness support them; they start a profitable commerce with Europe; they lay the foundations of representative government in the prophetic Assembly which gathers in the little church

THE SETTLEMENT OF JAMESTOWN

at Jamestown. Within four years these amazing men have organized a democracy and virtually issued their declaration of independence.

Again, in 1645, only fifteen years after the landing of the Puritans, Governor Winthrop declares : " The great questions that have troubled the country are about the authority of the magistrates and the liberty of the people." [1] Great questions indeed! The " authority of the magistrates " had troubled England from the time King John met his scowling barons at Runnymede until that fateful day when King Charles lost

---

[1] Winthrop, *History of New England, from 1630 to 1649*, II, 279 ff. (Savage's edition, 1853). The whole speech is well worth reading, as it contains the first (American) definition of liberty.

his head; and "the liberty of the people" had been a trouble, vague yet terrible, like the first rumble of an earthquake, which Europe had for centuries feared either to meet or to avoid. Yet these quiet, straight-thinking Puritans grappled the problem in their first General Court, and rested not till they had mastered it.

Here, then, is our first suggestion : the Colonists produced few great books because they were too busy with great deeds, too intent on solving the great problems of humanity. The man who makes history seldom writes it; the Beowulf who fights a dragon bare-handed does not turn gleeman to sing his own heroism. And never was history better made, never was more heroic work done for man than by these silent Colonists. They fashioned no sonnets because they were absorbed in the higher art of forming free states. ~no printing presses~

Another reason for the scarcity of Colonial literature was the lack of nationality. For it is the experience of all nations that **Lack of** letters flourish at a time when, as in the Age of **Nationality** Pericles or Elizabeth, all classes of people are bound together by patriotic enthusiasm, and by devotion to one leader who typifies the whole nation's welfare and greatness. At such a time men's hearts expand with emotion, and the emotion finds expression in good books. But the Colonies were not in any sense a nation. Each was isolate and self-dependent; separated from its neighbors by vast stretches of wilderness; separated also from England, which men still regarded as their country. There was little in Colonial life or thought to indicate an independent America, little to suggest a thrilling national anthem, and nothing whatever to create a national enthusiasm which should be reflected in a national literature. So two hundred years passed; the battles of the Revolution were fought and won, and the Constitution adopted, before America announced her destiny and became a nation among the nations. And then, like a herald proclaiming his mission, the new national spirit suddenly announced its quality in the poetry of Bryant and in the prose of Irving and Cooper.

Why study Colonial Literature? One who looks merely for entertainment will doubtless be disappointed in Colonial literature; but if one is interested in human life, and in records which reflect and interpret that life, then he shall find good reading. Only yesterday a traveler in Rome rested a moment beneath a crumbling archway, amid the ruins of the Colosseum. At his feet lay a brick, one of unnumbered thousands, hidden in the dust of centuries. A mark, a mere scratch, called attention to it; and then a story was revealed which touched the heart with something of the old sorrow and yearning of humanity. While the brick was yet soft a sparrow had lit upon it and left the faint outlines of his feet, which soon hardened into imperishable records. And then a man, seeing the record, had taken a flint and graved in rude letters beneath the sparrow's tracks: *Regulus the slave wrote this.* The sparrow was a passing accident; but the slave with his bit of stone, toiling obscurely amid a multitude of his fellows, was one of those very human beings, like ourselves, who desired to be known and remembered.[1] And the brick was no longer a dull thing of water and clay, but a living voice, telling a story of a bird that was alert and inquisitive, and of a man who strove for immortality.

Even so, these neglected records of the Colonists may become living voices from the past, and every voice has a story to tell, not of poor slaves but of free, indomitable spirits who conquered the wilderness, to whose heroism we owe the glorious land which we now call home and which stirs the heart to noble emotion whenever we sing " My Country." The object of all literature is to make us acquainted with humanity; and we shall never know our own forebears until we forget what others have written about them, in the histories, and learn from their own pages what they thought and felt, what they dreamed and dared, what they adored in God and honored in their fellow man. We shall

[1] A primitive belief, which takes us far back in the history of the race, is that a man is immortal so long as his name is remembered. Hence the first monuments; hence perpetuating a father's name in that of his son; hence also the terrible curse, " May his name perish! "

study Colonial literature with this single object : to know the men and women who founded this nation, and who are bound to us across the centuries by the ties of a common hope and a common fatherland.

II. COLONIAL ANNALISTS AND HISTORIANS

WILLIAM BRADFORD (1588?–1657)

At the beginning of American literature stands the chronicle history of Governor Bradford. It is a noble record, telling the story of the Pilgrim Fathers, and compares in historic value with the *Anglo-Saxon Chronicle* of King Alfred, which marks the beginning of English prose. Its style is a revelation of the Pilgrim mind, rugged and sincere, with a glint of humor lighting up its sternness ; and its subject is as fascinating as the story of pioneers and nation builders must ever be. Both in style and in matter, therefore, in its reflection of a fine personality against a background

GOVERNOR BRADFORD'S HOUSE

of prophetic history, Bradford's manuscript is, to American readers at least, one of the most significant to be found in the literary records of any nation.

Biographical Sketch. Never was a better illustration than Bradford of Carlyle's theory that history is essentially the story of great men. And never did a handful of emigrants go out on a momentous enterprise led by one who better deserved the title of nature's nobleman. From Mather's *Magnalia* we learn that he was born in the Yorkshire village of Austerfield probably in 1588, the year of the Spanish

Armada ; that he was a remarkably well-read man in five languages,[1] a student to the end of his days, and many other details. But it is the spirit of the man — brave, tender, loyal as a saint to high ideals — that impresses us ; and this the reader will find reflected in Bradford's own work. Though he lived at a time when all Europe believed in witches and devils, we shall find hardly a trace of superstition in this leader of the Pilgrims. Though the age was one of general intolerance, and though he had himself suffered grievously from religious persecution, he was singularly broad-minded and charitable. Whoever came to the Colony, whether Jew or Gentile, Catholic or Protestant,[2] was kindly received, was given land and opportunity to work, and was never disturbed because of his religious belief. This enlightened policy of the Pilgrims spread so rapidly among the Colonies that, within thirty years, we find Nathaniel Ward in his *Simple Cobbler* (1647) indulging in violent diatribes against the growing spirit of religious toleration.

So, for thirty-seven years Bradford was the very soul of that heroic little Colony which built its ideals so largely into the foundations of the American nation ; and it was largely his business sagacity and sterling honesty that made of their remarkable venture a more remarkable success. He died (1657), as Mather records, " lamented by all the Colonies of New England as a common blessing and father of them all." [3]

Works of Bradford. In literature Bradford is remembered by his *Of Plimoth Plantation*, a vivid, straightforward history of the Pilgrims, written by the chief actor in the stirring drama of colonization. We advise the reader to begin with the second

---

1 One who studies the Pilgrims is impressed by their almost sacred regard for learning. They had their own printing press in Holland ; they established schools wherever they went ; they insisted on having highly educated teachers and ministers. The *Mayflower*, though barely furnished with the necessities of life, had an abundance of good books. Bradford's library alone contained 300 volumes. If we consider how scarce and expensive books were in 1620, this would equal a library of perhaps 30,000 volumes in our day. And many another astonishing collection might be found in the log cabins of Plymouth. Thus, Brewster had over 400 volumes, including 6 philosophical works, 14 books of poetry, 60 histories, 230 religious works, and 54 miscellaneous treatises covering every branch of knowledge.

2 While the first Colonists were making a home and a nation here, the Jesuits were carrying on their heroic work among the Indians far to the north and west. In the *Jesuit Relations* there is a pleasant account of Father Druillette's journey through the American Colonies, and especially of his visit to Governor Bradford. A part of this record may be found in Parkman's *The Jesuits in North America*, chap. xxii.

3 *Magnalia*, Bk. II, chap. i.

chapter,[1] the flight from England, where the narrative glows with the suppressed feeling of a brave and modest man, one of the few in all literature who make history and also write it.

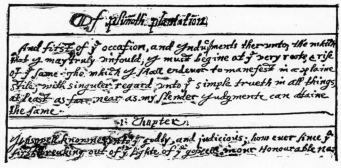

A PORTION OF THE BRADFORD MS.

" History of Plimoth Plantation "

We follow with sympathetic interest the story of their exile life in Holland till we come to the departure, which first made them Americans :

" And the time being come that they must departe, they were accompanied with most of their bretheren out of the city unto a towne sundrie miles off called Delfes Haven, where the ship lay ready to receive them. So they left that goodly and pleasant city [Leyden] which had been their resting place near twelve years; but they knew that they were pilgrimes, and looked not much on those things, but lift up their eyes to the heavens, their dearest countrie, and quieted their spirits. . . . The next day, the wind being faire, they went aboarde, and their friends with them, where truly doleful was the sight of that sad and mournful parting; to see what sighs and sobs and prayers did sound amongst them, what tears did gush from every eye . . . that sundrie of the Dutch strangers that stood on the key as spectators could not refraine from tears. . . . But the tide, which stays for no man, calling them away that were thus loath to departe, their reverend pastor falling downe on his knees, and they all with him, with watrie cheeks commended them with most fervent prayers to the Lord and his blessing. And then, with mutual embraces and many tears, they tooke their leaves one of another; which proved to be the last leave to many of them."

[1] The first is an account of religious dissent in England, and is interesting only to church historians.

Very different from this parting was their approach to the new land, with its " weatherbeaten face," and that terrible attack of savages upon Bradford and his first exploring party :

" So they made them a barricado with logs, stakes and thick pine boughs, the height of a man, leaving it open to leeward, partly to shelter them from the cold and wind (making their fire in the middle, and lying round about it) and partly to defend them from any sudden assaults of the savages, if they should surround them. So being very weary, they betooke them to rest. . . . Presently, all on the sudain, they heard a great and strange crie, and one of their company being abroad came runing in, and cried, *Men !* *Indeans*, *Indeans !* and withal, their arrows came flying amongst them. . . . The crie of the Indeans was dreadful, especially when they saw [our] men run out of the randevoue towards the shalop, to recover their armes, the Indians wheeling about upon them. But some, runing out with coats of maile on, and cutlasses in their hands, soone got their armes and let flye amongst them, and quickly stopped their violence. Yet ther was a lustie man, and no less valiante, stood behind a tree within halfe a musket shot, and let his arrows flie at them. He stood three shot of a musket, till one, taking full aime at him, made the barke or splinters of the tree fly about his ears, after which he gave an extraordinary shrike, and away they wente all of them. They left some to keep the shalop, and followed them about a quarter of a mile, and shouted once or twice, and shot off two or three pieces, and so returned. This they did, that they might conceive that they were not afraid of them, or any way discouraged. . . . Afterwards they gave God solemn thanks and praise for their deliverance, and gathered up a bundle of their arrows, and sente them into England afterwards by the master of the ship, and called that place the First Encounter."[1]

Napoleon had a profound respect for cockcrow courage ; and Indians, knowing that men are panicky when suddenly roused out of sleep, commonly attack at daybreak. Perhaps we shall better understand the Pilgrim brand of courage if we consider the very significant line that the attack came " after prayer, it being day dawning."

As an antidote to those historians who tell us that we have over-estimated the Pilgrim Fathers, we suggest the following paragraph from the story of the first winter, when most of the company were sore stricken with disease, and death stalked daily amongst them:

[1] Abridged, and slightly modernized, from chap. x *Of Plimoth Plantation.* A fuller account may be found in *Mourt's Relation* (see note on p. 18).

"And in the time of most distress there were but six or seven sound persons . . . who spared no pains night nor day, but with abundance of toil and hazard of their owne health fetched them woode, made them fires, drest them meat, made their beds, washed their loathsome clothes . . . in a word, did all the homely and necessarie offices for them which dainty and quesie stomachs cannot endure to hear named; and all this willingly and cheerfully without any grudging in the least, shewing herein their true love unto their friends and bretheren. A rare example and worthy to be remembered."

Still more worthy to be remembered is the fact that the Pilgrims showed kindness to their enemies also ; that when disease reached the brutal sailors of the *Mayflower* — who remained on board and took no part in the terrible struggle of the first winter — the Pilgrims cared for them with the same tenderness ; that when the Indians were stricken with smallpox they ministered unto them ; and that when a ship in distress put in for help they shared their food, though they were

OLD FORT, PLYMOUTH

themselves on short rations and threatened with starvation.

Doubtless, some of our present misconceptions of the Colonists arise from the fact that " Many wicked and profane persons were shipped off to the colonies by relatives who hoped thus to be rid of them." [1] And the transportation companies, as in our own day, seeing a chance for unholy gain, gathered together all sorts of undesirable emigrants and shipped them over :

"Some begane to make a trade of it, to transport passengers and their goods, and hired ships for that end; and then, to make up their freight and advance their profits, cared not who the persons were, so they had money to pay them. And by this means this countrie became pestered with many unworthy persons, who, being come over, crept into one place or another.'

[1] See *Of Plimoth Plantation*, record of year 1642.

Indeed, the modern reader, who thinks that our pressing problems arose yesterday, finds many surprising pages in Bradford's old history. Thus, the doctrine of free trade and "the open door" was not only promulgated but was upheld by arms on the Kennebec;[1] and socialism had an excellent chance to put its theories into practice. For three years the Colonists lived as a socialistic community, putting the fruits of their common toil into a common storehouse; and each year they battled anew with famine. Instead of reproaching them, or using his authority as governor, Bradford aroused their ambition:

" So they begane to thinke how they might obtaine a better crope . . . and not thus languish in miserie. At length, after much debate, the governor (with the advice of the cheefest among them) gave way that they should set corne every man for his own particuler, and in that regard trust to themselves, . . . and so assigned to every family a parcel of land, according to the proportion of their number. This had very good success, for it made all hands very industrious, so as much more corne was planted, and saved the governor a great deal of trouble, and gave far better contente. The women now went willingly into the field, and took their little ones with them to set corne, which before would alledge weakness and inability ; whom to have compelled would have been thought great tyranie and oppression.

" The experience that was had in this commone course and condition, tried sundrie years, and that amongst godly and sober men, may well evince the vanitie of that conceit of Plato's (applauded by some of later times) that the taking away of propertie and bringing in community into a commone wealth, would make them happy and flourishing. For this communitie was found to breed much confusion and discontente, and retard much imployment that would have been to their benefite and comforte. . . . Let none object, this is men's corruption and nothing to the course itself. I answer, seeing all men have this corruption in them, God in his wisdome saw another course fitter for them. . . .

" By this time harvest was come, and instead of famine, now God gave them plentie. And the face of things was changed, to the rejoysing of the hearts of many, for which they blessed God. And the effect of their particuler planting was well seen ; for all had, one way and another, pretty well to bring the year about ; and some of the abler and more industrious sorte had to spare and to sell to others. So as any general want or famine hath not since been amongst them to this day."[2]

[1] *Of Plimoth Plantation*, record of the year 1627–1628.
[2] Abridged from record of 1623, pp. 162–164, 177.

Some of the most luminous pages of Bradford are the biographical sketches, wherein his keen but kindly judgment of
Sketches   men is brightened by the play of a grim humor.
from Life   Here, for instance, is the salt maker from England,
who " knew only how to boil water in pans," but who made a
great mystery and hocus-pocus out of his art, making his helpers
do many unnecessary things "until they discovered his sutltie."
Here are Morton and his revelers at Merrymount, placing all
the settlements in danger, not simply by their evil living, but
by breaking the law against selling guns and powder to the
Indians. In a few terse pages Bradford makes us as well acquainted with Morton as if we had met him and his Indian squaws
around the Maypole; and the last scene, in which Myles Standish
"brake up the uncleane nest," and the only person injured "was
so drunk that he ran his owne nose upon the point of a sword
and lost a little of his hott blood," is worthy of a comedy.

There are many other little biographies of men and women,
some bad, some good, and all human ; but we can quote only a
few sentences from the story of Brewster. Here our historian's
feelings are deeply stirred by the loss of one with whom he had
shared joy and grief, labor and rest, for near forty years ; but he
writes with the simplicity and restrained emotion of the old
Greek dramatists :

" He was wise and discreete and well-spoken, having a grave and deliberate utterance ; of a very cheerful spirit, very sociable and pleasant amongst
his friends ; of an humble and modest mind, undervallewing himself and
his own abilities and some time overvallewing others ; inoffensive and innocent in his life and conversation, which gained him the love of those without
as well as those within. . . . He was tender hearted and compassionate of
such as were in miserie, especially of such as (like himself) had been of good
estate and ranke and were fallen into wante and poverty, either for goodness
and religion's sake, or by the injury and oppression of others. He would say,
of all men these deserved most to be pitied. And none did more offend and
displease him than such as would hautily carry themselves, being risen from
nothing, and having little els to commend them but a few fine clothes or a
little riches more than others." [1]

1 *Of Plimoth Plantation*, record of the year 1643.

One unacquainted with the source of this exquisite biography might easily assume that he was reading a chapter from North's *Plutarch*. And the ending, when Brewster "drew his breath long, as a man fallen into a sound sleepe, and so sweetly departed this life unto a better," is like a wreath of immortelles which a man leaves upon the grave of a dear and honored friend.

Our First Modern Historian. Before writing his History, Bradford had written a journal of important events, from the moment when the stirring cry of "Land Ho!" rang out from the *Mayflower* to the election of Carver as first governor of the colony. This journal, long known as *Mourt's Relation*,[1] is of extraordinary interest; but we must leave it to consider the quality of the single work upon which Bradford's fame as a writer must rest.

We shall appreciate the enduring basis of that fame if we remember simply that *Of Plimoth Plantation* belongs with the first works in English to which the name "history" may properly be applied. For there was very little scientific historical writing in 1620. If we examine Raleigh's famous *History of the World*, for instance, we find a mere jumble of story, legend and superstition, written with a view to entertain us, but without any conception of the essential difference between historical fact and fiction. In comparison with most other writers in the same field, Bradford impresses us as a real historian. He has, first of all, a profound reverence for truth, the fundamental quality of every great historian, and quotes letters, charters and other original records, that there may be no doubt of the accuracy of his narrative. He is scrupulously just, even to the enemies of the Colony; and when judgment must be uttered on men or on

[1] The so-called *Mourt's Relation*, consisting of Bradford's journal and some added narrative of Winslow, covers practically the first year of the Pilgrims' life in America. It was sent to England, as a kind of letter for friends to read; but the interest of the story led to its being published. Some one wrote a preface, signed G. Mourt (or Morton) and the book was issued as *Mourt's Relation*. It was used freely by John Smith in his *History* and part of it, much garbled, is found in *Purchase, His Pilgrimes* (1625). Various modern editions have appeared, the best by Dexter (1865), and it is reprinted in Young's *Chronicles of the Pilgrims*. Good selections from Bradford and other early annalists may be found in Masefield, *The Pilgrim Fathers*, in Everyman's Library.

methods, charity is always uppermost. Moreover, if we except the dry, original documents which he quotes, he is always readable, and his style is remarkable for a noble sincerity and simplicity.

If we ask, therefore, in the modern German way of criticism, What did Bradford write that was not as well or better written before him? the answer is simply this : He was the first to write the dream and the deed, the faith and the work of a company of men and women who founded a state and laid the deep foundation of a mighty nation. The result is a priceless book, such as any people might well be proud to count among its literary treasures.[1]

JOHN WINTHROP

JOHN WINTHROP
(1588–1649)

Next in importance to Bradford's History are the grave annals of John Winthrop, whom Mather calls "the Nehemiah of American history." He was a well-born and well-educated gentleman, the leader of that large

[1] Bradford's manuscript was practically lost for two hundred years. It was evidently used by Morton, Prince, and other Colonial historians ; but none of these men recognized the enormous value of the work, or even quoted it openly. It found its way to the library of the Old South Church in Boston, lay there for a century, and may have been stolen by some soldier when the British evacuated the city in 1776. In 1855 it was found uninjured in the Fulham Library of London. In 1897 it was presented to Massachusetts, and rests now in the State Library at Boston. The interesting story of the discovery and return of this manuscript may be found in the preface to the edition published by the Commonwealth in 1899. The fragmentary *Letters*, and various minor works of Bradford, may be found in *Collections of the Massachusetts Historical Society*.

band of Puritans who came to America in 1630, the governor of the Massachusetts Bay Colony, and the first "President of the United Colonies of New England."

We would gladly record here the whole story of Winthrop's life, and show from abundant records how kind, how unselfish, how wor- **Character** thy of our profound respect was this old Puritan, the first **of Winthrop** to hold the prophetic office of President in the American Colonies; but we must be content with a mere suggestion. This is found in the *Model of Christian Charity*, which was written by Winthrop and adopted by the Bay Colony:

" Now the only way to avoid shipwreck and to provide for our posterity, is to follow the counsel of Micah: to do justly, to love mercy, and to walk humbly with our God. For this end we must be knit together in this work as one man. We must entertain for each other a brotherly affection. We must be willing to abridge ourselves of our superfluities for the supply of others' necessities. We must uphold a familiar commerce together in all meekness, gentleness, patience and liberality. We must delight in each other; make others' conditions our own; rejoice together, mourn together, labor and suffer together, always having before our eyes our commission and community in the work, as members of the same body. So shall we keep the unity of the spirit in the bond of peace."

It is from this *Model*, which rises at times to the stateliness and melody of a prophetic chant, and from his exquisite letters to his wife, rather than by his hurried *Journal*, that we are to judge Winthrop both as a man and as a writer.

Winthrop's Journal. Winthrop began his story in 1630, before the Puritan fleet had left its last English harbor, and continued it until his death at Boston, nineteen years later. While on shipboard, having the leisure of a passenger, he gives a full account of the voyage; but on land, with a thousand new duties and interests to keep him busy, he must wait till candle-light to jot down a few unusual things that appeal to him during the day. From numerous blanks and queries left in the manu-script, it is evident that Winthrop intended to revise his notes and to publish them as a connected history; but the leisure never came. We read his *Journal* just as he left it; and that gives, if not a literary, at least a human interest to the story. Here is no literary disguise, such as authors generally assume; his notes are a window to his very soul.

Our first reading of the *Journal* leaves an impression of chaos; for Winthrop never tells a connected story, but runs on from Dixy Bull the pirate to Mr. Cotton the minister, or to Sagamore John the Indian. In one breath he makes us acquainted with the depravity of wolves or windmills, in the next with necromancers and the powers of darkness. We read on successive pages:

That Winthrop's son was drowned at sea; that a goat died at Boston from eating too much Indian corn; that wild pigeons ate up the crops, — this to remind us that God ordered man to eat bread in the sweat of his brow; that a phantom ship was seen in a storm at New Haven, soon after a vessel disappeared with all on board; that a boy shot his father with a pistol, which he did not know was loaded; that a man put several bags of powder to dry before the open fire, and "some of it went up the chimney"; that a poor demented woman was hung for killing her baby, to save it from future punishment; that the Pequots came to arrange a treaty of peace and free trade; that the ministers were called to advise the magistrates whether to receive a governor sent from England; that the elders met to consider whether the devil could indwell in the elect, or some other heresy of Anne Hutchinson; that the people protested to the court against high prices and the cost of living; that the whole town was violently divided over the ownership of a stray pig, which rooted up no end of trouble; that the magistrates were obliged to discipline certain merchants who had "cornered" all the available wheat and were scandalously putting up prices. . . .

All these and a thousand other details, trifling or important, are faithfully recorded. Some of the items contain the material for an excellent history; others are more suggestive of the morning newspaper:

"The 18th of this month [Nov., 1643] two lights were seen near Boston, as before mentioned, and a week after the like was seen again. A light like the moon arose about the N. E. point and met the former at Nottles Island, and there they closed in one, and then parted, and closed and parted divers times, and so went over the hill in the island and vanished. Sometimes they shot out flames and sometimes sparkles. This was about eight o'clock in the evening, and was seen by many. About the same time a voice was heard upon the water . . . calling out in the most dreadful manner: *Boy, boy, come away, come away!* And it suddenly shifted from one place to another a great distance, about twenty times. It was heard by divers godly persons."

Now Bradford would suspect will-o'-the-wisps and loons here, or would " leave the cause to the naturalists to determine " ; but Winthrop, like Cotton Mather, has a slant toward the preternatural. He suggests an explanation of the affair by saying that the lights appeared and the voice spake at a place where an evil wretch, " a necromancer," had blown up a ship with all on board. The bodies of the crew were found and buried ; but the wretch himself remained forever in the keeping of the restless tides.

Concerning special providences, of which Winthrop is inordinately fond, a whole chapter might be written :

How one Gillow, a mischief maker, troubled the cowherd, and by the special providence of God two of his own cows got into the corn that same night and died from over-eating. How a ship's crew refused to come on shore for Sunday service, and their ship blew up the next day. How two little girls were plucking wild pigeons under a great heap of logs, and the feathers flew into the house until their mother sent them to another place ; and immediately the logs fell down and would have crushed them like eggshells had they been there. How a man worked an hour on Sunday to finish his job, and his child was drowned that night in a well in the cellar. How a man in charge of a saluting cannon boasted, as he rammed home an immense charge, that he would " make her speak up," and the gun exploded, of course ; but, though many people stood about, only the fool was killed. How a woman's heart was set on a fine piece of linen, which she kept in a drawer ; and a bit of candlewick fell upon it, unnoticed ; and in the morning the linen was wholly burned, like a piece of punk, nothing else in the house being injured ; and the woman confessed in meeting that it was the judgment of the Lord, since she had been too fond of her fine linen. . . .

Here, to change the subject, is a story confirmed by other records, which we recommend to the psychologists :

" At Kennebeck the Indians, wanting food, and there being a store in the Plimoth trading house, they conspired to kill the English there for their provisions ; and some Indians coming into the house, Mr. Willet, the master, being reading in the Bible, his countenance was more solemn than at other times, so as he did not look cheerfully upon them, as he was wont to do ; whereupon they went out and told their fellows that their purpose was discovered. They asked them how it could be. The others told them that they knew it by Mr. Willet's countenance, and that he had discovered it by a book that he was reading. Whereupon they gave over their design."

Those who remember the high regard in which Puritan mothers were held will read with surprise this record of a woman with literary aspirations : [1]

" Mr. Hopkins, the governor of Hartford on Connecticut, came to Boston and brought his wife with him (a godly young woman, and of special parts) who was fallen into a sad infirmity, the loss of her understanding and reason, which had been growing upon her divers years by occasion of her giving herself wholly to reading and writing, and had written many books. Her husband, being very loving and tender of her, was loath to grieve her ; but he saw his error when it was too late. For if she had attended to her household affairs, and such things as belong to women, and not gone out of her way and calling to meddle in such things as are proper for men, whose minds are stronger, etc., she had kept her wits, and might have improved them usefully and honorably in the place God had set her. He brought her to Boston . . . to try what means might be had here for her. But no help could be had."

Of Winthrop's " modest little speech," as he calls it, we can give only a few sentences to show its prevailing spirit. But it should be read entire by every American, since it is the first expression of the fundamental principles of our government :

" . . . For the other point concerning liberty, I observe a great mistake in the country about that. There is a twofold liberty, natural, and civil or federal. The first is common to man with beasts and other creatures. By this, man, as he stands in relation to man simply, hath liberty to do what he lists ; it is a liberty to evil as well as to good. This liberty is incompatible and inconsistent with authority, and cannot endure the least restraint of the most just authority. . . . The other kind of liberty I call civil or federal ; it may also be termed moral, in reference to the covenant between God and man in the moral law, and the politic covenants and constitutions amongst men themselves. This liberty is the proper end and object of authority, and cannot subsist without it ; and it is a liberty to that only which is good, just, and honest. This liberty you are to stand for, with the hazard, not only of your goods, but of your lives, if need be. . . . Even so, brethren, it will be between you and your magistrates. If you stand for your natural corrupt liberties, and will do what is good in your own eyes, you will not endure the least weight of authority, but will murmur and oppose and be always striving to shake off that yoke ; but if you will be satisfied to enjoy civil and lawful liberties, such as Christ allows you, then will you quietly and cheerfully

[1] Only five years after this was written (1645) an American book of poems, by Anne Bradstreet, was extravagantly praised both in this country and in England (see p. 47).

submit unto that authority which is set over you, in all the administrations of it, for your good. . . . So shall your liberties be preserved, in upholding the honor and power of authority amongst you."

Characteristics of Winthrop's Journal. We have given a mere suggestion of this curious old book, which contains some eight hundred pages of matters as difficult to summarize as are the contents of a museum. It is generally known as *The History of New England*,[1] but the title is misleading. Winthrop was not a historian; he was a clerk, a reporter of news for the Bay Colony. Though he could write excellently, as his letters indicate, his style here is generally prosy, showing a sad lack of humor and imagination. Yet his work is interesting, often intensely interesting; and his *Journal* has an added value from the fact that Hawthorne, Whittier, Longfellow, and other writers have used it as a source book, finding in its pages the material for many of their stories and poems.

Historians also have used it; and to their profound misunderstanding of the work we owe many of our misconceptions of the early settlers, whose lives are reflected here, brokenly, imperfectly, like shadows in a troubled pool. For, in a word, there is too much journalism in this old *Journal;* and journalism, by recording largely the abnormal or unusual, might give some future reader an entirely wrong impression of our present life. So in reading Winthrop — who has something of the modern reporter's instinct for the sensational — it is well to remember that, though he is interesting as a newspaper, he is often misleading, and presents on the whole a very inadequate picture of the life and ideals of the Puritan commonwealth.[2]

---

[1] Winthrop's manuscript was neglected for over a century, until 1790, when it was first published as *The Journal of John Winthrop*. Early in the nineteenth century this *Journal*, with some added Winthrop papers, was republished as *The History of New England from 1630 to 1649*, and by a freak of the publishing houses it has been called a history ever since.

[2] There is no question here of Winthrop's sincerity or of his reliability in all strictly historical matters. The *Journal*, however, seems to us more the work of a reporter than of a historian. In fairness we add that Tyler (*History of American Literature*, Vol. I) and Jameson (*History of Historical Writing in America*) give the *Journal* high praise as a historical record.

SOME OLD LOVE LETTERS

As a supplement to the public records of the Colonists, we venture to present here a few old letters — dearer, and perhaps more significant, because they were never intended for publication. Here is life indeed, life that retains its sweetness and serenity in the midst of peril and hardship, as a flower retains its perfume though beaten by the wind and the rain. A fragrance as of lavender greets us as we open them, and their yellow pages seem to treasure the sunshine of long ago. Reading them, we forget the narrowness and stern isolation of the Puritans; we remember that ideals are eternal; that the hearts of men have not changed since the first settlers landed at Jamestown and Plymouth Rock; and that in their log cabins, as in our modern homes and workshops, love, faith and duty were the supreme incentives to noble living.[1]

(Nov. 26, 1624)

My sweet Wife, — I blesse the Lorde for his continued blessings upon thee and our familye; and I thank thee for thy kinde lettres. But I knowe not what to saye for myself. I should mende and prove a better husband, havinge the helpe and example of so good a wife; but I growe still worse. I was wonte heretofore, when I was longe absent, to make some supplye with volumes of lettres; but now I can scarce afforde thee a few lines. Well, there is no helpe but by enlarging thy patience, and strengtheninge thy good opinion of him who loves thee as his owne soul and should count it his greatest affliction to live without thee. . . . The Lorde blesse and keepe thee, and all ours, and sende us a joyful meeting. So I kisse my sweet wife and rest

Thy faithful husband

JO. WINTHROP

(1627)

My most sweet Husband, — How dearly welcome thy kinde letter was to me I am not able to expresse. The sweetnesse of it did much refresh me. What can be more pleasinge to a wife than to heare of the welfayre of her best beloved, and how he is pleased with her poore endeavors. I blush

---

[1] These letters, with many others, may be found in the Appendix to Winthrop's *History of New England* (edition of 1853), in Robert C. Winthrop's *Life and Letters of John Winthrop* (1864–1867), and in *Some Old Puritan Love Letters* (1894). In our selections we have abridged the missives and slightly modernized the spelling, keeping enough of the old forms, however, to preserve the flavor of the original.

to hear my selfe commended, knowinge my owne wants; but it is your love that conceives the best and makes all thinges seem better than they are. I wish that I may be allwayes pleasinge to thee, and that those comforts we have in each other may be dayly increased, as far as they be pleasing to God. I confess I cannot doe ynough for thee, but thou art pleased to accept the will for the deede, and rest contented.

I have many reasons to make me love thee, whereof I will name two: first because thou lovest God, and secondly because that thou lovest me. If these two were wantinge, all the rest would be eclipsed. But I must leave this discourse and goe about my household affayers. I am a bad huswife to be so long from them; but I must needs borrowe a little time to talke with thee, my sweet heart. It will be but two or three weekes before I see thee, though they be longe ones. God will bring us together in his good time, for which time I shall pray. Farewell my good Husband; the Lord keep thee.

Your obedient wife
MARGARET WINTHROPE

(On Shipboard, 1630)

My faithful and dear Wife, — It pleaseth God that thou shouldst once again hear from me before our departure, and I hope this shall come safe to thy hands. I know it will be a great refreshing to thee. And blessed be his mercy, that I can write thee so good news, that we are all in very good health. Our boys are well and cheerful and have no mind of home. They lie both with me, and sleep as soundly in a rug as ever they did at Groton. We have spent now two Sabbaths on shipboard very comfortably, and are daily more encouraged to look for the Lord's presence to go along with us.

And now, my sweet soul, I must once again take my last farewell of thee in Old England. It goeth very near to my heart to leave thee; but I know to whom I have committed thee, even to him who loves thee much better than any husband can, who hath taken account of the hairs of thy head, and put all thy tears in his bottle, who can and, if it be for his glory, will bring us together again with peace and comfort. Oh, how it refresheth my heart to think that I shall yet again see thy sweet face in the land of the living, — that lovely countenance that I have so much delighted in and beheld with so great content! I have hitherto been so taken up with business as I could seldom look back to my former happiness; but now, when I shall be at some leisure, I shall not avoid the remembrance of thee, nor the grief for thy absence. Thou hast thy share with me; but I hope the course we have agreed upon will be some ease to us both. Mondays and Fridays, at five of the clock at night, we shall meet in spirit till we meet in person. Yet if all these hopes should fail, blessed be our God that we are assured we shall meet one day, in a better condition. Let that stay and comfort thy heart. Neither can the sea drown thy husband, nor enemies destroy, nor any adversity deprive thee of thy husband or children. Therefore I will only take thee now and my sweet children in my arms, and kiss and embrace you all, and so leave you with my God. Farewell, farewell.

Thine wheresoever
JO. WINTHROP

SAMUEL SEWALL (1652–1730)

Sewall is generally known as one of the judges who pronounced sentence of death upon the Salem witches in 1692. Lest the reader look askance at him on this account, let us consider three things : that belief in witches was very general in Sewall's day; that he felt compelled by his oath of office to pronounce judgment according to law ; and that the English law, which prevailed also in America, condemned a witch to death.[1] Moreover, Sewall, unlike others who were concerned in that frightful tragedy, not only saw his error but acknowledged it, standing up before the whole congregation while the

SAMUEL SEWALL

minister from the pulpit read aloud his confession and repentance. "And that was a brave man," as the old Saxons would say in all simplicity.

[1] This law was not repealed in England till 1735, some forty years after it became a dead letter in America (see p. 62).

In literature Sewall is chiefly famous for his *Diary ;* but he wrote several other things, among them being "The Selling of Joseph," which was probably the first antislavery tract published in this country. Reading even these minor works, we see clearly that the author was a philanthropist, a friend of negroes and Indians, a pioneer in the work of establishing women's rights, and a just man in all his ways :

> Stately and slow, with thoughtful air,
> His black cap hiding his whitened hair,
> Walks the Judge of the great Assize,
> Samuel Sewall, the good and wise.
> His face with lines of firmness wrought,
> He wears the look of a man unbought,
> Who swears to his hurt and changes not ;
> Yet touched and softened, nevertheless,
> With a grace of Christian gentleness ;
> The face that a child would climb to kiss,
> True and tender and brave and just,
> That man might honor and woman trust.[1]

Sewall's Diary. This budget of old Colonial news begins in 1673, while a young instructor in Harvard is "reading Heerboord's *Physick* to the senior sophisters," and ends in 1729, while the same man, old and honored, is "making a very good match" for his granddaughter. Between these two entries are thousands of others, which would seem dreary and commonplace did we not remember that they mark, like monotonous clock ticks, the slow march of a human life across the field of light and into the shadows.

To summarize such a detailed story of over half a century is quite impossible. The book is like an old attic, filled with all manner of useless things, forgotten and dust-covered. Here, as in Winthrop, the small and the great affairs of life are jumbled in hopeless confusion. In one breath we are told that the weather is foggy ; in the next that war is declared between France and England — one of the fateful French and Indian wars which

---

[1] From Whittier, "The Prophecy of Samuel Sewall."

kindled in America the spirit of national unity. Of this, however, Sewall says nothing, but flits on to his favorite subject of
funerals, and ends with a mention of what they did with the
treasure of Captain Kidd the pirate. Merely as a suggestion of
his style and varied matter, we copy a few entries that attract
our attention as do certain faces in a crowd :

1676, Oct. 9. Bro. Stephen visits me in the evening and tells me of a
sad accident at Salem, last Friday. A youth, when fowling, saw one by a
pond with black hair and was thereat frighted, supposing the person to be
an Indian, and so shot and killed him : came home flying with the fright
for fear of more Indians. The next day found to be an Englishman shot
dead. The actor in prison.

1677, July 8. New Meeting House. In sermon time there came in a
female Quaker, in a canvas frock, her hair disshevelled and loose like a
periwigg, her face black as ink, led by two other Quakers, and two others
followed. It occasioned the most amazing uproar that I ever saw.[1]

1685, Nov. 12. Mr. Moody preaches, from Is. 57 : 1, Mr. Cobbet's
funeral sermon. After, the minister of this town come to the Court to complain against a dancing master who seeks to set up here, and hath mixt
dances, and his time of meeting is Lecture Day [Thursday] and 't is reported
he should say that by one play he could teach more divinity than Mr. Willard
or the Old Testament. Mr. Moody said 't was not a time for New England
to dance. Mr. Mather struck at the root, speaking against mixt dances.

1686, Feb. 15. Jos. Maylem carries a cock at his back, with a bell in 's
hand, in the main street. Several follow him blindfolded and, under pretence
of striking him or 's rooster with great cart whips, strike passengers and
make great disturbance.[2]

Apr. 22. Two persons, one array'd in white, the other in red, goe
through the town with naked swords advanced, with a drum attending each
of them, and a quarter staff, and a great rout following, as is usual. It seems
't is a challenge to be fought at Capt. Wing's next Thursday. *Apr. 28.*
After the stage-fight, in the even, the souldier who wounded his antagonist
went, accompanyed with a drumm and about seven drawn swords, shouting
through the streets in a kind of tryumph.[3]

[1] This entry, with other passages from Colonial literature, suggest that the Puritans
were not intolerant of another's faith, but only of disorderly or offensive methods of
proselyting.

[2] This was probably Shrove Tuesday (called also Pancake Tuesday, and in French
Mardi Gras), the day before the beginning of Lent. It was a merry holiday in England
at this time.

[3] Evidently this was not a duel but a kind of military roistering. In the record of
1717 (*Sewall Papers*, III, 208) two officers, because of dueling, were fined, imprisoned
and obliged to give bonds to keep the peace.

June 6. Ebenezer Holloway, a youth of about eleven or twelve years old, going to help Jno. Hounsel, another Boston boy, out of the water at Roxbury, was drowned together with him. I followed them to the grave; for were brought to town in the night, and both carried to the burying place together, and laid near one another.

1692, Apr. 11. Went to Salem, where, in the meeting-house, the persons accused of witchcraft were examined. Was a very great assembly. 'T was awfull to see how the afflicted persons were agitated. Mr. Noyes pray'd at the beginning, and Mr. Higginson concluded. *Aug. 19.* (Dolefull Witchcraft!) This day George Burroughs, John Willard, Jno. Proctor, Martha Carrier and George Jacobs were executed at Salem, a very great number of spectators being present. Mr. Cotton Mather was there, Mr. Sims, etc. All of them said they were innocent, Carrier and all. Mr. Mather says they all died by a righteous sentence. Mr. Burroughs by his speech, prayer, protestation of his innocence, did much move unthinking persons, which occasions their speaking hardly concerning his being executed.

Nov. 6. Joseph threw a knop of brass and hit his sister Betty on the forhead, so as to make it bleed and swell; upon which, and for his playing at prayer time, and eating when return-thanks, I whiped him pretty smartly. When I first went in (called by his Grandmother) he sought to shadow and hide himself from me behind the head of the cradle; which gave me the sorrowful remembrance of Adam's carriage.

1699, June 21. A pack of cards are found strawed over my foreyard, which, 't is supposed, some might throw there to mock me.

1702, Feb. 19. Mr. I. Mather preached from Rev. 22 : 16, — " Night and morning star." Mention'd sign in the heaven, and in the evening following I saw a large cometical blaze, something fine and dim, pointing from the westward, a little below Orion.[1]

1704, June 30. After dinner, about 3 P.M. I went to see the execution [of pirates]. Many were the people that saw on Broughton's Hill. But when I came to see how the river was cover'd with people, I was amazed. 150 boats and canoes, saith Cousin Moody of York. He told [counted] them. Mr. Cotton Mather came, with Capt. Quelch and six others for execution, from the prison. When the scaffold was hoisted to a due height the seven malefactors went up. Mr. Mather prayed for them, standing on the boat. When the scaffold was let to sink, there was such a screech of the women that my wife heard it, sitting in the entry next the orchard, and was much surprised at it; yet the wind was sou-west. Our house is a full mile from the place.

---

[1] Sewall has other records of comets, one of which (Aug. 17–23, 1682) may be a reference to Halley's comet, which recently (1910) caused such extraordinary commotion. There is nothing to indicate that the Colonists felt any fear or concern before this mysterious visitor; and the ministers generally welcomed every comet and used it to emphasize some special point in their sermons.

1706, Nov. 10. This morning Tom Child the painter [1] died.

> Tom Child hath often painted Death,
> But never to the life before:
> Doing it now, he 's out of breath;
> He paints it once and paints no more.

1713, Apr. 19. The swallows have come; I saw three together.[2]

1716, Feb. 6. Sloop run away with by a whale, out of a good harbor at the Cape. How surprisingly uncertain our enjoyments in this world are!

1720, Jan. 23. This day a negro chimney-sweeper falls down dead into the Governour's house. Jury sits on him.

May 20. In the evening I join the Revd. Mr. William Cooper and Mrs. Judith Sewall in marriage. I said to Mr. Stoddard and his wife [parents of the bride] " Sir, Madam, the great honour you have conferr'd on the bridegroom and the bride by being present at this solemnity does very conveniently supersede any further enquiry after your consent. And the part I am desired to take in this wedding renders the way of my giving my consent very compendious: There 's no manner of room left for that previous question, Who giveth this woman to be married to this man?

" Dear child, you give me your hand for one moment, and the bridegroom forever. Spouse, you accept and receive this woman now given you, &c." Mr. Sewall pray'd before the wedding, and Mr. Coleman after. Sung the 115th Psalm from the ninth verse to the end. Then we had our cake and sack-posset.

The three bulky volumes of this old *Diary* are not books which we would recommend to the general reader. They have absolutely no literary charm; they are mostly dull records of commonplace events, made gloomy by many funerals but never once brightened by the play of imagination or humor. Yet somehow we have grown deeply interested in them, following their endless windings as one follows a trout stream, with continual expectation of catching something in the next pool. Nor are we disappointed. Here and there, amidst dreary details,

---

[1] It is generally supposed that Peter Pelham (d. 1751) was the first American artist. He came to this country in 1726, and his portrait of Cotton Mather (1727) is the first authentic portrait produced in America. But in this record Sewall evidently refers to a painter who preceded Pelham by at least twenty years.

[2] Every year Sewall joyfully records the arrival of these little harbingers. The first swallow was eagerly looked for, but not till three or more were seen together was spring announced. Hence, probably, the expression, " One swallow does not make a summer." Within our own recollection, boys were allowed to go barefoot as soon as they had seen three swallows together.

are fleeting glimpses of the little comedies of long ago, when fashions were different but human nature quite the same as in our own day. Whether the record gives pleasure or weariness to others depends, like fishing, entirely upon the taste of the individual.

Aside from the question of interest, Sewall's *Diary* has a twofold value : it gives realistic pictures of habits, beliefs, political and social customs in one corner of America at an early period of our history ; and it is one of the most intimate and detailed records of a human life that we possess. It shows the author, not as the world knew him, but as he knew himself. Whoever has the patience to read this old record will meet a man who reveals himself without vanity or concealment, who follows the call of duty as he hears it, and who makes no attempt to win even our good opinion. As he says (May 9, 1690) : " Now the good God, of His infinite grace, help me to perform my vows, give me a filial fear of Himself and save me from the fear of man."

WILLIAM BYRD (1674–1744)

Pleasantest of our early annalists is William Byrd of Virginia. We fancy him sitting in an easy-chair in front of his open fire, elaborately dressed, pipe at lips, a glass of negus at his elbow, and smiling as he dictates his pleasantries to his secretary.[1] Meanwhile, in his Boston study, Cotton Mather scratches away industriously with his own goose quill, till the cry is forced from him, " The ink in my standish is frozen ; my pen suffers a congelation."

Almost on the first page we are struck by this personal contrast between Byrd and the Puritan writers. The latter were men profoundly educated along certain lines, and their experience of life was deep but narrow. Outside the three immediate interests of religion, trade and government, they had little regard

---

[1] Byrd's manuscripts are in a copyist's handwriting, with numerous notes and corrections inserted by the author.

for the ways of the great world. Byrd's education was broad but shallow; and to education he added the unmistakable polish of travel and of habitual contact with the best society. In consequence he has a certain air of cosmopolitanism, suitable to any civilized age or nation, and far removed from the provincialism and intense individuality of the Puritans.[1]

WILLIAM BYRD

Another contrast between Byrd and other annalists is **The Cavalier in Literature** found in the essential motive of his books. Most of our Colonial authors cared nothing for literary effect; their only object was to present the facts and to establish the truth. With Byrd, however, enters a new element into our literature. He has that indefinite but vitalizing quality which we call style; he seeks to make the form of his work attractive, and so becomes definitely artistic. Remembering that few will read a book unless it have the virtue of being interesting, he inserts a variety of observations and experiences with the sole idea of entertaining us. So far so good; but unfortunately Byrd has so little of the Puritan regard for truth that he is willing to sacrifice it cheerfully for a jest, even in his historical narrative.[2] He writes very much like certain

---

1 The prevalent idea that the Puritans were confined to New England is erroneous. A substantial part of the population of Virginia and Maryland, for instance, was made up of Puritans. Prominent among them was Alexander Whittaker, whose *Good News from Virginia* (1613) is as far removed from Byrd, both in style and matter, as are the journals of Winthrop and Sewall.

2 A case in point is his witty but unjust treatment of North Carolina; another is his ridicule of Germans and Huguenots — simple, God-fearing folk, who added a most desirable element to the mixed Southern society of the early days.

Cavaliers of Charles II in England. He is gay, witty, charming ; his mockery is invariably good-natured ; his stories, though sometimes a little scandalous, are told as a gentleman of those days would tell them ; but he is superficial, and often gives a wrong impression of the people he is describing. In one of his narratives he remarks, " Our conversation with the ladies was like whip-sillabub, very pretty but had nothing in it." It is hardly too much to say that Byrd has written here an excellent criticism of his own writings. Certainly, after Bradford and Winthrop, he furnishes a pleasant,whip-sillabub kind of dessert to a somewhat heavy dinner.[1]

Byrd's Journals. Byrd's best-known work, the *History of the Dividing Line*,[2] is largely the story of a surveying party which first penetrated the Dismal Swamp and some two hundred miles of unexplored wilderness beyond. It begins, however, with a breezy sketch of the history of Virginia and North Carolina ; and here we see the gay Cavalier who must have his jest at any cost, and who is more concerned to entertain us than to limn a true picture of the pioneers. He tells us that Virginia was settled " by reprobates of good families," whose character he judges from the fact that " they built a chapel that cost fifty pounds and a tavern that cost five hundred." And then, with the irreverence of Mark Twain, he argues that, for the good of both races, the whites should have intermarried with the Indians : " For after all that can be said, a sprightly lover is the most prevailing missionary that can be sent among them or any other infidels." When he comes to North Carolina his mirth overflows, and he

---

[1] No satisfactory biography of Byrd has yet appeared. A sketch of his busy, useful life is given in the Introduction to *The Byrd Manuscripts* (edition of 1866). The long and flattering epitaph on Byrd's tombstone — upon which questionable source his biographers largely depend — is quoted in Campbell's *History of Virginia*.

[2] Byrd was one of three commissioners appointed (1728) by Governor Gooch to fix the boundary line between Virginia and North Carolina. His journal of the expedition was written soon afterwards. The manuscript volume containing this, and other of Byrd's journals, is still preserved in the family mansion " Brandon," on the James River. The works were first published as *The Westover Manuscripts*, in 1841. In later editions (by Wynne, 1866 ; by Basset, 1901) they are called *The Byrd Manuscripts*. Byrd's interesting letters are collected in the *Virginia Magazine of History and Biography* (1902).

devotes a large part of his sketch to satirizing the barbarism and ignorance of people " that live in a dirty state of nature and are mere Adamites, innocence only excepted."

After such an introduction, we are skeptical of Byrd's fitness as a historian ; but we are delighted with him as a writer and camp companion in following the adventures of the surveying party. Scattered through the book, like plums in a pudding, are interesting bits of natural history, and passing comments, scintillating and evanescent as the sparks of his camp fire, on the appearance of the wild country and the habits of the Indians :

" *1729*, *Oct. 11*. But bears are fondest of chestnuts, which grow plentifully towards the mountains, upon very large trees, where the soil happens to be rich. We were curious to know how it happen'd that many of the outward branches of those trees came to be brok off in that solitary place, and were inform'd that the bears are so discreet as not to trust their unwieldy bodies on the smaller limbs of the tree, that would not bear their weight; but after venturing as far as is safe, which they can judge to an inch, they bite off the end of the branch, which falling down, they are content to finish their repast upon the ground. In the same cautious manner they secure the acorns that grow on the weaker limbs of the oak. And it must be allow'd that, in these instances, a bear carries instinct a great way, and acts more reasonably than many of his betters, who indiscreetly venture upon frail projects that wont bear them."

" *1729*, *Oct. 13*. In the evening we examin'd our friend Bearskin [the Indian hunter] concerning the religion of his country, and he explain'd it to us, without any of that reserve to which his nation is subject.

" He told us he believ'd there was one Supreme God, who had several subaltern deities under him. And that this Master-God made the world a long time ago. That he told the sun, the moon and stars their business in the beginning, which they, with good looking after, have perform'd faithfully ever since. . . .

" He believ'd God had form'd many worlds before he form'd this; but that those worlds either grew old and ruinous, or were destroyed for the dishonesty of the inhabitants.

" That God is very just and very good, ever well pleas'd with those men who possess those God-like qualities. That he takes good people into his safe protection. . . . But all such as tell lies, and cheat those they have dealings with, he never fails to punish with sickness, poverty and hunger; and, after all that, suffers them to be knockt on the head and scalpt by those that fight against them.

" He believ'd that after death both good and bad people are conducted by a strong guard into a great road, in which departed souls travel together for some time, till at a certain distance this road forks into two paths, the one extremely levil, and the other stony and mountainous. Here the good are parted from the bad by a flash of lightning, the first being hurry'd away to the right, the other to the left.

" The right-hand road leads to a charming warm country, where the spring is everlasting, and every month is May; and as the year is always in its youth, so are the people; and particularly the women are bright as stars, and never scold. That in this happy climate there are deer, turkeys, elks, and buffaloes innumerable, perpetually fat and gentle, while the trees are loaded with delicious fruit quite throughout the four seasons. That the soil brings forth corn spontaneously, without the curse of labour, and so very wholesome that none who have the happiness to eat of it are ever sick, grow old, or dy.

" Near the entrance into this blessed land sits a venerable old man on a mat richly woven, who examins strictly all that are brought before him; and if they have behav'd well, the guards are order'd to open the crystal gate, and let them enter into the Land of Delights.

" The left-hand path is very rugged and uneaven, leading to a dark and barren country, where it is always winter. The ground is the whole year round cover'd with snow, and nothing is to be seen upon the trees but icicles. All the people are hungry, yet have not a morsel of any thing to eat, except a bitter kind of potato. . . . Here all the women are old and ugly, having claws like a panther. . . . They talk much, and exceedingly shrill, giving exquisite pain to the drum of the ear, which in that place of torment is so tender that every sharp note wounds it to the quick.

"At the end of this path sits a dreadful old woman on a monstrous toad-stool, whose head is cover'd with rattle-snakes instead of tresses, with glaring white eyes that strike a terror unspeakable into all that behold her. This hag pronounces sentence of woe upon all the miserable wretches that hold up their hands at her tribunal. After this they are deliver'd over to huge turkey-buzzards, like harpys, that fly away with them to the place above mentioned. Here, after they have been tormented a certain number of years, according to their several degrees of guilt, they are again driven back into this world, to try if they will mend their manners, and merit a place the next time in the regions of bliss.

" This was the substance of Bearskin's religion, and was as much to the purpose as cou'd be expected from a mere state of nature, without one glimps of revelation or philosophy. It contain'd, however, the three great articles of natural religion: the belief of a god; the moral distinction betwixt good and evil; and the expectation of rewards and punishments in another world." [1]

---

[1] From " History of the Dividing Line," *Byrd Manuscripts*, I, 106–109.

Two other works of Byrd are worthy of our attention. *A Journey to the Land of Eden* [1] is an interesting journal of wilderness travel and mild adventure, very similar to *The Dividing Line*. *A Progress to the Mines* [2] is extremely valuable for its pictures of Southern society, and especially of Colonel Spotswood, that strong fighter for American democracy, who is here seen in his home, his sternness all laid aside, as an armor that a man uses only when he goes out to battle with the world :

" Here I arriv'd about three o'clock, and found only Mrs. Spotswood at home, who receiv'd her old acquaintance with many a gracious smile. I was carry'd into a room elegantly set off with pier glasses, the largest of which came soon after to an odd misfortune. Amongst other favourite animals that cheer'd this lady's solitude, a brace of tame deer ran familiarly about the house, and one of them came to stare at me as a stranger. But unluckily spying his own figure in the glass, he made a spring over the tea table that stood under it, and shatter'd the glass to pieces, and falling back upon the tea table, made a terrible fracas among the china. This exploit was so sudden, and accompany'd with such a noise, that it surpriz'd me, and perfectly frighten'd Mrs. Spotswood. But 't was worth all the damage to shew the moderation and good humor with which she bore this disaster. In the evening the noble Colo. came home from his mines, who saluted me very civilly; and Mrs. Spotswood's sister, Miss Theky, who had been to meet him *en Cavalier*, was so kind too as to bid me welcome. We talkt over a legend of old storys, supp'd about 9, and then prattl'd with the ladys, til 't was time for a travellour to retire. . . .

" *Sept. 22.* We had another wet day, to try both Mrs. Fleming's patience and my good breeding. The N.E. wind commonly sticks by us 3 or 4 days, filling the atmosphere with damps, injurious both to man and beast. . . . Since I was like to have thus much leisure, I endeavour'd to find out what subject a dull marry'd man cou'd introduce that might best bring the widow to the use of her tongue. At length I discover'd she was a notable quack, and therefore paid that regard to her knowledge as to put some questions to her about the bad distemper that raged then in the country. . . . But for fear this conversation might be too grave for a widow, I turn'd the discourse, and began to talk of plays, and finding her taste lay most towards comedy, I offer'd my service to read one to her, which she kindly accepted.

[1] There is a double play on words in this title. Byrd's wilderness journey here carried him into North Carolina, of which Charles Eden was then governor (1713–1719), and into a virgin country which many would consider a natural paradise.

[2] The title refers to the iron mines, which ex-Governor Spotswood was the first to develop in this country.

She produced the 2d part of the *Beggar's Opera*,[1] which had diverted the town [London] for 40 nights successively, and gain'd four thousand pounds to the author. This was not owing altogether to the wit or humour that sparkled in it, but to some political reflections, that seem'd to hit the ministry. . . . After having acquainted my company with the history of the play, I read 3 acts of it, and left Mrs. Fleming and Mr. Randolph to finish it, who read as well as most actors do at a rehearsal. Thus we kill'd the time, and triumpht over the bad weather."

Significance of Byrd's Work. After the sobriety, the didactic earnestness of Colonial writers, these cheery irresponsible books of Byrd seem to us to possess a threefold value. They interest us, first of all, by their style. No matter what he writes about,

WESTOVER, VIRGINIA — HOME OF THE BYRDS

this author never fails to entertain and surprise us by some unexpected playfulness. Thus, he says of his friend, who was afflicted with the "mining malady" which swept over our country like a pestilence early in the eighteenth century, "We cheered our hearts with three bottles of pretty good Madeira, which made Drury talk very hopefully of his copper mines." And of an old Indian he says, "To comfort his heart I gave him a bottle of rum, with which he made himself very happy and all the family miserable for the rest of the night."

[1] A popular opera by John Gay, produced in London in 1728.

Again, Byrd is an admirable supplement to the early annalists with whom we have grown familiar. The literature of any period must reflect the whole life of a people ; and Byrd reveals a side of Colonial life, a bright and most attractive side, which is seldom chronicled in our histories. And finally, Byrd is neither teacher nor reformer, as most other Colonial writers are, but simply an observer. Life of every kind seems good to him, as if indeed God had just created it. He delights to describe it just as it is, and to give happy pictures of settlers and Indians without wishing to reform either. His *Dividing Line*, especially, with its breezy, outdoor atmosphere, its lively interest in wild life, its rovings by day and its camp fires under the stars by night, marks an excellent beginning of that fascinating series of Journals of Exploration, of which Parkman's *Oregon Trail* is perhaps the best-known example.

Various Chronicles of Colonial Days

We have given comparatively large space to Bradford, Winthrop, Sewall and Byrd for two reasons : because they are excellent types of Colonial writers ; and because it is better to become well acquainted with one representative author than to name the hundred or more who contributed to our early literature. "A good plain dinner," says the *Simple Cobbler*, "is more wholesome than the taste of many dishes, which take away the appetite without satisfying the hunger." As a suggestion for further study, we add a list of books which, in our judgment, are best worth reading.

Annals. John Smith and John Josselyn are generally included in the history of our literature ; but they were sojourners, not settlers or citizens, and have scarcely more claim on our attention than have Hakluyt and Purchas, who also wrote fascinating accounts of American exploration. Smith's best works are *A True Relation of Such Occurrences and Accidents of Note as Hath Happened in Virginia* (1608), *A Description of New England* (1616), and *The General History of Virginia, New England and the Summer Isles* (1624). Josselyn wrote *New England's Rarities Discovered in Birds, Beasts, Fishes,*

Serpents and Plants of that Country (1672), and *An Account of Two Voyages to New England* (1674). He is bitter against the Puritans, and many besides Longfellow [1] have been misled by his ravings; but the chief interest in his book lies in his frequent excursions into natural history — a queer, jumbled kind of animal lore, in which facts and absurdities are related with the same gravity.

Alexander Whittaker, called by Cotton Mather " our incomparable Whittaker," and known generally as the " Apostle to Virginia," wrote a noble appeal to England in his *Good News from Virginia* (1613). This book is worth reading if only to show that the Puritans of the South were in all essentials exactly like their northern compatriots.

Edward Winslow was the companion of Bradford on the *Mayflower*. His *Journal*, written in connection with Bradford, and long known as *Mourt's Relation*, and his *Good News from New England* (1624) give vigorous and interesting accounts of the Pilgrims during the first three years of their American history. These books should, if possible, be read in connection with Bradford's *Of Plimouth Plantation*.

William Wood, one of the most interesting of our early writers, wrote *New England's Prospect* (1634). The book is in two parts, one describing the natural features of the country, its woods and waters, its plant and animal life; the other describing the life and customs of the various Indian tribes. It is remarkably well written, contains many vivid, picturesque descriptions, and its general style suggests that of the Elizabethan prose writers.

Edward Johnson came to America with Winthrop and his Puritans, in 1630. He was a fine type of the early settler — brave, self-reliant, religious; a little bigoted, to be sure, yet level-headed enough to oppose the witchcraft delusion. The title of his poem, *The Wonder-working Providence of Zion's Saviour in New England* (1654), suggests the character of its contents. It is a kind of modern *Book of Exodus*, in which the Colonists are pictured as under the direct leadership of the Lord of Hosts, fighting the Lord's battles against seen and unseen foes. And the work does not suffer in interest from the fact that Johnson was himself a vigorous fighter, and that the ax and musket were more familiar to his hand than the goose quill.

The *Burwell Papers* (*c.* 1700), by some unknown writer, are interesting for their first-hand descriptions of that dramatic episode of Virginia's history known as Bacon's Rebellion (1647). Another

---

[1] Whittier and Longfellow both found material in Josselyn. See for instance Longfellow's " Tragedy of John Endicott."

noteworthy feature is the style of the unknown writer, which is in marked contrast to the vigor and sincerity of early Colonial authors. He abounds in mannerisms, and attempts to be witty even in scenes which call for reverence and simplicity. This artificial style indicates that the French influence, which prevailed in England after the restoration of Charles II, was introduced from England to America at the close of the seventeenth century. These *Burwell Papers* include a dirge on the death of Bacon, which seems to us one of the best bits of verse written in the entire Colonial period.

Satire and Criticism. Nathaniel Ward is famous for one sensational book, *The Simple Cobbler of Agawam* (1647).

The author's purpose is evident in his subtitle, which tells us that England and America are a pair of old shoes, sadly in need of repair, **The Simple** and that he proposes to mend them to the best of his **Cobbler** ability. His idea of mending is, evidently, to knock everything to pieces; so he proceeds merrily to pound away at the women for their style of dress, at religious leaders for their toleration, and at everything else which savors of a change from the good old ways of the forefathers — all this, remember, only twenty-seven years after the landing of the Pilgrims. The work begins vigorously, " Either I am in an apoplexy, or that man is in a lethargy who doth not now sensibly feel God shaking the heavens over his head and the earth under his feet." Nor does the primal vigor wane even for an instant. Every blow is that of a hammer; every criticism has the pungency of red pepper. This *Simple Cobbler* was the most popular of all our earliest books; and it still affords the reader plenty of amusement, though of an entirely different kind from what the writer intended.

George Alsop is remembered for one book, of mingled seriousness and drollery, called *A Character of the Province of Maryland* (1666), which is worthy to be placed with Ward's *Simple Cobbler*. It is written partly in racy prose, partly in doggerel verse after the manner of Butler's *Hudibras*, which had just appeared in England and was immensely popular. Though probably written with a serious purpose of defending Maryland from certain evil reports which had been sent abroad, the book is chiefly noticeable for its fun and nonsense. The chief criticism against the latter is that the humor is often a little too broad for modern readers.

History. Three serious histories of New England were attempted in early days by Nathaniel Morton, William Hubbard and Thomas Prince. Morton's *New England's Memorial* (1669) and Hubbard's

General History of New England (written *c.* 1680, first published 1815) are both written in a good style, but concern themselves too much with commonplace events. Prince is remarkable as the first historian in the English language who wrote history on a large scale and on a scientific basis, that is, with an eye single to the facts, and with a dependence on original sources of information.[1]

This honor is usually given to Gibbon, but the latter's *Decline and Fall of the Roman Empire* appeared some forty years after Prince had published his *Chronological History of New England* (1736). Omitting the huge introduction, which, after the fashion of those days, attempts to give a summary of the world's history from Adam to James I, Prince's *History* is an extremely careful and scholarly work, but unfortunately a little dry. The work is a fragment, only one volume having been finished, which carries the history of the Colonies down to 1630.

Robert Beverly was the first native-born historian of the Old Dominion. His *History of Virginia* (1705) gives us not only a political history of the Colony, but also a first-hand description of the people, of the natural features of the country, of its plant and animal life and of the ways of the Indians. Beverly was a man of fine character, a gentleman by birth and breeding, and all unconsciously he reflects much of his own fine qualities in his writings. There is a very pleasing manliness and simplicity in his work, which is one of the most interesting of Colonial histories.

Indian Narratives. In almost every book of the Colonial period we find references to the Indians, and the large space given to them shows how profound was the impression made by these silent rovers of the wilderness. Of many books dealing exclusively with the Indians, the best were written by Daniel Gookin, the friend and companion of John Eliot.[2] Gookin was a grand old American patriot, whose life reads like a romance. He wrote *Historical Collections of the Indians of New England* (frequently quoted in Thoreau's *Journal*) and *An Historical Account of the Doings and Sufferings of the Christian Indians in New England* (written *c.* 1677, published 1836). Gookin

[1] Prince made a remarkably good collection of original documents. This collection, still known as " The Prince Library," is preserved in the Public Library at Boston.

[2] The very mention of the savages always suggests the name of John Eliot, the heroic " Apostle to the Indians," who wrote much about them. Unfortunately, a large part of his work was lost, and the rest is so scattered that the modern reader has no access to it. Eliot is famous in the literature of knowledge for two works, his *Indian Grammar* (1666) and his *Translation of the Bible into the Indian Tongue* (1663). These works represent America's first contribution to the original and scholarly books of the world For a suggestion of Eliot's greatness, see pp. 67–68

also wrote a history of New England; but the manuscript was burned before it was published. Our literature suffered a great loss in that fire; for Gookin, by his scholarship, his judicial mind and his intense love of truth, was admirably fitted to write our early history.

Other writers on Indian subjects are John Mason, a soldier and Indian fighter, who wrote *A Brief History of the Pequot War* (1677); Mary Rowlandson, who was dragged from her burning home and carried off captive by the Indians, and who relates her experiences in *The Sovereignty and Goodness of God, a Narrative of the Captivity and Restoration of Mrs. Rowlandson* (1682); and John Williams, who was carried to Canada by the savages when Deerfield was attacked and burned, in 1704, and who gives a vivid story of Indian atrocities in *The Redeemed Captive* (1707).

Many other such books were written, but the four mentioned enable the reader to see the Indian from many different points of view.

JOHN ELIOT

Gookin was the friend of the natives, and is the only one of our early writers who understands the Indian character. Mason was a fighter, and delighted to write of battle, murder and sudden death; while Williams and Mrs. Rowlandson were innocent sufferers at the hands of the savages, who treated their captives with alternate ferocity and indifference. The stories of the latter writers were immensely popular for over a century in America, while the better work of Gookin remained unknown. It is due largely to fighting stories like Mason's, and to pictures of savage atrocity as drawn in *The Redeemed Captive*, that hatred of the Indians was deeply ingrained into the popular mind. Even at the present day it is difficult to make the average American understand that the Indians were often actuated by noble motives and possessed some admirable native virtues.

III. COLONIAL POETRY

Our literary historians commonly begin their story of Colonial verse with the *Bay Psalm Book* (1640),[1] and after critically examining its jolting lines they conclude that our ancestors had no soul for poetry. This is a sad and also an erroneous beginning; for the simple fact is that the *Bay Psalm Book* was never intended as poetry, as the translators tell us plainly in their preface. The book is a mere curiosity, and we would ignore it here were it not for the fact that it has been so often quoted "as a pitiful indication of the literary poverty of the days and the land in which it was popular."[2]

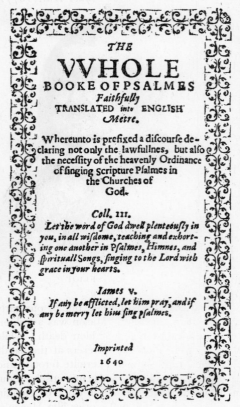

THE
VVHOLE
BOOKE OF PSALMES
Faithfully
TRANSLATED *into* ENGLISH
Metre.

Whereunto is prefixed a difcourfe declaring not only the lawfulnes, but alfo the neceffity of the heavenly Ordinance of finging Scripture Pfalmes in the Churches of God.

Coll. III.

Let the word of God dwell plenteoufly in you, in all wifdome, teaching and exhorting one another in Pfalmes, Himnes, and fpirituall Songs, finging to the Lord with grace in your hearts.

Iames V.

If any be afflicted, let him pray, and if any be merry let him fing pfalmes.

Imprinted
1640

TITLE-PAGE OF *THE BAY PSALM BOOK*

[1] This was the first book in English printed in this country. It was prepared by Richard Mather, John Eliot and several other learned ministers, and published by Stephen Daye, who in 1639 set up the first English press at Cambridge.

To the Franciscan monk, Juan de Zumarra, the first "Bishop of Mexico," whose vast diocese included a large section of the present United States, belongs the honor of introducing printing to America. The first book printed in the New World was probably a translation from Latin into Spanish of *The Spiritual Ladder*, by St. John Climacus, in 1535.

[2] See, for instance, Richardson, *American Literature*, II, 3-4, 6-7.

To understand this old relic, we must remember that the Colonists were a singing people, who used music in all their

Bay Psalm Book social gatherings. In their religious services they considered the wonderful poetry of the psalms most suitable for musical expression; and the first limitation placed on Richard Mather and his associates was that the Book of Psalms must be paraphrased in the meter of a few familiar tunes. The second limitation was even stricter. They were dealing with what they believed to be the Word of God, and their translation must give faithful account of every letter and accent, as a cashier is answerable for every penny that passes through his hands. Here is an average specimen of the result:

Aue Maria gratia

plena dominus tecũ.

FROM *DOCTRINA CHRISTIANA*, PRINTED IN MEXICO CITY BY JUAN PABLOS IN 1544

The first book printed in America that contained cuts to illustrate the text

> The earth Jehova's is
> and the fullness of it:
> The habitable world and they
> that thereupon doe sit.

It needs no greater critic than Touchstone to tell us that this is not poetry; but it can be smoothly sung to some grand old short-meter tunes, and it is a marvelously literal rendering of the Hebrew original — which was all that was desired or hoped for. We have perhaps forgotten that Bacon, of great literary renown, made a wretched failure when he attempted to put the psalms into English poetry ; that the Colonists attempted a new metrical translation simply because English poets had failed in the same task ; and that the makers of the *Bay Psalm Book* produced much better verses in Greek, Latin and English when they were free to follow their own invention.

Characteristics of Colonial Poetry. The first thing to strike the sympathetic reader is that these stern, practical settlers had a great hunger for poetry, a longing for ideal expression which suggests the man who cannot sing but whose feelings are deeply stirred when listening to a hymn by many voices. Practically all our Colonial writers felt the lyric impulse, and brightened their dull pages with poetry. That their verse is of poor quality may possibly arise from the fact that their thought was too high, their feeling too deep for poetic expression. God, freedom, duty, justice, immortality — these were the ideals of the Colonists ; and in all history we meet only two poets, Dante and Milton, who were fitted to express them. That the Colonists realized their limitation is often suggested, and is clearly expressed in a pathetic elegy by Urian Oakes, in 1667 :

> Reader, I am no poet; but I grieve.
> Behold here what that passiön can do
> That forced a verse without Appolo's leave,
> And whether the learned Sisters would or no.

A second characteristic — indicating that most of the settlers regarded themselves as Englishmen, and their writing as a part of English letters — is that our early poets all copy the prevailing fashion in England. Mrs. Bradstreet at first imitates Donne, Herbert and other " metaphysical " poets, whose influence dominated English literature in 1650. Richard Rich's *News from Virginia* (1610) is written in a popular English ballad style ; Benjamin Thompson's *New England's Crisis* (1675), an epic of Indian warfare, is modeled on the *Barons'*

Wars of Drayton; and Godfrey, most versatile of our early poets, copies in succession Chaucer, Spenser and Shakespeare. With the exception of Wigglesworth's *Day of Doom*, therefore, we shall find little that is original or distinctively American in Colonial poetry.

Less important, but still significant, is the classic tendency of our early poetry, suggesting that high regard for scholarship which is such a striking feature of the crude American settlements. The first poems written here (1621) were some excellent metrical translations of the poet Ovid, by George Sandys of Virginia. The first verses of our native scholars were in Greek or Latin; and judging their work by the specimens preserved in Mather's *Magnalia*, it was of excellent quality, comparing favorably with that of foreign universities of the same period. We may deplore this tendency of our first scholars; but it proceeded from a noble ideal of the early church, that literature, like religion, is of universal interest and must be preserved in a universal language.

ANNE DUDLEY BRADSTREET (1612–1672)

In 1650, when the Colonies were still in their infancy, there appeared in London an American book of poems with the following title:

"The Tenth Muse Lately Sprung up in America: or Several Poems, Compiled with Great Variety of Wit and learning, full of Delight, Wherein Especially is Contained a Complete Discourse and Description of the Four Elements, Constitutions and Ages of Man, Seasons of the Year; Together with an Exact Epitome of the Four Monarchies, viz., the Assyrian, Persian, Grecian, Roman; also a Dialogue between Old England and New Concerning the Late Troubles; with Divers Other Pleasant and Serious Poems. By a Gentlewoman in those parts." [1]

The Tenth Muse thus blazoned was Mrs. Anne Bradstreet, who is remarkable in three ways: as the author of our first book of

---

[1] This flattering title was not chosen by Mrs. Bradstreet, but by the London publisher, who was amazed that such poems could be written in the wilds of America.

poems, as the most extravagantly praised writer of Colonial times, and as the first literary woman to win a reputation among her American and English contemporaries.

Life. The author was a cultivated Puritan girl, daughter of Thomas Dudley, Governor of the Bay Colony. At sixteen she had married Simon Bradstreet, joined the company of wealthy Puritans who settled Boston, and from the refinement and comfort of her English home was suddenly transplanted to a cabin in the wilderness. Instead of the quiet English fields, she looked upon a rude clearing where corn sprouted amid the smoking stumps. Instead of the peaceful sounds that soothe all the senses in an English twilight, she heard the uncanny hooting of owls, the wail of the whippoorwill, the terrifying clamor of the wolf pack in the darkening woods. No wonder her sensitive nature rebelled at the change. Like Spenser in Ireland, she regarded herself as an exile, and like him she rose triumphant over her surroundings. " After I was convinced it was the way of God, I submitted to it," she tells us in one of her prose sketches.

In 1644 this frail exile held loyally at her husband's side as he pushed deeper into the wilderness. In the northern part of Andover, near the Merrimac, they made their pitch on a picturesque hillside, which is still known as the Bradstreet farm. Here she wrote her poems ; but though she was the first American to win a literary reputation, we can hardly think of her as a literary woman. She had eight children to care for, and her writing was done in brief intervals of rest from the day's labor. So we are reminded of another woman who, in the same town, amid the same ceaseless household cares, finished *Uncle Tom's Cabin*, a book which moved the whole civilized world, some two centuries later.

Our First Book of Poems. It is a curiosity of Mrs. Bradstreet's first book that it contains hardly a suggestion of that early American life which now seems so romantic. In her pioneer experiences there was abundant material for epic and lyric poetry ; but she never wrote them. The first touch of her pen sent her mind back to England on a holiday, and she simply copied what she had read there. So fully is she occupied with her English models that she does not see the wonderful nature about her, and writes of larks and nightingales instead of our familiar thrushes and bobolinks. Even in "A Love Letter" she speaks not by the heart but by the book :

> Phœbus make haste; the day 's too long; begone!
> The silent night 's the fittest time for moan;
> But stay this once, unto my suit give ear,
> And tell my griefs in either hemisphere.

Strange lines these from a woman who has just milked the cow and dropped the oaken door bar to protect the stock from wolves and Indians ; but they are found by hundreds in Mrs. Bradstreet's poems. Curiously enough, the only reflection of real life in our first volume of poetry touches the question of woman's rights. After describing the glories of Queen Elizabeth, she takes this sly shot at man's superior wisdom :

> Now say, have women worth, or have they none?
> Or had they some, but with our Queen is 't gone?
> Nay, masculines, you have thus taxed us long;
> But she, though dead, will vindicate our wrong.
> Let such as say our sex is void of reason,
> Know 't is a slander now, but once was treason.

In her later work our poet is plainly an American woman rather than an English exile. The Andover farm is now a home. Nature, at first wild and stern, grows intimate and kind ; and our poet is less dependent on a library for inspiration. Her verse in consequence becomes more simple, more true ; and though we may not call it excellent, we are interested in it as an early attempt to reflect life and human emotion in poetry. In the following lines from "Contemplation" the reader may note three significant things : that the thought and feeling are natural ; that the flow of the verse suggests the melody of Spenser ; and that we look not upon a foreign but upon the dear, familiar landscape of our own country:

> I heard the merry grasshopper then sing,
> The black-clad cricket bear a second part,
> They kept one tune, and played on the same string,
> Seeming to glory in their little art.

Shall creatures abject thus their voices raise,
And in their kind resound their Maker's praise:
Whilst I, as mute, can warble forth no higher lays?

. . . .

Under the cooling shadow of a stately elm,
  Close sat I by a goodly river's side,
Where gliding streams the rocks did overwhelm;
  A lonely place, with pleasures dignified.
I once that loved the shady woods so well,
Now thought the rivers did the trees excel,
And if the sun would ever shine, there would I dwell.

MICHAEL WIGGLESWORTH (1631–1705)

The first and probably the greatest " sensation " in American literature appeared, not yesterday in a popular novel, but two and a half centuries ago, when Wigglesworth published his *Day of Doom* (1662), a gloomy and terrible picture of the Last Judgment. Unlike the modern sensation, it had real power; it first startled attention and then held it firmly, and for nearly a century was the most widely read secular book in America. This in itself is warrant for us to examine it a little more closely than is commonly done.

Who was Wigglesworth? The author of the poem, Michael Wigglesworth, was minister of the church in Malden, Massachusetts. In a funeral sermon, Cotton Mather calls him " a feeble little shadow of a man "; but this is one of Mather's queer compliments. It minimizes the weak body to magnify the soul, which was mighty, and the imagination, which was tremendous. Wigglesworth was a lifelong sufferer from disease, and his own pain led him to study medicine, that he might relieve the pains of others. For years he was minister and physician to the frontier town; and in the mortal sins and sufferings of humanity his imagination saw only a forecast of eternal retribution — just as his English contemporary Bunyan brooded over future torments amid the flame and smoke of his tinker's forge. Occupied with the glory of the Lord, Wigglesworth was blind to the glory of his fellow men. For him earth had lost all its beauty when Adam wandered out of Paradise; it was an evil place, to be run through

The DAY of

DOOM:

OR,

A Poetical Defcription of the
Great and Laft

Judgment.

With a fhort Difcourfe about

ETERNITY.

By *Michael Wigglefworth*, A. M. Teacher of the Church at *Maldon* in *N. E.*

The Sixth Edition, Enlarged with
Scripture and Marginal Notes.

Acts 17. 31. *Becaufe he hath appointed a Day in the
which he will Judge the World in Righteoufnefs, by
that Man whom he hath Ordained.*——
Mac. 24. 30. *And then fhall appear the Sign of the
Son of Man in Heaven, and then fhall all the Tribes
of the Earth Mourn, and they fhall fee the Son of Man
coming in the Cloude of Heaven, with power and great
glory.*

Boston, Printed by *J. Allen*, for *N. Boone*
at the Sign of the Bible in *Cornhill.* 1715.

TITLE-PAGE OF THE *DAY OF DOOM*
By Michael Wigglesworth, 1715

quickly in order to get to heaven. We may infer his idea of life from the curt leave which he took of it:

> Now farewell, world, in which is not my treasure;
> I have in thee enjoyed but little pleasure.

In short, Wigglesworth was a man doubly acquainted with suffering. He saw no good in this life, no hope save for a chosen few in the future; and he let a powerful but morbid imagination play about one of the most powerful and morbid theological systems that have influenced humanity. Here is the secret of the man and his book.

The Day of Doom. Wigglesworth's chief work is generally regarded as a mere literary curiosity; but there is, perhaps, a deeper meaning to be read in it. Our first criticism is reflected in a smile, for this terrible poem, dealing with stupendous themes, is set to a measure that suggests jigging or whistling:

> With iron bands they bind their hands,
> and cursëd feet together,
> And cast them all, both great and small,
> into that Lake for ever;
> Where day and night, without respite,
> they wail, and cry, and howl
> For tort'ring pain which they sustain
> in body and in Soul.

It is obviously impossible to be impressed by anything that runs to the tune of "Yankee Doodle," and our first experience of the *Day of Doom* is like that of our first jack-o'-lantern — a frightful, demoniac face gleaming out of the darkness, which upon brave examination turns out to be a candle in a hollow pumpkin. So the poem seems ludicrous to us now; but two centuries ago it was very different, as were comets and other misunderstood things. Here was a theme with which all men and children were familiar. It had been drilled into them with their first reading lessons, in the *New England Primer*. They had heard it expounded in many a dreary sermon. They had brooded and trembled over it in the silence of the night. And suddenly, like a gorgeous moth out of an old gray cocoon, it appeared in new form, vivid, picturesque, and in a lively meter that set itself in the memory. It was this unusual combination of matter and manner, of a mournful theme and a jocund measure, that largely accounted for the popularity of the poem.

Our next impression is that, under the jigging lines and merciless theology of the *Day of Doom*, the soul of a poet is

TITLE-PAGE OF THE *NEW ENGLAND PRIMER*

struggling blindly for expression. We have not quoted the most familiar and ferocious stanzas, because our repugnance at the ideas expressed prevents a just appreciation of the power of their expression ; but one who can lay aside his prejudice finds many a fine line to suggest that, had Wigglesworth lived in a different environment, he might well have created a noble and enduring work. For he had the genius of an epic poet. His power is evident from the fact that he revived an old theme and made it live for a full century. Since the Miracle plays, which invariably ended with *Domesday*, many poets have written of the Last Judgment, and none of them compares in vigor or imaginative power with this " little feeble shadow of a man " in Malden.

Another characteristic of this poem is that it reflects the sternly logical trait which once dominated our politics as well **Essence of** as our theology, and which is reflected as strongly in **Calvinism** Adams or Calhoun as in Wigglesworth or Edwards. All these men disregard emotions, start with an accepted premise, and drive straight to a conclusion. In the *Day of Doom*, God is simply a judge who must interpret a law without pity or favor. He is not Father, or Creator, but simply Logic. All classes of men appear before him, and each makes argument based upon the proposition that

In Adam's fall
We sinnëd all,

which was the first sentence of the *Primer* in which Colonial children learned to read. The Judge refutes their claims by more logical arguments, and away they go to torment. Here is the nub of the whole poem. It confuses the true and the merely logical, forgetting that, if there be an error in the premise, every logical step leads farther away from the truth. The *Day of Doom* is, therefore, an epitome of the apparent strength and essential weakness of that mighty theological system which dominated a large part of our country in the early days. It shows the effect of such a system on a poet's imagination, just as *The Freedom of the Will* illustrates its influence on the human intellect.

Thomas Godfrey (1736–1763)

If one's sympathy is touched at the sight of Wigglesworth, shackled by a terrible theology, one's whole heart must go out to Thomas Godfrey, a poet by instinct, whose youth was compassed with difficulties, and who died, like Keats, just as his powers reached maturity. He is one of the poets whom we measure not by his achievement but by his unfulfilled promise.

Biographical Outline. Godfrey was the son of a poor Philadelphia glazier and mathematician, whom we meet occasionally in Franklin's *Autobiography.* His early education was of the most primitive kind ; and at thirteen, being left an orphan, he was " bound out " as an apprentice to learn the watchmaker's trade. For eight years he endured and hated this slavery, not because it made him work, but because it prevented him from following his poetic genius. At twenty-one he enlisted as a soldier in the French and Indian War, and served as a lieutenant under Washington. A few years later we find him, still wandering and unsatisfied, in North Carolina. Here, in intervals of hard labor, he wrote his *Prince of Parthia,* probably the first dramatic work printed on American soil ; and here he died, with all his soul's ambition unfulfilled, in 1763. He had contributed many verses to the *American Magazine,*[1] and these were collected and published by his friend and fellow poet, Nathaniel Evans.

Works. The slender volume called *Juvenille Poems, with The Prince of Parthia, a Tragedy* (1765), contains all of Godfrey's work. Judged simply as poetry, in comparison with the works of English masters, these verses are crude and immature ; but the student has other reasons for being interested in them. The very titles suggest that a new spirit has entered American literature. Here are odes, love songs, pastorals — very different, truly, from the gloomy fancies of Wigglesworth. One feels as if he had opened by mistake an English book of the early Elizabethan period. Here is " The Court of Fancy," evidently borrowed from Chaucer's " House of Fame " ; but the man who suggests Chaucer has at least entered the realm of good poetry. And here is " The Wish," which is interesting because Oliver Wendell Holmes may have borrowed or parodied it :[2]

[1] The first magazines in this country appeared in Philadelphia. These were the *General Magazine*, published by Franklin (1741), and the *American Magazine*, published by John Webbe, a few years later.

[2] Compare Godfrey's whole poem with Holmes, " A Modest Wish."

> I only ask a moderate fate,
>   And, though not in obscurity,
> I would not, yet, be placed too high;
>   Between the two extremes I 'd be,
> Not meanly low, nor yet too great,
>   From both contempt and envy free.

The Prince of Parthia is Godfrey's last work, and in reading it the student will feel most regret at the author's untimely death. For, considering all the circumstances, it is a remarkable dramatic poem. The plot is admirably constructed; the action is vigorous; the characters are well drawn and consistent; the interest advances steadily to the climax; and throughout the drama there are many suggestions of genuine poetry. It is written in blank verse, "Marlowe's mighty line," and is thoroughly Elizabethan in spirit. Note, in the first act, these men who plot treason in a setting of storm and darkness:

> *Vardanes.*   Heavens! what a night is this!
>
> *Lysias.*   'T is filled with terror,
> Some dred event beneath this horror lurks,
> Ordained by fate's irrevocable doom, —
> Perhaps Arsaces' fall; and angry heaven
> Speaks it in thunder to the trembling world.
>
> *Vardanes.*   Terror indeed! It seems as sickening Nature
> Had given her order up to general ruin:
> The heavens appear as one continued flame;
> Earth with her terror shakes; dim night retires,
> And the red lightning gives a dreadful day,
> While in the thunder's voice each sound is lost.
> Fear sinks the panting heart in every bosom;
> E'en the pale dead, affrighted at the horror,
> As though unsafe, start from their marble jails,
> And howling through the streets are seeking shelter.
>
> .   .   .   .
>
> Why rage the elements? They are not cursed
> Like me! Evanthe frowns not angry on them;
> The wind may play upon her beauteous bosom,
> Nor fear her chiding; light can bless her sense,
> And in the floating mirror she beholds
> Those beauties which can fetter all mankind.
>
> .   .   .   .

Lysias. My lord, forget her; tear her from your breast.
Who, like the Phœnix, gazes on the sun,
And strives to soar up to the glorious blaze,
Should never leave ambition's brightest object,
To turn and view the beauties of a flower.

- *Vardanes.* O Lysias, chide no more, for I have done.
Yes, I 'll forget the proud disdainful beauty;
Hence with vain love. Ambition, now, alone
Shall guide my actions. Since mankind delights
To give me pain, I 'll study mischief too,
And shake the earth, e'en like this raging tempest.

. . . .

Lysias. Then, haste to raise the tempest.
My soul disdains this one eternal round,
Where each succeeding day is like the former.
Trust me, my noble prince, here is a heart
Steady and firm to all your purposes;
And here 's a hand that knows to execute
Whate'er designs thy daring breast can form,
Nor ever shake with fear.[1]

Significance of Godfrey's Work. The publication of Godfrey's poems (1765) at the end of the Colonial period marks an epoch in the history of American letters. Our earliest writers were all men of affairs; they used literature as a means to an end — to record historic events, to teach moral and religious lessons. Godfrey regards literature not as a means but as a most desirable end in itself. He seeks beauty alone, and proceeds on the assumption of Emerson's " Rhodora," that " beauty is its own excuse for being." His little book suggests, therefore, that our writers had at last freed themselves from the Puritan's chief concern in otherworldliness, and it marks the definite beginning of artistic literature in America.[2]

[1] The bombast of some of these lines suggests the influence of Marlowe; a few others are plainly copied from Shakespeare.

[2] In the broadest sense, our literature includes all the written records of the nation; in the strict sense, only those books which may be considered as works of art properly belong to literature. Definition is difficult, but we may fairly sum up the subject by saying: all art is the expression of life in forms of truth and beauty; and literature is the particular art which expresses life in words that appeal to our own sense of the true and the beautiful.

IV. THEOLOGICAL WRITERS

From the many writers who reflect the dominant religious interest of Colonial life we select only Cotton Mather and Jonathan Edwards. These were giants in their own generation, and they are still, in widely different ways, the two most remarkable men in the whole history of our literature.

Cotton Mather (1663–1728)

Over the door of his study Cotton Mather wrote, "Be short," which is the only unadorned sentence we have found in all his writings. This was for other people, lest they should waste his precious time and obscure another motto which he had written on his heart, "Be fruitful." And a more fruitful man after his kind was never seen. He published some four hundred works, and left thousands of pages of manuscript, including a treatise on medicine and a huge commentary on the Scriptures, which are still waiting for a publisher. He was an extraordinary genius, whom to judge is ex-

COTTON MATHER

ceeding difficult, partly because his works and ways are often contradictory, partly because many of his biographers, in their eagerness to prove him a saint or a fanatic, have failed to make an impartial study of their subject. From desultory reading one

is apt to get the impression that Mather was an intolerant
dogmatist, and a monster in the matter of the Salem witches;
so we begin our story by recording two unnoticed details : that he
went fishing in Spy Pond and fell out of the boat; and that
whenever he visited a school he used his great influence to get
the girls and boys a half holiday. These trifles suggest that
Mather was at least quite human. Moreover, he wrote the first
book of American heroes, made the first conscious appeal to
American patriotism ; and that is no trifle, but a thing to honor
and to remember.

Life. Cotton Mather marks at once the splendor and decline of
the " Mather Dynasty " [1] in Boston. He was a precocious child, who
began at five years to display the wonderful memory of a Macaulay
and the intellectual curiosity of a Gladstone. At twelve he entered
Harvard, having an amazing acquaintance with Greek and Latin
authors ; at eighteen he had literally " compassed the whole field of
human knowledge " ; at twenty he was minister of the Old North
Church, and towered head and shoulders above all his learned
contemporaries.

For the next half century Mather's " fruitfulness " almost passes
the bounds of belief. In an average year he would produce a score
of books and pamphlets ; write and deliver some two hundred sermons and lectures ; keep up an enormous correspondence with great
men in foreign countries ; be incessantly active in politics, and attend
faithfully to the thousand small duties of a large parish. He was a
leader in all philanthropic work, in temperance reform, in forming the
earliest Young People's Society of Christian Workers, in ransoming
prisoners from Canada, in establishing schools for the education of
negroes, in sending missionaries to the heathen. And with all this, he
gave many hours each day to private devotion ; he studied and read

---

[1] Our first Mather, Richard, a learned Puritan from England, became a man of light
and leading in the Bay Colony. His son, Increase Mather, was for sixty years minister
of the Old North Church, the largest in the country, at a time when the church was the
center of Colonial life. He was, moreover, president of Harvard for sixteen years, and
a trusted agent of the Colonies in England. Our present hero was the son of Increase
Mather. We shall understand him better if we remember that he and his father opposed
the growing freedom of the churches and the liberal teaching of the colleges. Because
of their opposition, Increase was ousted from the presidency of Harvard, and Cotton
Mather never won it, thus failing in his dearest ambition.

prodigiously; he kept innumerable fasts, vigils and thanksgivings. One can only wonder how human nerves could stand such a strain for fifty years, and repeat with that heroic Jesuit, Bressani, who survived all manner of tortures among the Iroquois, "I could never have believed it was so hard to kill a man."

As we study Mather in the midst of his excellent activities, our feelings shift from one extreme to the other; for we are dealing with a man of contradictions, who fasts in secret like an ancient saint, and plays to the gallery like a modern politician. His course at the witch-craft trials was bitterly scored by his enemies, and critics ever since have cried fanaticism, as if it were the only part he played in the tragedy. Yet he was probably the only man in the country, or in the world, who made a scientific study of the alleged witches, taking some of the poor creatures to his own home, watching over them, recording their symptoms. And by strengthening their weak wills, by keeping them in a cheerful, hopeful atmosphere, he effectually cured some that else had been surely hanged. Moreover, in connection with twelve other ministers, he urged the judges to exercise compassion, and submitted rules of evidence, which if followed would have saved every witch from death. From one point of view he is a mere wonder-hunter, as credulous as a Hottentot; from another he is a scientist, upholding some theory far in advance of his age, or laying the foundations for what is now known as organized charity. So, though he loved applause as a miser loves gold, he flung popularity to the dogs when he urged inoculation against the regular scourge of smallpox; and this at a time when magistrates, people and almost every doctor in the Colonies were crying out against inoculation as the work of the devil.

In his inner life, also, Mather is still a puzzle. He is ascetic, spending whole days and nights fasting in his study, "knocking at the door of Heaven." There, he tells us, he is "irradiated with celestial and angelic influences, . . . rewarded from Heaven with communications that cannot be uttered." Yet he is as fond as another man of the good things of life, and commends this saying of Alphonsus: "Among so many things as are by men possessed or pursued, all the rest are bubbles beside these: old wood to burn, old wine to drink, old friends to converse with, and old books to read." Like Macaulay, he loves society, is cheerful and animated in public, attracting attention, charming everybody by his brilliant conversation. Yet he is a man of sorrows and acquainted with grief. The churches grow liberal, ignoring all his efforts to bind them; he fights a losing battle alone; he is thwarted in his dearest ambition, to become president of Harvard; his third wife is a terrible trial; his children die one by one; his dearest son Increase, the pride and joy of Cotton

HARVARD COLLEGE IN 1726

Mather's heart, is a reprobate. And this is the deepest sorrow, save one, that a man is ever called upon to bear. A cry as of mortal anguish breaks from his lips:

"Ah, my son Increase! My son, my son! My heart is water and my eyes are a fountain of tears. . . . Oh, my God, I am oppressed; undertake for me."

Here, one would think, is a winepress that Mather must tread alone. Next day he is out with a published sermon, parading in public the grief which another man hides deep in his soul, though it burn like coals of fire.

So, wherever we attempt to touch the real Cotton Mather, we are met and baffled by a contradiction, a jumble of piety and vanity, of wisdom and foolishness. One cannot judge such a man. We record simply that his last word was a paradox, like himself; that on his deathbed he cried out, "My last enemy is come; I would say, my best friend." A few hours later his contemporaries were saying that "the principal ornament of this country and the greatest scholar that ever was bred in it" had passed away.

Works of Cotton Mather. We merely suggest the variety of Mather's work when we say that for half a lifetime, of which the year 1700 is a dividing point, he was clerk, bellman and newspaper for a Colonial city, giving expression to all its thoughts and emotions. No matter what the event, nothing was complete till Mather, like an echo, had repeated it. In consequence, his pamphlets and sermons furnish a kind of history and detailed commentary of his age and neighborhood. One would suppose that an earthquake, which shook down houses and tumbled people out of their beds, might of itself make a reasonably strong impression ; but no, the echo is the main thing. Hardly has the last rumble died away before the press begins to labor with Mather's *Boanerges, an Essay to Strengthen the Impression Produced by Earthquakes*. This attempt to paint the lily, or put an extra terror on earth's convulsion, is typical of our author. Are witches abroad? Does a comet flame in the heavens? Is there rumor of a monstrous snake on Newbury marshes? Hard on the heels of the event,

> Cotton Mather came galloping down
> All the way to Newbury town,
> With his eyes agog and his ears set wide,
> And his marvelous inkhorn at his side ;
> Stirring the while in the shallow pool
> Of his brains for the lore he learned at school,
> To garnish the story, with here a streak
> Of Latin, and there another of Greek :
> And the tales he heard and the notes he took,
> Behold ! are they not in his Wonder-Book? [1]

We shall not weary the reader with even a list of the books that flowed from the pen of this ready writer. One of the most practical is *Bonifacius* (1710), sometimes called *Essays to Do Good*,[2] which influenced the life of Franklin. Other significant works are *Parentator*, a biography of his father, written in

---

[1] From Whittier, " Double-Headed Snake of Newbury."
[2] The title runs, " Bonifacius, an Essay upon the Good that is to be Devised and Designed by Those who Desire to Answer the Great End of Life."

pedantic style, but illumined by a lovely filial spirit; *Memorable Providences Relating to Witchcraft,* which established Mather's reputation as an authority in the uncanny subject, and *Wonders of the Invisible World,* consisting largely of the history of the Salem witches.

That this last work should be often reprinted and become the measure of Mather's mind seems to us little less than scandalous. **Witchcraft** For it is one of the least of his productions, and it has given readers a sadly distorted idea of Colonial life. Even our historians, misled by this work, still refer to witchcraft as a Puritan delusion which flourished chiefly in New England. As a matter of fact, witchcraft flourished for ages before the Puritans were heard of; and our Colonists were the first people in all the world to recognize the delusion, and to treat it as they treated wolves and rattlesnakes. When America was settled, belief in witchcraft was so general in Europe that no man dared openly deny it; witches were racked, burned and tortured by thousands; and the detection of witchcraft, with its following "kill or cure," was a regular profession. Yet it was denounced and opposed in New England from the beginning. Like many another noxious germ, witchcraft was brought over and widely planted in America, where the dark forests, the screaming of unknown beasts at night, the hideously painted savages, — everything external favored the increase of the superstition. And it speaks volumes for the character of our first settlers that this horrible fungus, which flourished all over civilized Europe, found root here in only one spot, — a soil made ready by numerous descendants of some feeble-minded immigrants, who were brought here for the profit of the early transportation companies.[1] There it grew weakly for a brief period, and was then rooted out and destroyed. Here, in a nutshell, is the real meaning of the Salem witchcraft.[2]

[1] Long after witchcraft was stamped out, William Douglass, a physician, characterized the Salem district in his day as "a place where hypochondriac, hysteric and other maniac disorders prevaile." Douglass was the author of a racy work called *A Summary Historical and Political, of the . . . British Settlements in North America* (1747–1751).

[2] It is significant that American historians make a mighty ado over the nineteen witches of Salem, while European nations are silent over the thousands they have slain. In the little city of Treves alone, over 7000 witches were put to death; and the number killed in European countries is estimated at 300,000. Moreover the torture, burning and unspeakable barbarism of European trials were all sternly suppressed at Salem. And though our writers still speak of the "burning of witches," there was never a witch burned in New England.

The Magnalia. The reader will do well to skip all minor
works, except *Bonifacius*, and begin with *Magnalia Christi
Americana, or The Ecclesiastical History of New England*
(1702). This is the heroic work over which Mather labors, fasts
and prays for nine years, like Fra Angelico on his knees painting the glorious face of Madonna. It is a strange book. Like
the *Anatomy of Melancholy* and *Sartor Resartus*, it cannot be
classified, since there is nothing like it in all literature.

Book I. *Antiquities*. It reports the design whereon, the manner wherein, and the people whereby the several colonies of New England were
planted.

Book II. *Ecclesiarum Clypei*. It contains the lives of the governors
and magistrates that have been shields unto the churches.

Book III. *Polybius*. It contains the lives of many divines by whose
ministry the churches have been illuminated.

Book IV. *Sal Gentium*. It contains an account of the New-English
University [Harvard] and the lives of some eminent persons therein
educated.

Book V. *Synodicum Americanum*, Acts and Monuments. It contains
the faith and order in the churches.

Book VI. *Thaumaturgus*. It contains many illustrious discoveries and
demonstrations of Divine Providence in remarkable mercies and judgments.

Book VII. *Ecclesiarum Prælia*, or A Book of the Wars of the Lord.
It contains the afflictive disturbances which the churches of New England
have suffered from their various adversaries.

One who reviews these books — for few ever read the
Magnalia systematically — gets the impression that he is
wandering through a museum. Here are odds and ends gleaned
from all the fields of human knowledge ; quotations from a
thousand works ; allusions to a hundred unknown authors ;
mottoes, puns, witticisms, biography, poetry, moral lessons
from Latin, Greek and Hebrew worthies. In a single paragraph,
relating to some local event, Mather introduces a story from
Suidas, a quotation from Gregory Nazianzen, and a motto from
Rabbi Kimchi. In a single book we have taled nearly a thousand
good mottoes, anecdotes and quotations. While this literary
shower falls upon us, Mather talks incessantly, like a guide in

a picture gallery. He has a marvelously stored memory, an elfish imagination, and he loves the queer, the fantastic, the unexpected. Every subject he touches is like a famous nursery pie ; no sooner does he open it than out come four-and-twenty blackbirds and straight begin to sing.

This is the first impression, from the first book of the *Magnalia*, — the impression of a pedant displaying his extraor-**Motive of** dinary knowledge ; and the majority of historians end **the Magnalia** here, more 's the pity. For this big book, with all its hotchpotch, is illumined by a great purpose. The monks of the Middle Ages had a motto, *Ad majorem gloriam dei*, which explains their own literary work and the loving care with which they illumined a missal or a manuscript of the Gospels. Mather, who feared and misjudged these monks, worked in the same spirit and added a significant word to their noble motto. " For the love of my country and the greater glory of God" is written across the greater part of the *Magnalia*.[1] So let us read the second book, giving the history of our early magistrates.

Here one may find that Cotton Mather has the root of the matter in him, and anticipates Carlyle in writing history. According to Carlyle, history is essentially the story of great men who have inspired every historical movement. That is Mather's idea precisely, and he writes in the same spirit. If we seek for his motive in the enormous labor of preparing these biographies, we shall find it noble and patriotic. " Their souls are in Heaven ; their names also should be written there," he says of his heroes with rare simplicity. And again :

" I please myself with the hope that there will yet be found among the sons of New England those young gentlemen by whom the copies given in this history shall be written again, and that saying of old Chaucer be remembered : ' To do the gentle deeds, — that makes the gentleman.' " [2]

[1] Critics vary greatly in their estimate of the *Magnalia*. Thus, Professor Wendell (*A Literary History of America*, p. 48) regards it as "a passionate controversial tract," written to uphold ancient doctrine and to prevent Harvard from becoming liberal. Some parts of the *Magnalia* doubtless support such a theory, but a candid reading of the whole work leaves us with a very different impression.

[2] *Magnalia*, I, 108.

Magnalia Christi Americana:

OR, THE

Ecclesiastical History

O F

NEW-ENGLAND,

FROM

Its First Planting in the Year 1620. unto the Year
of our LORD, 1698.

In Seven BOOKS.

I. Antiquities : In Seven Chapters. With an Appendix.
II. Containing the Lives of the Governours, and Names of the Magistrates
of *New-England :* In Thirteen Chapters. With an Appendix.
III. The Lives of Sixty Famous Divines, by whose Ministry the Churches of
New-England have been Planted and Continued.
IV. An Account of the University of *Cambridge* in *New-England* ; in Two
Parts. The First contains the Laws, the Benefactors, and Vicissitudes of
Harvard College ; with Remarks upon it. The Second Part contains the Lives
of some Eminent Persons Educated in it.
V. Acts and Monuments of the Faith and Order in the Churches of *New-Eng-
land*, passed in their Synods ; with Historical Remarks upon those Venerable
Assemblies ; and a great Variety of Church-Cases occurring, and resolved by
the Synods of those Churches : In Four Parts.
VI. A Faithful Record of many Illustrious, Wonderful Providences, both
of Mercies and Judgments, on divers Persons in *New-England :* In Eight
Chapters.
VII. *The Wars of the Lord.* Being an History of the Manifold Afflictions and
Disturbances of the Churches in *New-England*, from their Various Adversa-
ries, and the Wonderful Methods and Mercies of God in their Deliverance :
In Six Chapters : To which is subjoined, An Appendix of Remarkable
Occurrences which *New-England* had in the Wars with the *Indian* Salvages,
from the Year 1688, to the Year 1698.

By the Reverend and Learned *COTTON MATHER*, M. A.
And Pastor of the North Church in *Boston*, *New-England*.

LONDON:

Printed for *Thomas Parkhurst*, at the *Bible* and *Three
Crowns* in *Cheapside*. MDCCII.

TITLE-PAGE OF THE *MAGNALIA*

Such is the real purpose of the *Magnalia*, to cherish the memory of heroic Americans, and to inspire their descendants **A Book of** to noble living in the service of the Fatherland. **Patriotism** Here in the last word, moreover, is an entirely new ideal in our literature. Hitherto America has been only the Homeland, and its symbol is the hearth fire, which inspires hope ; now it is the Fatherland, and its symbol is the grave, which inspires loyalty. The first Colonists regarded England as their country. They had no love for America till they laid their heroes to rest in its soil ; and even now, when we visit Jamestown or Plymouth, it is Burial Hill, not the monument or museum, that stirs our deepest emotion. Among primitive people the tomb was everywhere the symbol of patriotism, and the deepest humiliation of the Indians, or of any other race with a spark of nobility, was to be driven from the graves of their ancestors. Cotton Mather was the first to recognize this universal truth, and from the graves and the heroism of the fathers to appeal to the loyalty of the sons and daughters. His purpose is written large in the second and third books of the *Magnalia*. They are our first books of heroes, our first appeal to American patriotism, and with them every student of our history and literature should be familiar.

After the fourth book Mather turns aside from biography, and the design of his history is lost in a maze of insignifi- **Fantastic** cant details. In one book he becomes a theolo- **Elements** gian ; in another he follows the endless trail of the Indian wars ; in a third he is a mere wonder-hunter, recording miraculous escapes, infamous crimes and the friskiness of witches :

" In the year 1679 the house of William Morse, at Newberry, was infested with daemons after a most horrid manner, not altogether unlike the daemons of Tedworth. Bricks and sticks and stones were often by some invisible hand thrown at the house : a cat was thrown at the woman, and a long staff danc'd up and down in the chimney ; and when two persons laid it on the fire to burn it, 't was as much as they were able with their joint strength to hold it there.

"While the man was writing, his inkhorn was by the invisible hand snatch'd from him; and being able no where to find it, he saw it at length drop out of the air down by the fire. A shooe was laid upon his shoulder; but when he would have catch'd it, it was rapt from him; it was then clapt upon his head, and there he held it so fast, that the unseen fury pull'd him with it backward on the floor. When he was writing another time, a dish went and leapt into a pail, and cast water on the man, and on all the concerns before him. His cap jump'd off his head, and on again; and the pot lid went off the pot into the kettle, then over the fire together.

"Once the fist, beating the man, was discernible; but they could not catch hold of it. At length an apparition of a Blackamoor child shew'd itself plainly to them. And another time a drumming on the boards was heard, which was follow'd with a voice that sang, *Revenge! revenge! sweet is revenge!* At this the people, being terrify'd, call'd upon God, whereupon there follow'd a mournful note, several times uttering these expressions: *Alas! alas! we knock no more, we knock no more!* and there was an end of all." [1]

One who likes such grotesque stuff may find plenty of it in Mather; but to judge the *Magnalia* by it, as is commonly done, is to estimate a medieval cathedral by its imps and gargoyles. So let us skip the witches and join the company of heroes:

Here are Bradford and Winthrop, whose lives are all gentleness and service. Here is Phips, the son of a Maine blacksmith, but a prince among men, whose life furnishes adventure enough for a dozen *Treasure Islands*. Here is Eliot, that gentle, charitable, heroic soul, of whom it was said, "The Colonies could not perish so long as Eliot was alive." He is the scholarly minister of the church at Roxbury, but he is first of all a teacher. He founds and endows a free school on the principle that "a country cannot fail whose children are educated." As if preaching and teaching were not enough, he goes out as a missionary among the Indians; lives and suffers with them, until he recognizes the real man under the grease and war-paint; and the savages love and trust him, as they never trusted a white man before or since. He learns their speech, translates the Scriptures into their language, gives them their first literature, gathers them into schools and churches, and sends the keenest of them to Harvard. He grows too old for such active work; but having, as he says, served the Lord eighty years and found him a good Master, he must still do Him service. So he gathers some negro slaves together, in the intervals of their labor, and goes once

---

[1] Much abridged from *Thaumatographia Pneumatica*, Wonders of the Invisible World, *Magnalia*, Bk. VI, chap. vii. By some strange perversity of judgment, Mather included this earlier, freakish work in his *Magnalia*.

a week to teach them to read. At last he is too feeble for even this effort; he can no longer walk abroad; but still he must serve God and man. So he sends for a poor blind boy to come to his study, and his last, love-inspired service is to lead a child out of darkness into the shining world of literature.

Aside from the questions of style or literary value, these old biographies wonderfully enlarge our horizon, giving us wider views of the men who founded our nation.

> Dear to me these far, faint glimpses of the dual life of old,
> Inward, grand with awe and reverence; outward, mean and
>   coarse and cold;
> Gleams of mystic beauty playing over dull and vulgar clay,
> Golden-threaded fancies weaving in a web of hodden gray.

Thus, we have been misled to think that Colonial magistrates and clergy had too much power, and were meddlesome and **Our First** intolerant. The fact is that their power, which was **Biographies** wholly democratic, lay in their superior education, for which they were greatly honored and trusted. As we meet them in Mather's pages, we find them gentle, tolerant, kindly, busy with serving humanity, leaders in the struggle for free government, but making every sacrifice to avoid religious controversy.[1] "Oh, mildness and cheerfulness, with reverence, how sweet a companion art thou!" cries John Rogers, whose *Form for a Minister's Life*[2] reflects the strong faith in God and loyal service to man which characterized the Colonial clergy.

Again, if we have thought of the Puritans as stern, hard, unlovely men, we are surprised to find that they regarded charity as the first of all virtues. A hundred examples might be quoted; but we have room for only one, showing a new side to a solemn old Puritan governor:

"'T was his custom also to send some of his family upon errands unto the houses of the poor, about their meal time, on purpose to spy whether they wanted; and if 't were found that they wanted, he would make that the

---

[1] Indeed, our chief grievance against Cotton Mather is that he fails to copy his models in their admirable tolerance. He is apt to castigate those whose faith differs from his own, and is especially hard on Roger Williams and the early Quakers. Yet he is more charitable than most English religious writers of the same period.

[2] *Magnalia*, Appendix to Bk. III, chap. xiv.

opportunity of sending supplies unto them. And there was one passage of his charity that was perhaps a little unusual : In an hard and long winter, when wood was very scarce at Boston, a man gave him private information that a needy person in the neighborhood stole wood sometimes from his pile; whereupon the Governor in a seeming anger did reply, " Does he so ? I 'll take a course with him ; go, call that man to me ; I 'll warrant you I 'll cure him of stealing." When the man came, the Governor considering that, if he had stolen, it was more out of necessity than disposition, said unto him, " Friend, it is a severe winter, and I doubt you are but meanly provided for wood; wherefore I would have you supply yourself at my wood-pile till this cold season be over." And then he merrily asked his friends, Whether he had not effectually cured this man of stealing his wood ? " [1]

The old unchanging comedy or tragedy of human life is often reflected in Mather's pages. We find the good and the bad, the wise and the foolish, the minister who gave his only coat to a man poorer than himself, and the charlatan who " bubbled the silly neighbors out of their money." We read of John Wilson that " his low opinion of himself was the top of all his other excellencies "; of Samuel Stone that he defined the Colonial church as " a speaking aristocracy in the midst of a silent democracy "; and of Eliot that he went into a store one day, found the merchant busy with a huge pile of account books, and noticed over his head a Bible and a few other works of devotion : " Sir," says Eliot, " here is earth on the table, and Heaven all on the shelf." Such records, even in their fantastic setting, suggest two things : that the hearts of the old Puritans were like our own hearts, and that the author of the *Magnalia* had a very human side to his strange nature. It is the humanity of Cotton Mather, rather than his pedantry, that we have tried to reflect in this study of his life and writings.

[1] From *Nehemias Americanus*, Life of John Winthrop, *Magnalia*, Bk. II, chap. iv.

Jonathan Edwards (1703–1758)

In the church of the wilderness Edwards wrought,
Shaping his creed at the forge of thought;
And with Thor's own hammer welded and bent
The iron links of his argument,
Which strove to grasp in its mighty span
The purpose of God and the fate of man.[1]

Those who read and understand Edwards point out his spiritual resemblance to Dante, greatest of Italian poets; but few find in him any suggestion of America's most famous practical philosopher. At first glance no two men could be more unlike than the worldly-wise Franklin and the childlike Edwards, who was so absorbed in thought that he could never tell whether he was driving his own or his neighbor's cow from the common pasture. The resemblance lay in this, as a modern critic has suggested, that to each the world was intensely real, and each aimed to conquer the world by knowing it. Franklin occupied himself with the outer world of sensible things; while Edwards undertook the greater task of exploring the invisible world of thought and ideas.

Life. Edwards was born (1703) in East Windsor, a little Connecticut settlement, where his scholarly father was pastor of the village church. His mother was a woman of noble character and education, who reared her children in a way most favorable to deep thought and fine feeling. This little house in the woods sheltered a large world; and though the fare was often scant, the real living was of the highest order.

Edwards was certainly an unusual boy. At nine we find him writing on "The Substance of the Soul," and at eleven a wonderfully interesting paper on the habits of spiders.[2] The handwriting of these papers is that of a child; but the deep thought and the clear, logical expression suggest a man, and a very unusual man, full-grown.

---

[1] From Whittier, "The Preacher." The whole passage, which we have not quoted, suggests the rare combination of logic and mysticism in Edwards.

[2] These papers may be found in Vol. I of Dwight's edition of Edwards (10 vols., 1829). A few extracts are given in Tyler, *History of American Literature*, II, 179–185.

As one reads the notebooks of his Yale college period, from his twelfth to his sixteenth year, it is hard to believe that they were written by a mere boy. Though naturally a philosopher, an explorer in the world of thought, he was not the kind to build a castle in the air without first putting a foundation under it; hence his remarkable scientific investigations, which show plainly that he was far in advance of his age. He anticipated Franklin's discovery of electricity, showed that some of the fixed stars are suns like our own, suggested a theory of atoms very much like that now accepted by chemists, and made endless observations and experiments with a view of preparing a reliable textbook on the physical sciences. In all his works, whether exploring the visible or the invisible world, Edwards sought two things: first, to know the fact, and then to find the law which expressed itself in the fact. And in all her history America has never produced a man more governed by the spirit of truth.

JONATHAN EDWARDS

Toward the end of his college course Edwards evidently went through a tremendous spiritual struggle, such as awaited Puritan youths in those days before entering the visible church. The result is best expressed in his own words, which might well be those of St. Francis:

"After this my sense of divine things gradually increased, and became more and more lively, and had more of that inward sweetness. The appearance of everything was altered; there seemed to be, as it were, a calm, sweet cast or appearance of divine glory in almost every thing. God's excellency, his wisdom, his purity and love, seemed to appear in every thing; in the sun and moon and stars; in the clouds and blue sky; in the grass, flowers, trees; in the water, and all nature; which used greatly to fix my mind. I often used to sit and view the moon for continuance; and in the day spent much time in viewing the clouds and sky, to behold the sweet glory of God in these things; in the mean time singing forth, with a low voice, my contemplations of the Creator and Redeemer." [1]

After graduation the boy spent four more years at Yale, preparing for the ministry and tutoring undergraduates. All the while he kept himself in the strictest mental and spiritual discipline, seeking knowledge like a Faustus and holiness like a monk; and at twenty-three he was ordained minister to the church at Northampton. The discipline of the period was lightened by his love for Sarah Pierpont — a curious romance, made up of theology, mysticism and tender human emotion:

" They say there is a young lady [in New Haven] who is beloved of that great Being who made and rules the world; and that there are certain seasons in which this great Being, in some way or other invisible, comes to her and fills her mind with exceeding sweet delight, and that she hardly cares for anything except to meditate on Him. . . . She has a strange sweetness in her mind, and singular purity in her affections; is most just and conscientious in all her conduct; and you could not persuade her to do anything wrong or sinful, if you would give her all the world, lest she should offend this great Being. She is of wonderful calmness and universal benevolence, especially after this great God has manifested Himself to her mind. She will sometimes go about from place to place singing sweetly; and seems to be always full of joy and pleasure, and no one knows for what. She loves to be alone, walking in the fields and groves, and seems to have some one invisible always conversing with her."

Here is a companion after Edwards's own mystic heart, and with his belief in Determinism, she must be reserved for him from the foundation of the world. So presently he goes down to New Haven and marries her. Never did a stern theological doctrine find more lovely illustration. She was a rare woman, helpful and sympathetic, with a strong practical sense to balance her mysticism and keep her household in order, while her husband explored the deeps of human experience. Long afterwards, as he lay dying at Princeton, Edwards's last thought was for her, and he sent her this whispered message: " Tell her that the union which has so long subsisted between us is spiritual, and therefore will continue forever."

We pass over his long ministry in Northampton, noting only two suggestive things. First, his preaching, with its vivid imagery and

[1] From " Nature and Holiness," Miscellaneous Papers, *Works*, Vol. I.

overwhelming sincerity, made a tremendous impression. As a result, the Great Awakening, that soul-searching religious revival which swept over the Colonies in 1740, began in Northampton, and was only intensified when the English evangelist Whitefield visited this country. Second, the literary works of this period, such as his *Faithful Narrative of the Surprising Works of God* (1736) and his *Treatise concerning the Religious Affections* (1746), are utterly different from those of the marvel-loving Mather. They are profound mental studies, strikingly like our modern psychological treatises, only better written and more interesting. So far as we know, Edwards was the first to attempt to explain certain universal religious experiences by a scientific study of the mind itself.

In 1750 Edwards left Northampton [1] and went to Stockbridge, as missionary to the Indians and pastor to a handful of white people on the edge of the wilderness. Here, amid the privations of frontier life, he labored heroically seven years, finding leisure meanwhile to write the work by which he is now remembered. His *Freedom of the Will* (1754) made a sensation among scholars, and was the first American book to influence profoundly the thought of the whole world. The fame of this book led to his call to be president of Princeton College; but he had hardly begun his work there when he died (1758), one of the first martyrs to the cause of inoculation.

We have given but a small outline of a great life, and those who know Edwards will complain that we have done scant justice to his **Character of** greatness and his heroism. But one must learn to know **Edwards** this man, as one knows a friend, slowly, from year to year. Even then he often surprises us by a dainty bit of fancy which suggests a poet's soul, or by a gentle mysticism which tells us that this intellectual giant had the heart of a little child. Dealing with such a life, we need hardly mention that he was poor, and that he accepted poverty cheerfully, well content with the inner wealth that was his. Also he suffered and sorrowed much; but he made no struggle, letting the great soul within him manifest its superiority to all outward affliction. In an age of intense theological discussion he could not escape being drawn into controversy; but, like Cardinal Newman in similar circumstances, he was too great to feel bitterness, and kept that serenity of spirit, that "inward sweet delight in God," of which he

[1] The cause of his leaving, which seemed almost a tragedy at the time, was a difference with his congregation in the matter of church discipline. Edwards was undoubtedly right; his position is clearly stated in his "Qualifications for Full Communion."

had written in earlier years. Touch Edwards where you will, and instantly you feel the influence of a master mind, illuminated by a light which suggests that of the heavenly city. " Second to no mortal man " was the judgment of his contemporaries, when the news of his death passed like a cloud shadow over the Colonies.

The Freedom of the Will. We shall hardly understand even the title of Edwards's famous work [1] until we reflect that every outward act of a man's life is the result of a previous inner act of the will; and that we are called upon every moment to choose one thing, in presence of several others that we might select. Our future seems to be largely in our own hands till we ask the question, Is my will entirely free to choose? that is, do I determine my own choice, or is it determined for me before I make it?

To illustrate the matter simply: if a score of lines are drawn from a common center, like the spokes of a wheel, and a man is asked to select one line instantly, he will naturally put his finger on one of the lower lines to the right, thus indicating right-handedness and the inclination to avoid unnecessary effort; indicating also that our wills are not in a state of perfect equilibrium, but are inclined to one thing rather than another. So the question arises, Are not all our choices more or less predetermined in a similar way, by love of ease or fear of discomfort, by force of habit or conscience or inclination, by the influence of others — in short, by a score of subtle influences which lead a man to his choice even when he thinks himself perfectly free?

Strangely enough, this metaphysical question seemed then of very grave import, second only to the question of liberty, which **The Question** Winthrop had defined as a choice of masters. The Colonists were men of strong religious natures, who believed profoundly in the future life and gave diligent heed to salvation. Now salvation, like liberty, was fundamentally a matter of choice, a choice of eternal rather than temporary good, of a divine rather than a human master. And no man was suffered to bide long in America without having the alternative

[1] The exact title is " A Careful and Strict Inquiry into the Modern Prevailing Notions of that Freedom of the Will which is supposed to be Essential to Moral Agency, Virtue and Vice, Reward and Punishment, Praise and Blame " (1754).

put sternly before him : Choose, man, either God and eternal life, or the world and eternal death. But was a man free to choose, even when his choice meant life or death ? That was the question which troubled not only scholars but plain working men and women, who had been trained to think for themselves, and who had heard the question of free will discussed from every backwoods pulpit.

We have given a mere outline of the subject, but enough to suggest that Edwards faced a problem of universal interest, to **Edwards's Answer** which every great religious and philosophical system of the world has attempted to give answer. By early training and by long study he was a Calvinist,[1] and in his *Freedom of the Will* he attempted two things : to establish the doctrine of Determinism — that man is not free, all his choices being part of a plan predetermined by the Supreme Will — and to refute every possible argument of the liberal Arminians. So thoroughly did he carry out this attempt that all the logicians of the next century were unable to find the weak spot in his argument, which seemed forged like an anchor chain from end to end. We would not attempt here to criticize the logic or the doctrine of the *Freedom of the Will*, which is an epitome of all Calvinistic reasoning. Perhaps the chief objection to it, and to all similar attempts, is that logic must give way to facts, which are more evident than any proof of them can possibly be. It would be difficult, for instance, to furnish logical proof of our own existence ; it is no less difficult to prove the freedom of the will, which is one of the basic facts of morality and of all human experience. So, when Edwards demonstrates that our will is not free, we instinctively reject his argument ; yet the rejection does not change our admiration for the man, for the grasp and power

[1] The Calvinists held, among others, the doctrines of (1) Determinism, that is, that man has no freedom of will, but is in bondage to sin since Adam ; and (2) Predestination, that is, that some men are foreordained to be saved and some to be lost. Opposed to the Calvinists were the Arminians, who held that man has freedom of choice, and that all men may be saved, and will be saved, if they accept the means that are freely offered. One can hardly read a book of the Colonial period without finding some suggestion of these two religious parties.

of his intellect, for the sincerity and reverence of his great spirit. Few of us may read the *Freedom of the Will*, but it broadens our conception of Colonial life to remember that, while Franklin made practical discoveries that startled the world, this obscure missionary on the edge of the American wilderness produced a work which for solid reasoning power has hardly a peer in the English language.[1]

Miscellaneous Works. As there are some fifty different works of Edwards, it seems a pity that he should be known in literature only by a quotation from his " Sinners in the Hands of an Angry God,"[2] or some other soul-racking sermon. Two of the most important are *The Religious Affections* (1746) and the *History of the Work of Redemption*. Edwards intended to make the latter a mighty work, a philosophical study of human life in its relation to heaven, earth and hell. In the broad sweep of his thought here, he reminds us of Dante and Milton; but his untimely death cut short his cherished plan, and all we have is a suggestion of the work in a few extracts published after his death by Dr. Erskine, of Edinburgh.

It is not in these heavy works, however, but rather in the short miscellaneous papers that the student will find most enjoy-

Quality of Edwards

ment. Here we meet the man rather than the theologian; and a very strong, helpful, inspiring man he is. The most remarkable thing about him is what has been well called his God-consciousness. To him God was the most real, the most lovable being in the universe; and one can hardly be with Edwards five minutes without being led reverently into the presence of the Eternal. Another interesting quality is

1 Naturally we do not recommend such a book for general study, for the reason that one is certain to find it tough reading. Nevertheless one should know something about it, as one knows about the *Institutes* of Calvin, the *Summa* of Thomas Aquinas, the *Critique* of Kant, and other great books that have profoundly influenced the thought of the world.

2 This was the famous sermon preached at Enfield, during the revival known as the Great Awakening, in 1741. In connection with this sermon we emphasize the fact that Edwards was not a hater but a lover of mankind; that his insistence on the awful consequences of sin was the result of his vivid sense of the greatness and goodness of God, and of man's consequent obligation to serve Him.

his nature-consciousness, his instant response to the changing beauty of earth and sky. To him, as to Ruskin, nature was another Book of the Lord, a vast open Bible in which to read divine messages. A third noteworthy thing is his idealism ; and here he should be read as a supplement, or rather an antidote, to Franklin ; for these two men give us the two sides of the native American mind.[1] Franklin is the man of sight, shrewd and practical, concerned for the tangible outer world ; Edwards is the seer, the man of vision, penetrating to the heart of things and revealing spirit and ideals as the only enduring realities. And the American who follows Franklin in his practical method is at heart a believer in the eternal ideals which have been emphasized by Edwards, Bushnell, Channing, Emerson, and indeed by all our profound thinkers.

There are many other significant things to be found in Edwards, including his wonderful catholicity ; but these the reader must find and appreciate for himself. His style, even in his philosophical works, is remarkably clear and transparent, reflecting his thought perfectly. It is unconscious also, entirely free from the affectation and pedantry of Cotton Mather. Here and there are vivid flashes of imagery which reveal a poet's soul, and bits of delicate satire and irony which suggest a literary power that Edwards was sternly repressing in the interest of truth. Altogether, he seems to us, both in style and matter, incomparably the greatest of all our early writers.

[1] In a remarkable essay on " National Literature " (1830) Channing finds only two authors, Edwards and Franklin, worthy to represent the American mind to foreign readers.

Summary of Colonial History. It is impossible to set definite limits or to give a satisfactory name to any literary period. We have used the general term " Colonial "[1] to cover the century and a half following the landing of the first English settlers at Jamestown in 1607. At some time during this period the greater part of the Colonists, who had at first regarded themselves as Englishmen living abroad, came to consider and to call themselves Americans; but they still remained loyal to England until the Stamp Act of 1765 turned them definitely, if unconsciously, into the way of union and nationality.

No unified history of the period has yet been written. In our historical reading the attention is divided among thirteen different organizations, which

The Separate Colonies
historians now group locally into New England, Middle and Southern, or politically into charter, royal and proprietary colonies, but which then had no outward semblance of unity. Each colony was separated from its nearest neighbors by vast stretches of forest, through which travel was difficult or dangerous or at times impossible. In consequence each pursued its own immediate ends, of agriculture or trade or liberty; each cleared the forest before its own door, and then explored the rich unknown lands that were calling men everywhere to enlarge their borders. The first problem that confronted every settler was to subdue the earth, to win shelter and support, to establish the comfort and peace of home in the midst of a savage wilderness. That in itself might well employ a man's full energy, but the second problem was even harder, namely, to settle the vexed matters of political and religious freedom with which the old-world nations had struggled for centuries in vain. It was due to their absorption in these two problems, one of vital interest to the present, the other of untold consequences to the future, that the Colonists produced comparatively few books, and that their works were practical and didactic rather than artistic in form and motive.

Though outwardly separate and independent, the people of all these colonies show the same spiritual characteristics. They speak the same noble language; they follow the same high ideals; they love liberty, and

Ideal Unity
are determined not only to enjoy it themselves but to secure it forever to their children. When occasion arises they unite readily, here to protect themselves from a general uprising of the Indians, there to secure a greater measure of self-government from England; and as early as 1643 we have " The United Colonies of New England,"[2] which endured forty years, and was a prophecy of greater things to come.

This tendency toward unity, though often interrupted by trading disputes, increased steadily with the growth of the Colonies. It was strengthened, moreover, by the influence of the American colleges, which were founded with

[1] Some writers divide the period into Early and Late Colonial; others into Colonial and Provincial. The latter period begins, chronologically, with the loss of the charter under James II, or with the arrival of the royal governor, Andros, in 1686, and ends with the Declaration of Independence.

[2] The twelve articles of this confederation should be read entire by those who would understand the history of the American Union. See Bradford, *Of Plimoth Plantation*, record of the year 1643.

the express purpose of furnishing teachers to all the people. The extraordinary success of these colleges suggests one of the chief characteristics of

The Colleges the first Americans, namely, their high regard for learning and their selection of educated men to be their leaders and representatives. During the Colonial period seven colleges — Harvard, William and Mary, Yale, New Jersey, Kings, Philadelphia, and Rhode Island, all maintaining a high standard[1] of learning — were firmly established here, and each was largely supported by a handful of settlers engaged in wresting a living from the wilderness. Search the history of the world, and you shall find no other such inspiring picture, of pioneers demanding a university, of colonization guided by scholarship. In these colleges young men of various colonies fraternized for a time, and returned to the distant settlements whence they had come, carrying the ideal of a common fellowship and a common destiny. And these young men, be it remembered, were trusted leaders in the Revolutionary struggle that changed certain English colonies into the American nation.

Summary of Colonial Literature. The literature of the Colonial period as a whole has two marked characteristics, one historical, the other theological or religious. Though the Colonists generally were loyal to England, their old annals indicate that their leaders north and south — and especially the Puritans, who were scattered through the colonies from Maine to Georgia — believed profoundly that they were leading a great revolution in the world, out of which should arise a new nation of freemen.[2] Hence the strong tendency toward historical writing, which began with the first Colonial records, and which has characterized American literature ever since.

As might be expected in a country which was largely settled by men who sought freedom of belief and worship, the theological note is constantly heard in our early literature. Indeed, a large part of that literature was made up of theological and controversial works which, with few exceptions, were soon forgotten. Far more significant than the theological is the sincerely religious spirit that shows itself in all our earliest prose and verse. The Colonists believed, and reflected their belief on almost every page of their records, that in founding a state, as in forming a character, religion and education are the two factors of supreme importance.

In our study we have confined ourselves largely to certain significant types of Colonial writers: (1) The annalists and historians, of whom Bradford, Winthrop and Byrd are the best examples. Among these we place also Sewall, whose diary might well be called a window in old Boston. (2) The poets, with their general tendency to copy English models. Chief of these minor singers

[1] The Earl of Chatham, amazed at the style and scholarship of the state papers sent from America, paid an eloquent tribute to Colonial culture on the floor of the House of Lords in 1775. Few college graduates of the present day could pass the examinations in the classics which were then required for entrance.

[2] The writings of Bradford, Winthrop, Morton, Prince, and indeed of nearly all our early annalists, make frequent reference to the future nation that " shall reap the liberty which these Colonies have planted."

are Anne Bradstreet, the first American woman to win general literary recognition; Wigglesworth, whose poetic genius was kept chained, like a prisoner in a dungeon, by his terrible theology; and Godfrey, who at the end of the Colonial period made a crude but unmistakable beginning of artistic literature. (3) The theological writers, of whom Mather and Edwards are the most notable. The former gave us our first book of national heroes; the latter produced a philosophical work which for solid reasoning power has never been surpassed in America.

Typical Writers

In addition to these typical writers we have reviewed a number of miscellaneous authors: Whittaker, "the apostle of Virginia"; Wood, the naturalist; Edward Johnson, maker of our first verse-history, or rhyming chronicle; Mary Rowlandson, and other writers on Indian life and warfare. All these were well known to Colonial readers, and we find their works still interesting. Among miscellaneous writers the greatest name is that of Eliot, a noble character, whose works on the Indian language, including a translation of the Bible into the Indian tongue, were America's first contribution to the literature of scholarship and original investigation.

Selections for Reading. Bradford, Of Plimoth Plantation, and Smith, Settlement of Virginia, in Maynard's Historical Readings (Merrill); Chronicles of the Pilgrims, in Everyman's Library (Dutton). A few well-chosen works of Bradford, Winthrop, John Smith, Eliot, Morton, Cotton Mather, Anne Bradstreet, etc., are published in Old South Leaflets.[1]

Representative selections from all authors named in the text may be found in Trent and Wells, Colonial Prose and Poetry; in Cairns, Early American Writers; in Stedman and Hutchinson, Duyckinck, etc. (see "Collections" and "Texts," in General References, at the beginning of this book).

Bibliography. For extended works on American history and literature, covering the whole subject, see General References. The following works are useful in a special study of the Colonial period.

History. Contemporaneous: Original Narratives of Early American History, a series of well-edited volumes reproducing the narratives of explorers and founders: Narratives of Early Virginia, edited by Tyler; Bradford's History, by Davis; Winthrop's Journal, by Hosmer; early narratives of New Netherlands, Maryland, Carolina, Pennsylvania, etc. (Scribner). Hart, American History told by Contemporaries, 4 vols. (Macmillan).

Modern Works: Fisher, The Colonial Era (contains a chapter on Colonial literature); Osgood, American Colonies in the Seventeenth Century; Doyle, English Colonies in America, 3 vols.; Thwaite, The Colonies, in Epochs of American History series; Fiske, Beginnings of New England, Old Virginia and her Neighbors, Dutch and Quaker Colonies; Lodge, English Colonies in America; Arber, Story of the Pilgrim Fathers; Eggleston, Beginners of a Nation.

---

[1] The "Leaflets" are of great value to teachers and students of our earliest history and literature. They average about sixteen pages each, with excellent notes, and are sold at four or five cents per copy, — which barely covers the cost of publication. For a list of over two hundred subjects, address Directors, Old South Meeting House, Boston.

Supplementary : Alice Morse Earle, Home Life in Colonial Days, Child Life in Colonial Days, Colonial Dames and Goodwives, Customs and Fashions, etc. (Macmillan) ; Fisher, Men, Women, and Manners of Colonial Times ; Whittier, Margaret Smith's Journal (fiction) ; Lowell, New England Two Centuries Ago ; Emerson, Historical Discourse at Concord.

Biographical : Lives of Higginson, Hooker, Winthrop, Peter Stuyvesant, the Calverts, Cotton Mather, Oglethorpe, in Makers of America (Dodd) ; in the same series, Griffis, Sir William Johnson and the Six Nations ; Walker, Ten New England Leaders ; Bowen, Life of Sir William Phipps (1834) ; Straus, Roger Williams ; Green, Pioneer Mothers of America, 3 vols. (Putnam). For other biographies, of Jonathan Edwards, Anne Bradstreet, etc., see below.

Literature. Tyler, History of American Literature 1607–1765, 2 vols., or Students' Edition, two volumes in one (Putnam), is the most complete and scholarly work on the Colonial period. Other works are Preston, Colonial Ballads ; Holliday, Wit and Humor of Colonial Days ; Jameson, History of Historical Writing in America ; Smyth, Philadelphia Magazines and their Contributors 1741–1850.

John Smith. Texts : Works, in Arber's Reprints, English Scholar's Library (Birmingham, 1884) ; selected narratives, in Tyler's Early Virginia (Original Narratives series) ; Winsor's America, Vol. III ; Hart's American History, Vol. I (see General References). Selections, in Old South Leaflets, Maynard's Historical Readings, etc.

Biography and Criticism : Life by Simms (1846) ; by C. D. Warner (1881) ; Fiske, Old Virginia and her Neighbors ; Poindexter, Capt. John Smith and His Critics ; Deane's edition of the True Relation (1866) ; Henry, Proceedings of the Virginia Historical Society (1882) ; Charles Francis Adams, in Chapters of Erie and Other Essays.

Bradford. Texts : Works, in Collections of Massachusetts Historical Society ; Of Plimoth Plantation, edited by Davis, in Original Narratives series ; various other editions, the best by Ford, 2 vols. (1913). Selections, in Chronicles of the Pilgrims, etc. (see Selections for Reading, above).

Biography and Criticism : Cotton Mather's life of Bradford, in Old South Leaflets, number 77 ; a good sketch in Leslie Stephen's Dictionary of National Biography ; others in Appleton, etc. (see " Biography " in General References). Walker, Ten New England Leaders ; Winsor's America, Vol. III, chap. viii ; Tyler, I, 116–126 ; C. F. Adams, Massachusetts : its Historians and its History ; Steele, The Chief of the Pilgrims (life of Brewster). For the story of the discovery and return of Bradford's manuscript, see Winsor, Governor Bradford's Manuscript ; also Introduction to the edition of Bradford's History published by the Commonwealth of Massachusetts, 1899.

Winthrop. Texts : Journal, called History of New England, edited by Savage, 2 vols. (Boston, 1853) ; in Original Narratives, edited by Hosmer (Scribner). Some Old Puritan Love Letters, edited by Twitchell (Dodd).

Biography and Criticism : Life, by R. C. Winthrop, 2 vols. (1864) ; by Twitchell, in Makers of America series ; Walker, Ten New England Leaders ; Adams, Massachusetts.

Supplementary: Alice M. Earle, Margaret Winthrop; Anderson, Memorable Women of Puritan Times (1862); Ellis, Puritan Age in Massachusetts.

Sewall. Texts: Works, in Collections of Massachusetts Historical Society.

Biography and Criticism: Chamberlain, Samuel Sewall and the World He Lived in; Lodge, A Puritan Pepys, in Studies in History; Whittier's poem, The Prophecy of Samuel Sewall.

Byrd. Texts: Byrd Manuscripts, edited by Basset (1901).

Biography and Criticism: Only fragments are available, in Virginia Magazine of History and Biography, 1902; Moses, Literature of the South; Campbell, History of Virginia; Holliday, Southern Literature, etc.

Anne Bradstreet. Texts: Works, prose and verse, edited by Ellis (Charlestown, 1867); Poems, edited by C. E. Norton (privately printed, Boston, 1897); Selected Poems, in Old South Leaflets.

Biography and Criticism: Helen Campbell, Anne Bradstreet and Her Time (Lothrop, 1891).

Wigglesworth. Texts: Day of Doom, reprint of sixth edition, with notes, memoir, etc., edited by Burr (American News Co., 1867). Minor prose works, in Proceedings of Massachusetts Historical Society.

Biography and Criticism: Dean, Memoir of Wigglesworth (1871).

Cotton Mather. Texts: Magnalia, last edition 1855. Lives of Bradford, Winthrop, etc., in Old South Leaflets. (No worthy book of selections from Cotton Mather has ever been made.)

Biography and Criticism: Life by Wendell (1891); by Marvin (1892).

Supplementary: A Daughter of Cotton Mather, in The Outlook, Oct. 7 and 14, 1905.

Jonathan Edwards. Texts: Dwight's edition, 10 vols. (New York, 1830); abridged edition, 4 vols. (1852).

Biography and Criticism: Life, by Allen (1889); Gardiner, Jonathan Edwards, a Retrospect (1901). Essays: by Leslie Stephen, in Hours in a Library; by Holmes, in Pages from an Old Volume of Life.

Supplementary: Whittier's poem, The Preacher.

Historical Fiction. *Early Romances of Colonial Times:* Mrs. Child, Hobomok; Miss Sedgwick, Hope Leslie, Redwood; Paulding, Dutchman's Fireside, Koningsmarke; Kennedy, Rob of the Bowl; Cooper, Satanstoe, Red Rover, Water Witch.

Later Romances: Hawthorne, Scarlet Letter; Motley, Merry Mount; Cooke, Virginia Comedians, My Lady Pokahontas; Eggleston, Pocahontas and Powhattan; Thompson, Green Mountain Boys; Caruthers, Cavaliers of Virginia; Bynner, Begum's Daughter; Goodwin, White Aprons (romance of Bacon's Rebellion); Barr, Black Shilling (witchcraft); Austin, Standish of Standish; Stimson, King Noanett; Mary Johnston, To Have and to Hold.

Books for Young People. *Colonial History:* Catherwood, Heroes of the Middle West, a book of early French explorers (Ginn and Company); Drake, Making of New England, Making of Virginia and the Middle Colonies, Making of the Great West, 3 vols. (Scribner); Baldwin, Discovery of the Old Northwest, Conquest of the Old Northwest, 2 vols. (American Book Co.);

Moore-Tiffany, Pilgrims and Puritans (Ginn and Company); Edgar, Struggle for a Continent, edited from Parkman's histories (Little, Brown); Helen Smith, The Colonies; Alma Burton, Story of the Indians of New England (Silver, Burdett).

Colonial Stories: Hawthorne, Grandfather's Chair, Legends of the Province House; Bass, Stories of Pioneer Life (Heath); Eggleston, Stories of Great Americans for Little Americans, Stories of American Life and Adventure (American Book Co.); Tappan, Letters from Colonial Children (Houghton).

Suggestive Questions. The following questions — which are fairly suggested by the text and by the selections usually read — are not to be considered as an examination. They are intended chiefly to stimulate the pupil's thinking, to encourage his independent judgment, and occasionally to lead him away into a field of pleasant research :

1. In what significant way does the early literature of America differ from that of England or Greece ? How do you account for the difference ? Why should American literature begin with prose, while that of older nations begins with poetry ? Give two good reasons why the Colonists produced comparatively few books.

2. The early Colonists regarded England or some other country as their fatherland; what effect did this have upon their writing ? Who was probably the first Colonial writer to emphasize America as home and fatherland ? How do patriotism and national enthusiasm aid literature ?

3. Colonial writers are often classified as annalists, poets and divines : name two or more writers in each class, and give the titles of their chief works. Explain the tendency of Colonial authors to write history. Explain also their tendency to combine history with theology.

4. Who were the great writers in England during the early Colonial period, and what was the general spirit of their writings ?

5. At a later period we shall find that our chief writers (Irving, Bryant, Cooper, etc.) were strongly influenced by the new romantic movement in Europe; how do you account for the fact that the Colonists were so little influenced by the romanticism of the Elizabethans ?

6. Do you consider Captain John Smith an English or an American writer ? What Elizabethan characteristics does he display ? How does his account of the new land compare with those of Bradford, Byrd and other Colonial writers ? Some historians regard the Pocahontas incident as an example of Smith's romancing ; others as a record of fact; what is your impression after reading the story ?

7. What differences have you found recorded (in various histories) between the settlers of New England and those of the South ? Now read the selections given in Cairns, Trent and Wells, etc., and compare the various writers, having in mind their style, their material, and their evident motive in writing. Judging by what you have read of Colonial literature, have the differences between North and South been exaggerated by historians ? Make a list of American characteristics displayed by Northern and Southern writers alike.

8. Of Bradford's History the scholarly Senator Hoar said, " I read again with renewed enthusiasm and delight the noble and touching story." Speaking of his search for the original manuscript he said, " It seemed to me then, as it now seems to me, the most precious manuscript on earth." Can you explain or understand his enthusiasm?

9. What is the historical and what the literary value of Bradford's work? What qualities are revealed and what virtues are emphasized in *Of Plimoth Plantation?* What Pilgrim ideals, as reflected in this work, are now national and American?

10. What is the general character of Winthrop's Journal? Why is it called a source-book of American literature? Read Winthrop's famous " Little Speech " (Old South Leaflets, number 66) and give in your own words his definition of liberty. What qualities are reflected in his Journal and in his letters?

11. Why should Sewall's Diary be called " a window in old Boston "? Why is the author called " A Puritan Pepys "? What is the value of his book? It is said that Sewall may be known better than any other man in American history or literature; what is the basis of such an assertion?

12. What new and important element did Byrd add to our early literature? What qualities are reflected in his writings? Read selections from Byrd and from his contemporary Cotton Mather, and write a brief comparison of the two men, having in mind their personal qualities, the interest of their subjects, their style and their motive in writing.

13. Explain the prominence given to Indians and to natural history in Colonial literature. Why is Eliot called " the Apostle to the Indians "? What was his character, and what his contribution to scholarly literature?

14. What is the general character of Ward's *The Simple Cobbler?* From the fact that it denounces feminine fashions, religious toleration and other " innovations," what do you judge of the author's spirit? What does it suggest of the early settlers?

15. What is the general character of the poetry of the Colonial period? Who was "The Tenth Muse," and what are her claims to distinction? The statement has often been made that *The Bay Psalm Book* is a measure of the poetic taste of the Puritans; criticize the statement.

16. What Puritan (or American) characteristics are reflected in the *Day of Doom?* Give a brief description of the author and his work. The *Day of Doom* (1662) and *Pilgrim's Progress* (1678) were both popular with the masses of people in their respective countries. What common qualities are reflected in these two works, and how do you explain their popularity?

17. Give your impression (from selections read) of the *Magnalia.* In what noble way did Cotton Mather appeal to patriotism? What is meant by " the Mather Dynasty "? In a recent newspaper editorial Cotton Mather was called " a persecutor and burner of witches "; criticize the statement. What work of Mather is mentioned in Franklin's *Autobiography?*

18. Who was Jonathan Edwards? What is the character of his chief work? What profound question does that work attempt to answer? What common

characteristic is reflected by Edwards and Wigglesworth? Edwards and Franklin (see next chapter) are said to represent the two sides of the American mind; explain and criticize the statement.

19. What is the object in studying or reading Colonial literature? How does this object compare with that of reading an adventure story or a newspaper?

20. It is often alleged that our literature as a whole is "provincial"; what does that mean? After agreeing upon a general definition, debate in class the question, Resolved, that American literature is provincial. Support your arguments by the book you have read.

Subjects for Pleasant Essays. (The following subjects are suggested with the conviction that when one begins to read widely in Colonial literature, he finds it vastly more interesting than it has been represented to be. Original material for essays or discussion may be found in the numerous collections named in the General References, or it may be had, at an expense of five cents, by sending for the appropriate number of Old South Leaflets.)

An old Colonial library. Permanent American characteristics in Colonial literature. Influence on national life of the first American colleges. A boy's entrance examinations two hundred years ago. My favorite book (or passage) in Colonial literature: what it tells me of my forefathers. Cotton Mather and the witchcraft delusion. Good anecdotes from the *Magnalia*. Mather's *Essays to Do Good*. Nature studies of Jonathan Edwards. Common qualities of early Northern and Southern writers. Anne Bradstreet and "votes for women." Early Indian narratives. The American hero in Cotton Mather's biographies. Natural history in Colonial days. John Smith: historian or romancer? Bradford's manuscript: how it was lost and found. What I thought of the Puritans before and after I read their own works.

CHAPTER II

THE PERIOD OF THE REVOLUTION (1765-1800)

By the rude bridge that arched the flood,
  Their flag to April's breeze unfurled,
Here once the embattled farmers stood
  And fired the shot heard round the world.

Emerson, " Concord Hymn "

I. HISTORICAL OUTLINES [1]

Social Development. Four historic movements, separate yet continuous, like the four acts of a mighty drama, and all having profound influence on our literature, are crowded into the latter half of the eighteenth century in America. The first is social and industrial; it is concerned with the rapid increase of trade and wealth as America's natural resources are discovered, with the spread of education, and with the phenomena of town as contrasted with country life. For America is no longer an experiment, a " trade venture " as England first regarded her; she is beyond all expectation a success, and has ambition of becoming a nation. Where once the forest stood, dark and silent, the sun now shines on prosperous farms; the frontier hamlet of log cabins is now a bustling town; and with the town come inevitably the newspaper, the high school, the theater, the beginning of music, poetry and all the fine arts. Very different this from the Jamestown of John Smith, the Boston of John Winthrop! Here are highways to follow, instead of the old buffalo and Indian trails. With prosperity and social pleasures, men begin to think less of theology and " other-worldliness," which were prominent in the early days, and more of this present life and opportunity. Whittier, who has the deepest insight into Colonial

---

[1] Any adequate history of the Revolution must consider the Loyalist as well as the Patriot side. It must also trace causes of separation that were operative long before the Stamp Act and other measures of taxation finally roused and united the Colonies in opposition to the mother country. In our summary we try simply to see events as the writers of '76 saw them, to get the Revolutionary view rather than to paint a picture of the Revolution itself.

life, notes the changing standards, in "The Preacher," as he looks
upon an old country church and considers the waning glory of Edwards:

> Over the roofs of the pioneers
> Gathers the moss of a hundred years;
> On man and his works has passed the change
> Which needs must be in a century's range.
> The land lies open and warm in the sun,
> Anvils clamor and mill-wheels run,—
> Flocks on the hillsides, herds on the plain,
> The wilderness gladdened with fruit and grain!
> But the living faith of the settlers old
> A dead profession their children hold;
> To the lust of office and greed of trade
> A stepping-stone is the altar made. . . .
> Everywhere is the grasping hand,
> And eager adding of land to land;
> And earth, which seemed to the fathers meant
> But as a pilgrim's wayside tent, . . .
> Solid and steadfast seems to be,
> And Time has forgotten Eternity!

The Stamp Act and what followed. The second great movement,
leading toward the climax of union and nationality, takes us into the
midst of tumult and upheaval which followed the Stamp Act of 1765.
And perhaps the most noteworthy thing in this fateful movement is
its unexpectedness. Only two years earlier the whole country had rejoiced with England over the Treaty of Paris, which meant two mercies
to the Colonies: that the raids, massacres and general barbarism of
the French and Indian War were all things of the past; and that English rather than French ideals had finally prevailed in America, leaving
man free here to work out his salvation, not in the shadow of military
despotism, but in the full sunshine of Anglo-Saxon liberty. To make
such peace, such opportunity possible, the Colonies had given twenty
thousand of their young men, and a sum equal to forty millions of our
present money; and they were content with their sacrifice.

Then, at the very season of their rejoicing, King George and his
ministers resolved, with colossal stupidity, on two measures: that the
Colonies were to be taxed by the British Parliament to support a
British army; and that no settlers should be allowed west of the Alle-
gheny Mountains. That the tax was small was of no consequence;
it was the big injustice that struck the loyal Colonists like a blow in

the face. And just as the rich Ohio and Mississippi valleys were cleared of French troops, our pioneers, pressing eagerly into the spacious country, must halt and turn back into a narrow land ; because, forsooth, an English king had covenanted with his "royal brother of France" that the whole splendid territory should be reserved forever for a handful of roving savages. Such things were not to be endured by free men. While towns and cities of the Atlantic coast were in an uproar over one proclamation, men of the woods and mountains quietly ignored the other. So loyalty was changed to distrust, and the Revolution began while Americans still treasured the memories of a war in which they had fought shoulder to shoulder with Englishmen against a common enemy.

The first effect of the Stamp Act, and of the uproar which followed it, was to unite the Colonies and prepare them for nationality. They **Union of** contained at this time only a million and a half of widely **Colonies** scattered people. There was no particular grouping of interests ; each colony stood firm by itself, zealously guarding its own rights ; and we have little excuse for dividing them into Northern and Southern, and so making false distinctions in our national life and literature. There were superficial differences among them, to be sure, and doubtless certain colonies had more frequent and intimate connection with England than they had with each other ; but when the first American or Continental Congress meets at Philadelphia, in 1774, our attention is focused, not on divisions and differences among the members, but rather on their unity, their concord, their amazing resemblances. Here are fifty-five delegates gathered from the four corners of a vast territory. Here are Cavaliers and Puritans, Catholics and Protestants, ministers, teachers, merchants, artisans ; and lo ! all these men speak the same speech, cherish the same ideals, and are instantly ready to elect and follow the same leader. For the words of Otis and Samuel Adams have been heard far beyond the borders of Massachusetts, and Patrick Henry's speech has rung like a bugle call through all the American settlements.

So, though there is as yet no nation on this side of the Atlantic, there is a prophecy in the air, and the prophecy is voiced by South Carolina when she declares, "The whole country must be animated with one great soul, and all Americans must resolve to stand by one another even unto death."[1] Of all the spoken or written words of

[1] Almost a century and a half earlier, Bradford, in the little colony of the Pilgrims, had voiced the same noble sentiment ; almost a century later, on the terrible field of Gettysburg, Lincoln reëchoed it.

the eighteenth century, these seem, to a literary man, the most significant. That "one great soul," all aflame with the love of freedom and justice, symbolizes the unity of aim and spirit among the Colonies immediately preceding the Revolution.

The Revolution. The third act of this stirring drama is the Revolutionary War, that epic struggle against odds, which makes the blood of an American tingle every time he reads it anew. We are so accustomed to think of it, and of our independence, as the result of a supreme effort of our whole people, that it occasions a shock of surprise to learn that the Revolution was fought and won by only a part, — perhaps the smaller and, in the matter of this world's goods, probably the poorer part of our Colonial ancestors. The heroism of the war consists partly in this : that the Continental army had to fight front and guard rear at the same time ; that while it faced a superior force of open enemies, behind it was a larger body of American Tories, foes of its own household, ready at any moment to give secret or open aid to the British. So also the prose and poetry that we cherish, as reflecting the spirit of '76, is only a portion, the Whig portion,[1] of Revolutionary letters. And the wedge which split our life and literature into two sections was the famous Declaration of Independence, which is commonly considered the symbol of national unity.

As we have noted, the year 1774, when the first Continental Congress assembled, found the American colonies singularly united in spirit. Declaration of Independence Up to that time, and even later, they were splendidly loyal to England, and only a few bold, visionary spirits, like Henry, and Samuel Adams, had dreamed of a separate national existence.[2] Then, sudden and startling as a thunderbolt to a great part of the country, came the Declaration of Independence ; and every man was called upon to make instant decision between the new and the old. It was a tense, dramatic moment, like that in which Elijah built his altar on Mount Carmel and cried aloud to his people : " How long halt ye between two opinions ? " It meant not only the separation of nation from nation ; it divided a man from his neighbors and friends, and sometimes a father from his own sons and daughters. Our histories are often eloquent — and well they may

---

[1] There is a large Tory literature of the Revolution which is now almost forgotten.

[2] At Bunker Hill, Ticonderoga, and Charleston, the Colonists were fighting, not for independence, but expressly for their rights as English subjects. Washington writes : " When I first took command of the Continental army (July 3, 1775) I abhorred the idea of independence." See also Jefferson's letter to John Randolph, August 25, 1775.

be —on the subject of Franklin's patriotism ; but they are silent concerning Franklin's son, who accepted a British office here, probably
also a British bribe, and was a Tory, a secret enemy of the cause for
which his father labored. There is a fine stirring story of Edmund
Randolph, and of many another young Patriot, whose hearts ran ever
ahead of their Virginia thoroughbreds as they hastened at the first.
call to join the army of Washington; but we hear little at this time
of the father, John Randolph, who followed the English governor
Dinsmore over seas, and remained a Tory exile during the Revolution.
And these are but types of thousands of such family divisions.

So, the ringing of the famous Liberty Bell, on July 4, 1776, divided
the country for the first time into two hostile parties : the Whigs, or
Whigs and Patriots, who supported the new government; and the
Tories Tories, or Loyalists, who remained true to old England,
as their fathers were before them.[1] There was no separation into
North, Middle, and South ; but every colony, every town and hamlet,
was a house divided against itself. The Patriots were the younger,
the more enthusiastic party, and speedily gained control of the state
governments. For them the bells rang, the cannon roared, the bon-
fires blazed to heaven ; but we must not assume that this voiced the
joy of a whole nation. For every man who ran out to join the jubila-
tion, there was another man who hurried into his house, in grief or
rage, and slammed the door behind him. Nor are we to conclude,
from the Revolutionary literature which survives on our bookshelves,
that the young Patriots monopolized the patriotism of the land. The
Tories were quite as sincere, quite as patriotic, quite as liberty-loving ;
only they sought liberty, as all the Colonists had done for a century
past, by maintaining their rights as Englishmen. Utterly misjudging
the new movement, they regarded the Patriots as ungrateful rebels ;
many of them took up arms to suppress the " unholy rebellion " ;
many more gave secret aid to the British. The Patriots, on the other
hand, sadly misjudged their opponents, calling them traitors to the
cause of liberty. Thousands of intelligent Loyalists were driven out
of the country, and their property was seized ; thousands more were
looked upon with suspicion or hatred. In Loyalist counties, a too-
zealous Whig was promptly ostracized, or hanged, as the case might be ;

---

[1] No accurate estimate of the relative strength of these two parties is possible. In
Georgia the Tories were the larger and more influential class. In New York, Pennsyl-
vania, and the Carolinas the parties seem to have been equally divided. In Virginia and
New England the Whigs probably predominated.

in Patriot districts, a suspected Tory might be ridden out of town on a rail, or else given a horrible coat of tar and feathers. Altogether it was a hard and bitter separation of old friends and neighbors, so bitter that in many places the Revolution seemed more like a barbarous civil strife than a united struggle against foreign oppression.[1]

The Constitution. The fourth great movement of this period is political, and includes the long struggle to form a national constitution. It is the most tense, the most critical, the most fateful movement in all our history. To understand this, we must remember that democracy in America has two essential elements: representation and federation. The first was inherited from England by the Colonists, who from the beginning showed their training and independence by electing their own representatives to the House of Burgesses, or Assembly, or General Court, as the Colonial legislatures were variously called. The second element, of federation, was new in the world. The problem of welding a number of free states into a single free nation had never been solved, or even attempted; and America, as she set herself to the mighty task, had no precedent to guide her. Alone and amid endless difficulties she began her work. Her people were hopelessly divided over questions of state and personal rights involved in or threatened by federation; and the effort to form a nation came perilously near to disrupting the Colonies just after the Revolution had united them. Again there were two parties: the Federalists, who thought first of the nation and sought as much power as possible for the national government; and the Anti-Federalists, who distrusted and feared the monarchial tendency of every centralized government since time began, and who were determined to keep the governing power as largely as possible in the hands of the individual states. The struggle reached a climax in Philadelphia, in 1787, when Washington called to order the leaders of the Colonies in thought and action, — "an assembly of demigods," Jefferson calls them,— and after four months' debate they produced the Constitution of the United States, "the noblest work," according to an English statesman, "ever struck off at a given time by the mind and purpose of man."[2]

[1] Simms's historical novels, *The Partisan*, etc., give vivid pictures of this civil strife in the Carolinas. Cooper's *The Spy* portrays the plots of Whig and Tory in New York.

[2] This fine tribute of Gladstone is often quoted, but the "struck off at a given time" is misleading. The Constitution did not come into the world full-grown, like Minerva. It was the result of two hundred years of experiment here in the matter of government, and is partly composed of fragments taken from our old state constitutions. For the clear, strong language of the Constitution we are largely indebted to Gouverneur Morris.

Somewhere in the midst of all this mighty struggle our national life began; but as a nation we have no natal festival, for the simple **Birth of the** reason that none can tell us when America was born. **Nation** Some date it at the first Continental Congress; some at the Declaration of Independence; some at the inauguration of Washington, whose noble personality held the discordant states together until the new government was established and organized; and a few follow Lowell, who, with fine poetic insight, places the birth of the new nation on the day when Washington took command of the army, no longer Provincial but Continental, on July 3, 1775:

> Never to see a nation born
> Hath been given a mortal man,
> Unless to those who, on that summer morn,
> Gazed silent when the great Virginian
> Unsheathed the sword whose fatal flash
> Shot union through the incoherent clash
> Of our loose atoms, crystallizing them
> Around a single will's unpliant stem,
> And making purpose of emotion rash.
> Out of that scabbard sprang, as from its womb,
> Nebulous at first but hardening to a star,
> Through mutual share of sunburst and of gloom,
> The common faith that made us what we are.[1]

II. LITERATURE OF THE REVOLUTION

General Tendencies. The effects of such mighty historic movements are seen instantly in Revolutionary prose and poetry; and we shall better appreciate these if we contrast them with the record of the preceding period. A wide reader of Colonial literature notes two general characteristics: its narrowness and its isolation. Almost every writer dwells apart from the world; his book is as a voice crying in the wilderness; and life seems to him only a pilgrimage, a brief day of preparation for eternity. Hence poetry, history and biography are all alike theological, that is, they interpret the human in terms

---

[1] From Lowell, "Under the Old Elm."

of the divine life. In Revolutionary literature there is no isolation, but rather a splendid sense of comradeship, strong and loyal. When the Colonies draw near together, after the Stamp Act, they find themselves one in spirit. Otis and Henry voice the thought and feeling of a multitude ; Hamilton and Jefferson appeal not only to the new nation but to the men of every land who have pondered the problems of democracy. Even in the satires of Freneau, in the ballads of Hopkinson against the Tories, and of Odell against the Patriots, there is no sense of solitariness ; for each writer is but the voice of a great party which cherishes the same ideals and follows the same leader.

As American literature thus emerges from its isolation, we note instantly that it has become more practical, more worldly, more intent on solving the problems of the present than of the future life. In nearly all books of the period the center of interest shifts from heaven to earth ; theology gives way to politics ; and the spiritual yearnings of an earlier age, which reached a climax in Jonathan Edwards, are replaced by the shrewd, practical " philosophy of common sense," with Benjamin Franklin as its chief apostle.

Not only the spirit but the form also of literature is changed in the Revolutionary period. The great social movement which **New Types** we have outlined gave rise to numerous newspapers **of Literature** and magazines,[1] with their poems, satires, essays, stories, — a bright and varied array compared with the Colonial product. More significant of the new social life are the crude plays of Royall Tyler and William Dunlap, which were immensely popular in the new playhouses, and the romances of Charles Brockden Brown, which at the close of this period mark the beginning of the American novel.

---

[1] At Boston, in 1690, appeared *Public Occurrences*, our first newspaper. Its editor promised that it should appear " once a month, or oftener if any glut of occurrences happen." This poor literary infant gave some political offense, and was promptly suppressed by the Legislature. The first regular weekly, *The Boston News Letter*, appeared in 1704, almost a century after the first English settlement; and as late as 1750 only a few weeklies could be found here. Then, within a few years, scores of newspapers and magazines made their appearance (see Thomas, *History of Printing in America*).

Just as the new social life brought forth this ephemeral writing — a kind of literature of amusement, to be enjoyed to-day and forgotten to-morrow — so the various political movements had each its distinctive form of literary expression. The years following the obnoxious Stamp Act saw the beginning of that brilliant oratory which was, and still is, one of the great molding influences in American life and literature. The strife of Whigs and Tories is mirrored in a host of ballads, songs and satires in verse ; and the struggle between Federalists and Anti-Federalists over the Constitution produced, in the writings of John Adams, Washington, Madison, Jay, Hamilton, Jefferson, and many others, a new form of political writing, the first true literature of Democracy, which had influence far beyond the borders of the American nation.

Revolutionary Poetry. One of the first things we note in the poetry of the Revolution is that it is often cheapened and vulgarized by being devoted to the service of politics, as was English literature in the days of Swift and Addison. We should expect an oration or a political essay of the period to bristle with arguments ; but in the realm of poetry we expect better things, and are disappointed to find that lyrics and ballads, satires and ambitious epics, are all alike intended, not to voice the emotions of a nation, but rather to serve as an arsenal in which Patriots or Tories sh... find weapons to hurl at the heads of their political enemies.

Another marked characteristic of the poetry of the age is its imitativeness, its bondage to fashion.[1] The thought is sometimes

Poetic Fashions original, and the setting is generally American, but the style and phraseology are usually only slavish copies of British originals. Thus, one of the most notable American poems of the eighteenth century was the *Philosophic*

---

[1] Literature, no less than dress, is often ruled by fashion. Many English prose writers of Elizabethan times thought that they must write in the wretchedly involved style of Lyly's *Euphues*. Later, poets must have a "metaphysical" style and write like Donne. In Revolutionary times English and American poets imitated Pope's rimed couplets, and essayists copied the "elegance" of Addison.

Solitude of William Livingston. The author was a soldier in the French and Indian Wars, a member of the Continental Congress, a war governor of New Jersey during the Revolution, — a rugged, Cromwellian kind of man, to be cherished as a friend and feared as an enemy. When he writes prose he speaks like a man, often like a soldier ; but when he turns to poetry he straightway simpers, and becomes the mere slave of a literary fashion :

> Lo! round the board a shining train appears
> In rosy beauty, and in prime of years!
> This hates a flounce, and this a flounce approves,
> This shows the trophies of her former loves; . . .
> Then parrots, lapdogs, monkeys, squirrels, beaux,
> Fans, ribbons, tuckers, patches, furbelows,
> In quick succession through their fancies run,
> And dance incessant on the flippant tongue.
> And when, fatigued with every other sport,
> The belles prepare to grace the sacred court,
> They marshall all their forces in array,
> To kill with glances, and destroy in play.[1]

A far cry this from the gloom and terror of Wigglesworth's *Day of Doom*, which has, at least, the two virtues of being sincere and of reflecting a true side of the Puritan imagination. These endless rimed couplets have two chief faults : they are artificial, and they give false impression of the mothers of the Revolution. One has hardly read a dozen lines before he knows that Livingston has merely taken Pope's *Rape of the Lock* and given it an American setting.

Because of the political turmoil of the age, a large part of Revolutionary verse is devoted to satire. Here again our writers follow the English poets of the eighteenth century — who were sometimes hired by Whigs or Tories to satirize political opponents — and their verses copy the style and methods of Dryden, Pope and Churchill. It was a beautiful case of "fighting the devil with his own weapons," for every one of these vigorous

---

[1] From *Philosophic Solitude* (1747). The same imitation of Pope is seen in another famous poem, Barlow's *Hasty Pudding* (1796).

American satirists used his British model as a club wherewith to belabor the mother country for her political blunders:

> With press and pen attacked the royal side,
> Did what he could to pull their Lion down,
> Clipped at his beard, and twitched his sacred hide,
> Mimicked his roaring, trod upon his toes,
> Pelted young whelps, and tweaked the old one's nose.[1]

To the student, the most interesting thing in Revolutionary poetry is the new and vibrant note of nationality. Songs and **National Songs** ballads appeared in countless numbers; satires fairly peppered the columns of every Patriot newspaper; and all alike voiced the national spirit of the first Continental Congress. A score of verses from different sections might easily be quoted, but a single illustration must suffice. At the period of which we are writing, one of the most popular songs in England was David Garrick's sailor chantey, the chorus of which ran:

> Hearts of oak are our ships,
> Gallant tars are our men;
> We always are ready;
> Steady, boys, steady!

In the *Virginia Gazette* of May 2, 1766, when the Colonies were all aflame over the Stamp Act, appeared a parody on this " English Hearts of Oak." Though the title remained intact, the verses warned England that crossing the ocean had not changed the Saxon spirit, and that a lion's whelp is a lion, no matter where he happens to be born. One of the stanzas ran:

> On our brow while we laurel-crowned liberty wear,
> What Englishmen ought, we Americans dare:
> Though tempest and terrors around us we see,
> Bribes nor fears can prevail over hearts that are free.
> Hearts of oak are we still,
> For we 're sons of those men
> Who always are ready —
> Steady, boys, steady! —
> To fight for their freedom again and again.'

[1] From Freneau, " The Country Printer."
Duyckink, *Cyclopedia of American Literature.*

Ten years later, on the eve of conflict, the song was parodied by another Virginian, and now it was called " American Hearts of Oak." The meaning of the changed title is obvious. The verses, and indeed all the songs of the period, are echoes of Patrick Henry's passionate declaration : " I am not a Virginian ; I am an American." [1]

Revolutionary Prose. Individuality is perhaps the first quality of Revolutionary prose. For the orators and statesmen have this advantage over the poets, that a man dares to be himself, instead of a copy of Pope or some other literary fashion. When we read such poems as Livingston's *Solitude*, or Dwight's *Conquest of Canaan*, or Barlow's *Columbiad*, there is nothing whatever in the style to suggest that the first was written by a doughty Whig champion, the second by a college president, and the third by a versatile minister, lawyer, land speculator and politician. If by some chance the poems had been found among Dwight's manuscripts, the world would never suspect, from internal evidence, that the godly Yale president had not written all three tiresome effusions. But one who reads Franklin's *Autobiography*, or Woolman's *Journal*, or Paine's *Common Sense*, knows instantly what manner of man is speaking ; knows also that Franklin could not by any possibility have written the spiritual *Journal*, or Paine the self-satisfied *Autobiography*. And so with the other prose writers, Lee, Adams, Quincy, Mayhew, Jefferson, Hamilton, — the revelation which each makes of himself in his style is far more interesting, because more human, than the political subject he happens to be expounding.

Almost as notable as this individuality of Revolutionary prose writers is another trait, a kind of " commonwealth quality," **Citizen** arising from community of interests on the one hand, **Literature** and from a man's profound sense of responsibility to his fellows on the other. If the lonely Colonial writers impress us as voices crying in the wilderness, the Revolutionary

---

[1] From a speech at the opening of the First Continental Congress, 1774.

authors seem like men speaking in a great assembly ; and their words have power because they voice the thought and aspiration of a multitude. For a new problem has been suddenly thrust upon the Colonies by the Revolution. It is the problem of forming one union out of many states, of making one government out of many factions, of bringing a multitude of all sorts and conditions of men into national peace and harmony. Hence the orators and prose writers, if they are to help solve that mighty problem, must appeal to the love of freedom and the sense of justice which lie deep in the hearts of men ; they must emphasize ideals which are acknowledged by rich and poor, wise and ignorant ; and, like Bradford, they must have an eye single to the truth in all things.

That they felt their responsibility, that they used voice and pen nobly in the service of the nation, is evident enough to one who reads even a part of the prose literature appearing between Henry's impassioned " Liberty or Death " speech and Washington's calm and noble " Farewell Address " to his people. Clearness, force, restraint ; here a touch of humor, when the crowd must be coaxed ; there a sudden exaltation of soul, when the old Saxon ideal of liberty is presented, — all the elements of a fine prose style are manifest ; but it is not so much the form as the substance that appeals to us, and especially the greatheartedness of the Revolutionary writers. They gave the world the first example of what has been well called " citizen literature," that is, the expression of the ideals of a whole commonwealth, and to this day their work remains unrivaled in its own political field.

This Revolutionary prose belongs largely to the " literature of knowledge " and is seldom found in literary textbooks ; but it is well to remember two things concerning it : that it began with our national life ; and that it reflects a strong, original and creative impulse of the American mind. It was as if Democracy, silent for untold ages, had at last found a voice, and the voice spoke, not doubtfully, fearfully, but in trumpet tones of prophecy. It gave the startled old world something new and vital to think about; and it is quite as remarkable in its way as are the forest and sea romances of Cooper, which surprised and delighted all Europe a half century later.

III. TRANSITION FROM COLONY TO NATION

BENJAMIN FRANKLIN (1706–1790)

It was a custom among certain Indians to place at the gate of their village a symbolic staff, carved in the likeness of some bird or beast. This was the totem pole, and it indicated three things: the tribe or clan to which the Indians belonged, the qualities of strength or cunning which they admired, and the bond of unity and peace among those who followed the same symbol. Had America adopted this custom at the close of the Revolution, and set up totem poles instead of flag-staffs on her village greens, it is probable that many of them would have been carved in the semblance of a human head, with fur cap and spectacles, which would have suggested

BENJAMIN FRANKLIN

to every visitor the name, the quality and the influence of Benjamin Franklin, the man who symbolized success.

In many ways this one citizen was typical of the new American nation. He was a self-made man, who had risen by his own effort from poverty to wealth, from obscurity to world-wide honor; he was an epitome of the shrewdness and practical sense that win reward in the business of life; and when he had signed the four notable documents of our early history,[1] and represented us with marked success in the courts of Europe, he became a bond of unity among the people. For a quarter of a century his almanac had been their daily counselor; they read newspapers which bore the stamp of his genius; they comforted themselves about his new stove; they lost fear of the tempest under the protection of his lightning rods. In all these ways Franklin had entered into the warp and woof of American life. At home he was more widely known than any other man save Washington; abroad he was famous for his electrical experiments, and his maxims were household words in many places where the name of the great Virginian had never been heard. He seemed, therefore, and to many he still seems, a kind of totem or symbol of his age, the most representative American of the eighteenth century.

Life. Franklin's life began (1706) when America consisted of a few scattered settlements, in only one of which was a newspaper; it ended (1790) when the same settlements had become a united and progressive nation under one great leader. He marks the rapid transition from the Colonial to the National period, and when we study the spirit of his life we are struck by the contrast between the old order and the new.

Thus, he was a contemporary of Jonathan Edwards; but while Edwards marks the end and glory of one age, Franklin is unmistakably the beginning of another. Contrast these two men in any way, and they are as different as the *Freedom of the Will* and *Poor Richard's Almanac*, as a Greek temple and a modern workshop. He was born and bred in Boston, the stronghold of Puritanism, while Cotton Mather was in the autumn splendor of his influence; but there was nothing of the Puritan in Franklin, and Mather he regarded with mild curiosity. "There came in my way," he tells us, as if he were meeting a stranger, "a book of Dr. Mather's, called *Essays to Do Good*, which gave me a turn of thinking"; but we note that it was one of the least of Mather's works, and that Franklin did not get even the title right. All the rest

Franklin's Contemporaries

---

[1] These are the Declaration of Independence, the treaty of alliance with France, the treaty of peace with England, and the Constitution of the United States.

of the Puritan's mighty interests, like outgoing ships, had already dropped below the rim of Franklin's horizon. Some five years before Mather died Franklin ran away to Philadelphia, and Boston lost in the same decade two prominent citizens; one departing broken-hearted because the city had become too liberal, the other shaking the dust gladly from his feet because the same city was too strait and narrow for his way of thinking. " I had already made myself a little obnoxious to the governing party," he tells us, without a smile at the conceit of this youth of seventeen, who takes issue with the Governor in affairs of statecraft, and with Doctors of Divinity in matters of religion and morals. His attitude toward his superiors reminds us strongly of the young Omar:

> Myself when young did eagerly frequent
> Doctor and saint, and heard great argument
> About it and about: but evermore
> Came out by the same door wherein I went.

Our first impression, therefore, is that Franklin and his contemporaries have parted company; that he seems less a product of New England, with her faith and idealism, than of eighteenth-century Old England, with her skeptical philosophy and worldly manner of living.

From his life story we glean the following facts: that he was poor and obscure; that he had only two years of schooling; that he liked **Early Life** to read, but had very few books.[1] At ten he was working in the shop of his father, who made soap and candles; at twelve he was apprenticed to his brother, who was a printer, thereby spoiling his own plan to run away to sea, and his father's ambition to make a minister of him.

When he entered the printing house, Franklin set his foot promptly on the first rung of the ladder of fame and fortune. For a short time he was the odd-job boy of the place; then he determined to improve the newspaper by writing essays after the manner of Addison. He had studied this master of style in an odd volume of the *Spectator*, and thought that he " could improve the matter or the language." These essays, on such timely subjects as " Freedom of Thought " and " Hoop Petticoats," he slipped under the door, and listened with delight when the printer asked who could have written them. Here,

---

[1] Franklin's library consisted of *Pilgrim's Progress*, Plutarch's *Lives*, Burton's *Historical Collection*, Defoe's *Essay on Projects*, a translation of Xenophon's *Memorabilia*, a volume of the *Spectator* essays, and a few unread volumes on " Polemical Divinity."

at the outset of his career, we find him cultivating the talent to which, as he tells us, he owed most of his success, namely, his " little ability in writing." He seemed on the point of making a name for himself, when he quarreled with his brother, broke his articles, and ran away to Philadelphia. There he arrived, after an adventurous journey, with one Dutch dollar and a few coppers in his pocket.

From the *Autobiography* we form a picture of him as he trudges up Market Street. Here he is, the future foremost citizen of Pennsylvania, the man who shall stand before princes. His clothes are soiled, his hair unkempt from sleeping in the fields; his pockets bulge out with his spare shirt and stockings; he is eating a puffy roll of bread, and holding another roll under each arm. No one recognizes the future great man. A girl on a stoop turns, glances at him, smiles at his awkward appearance; and this smiling girl is his future wife. What a chance for romance, for poetry, for sweet and tender recollections when they shall look back on the scene together! But alas! there is no sentiment in Franklin; to him poetry is a book with seven seals; and never, not even in the memory of a woman's smile, shall he look in at the golden door of romance. Interested in his new surroundings and wholly unconscious of self, he goes on his way, eating his roll, his keen eyes taking in the world as his mouth takes in the bread. When his hunger and curiosity are satisfied, he follows some well-dressed people into the Quaker meetinghouse and takes a comfortable nap during divine service.

Next day he was looking for work, and straightway found it. For a year or more he followed his printer's trade, exercising meanwhile his remarkable faculty for making influential friends. One of the latter, Governor Keith, sent him on a wild-goose chase to London, where he made the best of misfortune by learning improved methods of printing. Then he returned to Philadelphia, and was clerk in a store till fate drove him from the counter to the printing house again. This time he stayed to make his fortune.

The rest of the story is one of unbroken triumph. He succeeded rapidly in business, largely by industry and thrift, but occasionally advancing his own interests by methods which cannot stand for an instant in the white light of honor. At forty he had enough money, knew it, and retired from business to devote himself to the public welfare.

With his genius for practical leadership, he was appointed or elected to various offices, and in every case he revolutionized the methods of the public service. The modern post office dates from the day he was appointed postmaster at Philadelphia, and made it for the first time a useful and paying institution. He created the modern police force, **Public** to replace the ridiculous old night watch; he organized the **Service** first fire company, instituted the modern militia, started the American Philosophical Society, began a circulating library, founded an academy which became the University of Pennsylvania. Also he made inventions, like the iron stove, the first advance on the clumsy brick oven of the Romans, which added enormously to the comfort of the common people. All the while he wrote essays, using literature to serve some practical end. The result of his work and writing was that he soon became the leading citizen of a great colony. Not a project, from cleaning streets to starting a hospital, could succeed unless he indorsed it. Though ignorant of military affairs, he furnished transportation and food for Braddock's army; and after the rout of the British troops (1755) he was sent to build forts on the frontier to protect settlers from the fury of the savages.

While Franklin was debating whether to devote himself to science or to writing his cherished *Art of Virtue*, fate again interfered to push him away from the book, which he was hardly fitted to write, into an unexplored region where a great revelation was awaiting the time when he should apply his common sense to the clouds instead of to Braddock's army. Into his discovery, that the blinding flash from the thunder cloud and the amusing spark from a cat's back are one and the same thing, we cannot enter here; it is a matter of science rather than of literature. We note only that, when the discovery was quietly announced, this obscure tradesman was known and honored from one end of the civilized world to the other. He was then ready for his mission, and Europe was ready to listen to every message he might bring from America.

In 1757 he began his eighteen years' residence in England, going abroad as agent of his state. Here again he made influential friends, **Franklin** used the newspapers, till he became almost as well known **Abroad** in London as in Philadelphia. Meanwhile he did splendid service for the Colonies, securing the repeal of the Stamp Act, postponing and trying to avert the Revolution. When war seemed inevitable, England apparently offered liberal inducements to hold him to the British cause, but he sided squarely with the Patriots, while his own son went over to the Tories. There is sterling metal in this American, and it rings true when he rejects England's offer, and comes home to sign the Declaration of Independence.

Franklin was then an old man and longed for peace, but almost immediately he was sent to France as ambassador of the Colonies. His reception in Paris was perhaps the most remarkable ever accorded to a foreigner. Enthusiastic crowds followed him on the streets; his words were on every tongue, his picture in every shop window — curious pictures, with lightning flaming around his old fur cap and illuminating Turgot's poetic line: *Eripuit coelo fulmen sceptrumque tyrannis.* Taking shrewd advantage of the enthusiasm, he pleaded the cause of his country, used the newspapers, made powerful friends; and it is due largely to his personal influence that money and a fleet were sent to aid us in the Revolution.

When the treaty of peace was signed, in 1783, Franklin's great work for his country was practically done, and he seems for the first time a little weary, a little sad, as he writes home to an old friend:

" At length we are at peace. God be praised, and long, very long, may it continue. All wars are follies, very expensive and mischievous ones. When will mankind be convinced of this, and agree to settle their differences by arbitration? Were they to do it even by the cast of a die, it would be better than by fighting and destroying each other."

He had often asked to be recalled, but it was not till 1785 that he was allowed to return home in triumph. He had served his state and nation for a full half century, and looked forward to ease by his own fireside and to writing his *Art of Virtue;* but hardly had he landed before he was elected Governor of Pennsylvania, and again took up the burden of public office. He lived long enough to help frame the Constitution, and to see his friend Washington made President of the new nation. His last years, when he met suffering and death with undiminished cheerfulness, seem to us the most heroic of his long career. His attitude toward life is summed up in a paragraph of the *Autobiography*, which tells us that he would be glad of the chance to repeat his course from the beginning, " only asking the advantage authors have in a second edition, to correct some faults in the first." His attitude toward death is summed up in a sentence:

" Death I shall submit to with the less regret as, having seen during a long life a great deal of this world, I feel a growing curiosity to be acquainted with some other."

Works of Franklin. In ten large volumes we have only a part of Franklin's writings; but these are enough. We do not read them for the simple reason that they have no beauty, no enduring interest. For sixty years he had been industrious with his pen, using it only as a tool, as a means to some practical and immediate end. Like Swift, he seldom signed his work, letting it stand or fall on its own merits. He made no effort to collect his writings, and the most important of them was forgotten and thrown into the street. In declaring, therefore, that the bulk of Franklin's work is of small literary value, we are merely repeating his own shrewd judgment. An exception must be made, however, of his almanac, his *Autobiography*, and a few of his letters and essays.

Poor Richard's Almanac was begun in 1732, the year of Washington's birth, and for twenty-five years was known throughout the Colonies. Franklin's work here, though not original,[1] was notable in this respect, that it produced our first typical character, Poor Richard,—who ranks with Leatherstocking and Uncle Remus among the enduring creations of American fiction.

Poor Richard's Almanac

> *Poor Richard, 1733.*
>
> AN
> # Almanack
> For the Year of Chrift
> # 1733,
> Being the Firft after LEAP YEAR.
>
> *And makes fince the Creation* Years
> By the Account of the Eaftern Greeks 7241
> By the Latin Church, when ☉ ent. ♈ 6932
> By the Computation of W W 5742
> By the Roman Chronology 5682
> By the Jewifh Rabbies 5494
>
> *Wherein is contained*
> The Lunations, Eclipfes, Judgment of the Weather, Spring Tides, Planets Motions & mutual Afpects, Sun and Moon's Rifing and Setting, Length of Days, Time of High Water, Fairs, Courts, and obfervable Days Fitted to the Latitude of Forty Degrees, and a Meridian of Five Hours Weft from London, but may without fenfible Error ferve all the adjacent Places, even from Newfoundland to South-Carolina.
>
> By RICHARD SAUNDERS, Philom.
>
> PHILADELPHIA:
> Printed and fold by B. FRANKLIN, at the New Printing Office near the Market.
> The Third Impreffion.

TITLE-PAGE FROM *POOR RICHARD'S ALMANAC*

[1] Long before 1732 the yearly almanac was a welcome visitor in every Colonial home. The best, not excepting Franklin's, was the *Astronomical Diary and Almanac* of Nathaniel Ames, of Dedham, Massachusetts. This appeared in 1724, and for forty years preached the gospel of work and cheerfulness. Franklin's general plan suggests that of Ames; his title, "Poor Richard," was taken from an English almanac.

Another detail is worthy of notice. At that time Pennsylvania's only almanac, a poor affair, was published by a quack astrologer named Titus Leeds. Franklin, in the guise of Poor Richard, informs the public that he would not start a second almanac but for this reason: the author of the first is doomed; the stars have been consulted, and by their infallible decree Leeds must die on October 17, after which his excellent almanac will be no more. Evidently Leeds had no sense of humor, for in his next almanac he replied hotly, insisting that he was alive, and abusing Poor Richard. In the following year Richard sadly informs his readers that Leeds must be dead for two reasons: first, the stars could not lie, as Leeds had often declared; and second, if that illustrious man were living, he would not use such unchristian language, nor publish such a wretched almanac. It was a good-natured kind of fooling, which we might better enjoy if we did not know that it was copied from Swift's *Bickerstaff Almanac*. But the public knew nothing of Swift; it applauded Poor Richard's stolen wit, and bought his almanacs as fast as he could print them.

Surprised at the success of his venture, Franklin resolved to make his almanac useful as well as profitable, and filled it with wise saws, anecdotes and moral precepts, till its pages were like a boy's pocket:

" Better slip with foot than tongue. Doors and walls are fools' paper. Diligence is the mother of good luck. Honesty is the best policy. Great talkers are little doers. God helps them that help themselves. Experience keeps a dear school, but fools will learn in no other. If you would know the value of money, go and try to borrow some, for he that goes a-borrowing goes a-sorrowing. . . . "

These and hundreds of similar aphorisms, scattered among the calendars and weather predictions, indicate the character of Franklin's philosophy.[1] In thousands of homes his almanac

1 Franklin's wisdom is part of the so-called gnomic philosophy, and most of his maxims may be traced back to the Seven Sages, the gnomic poets of early Greece. These were men famous for making proverbs, and their wise saws are still repeated in every civilized language.

BENJAMIN FRANKLIN

From the portrait by Duplessis

was read over and over again by the winter fire; his proverbs were repeated by fathers to children, until his thought became almost a part of the national consciousness.

Before Franklin went abroad, in 1757, he made a last powerful impression on his countless readers. Reviewing all his **The Way to Wealth** almanacs, he packed their best wit and wisdom into the form of a speech heard at an auction — a remarkable homily on industry and thrift, seasoned with the salt of Poor Richard's maxims. As this famous speech is a short one, we forbear quotation, leaving it entire to the reader. It made a sensation, next to the *Day of Doom* probably the greatest in our literary history. Under various names, such as "Father Abraham's Speech" and "The Way to Wealth," it was reprinted in every American newspaper. It went abroad on the first ship; was displayed in English stores and factories; two translations of it were made in France, where the clergy used to distribute it to their parishioners, and from France it spread through every other civilized country.

The *Autobiography* was begun in 1771, while Franklin was visiting his friend Bishop Shipley, at Twyford, England. He **The Autobiography** was then sixty-five years old, and thinking, possibly, of his death and of newspaper obituaries, he wrote a letter to his son, at that time Governor of New Jersey. It opens as follows:

"Dear Son: I have ever had pleasure in obtaining any little anecdotes of my ancestors. . . . Imagining it may be equally agreeable to you to know the circumstances of my life, . . . I sit down to write them for you. To which I have besides some other inducements. Having emerged from the poverty and obscurity in which I was born and bred to a state of affluence and some degree of reputation in the world, and having gone so far through life with a considerable share of felicity, the conducing means I made use of, which with the blessing of God so well succeeded, my posterity may like to know, as they may find some of them suitable to their own situations and therefore fit to be imitated. . . .

"Hereby, too, I shall indulge the inclination, so natural in old men, to be talking of themselves and their own past actions. . . . And lastly (I may as well confess it, since my denial of it will be believed by nobody) perhaps I shall a good deal gratify my own *vanity*. . . . Most people dislike vanity in others, whatever share of it they have themselves; but I give it fair quarter wherever I meet with it, being persuaded that it is often productive of good to the possessor, and to others that are within his sphere of action; and therefore, in many cases, it would not be altogether absurd if a man were to thank God for his vanity among the other comforts of life."

Here, on the first page, we have the author's three motives in writing : he will gratify a little natural vanity, record such family history as a son would like to remember, share the secret of his worldly success and so instruct others in the conduct of life. He has no thought of literary fame, and this explains the greatest charm of his book, its straightforwardness.

The son evidently cared little for this letter, which was lost for twelve years and rescued on its way to the bonfire.[1] At the urgent request of friends Franklin wrote another chapter in Paris, and a third in Philadelphia, bringing the record down to 1757; but he cared so little for the story that he never completed it, and died without arranging for the publication of any of his writings.

The literary world has dealt more kindly with the *Autobiography*, which has been widely read at home and in many foreign countries. The secret of its popularity lies partly in the glamor which surrounds the author's worldly success, partly in the interest which we take in the story of any life, if it be told frankly from within. Here is a man who has "warmed both hands before the fire of life." He has risen from obscurity to fame ; on his upward way he has met the heroes and shared in the fateful incidents of our national history. He tells us just how he did it, and somehow gives the impression that others may win the same success by the same methods. As the vast majority of readers are, like Franklin, born poor and ambitious,

[1] Abel Jones, a Quaker, rescued Franklin's letter, recognized its value, and sent a copy to Franklin, urging him to complete the work. The *Autobiography* was first published in France, immediately after Franklin's death, in 1790. The first edition in English was a retranslation of this garbled French version. Not until 1868 was the work published as Franklin wrote it. The long delay is attributed to the carelessness of a grandson, Temple Franklin, who had charge of Franklin's manuscripts. It has been suspected, however, that this grandson was bribed by some stupid official to suppress all of Franklin's papers relating to his dealings with the English government.

his story made a lasting impression, especially in a country where every man may set his own goal and win it by his own effort.

On these three accounts — the human interest of the work, its historical background, and its tonic influence on the reader's will power — Franklin's *Autobiography* has become a classic in our literature. This is the fact, though some of us may doubt the value of the work and the judgment of those who praise it extravagantly. Regarded as a matter of self-portrayal, simple, clear, without affectation or concealment, it is an excellent piece of work ; but the spirit of the author is too worldly and mechanical, too negligent of the higher attributes of humanity to rouse our enthusiasm. Many excellent critics commend the work nevertheless. They would give the *Autobiography* to young people as a stimulus in the prosaic matter of getting a living, just as poetry is given to educate their sense of beauty, and the *Iliad* and *Morte d'Arthur* to develop their heroism and chivalry.

The remaining works of Franklin cover such a variety of subjects that the beginner will do well to read a small book **Various** of selections. Such a collection should include some **Minor Works** of the *Silence Dogood* and *Busybody* papers, which are brief essays modeled on the *Spectator ;* a few dialogues, after the manner of Xenophon, like "Franklin and the Gout"; and a dozen of the later essays, like "The Ephemera" and "The Whistle." The last are of no consequence ; but they indicate the curious fact that Franklin, at seventy-five, was writing with more vivacity than at any other period of his life. In an entirely different vein are the satires, like "Rules for Reducing a Great Empire to a Small One," "An Edict by the King of Prussia," and "From the Count de Schaumburgh" — keen, penetrating little works, suggesting a favorable comparison with Swift, the greatest master of satire that the English race has produced. The selections should include also some of Franklin's *Letters*, which are, in our judgment, the best of all his writings.[1]

---

[1] An excellent book for the beginner is Bigelow's *Life of Franklin Written by Himself.* Here the *Autobiography* is supplemented by numerous letters.

The Quality of Franklin. The style of Franklin is in marked contrast to that of other Colonial and Revolutionary writers. Aiming in his first essays at clearness, force and brevity, he grows steadily clearer, more forceful, more pithy, until he can say more in a sentence than other writers in a paragraph. His English is, like that of Swift and Defoe, remarkable for simplicity, for absence of all rhetorical effort. Best of all, his style is

pervaded by a kindly humor, which is often called American, but which, like all humor, is an individual not a national quality. As Tyler points out, it answers Thackeray's description of real humor as being made up of wit and love, "the best humor being that which contains the most humanity and is flavored throughout with tenderness and kindness." Even in his satires, which attack injustice, Franklin's humor is always kindly; and here he is in contrast

FRANKLIN'S PRINTING PRESS

not only with his master Swift, but also with Freneau, Odell and other satirists of the Revolutionary period.

Omitting Franklin's political and scientific writings, the bulk of his work is a kind of homily on the art of living; and here, **His Philosophy** we must remember, he marks the transition from the theological to the worldly period of American life. Unlike the Colonial writers, he looked at men steadily from a workaday viewpoint, and aimed to make the humdrum life of this world more comfortable and contented. To accomplish this desirable end, two things seemed to him essential, virtue and prosperity, and either of these must lead to the other. Thus he tells us in one work that " virtue is the best means of success," in another that " prosperity is the road to virtue." The chief fault of such a philosophy, if we may dignify worldly wisdom by so noble a name, is that it estimates virtue and human life on too low a plane. Virtue is not a means, but an end in itself; it is an immortal ideal which lightens the soul of every man coming into the world; it has nothing to do with riches or poverty, with present success or failure. As Tennyson writes:

> Glory of warrior, glory of orator, glory of song,
> Paid with a voice flying by to be lost on an endless sea.
> Glory of Virtue, to fight, to struggle, to right the wrong —
> Nay, but she aim'd not at glory, no lover of glory she:
> Give her the glory of going on, and still to be.

We can honor Franklin heartily for his inventions and scientific discoveries, his patriotism and service to his country; but we are considering now his moral philosophy and his literary work. The philosophy seems to us an affair of policy, rather than of enduring principle. It is shortsighted, being bounded by earth's horizon. It lacks the tremendous emphasis of the eternally right. In his writings we find abundant sense and humor, but nothing of delicacy or culture, of sentiment or chivalry. In a word, he lacks idealism — that exquisite sense of unseen reality, of the eternal in the temporal, of the divine in the human, which is the glory of our life and literature.

IV. ORATORS AND STATESMEN OF THE REVOLUTION

In studying that unrivaled group of orators and statesmen who made our nation what it is, one is often reminded of the words of De Tocqueville, who, viewing them from an impersonal vantage ground — as one must ever study a varied group of men or a complex movement in history — loses sight of the individual and notes only the big, significant qualities that characterize them all alike:

I can conceive nothing more admirable or more powerful than a great orator debating great questions of state in a democratic assembly. As no particular class is ever represented there . . . it is always to the whole nation, and in the name of the whole nation, that the orator speaks. This expands his thoughts and heightens his power of language. As precedents have there but little weight, the mind must have recourse to general truths derived from human nature to resolve the particular question under discussion. Hence the political debates of a democratic people, however small it may be, have a degree of breadth which frequently renders them attractive to mankind. All men are interested by them because they treat of Man, who is everywhere the same.

No better estimate of the Revolutionary fathers has ever been made. These men have a national, not a sectional spirit. They appeal directly to the ideals of liberty and justice which glorify the souls of men wherever man is found. And that, in a word, is the secret of their power and influence.

Typical Revolutionary Speeches. It is difficult to name the best speeches of such an age of oratory, when patriotism glowed

James Otis
 in every pulpit and flamed in every legislative hall throughout the Colonies, and with some hesitation we have selected two that seem typical of all the rest. The first is the speech of James Otis, in the Town House at Boston, in 1761. His subject was the Writs of Assistance, which he enlarged to the general proposition that "taxation without representation is tyranny." He began with a legal argument, but from the advocate he changed to the prophet — a very Isaiah, Adams calls him — and boldly asserted that no law could stand which violated the fundamental rights of humanity. Fragmentary as it is,[1] this speech, with its logic, its passionate appeal, its prophetic warning, is an epitome of the political thought of America during those tense years when revolution, a little cloud like a man's hand, rose darkly above the horizon. "On that day Independence was born," says John Adams; and again, writing from Philadelphia after signing the Declaration of Independence, he calls this speech the beginning of the struggle between England and America.

---

[1] The address was probably never written, for Otis, like Henry, depended on his audience for inspiration. Full notes were taken by John Adams, then a young lawyer, and they are found in his collected works.

The speech of Patrick Henry, in 1775, marks the end and climax of Revolutionary oratory. Fifteen years have passed

Patrick Henry since Otis defined the question at issue, stated the American argument, and voiced the American spirit. During these years the Colonies were buzzing like a beehive with legal argument and political oratory; but every argument had failed, every petition had been slighted, every solemn warning to England fell on ears as deaf as Pharaoh's to the voice of justice. As that fiery old patriot Samuel Adams declared :

PATRICK HENRY

" We have explored the temple of royalty, and found that the idol we have bowed down to has eyes that see not, ears that hear not our prayer, and a heart like the nether millstone."

Down in Virginia the House of Burgesses has been roughly dissolved by the royal governor. As the delegates gather again, in old St. John's Church, there is a feeling in the air that further argument is idle; that there is nothing left for a free man but to submit quietly to injustice or to reach for his weapons. At this critical moment Henry rises to speak. His first words imply that the day of speech is past; it is the time for action. Then, with the power of a master musician, he plays upon the emotions, rouses the fighting blood of his hearers, till all doubts are dissolved, prudence swept aside, and they grow eager, impatient of delay, like cavalry horses at the sound of the bugle. Hear this peroration, and for a moment put yourself back among the aroused delegates, for whom

Henry's prophecy was startlingly verified in the tidings from Lexington and Concord :

" It is in vain, sir, to extenuate the matter. Gentlemen may cry, peace, peace, but there is no peace. The war is actually begun. The next gale that sweeps from the North will bring to our ears the clash of resounding arms. Our brethren are already in the field. Why stand we here idle? What is it that gentlemen wish? What would they have? Is life so dear, or peace so sweet, as to be purchased at the price of chains and slavery? Forbid it, Almighty God. I know not what course others may take; but as for me, give me liberty or give me death!" [1]

We have read this speech and heard it declaimed many times. We know that it is perfervid, illogical ; that our reason ought to detect and criticize its weaknesses ; yet we confess that we have never read or heard it without a tingling of the nerves, a tightening of the muscles for action. There is something irresistible in the appeal, which stamps it as a masterpiece of popular oratory.

The Statesmen. There are at least twelve Revolutionary statesmen, each one remarkable for some written word that has given inspiration to America for a century past, who deserve a place in our literature. Even a list of their names suggests how vain were the attempt to do them justice in this brief history. Towering above the rest is Washington, whom " Light-Horse Harry " Lee described as " first in war, first in peace, first in the hearts of his countrymen." Washington's mother calls him simply " a good son " ; all his contemporaries unite in calling him a good " father of his country," and these two tributes sum up his qualities as a man and as a statesman.

No other American has been so bepraised ; hardly another seems so vague as Washington, and this because we are content to receive our impressions at secondhand, from Washington biographers who make of him " a frozen image," or else a model of superhuman excellencies. Washington was primarily a man, and the only way to know him now is to read

---

[1] Henry's speeches were never written. He seems to have been like the old Greek rhapsodists in being able to give himself wholly to the inspiration of the moment, and his words pour from him like water from a living spring. The account of his famous speech is found in Wirt's *Life of Patrick Henry* (1816).

his own record. We would begin with his Journal, especially that modest record of his heroic journey through the wilderness to the French forts on the upper Ohio, in 1753. Here we meet a youth going about a strong man's work with courage and profound sagacity, estimating the value of this western wilderness, showing the judgment of a soldier and a statesman in concluding that the distant French and Spanish possessions are a menace to liberty and to the expansion of the American people. In this youthful record we hear, faint but clear, the trumpet note of nationality that is to ring through all his later writings.

GEORGE WASHINGTON

Aside from his personal quality, Washington was **Farewell Address** fitted to be a national leader largely because by travel and observation he knew his whole country, — the common spirit of New England, the Old Dominion and " the land beyond the mountains." And for North, South and West he advocated a national university, where youths from every section should meet one another and learn devotion to a common ideal. His journals, his letters, his message to the states after disbanding the Revolutionary army, — all these speak first of the man, and then of the patriot animated and dominated by the new national spirit.[1] Hardly

[1] We would recommend to the student Washington's *Journals*, *Letters*, his note " To the Governors of all the States " (1783) and his " Farewell Address " (1796).

is the nation formed, when he sees it doubly divided, first by those who side with France or England in their European war, and second by the bitter struggle between Federalists and Anti-Federalists. Then he writes his "Farewell Address," still sounding the same note of nationality, pleading with the American people to be a nation after their own fashion, avoiding alike the "entangling alliances" with foreign nations and the dangers of partisan strife among themselves :

" . . . Citizens by birth, or choice, of a common country, that country has a right to concentrate your affections. The name of American, which belongs to you in your national capacity, must always exalt the just pride of patriotism, more than any appellation derived from local discriminations. With slight shades of difference, you have the same religion, manners, habits and political principles. You have, in a common cause, fought and triumphed together; the independence and liberty you possess are the work of joint counsels and joint efforts, of common dangers, sufferings and successes. . . .

"Observe good faith and justice toward all nations; cultivate peace and harmony with all. Religion and morality enjoin this conduct; and can it be that good policy does not equally enjoin it? It will be worthy of a free, enlightened and, at no distant period, a great nation to give to mankind the magnanimous and too novel example of a people always guided by an exalted justice and benevolence. . . ."

From that pioneer band of statesmen who upheld Washington's hands as he formed and presided over a nation, we select only two, Hamilton and Jefferson, not because they were the best writers, but because they reflect two opposing tendencies, which had and still have an important influence on American life and letters. We shall never understand these two men, who represent permanent types of statesmen, unless we have some clear idea of the parties they were leading.

Permanent Political Parties. When Winthrop made his notable speech on Liberty, in 1645, he faced two distinct parties, which are best described in his own faithful words :

" Two of the magistrates and many of the deputies were of the opinion that the magistrates exercised too much power, and that the people's liberty was thereby in danger; other of the deputies (being about half) and all the rest of the magistrates were of a different judgment, and that authority was overmuch slighted, which, if not timely remedied, would endanger the Commonwealth and bring us to a mere democracy." [1]

Ever since Winthrop's day the same parties have been in opposition in America. As no strict definition has ever been made, we endeavor simply to point out their chief characteristics.

The first party, which a theorist might call " Maximarchist," aims to increase the functions and powers of government. It strives continually to regulate by legislation, multiplying the number and the complexity of laws, bringing under supervision many affairs that formerly were left to the will of the individual. Also it tends strongly toward centralization. As many different state legislatures are bound to run counter to one another, this party would leave all important matters to the central government, letting it control our business and railroads as well as the tariff, our divorces and old-age pensions no less than the post offices. It would strengthen the hands of President and Congress, till all our affairs are controlled by one strong, paternalistic government.

The other party, which might be called " Minimarchist," regards government as, at best, an unfortunate necessity, and would reduce lawmaking to its lowest and simplest terms. It holds that we already have too many laws, some of which are mere experiments, or else benefit one class at the expense of another. Its fundamental position is that a country is best governed which is least governed; that men should be left free as possible to manage their own affairs, without legislative interference. And because government, which is in theory a servant, has in past ages inclined to become a master and a tyrant, this party opposes all centralizing tendencies. It would leave legislation as largely as possible to local governments, which are more easily held in check, more sensitive to the will of the people.

These two parties became national and sharply defined after the Revolution, when thirteen independent states sought to unite under **Federalists** a common government. At that time America followed **and Anti-** English political methods of the age; in consequence her **Federalists** various governments inclined to the privileged classes, manhood suffrage was almost unknown, and Winthrop's old fear of a " mere democracy " was still widely prevalent. [2] Every state that

[1] Winthrop's *History of New England* (Savage's edition, 1853), II, 277. This speech, in 1645, opens one of the most significant chapters in our political history.

[2] The latter statement is amply supported by the comments of the Federalist press after Jefferson's election in 1800.

entered the Union had its Federalists and Anti-Federalists, —its Monocrats and Mobocrats, as they called each other,—one party advocating a strongly centralized government, the other concerned for state and individual rights, seeking to curb the central government and make it answerable to the popular will. Hamilton and Jefferson are symbolical of these two parties, and of the mighty struggle that resulted in the compromise Constitution of 1787. The remarkable success of that Constitution is due largely to the fact that the same parties are still with us, though no longer strictly defined, and that the Constitution preserves a just balance between them.[1]

ALEXANDER HAMILTON

ALEXANDER HAMILTON
(1757–1804)

To write an adequate account of either Hamilton or Jefferson is very difficult, for two reasons : First, there are no authentic biographies, those we have being mostly written with an eye to party politics rather than to truth and humanity, which are the only concerns of literature. Second, to follow these men is to enter a mighty political struggle and discuss issues outside our present interest. We confine ourselves, therefore, to a brief outline ; and this will be more luminous if we keep in mind the governing motive in each man's life. Hamilton aimed at a powerfully centralized government, which should be largely in the hands of

---

[1] "Coleridge once said that in philosophy all men must be Aristotelians or Platonists. So it may be said that in American politics all men must be disciples either of Jefferson or of Hamilton. But these two statesmen represented principles that go beyond the limits of American history, principles that have found their application in the history of all countries and will continue to do so " (Fiske, *Essays Historical and Literary*, I, 170).

the privileged classes. He distrusted the common people, denied their right or ability to govern themselves, and regarded democracy as the dream of demagogues or visionaries. The keynote of Jefferson's life was his patient faith in the whole American people. He aimed at a democracy, pure, just, enlightened, and opposed all centralizing tendencies in the national government. Both men were patriotic; both rendered vast and disinterested service to the American nation; but they sadly misunderstood one another, and this personal misunderstanding spread through

EARLY VIEW OF KING'S COLLEGE (COLUMBIA)

their respective parties and discolored our political literature for a generation following the adoption of the Constitution.[1]

Biographical Outline. Hamilton was born on the island of Nevis, West Indies, in 1757. At twelve years he was earning his living as a clerk; at fifteen he came alone to this country, entered King's College (Columbia), and presently became a leader of the young Patriots in their political debates with the college Tories. Anticipating the Revolution, he plunged into military studies, entered the army at the head of a well-drilled company, served on Washington's staff, and fought bravely to the end of the war. Then he studied law, went

[1] Hamilton was an acknowledged leader of the Federalists. Jefferson's party was first called Anti-Federalist, then Democratic-Republican, and finally Democratic.

to Congress, and was a leader of the New York delegates at the Constitutional Convention of 1787.

When our Constitution was finally framed — after endless debates between two parties, one of which demanded more and the other less power for the central government — Hamilton was deeply disappointed. He had fought hard for a different instrument,[1] yet with rare self control he accepted a government which seemed to him weak and dangerously democratic, supported it loyally, and it was due largely to his efforts that the Constitution was ratified by his own state.

Recognizing Hamilton's service, knowing also his remarkable financial ability, Washington called him to be our first Secretary of the Treasury. We had then no settled currency, no national revenue, no responsibility for large debts incurred during the Revolution. Hamilton's first duty was to create out of this financial chaos a firm national credit, without which the new government must have speedily gone to pieces. How he accomplished this herculean task is a matter of history.[2] Webster summed it up in his oratorical fashion by declaring, " He smote the rock of national resources and abundant streams of revenue gushed forth ; he touched the dead corpse of public credit and it sprang upon its feet."

Hamilton's leadership slipped away from him during the presidency of John Adams, when he became involved in political intrigues, and after the rout of the Federalist party by Jefferson, in 1800, he retired to private life. Four years later he was shot in a duel by Aaron Burr — a terrible and needless sacrifice, for Hamilton disapproved of dueling and made no effort to defend himself.

Works of Hamilton.

In the literary battles of the Revolution two weapons were employed : the light verse satire, which Freneau used with the skill of an Indian shooting his arrows ;

[1] The constitution which Hamilton favored provided for (1) a House of Commons with insignificant powers, elected by general suffrage ; (2) a powerful Senate for all important legislation, elected from and by property owners, its members holding office for life ; and (3) a President with immense powers, holding office for life, and having authority to appoint governors for the several states. Even this was not centralized enough to suit him, but was " the best I may hope to obtain at present."

[2] The three prominent features of his work were : the assumption of the various state debts by the nation, the funding of this national debt by issuing bonds against the revenue and the sale of public lands, and the establishment of the United States Bank. The mint, tariff, excise tax, management of public lands, and other features of our government still follow the general direction laid down by Hamilton at a time when he was under thirty-five years of age.

and the heavy prose pamphlet, the war club of the period, of which Hamilton was a master. Soon after his arrival in America public attention was centered on Seabury's *Westchester Farmer* (1774–1775), a series of powerful essays upholding the Tory or Loyalist cause, and shattering the arguments of young Patriots who were advocating armed resistance to England. A score of answers to the *Westchester Farmer* appeared, but the Loyalist position remained unshaken till Hamilton, a mere boy and a stranger, published " A Full Vindication of the Measures of Congress" and " The Farmer Refuted " — papers of such remarkable ability that they were generally attributed to Jay or Livingston, or some other statesman of wide experience and profound learning. With the exception of Paine's *Common Sense*, all such works were soon forgotten ; but the student who would understand the spirit of the age will read the pamphlets of Hamilton and Seabury for their steady light, and the satires of Freneau and Odell for their sputter and sparkle.

At the present day Hamilton's literary fame rests largely on his essays known as *The Federalist*.[1] They began to appear in

The Fed- 1787, when each state was divided on the question
eralist   of ratifying the Constitution, when the whole country was agitated over problems of state and national rights involved in the new Union. As their name implies, they advocated a strong centralized government ; but their chief object was to explain and defend the Constitution, as a just compromise between the radically different parties, and as a safe solution of the difficult problem involved in making one nation out of many independent states.[2]

Concerning the matter of these essays we hesitate to offer an opinion. They crystallize the results of two centuries of

[1] Several of these essays appeared first in the newspapers, over the name of " Publius " ; later they were increased to the number of eighty-five and published in book form. Hamilton originated the work, and wrote some fifty of the papers ; but he was ably assisted by James Madison and John Jay, who completed the series.

[2] For the other side of the argument, see Richard Henry Lee's *Letters of a Federalist Farmer*, and Patrick Henry's speeches in the Virginia Convention. These opposed ratifying the Constitution.

experiment in the matter of free government, and properly belong to political science rather than to literature. Moreover, a fair judgment is rendered difficult by the fact that, even at the present day, one party regards Hamilton as the fountain of political wisdom, while the other sees chiefly the dangerous tendency of his principles and methods. As literature knows no partisanship and no interests save those of humanity, we forbear discussion of what is largely a political problem. We simply record two facts : that, at a critical moment in our history, *The Federalist* essays exercised a powerful influence in establishing the Constitution ; and that they have since been widely accepted as expressive of the fundamental principles of confederation, — principles which great legal minds, like Story and Marshall, expanded later into our constitutional law.

The style of these papers would alone make them remarkable. They have clearness, force, polish — all the good qualities of eighteenth-century prose — and are, both in style and matter, probably the highest examples of modern political writing. They imply, moreover, a splendid tribute to the intelligence of the age which first received and appreciated them. As Fiske says :

" The American people have never received a higher compliment than in having such a book addressed to them. That they deserved it was shown by the effect produced, and it is in this democratic appeal to the general intelligence that we get the pleasantest impression of Hamilton's power."

Thomas Jefferson (1743–1826)

Ask the first educated (and unprejudiced) man you meet, Who was Thomas Jefferson ? and he will answer, in effect, that he was one of our greatest statesmen, the author of the Declaration of Independence, the third president of the United States, our first conspicuous Democrat, and to all ages the apostle of democracy in America. All that is true and interesting, but it misses Jefferson's most significant trait, — his romantic idealism, which allies him with Coleridge, Southey and the band of young poets who were joyfully expectant after the first success of the

French Revolution, as if the trumpet must sound and the millennium follow with the next sunrise. We shall appreciate him
better if we remember that in his youth he was an enthusiastic
reader of the new romantic literature, and that he accomplished
his work for democracy and education here while the romanticism
of Wordsworth, Scott and Byron was most influential in Europe.

Unlike other Revolutionary leaders, Jefferson won recognition not by oratory or military success, but by his pen alone. In

Jefferson's Idealism a tumultuous time
he was the one
man in America, of power-
ful, sympathetic imagination,
who could express at any
moment what the multitudes
were thinking and feeling.
That is why the eager young
Patriots hailed his startling
Summary View of 1774;
why the sagacious old leaders
of the Continental Congress
turned to him instinctively
for their Declaration of Independence. Though occu-
pied forty years with public
affairs, his heart was most at
home in the quiet country,

THOMAS JEFFERSON

cherishing the love of birds, the delights of nature, the simple
joys of domestic life. All the while, whether in field or forum,
he was not simply a man of fact, as practical and helpful as
Franklin, but a man of vision, and of enthusiastic faith in his
fellow men. He was both a doer of deeds and a dreamer of
dreams, the quality of the latter showing that he was far ahead
of his age, and even in advance of our own.

Now vision and dreams, love of nature and faith in man, were
the heart and soul of the new romantic movement in literature.

Jefferson belonged to it, was part of it, as truly as he belonged to the new political party. But while he dreamed for the future, he worked and wrote for the present. He aimed to educate men, to lead them up to the point where they must share his vision of a free and equal manhood. So his literary work is subordinate to his practical purpose. A romanticist who applied his high ideals to common men and to the problems of humanity ; a builder at once of air castles and foundations ; an idealist who was an educational reformer, a constructive statesman and the most successful of politicians ; a revolutionary enthusiast, like Shelley, who instead of a chaotic *Prometheus Unbound* left us the Democratic Party, the University of Virginia and the Declaration of Independence as his enduring monuments, — such was the genius we are trying to understand.

Sketch of Jefferson's Life. At a plantation called Shadwell, on the Indian-haunted frontier of Virginia, Jefferson was born in 1743. He had an admirable early education, his father teaching him the practical affairs of life, his mother, Jane Randolph, leading him to the delights of literature. Glimpses of the boy's early life show that he was fond of reading, hunting and all outdoor sports ; that he studied hard, worked hard, played hard ; was a lover of nature and humanity, and practiced the fiddle, as he called it, three hours every day. This ideal life, of study and work and play, lasted until he was seventeen.

From the farm he rode to William and Mary College, where he worked faithfully at science and modern literature, as well as at the classics. Then for five years he studied the principles of law under a famous teacher. When at twenty-six he first **Education** appears in public life, as a delegate to the House of Burgesses, we are impressed by his splendid development. He is an athlete, a scholar, a trained lawyer, a practical farmer, an experimenter in natural science. And he knows Virginia society from top to bottom, from the planter's mansion to the slave's cabin, from the famous ballroom at Williamsburg to the smoky Indian wigwam hidden far away in the forest. Knowing men as they are, and dreaming of their future, he is a democrat, an idealist, a forerunner of the same mighty movement which produced romanticism in literature and the American and French Revolution in politics.

In reading even an outline of Jefferson's public service the chief thing to note is this: that whatever he does or attempts, he always **Public** looks far ahead of his contemporaries, and plants a crop **Service** that will mature after his death. For dreams, especially great dreams, take no heed of time; they partake of eternity. He saw that the great need of democracy is intelligence, and straightway laid a broad foundation for free popular education. Though a slave-owner, he recognized the evil of slavery and set bravely to work, first to suppress the slave traffic, then to find a just way of general emancipation. "I tremble for my country," he said, "when I think of the negro and know that God is just"; and again, with perfect faith in humanity, he declares, "Nothing is more certainly written in the book of fate than that these people are to be free." With a few enthusiastic young Virginians, he formed the historic Committee of Correspondence, which anticipated the Revolution and united the Colonies in preparation for it. As our ambassador to France, where he was consulted by leaders of the French Revolution, he was more interested in the common people than in courts or society; he grieved over their oppression, and renewed his vow to oppose every attempt at aristocracy and class privilege in government. So, as Secretary of State in Washington's cabinet, he set himself against Hamilton, and quietly began to organize a democratic party in opposition to what he believed to be the monarchial tendency of the Federalists. He was twice elected President; he came into office as a radical reformer, feared and hated by the old party as one who would plunge the country into anarchy; and he led the nation steadily onward in a career of unexampled prosperity.[1] Then he retired to his Virginia home, "Monticello," where he quietly exercised a profound influence over a large party of his countrymen, whose confidence in his judgment was increased by the fact that he opposed as dangerous their desire to elect him for a third term to the presidency.

To the end he worked faithfully for his three supreme objects: for popular education, for civil and religious liberty, and for a democ-**Jefferson's** racy which should be in truth a government of the whole **Aims** people. He cherished the ideal that America should follow her own ways, as a new nation of freemen, avoiding as a plague the barbarous strife of the world for riches, and the insane competition of European nations for military or commercial supremacy. For he

---

[1] For an outline history of the period, see introduction to the next chapter.

had the conviction—which Ruskin adopted later—that the wealthiest nation is that which has, not the greatest fleets and factories, but the largest number of happy and intelligent people. He died, full of years and honors, on July 4, 1826. On the same day died John Adams. These two old patriots and signers of the Declaration, thinking of each other and stretching out their hands to each other across a united country, passed away together on the birthday of the nation they had helped to establish. And the last words of Adams, "Thomas Jefferson still lives," seem to us at once a tribute and a prophecy.

STREET FRONT OF THE UNIVERSITY OF VIRGINIA (1819–1826), DESIGNED BY THOMAS JEFFERSON

Works of Jefferson. The life of this man is so interesting that one is bound to be disappointed in his writings. Not that they are scant—a small part of them fills ten volumes [1]—but because they are so practical and didactic in purpose that they obscure Jefferson's romantic idealism, which is, in our judgment, the most significant thing about him. First in importance we would place the *Letters*, which furnish a critical commentary on the men and events of a stirring historical period. The chief

---

[1] Jefferson was an inveterate writer, on a great variety of subjects, but he had no literary ambition and published only a few works which his friends deemed of great public importance. After his death a large number of manuscripts were found, some of which (like the unfortunate *Anas*) were of a private nature and were never intended for the press. The editors used their own judgment, which was sometimes influenced by politics in their selections for publication.

trouble with these letters is their abundance. There are thousands of them, and until they are all explored and the best collected into a single volume, we shall hardly appreciate their value. Meanwhile, one must read them as one goes through a mine, avoiding the rubbish and stopping only when one finds a nugget. Here, for instance, is the letter that Jefferson the President wrote to lonely old Samuel Adams, — a generous, glowing tribute from one patriot in his hour of triumph

MONTICELLO, JEFFERSON'S HOME

to another patriot, poor and neglected, which would make us honor the author, even if he had never written anything else.

Two other works belong to the borderland between literature and history. The *Autobiography*, with its keen observation, its pictures of the men he had known and of the great events in which he had taken part, is extremely valuable to the historian, and many general readers find it more interesting than Franklin's better-known story of his life. The *Notes on Virginia* is a series of essays written in response to questions of the secretary of the French legation, who was collecting information about America for his home government. These essays, with their descriptions of nature, their pictures of Indian and slave life, their discussion of political, religious and economic questions,

are invaluable to the student of our early history. They outline
a picture of the country as it was at the beginning of its national
career, and, in their aim at least, carry a suggestion of Bryce's
The American Commonwealth, of a century later.[1]

Of Jefferson's numerous political works we recommend only
two, his *Instructions to the Virginia Delegates to the Congress*
The Sum-   *of 1774*, and his first *Inaugural Address*. The former,
mary View   which was republished as *A Summary View of the
Rights of America*, exercised a powerful influence in uniting
the Colonies for the Revolution. It was reprinted in England,
and furnished Burke with the chief argument of his speeches
in favor of America. At that time it was a revolutionary work,
but the modern reader can hardly appreciate its boldness and
radicalism. The king is told bluntly that the Colonies are asking for rights, not favors; that his duty is " simply to assist
in working the great machine of government erected for the
people's use and subject to their superintendence." England is
informed that all men must and shall have " equal and impartial right"; that "the whole art of government consists in being
honest," and a deal more of what to us seems commonplace but
what was then heroism in rebellion :

> Thoughts that great hearts once broke for, we
> Breathe cheaply in the common air ;
> The dust we trample heedlessly
> Throbbed once in saints and heroes rare,
> Who perished, opening for their race
> New pathways to the commonplace.[2]

The Declaration of Independence. Every American should read
this noble document, not only in its present form, but as it first
came from Jefferson's soul, glowing with ardor for liberty and

---

[1] Unfortunately, in order to answer all the questions, Jefferson included a deal of
dry statistics. Until these are relegated to an appendix, and the whole work judiciously
edited, the *Notes* will hardly appeal to the general reader.

[2] From Lowell's " Masaccio." The *Summary View* of 1774 is sufficient answer to the
common allegation that Jefferson's work for democracy here was inspired by the French
Revolution. All the principles for which he worked in later life are clearly expressed in
his earlier writings.

humanity ; and especially should we read and consider it, not as political science, but as literature. For it is the most powerful, the most significant piece of literature that ever came from a statesman, — a prose chant of freedom that echoed round the world ; a passionate cry against injustice, which Burns caught up instantly and set to music ; a declaration not of American independence but of human brotherhood, which inspired all the romantic poets and proved its power by hastening on the French Revolution.[1]

We are told by the wise that the Declaration is not original, and by the prudent that its political theories are unsound, espe-**Represent-** cially its "self-evident" truth that "all men are cre-**ative** ated equal." But originality was the last quality that **Character** a great man would have desired in that fateful hour when the Continental Congress reached its decision. As Jefferson said long afterwards, he had no wish to be original but to be representative. It is true that some of its expressions, like "unalienable rights" and "consent of the governed," are taken from Locke's *Essay on Government;* true that many of its statements are found in earlier records of the Virginia Assembly ; true that all its principles were familiar as the Commandments, having been preached in the churches, argued in the legislatures, and published in every newspaper. After years of anxiety and hesitation, the crisis has at last arrived—" now's the day and now's the hour " —when the Colonies stand face to face with the most momentous decision in their history. Before they take the step that shall plunge the country into war, the delegates at Philadelphia must proclaim their principles, must speak the word that shall hearten the timid ones, convince the doubtful, and electrify the brave by a call to action. They turn instinctively to the young Virginian and say : " Write it for us. Tell England and the world what we think and feel, what multitudes

[1] All this is not figure but fact. American newspapers, diaries, letters and sermons of the period bear witness to the electrical effect of Jefferson's masterpiece at home. In Buckle's *History of Civilization* may be found a tribute to its remarkable influence abroad.

of free American men have thought and felt these twenty weary years." And he did it. If ever statesman forgot himself and gathered the ideals, the arguments, the indignation and defiance of a people into a broadside and hurled them with the directness of a cannon ball against the enemy, that statesman was Thomas Jefferson when he wrote the *Declaration of Independence*. Its power lies in the fact that it is not new but old, old as man's dream of freedom; that it is not the weak voice of a man, but the shout of a nation girding itself for conflict. As old Ezra Stiles, president of Yale, declared in 1783, Jefferson "poured the soul of the whole continent" into his *Declaration*.

Criticisms against it are mostly based upon the assumption that it is a state paper. We prefer to think of it as a prose war **Emotional** song. Even mollified as it was by a cautious Con- **Quality** gress, it is still vibrant with suppressed emotion. That Jefferson began it as a state document is evident from the noble, rhythmic prose of its opening sentence; but as he wrote rapidly, forgetting himself to speak for his country, he must have remembered the burning of Norfolk, the battle of Bunker Hill, and heard as an echo the shout of Washington's victories at Boston. Then the war song began to throb like a drum in his heart and to vibrate in his fingers. And we imagine — nay, we need not imagine, since contemporaries bear witness to the outburst of enthusiasm which followed — that the *Declaration* stirred these quiet Colonials as Scottish clansmen are stirred by "Scots, wha hae," that most magnificent of all battle songs. Very appropriately, it was first read aloud in Independence Square before an immense throng of people, and the reader was Captain John Hopkins, of the new American navy. As he rolled it out in his powerful seaman's voice, now with the swing of a deep-sea chantey, now with the ringing summons of *Clear ship for action!* the words thrilled that vast audience like an electric shock. They knew, as we can never know, just what the *Declaration* was, — a call to battle for the rights of man. And they were ready to answer.

We shall not, therefore, criticize the *Declaration of Independence* as a work of political science, or analyze its prose style, or otherwise maltreat and misunderstand it. We see its faults, but we love it for its virtues; for its elemental and unchanging

INDEPENDENCE HALL, PHILADELPHIA

manliness; for its deep emotion, more convincing than argument; for its moral earnestness; for its bold, unproved assertion of the fundamental rights of humanity:

"We hold these truths to be self-evident: That all men are created equal; that they are endowed by their Creator with certain unalienable rights; that among these are life, liberty and the pursuit of happiness. That, to secure these rights, governments are instituted among men, deriving their just powers from the consent of the governed; that, whenever any form of government becomes destructive of these ends, it is the right of the people to alter or to abolish it, and to institute a new government, laying its foundation on such principles, and organizing its powers in such form, as to them shall seem most likely to effect their safety and happiness."

Terrible words to a king and a tyrant! Brave, faithful, inspiring words to men who toil and hope and are still oppressed! But are they true? The answer is found not in political economy but in the heart of man, which cherishes ideals as the only permanent realities. For a hundred years now that *Declaration* has been read on the nation's birthday, in town halls, in city churches, on thousands of village greens; and wherever it is really heard, eyes glisten and hearts are lifted up from the noise of the day to its silent, solemn meaning, as one sees above the bursting skyrockets the steady light of the eternal stars. For

Wherever Columbia's stars have shone, since ever their course began,
The lowly ones of the earth have known they stood for the rights of man.

During that hundred years our nation has been steadily breaking the shackles of men and bidding the oppressed go free; and still the *Declaration* goes before us, like the pillar of fire, to show the way. In its light all our political problems are seen to be one, and that is to realize a democracy which shall be in truth a brotherhood of men. The reform of yesterday, the work of to-day, the hope of to-morrow, are all builded on the dream of '76, that men shall be equal, free and happy. Our whole history, if it have any significance, means simply this : that we remember our high calling ; that we obey a mighty impulse ; that we press forward to realize the ideal to which our first representatives pledged " our lives, our fortunes and our sacred honor."

V. THE POETRY OF THE REVOLUTION

It is a literary rule that the spirit of any age is measured by the poems which it inspired ; but as we study this Homeric period of American history we are confronted by the startling fact that its heroism has never found adequate expression. It appeals to the young American as an age of great ideals and noble action, like the age of Elizabeth ; yet no poet caught the inspiration and expressed it so as to make us feel the national enthusiasm. Much was attempted, in ballads, lyrics, dramas,

even epics ; but little remains save the remembrance of failure.
We shall confine ourselves, therefore, to an outline of the forms
which verse assumed, and to the work of one man, Philip
Freneau, who marks the beginning of a new and important
movement.[1]

Songs and Ballads. Moore's *Songs and Ballads of the
American Revolution* and Sargent's *The Loyalist Poetry of the
Revolution* contain the best of our early ballads ; but one must
search a dozen collections, and the files of century-old newspapers, to appreciate the quantity and variety of this particular
form of poetry. Every town had then its ballad maker, every
newspaper its poet's corner, and every important event on land
or sea was immediately celebrated in song. Merely as a suggestion, we name "The Volunteer Boys," "The Old Man's
Song," "The Battle of Trenton," "The Dance," "A Fable,"
"The Battle of the Kegs," "Bold Hathorne," "King's Mountain," and "The Present Age," which are types of all the rest.
As we read them, we hear again the toot of a fife, the rattle of
a drum, the tread of marching soldiers ; for whatever their literary faults, they still preserve something of the warlike spirit
that inspired them. And there is at least one, "The Ballad of
Nathan Hale," which we can never forget :

> The breezes went steadily through the tall pines,
>   A-saying "Oh hu-ush !" a-saying "Oh hu-ush !"
> As stilly stole by a bold legion of horse,
>   For Hale in the bush, for Hale in the bush.
>
> "Keep still," said the thrush, as she nestled her young,
>   In a nest by the road, in a nest by the road ;
> "For the tyrants are near, and with them appear
>   What bodes us no good, what bodes us no good."
>
>   .   .   .   .
>
> No mother was there, nor a friend who could cheer,
>   In that little stone cell, in that little stone cell ;
> But he trusted in love, from his Father above :
>   In his heart all was well ; in his heart all was well.

[1] For the general characteristics of Revolutionary poetry, see pp. 94-97.

Partly because of our sympathy for the brave young patriot who suffered the meanest of deaths for his country, and partly because of the peculiar melody and the fine natural setting, "Nathan Hale" rises above all others of its class into the realm of poetry. It is, in our judgment, the best of a thousand ballads produced during the Revolutionary period.

JOEL BARLOW

The Hartford Wits. This unfortunate pseudonym was given to a group of clever college men, living in Hartford, who wrote newspaper verses to support the government or to satirize the follies of the age. Their chief aim, however, was not political but literary, and we have not yet done justice to their endeavor. Barlow, Dwight and Trumbull, the leaders of these "wits," are remarkable for two things: they were the first group of men who made a definite attempt to create a national poetry in America, and they were probably the pioneers of our modern English studies.[1] There were no teachers of modern literature in those days; Dwight and Trumbull, both tutors at Yale, were regarded as innovators when they formed classes for the study of English letters. Meanwhile Trumbull wrote his "Progress of Dulness" (1772), a famous

[1] Trumbull's English studies had a curious beginning. He was a precocious child, who passed his entrance examinations to Yale when he was seven years old. He was not allowed to enter till he was thirteen, and by that time he had read so much Greek and Latin that there was nothing left to do in college. He was advised to take up mathematics and astronomy, but turned to the new field of English literature instead.

satire ridiculing, among other things, the college fashion of
stuffing men's heads with Latin, Greek and Hebrew to the
exclusion of their own noble literature.

The attempt at a literature which should be national rather
than provincial is shown in *The Columbiad* of Joel Barlow

Barlow (1754–1812). This is an epic of ten books, so long
and dull that
few persons ever finish the
task of reading it. Yet
the motive is magnificent,
and there is enough heroic
material in the poem to
make us sympathize with
Hawthorne, who wanted to
make a melodrama of *The
Columbiad* and put it on
the stage to the accom-
paniment of thunder and
lightning. The epic is now
forgotten, and Barlow is
known as the author of
" Hasty Pudding " (1796).
This burlesque poem was
very popular in its day,
and is still worth reading.
But it seems a pity that
this ambitious man, who

TIMOTHY DWIGHT

aimed to create a national literature, should now be remembered
as the singer of the joys of mush and milk.

Timothy Dwight (1752–1817) was another poet who attempted
to express the new national spirit, first by patriotic songs like

Dwight " Columbia," then by a huge epic called *The Conquest
of Canaan* (1785). The few who have patience to
read this work will feel here and there the thrill of nationality,
like the stir of a slumbering giant; may feel also the spirit of

this noble teacher, the first of our great college presidents, who became so much a part of our life that his death " seemed to leave a gap in the solar system."

YALE COLLEGE IN 1820

John Trumbull (1750–1831) is the most brilliant of this significant group of literary men. His youthful essays, in the Connecticut Journal, are in many ways superior to Franklin's, and some of his early poems, such as the " Ode to Sleep," are full of promise :

Trumbull

> Come, gentle Sleep,
> 　Balm of my wounds and softener of my woes,
> 　And lull my weary heart in sweet repose,
> And bid my saddened soul forget to weep,
> 　And close the tearful eye ;
> While dewy eve with solemn sweep
> 　Hath drawn her fleecy mantle o'er the sky,
> And chased afar, adown th' ethereal way,
> The din of bustling care and gaudy eye of day.

Like Freneau, he has the instinct of a poet ; but when the Revolution approaches he throws himself into the strife of the hour, using a valiant pen instead of a sword for a weapon. Farewell, greatness ! Trumbull is henceforth a mere satirist, a slave to literary fashion, wasting his genius on the three subjects of the hour, " Tea, Toryism, and Taxes."

THE TORY'S DAY OF JUDGMENT

An illustration from John Trumbull's *M'Fingall*, New York, 1795

Because of this absorption in political satire, Trumbull's extraordinary promise came to naught; his good work for modern literature is forgotten, and he is remembered only as the author of *M'Fingal* (1775–1782). This is a burlesque poem, modeled after *Hudibras*, ridiculing the principles of a Tory squire, and describing his punishment by a jeering mob of Whigs. It is something to be popular even for a day, and *M'Fingal* was the most popular and widely quoted work of the entire Revolutionary period. Aside from this, it has three merits : it is a good example of a rough type of American humor ; it is an excellent picture of the political hurly-burly of the age ; and it ranks with Paine's *Common Sense* among the literary forces which hastened the Declaration of Independence. Merely as a suggestion of the style, we add a few doggerel couplets from the third canto :

> Not so our 'Squire submits to rule,
> But stood, heroic as a mule.
> " You 'll find it all in vain," quoth he,
> " To play your rebel tricks on me.
> " All punishments the world can render
> " Serve only to provoke th' offender ;
> " The will gains strength from treatment horrid,
> " As hides grow harder when they 're curried.
> " No man e'er felt the halter draw
> " With good opinion of the law ;
> " Or held, in method orthodox,
> " His love of justice in the stocks ;
> " Or failed to lose by sheriff's shears
> " At once his loyalty and ears." . . .
>
> Forthwith the crowd proceed to deck
> With halter'd noose M'Fingal's neck,
> While he, in peril of his soul,
> Stood tied half-hanging to the pole ;
> Then lifting high the ponderous jar,
> Pour'd o'er his head the smoking tar. . . .
> And now the feather-bag display'd
> Is waved in triumph o'er his head,
> And clouds him o'er with feathers missive
> And down, upon the tar adhesive.

Philip Freneau (1752–1832)

In Freneau we have an example of the fact that the literary world is not divided by national barriers, for he is unmistakably a part of that important movement known as Romanticism,[1] which influenced all Europe toward the close of the eighteenth century. We shall never appreciate Freneau at his best until we see him, not as the political satirist of his age, but as a fore-runner of Wordsworth and Coleridge, in whom the romantic movement in English poetry made a definite and glorious beginning.

Life. Freneau was a man of contrasts. As we follow his career — as student, rebel, journalist, trader, poet, privateer; now afloat on the spacious deep, now scribbling in the narrow cell of a government clerk; to-day a captain on his own deck, to-morrow a captive in a loathsome prison ship — we have occasional memories of Walter Raleigh, that restless adventurer on unknown seas, in whom the Elizabethan age is personified.

He was of French-Huguenot descent, and was born in New York in 1752. His father was a wine merchant, like the father of Chaucer, and growing prosperous the family removed to a farm near Monmouth (now Freehold) in New Jersey. Here his boyhood was spent; hither he returned to rest after toil, and here he perished in a storm, three quarters of a century later.

---

[1] In English literature the Romantic is generally contrasted with the Classic period. Classicism, which prevailed during the eighteenth century, was cold, precise, formal; it followed set rules, and regarded the plays of Shakespeare and the enthusiasm of Elizabethan writers as "monstrously irregular." It appealed to the head, and glorified the intellect to the neglect of the imagination. Its leaders were Dryden and Pope, and its oracle was Dr. Johnson. Romanticism, which occupied the nineteenth century, gave literary expression to the ideals of common men, just as their importance was recognized politically by the triumph of democracy in America, France and England. It was warm, tender, human; it followed original genius rather than set rules; it appealed to the heart rather than the head, to the imagination rather than the intellect. Some of its leaders were Wordsworth, Coleridge, Shelley, Scott and Byron.

Like most generalizations, the above is open to objections. Thus, the coldness and formality of much eighteenth-century literature indicate pseudo-classicism, that is, Classicism gone to seed. Goethe made a suggestive generalization when he said, "Everything that is good in literature is classical." So also Romanticism is often associated with excess, with unbalanced imagination. In reality, Classicism and Romanticism when good approach each other and touch; when bad they fly to opposite extremes, and it is against these extremes that most criticisms are leveled.

When Freneau entered Princeton College, in 1768, he was already writing verses in imitation of Milton; but the turmoil of the age

A Revolutionary Enthusiast speedily drove him from poetry to politics. Among his classmates at old Nassau were Madison, who became President of the United States; Aaron Burr, that strange genius who did many extraordinary things besides shooting Hamilton; and Hugh Brackenridge, the dramatic poet. In the revolutionary aims of these enthusiasts we note a curious parallel to Wordsworth, Coleridge and Southey, who planned their famous "Pantisocracy on the banks of the Susquehanna," which should change the natures of men and establish a new order of society. We note also the resemblance

EARLY VIEW OF PRINCETON COLLEGE, N.J.

to Jefferson, who had just completed his college course, and who became closely associated with Burr and Freneau in the public service.

After graduation Freneau taught school, studied law, and incidentally lashed the British and Tories in his satiric verse. Next we find him in the West Indies, writing poems like "The Beauties of Santa Cruz," and giving little heed to the Revolution for which he had clamored. When he returned, in 1778, he was amazed at the havoc wrought here by the war. It was a sad, almost a hopeless time; but Freneau poured out a flood of confident satires, jeering at English generals, cheering on the fainting Patriots, and exulting over the coming treaty with France. After an unsuccessful venture with the *United States Magazine*, he seems to have fitted out a privateer; but the vessel was captured and Freneau was thrown into a horrible prison ship, from which he escaped, after a few months, reduced almost to a skeleton. Those who would see the vinegar of his early satire change to vitriol may find it in "The British Prison Ship," written after his escape, while his anger was hot within him.

Into the details of his later career we shall not attempt to enter. We note only that he was always a radical, attacking Hamilton and the Federalists as savagely as ever he assailed the Tories, and that his satires and newspaper articles form a red-peppery sauce to our history till after the War of 1812. Then all bitterness left him, and he rejoiced in a united democracy. Several editions of his poems appeared during his lifetime, two of which were published from his own press. As we read them now, our chief feeling is one of regret that such a man should have wasted his talents. He was capable of real poetry, and his quiet verses, scattered among rough satires, are like violets in a stony field.

Works of Freneau. The important works of Freneau fall naturally into two classes, — political satires and occasional poems of nature and humanity. The spirit of the former may be judged from four lines of one of his earliest efforts:

> Rage gives me wings and, fearless, prompts me on
> To conquer brutes the world should blush to own;
> No peace, no quarter to such imps I lend,
> Death and perdition on each line I send.

Here we feel not simply the rancor of a Patriot against Hessians and Tories, but the added hate of one whose ancestors had waged war for a hundred years against England. Nor was the bitterness all on one side. Opposed to Freneau were the clever Tory satirists, chief of whom was Jonathan Odell, who loved the cause that Freneau hated, and who flayed the Whigs on every occasion. "The Prison Ship," "The Midnight Consultation," describing an imaginary meeting of British generals after Bunker Hill, "America Independent," with its hatred of kings and Tories, — these three will give a good idea of Freneau's satiric power. We may appreciate them better if we remember that satire was a legitimate and powerful weapon in the

struggle that made us a nation ; and that Freneau used satire
simply because it was the form of poetry that most strongly
appealed to his readers :

> With the Muse of Love in no request,
> I 'll try my fortune with the rest.
> Which of the nine shall I engage
> To suit the humor of the age?
> On one, alas! my choice must fall,
> The least engaging of them all.
> Her visage stern, severe her style,
> A clouded brow, a cruel smile,
> A mind on murdered victims placed, —
> She, only she, can please the taste.

It is a relief to turn from this bitter war of Whig and Tory
to the poems of nature and humanity, which are as dear to us
as to those who first read them. Such are " The Indian Burying Ground," suggesting that the savage has lost his fearsome
aspect of earlier days and become a subject for romantic poetry;
and "The Wild Honeysuckle," with its Wordsworthian appreciation of flowers and common things :

> Fair flower, that dost so comely grow,
> Hid in this silent, dull retreat,
> Untouched thy honied blossoms blow,
> Unseen thy little branches greet:
> > No roving foot shall crush thee here,
> > No busy hand provoke a tear.
>
> .   .   .   .
>
> From morning suns and evening dews
> At first thy little being came ;
> If nothing once, you nothing lose,
> For when you die you are the same:
> > The space between is but an hour,
> > The frail duration of a flower.

Other significant works are " Fancy and Retirement," " House of
Night," " Beauties of Santa Cruz," " Eutaw Springs," " Ruins
of a Country Inn," " Indian Student," "Death's Epitaph," " The
Parting Glass " and " To a Honey Bee," — none of them great

poems, but all good, and remarkably original when we consider the fact that on both sides of the Atlantic many poets were still imitating Pope's heroic couplets.

Beginning of Romantic Poetry. Freneau's satire is part of the general eighteenth-century classicism, which prevailed in England as well as America. His occasional poems are remarkable for this, that they indicate an independent beginning of romantic poetry here, at the same time that we began our national existence. Just as Brockden Brown made an original beginning in American fiction, so Freneau broke away from English satirists to speak in his own way to the hearts of his countrymen. And here he is closer than we have imagined to the greatest of all song writers. Thus, in 1786 Burns published his first volume, that famous Kilmarnock edition, which marks an epoch in the history of English poetry. In the same year Freneau published his *Poems*, and many of the latter are inspired by the same spirit that so deeply moved the Scottish plowman. Indeed, if we had found "Fair Flower that dost so comely grow" beside that other "Wee modest crimson tippet flower," we might easily assume that the same poet had written both ; or that these lines from Freneau's "To a Honey Bee" had been taken from one of Burns's drinking songs :

PHILIP FRENEAU

> Welcome! I hail you to my glass :
> All welcome here you find ;
> Here let the cloud of trouble pass,
> Here be all care resigned.

Again, the year 1798 is famous because Wordsworth and Coleridge then produced an inspiring volume, *Lyrical Ballads,* which marks the dawn of the romantic day in English poetry. But long before that time Freneau had published " The House of Night " (1779), which is strikingly suggestive of Coleridge. And here is another suggestion :

> A hermit's house beside a stream
>   With forests planted round,
> Whatever it to you may seem,
> More real happiness I deem
>   Than if I were a monarch crowned.

We can hardly get rid of the impression that these lines were taken from Wordsworth ; yet they were written by the boy Freneau, about the time that Wordsworth was born, in 1770. That the *Lyrical Ballads* were reprinted here, in 1802, and were much better appreciated than in England, may possibly be due to the fact that Freneau had prepared the way for romantic poetry. Moreover, he had influence abroad, as is shown by the fact that Campbell and Scott both "cribbed " his lines; which is an honor they never accorded to the *Lyrical Ballads.* We would not imply that Freneau is the equal of Burns or Coleridge or Wordsworth ; we simply note the remarkable fact that the romantic movement, the most important since the age of Elizabeth, had an independent origin in this country. The spirit of the new movement is reflected in a poem of Freneau's boyhood :

> Fancy, thou the Muses' pride,
> In thy painted realms reside
> Endless images of things,
> Fluttering each on golden wings,
> Ideal objects, such a store
> The universe could hold no more :
> Fancy, to thy power I owe
> Half my happiness below ;
> By thee Elysian groves were made,
> Thine were the notes that Orpheus played ; . . .
> Come, O come, perceived by none,
> You and I will walk alone.

If one has read *L'Allegro*, there is no mistaking the inspiration here. It is imitative, to be sure; but in an age of imitation Freneau, like Godfrey, was remarkable for this, — that he followed an ideal instead of a fashion. The delicate fancy of this little poem, its melody, its appeal to the imagination, its conscious following of Milton rather than of Pope, — all this suggests that the romantic movement in poetry began here, as in England, by a deliberate return to the old masters. And Freneau, the man who led the movement that gave us Bryant and Poe, Longfellow and Lanier, is worthy of more appreciation than our historians have thus far given him.

Miscellaneous Verse. With the crude songs and ballads inspired by the war, the attempt of the Hartford Wits to establish a national literature, the political satires of Patriots or Loyalists, and the romantic verse of Freneau, we have outlined the main forms of poetry during the Revolutionary period. In addition, one finds considerable " vagrom " verse, of small intrinsic value, but indicating that the Colonial era with its isolation and intensity was passing away, and that a new spirit of song was manifest, " like the first chirping of birds after a storm." The nearest approach to a definite literary type is found in the " society verse " of James McCloud and St. George Tucker, two graduates of William and Mary College, whose verses show the influence of the English Cavalier poets. In this significant group we include Francis Hopkinson, of Philadelphia, a stanch old Whig, who could unbend from his severity to write the rollicking " Battle of the Kegs," or dash off Cavalier lyrics like " My Love is Gone to Sea," and the jaunty love song beginning,

> My generous heart disdains
> The slave of love to be.

Very different these from the slashing satires of Trumbull, and from the ponderous epics of Dwight and Barlow! They suggest that all types of English poetry had taken root, like wind-blown seeds, on this side of the Atlantic; and that in any study of early American life or literature we must consider the gayety of the Cavalier as well as the seriousness of the Puritan.

Dramas also were written in this period by John Burk, Royall Tyler and William Dunlap ; but, though they were once played to crowded houses, they are now forgotten. Much more interesting are the dramatic poems of Hugh Brackenridge, *The Battle of Bunker's Hill* (1776) and *The Death of Gen. Montgomery* (1777). In style both poems show the influence of Shakespeare ; but in matter they are wholly American, and reflect a magnificent national patriotism. The dramatic satires of Mrs. Mercy Warren and **the** huge chronicle play, *The Fall of British Tyranny* (1776), are also significant, as a reflection of the dawning national consciousness.

Prominent among the minor versifiers who enjoyed a day's favor was Phillis Wheatley, the negro slave girl. In 1761 she **Phillis** stood, a trembling girl without name or speech, in **Wheatley** the open slave market of Boston. Twelve years later she published, in London, a book with the following title : *Poems on Various Subjects, Religious and Moral, by Phillis Wheatley, Negro Servant to Mr. John Wheatley of Boston, in New England, 1773.* The book created a mild sensation on both sides of the Atlantic, and no wonder ! Even the inspired Psalmist once cried out, " How shall we sing the Lord's song in a strange land ? " This stranger among us was violently taken from her savage mother in Africa. She remembered the horror in that mother's face as her child was snatched away. She could recall the wild, free life of the tribe, — chant of victory or wail of defeat, leaping flames, gloom of forest, cries of wild beasts, singing of birds, glory of sunrise, the stately march of the wild elephants over the silent places. Here was material such as no other singer in all the civilized world could command, and she had the instinct of a poet. We open her book eagerly, and we meet " On the death of an Infant " :

> Through airy roads he winged his instant flight
> To purer regions of celestial light.

This is not what we expected. We skip the rest, and turn the leaves. Here is something promising, " To Imagination " :

> Imagination ! who can sing thy source,
> Or who describe the swiftness of thy course?
> Soaring through air to find the bright abode,
> The empyreal palace of the thundering god,
> We on thy pinions can surpass the wind,
> And leave the rolling universe behind.
> From star to star the mental optics rove,
> Measure the skies and range the realms above;
> There in one view we grasp the mighty whole,
> Or with new worlds amaze the unbounded soul.

It is vain to seek further, for the end is disappointment. Here is no Zulu, but drawing-room English ; not the wild, barbaric strain of march and camp and singing fire that stirs a man's instincts, but pious platitudes, colorless imitations of Pope, and some murmurs of a terrible theology, harmless now as the rumbling of an extinct volcano. It is too bad. This poor child has been made over into a wax puppet ; she sings like a canary in a cage, a bird that forgets its native melody and imitates only what it hears. We have called attention to her simply because she is typical of scores of minor poets of the Revolutionary period who, with a glorious opportunity before them, neglected the poetry and heroism of daily life in order to follow a literary fashion.

VI. MISCELLANEOUS WRITERS OF THE REVOLUTION

A careless glance at Revolutionary literature leaves the impression that America was like Bethesda in those days, and that the multitudes about its troubled pools had no thought but to be healed of their political infirmities. There were many writers, however, who were undisturbed by the general excitement, and whose works have enduring charm from the fact that they deal with life, which is old as the earth, rather than with political problems which arose but yesterday. Crèvecœur's *Letters from an American Farmer*, for instance, is a joyous, a charming bit of literature, giving idyllic pictures of nature and human life in the Colonies. Here also is Jonathan Carver's

Travels through the Interior Parts of North America, a brave book, as fascinating as Parkman's story of the Jesuit explorers. Among the historical writers are Hutchinson, who carries out the work of Bradford and Prince; Ramsay and Belknap,[1] who are precursors of our modern historians. Among biographies are Wirt's admirable *Life of Patrick Henry*, and Marshall's judicious estimate of the father of his country. The latter is in marked contrast to Weems's *Life of Washington* (1800), a grossly inaccurate work which was once more widely read than any other American biography. For naturalists there are the works of John Bartram and of Alexander Wilson; and for those interested in what we may call personal literature, there are the letters of Abigail Adams, of Eliza Wilkinson, and of Dolly Madison — delightful letters, reflecting clearly the spirit of the women of the Revolution.

Here is variety enough to tempt one who loves to explore outside the beaten trails of literature. We offer these books merely as a suggestion. Our work here is to consider two unclassified writers, the one a stormy product of the age of revolution, the other a gentle soul who belongs to no age or nation but to all humanity.

THOMAS PAINE (1737–1809)

One who knew Paine well refused to write about him, saying that he was such a mixture of vanity and greatness, of frankness and concealment, that it was impossible to tell the story of his life.[2] That was a century ago, and time in its merciful way has softened the man's offenses and magnified his service; but we still have no mind to attempt a biography. We note that Paine, who served three countries, was always the man without a country, "a citizen of the world," as he called himself; that he was at home everywhere, and had a home nowhere; that he was always helping others, always in sore

---

[1] Ramsay's most interesting work is his *History of the Revolution in South Carolina*. His twelve-volume work, *Universal History Americanized*, is as suggestive as Noah Webster's *Dictionary*, or Brown's novels, of a strong tendency in the new nation to look at life and letters from an independent viewpoint. Belknap's *New Hampshire* is one of the best of our early histories.

[2] See Joel Barlow's letter to James Cheetham (1809). A part of this letter is quoted in Stedman and Hutchinson, *Library of American Literature*, IV, 56.

need of help himself; forever looking for trouble and, as trouble is accommodating, forever finding it. He wrote his most inspiring message in the midst of a disastrous rout; he merrily knocked theology to pieces while starving in prison, with the guillotine waiting for his head. So he reminds us of the stormy petrel, a restless bird that appears with the first white-caps of a gale, and that chippers most contentedly in the midst of turmoil and danger.

Paine arrived here in 1774, just as the storm was gathering. No one missed him when he left England; no man welcomed him to America; but with a letter in his pocket from Franklin, recommending him as "an ingenious, worthy young man." he went to Philadelphia, found work on the *Pennsylvania Gazette*, and was presently up to his ears in political agitation. As we study him there, with his shady past and resourceful present, his journalistic sense and his extraordinary talent for interesting the public, we are reminded constantly of Defoe, whom of all writers Paine most closely resembles.

Common Sense. Paine's first work shows that, like other writers of the period, he was in favor of union with England; but after the battle of Bunker Hill and the burning of Portland and Norfolk, he declared that "the country was set on fire around my ears, and it was time to stir." He opened the new year (1776) with his *Common Sense*, the first open assertion of American independence, and probably the most powerful pamphlet that ever influenced a nation's history. Every paragraph of this stirring appeal bristles with epigrams sharp as bayonets; every argument suggests the thud of a ramrod driving home a charge, and the ending is like the brattle of a trumpet calling to action:

"O ye that love mankind! Ye that dare oppose not only tyranny but the tyrant, stand forth! Every spot of the old world is overrun with oppression. Freedom hath been hunted round the globe. Asia and Africa have long expelled her. Europe regards her like a stranger, and England hath given her warning to depart. Oh, receive the fugitive, and prepare in time an asylum for mankind!"

Reading it now, in peace and serenity, we are unable to appreciate the effect of this pamphlet, which brought men to their feet like the waving of a torch over a powder magazine. Unnumbered thousands of copies were sold as fast as they could be printed; every Whig newspaper in the Colonies was aflame with its spirit. Odell, the Tory satirist, winces as he writes:

The work like wildfire through the country ran.

That describes it exactly. Within a few months its words were repeated in almost every home within the vast circle of frontier cabins, and the unknown author was for a moment the most talked of person in the whole country.[1]

It is hardly too much to say that this one pamphlet changed the whole character of our Revolution. Though the Colonies were in arms at this time, they were fighting not for independence but for their rights as English subjects. When *Common Sense* appeared, men faced a new issue, and by hundreds and thousands they accepted Paine's fiery assertion that America must be free. When the Continental Congress met, some six months later, a large Patriot party had arisen, and the Declaration of Independence was inevitable. The estimate of Paine's contemporaries, that *Common Sense* was worth an army of ten thousand men to the Continental cause, hardly exaggerates its influence.

The Crisis. While serving in Washington's army, during the terrible retreat across New Jersey, Paine began hastily to write *The Crisis*, and finished this inspiring appeal while his company dodged about like hunted foxes, hoping to escape capture or annihilation:

"These are the times that try men's souls. The summer soldier and the sunshine patriot will in this crisis shrink from the service of his

[1] "Who the author of this production is," Paine writes in answer to a flood of inquiries, "it is wholly unnecessary to the public to know, as the object of the attention is the doctrine, not the man." As the author would have been hanged by the first squad of British soldiers that laid hands on him, he had reasons other than modesty for remaining unknown. In America the work was attributed to Samuel Adams; in England, where *Common Sense* made a sensation, it was credited to Franklin.

country; but he that stands it now deserves the love and thanks of men and women. Tyranny, like hell, is not easily conquered; yet we have this consolation, that the harder the conflict, the more glorious the triumph."

So begins *The Crisis*, and one must perforce read to the end. Its cheerfulness even in defeat, its indomitable optimism, its faith in God and in the American spirit, uplifted the nation like the news of victory. Washington himself was so moved that he ordered it to be read before every company of his soldiers. Unfitted as he was for military service, Paine accepted a lucrative civil office; but he never forgot the fighting soldiers. Sometimes *The Crisis* appeared after a victory, more often after a defeat; and occasionally it ridiculed the proclamation of some pompous English general in a way that made men laugh and cheer in the same breath. The first number appeared in 1776, the last in 1783, and with peace in full sight Paine ends his work with a prophetic look into the future and a plea for a union of all the states into an American nation. His plea was answered, four years later, by the adoption of the Constitution.

The *American* CRISIS.

NUMBER I.

By the Author of COMMON SENSE.

THESE are the times that try men's souls: The summer soldier and the sunshine patriot will, in this crisis, shrink from the service of his country; but he that stands it now, deserves the love and thanks of man and woman. Tyranny, like hell, is not easily conquered; yet we have this consolation with us, that the harder the conflict, the more glorious the triumph. What we obtain too cheap, we esteem too lightly:—'Tis dearness only that gives every thing its value. Heaven knows how to set a proper price upon its goods; and it would be strange indeed, if so celestial an article as FREEDOM should not be highly rated. Britain, with an army to enforce her tyranny, has declared, that she has a right, (*not only to* TAX) but "*to BIND us in* ALL CASES WHATSOEVER," and if being *bound in that manner* is not slavery, then is there not such a thing as slavery upon earth. Even the expression is impious, for so unlimited a power can belong only to GOD.

WHETHER the Independence of the Continent was declared too soon, or delayed too long, I will not now enter into as an argument; my own simple opinion is, that had it been eight months earlier, it would have been much better. We did not make a proper use of last winter, neither could we, while we were in a dependent state. However, the fault, if it were one, was all our own; we have none to blame but ourselves*. But no great deal is lost yet; all that Howe has been doing for this month past is rather a ravage than a conquest, which the spirit of the Jerseys a year ago would have quickly repulsed, and which time and a little resolution will soon recover.

I have as little superstition in me as any man living, but my

* "The present winter" (meaning the last) " is worth an " age, if rightly employed, but if lost, or neglected, the whole " Continent will partake of the evil; and there is no punish- " ment that man does not deserve, be he who, or what, or " where he will, that may be the means of sacrificing a season " so precious and useful." COMMON SENSE.

FIRST PAGE OF "*THE CRISIS*, BY TOM PAINE"

The rest of Paine's career belongs to European literature. The Colonies were grateful, giving him money and an estate at New Rochelle; but he was essentially an agitator, as uneasy in peace as a fish out of water, and presently he went abroad to exhibit an iron bridge which he had invented. Fox and Burke received him kindly in **Paine's Last** England; but after the latter's apparent desertion of de-**Years** mocracy in his *Reflections on the French Revolution*, Paine seized his pen, as one would take a musket, and fired his *Rights of Man* (1791) at Burke and the English Constitution. This brave, outspoken book produced such a terrible sensation that the alarmed government outlawed the author. Before the storm broke over his head, Paine flitted away to Paris, where he arrived in the midst of the French Revolution.

We can only outline the rest of the story — his career as French citizen and deputy to the National Assembly; his noble plea for mercy for Louis XVI; his imprisonment and narrow escape from the guillotine; his ill-judged and ill-written *Age of Reason;* and his sad last years, when he was at war with himself, with his friends, and with the only country which had appreciated him. From his poverty and obscurity in Paris he was brought home by Jefferson, who in his hour of triumph remembered all the neglected patriots that had served America in her hour of need. He died in 1809, and an empty tomb and monument at New Rochelle still mark the spot where he once was buried. For his body was removed to England, as if to remind us that in death as in life he was a man without a country.

JOHN WOOLMAN (1720–1772)

When Franklin in the flush of worldly success began his *Autobiography*, the modest *Journal of John Woolman* was just drawing to its close. One author begins by telling us that he writes largely to gratify his vanity; the other, writing as he had lived with no thought of self, shows in his first line the spirit of the old monks, who worked or wrote or taught their fellow men alone for the glory of God :

" I have often felt a motion of love to leave some hints in writing of my experience of the goodness of God, and now, in the thirty-sixth year of my age, I begin this work."

Both books hold the **mirror up to human nature** ; both contribute to the chief end of literature, which is to know men ; but while one makes us think of man in his body and estate, the other is the tender, exquisite story of a human soul, " the sweetest and purest autobiography in the language." [1] As the latter is a book that few discover or appreciate, we cull a few paragraphs, that the reader may decide for himself whether he belongs with the simple-minded folk who like *The Journal of John Woolman:*

" My mind, through the power of truth, was in a good degree weaned from the desire of outward greatness, and I was learning to be content with the real conveniences, that were not costly, so that a way of life free from much entanglement appeared best for me, though the income might be small. I had several offers of business that appeared profitable; but I did not see my way clear to accept of them, believing they would be attended with more outward care and cumber than was required of me to engage in. I saw that an humble man, with the blessing of the Lord, might live on a little, and that where the heart was set on greatness, success in business did not satisfy the craving; but that commonly, with an increase of wealth, the desire of wealth increased. There was a care on my mind so to pass my time that nothing might hinder me from the most steady attention to the voice of the true Shepherd."

In a letter to his wife he writes thus of his missionary journeys and labors:

" Of this I may speak a little, for though since I left you I have often an engaging love and affection toward thee and my daughter and friends about home, and going out at this time is a trial upon me, yet I often remember there are many widows and fatherless, many who have poor tutors, many who have evil examples before them, and many whose minds are in captivity; for whose sake my heart is at times moved with compassion, so that I feel my mind resigned to leave you for a season and to execute the gift which the Lord hath bestowed upon me, which though small compared with some, yet in this I rejoice, that I feel love unfeigned toward my fellow creatures. . . ."

While Woolman is at home, tending his little shop and cultivating his fruit trees, an alarm flames out on the frontier: Indians are on the warpath, and brave men are hastening with their families to the protection of the towns. At such a time he thinks only of the misguided savages, and with a " tender concern " he pushes westward through the wilderness to meet them.

---

[1] This is Channing's estimate, quoted in the Introduction to Whittier's edition of Woolman's *Journal.*

"My companion and I, sitting thus together in a deep inward stillness, the poor [Indian] woman came and sat near us; and, a great awfulness coming over us, we rejoiced in a sense of God's love manifested to our poor souls. After a while we heard a conch shell blow several times, and then came John Curtis and another Indian man, who kindly invited us into a house near the town, where we found about sixty [Indians] sitting inside. After sitting with them a short time I stood up, and in some tenderness of spirit acquainted them in a few short sentences with the nature of my visit, and that a concern for their good had made me willing to come thus far to see them; which some of them, understanding, interpreted to the others, and there appeared gladness among them. . . ."

After hearing a soldier's story of war and barbarism his heart is moved to compassion, and his record reminds us of the treasured old volume of Thomas à Kempis:

"This relation affected me with sadness, under which I went to bed; and the next morning, soon after I woke, a fresh and living sense of divine love overspread my mind, in which I had a renewed prospect of the nature of that wisdom from above which leads to a right use of all gifts both spiritual and temporal, and gives content therein. . . . Attend then, O my soul, to this pure wisdom as thy sure conductor through the manifold dangers of this world.

"Doth pride lead to vanity? Doth vanity form imaginary wants? Do these wants prompt men to exert their power in requiring more from others than they would be willing to perform themselves were the same required of them? Do these proceedings beget hard thoughts? Do hard thoughts when ripe become malice? Does malice when ripe become revengeful, and in the end inflict terrible pains on our fellow creatures and spread desolations in the world? . . . Remember then, O my soul, the quietude of those in whom Christ governs, and in all thy proceedings feel after it. . . ."

To some readers the above quotations are enough to indicate that Woolman has for them no vital interest; but others will The Quality surely ask, Who is this man that writes with such of Woolman exquisite simplicity, with the refinement of gentleness and the purity of the pure in heart? There is little to say in answer: that he was an obscure, self-educated Friend or Quaker of Mount Holly, New Jersey; that his early years were spent on the farm, as a clerk, and as a teacher of poor children; that he was a tailor "by the choice of Providence," and kept a little shop; that his honesty brought many customers, but he avoided as " cumber " all business beyond a simple living for his family, having, as he said, seen the happiness of humility and formed the earnest desire to enter deeper into it; that he went up and down the land on missionary journeys to rich and poor, to slaves and slave owners, preaching mercy and justice as the rule of life, and love as the solution of all earthly problems; that he often did heroic things but always concealed his heroism; that in the excitement of the days before the Revolution he went on a mission to the Friends in England with the same message that he had carried to his countrymen; and that on this last journey of love he died among strangers, who cared for him as their own. Having told this, we leave the reader with the book, as we would leave him with a child or a friend; such a friend as we have sometime known, who is in the world but not of it, who is wise from his very artlessness, who lives with God and loves his fellow men, and whose counsel has no taint of earthliness — in a word, a friend who makes us know and trust the saints of all ages.

VII. THE BEGINNING OF AMERICAN FICTION

CHARLES BROCKDEN BROWN (1771–1810)

Brown occupies a curious position in our literature. He seems historically important, but personally of small consequence; he marks an important literary epoch, but is unknown to modern readers. So he reminds us of the pioneer who blazed a trail through the Indian-haunted forest and cleared the space where the town hall stands, — a most important work, though we have carelessly forgotten who did it. This unknown author is remarkable for three things: he is the first American who believes enough in literature to adopt it as a profession; he is the founder of the American novel; [1] and he starts a revolution against the

[1] A few attempts at novel writing were made by other authors of the same period. Thus Susanna Rowson's *Charlotte Temple* (1790) and Tabitha Tenney's *Female Quixotism, Exemplified in the Romantic Opinions and Extravagant Adventures of Dorcasina Sheldon* (1808) represent two distinct tendencies in our earliest fiction. Mrs. Tenney

English fiction of his age by declaring his purpose to write of American life in his own way. If we begin by comparing Brown's *Wieland* with *The Scarlet Letter*, or his *Edgar Huntley* with *The Last of the Mohicans*, we shall see only our author's limitations ; but if we can imagine ourselves back in an age when there were no novels here, and when England was occupied with grotesque "Gothic" romances, then the work of this poor consumptive will appear to us heroic. And if we read more carefully, we shall discover a fourth remarkable fact, — that Brown's work anticipates the material or method of our greatest writers of fiction : the stirring adventures of Cooper, the weird horror of Poe, and the psychological analysis of Hawthorne. For Brown was a pioneer in a new realm of literature ; and though he failed to win permanent success, his failure, like that of most explorers, may have served effectually to point out the way by which others might reach the goal.

CHARLES BROCKDEN BROWN

Life. Some men put themselves so completely into their work that the only way to get acquainted with them is to read what they have written. With Brown the case is reversed ; he hides behind his books, and we must study his life before we can understand his writings.

wrote to counteract the false sentiment of Mrs. Rowson's *Charlotte Temple*, very much as Fielding, in English literature, had written to burlesque the sentimentality of Richardson's *Pamela*. Notwithstanding its stilted style and lugubrious matter, *Charlotte Temple* has been read for over a century. The editor of the last edition (1905) found that at least one hundred and four editions had already been published. For a study of American fiction before the year 1800, see Miss Loshe, *The Early American Novel* (New York, 1907).

He was born in Philadelphia, in 1771. Like Woolman, he was of Quaker descent and training; but he soon broke away from the gentle discipline, being influenced by the writings of Godwin, that same English radical who exercised an unfortunate influence over the poet Shelley.[1] As a child he was precocious, and in his first school made havoc of his health by overstudy. Exiled by disease from the sports of vigorous boys, he had two unfailing resources, — to pore over books by the hour, and to ramble alone in the big woods. Here his imagination, set loose from his frail body, led him away to glorious adventures with wild beasts and Indians. But wherever he went, like Wigglesworth he dragged the two millstones of disease and morbidness along with him.

Schooldays over, and with them the golden age, Brown took up the burden of life in a lawyer's office. Presently he wearied of the law, as did Irving later, and abandoned it to commit himself definitely to literature, beginning with essays and poems for the new magazines. Philadelphia now seemed to him strait and narrow — though Franklin had found it broad enough when he ran away from Boston — and Brown migrated to New York. Here all his important work was crowded into a few years, during which he battled daily for health, with a heroism that suggests Lanier. He produced his first complete novel, *Wieland*, in 1798. The next year, while publishing the *Monthly Magazine*, he wrote *Ormond* and the first part of *Arthur Mervyn;* and in 1801 appeared three novels, *Edgar Huntley*, *Clara Howard* and *Jane Talbot*. It was a large amount of work, and we still feel the haste, the fever, the anxiety of it. Whether his genius had burned itself out like a candle, or whether he sought to turn his fame into fortune by publishing a successful magazine, we do not know. Suddenly he abandoned romance, went back to Philadelphia to establish the *Literary Magazine* (1803–1808), and spent his failing energy on essays and sketches of no consequence.

The tragedy of Brown's life is suggested by the fact that he died of consumption, in 1810, before his powers had reached maturity; the heroism of it may be inferred from one of his last letters, in which he says that a single half-hour of health was all that he could remember.

---

1 It is worthy of note that Brown and Shelley had much in common, and that the English poet was a reader and admirer of the American novelist. To the influence of Godwin we owe the shallow notions concerning women and divorce to be found in Brown's *Alcuin* (1797). Such notions were quietly ignored here, but they raised a tempest about the ears of Shelley in England.

And he adds, with a touch of infinite pathos, that had his pilgrimage been longer he might have lighted at last on hope.

Works of Brown. Of the six novels mentioned, the beginner will do well to choose *Edgar Huntley*, which is, on the whole, the best of Brown's works. In the preface, which is well worth reading, we find that our first novelist is actuated by two motives. The first was to oppose the prevailing " Gothic " romances, with all their ghostly claptrap ; and here, all unconsciously, Brown was working with the same intent and purpose as Jane Austen.[1] His second motive, also original and independent, was to make an American book, to lay the scene in his own country, and to use the romantic material of Colonial life which had lain neglected for two centuries. In the latter motive he anticipated Cooper, who, after trying one novel of English society, plainly followed Brown's lead in finding his literary material on our own frontier.

The story of *Edgar Huntley* is a strange combination, — a minute analysis of human emotion, set in a rush of stirring incidents and hairbreadth escapes. The one sug-
Edgar Huntley gests the earlier work of Richardson, who gave us the first modern novel ; the other sets our feet in the trail which Cooper followed in his Leatherstocking romances. A single adventure may serve to show the spirit of the entire work. The hero goes to sleep in his bed, and knows that he slept as usual, for he remembers every detail :

" I have said that I slept. My memory assures me of this ; it informs me of the previous circumstances of my laying aside my clothes, of placing the light upon a chair within reach of my pillow, of throwing myself upon the bed and of gazing on the rays of the moon reflected on the wall and almost obscured by those of the candle. I remember my occasional relapse into fits of incoherent fancies, the harbingers of sleep. I remember, as it were, the instant when my thought ceased to flow and my senses were arrested by the leaden wand of forgetfulness."

[1] One motive of Miss Austen was to counteract the evil influences of the same " Gothic " romances. Her greatest novel, *Pride and Prejudice*, was written in 1797 (a year before Brown published his first romance, *Wieland*), but it did not find a publisher till sixteen years later.

Here is a mental picture which we instantly recognize as true. When the hero wakes from his natural sleep, he is bruised and sore, as if beaten with a club ; he is at the bottom of a pit in gross darkness. As he feels his way out, in a chaos of doubt and fear, he meets a ferocious panther and slays the beast. Then, attracted by a dim light, he stumbles upon a band of Indians with a captive white girl, sleeping around a fire in a gloomy cave. So far this is almost as good as the *Arabian Nights,* wherein castles grow like toadstools, and marvels come and go like the clouds. We enjoy the adventures, and especially the Indians, who are somewhat truer to nature than are Cooper's smoky philosophers ; but there is a mystery about this hero, who goes to sleep in his bed and wakes up in " antres vast and desarts idle," which is not cleared up till we learn that he is a somnambulist — a lame and impotent conclusion.

The same weakness is shown in all of Brown's novels. We find dark and direful strangers, secret murders, conspiracies galore ; and at the end some wretchedly inadequate

Wieland

motive to account for them all. In *Wieland,* for example, a man in the midst of ideal happiness is called by a supernatural voice to murder his wife and children. Horrors upon horrors attend this awful mystery ; and at the end we find only the " squeak and gibber " of a ventriloquist. Yet there is a dramatic power and intensity in the story which makes us read on :

" I now come to the mention of a person with whose name the most turbulent sensations are connected. It is with a shuddering reluctance that I enter on the province of describing him. . . . My blood is congealed and my fingers are palsied when I call up his image. Shame upon my cowardly and infirm heart ! Hitherto I have proceeded with some degree of composure ; but now I must pause. I mean not that dire remembrance shall subdue my courage or baffle my design ; but this weakness cannot be immediately conquered. I must desist for a little while."

After such an introduction we insist on knowing what happened. Our interest is aroused, first, by the fact that the hero is introduced under startling conditions, and then is allowed to tell his own story. Just as in *Othello* we read with a more lively interest when the Moor begins to relate his adventures, so in all Brown's stories the characters make a direct appeal to the reader. Another device, which he uses excellently, is to paint a scene so vividly that we expect some adventure to follow. As the oldest teller of ghost stories put his hearers on tiptoe for the specter by describing the dark night, the fearsome old house, the moaning wind, so Brown plays upon our imagination to make us anticipate the horror before it appears. Though he lacks the highest qualities as a writer, it is much to say of a first novelist that he knows how to attract attention, and to paint vivid pictures of human emotion against a suitable natural background.

General Characteristics. Brown's faults are so obvious that we may pass over them silently and give attention to certain significant qualities that are reflected in all his romances. The points to be emphasized are these : that these books, now dead, were once very much alive ; that this forgotten prophet was once honored in his own country and in England ; and that he won success by reflecting in an original way two marked characteristics of his age. These are summed up in the words " sensibility " and " mystery," which furnish the key to Brown's novels and to practically all the fiction of the age in Europe and America.

Now "sensibility " is defined as the ability to feel sensations and emotions ; in literature it means unusual sensitiveness, delicacy of feeling, responsiveness to every emotion of pleasure or pain. At the close of the eighteenth century "sensibility" was a kind of fetish, just as "humor" was in the days of Ben Jonson. In the romances of this period men were not simply glad or sorry ; they had transports of joy, paroxysms of grief ; they danced up and down the gamut of feeling as if human nature were a stretched nerve, vibrating to every breath of emotion. Coupled with this sensibility was a mawkish and garrulous sentimentality, repulsive to us now, but very dear

Sensibility

to an age that considered it proper for a lady to talk like Richardson's *Pamela*, to "fall senseless on the sofa," or "sink
fainting into the arms of an attendant" at every unusual
announcement.[1]

That Brown was influenced by the prevailing literary fad is
shown by the interest which his characters take in their sensibil-
ities. The hero may be rescuing a girl from Indians, or dozing
in front of his own fire; but always, everywhere, he is making
minute analysis of his own feelings. So far Brown follows the
fashion. His independence is shown by his choice of American
themes, and by the fact that, in portraying human feeling, he
is more of a psychologist than a sentimentalist, more interested
in the scientific explanation of an emotion than in the prevailing
book of etiquette. It was this new variation of an old theme that
made him popular, and if we read him candidly, we shall find that
he was probably in advance of most of his English and German
contemporaries.[2]

The second characteristic of Brown's novels is the sense of
horror that pervades them; and here our author reflects, not
Mystery simply the fashion of his age, but the tendency of
and Horror humanity in all ages to create for itself imaginary
fears. Wherever you find him, whether in a primitive cave or
in a modern office, man is always surrounded by mystery. He
stands, as the first Colonists stood, fronting an unknown sea
with an unknown wilderness at his back; and his imagination

---

[1] Mackenzie's *Man of Feeling* (1771) is an epitome of this literary fad. Sheridan
burlesqued it in the character of Lydia Languish, in *The Rivals* (1775). At this time
the "Gothic" romances of Mrs. Radcliffe and the sentimental romances of Frances
Burney were immensely popular on both sides of the Atlantic. In this country about
twenty novels were published before Brown's, and they are all stories of "sensibility"
and sentimentality.

[2] To be specific: Mrs. Radcliffe's *Mysteries of Udolpho* (1794) and Goethe's *Sorrows
of Werther* (1774) seem to us more mawkish than anything Brown ever wrote; though
the first was written by the most popular English novelist of that day, and the second
by the greatest of all German writers. (See, in this connection, Richardson, *American
Literature*, ii, 288–289; also Goodnight, *Schiller in America*, a monograph published by
the University of Wisconsin.) In German romances of the period the keynote is generally egoism; there are the same sentimentality and horror as in Brown's romances,
and the mystery is psychologically explained.

always peoples the unknown with fantastic terrors. Dragons and *doppelgänger* were very real to the Anglo-Saxons; enchantment and witchcraft to all peoples of the Middle Ages. In Brown's day English romancers, after a period of general skepticism, were filling the unknown with ghosts, supernatural voices, and other horrors as artificial as their own periwigs. He had a vivid imagination, well suited to creating terror out of mystery; but he had also a practical balance-wheel from his Quaker forbears, and he shared the common-sense spirit of his nation. The result was that he first created a mysterious horror, and then explained it by somnambulism, or ventriloquism, or some other *ism* dear to a people that had just begun to dabble in science — a people who demanded a sign, like those of old, but who wanted also some kind of explanation. So Brown was hailed abroad as the man who had "Americanized" their "Gothic" romance, as Franklin's lightning rods had "Americanized" their houses.[1]

There are other things worthy of note in Brown's neglected romances: their stilted dialogue, so characteristic of an age **Our First** which insisted that literary persons must speak unnat-**Novelist** urally; their photographic reproduction of the dress and manners of the gentlefolk of those days; their keen observations and admirable descriptions of nature; their vivid pictures of the yellow-fever horror, which compare favorably with Defoe's famous description of the plague in London. All these are interesting; but we emphasize only the "sensibility" and the horror of mystery which give the keynote to all his work. And instead of criticizing Brown for his evident faults, we are impelled to praise him for his unnoticed virtues. It is no small triumph for any novelist, while reflecting the literary fashions of his age, to go beyond his contemporaries in the direction of truth and naturalness. He was, we repeat, the founder of the American novel, and his successors were Cooper and Hawthorne.

[1] The hideous mystery which overshadows Brown's pages has hardly yet vanished from our fiction. It reappears in the work of Poe and Hawthorne especially. For a study of Brown in comparison with later novelists, see Morse, *Century Magazine*, XXVI, 289.

Summary of the Revolutionary Period. If we include in our view not only the war but also its immediate causes and consequences, the Revolutionary period extends from the Stamp Act of 1765 to the close of the century. In our analysis of the period, we found four important historical movements. The first was social and industrial; it was concerned with the rapid growth of the country, the increase in trade and wealth, and the appearance of many towns, each a center of social life. The second was the intense agitation over the Stamp Act and other measures of taxation, which aroused and united the Colonies in opposition to England. The third was the Revolutionary War, which established American independence. During the war there were two great parties in violent opposition: the Whigs or Patriots, who demanded independence; and the Tories or Loyalists, who were in favor of continued union with England. The fourth movement was the adoption of the Constitution, the merging of the Colonies into the United States of America. This union was accomplished only after a long struggle between two antagonistic parties: the Federalists, who sought a strongly centralized national government; and the Anti-Federalists, who sought to keep the governing power as largely as possible in the hands of the individual states. The Constitution was regarded as a balance or fair compromise between these two parties.

The literature of the period shows the effect of all these historical movements. The new social life demanded newspapers, magazines, brighter and

Literature   more varied types of literature than had prevailed during the Colonial period. The turmoil after the Stamp Act led to a rapid development of popular oratory; the strife between Patriots and Tories produced numerous ballads and satires; the struggle over the Constitution developed a new type of political writing which has been well called "citizen literature." In general, the literature of the Revolution has a practical and worldly bent, in contrast to the religious spirit of Colonial writings.

In our study we noted, first, the general characteristics of Revolutionary literature, the contrast between its imitative poetry and its individualistic prose. The citizen literature especially reflects a strong, original and creative impulse of the American mind. Next we considered the life and works of Benjamin Franklin, who marks the transition from the Colonial to the Revolutionary age. He was a voluminous writer, but his aim was always practical, or utilitarian, rather than artistic. He is remembered in our literature chiefly by his *Autobiography*.

Of the Revolutionary orators, James Otis and Patrick Henry were chosen as typical of the period. The typical statesman was Washington, the object of whose life and work was to establish nationality in America.

Typical Writers   Two other statesmen, Hamilton and Jefferson, were studied at length, because they were leaders, and are still the types, of the two great parties that are found in every free government. The most memorable literary work of Jefferson was the Declaration of Independence, which we considered as a piece of literature rather than as a state paper. The chief work of Hamilton was a series of political essays included in *The Federalist*.

In studying the poetry of the Revolution we noted, first, the songs, ballads and verse satires in which Patriot and Loyalist reflected their political convictions and animosities; second, the efforts of the so-called Hartford Wits to establish a national rather than a provincial poetry; and third, the life and works of Philip Freneau. The latter's poems fall into two significant classes: political songs and satires, reflecting the turmoil of the age; and occasional poems of nature and humanity, which reveal Freneau as an American forerunner of the romantic movement in modern poetry.

Of the many miscellaneous writers of the Revolution the two most notable are Thomas Paine, whose *Common Sense* and *The Crisis* are among the most powerful pamphlets that ever influenced a nation's history; and John Woolman, whose *Journal* has been called "the sweetest and purest autobiography in the language."

At the end of the Revolutionary period we note the definite appearance of the American novel. Some thirty-five works of fiction, mostly of the exaggerated romantic type, were written before 1800; but their authors are now unknown even by name to most readers. The one fiction writer of the period who deserves recognition is Charles Brockden Brown. He was the first professional man of letters in America, and he may be regarded as the founder of the American novel. His models were the German and English authors of the so-called Gothic romances, — harrowing stories that combined mystery with ghostly horror, sensibility with sentimentality, and romance with gross exaggeration. Brown showed considerable originality, and gave a distinctly American color to his work by laying the scene of his romance in his own country, by using the incidents of Indian and Colonial life for his literary material, and by giving a practical or scientific explanation of the mysteries and horrors which filled his pages. In his work we find suggestions of Poe, Cooper and Hawthorne, the three greatest American writers of fiction.

First American Novels

Selections for Reading. Franklin's Autobiography, edited for class use by Trent and Wells, in Standard English Classics (Ginn and Company); the same work in Maynard's English Classics, Holt's English Readings, and other series. Poor Richard's Almanac and other Papers (a good selection) in Riverside Literature series. Washington's Farewell Address, in Standard English Classics, etc.; the same, with Washington's Journal, Circular Letters to the Governors, and other selections, in Old South Leaflets. In the same series, selections from Hamilton and Jefferson. The Federalist, in Everyman's Library. Woolman's Journal, in Macmillan's Pocket series, etc. Crèvecœur's Letters from an American Farmer in Everyman's Library.

There are no convenient editions of Brown, Paine or Freneau. Selections from these authors, and from all others mentioned in the text, may be found in Trent and Wells, Cairns, Carpenter's American Prose, Bronson's American Poems, etc. See "Selections" in the General Bibliography.

Bibliography. Historical textbooks: Montgomery, Muzzey, Channing, etc. For extended works in history and literature, see the General Bibliography. The following special works are useful in studying the Revolutionary period.

History. Winsor, Reader's Handbook of the American Revolution; Fiske, American Revolution, and Critical Period of American History; Hart, Formation of the Union; Walker, Making of the Nation; Fisher, Struggle for American Independence; Sloane, French War and the Revolution; Lossing, Field Book of the Revolution.

Political. Gordy, Political Parties, 1787–1828, 2 vols.; Stanwood, History of the Presidency.

Biographical. Lives of important historical characters, each in one volume as a rule, in American Statesmen series; Parton, Life of Franklin, of Jefferson, of Burr; Rives, Life and Times of James Madison, 3 vols.; Trent, Southern Statesmen of the Old Regime (Washington, Jefferson, Randolph); Sparks, Men who made the Nation; Parker, Historic Americans; Green, Pioneer Mothers of America, 3 vols.; C. F. Adams, John Adams's Diary.

Supplementary. Parkman, Half Century of Conflict, Montcalm and Wolfe; Hinsdale, The Old Northwest; Fiske, American Political Ideas; Earle, Stage Coach and Tavern Days, Diary of Anna Green Winslow, a Boston School Girl of 1771; Crawford, Romantic Days in the Early Republic.

Literature. Tyler, Literary History of the American Revolution, 2 vols.; (Putnam), includes all the writers of the period. Miss Loshe, Early American Novel (1907); Magoon, Orators of the American Revolution (1848); Sears, American Literature in the Colonial and National Periods (1892). For works on individual writers, Franklin, Freneau, etc., see below.

Collateral Reading. Women of Colonial and Revolutionary Times : Martha Washington, by Anne Wharton; Mercy Warren, by Alice Brown; Dolly Madison, by Maud Goodwin; Catherine Schuyler, by Mary Humphreys, etc. (Scribner); Green, Pioneer Mothers of America; Mills, Through the Gates of Old Romance (a book of the love stories of Freneau, Benjamin West, and other notable men of Revolutionary times).

Franklin. Texts : Works, edited by A. H. Smyth; by Bigelow (1887). Sayings of Poor Richard, edited by Ford (Putnam). Autobiography, etc. (see Selections for Reading, above).

Biography and Criticism : Life (including the Autobiography supplemented by many letters), edited by Bigelow, 3 vols.; Life, by McMaster, in American Men of Letters; by Morse, in American Statesmen; by Parton, 2 vols.; Ford, The Many-Sided Franklin; Fisher, The True Benjamin Franklin, in " True " Biographies. Franklin bibliography, by Ford (Brooklyn, 1889).

Hamilton. Texts : Works, edited by Lodge, 9 vols. (1885). The Federalist, edited by Dawson; by Ford; by Lodge.

Biography and Criticism : Life, by Morse, 2 vols.; by Lodge, in American Statesmen; Sumner, Alexander Hamilton (a critical study, in Makers of America series); Culbertson, Alexander Hamilton (Yale University Press, 1910); Basset, The Federalist System, in the American Nation, edited by Hart, Vol. II.

Jefferson. Texts : Works, 10 vols., edited by Ford (1892–1899).

Biography and Criticism : Life by Schouler, in Makers of America; by Morse, in American Statesmen; by Curtis, in " True " Biographies; by Parton, by Watson, etc.; Trent, Southern Statesmen of the Old Regime; Channing, The Jeffersonian System, in Hart's American Nation, Vol. XII.

The Hartford Wits. Texts: No complete editions are available. Dwight's Conquest of Canaan (Hartford, 1875) and Travels in New England and New York, 4 vols. (New Haven, 1821); Trumbull's Works, with Memoir, 2 vols. (Hartford, 1820); Trumbull's M'Fingal, edited by Lossing (1881).

Biography and Criticism: Tyler, Three Men of Letters (1895); Todd, Life and Letters of Joel Barlow (1895); Sheldon, Pleiades of Connecticut (Atlantic Monthly, 1865); Trumbull, Origin of M'Fingal (Historical Magazine, 1868).

Freneau. Texts: No complete edition of works; Poems, edited by Pattee, 3 vols. (Princeton University Library, 1902–1907); Poems of 1786, in Library of Old Authors; Poems of the Revolution, edited by Duyckinck (1865).

Biography and Criticism: Life, by Mary Austin (1901); Forman, Political Activities of Philip Freneau (Johns Hopkins University Studies); More, in Shelburne Essays, Fifth Series (1908); Greenslet, in Atlantic Monthly (December, 1904).

Brown. Texts: Works, 6 vols. (Philadelphia, 1857, revised 1887).

Biography and Criticism: Life, by Dunlap, 2 vols. (1815); by Prescott, in Biographical and Critical Miscellanies; and in Spark's Library of American Biography. Miss Loshe, Early American Novel; Erskine, Leading American Novelists; Morse, in Century Magazine, Vol. XXVI; Brown's connection with Shelley, in Dowden's Life of Shelley.

Historical Fiction. *Older Romances of the Revolution:* Catherine Sedgwick, The Linwoods; Lydia Child, The Rebels; Cooper, The Spy, The Pilot, Lionel Lincoln; Kennedy, Horse-Shoe Robinson; Paulding, Old Continental; Simms, The Scout, The Partisan, Katherine Walton.

Later Romances: Hawthorne, Septimius Felton; Cooke, Henry St. John; Winthrop, Edwin Brothertoft; Butterworth, Patriot Schoolmaster; Ford, Janice Meredith; Thompson, Alice of Old Vincennes; Frederick, In the Valley; Mitchell, Hugh Wynne; Harrison, Son of the Old Dominion; Coggeswell, The Regicides; Eggleston, A Carolina Cavalier; Churchill, Richard Carvel.

Books for Young People. *Revolutionary History:* Fiske, Irving's Washington and His Country (Ginn and Company); Dickson, Hundred Years of Warfare, 1680–1789 (Macmillan); Fiske, War of Independence (Houghton); Baldwin, Conquest of the Old Northwest (American Book Co.); Jenks, When America Won Liberty (Crowell); Hart, Camps and Firesides of the Revolution (Macmillan).

Revolutionary Stories: Hawthorne, Grandfather's Chair; Coffin, Boys of '76; Helen Cleveland, Stories of the Brave Old Days; Lillian Price, Lads and Lassies of Other Days.

Suggestive Questions. (Note: Questions in class should be based, first, on selections read from the various authors, and second, on parts of the text marked for study. It is not expected that the student should be able to answer all the general questions below. They are intended, chiefly, to stimulate his thinking and to arouse his patriotic interest in American literature and history.)

1. The period in which our independence was won is called the Age of Revolution: what events in European history and literature justify the title? What did America contribute to the age, in matters of government and literature?

2. Read the historical introduction to the Revolutionary period, and tell in your own words what effect each historic movement had upon our literature. It is said that, in passing from Colonial to Revolutionary times, our literature shifted its center of interest from heaven to earth; explain, criticize, challenge the statement. What common characteristics do you find in Colonial and Revolutionary literature?

3. What is meant by citizen literature? Why should it appear during the Revolutionary period? What are its qualities? What works of the present day belong to this class? How do they compare in spirit and motive with the earlier works?

4. Explain the prevalence of satire and of ballads in Revolutionary poetry. Describe the two main parties during the Revolution, and name some of the literary works of each. Why are Patriot ballads in general better known than ballads of the Loyalists? How do you account for the fact that the wretched doggerel of "Yankee Doodle" is remembered, while better ballads are forgotten?

5. How do you account for the fact that Revolutionary prose is better, more original and independent, than Revolutionary verse? (Note that Franklin's early prose is imitative.) In what ways does "the American spirit" reveal itself in both prose and poetry?

6. Quote from any of Washington's later and earlier works to show that he was animated by the national rather than by the provincial spirit. What is the value of his Farewell Address? Why should it be studied as a "classic"? It is said that the Farewell Address was the work of Washington and his friends, Hamilton being prominent among the latter: what evidence of composite authorship do you find in the work itself?

7. What two parties were prominent at the time of the adoption of the Constitution? Do you see any connection between these two parties and the Whigs and Tories of the Revolution? or between them and the two main political parties of the present day? Fiske has said that in politics all men are followers of either Hamilton or Jefferson; criticize the statement.

8. In what ways were Hamilton and Jefferson typical of two great parties? Give a brief sketch of Hamilton's life, and of his service to America. What literary work made him known before the Revolution? By what is he now remembered? What is the general character of *The Federalist?*

9. Sketch briefly Jefferson's life and service, and note the contrast with Hamilton. What qualities in Jefferson led to his being called at various times to speak for a large party or for the nation? What are his chief literary works? The Declaration of Independence has been called an Anglo-Saxon battle song; why? What national and race qualities does it reveal?

10. *Franklin.* (a) In what way does Franklin mark the transition from the Colonial to the Revolutionary age? He has been called "the teacher of a new order in America"; give your reasons for upholding or denying the allegation.

(*b*) What typical character, and of what sort, did Franklin introduce in his almanac? Show any resemblances between this character and the hero of any modern story, such as *David Harum* or *Eben Holden*. Make a list of Franklin's maxims that are, still in daily use. Show the mixture of truth and error in these sayings.

(*c*) Quote from some of the minor works you have read to illustrate Franklin's humor. Do you find any definite resemblances between Franklin's humor and that of later writers, Holmes, Stockton or Mark Twain for instance? It is customary to speak of "American humor"; what is meant by this? And how does American differ from English or German humor?

(*d*) Why should Franklin's *Autobiography* be studied as a "classic"? What are its qualities of style? How do you account for Franklin's careless disregard of the work, and for the world's keen appreciation of it? As a matter of speculation, if such a book had been written by an unknown author, would you be interested in it?

(*e*) Make a brief comparison between Franklin and Edwards, having in mind the careers of the two men, the interest of their works, their style, their motive in writing, and the different classes of readers to whom they appealed. Explain the statement that these two men represent the two sides of the American mind.

11. Who was John Woolman? An English critic, Charles Lamb, wrote, "Get the writings of John Woolman by heart, and love the early Quakers"; why should one exhortation suggest the other? What is the general character of Woolman's *Journal?* Can you explain why a modern college president should place it among the great and ennobling books of the world?

12. What influence did Paine exert upon the American Revolution? Describe briefly *Common Sense* and *The Crisis*. To what American traits did they appeal? Hundreds of strong political pamphlets appeared before the Revolution; how do you account for the extraordinary success of *Common Sense?*

13. Divide Freneau's poems into two main classes, and show that in each class Freneau was a reflection of his age. What is the present value of his satires? of his romantic poems? Who were his English models? In what ways did he show originality and independence?

14. Who were the Hartford Wits? What noble motive bound them together? What are the chief works of each? How do you account for the fact that their minor poems (Dwight's hymns and Barlow's "Hasty Pudding" for instance) are remembered, while their ambitious works are forgotten? What is the general character of *M'Fingal?* Account, on historical grounds, for its great popularity.

15. Why is Brown called our first professional man of letters? In what other respects is he notable? Give three characteristics of his romances, and show how they reappear constantly in later American fiction. What general literary tendencies of this age are reflected in his works? How do his romances compare with contemporary English and German romances? In what way does he show an advance in novel writing?

Subjects for Pleasant Essays. Why the Indian became a romantic figure in Revolutionary poetry and fiction. The Revolutionary drama. Earliest American fiction (not including Brown's works). Common elements in Brown, Poe, Hawthorne and Cooper. Original source of Franklin's maxims. The almanac in American life and literature. The first American magazines. The Loyalist side of the Revolution. *M'Fingal* and *Hudibras*. Franklin and Voltaire. Paine and Defoe. Freneau and the early English romanticists. Prose pamphlet and verse satire in the Revolution. European echoes of the Declaration of Independence. Two life-stories (Franklin's *Autobiography* and Woolman's *Journal*). What is American humor?

CHAPTER III

THE FIRST NATIONAL, OR CREATIVE, PERIOD (1800-1840)

O you youths, Western youths,
So impatient, full of action, full of manly pride and friendship,
Plain I see you, Western youths, see you tramping with the foremost,
Pioneers! O pioneers!

Have the elder races halted?
Do they droop and end their lesson, wearied over there beyond the seas?
We take up the task eternal, and the burden and the lesson,
Pioneers! O pioneers!

Whitman, " Pioneers "

I. THE BACKGROUND OF HISTORY

Reading for the first time the history of this period is like venturing on the open plains in a snowstorm; one may easily be confused by a multitude of rapidly shifting events and lose all sense of direction or perspective. Our attention is distracted by wars and rumors of wars, here by great prosperity, there by a great panic. We hear boasts of patriotism and national unity, followed hard by threats of secession. We see in rapid sequence the harmonious election of Monroe, the bitter strife which placed John Quincy Adams in the White House against the will of the majority of the people, and then " Old Hickory " Jackson " riding the whirlwind of democracy." In the midst of these crowding events, masses of men in motion suddenly arrest out attention. There on the east they come, thousands of eager foreigners from every clime and nation, breaking on our shores like a tidal wave that threatens to overwhelm us; and there opposite, as if pushed out by the newcomers, appears another multitude of men, toiling over mountains or whirling down the swollen rivers, all with rifles in hand, eyes alight and faces set resolutely to the western wilderness. And what does it all mean?

We shall never answer our question till we escape from the chaos of events and try simply to ascertain in what important respects the

America of Jackson differs from the America of Washington. Then we may see that the period which began with the election of Jefferson (1800) and ended with the defeat of his party in 1840,[1] instead of leading to mob rule and anarchy, as the Federalist party feared, was in reality a time of rapid national development, a lusty, expanding time, with only such pains as invariably accompany the growth of a young giant. It began with a fringe of states along the Atlantic coast; it ended in a mighty empire, spreading over the rich Mississippi valleys and pushing its borders westward to the Pacific. It began with grave doubts at home and open sneers abroad; it ended with invincible faith in democracy, and with our flag respected in every port of the seven seas. Bryant, who begins his career early in this period with the doubts and fears of " The Embargo," ends with a triumphant " O mother of a mighty race," which voices the faith and enthusiasm of the young republic.

National Unity. Four great movements are discernible in the rush of minor events which fill this period. The first and most important is the development of our national unity. The war with the Barbary States, which first made our flag respected, and the naval victories of 1812 vastly increased our confidence and solidarity as a nation. Thereafter we were not a mere confederation of states, as in the Revolution, but a united people animated by a national spirit. One reason for our earlier lack of unity was that the states were divided by vast stretches of forest, through which travel was both difficult and dangerous. Now invention set to work to break down the barriers. First came the national road, stretching from the Chesapeake to the Ohio; and as we think of the multitudes that passed over it we are reminded of Isaiah's magnificent prophecy of a highway in the wilderness, over which should come a free people, redeemed from all oppression, " with songs, and everlasting joy upon their heads." Next appeared Fulton's steamboat (1807), the first of a thousand craft that soon went up and down the American rivers, binding the north to the

---

[1] There are no distinctly marked periods in our history or literature. We recognize, however, a difference between the literature of Irving's contemporaries and that which follows the lead of Lowell, and a startling contrast between the " era of good feeling " and the turmoil which led to the Civil War. We have chosen the date 1840, which marks the election of Harrison after a most tumultuous campaign, as the dividing point between the two periods. At that time Bryant, Cooper, Irving and Poe were at the height of their influence, and the work of Longfellow, Whittier and Hawthorne was just beginning to be recognized. Some writers end the First National Period with the Civil War; others regard the entire nineteenth century as a single literary period.

south and the east to the west. Then followed the Baltimore and
Ohio Railway (1828), and within a few years three thousand miles of
road were spread like a web of steel over the country.

The effect of this new national unity is shown clearly in Monroe's
famous "era of good feeling," when the world saw the astonishing
spectacle of a nation of ten millions of freemen electing their president by a practically unanimous vote. Fifteen years later, in 1835,
the world was treated to another spectacle, a nation without a debt ;
for the country had prospered greatly, had paid all its obligations,

EMIGRATION TO WESTERN COUNTRY

and, to avoid the danger of an immense surplus, had distributed a
part of its revenue among the states for internal improvements.

Expansion. A second notable movement is the rapid growth of
America in territory and population. The Louisiana Purchase and
the acquisition of Florida doubled our territory, and the population
increased from five to seventeen millions in the space of forty years.
The vast Louisiana territory was cleared of hostile savages and settled
with almost bewildering rapidity. It was a second era of colonization,
and it differed in two important respects from the first. The earlier
colonists were all foreigners, men who knew nothing of America,
who had to win their slow way by experiment and failure. The later

colonists were mostly Americans, men born and bred in the spirit of the New World, who carried their ideals of democracy, as they carried their long rifles, wherever they went. The first colonists stood in awe of the vast, mysterious forests that stood between them and the unknown West; they dreaded its hunger, its solitude, its wild beasts and savages. The second colonists loved it; they rejoiced in its freedom, its teeming game, its wide, untrodden spaces; they saw in imagination a home by every spring where they quenched their thirst, a field of wheat or corn in every fertile glade, a town and a busy mill wherever a waterfall thundered its invitation. So they passed westward, ever westward, with the keen eye and confident step of men who were lords of the wilderness. The splendid states which they gave to the nation [1] are the best witnesses of the character and ideals of this new generation of colonizers.

Democracy. A third unmistakable movement is the growth of the democratic spirit over the whole country. In the days of Washington there had been a decidedly aristocratic tendency among our political leaders, — and we may not now question their patriotism or sincerity. All governments had always been in the hands of the privileged classes, and there was a widespread feeling, even in America, that a government of common people was a mere dream or, at best, a very doubtful experiment. Long before the end of this period such doubts and fears had been swept aside as by a tempest. The labors and triumph of Jefferson; the common-school education of the masses; the French Revolution, which shook the whole aristocratic world as by an earthquake; the electric influence of the English Reform Bill and of the liberation of all slaves in the English colonies; the steadily growing conviction that the brave American experiment of popular government was destined to success, — all these undoubtedly contributed to the spread of democracy. First on the list of causes, however, we are inclined to place the mighty westward movement and the building of new states by common men on the common principles of humanity. The wilderness, the farm, the forest, the prairie, — all these were levelers of false or artificial distinctions. Here every man had his chance and his vote; every executive was first of all a natural leader, chosen for his proved ability and for his sympathy with men who do

---

[1] Three states, Vermont, Kentucky and Tennessee, had joined the original thirteen before 1800. During the next forty years Ohio, Louisiana, Indiana, Mississippi, Illinois, Alabama, Maine, Missouri, Arkansas and Michigan were added, in the order named, to the nation.

the daily work of the world. And when from the very heart of this newer America came Andrew Jackson, a rough, primitive, original kind of man, with the petty faults and the big virtues of his kind, there was no longer any doubt that this whole country was irretrievably committed to the plain principles of democracy.[1]

Industrial Development. The fourth historic movement is the social and industrial development of the new land. At the beginning of the nineteenth century we were a nation of farmers and small traders, having no settled currency, bartering most of our products as in the days of the patriarchs. In the few large centers, by courtesy called cities, there was a pleasant, neighborly kind of social life; but just outside the town limits stretched an immense country of field and forest. A boy could leave the center of Richmond or New York and in a few hours' walk find good hunting or fishing, and perchance see a bear or hear a wolf howl as he turned homeward in the twilight. Within half a lifetime the whole Eastern country had changed its face and its ways. Towns sprang up as if by magic; cities overflowed their borders; hundreds of mills and factories were busy as beehives; money circulated freely, and fleets of our own ships were carrying our merchandise on every sea.[2]

We need not go into the subject of manufactures, or attempt to express the boundless enthusiasm of the new nation when our natural wealth of coal and iron was at last exposed, and our soil began to yield its increase of cotton and grain for the nations. We note only that with the increase of wealth came the growth of cities and the mental stimulus of social intercourse; that the common-school system of the Pilgrims became a national policy: and that the forty years which saw the growth of eight hundred mills saw also the establishment of unnumbered high schools, and of more than fifty colleges, seminaries and higher institutions of learning.

With the growth of nationality and democracy, the increase of wealth and education, and the unexampled development of our industrial life, we would gladly end our summary of this period; but another factor enters, like the ghost of Banquo, to disturb the feast. The panic

[1] Before Jackson our presidents were all men of superior birth and education; since his day about half of them have sprung from the common people.

[2] We suggest here two interesting topics for the historical student: first, the policy of England toward American industries before the Revolution; second, the effect on America of two inventions, — the jenny of Samuel Slater (1790) and the gin of Eli Whitney (1793).

of 1837, brought on by speculation and by the poor financial policy
of Jackson's administration, checked for a time our industrial prog-
The Seeds   ress. At the same time the tariff, the slave problem and
of Division   the unsettled question of state rights began to separate
a united country into two hostile sections. In the midst of great
peace came a sudden tremor, faint yet unmistakable as the rumble of
distant cannon ; and again the storm cloud, this time larger than a
man's hand and black as the pit, appeared on our national horizon.

II. LITERATURE OF THE PERIOD

The half century which witnessed the Declaration of Independence, the French Revolution and the English Reform Bill
is one of universal interest. It is generally called the age of
revolution, and is remarkable for two things : for the establishment of democracy in government, and for the triumph of
romanticism in literature. Just as our political independence
was the beginning of a world-wide struggle for human liberty,
so our first national literature was part and parcel of the great
romantic movement which swept over England and the Continent. Its general romantic spirit is in marked contrast to the
historical and theological bent of Colonial writers, who believed
they were writing a new page in the world's history ; and to the
political genius of Revolutionary authors, whose chief concern
was to establish a new nation on democratic foundations.

General Tendencies. It was Sydney Smith, a famous English
wit, who voiced a general opinion of our early literature in the
scornful question, " Who reads an American book ? " We may
understand his attitude, which was that of our own critics, if we
remember that in this, as in every other period, there were two
literary movements, a major and a minor ; and that it was the
work of minor writers which first received notice in English
newspapers and magazines. Here, for instance, is our poetry as
exemplified in the popular "Annuals" of that day, *The Talisman*,
The Token, Friendship's Offering, and many other favorites, —
dear old collections, full of new-made graves, urns, weeping

willows, tears and sentimentality.[1] Here are the fifty-odd volumes of Lydia Sigourney and a few romances of Catherine
Sedgwick, such as *Hope Leslie* and *Redwood*, — sentimental
stories which were republished in England and translated into
various European languages. The common people on both sides
of the Atlantic read these stories gladly, but the critics saw in
them only weak copies of English originals. In this country
Noah Webster anticipated foreign criticism when he declared
(1792) that "a hundred volumes of modern novels may be read
without acquiring a new idea."

When the work of our major writers appeared, a multitude
of delighted English readers stood up to answer the irritating
Originality question. Critics more thoughtful than Smith, knowing that national enthusiasm finds voice in a national
literature, had expected something pristine and vigorous from
the new nation,[2] and when Cooper's books began to be published
abroad these critics found what they had expected. Here were
good stories, a little crude perhaps, but fresh and genuine, —
stories with the breath of sea and forest in them, and with a
rush of adventure that reminded Englishmen of *Rob Roy* and
the *Heart of Midlothian*. So, having enjoyed the tales and being in a condescending humor, they christened Cooper "the
American Scott." A little earlier had appeared Irving, with a
grace and charm that recalled the best productions of their beloved *Spectator*, and him they called "the American Addison."
Then followed Bryant, with his natural refinement and his deep
understanding of nature, and he became known to a few as
"the American Wordsworth." Only Poe escaped, for the simple
reason that England had no writer with whom to compare him.

---

[1] In England, as in America, the poetry of the age reveals an abnormal interest in
funereal subjects. Note the influence of this interest on Bryant and Poe, p. 201, and on
Irving, p. 192.

[2] The state of England's expectancy may be judged from the wonder produced by
Irving's *Sketch Book* (1819). "It has been a matter of marvel to my European readers,"
he writes, "that a man from the wilds of America should express himself in tolerable
English. I was looked upon as something new and strange in literature, a kind of demi-
savage with a feather in his hand instead of on his head."

Though the names thus given to our writers are pleasantly suggestive, the fact remains that the first quality of our national literature is its originality. Irving's first work, the *Knickerbocker History*, is a unique book; there are no other tales like *The Spy*, *The Red Rover* and *The Last of the Mohicans;* and if there be any other poem than " A Forest Hymn " which reflects the instinctive reverence of primitive man in the presence of nature, we have never found it.

EARLY VIEW OF CHICAGO

A second characteristic of our literature in this period is its harmony with our natural environment. Nature had been sadly **Harmony** neglected in the greater part of the literature of the **with Nature** eighteenth century; when it was mentioned, for effect, every bird was apt to be a nightingale, every flower a primrose, and stock expressions such as " vernal winds " and "sylvan beauties" had been worn threadbare by repetition. Our first national writers changed all that, and the change was as welcome as rain to the parched grass. Bryant was by far our best observer, and his poetry reflects the spirit of nature and of the man who stands silent and reverent before her revelation. Cooper, though inaccurate in details, reflects something of the charm and mystery of the great wilderness, and he is the first in modern literature to use the ocean as the scene of romance and adventure. Irving has less love of nature than either Bryant or Cooper; but in much of his work he remembers the influence of the hills and the Hudson, and is at his best in "Sleepy Hollow" and "Rip Van Winkle," where he puts himself in harmony with the American landscape.

A third noticeable quality of our first national literature is its intense patriotism. This appears in many forms: in the national songs of Pinkney,

Patriotism Halleck, Drake and Percival; in the restrained passion of patriotism, cold as a star but clear and steadfast, which shines in Bryant's verse; in numerous popular lyrics, like "Adams and Liberty," "Warren's Address," "The American Flag," "The Star-Spangled Banner" and "Home, Sweet Home"; in dramas like "Eutaw Springs," "Marion," "Siege of Boston," "Washington at Valley Forge," and many others of the same kind. In these early melodramas, which quickened American patriotism by recalling the heroic age of the Revolution, we have a parallel to the popular chronicle plays which voiced the

STREET SCENE IN MODERN CHICAGO

pride and the national enthusiasm of the early Elizabethans.

Even more significant are the legendary and historical tales which appeared in this period. Crude as they are, we are interested in them as a reflection of the first national consciousness. As a result of the long struggle of the pioneers, of the faith and the work of colonizers and state builders, America had become a nation; she felt reverence for the past, confidence in the future, the thrill of national unity, — all of which are essential to national literature. She had, moreover, a history of two hundred years, a history of brave men and epic achievement; and our writers, like those of the older nations, could now look backward to a golden age of heroism. Irving created an old world of legend, the first to appear in American letters. Cooper glorified the old frontiersman and the soldier and sailor of past conflicts. Other writers heard the *sursum corda*, and a host of historical romances reflected the joy of the young nation in its old heroes. Kennedy's *Horse-Shoe Robinson*, Simms's trilogy of Revolutionary novels beginning with *The Partisan*, Paulding's *The Dutchman's Fireside*, Lydia Child's *Hobomok* and *The Rebels*, Bird's *Nick of the Woods*, — these are but a suggestion to the reader who would learn for himself what kind of tales delighted American readers of a century ago, when the nation was young, when art seemed of less, and enthusiasm of more, consequence than they do now.

We must note also the emphasis laid on moral and religious sentiments by practically all the writers of this period, and the first appearance of literary criticism, — a very significant detail, since criticism cannot begin until critics are assured of a considerable body of native literature to work upon.[1] There are doubtless other general characteristics,[2] but we emphasize only these three: the originality of the new writers, their rare harmony with nature, and their ardent patriotism born of reverence and faith, — that reverence for the past and faith in the future which ennobles a man's love of his home and country.

[1] American criticism was greatly encouraged by the new literary magazines. The *North American Review* (1815), the *New England Magazine* (1831), the *Knickerbocker Magazine* (1832) and the *Southern Literary Messenger* (1834) are a few of the best. The critical work of Poe and of the so-called " Knickerbocker School " will be considered later.

[2] The general romantic tendency of our first national literature should not be overlooked. For this tendency our writers were, indirectly, more influenced by Germany than by England.

Washington Irving (1783–1859)

Most readers welcome Irving for his cheerfulness, as they welcome the sunshine, without thinking of his quickening influence on American life and letters. It is significant that his first aim was always to please rather than instruct his readers. Unlike the Colonial and Revolutionary authors, who wrote for some practical purpose, Irving regarded literature as a desirable end in itself. He reflected life chiefly for the joy of it, as a painter reflects a face or a landscape, and the pleasure which his book gave was its sufficient excuse for being. In a word, he regarded literature as an art, and his success laid a broad foundation for all subsequent artistic writing in America.[1]

WASHINGTON IRVING

That Irving developed the modern short story[2] is in itself a notable achievement, but this is only one of his honors. He was the first to reveal America as a land of legend and romance. In his *Bracebridge Hall* he showed England that the literary possibilities of country life had only been touched, not exhausted, by Addison's *Sir Roger de Coverley*. He went to Spain, and there found a mine of literary treasures which the Spaniards themselves had

[1] For the earlier work of Godfrey in the same direction, see p. 56.
[2] Some of our present critics make a distinction between the Short-story and the story that is merely short. They regard Poe as the inventor of the American Short-story (see note on p. 235).

well-nigh forgotten. He crossed the Mississippi with hardy explorers, and again revealed a world of romance where others had seen only a wilderness. So, wherever he went, Irving was a discoverer, having the seeing eye and the understanding heart. Every old castle opened a secret door to his *sesame;* every wild prairie offered him the blue flower of sentiment; every hill and mountain told him its unspoken legend.

And what a surprise, what a delight he was to the readers of a century ago! At that time we had no writer whose genius was generally acknowledged. We were self-conscious, eager for praise, but England looked askance at our literature, thinking that only the strange and uncouth could proceed from this supposed wild land of democracy and buffaloes. Then appeared Irving's stories, not wild or strange at all, but natural as the landscape, familiar as the tales that men had loved in childhood. Their matter was fresh and original; their graceful style was unequaled by any living writer of English. At a time when Scott and Byron were literary heroes, this American was immediately given an honored place beside them; and the favors showered upon him by English critics produced deep gratification here, as if Irving were one of our national institutions. He bridged the gap created by the Revolution, united the two great nations in spirit, and showed that our American books are forever a part of the great body of English letters. Thackeray calls Irving " the first ambassador whom the New World of letters sent to the Old," and our own critics are almost unanimous in considering him the father of American literature.

Life. Those who are fond of finding the explanation of books in the author's environment will be disappointed in Irving. Though the New York in which he was born (1783) was a straggling town of quaint houses, orchards and cabbage gardens, he began to write his *Salmagundi* essays as if he were recording gossip from the clubs and coffeehouses of a great city. The country at large was growing and exulting; there were wars, bitter political strifes, discoveries that set the world agog; but Irving's pen reflected nothing of the excitement.

He was in England after the Battle of Waterloo, and again during the uproar attending the Reform Bill; he arrived in Spain at a time of revolution; but we look in vain for any suggestion of these stirring events in his pages. For Irving dwells in the romantic past, not in the present or future.

His father was a Scotchman of the Covenanter type, his mother an Englishwoman, gentle and indulgent to her children. They had settled in America long enough before the Revolution to catch the spirit of the new land, and had been stanch patriots during the occupation of New York by the British soldiers. To these parents, who still cherished a love for their old home, our author owed that rare sympathy which made him understand and revere England, while he remained splendidly loyal to his own country.

Unlike his brothers, who were college trained, Irving had but a scant education. This was due partly to delicate health, and partly to **Education** his dislike of routine work of any kind. He was naturally an idler, like his old Mateo of the *Alhambra*, and took many holidays that were not on the calendar. He explored the Hudson, shot squirrels in the woods of Harlem, or loafed in the sunshine on the Battery watching the ships go out to sea, taking the long thread of his dreams with them. At sixteen he was through with school and began with a wry face to study law. Also he began to write, and in 1802 first published, in his brother's newspaper, some light essays in imitation of Addison. Then he was seriously threatened with consumption, and his brothers sent him abroad in the hope that the long sea voyage might save his life.

One must read Irving's letters to appreciate his joy and wonder in the Old World. Fate was unusually kind to this lover of the romantic; **First Journey Abroad** for besides giving him a happy time, she arranged that he should see Nelson's fleet sweeping the sea to Trafalgar, that he should be arrested as an English spy at Nice, and that his ship should be boarded by pirates in the Mediterranean. After eighteen months of travel he returned home in excellent health, dabbled in Blackstone again, and was presently admitted to the bar. To this period, when his head was busy with law and his heart was on a literary vacation, belong his *Salmagundi* papers, which first gave him a local reputation, and which probably led to his appointment as one of the attorneys at the famous trial of Aaron Burr,—an event which at that time (1804–1807) occupied the attention of the entire country.

The date 1809 is noteworthy, for in that year Irving published his *Knickerbocker History*.[1] This book met with instant success at home, and its fame spread to England, where Scott was one of its delighted readers; but the surprised young author was still afraid to follow his spirit and commit himself wholly to literature, as Brown had done. Instead, he went into partnership with his brothers, who were importers of hardware. The War of 1812 broke out, but not until the burning of Washington was Irving roused. Then he offered his services to the Governor of New York, and for a time did the inglorious work of a military secretary. Under the genial, ease-loving exterior there was a heroic strain in Irving, and he was sorely disappointed when he was not allowed to accompany his friend, the gallant Decatur, in the naval expedition against the Algerian pirates. Failing in this ambition, he went on a business trip to England, intending to be gone a few months. Seventeen years passed before he saw his native land again.

In England our young author was speedily enmeshed in the affairs of the Irving Brothers, whose trade had been almost ruined by the **Irving in** war. The firm failed in 1818, which is another memora- **England** ble date in Irving's life. Up to that time he had perhaps taken life too easily, depending on his generous brothers. The common calamity roused him, and he turned seriously to literature with the determination to earn a living by his own effort. Through the influence of Walter Scott, "that golden-hearted man," he was offered pleasant employment as an editor; but distrusting his fitness for routine work he declined the offer, finished a few essays and sent them to America. This was the beginning of the *Sketch Book* (1820), which definitely settled Irving's career as a writer. At this time Brown was dead, Poe was at school in Richmond, Bryant was struggling with the law, and Cooper had not yet planned *The Spy*. Irving was therefore our only professional man of letters, and he depended at first as much upon English as upon American readers. *Bracebridge Hall* (1821) and *Tales of a Traveller* (1824) are two more important results of this English period of his life. Then, welcoming the suggestion of Alexander Everett, our minister to Spain, that he should translate Navarrete's *Voyages of Columbus*, he hastened to Madrid, where he proved himself as much of an explorer in the Old World as was ever De Soto in the New.

---

[1] Those who remember only the hilarity of this work will learn with a shock that it was written during the only great sorrow of Irving's life, a sorrow occasioned by the death of Matilda Hoffman, a lovely girl to whom he was engaged.

The next three years (1826–1829) were the most fruitful of Irving's life. He had intended to make a translation, but the mass of **Spanish Discoveries** unused material in the Spanish archives presently led him to attempt his own story of Columbus. Soon the romantic history, the legends and traditions of this old land of cross and crescent, began to fascinate Irving, as the first book of fairy stories fascinates a child. The very names had magic in them. Granada, Guadalajara, Andalusia, — who can read them, even now, without the desire to mount and away to the land of enchantment? Irving spent his mornings in the Jesuit College at St. Isidoro, an exquisite old place, refined by years of study and meditation, where every shelf of parchment-bound books opened to him a wonderland. It was the first scholarly discipline he had ever known, and he responded as a plant that is taken out of its earthen pot and set in its native soil and air. The *Life and Voyages of Columbus* (1828), *Conquest of Granada* (1829), *Spanish Voyages of Discovery* (1831) and *Alhambra* (1832) were the immediate results of his first visit; and to his study of Spanish records we owe also the later *Moorish Chronicles, Legends of the Conquest of Spain* and *Mahomet and his Successors*.

This busy, happy Spanish period was ended by his appointment as Secretary of the American Legation in London. He held this position for two years, receiving such attention as England gave to her own great writers; then the call of his country became irresistible, and he turned homeward in 1832. His reception here was all that an author could desire. He had quietly answered the galling question, " Who reads an American book? " and the whole nation delighted to do him honor.

One who reads Irving's letters of this period finds two significant reflections of the author: his modesty, which was proof against the **With Western Explorers** perils of success; and his amazement at the changes which had taken place here, and which made him feel like Rip Van Winkle after a long sleep. He had left New York a country town, over which drowsy Dutch traditions still hovered; he found it a city of two hundred thousand people, stored with wealth, buzzing with tremendous energy; and this local transformation was typical of the entire country. He felt the excitement of the mighty Western movement, and went to see for himself the wonders of the great plains. The *Tour of the Prairies* (1835), *Astoria* (1836) and *Adventures of Captain Bonneville* (1837) are the literary results of his journey. In reading them we are again conscious of the manly soul that is hidden in this dreamer and story-teller. He is enthusiastic over a good horse; he enters headlong into the excitement of buffalo running, forgetting the danger till he is almost thrown under the feet of a charging bull; he loves the vast open spaces, the march with adventurous men, the bivouac under the stars. Moreover, he is the original discoverer of that stirring romance of the West, which has inspired so many writers ever since.

Tired of his wandering, Irving now bought a little Dutch cottage at Tarrytown overlooking the Hudson, remodeled it till it was all nooks and gables, and called it Sunnyside. He lived there with his relatives in great happiness for the remainder of his life, with the exception of four years which he spent abroad as our ambassador to Spain. He had declined many political offices which were offered him by a grateful nation, knowing his unfitness for the work involved; but he accepted this mission, which was urged upon him by Webster and President Tyler, modestly thinking that the honor was offered to the profession of letters. He proved, on the whole, a worthy member of that splendid group — Franklin, Randolph, Laurens, Jefferson, Motley, Everett, Bancroft, Lowell, and other literary men — who have at various times represented America at the courts of Europe.

To the last period of Irving's life, after his return from Spain, belong his Sunnyside sketches known as *Wolfert's Roost* (1855), and the **His Last** three important biographies: *Life of Goldsmith* (1849), **Years** *Mahomet and his Successors* (1850) and the monumental *Life of Washington*, the last volume of which was published only a little while before Irving's death, in 1859. Loved as he was in his own home and honored by the nation, his closing years were like an October day, mellow, serene and fruitful. In one of his *Easy Chair* papers Curtis describes Irving as men met him tripping along Broadway, affable, happy, courteous, with a suggestion of the "old school" in his dress and manners, as if he had "just stepped out of his own books." As he had once accepted the mission to Spain, not as a personal gift but as a mark of respect to literature, so now he received the honors that were showered upon him, as a generous tribute of youth to age. He was delighted with the thought that old gentlemen were still respected " and were even becoming fashionable."

Earlier Works of Irving. There are various classifications of our author's works, but one who depends upon them is speedily brought to confusion. Irving's spirit is constant; the romantic always appeals to him ; and while one may safely call the *Knickerbocker History* a work of humor, and the *Life of Columbus* a biography, other productions like the *Sketch Book* defy classification. Simply for convenience, therefore, we divide his twenty-odd volumes into three parts, corresponding to the early, middle and later periods of his life.

The chief works of the early period are the boyish *Jonathan Oldstyle* essays, *Salmagundi* and the hilarious *Knickerbocker History*. The general character of the *Salmagundi*

NEW AMSTERDAM, 1664

papers[1] may be inferred from the name (which is that of an appetizing hash, compounded of meat, smoked fish, eggs, onions and spices) and from the startling announcement of the young authors :

" Our purpose is simply to instruct the young, reform the old, correct the town and castigate the age. This is an arduous task, and therefore we undertake it with confidence."

Of these airy papers, which were begun and ended as a jest, we may simply say, " They had their day and ceased to be."

[1] The correct title was *Salmagundi, or the Whim-whams and Opinions of Launcelot Langstaff, Esq., and others.* The "others" were Irving's brother William, and James K. Paulding. Irving follows the fashion of his age in using assumed names. He appears first as Jonathan Oldstyle, then as Launcelot Langstaff, Diedrich Knickerbocker and Geoffrey Crayon.

A few readers, however, are still interested in them ; and such readers cite the " Chronicle of the Renowned and Ancient City of Gotham," as an instance of Irving's power to create a lasting tradition.[1]

The most notable work of this period was *A History of New York from the Beginning of the World to the End of the Dutch Dynasty, by Diedrich Knickerbocker* (1809),
The Knicker-bocker History
which some critics regard as the first literary work of national importance produced in America. If the critics are right, then our national literature began with a joke. The alleged historian was a queer Dutch antiquarian, who suddenly disappeared, leaving an unpaid board bill and a package of manuscript. After advertising for him in the newspapers, Irving professed to publish the manuscript in order to pay the board bill.

Opening the *Knickerbocker History*, we find that the first book is merely a burlesque of a popular history of New York, which began, in the historic fashion of those days, with the creation of the world. The second book consists largely of making fun of the New Jersey settlers. We advise the reader to skip these two books, the humor of which now seems tedious, and to read (in an abridged edition) the last three books, which chronicle the doughty deeds of three Dutch governors : Wouter Van Twiller, William the Testy, and Peter the Headstrong. The whole work is a huge farce, and Irving increased the ridiculous effect by dedicating it to the Historical Society, gravely announcing that its one merit was its scrupulous accuracy. Its boisterous fun is directed against the Dutch colonists, with here and there a somewhat malicious fling at the Yankees, showing that Irving was influenced by an English fashion and

[1] Occasionally residents of New York still call themselves " Gothamites," but few who use the name realize its significance. The modern slang equivalent is " hayseeds." The old English town of Gotham was the butt of city jokers in the Middle Ages. Its rustic people are ridiculed in an old Miracle play and in the nursery rime beginning, " Three wise men of Gotham went to sea in a bowl." So also the name " Knickerbocker," which is now proudly applied to hotels, banks, and even " first families," refers to a crazy old bachelor invented by Irving.

THE EDICT OF WILLIAM THE TESTY

Knickerbocker's History of New York. From the painting by Boughton; property of the Metropolitan Museum of Art

by a local prejudice.[1] The latter leads him into an occasional display of bad taste, which is in marked contrast to the refinement of his life and of all his later writings.

Aside from these blemishes, the book is characterized by rollicking good nature, though the fun is often carried to a point where, like children's fooling, it becomes tiresome. The humor consists largely in relating fact and absurdity, the obvious and the impossible, in the same strain of sober gravity. Irving holds close enough to historical dates and personages to give an impression of reality ; then he leads his characters into the most ridiculous and outrageous adventures. It is the grain of truth in the bushel of nonsense that gives point to his humor, and that makes his Dutch heroes at once familiar and grotesque, like faces seen in a doorknob.

Middle Period. The works of Irving's middle period may be grouped in three divisions, showing the influences of England, Spain and America respectively. In the first are the *Sketch Book* (1820), *Bracebridge Hall* (1822), *Tales of a Traveller* (1824) and a part of the *Crayon Miscellanies* (1825). These are all of the same sketchy character, revealing the author's impressions as traveler, critic, essayist, and story-teller. They are all characterized by a mingling of humor and pathos, sentiment and sentimentality.

The *Sketch Book* is probably the best known and loved of all Irving's works. One might analyze the romantic sentiment The Sketch and the Addisonian style of these delicate sketches Book of English and American life, but the book is one to read and enjoy, not to criticize as we criticize the *Knickerbocker History*. Every reader must find his own favorite sketches, and we merely indicate our own in naming the following : " Rip Van Winkle " and " Sleepy Hollow," which have made the Hudson more renowned for its legends than for its commerce ; the

[1] It was an English fashion at that time to ridicule the Dutch, — possibly to make men forget that the gallant little Dutch squadron had once swept the English from the sea. Irving's prejudice against New England was shared by Cooper and by many other New York writers of the period (see p. 216).

Christmas stories, which inspired Dickens and which mark the beginning of our modern joyous celebration of the festival; "Stratford" and "Westminster Abbey," which may be likened to a pair of romantic spectacles that every American puts on when he visits these literary shrines; and for variety, the "Spectre Bridegroom" and "The Angler." One should not attempt this last, however, unless he likes fishing and understands Isaac Walton.

Copyright, 1898,
by Edward Moran

HENRY HUDSON ENTERING NEW YORK BAY

Bracebridge Hall, one of the most charming of Irving's works, is a series of sketches and stories of English country life suggesting Addison's *Sir Roger de Coverley*. Our own favorites in *Bracebridge Hall* are the Introduction, the May-Day and Christmas sketches, the stories of "Dolph Heyliger," "The Stout Gentleman" and "Annette Delabre." The *Tales of a Traveller*, which Irving thought the best of his works, is on the whole inferior to the two we have just mentioned; but after reading "Wolfert Webber" (which may have influenced Poe to write "The Gold Bug") and "The Bold Dragoon," which delighted Scott by its grotesque imagination, we understand Irving's place as the first, and still one of the best, of our short-story writers.

The remarkable series of books on Spanish themes belong also to the middle period. Irving began with the *Life of Columbus* (1828), a readable book, having the rare combina-
Spanish
Themes tion of historical accuracy and warm human interest. It remains, after a hundred years, probably our best biography of the great explorer. Columbus naturally suggested his patrons, Ferdinand and Isabella, and all the chivalry and romance of Spanish history. Here Irving lost himself in a wonderland, and even his serious works, such as the *Conquest of Granada* (1829), have an atmosphere of romance rather than of history.[1] The best of his Spanish books is *The Alhambra* (1832), a collection of descriptive essays, legends and stories, all clustering about the last stronghold of the Moors. When Prescott called this " the beautiful Spanish Sketch Book," he said enough in its favor. Indeed, one who reads the *Sketch Book* and *The Alhambra* meets Irving at the highest point he ever reached as a writer.

The series of books on American pioneer themes completed the work of this fruitful middle period. The *Tour of the Prairies*
The Romance
of the West (1835) describes Irving's wanderings with a party of explorers through the unknown region between the Arkansas and the Red rivers. Hitherto he had been absorbed in the past, but when he crossed the Mississippi he was instantly inspired by the romance of the present. Though apparently a lazy observer, he is at times keener or more accurate than Cooper, and there is a zest, a hearty joy of wild life, in his pages which probably influenced Parkman in his *Oregon Trail*. Altogether, this *Tour*, though generally neglected, will appeal to a few readers as one of the most significant of Irving's works. It reveals an entirely new side of the author's character and his rare power of finding a romantic interest in the silent places, as once before, in " The Voyage," he had found it even on the lonely sea.

[1] In all his Spanish themes, Irving is perhaps too much of the romanticist. He looks only at the good side of his heroes, and fails to note the barbarities of the Spanish conquerors.

Astoria, a jumbled, chaotic account of the fur house at the mouth of the Columbia, is plainly hack work and of no consequence. Much better is the *Adventures of Captain Bonneville*, compiled largely from the journal of that daring explorer. Here is a helter-skelter story of pack trains, exploration and fighting, with side excursions among the " free trappers " of the Rocky Mountains. It has small literary value but plenty of adventure, and we have known at least one reader to be wide-awake over its camp fires at midnight who might have grown sleepy in *Bracebridge Hall*.

Late Period. To the last period of Irving's life belong the volume of sketches known as *Wolfert's Roost* and the three biographies of Mahomet, Goldsmith and Washington. The *Life of Goldsmith* is a tender, uncritical appreciation of one of the most lovable geniuses in English literature. The *Life of Washington* was in its day [1] a notable work, in that it combined a lover's enthusiasm with a historian's desire for fact and truth ; but the theme was too great for Irving's failing powers. He was at his best in the sketch ; and the career of Washington offered a vast panorama of history, filled with complex movements and contending forces, through which one great figure moved steadily to its appointed end. Perhaps, from this viewpoint, the life of Washington has not yet been written ; the puzzled reader must sometime choose between earlier biographers, who emphasize Washington's superhuman virtues, and later writers, who seem somewhat too diligent to discover his faults. We suggest, therefore, that though Irving was not a critical scholar, his abridged *Life of Washington*, as edited and supplemented in a sympathetic way by John Fiske, is still a very good book to read.

The Life of Washington

---

1 Irving was often misled by Weems's popular but fictitious biography of Washington, and a large mass of material discovered by modern historians was unknown to him. Irving had been named after Washington, and in his childhood was presented to the great soldier. " I was but five years old," he said long afterwards, " but I feel that touch on my head even now." It was probably this cherished memory of childhood which led Irving in his old age to write the life of his hero.

General Characteristics. Irving signed his first essays
"Jonathan Oldstyle," and the name is pleasantly suggestive
Irving's of his literary masters, Addison and Goldsmith, who
Style were going out of fashion when he began to write.
The most pervasive quality of his style is its charm, an indefinite
word, which means simply that his manner is attractive, that
it is a pleasure to read or to listen to him. If we analyze his
work more minutely, we find that the first definite quality of his
style is its naturalness. He writes without effort, and finds
without seeking the most felicitous word and the most expressive metaphor. The naturalness is increased, moreover, by the
harmony between tone and theme, and by Irving's rare ability to
give "local color" to his narrative. Though he writes of many
things, of Old-World castles and New-World prairies, of men
and women, ghosts and goblins, we feel in each of his stories
the very atmosphere of his scene and the harmony between his
manner and his subject.

Next in importance is the clearness, the transparency of Irving's style, which is so marked that the poet Campbell declared
he had "added clarity to the English tongue." By "transparent" we mean that his thought is so well expressed that we
are never in doubt of his meaning, and that he always keeps
modestly out of our way, calling attention not to himself but to
what he is saying. Added to these qualities are a certain balance
and melody of his sentences, and an unmistakable refinement,
as of culture and wide reading, which commands respect wherever heard. This last quality seems more remarkable in view of
the fact that Irving could hardly be called a scholar, or even a
disciplined reader. It is evidently from within, like a child's
singing, and we are content to appreciate without trying to
explain it.

To Irving's humor, boisterous and crude in the *Knickerbocker
History* but becoming more and more delicate in his later works,
and to the love of romance and sentiment which are reflected
even in his serious works, we have already called attention. His

sentiment is generally wholesome, but, like Brown, he shows the influence of literary fashion by occasional lapses into sentimen-

Humor and Sentiment tality. Here, for instance, are "Rural Funerals," "The Widow and Her Son" and "The Broken Heart," which Byron and many others found an occasion for tears but which will hardly stand our critical analysis. They aim rather too obviously to make us cry; and many readers resent such a deliberate attempt at their emotions, knowing that the world's grief — which Irving never felt very deeply — is too simple and sacred a thing for sentimentality. We are to remember, however, that Irving wrote to please, not to reform; that his readers loved tears, urns and new-made graves in their stories and poems; and that a sentimental interest in sad or funereal subjects was a marked characteristic of English and American literature for a full century following Gray's *Elegy*.[1]

Irving's Message. There are critics who say that Irving has no message, but they belong with those who never detect a sermon unless it begins with a text and ends with a "finally." There are many kinds of sermons, the best of which are not too obvious; and some messages, like the bluebird's song, might suffer harm from too definite expression. It is true that Irving, like his historian of *Bracebridge Hall*, is merely an observer of life. He has neither problems nor ambitions; he enters not into the doubts and struggles of humanity; he never takes sides in strife, having, as he says, "a most melancholy good opinion of all my fellow creatures." But in a world of reforms and reformers, and in a literature that welcomes the "problem" novel, it is rather refreshing to find one to whom life seems good, and whose work always suggests the legend written on the old sundials: *horas non numero nisi serenas*, "I count only the sunny hours."

We can accept, therefore, the dictum of the English critic Hazlitt, that Irving is "a filigree man," remembering that the

[1] For the influence of this taste, or fashion, on Brown's novels, see p. 159. For its influence on Bryant's poetry, see p. 201.

RIP VAN WINKLE

A portrait of Joseph Jefferson as Rip Van Winkle by Marion Swinton

old Greek and Etruscan filigrees were of exquisite beauty and sometimes inclosed a jewel. We accept also a general judgment of our own writers, that Irving is the companion of an idle hour rather than the friend to whom we turn in adversity. But let us not leave him with this negative tribute. He was, first of all, remarkable as a discoverer of literary material, and his discoveries have been freely used by writers on both sides of the Atlantic.

"SUNNYSIDE," IRVING'S HOME ON THE HUDSON

Again, by his delicate sympathy he found his way to the hearts of America, England and Spain successively ; and he established the famous principle, which De Quincey formulated, that " not to sympathize is not to understand." Finally, by his style, his attention to artistic form, his development of the essay and the modern short story, he exerted a strong and wholesome influence at the beginning of our national literature. Though he died half a century ago, he is still to thousands of men and women a cheerful comrade, whose message is that we live in a good world, and that the best way to show our appreciation is to give thanks and enjoy it. As he wrote modestly in " The Christmas Dinner " :

" If I can by any lucky chance in these days of evil rub out one wrinkle from the brow of care, or beguile the heavy heart of one moment of sorrow ; if I can now and then penetrate through the gathering film of misanthropy, prompt a benevolent view of human nature and make my reader more in good humor with his fellow beings and himself, — surely, surely, I shall not then have written entirely in vain."

WILLIAM CULLEN BRYANT (1794–1878)

The groves were God's first temples. Ere man learned
To hew the shaft and lay the architrave,
And spread the roof above them — ere he framed
The lofty vault, to gather and roll back
The sound of anthems ; in the darkling wood,
Amid the cool and silence, he knelt down,
And offered to the Mightiest solemn thanks
And supplication. For his simple heart
Might not resist the sacred influences
Which, from the stilly twilight of the place,
And from the gray old trunks that high in heaven
Mingled their mossy boughs, and from the sound
Of the invisible breath that swayed at once
All their green tops, stole over him, and bowed
His spirit with the thought of boundless power
And inaccessible majesty. Ah, why
Should we, in the world's riper years, neglect
God's ancient sanctuaries, and adore
Only among the crowd, and under roofs
That our frail hands have raised? Let me, at least,
Here, in the shadow of this aged wood,
Offer one hymn — thrice happy, if it find
Acceptance in His ear. . . .

In this introduction to the noble " Forest Hymn " may be found two suggestions of the life and work of one who is often called our first national poet. First, he is skillfully using blank verse, that wonderful instrument of old Latin and English poets ; and second, he appears as the high priest of Nature, offering his hymn at her altar, as one might leave a cherished possession reverently at the shrine of a saint.

The latter suggestion is emphasized in the portraits with which we are all familiar. Bryant was a young man when he wrote his best poetry ; but who can recall any picture of his smooth, boyish face, with its fair curls and eyes innocent of experience ? Or who that reads in succession " Thanatopsis " and " The Flood of Years " finds anything to indicate that one was written by a mere boy and the other by a man of eighty ?

Bryant seems to have been always old, like our grandfathers. That grave, strong, patriarchal face, with its deep-set eyes, shaggy eyebrows and snowy drift of hair, is the only one that could satisfy us after reading his poetry.

Life. Bryant was of Pilgrim stock and counted himself among the descendants of John and Priscilla Alden, who are immortalized in a poem written by another descendant and called " The Courtship of Miles Standish." His father was a country doctor, a lover of books and poetry ; his mother was a Puritan, with all that the name implies of devotion to lofty ideals and practical duty :

> A virtuous woman who can find?
> For her price is far above rubies.
> The heart of her husband trusteth in her. . . .
> She doeth him good and not evil all the days of her life. . . .
> She openeth her mouth with wisdom,
> And in her tongue is the law of kindness.
> She looketh well to the ways of her household,
> And eateth not the bread of idleness.
> Her children rise up and call her blessed.

That Bryant's mother merited every line of this fine old eulogy is shown by her diary and by the testimony of the poet, who attributed his ideals and his success largely to his mother's influence.

He was born (1794) in Cummington, a frontier village in the rugged hill country of Massachusetts. There his boyhood was passed, **A Poet's** attending the district school or working on the farm by **Childhood** day, and reading before the open fire at night. A dull, secluded, heavy-laden life it may seem to us now, with its days of anxiety and pain ; but it was ennobled by the companionship of good parents and good books, and dignified by the Puritan spirit, which regarded small duties by the light of great principles. Nor must we forget the curtain of the day, when the whole family was accustomed to kneel together in prayer. As the grandfather offered his petition for a blessing on home and friends and nation, the small boy would whisper the desire of his own heart that he might some day be his country's poet. Later he will leave this lonely farm, will study, travel, become a leader of affairs in a great city ; but he will ever do his best work in the remembrance of his childhood. There is only one way to get the spirit of Bryant's poetry, and that is to put yourself in sympathy with a Puritan boy looking up at the eternal hills.

He fitted for college in the old-fashioned way, by studying with the learned ministers of the neighborhood. For one dollar a week, so **His** the record runs, he obtained his scanty fare of bread-and-**Education** milk and his liberal mental pabulum of Latin, Greek and mathematics. He learned quickly, and in his sixteenth year easily passed his examination for the sophomore class in Williams College. Even at this early age he had won local recognition; some of his boyish verses were printed in the newspapers, and " The Embargo,"

WILLIAM CULLEN BRYANT

a bitter satire directed against Jefferson's administration, was published in Boston and ran through a second edition.

Bryant left Williams after two terms, intending to enter the junior class at Yale. Alas! his father had no money, and the boy went sorrowfully back to the farm. It was at this time, when he grieved in secret over the failure of his college plans, that he wrote "Thanatopsis," which takes an added luster from the fact that it was written by a youth of seventeen. Then followed a long period of law studies, and of practice as a country lawyer at Great Barrington. That he disliked this work is evident from his letters and from the closing lines of " Green River "; but there was no chance to earn one's bread by poetry in those days, and Bryant held faithfully to the law until he had mastered it, still following the Puritan ideal of duty. Meanwhile his reputation as a poet was established by the publication of his early poems in the *North American Review*.[1] In 1821 appeared his first modest little volume called *Poems*. The date marks the definite appearance of national poetry in America.

---

[1] The originality of these early verses attracted instant attention. Dana, one of the editors of the *Review*, assured the other editors that they had been imposed upon; that there was " no one on this side of the Atlantic capable of writing such verses." The remark is suggestive of the state of poetry in America at that time.

Three years later, in 1824, Bryant abandoned the law and followed his heart into the world of letters. He moved to New York, which was then becoming famous as a literary center, and became an editor of the *New York Review*. Magazines led a will-o'-the-wisp kind of life in those days, and after a few sparkles generally went out in darkness. The *Review* failed, and Bryant, the lover of solitude and poetry, was glad to find work with the *Evening Post*, where he was plunged into the turmoil of news and politics. In three years, such was his ability, he was editor-in-chief of this newspaper, and held the position for more than half a century.

The rest of Bryant's life belongs to journalism rather than to literature, and we note only a few significant characteristics. At that time **The Journalist** our newspapers were generally devoted to party politics, but Bryant determined to make his work national and to speak the truth fearlessly, without regard to party or prejudice. In consequence, many regard him as the first of our great editors and the father of modern journalism. Naturally his poetry suffered from his absorption in temporary affairs; though he published a slender volume of verse every few years, he made little or no improvement on his earliest work. His business prospered greatly; he traveled much at home and abroad; he was a recognized literary leader, and was called upon to make an address at many a public function.[1] His home life during all these years of prosperity was beautifully serene and happy. He kept his scholarly interests to the end, and his last important achievement was the translation of the *Iliad* and the *Odyssey* into blank verse. This translation, a notable work in itself, is especially remarkable in view of the fact that it represents six years' labor on the part of a man already past his threescore years and ten.

Looking back on his long, quiet life, the first work of the historian is to account, not for his poetry or journalism, but for the place which **His Commanding Position** he holds in our national literature, — a place much higher than the quality of his poetry would seem to warrant. His position was well indicated by Cooper, who said, " The rest of us " — meaning himself, Irving, Poe, and the Knickerbocker School — " may be mentioned now and then, but Bryant is the real American author." In New York especially he towered above the minor poets of his age; and throughout the country he was, until

---

[1] Some of his speeches, especially his memorial addresses on Cooper, Irving, Halleck and Verplanck, are still worth reading. His other prose works, such as *Letters of a Traveller* (1850) and *Letters from the East* (1869) are quite neglected.

the triumph of Longfellow, generally regarded as the first of our national singers. The glamour of worldly success was about him, as it was about Franklin, and this made men more ready to applaud his poetic talent. He had won fame and fortune as the most successful journalist of his day ; he was recognized not simply as poet and scholar, but as a successful business man, the first citizen of a great city and a leader in national affairs. In this last respect he completely overshadowed Irving and Poe, who took little or no interest in public matters. Moreover, his life was noble, in all respects worthy of his place and art. Whittier and Emerson both paid generous tribute to his greatness of soul, and Lincoln, after his memorable visit to New York in 1855, declared that " it was worth the journey East to see such a man."

Sentiment also played a leading part in Bryant's honors. His life began in the days of Washington, and he lived to celebrate the one-**The Pioneer** hundredth birthday of the nation in 1876. Men saw in **Poet** him a living bridge which joined the old to the new ; a reminder, in the days of Calhoun and Webster, of the old struggle between Jefferson and Hamilton ; a literary leader whose work began with the attempts of the Hartford Wits to establish a national literature, and who lived to give a generous welcome to Longfellow and Lanier, who were greater poets than himself. To the solid achievement of the present, therefore, was added a romantic glamour from the past, and America, as the criticism of the period clearly shows, could find nothing too good in the way of praise to offer to her noble old pioneer who had outlived his great contemporaries.

On all these accounts — his talent, his poetry, his worldly success, his leadership in public affairs, his sterling character, his association with the remote past — Bryant held a prominent position for more than fifty years. North and South, East and West, Canada, Cuba and Mexico as well as the United States, — all honored him as the New World's poet. Later singers undoubtedly produced better work ; probably no other ever won quite so commanding a place in American letters as Bryant occupied in the middle of the nineteenth century.

Bryant's Work. As it is easy to misunderstand Bryant or to misjudge the value of his verse, we venture at the outset to call attention to three general considerations :

First, though he wrote for seventy-odd years, his collected poems, aside from his translation of Homer, fill only one volume ;

and of these poems all that are permanent might easily be printed on fifty pages. We have our own opinion that, as Brooke said of Coleridge, these few pages should be bound in gold ; but if we compare our aged poet with Keats or Shelley, who died under thirty, we must admit frankly that both in quantity and quality he falls below the standard of the English masters.

Second, in reading Bryant one is conscious after a time of a certain monotony, which is due to the fact that our poet holds

Quality of his Verse

always to the same level. He never touches either the heights or the deeps of human life. He produces no epic, no comedies or tragedies, no passionate outcry, no glorious romance. He has a few simple themes, which he treats with such classic simplicity that we are apt to overlook his restrained emotion, just as the careless reader never feels the fire that lurks in the calm, Puritan verse of George Herbert. To many readers, indeed, who know Bryant only as the author of the melancholy " Thanatopsis," he seems cold and didactic ; but to the few, who have stood alone among the hills or under the stars, Bryant is a true poet, second only to Wordsworth in his ability to express man's thought and feeling in presence of the mighty life of nature.

Third, Bryant's work, aside from its intrinsic merits, is remarkable for this, — that it definitely establishes a standard of American verse. In his first boyish attempts Bryant was plainly a provincial, copying English models as all other American poets had done before him ; but when he abandoned these models to follow his own spirit he became the founder of a new national poetry. Before 1821, the year of his first volume, our poets generally thought that they must write like Pope, or some other English master, to win success ; after that date, encouraged by Bryant's example, they dared to be themselves. His place in our poetry, therefore, is comparable to that of Jefferson in the history of democracy. Though he established no school and had no follower, all our modern poets are his debtors.

Indeed, in view of his work, his contemporaries were probably justified in calling him " the father of American poetry."

Poems on Death. Of the first thirty poems in our edition of Bryant, it happens that twelve deal with death in some form, and twelve with nature, — a chance arrangement, we might think, until we examine the book and find that four fifths of the poems are devoted to these two subjects. One can explain the nature poems on the ground that a man's pen, like his face, generally reflects what he loves best ; but the thoughtful reader will surely ask, Why should a young poet be interested in death, or a young man winning his fame and fortune be forever thinking of the grave ? The answer leads us at once to the secret of Bryant's work, and to the general literary influences which surrounded the beginning of our national poetry.

We are to remember, first of all, that though Bryant became a liberal in matters of theology, he never outgrew his Puritan training. We may remember also that the Puritan took no shortsighted view of life, as bounded by earth's horizon ; he worked in time for eternity, and settled the problems of this world by principles that should make him feel at home in heaven. The two greatest Puritan books are *Paradise Lost* and *Pilgrim's Progress ;* and both are more deeply concerned with the future than with the present life. Our poet, as the result of his early training, shared the abiding Puritan interest in the hereafter, and always looked upon death, the gateway between two worlds, with supreme interest. Moreover, he was a delicate child, and was threatened with consumption ; he had seen a beloved sister taken away by the same dread disease, — that little sister whom he remembers with such tenderness in " The Death of the Flowers." At an age when other boys are joyously interested in life as an eternal springtime, he often faced the great question of immortality. Though he grew strong and lived to a hale old age, he never quite lost the bearing of one who had seen the majesty which death gives to the humblest dwelling, and who had

The Puritan's Interest

accustomed himself to look without fear or trembling into the Reaper's face, as one who asks a question.

So far, Bryant's peculiar interest seems to be personal, but we must reckon also with the poetry of his age, with the *Garlands*, *Tokens* and other collections that appeared in America and England. All these reflect a deep interest in funereal subjects, an interest which chills or repels us now, but which then amounted almost to enthusiasm. Probably the best-known English poem in his day was Gray's *Elegy Written in a Country Churchyard* (1750). Amid a thousand poems on the grave it retained its popularity for a full century. Next to the *Elegy*, we would place Young's *The Complaint, or Night Thoughts* and Blair's *The Grave;* terribly gloomy poems they seem to the modern reader, but they were widely read and quoted on both sides of the Atlantic during this entire period. Bryant's poems on death and the grave are, therefore, like those of Poe, largely a reflection of the literary taste or fashion which influenced English and American poets from the middle of the seventeenth to the middle of the eighteenth century. If we read, for instance, that part of Blair's *Grave* beginning :

Poetry of his Age

> What is this world?
> What but a spacious burial field unwalled?

we shall find an interesting parallel to the following passage from " Thanatopsis " :

> The hills,
> Rock-ribbed and ancient as the sun ; the vales
> Stretching in pensive quietness between ;
> The venerable woods ; rivers that move
> In majesty, and the complaining brooks
> That make the meadows green ; and, poured round all,
> Old Ocean's gray and melancholy waste, —
> Are but the solemn decorations all
> Of the great tomb of man.[1]

[1] Probably both Bryant and Blair borrowed this conception from Thucydides, who declared that the earth is but a sepulcher of famous men. The influence of Homer in " Thanatopsis " is shown in such sounding expressions as " the all-beholding sun." In the first stanza, in the " communion " with nature, her " healing sympathy," etc. some critics detect the influence of Wordsworth.

This "Thanatopsis" (A View of Death) is generally placed at the head of Bryant's works, — unfortunately, we think, for it is less imaginative than other poems of his on **Thanatopsis** the same subject. If we dared criticize this old favorite, we would confess frankly that the hills and trout streams which we have loved since childhood have never once appeared to us as decorations on the universal tomb. Such a conception of nature seems to us hardly more poetic than that of Alaskan Indians, who say that the earth is a huge animal, vegetation is its fur, and men and animals are parasites on its back. Notwithstanding the majestic sweep and harmonious verse of "Thanatopsis," we find it very cold comfort. Bryant also found it so, as is evident from the two additions which he made to his original work : the opening stanza, giving a more cheerful view of nature, and the ending with its pleasant hope of dreams. One who begins with "Thanatopsis," therefore, should not end the subject with this pagan view of death, but should read also "The Return of Youth," with its golden promise, and especially "Tree-Burial," reflecting the sorrow and immortal hope of a mother's love.

Nature Poems. The numerous nature poems of Bryant ally him with Thomson, Cowper, Wordsworth and other leaders of the romantic movement in English literature. The reader will soon understand Bryant's prevailing mood if he begin with "A Forest Hymn" and read in succession the "Winter Piece" (with its suggestion of Wordsworth's "Tintern Abbey"), "A Rain Dream," "The Prairies," "The Yellow Violet," "To a Fringed Gentian," "Green River," "Autumn Woods," "Summer Wind" and "The Night Journey of a River." All these are rather somber, and for a pleasant contrast we add "The Gladness of Nature" and the rollicking "Robert of Lincoln." One who has any appreciation of nature will surely find his own mood somewhere reflected in these poems, though they are all more in sympathy with the stern and majestic than with the gladsome aspects of the outdoor world.

STATUE OF WILLIAM CULLEN BRYANT, NEW YORK PUBLIC LIBRARY

Miscellaneous Verse. Many readers find more satisfaction in the lyrics [1] of Bryant than in his poems of death or nature. Prominent among these lyrics are " The Evening Wind," " June," " Death of the Flowers " and " Song of Marion's Men." To the student who has read all the above poems, and found their range somewhat narrow, we suggest also, by way of variety, a few unclassified poems such as " The Poet," " Antiquity of Freedom," " O Mother of a Mighty Race " and " The Planting of the Apple Tree." Strangely enough, this stern singer attempted two long journeys into Fairyland ; but his mind was too Puritanic to find itself at ease in Oberon's country, and we are loth to recommend " Sella " and " The Little People of the Snow " except to the most inquisitive readers.

Last but not least on our list comes " To a Waterfowl," the most artistic of all Bryant's works. In this little poem one may
To a Waterfowl find three things : a single strong impression, a question such as the human heart instinctively asks, and the profound answer, all reflected without an unnecessary word, with an attention to form and melody rarely equaled, and then only by a master of poetry. That the reader may better appreciate this gem we venture to give its history.

Bryant had just finished his law studies (1815) and was journeying on foot through a sparsely settled country, seeking a village without a lawyer wherein he might begin his work among men. He was unknown and poor ; his dearest plans had failed ; he was doubtful of himself, of his health, of the profession he had chosen, of the big world itself, which he faced there alone in the sad twilight. Suddenly, across the afterglow of sunset, a solitary wild duck passed swiftly and was gone. Many of us have noted that sunset flight of the black mallard — the pulsating

---

[1] Lyric poetry — so called because originally it was intended to be sung to the accompaniment of a lyre — now refers to verse which expresses the poet's own mood or feeling. It is contrasted with epic, dramatic, and descriptive poetry, which are concerned with external events or persons. A lyric is a short poem, reflecting some single mood or feeling of the poet himself. Bryant rarely writes a true lyric, but generally includes more or less description of external things, and adds a moral lesson.

wings, the arrowy line drawn for an instant against the golden splendor, the tiny speck of life swallowed up in the immensity of the dusk — and we understand perfectly the question that rose unbidden from this man's lonely heart :

> Whither, midst falling dew,
> While glow the heavens with the last steps of day,
> Far, through their rosy depths, dost thou pursue
> Thy solitary way?

Line by line he draws the picture, as he sees it there on the rugged hillside, till it is all clear and sharp as an etching ; then, as an artist gives the ultimate personal touch by signing the canvas he has painted, Bryant writes himself down in the last stanza :

> He who, from zone to zone,
> Guides through the boundless sky thy certain flight,
> In the long way that I must tread alone,
> Will lead my steps aright.

Here, in a few exquisite lines, we have not simply the picture of a wild duck against the twilight, but an intensely human experience ; and the experience ends with a word of faith so simple and sincere that, after the lapse of a century, thousands of human hearts are still uplifted by it. Matthew Arnold, who was a very cold critic, grew almost enthusiastic over " To a Waterfowl " ; and Hartley Coleridge, another English poet and critic, praised it extravagantly as " the best short poem in the English language."

General Characteristics. There are two achievements of Bryant which deserve special attention : he is our first poet of nature, and the first to embody in his work the national spirit. As Emerson said of him, " He is our native, sincere, original, patriotic poet. . . . He is original because he is sincere, — a true painter of the face of the country and of the sentiments of his own people." This condensed criticism suggests an analysis of Bryant as the poet of nature and the nation.

In addition to the songs of birds there are many harmonies, tones and overtones in nature, though few men be silent and **Nature's** attentive enough to hear them. The tinkle of a brook, **Undertone** the rush of a torrent or a tempest, the murmur of waves, the hum of innumerable insects, the soft breathing of the pines, the rustling of the aspens, the faint vibration of certain forest trees grown dry and resonant as violins, — all these sounds are in the air incessantly, producing a universal melody and music,

Such as never was by mortal fingers strook.

Musicians declare that all these musical sounds are pitched upon and harmonize with one deep undertone, which is a kind of keynote to all nature. Though many of our poets have been conscious of this mighty symphony, only two of them, Bryant and Lanier, have tried deliberately to reflect it in verse. By the music of his lines Lanier tries to suggest, and often does suggest to a remarkable degree, the subtle, changing harmonies which his sensitive musical soul had detected. Bryant hears nothing of the joyous melody which fascinated the Southern poet, but only the keynote, the deep undertone as of a church organ, which rolls through his " Forest Hymn " like a summons to praise and prayer.

For Bryant was, we repeat, in a superlative way the high priest of Nature. Perhaps if we call him the druid of nature, we shall better express our thought. His religion was not theological but instinctive. There is something elemental in his verse, which reflects the feeling of the primitive man in presence of the wilderness or the sounding sea. Unlike Blake, who found elves, fairies and blithe spirits revealing themselves in flowers and stars, Bryant saw in Nature a manifestation of the one living God. Nature's grandeur, her immensity, her sublimity appealed to him profoundly. In her presence he bowed down his soul as one who worships. The deep organ tone of his blank verse is characteristic of his own attitude of devotion.

Though he wrote mostly of the rugged Northern landscape, and though he is called by some critics " the New England poet," a broad nationality which knows no sectionalism and no prejudice is perhaps the chief quality of Bryant's poetry. This **The National Spirit** is shown, first, in the perfect naturalness of his impressions, his "Hymn" sounding equally well in the spruce forests of Maine or under the mighty redwoods of California; and second, in a certain moral and didactic tendency which we call "Puritanic" and which has influenced the national spirit. If we were to sum up the Puritan influence, we should say that it reveals itself in four ways: in an insistence on facts, in a devotion to high moral and spiritual ideals, in a strong sense of responsibility which made the Puritan everywhere a teacher, and in the fundamental belief in God and man which made him a theologian and a democrat. In Bryant's verse all these qualities are manifest. He takes no liberties with the facts of nature, but is the most accurate and reliable of our poets; he never wavers from a high moral ideal, and he generally adds to his poems some lesson of faith or duty, of freedom or patriotism. In all this Bryant shows himself the true Puritan; and because the Puritan quality has entered deep into American life, he is the poet of the whole nation.

As for Bryant's style, it is as simple and as forceful as the man himself. Occasionally, as in "June," he tries an elaborate **Bryant's Style** versification, but for the most part he confines himself to the four-line stanza and to blank verse. Though a classical scholar, he uses Anglo-Saxon words whenever possible, — strong, homely words, suggestive of dear old things like poker and tongs, which our fathers found old and our children find delightfully new. Two other qualities of his style should be mentioned: its harmony with the subject, and its transparency. It reveals not only Bryant's thought but the nature and quality of his mind, — a little austere, perhaps, but fundamentally noble and sincere. As a contemporary wrote of him, "It is the glory of this man that his character outshone his great talent and his large fame."

James Fenimore Cooper (1789–1851)

" The hunter prepared himself for his journey, drawing his belt tighter and wasting his moments in the little reluctant movements of a sorrowful departure. Once or twice he essayed to speak, but a rising in his throat prevented it. At length he shouldered his rifle and cried, with a clear huntsman's call that echoed through the woods, ' Here, here, pups; away dogs, away; ye 'll be footsore afore ye see the ind of the journey.'

" This was the last that they ever saw of the Leatherstocking. . . . He had gone far towards the setting sun, — the foremost in that band of pioneers who are opening the way for the march of the nation across the continent."

The Pioneers, Chapter XLI

In this farewell of the old woodsman we have several suggestions of Cooper and of his work for American literature. The author is as slow as Leatherstocking in making a start; but once *au large*, as the voyageurs say, he is off on a long trail, and over him brood the lure and mystery of the great wilderness.

JAMES FENIMORE COOPER

Again, Cooper is at his best in portraying simple characters. We have no patience with his stilted gentlemen, but we feel the touch of nature that makes us kin with Harvey Birch, Tom Coffin and Natty Bumppo. These obscure men, vigorous and sincere, are his real heroes ; in them he reflects the spirit of the young American nation, and at the same time appeals to a universal interest. Though he writes in prose, there is an epic strain of poetry and heroism in his

best work. His hero battles against odds and embarks on peril-
ous adventure; he has physical strength and moral fiber; he is
loyal to friend, generous to enemy, chivalrous to woman. He is
not only a brave fighter, like Beowulf; he is always a knight
and a gentleman, like Ivanhoe. So the stories which delighted
America, because they were national, were welcomed abroad
because they reflected the world's ideals of heroism and chivalry.

A third suggestion from this scene may explain the keen interest with which Europe listened to the first American tale-
The Pioneer bringer, as the old Saxons would call him. We must
Interest remember that other nations also had their pioneers;
that the interest in colonization is as ancient and inclusive as
the original command to replenish the earth and subdue it. In
the same adventurous spirit that led the Saxons to England
and the Norsemen to France, all Europe had sent hither its
sons and daughters. During two hundred years they had gone
forth, like birds that flock to unknown lands, and still America
remained a silent country, as little understood as is Tibet or
Patagonia. For a nation is never known till it expresses its own
spirit in literature. "They had no poet and they died" is written
on the tombs of all forgotten races. Then appeared *The Spy*,
The Red Rover, *The Last of the Mohicans*, revealing America
not as a savage wilderness but as a new stage for the old heroic
drama of human life, — a life that Europe understood and honored because it was like its own. In all his best work Cooper
proclaimed this one truth, so easily forgotten in our barbarous
wars : that men of all nations are fundamentally alike ; that love
and heroism have no nationality, nor any bounds save those of
humanity. In his outdoor romances all men felt vigorous again,
sharing the mighty life of nature ; in the manly soul of his hero
the reader of Norway or Germany or England recognized with
joy the spirit of his own ancestors, the pioneers of the world's
free people. It is this daring pioneer spirit, with its appeal to
elemental manhood, which may best explain Cooper's success
at home and abroad.

Life of Cooper. Our novelist was born (1789) in Burlington, New Jersey, but his life is largely associated with central New York. Here his father settled in 1790, building his manor house by Otsego Lake, and founding the village which is still called Cooperstown. In this frontier settlement with its noble surroundings,[1] where all the works of man seemed like ugly scars on the face of nature, Cooper passed his childhood. Here he met his two romantic heroes, the buckskin-clad trapper and the silent-footed Indian, trailing in from the wilderness to trade furs for powder. A rude backwoods school held him for a time; then he was sent to Albany to study with a minister. At thirteen he entered Yale College, where he thought so much of play and so little of study that he was presently expelled for some youthful frolic.[2]

The practical side of Cooper's education began when he shipped aboard a merchantman as a preparation for the American navy, which he soon entered as midshipman. Of his short naval service, we know very little. He was sent to help build a warship on Lake Ontario, where he picked up the knowledge and " local color" which appear in *The Pathfinder;* and he was for a time in command of a gunboat on Lake Champlain, where he learned of the old Indian war-trail to Canada, which is followed in *The Last of the Mohicans*.

Naval Training

At twenty-one, Cooper married and resigned from the navy, just before our second war with England. His wife was the daughter of a Loyalist, and it is due partly to her influence that Cooper is so unusually considerate to the Tories in his Revolutionary stories. For the next ten years he was a farmer in the Hudson valley, and not till he was thirty-one years old did he show any indication of his literary power. His first book, *Precaution*[3] — a tedious, artificial romance of English society, of which Cooper knew little or nothing — was of no consequence, but the fact of having written it proved a tonic to his imagination. Led by his wife, he resolved to write an American story, and discovered that a novelist does

His First Romances

---

[1] For a description of the place, see *The Pioneers*, chap. xxi. In the character of Judge Templeton the novelist has portrayed some characteristics of his own father.

[2] In later years Cooper affected to despise college education. In the preface to *Lionel Lincoln* he says scornfully that what little he learned in college had been long since forgotten.

[3] This story was not signed, and it was supposed to be the work of an Englishman. At this time (1820) a book written by an American had small chance of success either at home or abroad.

best when he "paints the scene from his own door." He located his story in Westchester County, where he was then living and where a thousand memories of the Revolution still lingered, and he chose an obscure American spy of that region for his hero. The Waverley novels had prepared the public for the historical romance, and when *The Spy* appeared (1821) it was instantly successful. The next year it was published and praised in England, and it was speedily translated into several European languages.

This unexpected success determined Cooper's career as a literary man. In his second noteworthy novel, *The Pioneers* (1823), he abandoned the literary treasures of the Revolution to write the romance of the wilderness. Here was something entirely new in fiction; not even Scott had produced anything like it; and the reading world gave it enthusiastic welcome.

Not content with conquering in two new regions, Cooper opened yet another realm to fiction. He had by this time moved to New York City, where he founded a famous club, the "Bread and Cheese Lunch," which included the poets Bryant and Halleck, Verplanck the editor of Shakespeare, Morse the inventor, and other celebrities of the period. One day some members of this club were discussing the unknown author of the Waverley novels. *The Pirate* had just appeared, and one critic asserted that Scott could not possibly be the author of such a work, which only a sailor could have written. Cooper declared, on the contrary, that *The Pirate* was the work of a landsman; and to convince the critic he resolved to write a sea tale as it should be done. The result was *The Pilot* (1823–1824), our first modern romance of the sea.

A sad change began in Cooper's life (1826), when he packed his penates in a trunk and sailed away to Europe. He was gone seven His Life years, at a time when America was changing with bewil-Abroad dering rapidity, and the effect was disastrous. Being naturally a conservative, he dropped easily into the indolent ways of the Old World, grew out of sympathy with the restlessness of his native land, and began that long series of criticisms which ended in general ill temper and misunderstanding.

Wherever Cooper went, the fame of his *Spy* and *Pioneers* had preceded him, and he received the honor which European nations offer freely to men of letters. Unfortunately he was drawn into controversy, at first unwillingly, when he loyally defended Lafayette in a political dispute, and then eagerly when he denounced certain false notions of America that were and still are prevalent in Europe. A prejudice has more lives than a cat, and Cooper was soon fighting the same old falsehoods that Franklin had slain in vain. His *Notions of Americans picked up by a Travelling Bachelor* (1828) offended Europe and America alike, and the author became instantly a storm center of newspaper controversy.

Aside from the controversial works of this period, Cooper wrote *The Prairie, The Red Rover, The Wept of Wish-ton-Wish* and *The Water Witch.* The first two novels are among his best, and we never think of them as belonging to his European period. More significant are *The Bravo, The Heidenmauer* and *The Headsman,* which were occasioned by the expulsion of the Bourbons from France and by the Polish struggle for independence.

With his return home, in 1833, began another long period of controversy, occasioned partly by Cooper's attempts to reform his coun-**Period of** trymen[1] and partly by his *History of the Navy* (1839). **Controversy** The latter was a painstaking work, but because it spoke the truth frankly it offended partisans on both sides of an acrid dispute which was then waging over the rival commanders Perry and Elliott at the Battle of Lake Erie. We would ignore this controversy were it not for the fact that it marks a forward step in the history of newspaper criticism. On one side was Cooper, with too little charity and humor, perhaps, but sincere and truth-loving; on the other was the public press, with its fickleness and love of sensation. Papers that never heard of Cooper, save as a writer of stories, rushed to take sides, read a word hastily, found that he had criticized America and the Whig party, and straightway began reviling him and all his works.

Perhaps it would have been better if Cooper had ignored such attacks; certainly he injured himself and stopped the sale of his books; but there are authors and authors, and a fighter cannot tarry to count his profits when the cry is raised, " The Philistines be upon thee!" To every attack he responded, first by presenting the facts and demanding an apology, then by bringing libel suits. Alone he fought the entire Whig press of the country. The smaller papers were first disposed of, and when the *Albany Journal* and the *New York Tribune* were fined and silenced, Cooper's victory was complete. It is generally alleged that he aimed to vindicate himself, but that is only

---

[1] Those who would understand his attempt may read, if they have patience, his *Letter to his Countrymen* (1834), *The Monikins* (1835) and especially *Home as Found* (1857).

half the truth. The principle he laid down was that personalities form no part of legitimate criticism, and in winning his case he conferred unmixed blessing upon others. The more considerate tone of present-day criticism is due largely to Cooper's heroic struggle. The press, no less than the author or critic, owes a debt of gratitude to the man who fought for the sacredness of private character in all public discussion.

For the rest of his life our author returned to the peace of the old home at Cooperstown. The echoes of controversy died away; a new **In the** generation read the Leatherstocking tales with renewed **Old Home** delight, and Cooper regained something of his lost popularity. All the while love, like a cheerful fire, brightened his home; his old friends remained loyal; his own character, always rugged and true, grew more gentle and charitable as age brought its sad wisdom. But he never became reconciled to the public which had treated him so harshly, and one of his last commands was that his letters be kept secret and that no one should be authorized to write his biography.

Classification of Cooper's Works. A man who plans his first vacation in the woods generally asks two questions : What must I take for necessity, and what useless baggage of civilization may I leave behind for convenience ? Facing an outing among Cooper's sixty-seven volumes, one may well repeat the same questions, since the greater part of his work belongs in the literary attic, as any librarian will tell you.

We first divide the works into two almost equal parts, fiction on one side, miscellaneous subjects on the other. Of the latter, the *History of the Navy* (1839) and *Lives of Distinguished Naval Officers* (1846) are still readable. The rest of his miscellanies are headed toward oblivion, and may well be left to follow their own ways.

Of the thirty-two books of fiction, we again make equal division and cast the half aside. There remain sixteen romances, which fall naturally into groups suggested by the author's first three notable works, *The Spy*, *The Pioneers* and *The Pilot*. The first group consists of historical romances, the second of the inimitable Leatherstocking tales, and the third of romances of the sea.

As many of these stories appeared while Scott occupied the center of the literary stage, it was inevitable that the two writers **Cooper and Scott** should be compared. Almost from the beginning our novelist was called "The American Scott," but the implied criticism seems to us unwarranted. Cooper was the kind of man to follow his own compass and blaze his own trail, and in his forest and sea tales especially he was a leader, not a follower. In his historical novels he aimed at a romantic and perhaps exaggerated portrayal of the heroism of his own country in times past; and in this he was undoubtedly influenced by Scott, who had done the same for Scotland and England; but as the latter novelist's range was wider, he described a larger number of enduring characters and appealed to a more universal interest than was possible to his American contemporary. Except in their aims, therefore, there can hardly be any fair comparison of the two writers.

In one important respect, which is generally overlooked, Cooper seems to have depended on earlier novelists, and his work suffers in consequence. We refer to the majority of his "females" as he calls them, — weak, garrulous, sentimental creatures, unlike any known types of American women, but bearing a strong resemblance to the heroines met in nearly all romances of "sensibility."[1] Perhaps the most noticeable point of resemblance between Scott and Cooper is that both alike were too much influenced by the prevailing literary fashion of making a heroine of fiction as unlike the natural woman as possible. Otherwise our novelist was a vigorous and original genius who told a tale in his own way, without much regard to any other writer.

The Historical Romances. The publication of *The Spy* (1821) was an important event in our literary history.[2] Up to that time America had been, in the matter of fiction especially, almost

---

[1] See our study of Charles Brockden Brown, p. 159.

[2] Critics have called this book "our literary Declaration of Independence." A few years later Emerson's "The American Scholar" (1837) was characterized by Holmes as "America's intellectual Declaration of Independence."

slavishly dependent on England in literary matters. Our authors often affected foreign ways and names ; our critics echoed the opinions they had read in English magazines. The coming of *The Spy* was like the ringing of another Liberty bell. Our own critics, roused to independent enthusiasm, called it the foundation of American romance ; while English reviewers began to speak of Cooper, of whom they had never before heard, as "the distinguished American novelist." The *Sketch Book* had just made Irving known in England, but *The Spy* passed the bounds of language as well as of nationality. It repeated its success in many of the countries of Europe and South America, and is still probably more widely known than any other American work of fiction with the exception of *Uncle Tom's Cabin.*

At first reading *The Spy* seems hardly worthy of such honor. It has glaring faults ; its crude style and stilted dialogue suffer

The Spy by comparison with the work of our later novelists ; but the chief thing to remember is this: that our first contribution to international fiction stands the hard test of time ; that it is still widely known and read, while hundreds of better-written novels are forgotten. And this suggests that *The Spy* owes its place to real power, not to chance or the passing humor of the age which first welcomed it.

The reasons for its enduring interest are threefold. It is, first of all, a good story of vigorous action and undaunted personal courage. With the young, at least, such a story can never grow old. It throws the glamour of romance over the men and women of the Revolution, standing in this respect almost alone ;[1] and it creates one original character, Harvey Birch, whose patriotism appeals powerfully to men of every nation. "When war comes men stand by their chief" says the old Saxon proverb. It is easy to do that, to serve chief or country knowing that the service will be known and honored ; but here is a patriot who serves

---

[1] Many other romances of the Revolution have been published from time to time, from Simms's *The Partisan* (1835) to Mitchell's *Hugh Wynne, Free Quaker* (1897). None of these, with the possible exception of Kennedy's *Horse-Shoe Robinson,* seems destined to a permanent place in literature.

without hope or possibility of reward. In order to help Washington he becomes known as a spy for the British army.[1] He is hated by the Patriots; a price is set upon his head; several times he barely escapes death at the hands of the soldiers whom he is secretly serving. His courage is proved to the uttermost when he destroys the paper, given him by Washington, which would make known his loyalty to the very men who were preparing to hang him. The last battle is fought and won; America is free; the nation heaps rewards and honors upon its heroes; but Harvey Birch goes on his lonely way, branded and despised as a traitor. And the last scene, where the old man haunts the battlefields of a later war, still hiding his mighty secret, reminds us again that the real heroes of every conflict are mostly unknown:

> The bravely dumb that did their deed,
>   And scorned to blot it with a name,
> Men of the plain, heroic breed
>   That loved Heaven's silence more than fame.[2]

There is wide difference of opinion concerning the relative merits of Cooper's other historical romances, and in selecting a few of them we are guided largely by a personal preference. First in historical order, though not in interest, comes *Mercedes of Castile*, a story of the discovery of America. This still interests many readers by its ocean pictures and by its portrayal, in a romantic way, of the character of Columbus.

The Wept of Wish-ton-Wish, a narrative of Colonial life in Connecticut, attracts and puzzles us by its musical title. "Wish-ton-Wish" (an Indian term for the whippoorwill) is **Wept of Wish-ton-Wish** the name given to the home of Mark Heathcote, an old Quaker whom Cooper calls "the venerable religionist." The "Wept" (that is, the bewept, the one mourned for) refers to a little girl who is stolen by the savages, and who

---

[1] *The Spy* reflects the civil discord of Patriots and Tories, which was especially bitter in Westchester County, where the scene is laid (see p. 90).
[2] From Lowell, "All Saints."

returns later as the bride of an Indian chief. This narrative shows astonishing creative vigor. It has adventure enough for a dozen novels ; it introduces one romantic figure, the old regicide, hiding in the wilderness from the wrath of King Charles ; and it has many dramatic situations, notably that in which a mother tries to make herself known to her own child, who has forgotten her people and even her native language. With all these possibilities the story is ruined by careless observation, artificial talk, and especially by the characters, which have scarcely more naturalness than the wooden animals of a Noah's ark. Nevertheless the book is worth reading, if only to show how Cooper could spoil an excellent story by neglecting the essential details.

In *Lionel Lincoln* our novelist returned to the Revolution, and planned a series of romances to be called " Legends of the Thirteen Republics," of which this should serve as an introduction. He worked hard on this book, reading endless documents in order to make his narrative true to the facts ; but unfortunately he did nothing to remove his own prejudice against New England, and this prejudice is largely responsible for a very dull story. The most vivid parts of the book are the descriptions of the battles of Lexington and Bunker Hill ; the latter, according to Bancroft, being the best account of the fight that has ever been written. In a different and better spirit is *Satanstoe*,[1] a tale of Colonial life in New York. The book is marred by Cooper's political theories, and again he shows his prejudice by dragging in a villain from New England ; but for the most part he sticks to his real work, which is to tell a tale. *Satanstoe* has still power to interest many readers, partly by its adventures, partly by its vivid pictures of American life in the middle of the eighteenth century.

Legends of the Republics

---

[1] This was one of a series of political novels inspired by the frenzy of reform in America (1840–1846) which culminated in Dorr's Rebellion and the Anti-rent War. Other novels of this series are *The Chain Bearer* and *The Redskins*. The same Anti-rent War which inspired *Satanstoe* produced also Ruth Hall's *Downrenter's Son*.

The Leatherstocking Tales. If the beginner must choose among these stories, we suggest *The Last of the Mohicans*, which presents Natty Bumppo, a favorite character in American fiction, in the most favorable light. As the five books constitute a single drama in five acts, they should all be read, if possible, in this natural order, which happens also to be alphabetical : *The Deerslayer, The Last of the Mohicans, The Pathfinder, The Pioneers* and *The Prairie.* In our analysis we shall interrupt this natural order and begin with *The Pioneers* (1823), which was the first to be written.

OTSEGO LAKE, COOPERSTOWN, N.Y.

When Cooper wrote this book he probably had no idea of a series of romances ; otherwise he would hardly have painted such a shabby picture of his heroes. He aimed simply to portray the life of a frontier village, with its restless characters that hovered like skirmishers in advance of American civilization. One of these characters was Natty Bumppo, an old woodsman with an inborn love of the wild ; another was Chingachgook the Indian, a sad relic of the past, despised and neglected in a land that once shivered at the sound of his war whoop. Both these characters seemed strange yet familiar to American readers ; strange, because they

(Heroes of the Leatherstocking Drama)

had never appeared in romantic literature; familiar, because their doubles were to be seen in almost every village. We have met such characters even in our own day. We remember how we watched and followed them at a distance; how we went tiptoe through the woods where they set their traps; how our wild instincts were stirred by the report of their old rifles, or by the smoke that rose from their camp fires. So we can understand why the young readers of that age, having detected a world of romance and adventure in these two old men, begged Cooper to tell them the whole story. Led by this widespread interest he rejuvenated Natty and Chingachgook, and made them the central figures of the Leatherstocking drama.

Unlike most of Cooper's works, *The Pioneers* interests us by its scenes and characters rather than by its adventure. The **The Pioneers** story element is comparatively weak, but the backwood scenes are strongly realistic and the characters are, on the whole, the best that Cooper has drawn. He gathers together some thirty people — the squire, the foreigner, "the quality," the odds and ends of a frontier village — and, excepting only his inane heroines, they impress us, in contrast with the minor characters of his other romances, as being remarkably true to life. Cooper is so deficient in humor that his attempts at fun generally bore us; but in Ben Pump we have a rough suggestion of Sam Weller, and one scene especially, where Ben shares Natty's punishment by placing himself in the "bilboes," is worthy of a place in the *Pickwick Papers*.

The Deerslayer (1841) should be read first by those who intend to enjoy the whole drama of Leatherstocking. The action **The Deerslayer** takes place on the shores and waters of Otsego, at a time when lake and forest are still Indian country. Here we meet Natty and his friend Chingachgook as young men on their first warpath. The main figures are well drawn,— even the two feminine characters, the beautiful Judith and the simple Hetty, are far above Cooper's average,— but the interest of the story lies almost entirely in its pioneer scenes and adventures.

In *The Last of the Mohicans* (1826) we find the same two heroes in the vigor of manhood, and our interest in Chingach-

Last of the Mohicans gook is heightened by the presence of his son Uncas, the last of the Mohican chiefs. The nobility of these two savages is emphasized by the treachery of their Huron enemies, and Cooper evidently intended to present here both sides of the Indian character. The scenes of the story follow the old Indian war trail to the St. Lawrence, and from beginning to end we are in the midst of stirring adventure. That Cooper knows little of Indians and less of woodcraft, that many of his incidents are impossible, — all this seems of small consequence. The lure of the trail is upon us; the excitement of moving incidents makes us forget probabilities; we hurry on to the end, and lay down the book with the criticism that it is one of the best adventure stories we have ever read.

Next in the series is *The Pathfinder* (1840), which takes us through the wilderness to the Great Lakes. Cooper considered

The Prairies this the best of his novels; which is only another indication that authors, like mothers, have incomprehensible favorites among their children. Then comes *The Pioneers*, which we have already examined. At the end of this book the old hero turns his face westward, and we follow his last trail in *The Prairie* (1827). Leatherstocking is now a mere relic of the past; his eye is too dim to sight his famous rifle; he no longer follows a savage enemy; and instead of his love of adventure we find the gentleness, the patience, the profound wisdom of old age. Contrasted with him are the restless squatters who disturb his solitude; and to keep up our interest in good Indians we have the young Pawnee chief, a reincarnation of the vanished Uncas. There is an abundance of action and adventure; over the scene broods the mystery of the illimitable prairies; and the old woodsman's last days among friendly Indians seem a fitting conclusion to the whole Leatherstocking drama, — which ends, as it began more than half a century earlier, on the outer verge of the American frontier.

In this romance Cooper treats us to a bit of psychology which almost startles us by its truth to life, by its contrast with his usual, unsatisfactory method of explaining human action. We refer to the rough-handed justice of old Ishmael and the terrible punishment of the criminal. That scene in which the old squatter returns at night to the place of judgment, his harsh nature subdued by the silent majesty of earth and heaven, is perhaps the strongest to be found in Cooper's sixty-odd volumes. Notwithstanding various inconsistencies in the portrayal, the figure of Ishmael stands out at the end, bold, vigorous, commanding, like the silhouette of a blasted pine against the sunset.

The Sea Stories. It was a daring venture in the early part of the last century, before Cooper and Herman Melville had begun to write the romance of the deep, to lay the scene of a story at sea. To the readers of that age it seemed incredible that any romantic interest could attach to a place that was associated in their minds with dangers or dizzy heads, with storm or wreck or loneliness unspeakable. In polite literature the ocean, except as one watched it safely from the shore, had been represented as the lifeless, maddening waste of " The Ancient Mariner "; in all churches it was coupled in hymns and litanies with perils and afflictions from which men prayed to be delivered; in the Apocalypse one who had a vision of a new heaven and a new earth had written the significant line, " And there was no more sea." That Cooper should overcome this general apprehension, making the ocean a place of romance rather than of fear, was in itself no small triumph. That he shared the general doubt of the success of his first sea venture appears from the fact that he " backed his anchor " by locating the half of his romance on solid ground, where his audience felt more at home. Fate, however, seems to have played with the author; the land incidents and the heroines which he inserted with the hope of interesting his readers only served to bore them, while his ships and seamen roused them to a new enthusiasm.

This first sea tale, *The Pilot* (1823), is by many critics regarded as Cooper's best. The scene is laid off the English **The Pilot** coast, which at a critical period in our Revolution was thrown into a state of terror by the daring raids of one man in a swift ship, who alternately played with and defied the whole British navy. Interest in *The Pilot* is supposed to center in the mysterious Mr. Gray, who turns out to be the famous John Paul Jones in disguise. We confess, however, to finding him a foggy kind of character, utterly unlike our ideal of the gallant naval officer who first sent aloft the stars and stripes to float over a man-of-war, and who startled old England at her very gates as Coriolanus " fluttered the Volscians." Far more interesting are the common sailors, especially Long Tom Coffin, a splendid type of the Nantucket seaman, and the most original of Cooper's characters. Aside from this vigorous figure, our interest is held by a succession of vivid sea pictures, such as working the ship offshore against the pressure of a landward gale, and the stirring flight of the American frigate.

The Red Rover is our own favorite among the sea tales.[1] Indeed, if we were asked to recommend only one of Cooper's **The Red Rover** books, we should name this in preference even to the best of the Leatherstocking romances. The plot is an absorbing one, and the action keeps us continually on the sea. The hero is an original and refreshing kind of pirate, and the minor characters, if not quite natural, are better than we commonly find in Cooper's romances. Among them we are glad to find one real woman, disguised as a boy but very different from the gay Rosalind, from whom Cooper may have taken the suggestion for his character. To many readers, however, the greatest charm of *The Red Rover* is found in its pictures of the sea, pictures so vividly, powerfully drawn that they fairly take us off-soundings ; we lose grip on solid ground and seem to view the scenes from the deck of a reeling ship.

[1] Other notable sea stories are *Wing and Wing*, *The Two Admirals*, *Afloat and Ashore* and *The Water Witch*.

General Characteristics. It is hardly too severe a criticism to say that, next to the vigor of Cooper's style, its most prominent quality is carelessness, — a confident, attractive kind of sang-froid, like that of the voyageur who steps into any canoe and takes up any kind of paddle, trusting his own strength and skill rather than his instruments to carry him to the end of his journey. His matter is chiefly romantic and adventurous. The adventures are such as delight healthy and vigorous young people, but they seldom appeal to mature readers who have accustomed themselves to the best work of English and American novelists.

Aside from his careless style, his tedious moralizing and his insipid " females," our chief criticism of Cooper is leveled at Cooper's   his inaccuracy, his lack of harmony with his own Inaccuracy   incidents and characters. We may overlook the fact that Leatherstocking talks at one moment like a book of etiquette and then slips into the backwoods dialect ; but we can hardly forgive a novelist for making a master of Indian woodcraft do impossible feats at one point and flounder at the next like a tenderfoot on his first trail. The fact is that Cooper can give a splendid impression of sea and forest as a whole, but he is slovenly and inaccurate in details ; and to analyze his work is to spoil our first good impression.

In *The Last of the Mohicans*, for instance, we see Indians trailing an enemy through an unbroken forest at midnight. Wonderful skill ! But the depths of a primeval forest are black as the pit at night ; one can hardly discern a moose there at arm's length, much less the print of a moccasin ; and the keenest woodsman is at a loss until he learns to look up, not down, and shape his course by the black bulk of trees against the lighter sky. Again, Chingachgook draws a beaver skin over his head, goes into a beaver lodge, and looks out of the door while his enemies pass by. Rare cunning ! But the beaver's lodge has no door or window ; its only entrance is a muddy tunnel under water ; there is no possible way for a man to get in without tearing the structure to pieces. In another chapter Natty Bumppo, in order to save Uncas from torture, disguises himself in the skin of a black bear, waddles into the Huron camp, and readily fools the keen-eyed warriors. Marvelous! But aside from the difficulty of fitting a man's long legs into the short stockings of a bear, we wonder what tailor-bird Natty found in the woods to sew him up in the skin, since safety pins were surely not among pioneer inventions.

Enough of Cooper's faults! They are many and easily seen, and the question arises, How does he find so many enthusiastic **His Power** readers? The answer is, simply, that his virtues are **as a Writer** great enough to outweigh his faults; we overlook the latter as we forget the peculiarities of a relative who leaves us a goodly legacy. With all his shortcomings, he claims a leading place among American romancers, and his claim rests upon four solid foundations: First, he has a tale to tell, a stirring **tale** which moves the dullest reader out of his lethargy, making him long to do brave deeds and play his part manfully in the world. Second, he adds the two realms of sea and forest to fiction, and creates three new types of characters which never lose their charm. These are the noble Indian in Chingachgook, the woodsman in Natty Bumppo, and the American sailor in Long Tom Coffin. Third, he has a vivid imagination; he invents new plots and adventures as easily as Longfellow makes rimes; he paints the changing panorama of ocean and forest with a power that knows no doubt and feels no weariness. Follow, for example, the flight of that ship through five long chapters of *The Red Rover*. From the moment she clears the harbor, a stately, beautiful vessel, until she rolls as a helpless tub on the billows, while the pirate craft sweeps by like a storm-driven cloud, we have a series of descriptions of sea and storm which for sustained vigor have hardly a parallel in literature. Reading such scenes we appreciate Balzac's criticism: "If Cooper had succeeded in the painting of character to the same extent that he did in the painting of the phenomena of nature, he would have uttered the last word of our art."

Finally, all these romances have, like those of Scott, a bracing, healthful atmosphere. In the sixteen books upon which his fame rests, Cooper leaves the "problem" novel to others; he writes in a hearty, wholesome way for young people who have no problems, and for men and women who would fain forget them. Here are no false situations, no forbidden topics, no shadows of impurity. When with Cooper, we travel the open spaces, warmed with the sunshine, swept clean by the winds of God. Here are characters with the tang of brine and wood smoke in them; stories of love, brave fighting and loyal friendships, which boys and men like to read because they deal in honest human nature. Since heroism and human nature are of abiding interest, Cooper's romances bid fair to justify Bryant's prediction, that they will last as long as the English language.[1]

Edgar Allan Poe (1809–1849)

Poe is a solitary figure, the Ishmael of letters. He stands apart in the peculiar quality of his work and in the tragedy of his life. A study of other notable American authors reveals four common characteristics: a reflection of the natural and social environment in which they lived, an embodiment of the national spirit, an emphasis on the moral and spiritual side of life, and generally a strength of character which makes us honor the man as well as his work. In Poe all these qualities are weak or wanting. Though he was a genius, his life saddens or repels us. One might rejoice in his suffering had anything been gained by it; but lacking the noble, the vicarious element of human suffering, it fills us with profound regret. He belongs by ancestry

---

[1] Some of Cooper's works, notably *The Spy* and the Leatherstocking tales, are still widely read in practically every country of Europe and South America, as well as in his own country. As an indication of the widespread interest in his earlier romances we quote from S. F. B. Morse, the inventor of the telegraph, who writes (1833) as follows: " In every city of Europe that I visited the works of Cooper were conspicuously placed in the windows of every bookshop. They are published, as soon as he produces them, in thirty-four different places in Europe. They have been seen by American travellers in the languages of Turkey and Persia, in Egypt, at Jerusalem, at Ispahan."

and training to the South, but there is no reflection of place
or of the American spirit in his work. He seems to have
arrived among us not from patriotic ancestors, not from sunny
Maryland, but as a wanderer from some outlandish region,
saying as he comes:

> By a route obscure and lonely,
> Haunted by ill angels only,
> Where an Eidolon, named Night,
> On a black throne reigns upright,
> I have reached these lands but newly
> From an ultimate dim Thulë —
> From a wild weird clime that lieth, sublime,
> Out of Space, out of Time.[1]

As Poe is the most solitary, so also is he the most debatable
figure in American letters. A tempest of criticism has raged
around him for half a century, and as the storm is
not yet stilled, we venture to offer certain suggestions
to the beginner. The first is, that criticism of Poe's character
is no part of our literary business. Though a dozen biographies
have appeared, and in hundreds of essays Poe has been bewrit-
ten and befogged more than any other American author, the
simple fact is that we do not yet know the details or motives of
his life. How then should we judge him? In a brief, tragic
career he accomplished certain works, unique in quality, remarkable even in quantity, considering the number of his days. These
we may criticize freely, as part of our literary inheritance; but
we leave judgment of the man to one who knows all the facts
and the motives from which human actions proceed.

A second suggestion is that Poe's life might seem more
heroic if certain facts were simply recorded and understood,
instead of being hidden by one and emphasized by another
biographer. It is plain that he was brought up to luxurious living; that he was afterwards thrown on the world to battle with
poverty, and to see the woman he loved suffer from cold and

The Poe Controversy

---

[1] From Poe, " Dream Land." The whole poem should be read in this connection.

hunger. By inheritance and early training he had an appetite for strong drink, and when the inevitable struggle came his will was like a broken reed. He had the sensitiveness of genius, the pride of a gentleman ; yet he was compelled to accept charity from a world which then had no place for a poet, unless he became a teacher, like Longfellow, or had Bryant's ability to run a newspaper and make shrewd investments. That Poe created any enduring works while he fought a losing battle with himself or the world or the wolf at his door, and wandered like a laborer seeking a job from city to city, seems to us little short of marvelous. It is a glorious thing to strive, to run, when victory flits just ahead in plain sight ; but it

EDGAR ALLAN POE

requires a grimmer courage to struggle on, as Poe did, with no companion but failure. " So have I wondered at seeing a delicate forest bird leagues from the shore, keeping itself on the wing above relentless waters into which it was sure to fall at last." [1]

A third suggestion may occur to one who studies a portrait of Poe and compares the two sides of the face :

> God be thanked, the meanest of His creatures
> Boasts two soul sides, — one to face the world with,
> One to show a woman when he loves her !

The last two lines, from Browning, fit Poe as if they were written for him. He had one unsympathetic side for the world ;

---

[1] Stedman, *Poets of America*, p. 236.

but he showed another, tender and chivalrous, to the noble women who made his home and whose love was of the kind **Poe's Double** that beareth and believeth and hopeth and endureth **Nature** all things. This double nature is indicated in the prose tale "William Wilson," and is suggested in nearly all of Poe's works; for, like Byron, he had but one subject, all his characters being so many different reflections of himself. Note this description of the hero, in "The Fall of the House of Usher":

"Yet the character of his face had been at all times remarkable. A cadaverousness of complexion; an eye large, liquid, and luminous beyond comparison; lips somewhat thin and very pallid, but of a surpassingly beautiful curve; a nose of delicate Hebrew model, but with a breadth of nostril unusual in similar formations; a finely moulded chin, speaking in its want of prominence of a want of moral energy; hair of a more than web-like softness and tenuity; these features, with an inordinate expansion above the regions of the temple, made up altogether a countenance not easily to be forgotten."

That is a fair description of the face which Poe saw in a looking-glass,[1] and it foreshadows tragedy, as certain children's faces haunt us by the sad prophecy that is in them. The tragedy of his life consists not in poverty or suffering — for many great and noble men have endured these and glorified them — but in the fact that, having two natures, he allowed the weaker to triumph; that, seeing the celestial vision, he despaired of attaining it and fell in the dust of the roadside. The vision and the failure are symbolized in the opening and closing stanzas of "Israfel," one of the most suggestive of Poe's lyrics:

> In Heaven a spirit doth dwell
>   ' Whose heart-strings are a lute';
> None sing so wildly well
> As the angel Israfel,
> And the giddy stars (so legends tell),
> Ceasing their hymns, attend the spell
>   Of his voice, all mute.

[1] Note also Higginson's description, in *Short Studies of American Authors*, p. 13.

> If I could dwell
> Where Israfel
>   Hath dwelt, and he where I,
> He might not sing so wildly well
>   A mortal melody,
> While a bolder note than this might swell
> From my lyre within the sky.

Life. One who plants a garden must have some preference for flowers or fruit and a willingness to work out his purpose ; else will the weeds, which require no cultivation, crowd in riotously to fill all vacant places. Even so, one who rears a child should from the beginning take some thought and do some faithful work in the direction of his moral education. This homily is founded on the text of Poe's life. Its tragedy was set in motion, its catastrophe made inevitable, long before Poe was old enough to know anything about such matters.

His father — a descendant of patriotic ancestors in Maryland — had abandoned the study of law to become an actor. He married an **Early Life** English actress, and while the two were playing an engagement in Boston their son Edgar was born, in 1809. The poor mother, on whose shoulders the burden of family support lay heavily, seems to have fought a hard and losing battle. Both parents died destitute in Richmond ; their children were adopted by different families, and Edgar found a home in the house of John Allan, a tobacco merchant. The next scene, foreshadowing the tragedy, shows a bright, attractive child standing on a chair, a glass of wine in his hand, offering a toast or a pretty speech to a thoughtless dinner company.

The boy's education began in a private school. He went abroad with his foster parents, and for five years was a pupil in the Manor House School at Stoke Newington, near London. Then followed several years with private tutors in Richmond, and at seventeen he entered the University of Virginia.

A study of Poe during these early years leaves certain impressions, which grow upon us as we read his works. At home he was treated **First Impres-** indulgently, and in the Virginia society of those days he **sions of Poe** acquired a polish, a neatness of appearance, a deference towards women, in a word, the indelible stamp of a gentleman ; but neither at home nor in society did he receive the sympathy which his soul craved, and he was always forming romantic attachments to women older than himself. Here, for instance, is his boyish love for the mother of one of his schoolmates, and his frantic despair at her untimely death. She was the first of many Helens to whom he went for sympathy, and who reappear vaguely in his tales and poems.

A second impression is that of Poe's aloofness. In school he made many acquaintances but no real friends; for friendship requires giving, the giving of one's self, and Poe was too self-centered to give himself unreservedly to anybody. The morbid unreality of his work, which critics explain as a manifestation of his strange genius, seems to us largely the result of his self-absorption, which kept him from knowing his fellow men. Like Manfred, he walked through the world without ever seeing humanity:

> From my youth upwards
> My spirit walk'd not with the souls of men,
> Nor looked upon the earth with human eyes;
> The thirst of their ambition was not mine,
> The aim of their existence was not mine;
> My joys, my griefs, my passions and my powers
> Made me a stranger; though I wore the form,
> I had no sympathy with breathing flesh.[1]

Poe's college life was short and unsatisfactory. He made a brilliant record in some studies, but he drank, gambled and ran deep into debt. **Poe's Wanderings** At the end of the first year Mr. Allan took him from the university and set him to work in the tobacco business. He stayed at his desk only a few months before he broke with his foster father and wandered out into the world.

In Boston he signalized his new freedom by publishing a handful of poems;[2] then, knowing no other way of earning a living, he enlisted in the army and served honorably for two years. At the death of Mrs. Allan he became reconciled to his foster father, who secured his appointment as a cadet to West Point. Here he made an excellent beginning, but presently he neglected his duties, was dismissed from the Military Academy, and drifted into the world again. Why he left an honorable career to starve on hack work has never been explained. We have only his own account of the matter, and that is untrustworthy.

To the next few years belong the popular accounts of his wanderings abroad and of his fighting with the Greeks, like Byron, — a myth for which Poe himself is largely responsible.[3] The facts are that he went

---

[1] From Byron, *Manfred*, II, 2.

[2] *Tamerlane and other Poems, by a Bostonian.* Boston, 1827.

[3] In his correspondence with Lowell, Poe characterized a biographical notice containing this myth and others as "correct in the main."

to Baltimore and supported himself by writing for the newspapers, but not until he had tried and failed to secure a political appointment. His literary career may be dated from 1833, when his "Manuscript Found in a Bottle" won him a money prize[1] and the friendship of John P. Kennedy, who presently found a place for Poe on the staff of the *Southern Literary Messenger*.

Poe now settled in Richmond, and a splendid career opened before him. While in Baltimore he had lived with his aunt, Mrs. Clemm, and her daughter Virginia, of whom he wrote long afterward:

> And this maiden she lived with no other thought
> Than to love and be loved by me.

This cousin was but a child in her fourteenth year when Poe married her, in 1835. Her mother came with her to the new home in Rich-
Life in Richmond mond, and in the lean years that followed, these two women were "as rivers of water in a dry place, as the shadow of a great rock in a weary land." But the sky was blue and serene in those first days, the happiest that Poe ever knew. He had a home where love was; his friends appreciated his ability; the *Messenger* published his work and gave prominence to the criticisms that soon made him known in the literary world. Everything pointed to fame and fortune, when suddenly he left or was dismissed from the magazine and became a wanderer once more.

Again we have conflicting accounts of the calamity. We do not know the facts; we merely infer that a touchy humor, an ambition to run a magazine of his own, the curse of drink,[2] — all these entered into it. He moved to New York, to Philadelphia, then back to New York, repeating in each new abode the old story of failure. He joined the staffs of various magazines and newspapers, only to lose or resign his place just as success hovered over his head. He revised and republished his little volume of poems; he sold and resold his tales

---

[1] Prizes were offered by the *Baltimore Saturday Visitor* for the best story and the best poem. Poe easily won the first, and would have won the second by his fine poem "The Coliseum," had the conditions allowed a writer to win both prizes. Kennedy was one of the judges (see p. 248).

[2] Poe was not a habitual drinker. He would go for months, even years, without touching liquor. Then he would drink at some convivial gathering; the drink became a spree, and was followed by a long period of suffering. For liquor always poisoned him. In the intervals he worked hard, and discharged his duties faithfully. Willis, editor of the New York *Evening Mirror*, records of Poe (1844) that he was "a quiet, patient, industrious, and most gentlemanly person, commanding the utmost respect and good feeling by his unfailing deportment and polish."

and criticisms for a pittance; when Cooper or Irving made a popular "hit" he would try a book in the same vein;[1] and, like Goldsmith, he wrote textbooks on subjects of which he had only a smattering of knowledge. We mention these shifts and makeshifts simply to suggest that Poe's life was a struggle for daily bread, — a weary, anxious, heartbreaking struggle, unrelieved by comforts, made harder by lack of plain necessities. When his industry failed of reward Mrs. Clemm kept boarders. Only for that noble woman, genius must have starved and love gone cold. Meanwhile Virginia, the beautiful child wife, grew pale and paler before their troubled eyes.

We pass rapidly over the remaining years, as one reads a tragedy which has reached its climax and hastens on to the catastrophe. In **In New York** 1844 he went with Virginia to New York, and his first letter to Mrs. Clemm is profoundly suggestive. He speaks of the journey; of leaving "Sis" in the boat, because it was raining and her lungs were weak; of his refusal to hire a cab because the driver, seeing his necessity, demanded a dollar for a ten-cent job; of buying an umbrella, and of the boarding house they found in Greenwich Street. With the zest of a boy he goes on to describe the supper, its "great dish of elegant ham," its slices of other good things "piled up like a mountain." It is said that geniuses are great eaters; but here is a genius who is hungry, who has worked and despaired, who eats and is hopeful, and who rejoices because he can jingle a few coins in his pocket which may suffice till he find work again. It is all simple, natural, human. Unlike his elaborate tales, which fly off into the region of shadows, this poor letter [2] touches the heart of humanity.

A new home was established in a little cottage in Fordham (now the Bronx) where Poe worked hard on a proposed history of American **The Child Wife** literature. This curious work, which began with the present, was never finished; a part of it appeared serially in *Godey's Lady's Book* in 1846, and was published later as *The Literati* (1850). It consisted largely of critical or personal estimates of writers who were then living; its chief effect was to make a number of petty enemies and raise a storm of hostile criticism that followed Poe to his death, and afterwards. Meanwhile Virginia grew very ill. There were no comforts in the house; the desperate condition of the family may be judged from the fact that some friend, with more zeal than discretion,

---

[1] Thus, Poe's *Journal of Julius Rodman* appeared (1838) the year after Irving's *Captain Bonneville*. There are several other instances of his "following the market."

[2] Quoted by Woodberry, *Edgar Allan Poe*, p. 201.

made an appeal in the newspapers for charity. It was but a last drop added to a bitter cup, and Poe drank it to the dregs. Two letters of this period deserve attention for the light they throw on the author's home life. The first is from Poe to his wife:

" My Dear Heart — My Dear Virginia — Our mother will explain to you why I stay away from you this night. I trust the interview I am promised will result in some substantial good for me — for your sake and hers. Keep up your heart in all hopefulness, and trust yet a little longer. On my last great disappointment I should have lost my courage but for you — my little darling wife. You are my greatest and only stimulus now, to battle with this uncongenial, unsatisfactory and ungrateful life.

" I shall be with you to-morrow P.M., and be assured until I see you I will keep in loving remembrance your last words and your fervent prayer.

" Sleep well and may God grant you a peaceful summer with your devoted

" EDGAR."

The second is from a friend who visited the family in the bleak winter season :

" . . . There was no clothing on the bed, which was only straw, but a snow-white counterpane and sheets. The weather was cold, and the sick lady had the dreadful chills that accompany the hectic fever of consumption. She lay on the straw bed, wrapped in her husband's greatcoat, with a large tortoise-shell cat on her bosom. . . . The coat and the cat were the sufferer's only means of warmth, except as her husband held her hands and her mother her feet. Mrs. Clemm was passionately fond of her daughter, and her distress on account of her illness and poverty and misery was dreadful to see."

Such a picture is fortunately unique in our literary history. When a strong man goes down in the waste of the far North, battling alone with cold or hunger, the natives speak of it as " cruel hard " ; what it was for a poet, in a wealthy city, to watch an idolized woman die without suitable food or clothing must be left to the imagination.

> Fear no more the heat of the sun
> Nor the furious winter's rages.[1]

We quote the lines softly to ourselves when the curtain falls on the terrible scene, early in 1847. But our eyes still follow that lonely, grief-stricken figure which follows on foot to the grave, wrapped in the same coat that had kept his Virginia warm when living.

[1] From the Dirge, in *Cymbeline*, IV, 2.

Into the details of the next few frenzied years we do not care to enter. That Poe was ill and suffering is evident enough ; that he was also mentally unbalanced has not occurred to some of his critics. We hear it in the ravings of his speech and letters ; we suspect it in "Ulalume" and "Annie," with their mixture of genius and madness, and even in "Annabel Lee," which voices his love and grief for his dead wife, but which runs to a measure that is gay rather than sorrowful.

The Tragedy

After two unmanly years, which we would fain forget, Poe became engaged to a widow (Mrs. Shelton) of Richmond. Generous friends raised a fund to give him a new start, and hopefully, with money in his pocket, he began the journey to New York, intending to settle his affairs and return quickly to Richmond, to love and a new life. Three days later he was found unconscious in Baltimore and died in the hospital there without telling what had happened. It was Longfellow who suggested that these two lines should be written on his monument:

> And the fever called Living
> Is conquered at last.[1]

Poe's Critical Work. For a long period after Poe's death our critics, in their zeal to judge the man, overlooked the originality and power of his writing. At the present time the pendulum swings the other way ; the tendency is to forget the weakness of the man and to overestimate the value of his work. Between the first and the latest judgment sixty years have passed. During practically all that time Poe has challenged attention. Many critics have assailed, but none could have safely ignored him. He has also, perhaps, to a greater degree than any other American author, laid his spell upon writers at home and abroad. Therefore, though the greater part of his work repels the ordinary reader, let us go softly about the task of judging it. His various productions fall naturally into three classes, — literary criticisms, prose tales, and lyrics. By the first he was chiefly known while living ; by the last he will probably be longest remembered.

[1] From Poe, "For Annie," a half-mad lyric, written after the loss of Virginia. The monument was erected in Baltimore, many years after Poe's death.

In his critical work, beginning about the year 1835, Poe attempted to carry out in this country the purpose of Coleridge.[1] By that time America's opinion of her own literature was very different from what it had been in the days when the editors of the *North American Review* refused to believe (1817) that "Thanatopsis" was the work of an American, and when Cooper, in order to gain favorable notice of his *Precaution* (1820), published it as the romance of an alleged English author. Influenced by the success of Bryant, and perhaps excited by the honors awarded to Irving and Cooper in Europe, our writers went to the opposite extreme in glorifying our literary productions. The critical faculty began to be exercised by a few men, each in his local "school" at New York or Charleston, who praised each other's work immoderately, with somewhat more of patriotic pride or generosity than of discernment. In the *Southern Literary Messenger,* Poe characterized such efforts as the work of a mutual admiration society; he declared his purpose to criticize "independently and fearlessly, in accordance with established literary standards." So far he did well, and he marks the beginning of true criticism in this country. He was certainly independent and fearless; he had also the insight to recognize such writers as Hawthorne, Tennyson and Mrs. Browning before the world was aware of their genius. We wish we could add that he was also wise, impersonal and just, but such is not the fact. His own conception of poetry [2] made him narrow-minded, and he let personalities prejudice his judgment. This part of his work, therefore, is of little interest except to critics, who consider that his theory of composition — of the short story especially — is worthy of careful attention.

[1] Wordsworth and Coleridge were among the leaders of the Romantic movement in English literature. Bryant, by his nature poetry, carried out the purpose of Wordsworth; while Poe seems to have been more or less a follower of Coleridge. This shows itself in his literary criticisms, and especially in his phantasmal themes, which suggest Coleridge's *Christabel* and *The Ancient Mariner.*

[2] See, for instance, his " Poetic Principle " and the " Rationale of Verse." Poe held that a poem should produce a single impression; that it should deal with beauty alone; and that it must be short.

Poe's Tales. It is said that America's most significant contribution to general literature is the short story. Whatever honor is due us on that account should be offered largely to Irving and Poe. If the latter is not the actual discoverer of the modern short story,[1] as some critics allege, he at least brought it by his own effort to a high state of development. At the present time his influence extends to numberless writers, at home and abroad, who are making the short story the most popular form of literature. This influence is the more remarkable because it is due wholly to Poe's method of work, not to any interest attached to his subject; for unlike Irving, whose subjects were mostly attractive, Poe's matter is generally abnormal and repulsive. We shall examine here a few groups of stories that illustrate the author's peculiar genius.

" The Gold Bug " is the most readable of the so-called analytical stories, that is, stories which center in a mystery to be Analytical solved, and which are supposed to stimulate that Tales peculiar form of mental activity suggested by the words " following a clue." In such stories Poe was in his element; he had a keen, analytical mind that delighted in solving puzzles and cryptograms. This appears in " The Gold Bug," in which he uses his expert knowledge of cipher writing to find a pirate's buried treasure. The theme is old, but Poe shows his originality by making our interest center not in the greed of finding an immense store of gold and jewels, as a lesser writer would surely have done, but in the reading of Captain Kidd's cryptic message, which tells where the treasure is hidden.

Three other notable stories of this mental-puzzle class are " The Murders in the Rue Morgue," " The Mystery of Marie Roget " and " The Purloined Letter." These are remarkable

[1] Certain critics regard the Short-story (written with capital and hyphen) as a distinct, modern type of literature, differing in structure and essentials from a short romance or a short novel. Its chief characteristics are " ingenuity, originality and compression." Most of these critics regard Poe, rather than Irving, as the discoverer of this type. See Matthews, *The Philosophy of the Short-story* (1901), and Smith, *The American Short Story* (1912). The latter includes a good bibliography of the subject.

for two things : they portray the only real character, Dupin, to be found in Poe's writings ; and they mark the beginning of the flood of modern detective stories. Old Sleuth, Sherlock Holmes and all the rest of the tribe are copies of Dupin ; and Kipling's " Bimi " was probably suggested by a grotesque incident in Poe's " Murders in the Rue Morgue."

In his allegorical tales Poe uses some external object or event to symbolize a mental experience and, incidentally perhaps, to point a moral lesson.[1] " The Black Cat " and "The Telltale Heart " are good examples of this class. They illustrate the author's ability to grip and horrify his readers ; but they are repulsive stories, though cunningly worked out, and their characters are not human beings but rather faces, — wild or expressionless faces, upon which insanity has set its awful seal.

Allegories

" William Wilson " seems to us the most suggestive and wholesome of the allegorical tales. It contains some biographical material from Poe's English schooldays, and in this respect, as being even remotely connected with his own experience, it is unique among his stories. Conscience here assumes the form and substance of a man, who appears at every crisis of the hero's life and points out to him the ways of good and evil. The tale is an allegory of man's double nature ; one who reads it must recognize Poe's influence over Stevenson (in *Dr. Jekyll and Mr. Hyde*) and other writers who make use of the dual personality as a motive of their stories.

The pseudoscientific tales, with their smattering of science and their extravagant adventure, are a type of romance associated with the name of Jules Verne, who belongs unquestionably to Poe's school. Two of the best of these tales are " A Descent into the Maelstrom," a wonderful bit of imaginative and descriptive writing, and " The Unparalleled Adventure of One Hans Pfaal," describing a trip to the moon.

Science and Adventure

---

[1] The moral is evident, but we do not wish to imply that these stories were written with a moral purpose. Poe's only aim was to produce a startling " effect." See " The Tale Writer and His Art," in *The Literati.*

There is a parade here of some superficial scientific knowledge, but this is quickly forgotten by one who feels the power of Poe's imagination, who hears the appalling roar of waters, or looks down with reeling senses from a stupendous height. We can readily believe that the hero's hair turned white in the maelstrom; our own hair feels a shade lighter after merely reading about it.[1]

We have examined enough of Poe's stories to appreciate the title *Tales of the Grotesque and Arabesque* (1839) which he gave to his collection. The climax of his uncanny power is reached in his tales of preternatural horrors. In some of these he makes use of the fascination of terror, of the hypnotic spell which fear casts upon certain minds; in others he appeals to that morbid interest which leads some men to read the revolting details of a murder, for instance, or to carry away ghastly souvenirs of a holocaust. Perhaps the most typical of these gruesome stories are "The Fall of the House of Usher" and "Ligeia," in which he makes use of a favorite theory, or hallucination, that the will survives for a time in the body of a person after death. There are two widely different ways of looking at these and all other stories of the same class; which are, in general, realistic descriptions of morbidness or insanity, and of the spectral horrors which are ignorantly associated with groans and graveyards at midnight. One critic sees in them Poe's wonderful mastery of technic, and his artistic handling of two legitimate motives: the fascination of fear, and the appeal of the horrible. Another sees, chiefly, an indication of Poe's abnormal imagination, of his lack of sanity and moral balance; and to such a critic the "art" of these stories resembles a mere artifice, a stage trick to produce an effect. It is obviously impossible to reconcile such views; hence the endless controversy over Poe's works. Considered

(marginal note: Tales of Horror)

---

[1] To the same pseudoscientific class belong Poe's two attempts at sustained story: *The Narrative of Arthur Gordon Pym of Nantucket,* a bloodcurdling sea story; and *The Journal of Julius Rodman,* a story of Western adventure. In *Eureka, a Prose Poem,* with an amateur's knowledge of astronomy and metaphysics, Poe attempts to explain the creation and present state of the universe.

not as an ordinary story but as an impression, the "House of Usher" is a remarkable piece of literary work; and even one who dislikes the somber impression is forced to admire the skillful way in which it is produced. It is one of the best examples of the so-called story of atmosphere to be found in English or any other language.

A little more wholesome, but still moving in the realm of phantoms, is the "Manuscript Found in a Bottle." This is a powerfully realistic story of a man who found himself aboard a specter ship with a silent crew of ghosts — a veritable Flying Dutchman of the Antarctic — cruising endlessly over seas of eternal darkness and desolation. To the same class, but suggesting the more delicate imagination of some of his poems, belong the strange group of tales concerning disembodied spirits, such as "The Colloquy of Monas and Una," and also the two little sketches, "Shadow" and "Silence," which lay a spell upon us but which we do not attempt to classify or to explain.

Poe attempted many humorous stories such as "The Devil in the Belfry," but they do not attract us. Unlike the true **Miscellaneous Tales** humorist, who laughs with men, Poe laughs at them; he lacks the deep undercurrent of sympathy and human kindness, without which humor is artificial and without understanding. Much more interesting than these humorous attempts are certain miscellaneous stories: "The Masque of the Red Death," a powerful but meaningless story of pestilence; "The Pit and the Pendulum," describing the horrors of torture during the Inquisition; "The Cask of Amontillado," a study of revenge as practiced by the Italians; and "The Assignation," a melodramatic story of love as it might have been in Venice. In the last-named story Poe's originality is strikingly evident. The theme is an old one, which has been used in the same way over and over again by Italian and French romancers; but Poe avoids the usual, vulgar intrigue and makes the interest of his story center in the utterly unexpected character of the meeting between two lovers.

The Poetry of Poe. Recently a cultured woman was found reading Poe's " Ulalume" and a few other lyrics, which she thought
very beautiful. "And what do they mean to you?" was asked.
"Nothing, absolutely nothing," she said; "I don't understand a
word of them. I read them just for the mood or the melody."

This criticism is so nearly perfect that we are tempted to
leave the subject here; but we must try to understand, if possible, Poe's motive in writing beautiful but apparently meaningless verse. His theory was that poetry must concern itself, not
with life or truth or nature, but with beauty alone; that the
beauty, because it is of a "supernal" kind, must always be
associated with melancholy; that the most beautiful imaginable
object is a beautiful woman, and the greatest possible sorrow is
the loss of such a being; that the true poem, therefore, must
be a kind of dirge, a lament for the death of beauty in the form
of woman. Hence Poe's succession of shadowy Helens and
Lenores; hence his despair and lamentation at their untimely
death. To the mature mind this is an abnormal, a diseased
conception of poetry, but we must harbor it for a moment if
we are to appreciate Poe's verse; for with a few brilliant exceptions, like "The Coliseum" and "The Bells," he follows
his theory and has but two subjects: his lost beauty, and his
own woe.

With this introduction, we leave the reader with the melodious
lyrics in which Poe has added variety and color to our poetry.
For an expression of his prevailing mood, we suggest "To
Helen," [1] "Ulalume," "The Raven," "To One in Paradise,"
"Lenore," the song "Ligeia" (from *Al Aaraaf*), "A Dream
within a Dream," "Eulalie," "For Annie," "The Sleeper"
and "Annabel Lee." For variety we add "Israfel," the noble
"Coliseum," [2] the melodious "Bells," the lurid "City in the

---

[1] This refers to the first of the "Helen" poems, beginning, "Helen, thy beauty is
to me." We know not who inspired this exquisite lyric. There is another "To Helen,"
inspired, it is said, by Poe's first sight of Mrs. Whitman.

[2] This poem is more remarkable from the fact that Poe never saw the Coliseum.
See Byron's description of the same ruins in *Childe Harold*, Canto IV, stanza 114.

Sea," the phantasmal " Haunted Palace " and the terrible alle gory of " The Conqueror Worm."

Here, in a dozen pages, we have the quintessence of Poe's genius. Aside from the melody, the first thing to attract us is the variety of verse forms. Poe maintained that each poem must have a distinct individuality, which he secured by varying the rime, meter and refrain. The second noticeable quality is the narrow range and monotony of the subject ; for nearly all these poems are but variations of a single mood, — a dull, helpless, hopeless mood, suggesting Coleridge's " Ode to Dejection." Love, loss, despair ; love, loss, despair, — the melancholy burden runs through the verse like the drip, drip of rain from a roof. Poe makes a lyric out of his despair, just as Chopin weaves the monotony of falling raindrops into his most perfect " Prelude " ; but exquisite as they are, lyric and prelude are alike unbearable if long continued. The charm of these poems, which rank with the greatest of their kind in our literature, is that their form is exquisitely finished ; that they are a true reflection of the despairing mood which produced them ; and that, long after our reading, they haunt us like a strain of sad, wild music. Their weakness lies in the fact that their impulse came not from healthy life but from nerves ; and that, unlike most of the poems which we cherish, they have no message or inspiration for humanity.

General Characteristics. In a book of rhetoric Poe's style would probably be termed " adequate," but the word does not satisfy us. His aim in every work was to make a single strong impression. In this aim he is like the sensational writer of our own day, though his method is entirely different. Any shouting will attract attention, but Poe never shouts. He first decides what effect or impression he wants to create ; then from first word to last he makes every incident, every character, every description bear steadily upon that predetermined impression. When the effect is so vivid that even the dullest readers must feel it, the tale ends. Herein Poe is utterly unlike Hawthorne, who when he began a tale often had no idea how it would turn out. If we remember how an artist finishes a portrait, with here a touch of light or there a deeper shadow, and then think of Poe as painting a mental picture of horror, with lurid lights and shadows of gross darkness, we shall have a suggestion of his method. His impression is seldom a wholesome one ; what he does may not seem worth doing ; but we must confess that it is invariably well done. Effectiveness, therefore, is the chief quality of his style ; and it is this effectiveness, this almost perfect accomplishment of what he aims to do, that leads critics to rate Poe as a master of the short story.

In view of this analysis of Poe's method it seems ridiculous, as if one were to bump his head against a moonbeam, to say **His Material** that the chief characteristic of his matter is its unreality ; but such is the fact. There are no such things as his cats, ghouls, demons, and mere ghosts of characters ; and the only way to account for their effect is to remember that unrealities may make a strong impression in a lonely old ruin at night, — which is where we commonly imagine ourselves to be while reading Poe. He dwells in a land of phantoms that flit about like bats in the darkness ; he is chiefly occupied with shadows, not natural shadows, suggestive of substance and light, but spectral shadows that do perverse things,[1] — as in his famous " Raven," for instance, where the shadow comes down to the floor instead of remaining on the ceiling, where it properly belongs :

And the Raven, never flitting, still is sitting, *still* is sitting
On the pallid bust of Pallas just above my chamber door ;
And his eyes have all the seeming of a demon's that is dreaming,
And the lamplight o'er him streaming throws his shadow on the floor ;
And my soul from out that shadow that lies floating on the floor
    Shall be lifted — nevermore ![2]

[1] Note the shadows in the tale " Ligeia," and in " Shadow, a Parable."
[2] Poe has described the elaborate way in which he prepared " The Raven " (see his " Philosophy of Composition "). A controversy arose immediately over the question of how much Poe was indebted in this poem to another Southern poet, Dr. Chivers of

Generalization is always dangerous, and often unjust, but it would seem, as Lanier suggested, that Poe's work as a whole is lacking in some necessary intellectual quality. Great literature owes its power to a combination of ideas and imagination, of strong intellect and profound emotion. It has meaning as well as form, truth as well as beauty; and to read it is to have a better understanding of life. A candid study of Poe's work shows that the greater part of it is simply emotional and, therefore, more or less unbalanced and disordered.

It is hardly necessary to point out that, since Poe deals with unrealities, nature and humanity are not reflected in his work. He gives us many descriptions, but the light is ghastly **His Model** and the landscape not of earth. He depicts a hundred characters, but, with the possible exception of Dupin, there is not a man or a woman among them. Perhaps the chief reason for his weakness here is that he seeks not truth but an effect; he never stands aside to let nature or man or history speak its own message, but uses these as looking-glasses or sounding boards to reflect himself or his own voice. Another reason is that Poe is so self-centered that he cannot put himself in the place of another; his chief characters are all repetitions of himself or of his shadow. He is like a modern illustrator who draws one picture that interests us, and then a hundred more that soon grow wearisome, since they are all from the same model, and all like the first save for the pose or the clothing. In the story of "The Gold Bug," for instance, there are two chief characters, the hero and his negro servant Jupiter. The hero is Poe with his love of cryptograms, and Jupiter is as much a Bushman or an Eskimo as a Southern negro. So in all his works, Poe's hero is invariably himself; the rest of his characters are shadows or nonentities.

Georgia. (See Woodberry, "The Poe-Chivers Papers," in *The Century*, January–February, 1903; also "Poe and Chivers," in the Virginia edition of Poe's *Works*, Vol. VII.) It was Stedman, we think, who first pointed out that Poe evidently borrowed from Mrs. Browning rather than from Chivers. Compare, for instance, the third stanza of "The Raven," beginning, "And the silken, sad, uncertain rustling of each purple curtain," with that stanza in "Lady Geraldine's Courtship" beginning, "With a murmurous stir uncertain, in the air the purple curtain."

Our final characterization takes the form of a question, which the student must answer for himself. As we have noted, many **Artist or** critics at home and abroad regard Poe as a great lit-**Craftsman?** erary artist; others regard him as a cunning worker in stage effects; and these men honestly differ because of their different conceptions of art, one being content with " art for art's sake," the other insisting that art must be steadily viewed in its relation to humanity. Those who regard art as inspired first of all by a vision of truth, and who would define art as the expression of life in forms that give pleasure by appealing to our sense of the true, the good, and the beautiful, will probably hesitate over the greater part of Poe's work. With normal life his prose has little or nothing to do ; and his poetry was the result of a theory of beauty that hardly included either truth or goodness.[1] That his work was " beautifully done," meaning that it was adequately or effectively done, cannot be questioned. Shall we therefore class it with the great pictures and the great poems which, in addition to their excellence of form, have the power to inspire humanity by revealing the glory of the imperfect and the beauty of the commonplace ? And shall we apply the term " art " or " craft " to Poe's expression of our human life in literature ?

WILLIAM GILMORE SIMMS (1806–1870)

Simms, like Bayard Taylor, is an author who impresses us more by the greatness of his aim than by his achievement. The bulk of his work is now almost forgotten, but there are three things concerning the man that are worthy to be remembered : his brave struggle against adversity ; his devotion to the profession of letters, at a time when only two other men in America were living by their pens ; and the influence of his work in the direction of a national rather than a sectional literature. We shall

---

[1] Poe's theory of art should be compared here with that of another Southern poet, Lanier (see following chapter).

study him here as an American, rather than a Southern, writer who deserves an honored place in our literary records. [1]

Biographical Outline. Simms was born and reared in Charleston, South Carolina. He was a poor boy who, unlike Poe or Kennedy, knew little of the comfort and social culture which we associate with Southern life. His mother died when he was a child; his father moved westward with the pioneers, leaving him in the care of a grandmother, who told him stirring tales and sang to him many a ballad of the Revolution. In this way was his ambition first stirred to write the romance of his country. We remember in this connection the childhood of another romanticist, Walter Scott, whose impulse to literature came from listening to his grandmother's tales and ballads of the Scottish border. There is another parallel nearer home. Like his Northern contemporary Bryant, the young Simms was well acquainted with hard work; like him he studied law, while cherishing the ambition to become his country's poet; and like him he abandoned the courts (1827) to follow his heart into the wide world of letters. For the next forty years he was both creator and encourager of literature, doing his best by lectures and essays to promote the appreciation of good books among his countrymen. He was for a long time the central figure in the Charleston "school," a group of literary men which included Timrod and Hayne, who later became famous as Southern poets; and he was always in the best sense a citizen, playing his part manfully in the affairs of his native state. We cannot enter into the details of his career; but one who reads the story of his life will find it an epitome of the history of the Carolinas, from the "great debate" between Calhoun and Webster to the close of the Civil War.

Variety of Simms's Work. The breadth of Simms's literary taste stamps him as one of the notable men of our First National period. His thirty-odd romances of Colonial and Revolutionary days represent only a small part of his accomplishment. By constant study and travel he made himself an authority on local history, and his *History of South Carolina* and his *South Carolina*

---

[1] The student may doubt the propriety of placing Simms in a period which ends, nominally, in 1840, since a large part of his work was published after that date. The same is true of Bryant. As we have noted, literary periods cannot be strictly defined or observed. We study Simms here simply because he seems to belong with the earlier rather than with the later national writers. Hawthorne, who is often studied in the earlier group, will be considered in the next chapter.

in the Revolution are still standard works. As a biographer, Irving is the only man of this period to be compared with him. While Irving, with one conspicuous exception, went abroad for his heroes, Simms was content to bide at home and, in such works as his lives of Marion and Greene, to show the heroism that glorified his own people. He was a poet also, with several volumes to his credit, and desired to be remembered as a bard rather than as a novelist. In addition to all this he wrote plays, short stories, literary and political essays ; he edited magazines, and was an editor also of some of Shakespeare's dramas.

One good result of all this work was to broaden and nationalize the spirit of our literature. We are to remember that there was at this time a New England, a Knickerbocker, and a Southern "school"; that "literary centers" were emphasized, and that each of a dozen cities considered itself the real hub of the American world of letters. Against all this narrowness and provincialism Simms's efforts were quietly, steadily directed. His border tales cover a dozen states and have a national rather than a sectional appeal. His Revolutionary romances are all laid in the South ; but in this he rightly followed the example of most novelists, who present general truths or ideals under local conditions, and who do their best work amid scenes and characters with which they have been familiar from childhood. He has been called "the Cooper of the South"; but the criticism proceeds on the unwarranted assumption that Cooper belongs to the North exclusively. It is not the Southerner or the Northerner but the American that appeals to us in the heroes of Simms and Cooper. Moreover, Simms lived for a time in the North, where many of his books were published ; he had readers in every state ; he was in friendly correspondence with all the important literary men of the nation. He exercised, therefore, a wholesome unifying influence on our sadly divided world of letters.[1]

---

[1] During the Civil War, Simms shared the loss and suffering of his native state. Some of his late works follow the spirit of the minor writers, who ally literature with politics or geography, and so make it sectional.

It is a pity, in view of Simms's aim and endeavor, that we cannot heartily recommend his books; but the fact is that he wrote too hurriedly, too carelessly, too sensationally at times, to produce a work of enduring interest. He has many of Cooper's faults, of slipshod style and tedious moralizing; but he has also some of Cooper's virtues: an eye for picturesque effects, a love of stirring adventure, an ability to find sentiment and chivalry under a rough exterior. In addition, he can portray the character of a gentleman, which Cooper could never do, and some of his heroines are in pleasant contrast to Cooper's "females"; but he lacks the rugged strength, the epic interest of Cooper's best work, and his books have never received or deserved such attention as is given to *The Spy*, *The Red Rover* and the drama of Leatherstocking.

Quality of Simms

The Yemassee (1835), a story of Indian warfare in Colonial days, and *The Partisan* (1835), a romance of the Revolution, are generally considered the best of Simms's romances. The reader will find some highly colored sketches of frontier life in his short stories, such as are included in *The Wigwam and the Cabin;* and in "The Lost Pleiad" and "The Poet's Vision" a suggestion of Simms's talent and of his limitation as a poet. The last sonnet is so characteristic of the author, and so good in itself, that we quote it entire:

> Upon the Poet's soul they flash forever,
> In evening shades, these glimpses strange and sweet;
> They fill his heart betimes, — they leave him never,
> And haunt his steps with sounds of falling feet;
> He walks beside a mystery night and day;
> Still wanders where the sacred spring is hidden;
> Yet, would he take the seal from the forbidden,
> Then must he work and watch as well as pray.
> How work? How watch? Beside him, in his way,
> Springs without check the flow'r by whose choice spell —
> More potent than "herb moly" — he can tell
> Where the stream rises, and the waters play.
> Ah! spirits call'd avail not. On his eyes,
> Sealed up with stubborn clay, the darkness lies.

III. MINOR FICTION OF THE FIRST NATIONAL PERIOD

With the tales of Irving, Cooper and Poe we have considered all the fiction of the period that seems destined to a permanent place in our literature. There were many other romancers, however, some with ten, others with fifty volumes to their credit. A few of their works, such as Miss Sedgwick's *Redwood* (1824), were more widely read in Europe than were the works of Poe or Irving; many others were as dear to our grandmothers as are the romances of Crawford or Louisa Alcott to the present generation. Among these dust-covered books one may still find many suggestive pages. Susanna Rowson's *Charlotte Temple* is a type of the early novel of " sensibility," once extremely popular but now forgotten.[1] Catherine Sedgwick's *Redwood, Hope Leslie* and *The Linwoods* contain excellent pictures of American home life, and are notable as the beginning of the novel of character and manners, so finely developed in our time by Miss Jewett and Miss Wilkins. And here are the stirring *Typee, White Jacket, Moby Dick* and other stories of the deep by Herman Melville,[2] of whom a modern sea novelist, Clark Russell, writes enthusiastically :

" A famous man he was in those far days when every sea was bright with the American flag, when the cotton-white canvas shone star-like on the horizon. . . . Famous he was; now he is neglected; yet his name and his work will not die. He is a great figure in shadow; but the shadow is not that of oblivion."

Better known than Melville's work is a veritable classic of the sea written by R. H. Dana, Jr., and called *Two Years before the Mast* (1840). This book, which deals with the author's experience in such a graphic way that it reads like a romance, was officially recognized abroad when the admiralty adopted it for use in the British navy. At home its great popularity has hardly yet waned; after more than half a century we can still recommend

[1] See p. 159 and p. 160, note.
[2] Melville grew up in this period and shared its spirit; but the student will note that his books were published after 1840.

it as a virile, wholesome story, and as probably the best reflection of sailor life in the old days when American ships and seamen were known and honored the world over.

The two chief characteristics of all these story writers — Simms, Kennedy, Paulding, Ware, Judd, Dana, Sarah Hale, Lydia Child and many others — were their intense patriotism and their interest in national history which led them to seek literary material in the annals of Colonial and Revolutionary days. Among a hundred of their books, we would especially recommend the *Swallow Barn* and *Horse-Shoe Robinson* of John Pendleton Kennedy (1795–1870), who is personally interesting to us for two reasons : for having befriended Poe and given him a start in literature, and for furnishing Thackeray with some material for *The Virginians.*[1] His *Swallow Barn* (1832) is a series of sketches rather than a connected story, describing country life in Virginia in the olden time. The idea is plainly borrowed from *Sir Roger de Coverley,* and the style suggests the influence of Irving, to whom the book is dedicated ; but one must not conclude from this that Kennedy's work is merely imitative. *Swallow Barn* is a kindly, human book, reflecting the fine personality of the author and the charm of old-fashioned plantation life, which was even then passing away. Of all the minor works of the period, it seems to us the best worth reading.

Horse-Shoe Robinson (1835) is a romance dealing with the Revolution in South Carolina. It is somewhat crudely and hurriedly written, but its patriotic interest and stirring adventure made it instantly popular. It was speedily dramatized, and for years held an honored place on the American stage. It should be read, if possible, in connection with *The Spy* of Cooper, as these are the only two romances of the Revolution that have ever won general recognition.

Kennedy

---

[1] The friendship of Thackeray and Kennedy began in Paris. When *The Virginians* was appearing, in serial form, Kennedy is said to have written the fourth chapter of the second book, describing Warrington's escape in the region of the Cumberland. Kennedy knew this region well ; but whether he actually wrote the chapter or merely furnished the material is undecided.

IV. MINOR POETRY

In an old book, *The Arte of English Poesie*, there is an excellent criticism of Wyatt, Surrey and other "courtly makers" who brought new verse forms to England :

> "They traiveled into Italie, and there tasted the sweete and stately measures and stile of Italian poesie. . . . They greatly pollished our rude and homely manner of vulgar poesie from that it had bene before, and for that cause may be justly sayd the first reformers of our meetre and stile."

If we substitute England for Italy, and Burns, Byron, Moore and Shelley for the Italian poets, this old criticism applies perfectly to the minor American poets of the early nineteenth century. They studied the popular English poets of the age, and introduced here brighter and more varied verse forms to reflect the spirit of the growing nation. Pinkney, Wilde and Cooke in the South ; Allston, Dana, Sprague, Pierpont, Percival, Willis, Brainard, Mrs. Sigourney and Maria Brooks in the North, — here are a dozen poets, popular and widely read in their own day, but now forgotten. In all their works one might perchance find a dozen poems that are worth reproducing. Occasionally a single lyric, such as Wilde's "My Life is like the Summer Rose," makes us thoughtful ; but the grain is too scant, the chaff too abundant, to warrant the winnowing. The best that can be said of these poets is that they made new verse forms familiar to American readers ; the worst, that they lacked imagination, and that they regarded their art merely as a pastime. The fiction writers of the period were moved by a patriotic or historic interest, and a fine national enthusiasm is reflected in their pages ; but these poets have no common, ennobling characteristic. The only semblance of unity, which was local rather than national, is found in two groups of writers known as the Knickerbocker and the Charleston "school." The former may properly be considered here ; but the finer work of the latter, especially the poetry of Timrod and Hayne, belongs to a later period, and will be studied in another chapter.

The Knickerbocker School.[1] This unfortunate term is used here to designate a small group of writers who were associated with the common idea of making New York a literary center, and whose work is now forgotten, largely because of its local and temporary character. A book, to have any chance of permanence, must do one of two things : it must emphasize universal ideals under peculiar local conditions — as in the stories of Cable or Bret Harte, for instance — or else it must proceed on the principle that there is no Mason and Dixon's line in literature, and appeal to the whole country by reflecting the national ideals and enthusiasm.

With two of these Knickerbockers, Paulding and Willis, we may well be content to have a bowing acquaintance. Paulding's *Salmagundi* essays, written in connection with Irving,[2] and his numerous stories, plays and sketches, are now wholly neglected. A few of his romances, however, notably *The Dutchman's Fireside* (1831) and *Westward Ho !* (1832), still find a few interested readers.

Nathaniel Parker Willis (1806–1867) came to New York from his birthplace in Portland, Maine. He was a versatile

Willis genius who attempted almost every kind of literary work, and did it well enough to win immediate praise. It is evident from his numerous works in prose and verse that he was a graceful, often an entertaining writer ; but he was too eager to please his own age, which, judged by its *Tokens* and *Garlands*, was abnormally fond of sentimentality. Yesterday he was popular throughout the country, and from his vantage ground looked with pity upon the struggling Poe ;

[1] The name is often used loosely to designate all New York literary men, — not only Irving, Cooper and Bryant, who first made the city a " literary center," but later writers such as Bayard Taylor and Stedman. Aside from furnishing the name and a few trivial essays, Irving had little to do with the " school " ; Cooper was always a man of the sea and of the open country ; Bryant a New England Puritan ; Poe a Southerner ; Taylor from the Middle West, and Stedman from Connecticut. These men were too deeply concerned with literature in its human or national aspects to be claimed by any local school, and the name, as applied to them, is misleading.

[2] See p. 185.

WASHINGTON IRVING AND HIS LITERARY FRIENDS AT SUNNYSIDE
Upper row: Holmes, Hawthorne, Longfellow, Willis, Paulding, Bryant, Kennedy
Lower row: Simms, Halleck, Prescott, Irving, Emerson, Cooper, Bancroft

to-day his works are unknown even by name. A few readers still find pleasure in his verses; others may be attracted by his *Pencillings by the Way*, a series of fleeting impressions of travel and of the noted men and women whom Willis met in Europe. Here, for instance, is his account of an interview with Lady Blessington, — a leader of London society, a literary woman widely known in her own day, and still remembered for her *Conversations with Lord Byron*. She had expressed great surprise that she and other authors received so many kind letters from America, where, she supposed, few people had any acquaintance with books. The answer of Willis indicates that remarkable appreciation of literature which one still finds in thousands of American towns and villages :

" I accounted for it by the perfect seclusion in which great numbers of cultivated people live in our country, who, having neither intrigue, nor fashion, nor twenty other things to occupy their minds, as in England, depend entirely upon books, and consider an author who has given them pleasure as a friend. 'America,' I said, ' has probably more literary enthusiasts than any country in the world; and there are thousands of romantic minds in the interior of New England who know perfectly every writer this side the water, and hold them all in affectionate veneration, scarcely conceivable by a sophisticated European. If it were not for such readers, literature would be the most thankless of vocations. I, for one, would never write another line.' "

In the life of Joseph Rodman Drake (1795–1820) there is a strange parallelism to that of the poet Keats. They were born **Drake** in the same year, and were of the same delicate, beauty-loving temperament. Both were early acquainted with toil and poverty; both loved poetry, but studied medicine to earn a livelihood; both had consumption and journeyed southward in search of health; and both died at twenty-five, before their powers had reached maturity. To carry the comparison further and include their works would be unjust to Drake, who cannot possibly be classed with the major poets. He is remembered now by two poems : " The American Flag," a patriotic but grandiloquent effusion; and "The Culprit Fay," a unique poem recounting the adventures of a fairy knight who had fallen in love with a mortal maiden.[1] The following selection may serve to illustrate Drake's work and to suggest the poetic taste of his age, which was satisfied with prettiness rather than with beauty :

> The stars are on the moving stream,
>   And fling, as its ripples gently flow,
> A burnished length of wavy beam
>   In an eel-like, spiral line below ;
> The winds are whist and the owl is still,
>   The bat in the shelvy rock is hid,
> And naught is heard on the lonely hill
>   But the cricket's chirp, and the answer shrill
>   Of the gauze-winged katy-did ;
> And the plaint of the wailing whippoorwill,
>   Who moans unseen, and ceaseless sings,
> Ever a note of wail and woe,
>   Till morning spreads her rosy wings,
> And earth and sky in her glances glow.
>
> .   .   .   .   .   .
>
> They come from beds of lichen green,
> They creep from the mullein's velvet screen ;
>   Some on the backs of beetles fly
> From the silver tops of moon-touched trees,
>   Where they swung in their cobweb hammocks high,
> And rocked about in the evening breeze ;
>   Some from the hum-bird's downy nest —
> They had driven him out by elfin power,
>   And, pillowed on plumes of his rainbow breast,
> Had slumbered there till the charmèd hour ;
>   Some had lain in the scoop of the rock,
> With glittering ising-stars inlaid ;
>   And some had opened the four-o'clock,
> And stolen within its purple shade.
> And now they throng the moonlight glade,
> Above, below, on every side,
> Their little minim forms arrayed
> In the tricksy pomp of fairy pride !

[1] This delicate bit of fancy was written, it is said, after a conversation with Cooper and Halleck, who had declared that our American rivers, unlike those of Europe, were not fit subjects for romantic treatment.

The friendship between Drake and Fitz-Greene Halleck (1790–1867) of Guilford, Connecticut, might well be the subject of a very interesting chapter in American literature.

Halleck We can only note here that a memorial of their friendship, Halleck's "Green be the turf above thee," is one of the best-known poems surviving from this period. The association of the two men, who were of the type described as "free lances," began on the Hudson, in a common love of poetry; and presently both were engaged in writing *The Croakers*, a series of bright satires in verse, directed at men, manners and customs of New York society in the early part of the nineteenth century. Happy, good-natured satires they were, though their delicate point is now hardly discoverable unless one has an intimate knowledge of the period. Halleck's longest poem, *Fannie* (1819), is of the same general character, being a gay commentary on the fashions, books, social and political doctrines that interested our grandfathers and grandmothers.

FITZ–GREENE HALLECK

More lasting, and more suggestive of Halleck's power, are many of his lyrics, such as "On the Death of Drake," "Alnwick Castle" and "The Field of the Grounded Arms," which are well worth reading. Here also are "Red Jacket," a shrewd criticism of Cooper and his Indians; "Burns," a fine appreciation of the Scottish poet; and the immortal "Marco Bozzaris," beloved of every schoolboy. This last is not so much a national as a race war-song, suggesting as it does the primeval vigor of the old Anglo-Saxon "Fight at Finnsburgh." It is said that King Olaf once called for a song "with a sword in every line."

The old Viking would have been satisfied had his gleeman
responded with :

> An hour passed on — the Turk awoke;
> That bright dream was his last;
> He woke — to hear his sentries shriek,
> " To arms! they come! the Greek! the Greek!"
> He woke — to die midst flame and smoke,
> And shout and groan and sabre-stroke,
> And death-shots falling thick and fast
> As lightning from the mountain-cloud;
> And heard, with voice as trumpet loud,
> Bozzaris cheer his band:
> " Strike — till the last armed foe expires;
> Strike — for your altars and your fires;
> Strike — for the green graves of your sires;
> God — and your native land! "

V. ORATORS OF THE FIRST NATIONAL PERIOD

It is commonly assumed that the oratory of this period, as
exemplified by Calhoun, Webster and several others scarcely
less famous, is the best that America has produced. Once more,
as in the Revolution, politics was the dominant issue; but instead of the passionate, whole-souled devotion to liberty which
united the Revolutionary orators, we find now a bitter partisanship sweeping over the country like a plague, dividing orators
and people into two hostile camps. Aside from the tariff, which
is always with us, there were two great questions, slavery and
state rights, that called for endless debate. Both parties appealed
to the Constitution, which was studied and expounded as never
before; and we have the curious spectacle of orators proclaiming radically different opinions from the same ground, profess-
ing to settle a question by appeals to a document which purposely
left that very question unsettled. This fundamental error, or
inconsistency, is bound to produce disappointment when we study
the speakers of this period from the viewpoint not of transient
politics but of abiding literature.

Choice is difficult among so many that were excellent, especially if we remember that the power of oratory depends largely on personality, and that the speaker who rouses one man to enthusiasm leaves his neighbor cold and doubtful. We shall not go far wrong, however, if we select, as the four representative orators of this period, Clay, Calhoun, Everett and Webster.

Clay. Judged by his success in holding men of different convictions, Henry Clay (1777–1852), the "silver-tongued orator" of Virginia and Kentucky, "the great compromiser" as he was called, seems to have been the most persuasive of our public speakers. Apparently his power was based upon a wonderful personality, for the speeches that once stirred thousands to enthusiasm have now little influence over us. They seem like pressed flowers, out of which life has departed. That Clay was eloquent we must admit, on the testimony of those who heard him; but that his work is no permanent part of our literature will be evident to any candid reader who attempts even a single volume of his speeches.

Calhoun. John C. Calhoun (1782–1850) of South Carolina, "the philosopher of statesmen," was the most logical and acute thinker of this remarkable group. His eloquence, unadorned and severe as a Greek statue, was a part of his wonderful character. He was the kind of speaker who needed no rhetorical ornament; the fundamental sincerity of his life gave force to every word he uttered. Though a radical, carrying the doctrine of state rights to extremes, there is in his argument, as in that of Jonathan Edwards, a logical power from which there seems to be no escape. Start with him on the Constitution and its early history, and you are drawn on, bound as a captive, to his conclusion. You resist, nevertheless; you feel, as one must feel with Edwards, that the premises are wrong or the logic perverted, since the conclusion violates the history and spirit of the American nation. His speeches read better than those of Clay; but the modern reader, missing both the personality of the orator and the pressure of the great problem which he tried to solve by logic, soon wearies of them. Of more permanent value are two works classed with the literature of knowledge, his *Disquisition on Government* and his *Discourse on the Constitution and Government of the United States*. These are two remarkable essays on the Jeffersonian doctrine of the rights of the minority.

Everett. Edward Everett of Massachusetts (1794–1865), "the scholar in politics," was the most polished and scholarly speaker of his day, and probably the best public lecturer that America has produced. Though he gave a large part of his life to his country, we are less interested in his political career than in his lectures on Greek and German culture, which had a deep and lasting influence on the intellectual life of our country. From the four large volumes of his works we select, as the most suggestive oration, that on "American Literature" (1824). If we read this in connection with Channing's fine essay on "National Literature," we shall have an excellent idea of the aims and ideals which inspired American writers in the early part of the nineteenth century.

Other famous orations of Everett are "Washington,"[1] "Early Days of Franklin," and the "Gettysburg Oration." Though this last is polished and ornate enough to deserve all the flattering adjectives which critics have applied, it suffers grievously in comparison with the speech of Lincoln, plain, simple, heroically sincere, which was delivered on the same occasion.

Webster. Daniel Webster of New Hampshire and Massachusetts (1782–1852), "the godlike Daniel, the orator of the nation," as his contemporaries called him, is by many critics considered the foremost American orator, and the peer of Burke, Cicero and Demosthenes. The latter comparison, which springs from our pride in Webster's power and from our gratitude for his patriotic service, should be received with caution. Like all heroes,

---

[1] This was heard by large audiences in every section of the United States. By this single oration Everett earned nearly $100,000, which was devoted to the purchase and preservation of Washington's home at Mount Vernon.

whether of camp or forum, Webster is bound to loom large so long as he is near. His relative rank can be more accurately judged when he shall be viewed, with Burke and Cicero, in the long perspective of the centuries. Meanwhile, we note that a part of his work seems to stand the hard test of time ; that a few of his orations still impress the reader with something of their original force. If we could only add the personal element — the magnificent presence which startled Carlyle,[1] the sonorous voice, the consciousness of his own dignity and importance — then the effect of these speeches would be overwhelming, and we might join with his contemporaries in giving Webster a place among the world's four greatest orators.

DANIEL WEBSTER

Looking through the six large volumes of Webster's speeches, we divide them — with some hesitation, for many critics disagree with us — into two parts. Here on the one side is the great bulk of his political and legal speeches. Though many claim for them a place in American prose because of their diction and imagery, we confess that we have found it hard to become interested in them, — perhaps because the high-flown and somewhat artificial style, which was then considered essential to an orator, does not please our changed modern taste. There is everywhere a suggestion of power, of a commanding personality, in these speeches, which mark the climax of forensic oratory in America ; but they should probably be classed not as literature but

---

[1] Carlyle's impression of "the American Hercules" is vividly recorded (June 24, 1839) in one of his letters to Emerson.

rather as examples of a certain kind of rhetoric, " an extremely
elaborate rhetoric based partly on the parliamentary traditions
of eighteenth-century England, and partly, like those traditions
themselves, on the classical oratory of Rome and Greece." [1]

To the second class belong Webster's occasional speeches :
the " Plymouth Oration " (1820) delivered at the two-hundredth
anniversary of the landing of the Pilgrims ; the first
" Bunker Hill Address " (1825), at the laying of the
corner stone of the battle monument ; " Adams and Jefferson "
(1826), in memory of the two old statesmen who died on July 4 ;
and the " Reply to Hayne " (1830). The first three are historical addresses, inspired by a great love and veneration for American patriots ; the fourth, though a political address, rises at
times far above the turmoil of party politics in which Webster
was engaged. It first defends Massachusetts with noble sincerity,
and then pleads for a united country in words which will be
remembered as long as the nation endures :

Typical Orations

> " When my eyes shall be turned to behold for the last time the sun in
> heaven, may I not see him shining on the broken and dishonored fragments
> of a once glorious Union ; on States dissevered, discordant, belligerent ; on
> a land rent with civil feuds, or drenched, it may be, in fraternal blood ! Let
> their last feeble and lingering glance rather behold the gorgeous ensign of
> the Republic, now known and honored throughout the earth, still full high
> advanced, its arms and trophies streaming in their original lustre, not a stripe
> erased or polluted, nor a single star obscured, bearing for its motto, no such
> miserable interrogatory as ' What is all this worth ? ' nor those other words
> of delusion and folly, ' Liberty first and Union afterwards,' but everywhere,
> spread all over in characters of living light, blazing on all its ample folds,
> as they float over the sea and over the land and in every wind under the
> whole heavens, that other sentiment, dear to every true American heart, —
> ' Liberty and Union, now and forever, one and inseparable.' "

Here is rhetoric certainly ; but here also is an emotional appeal
which stirs all hearts in patriotic devotion to a common country.
It is idle to prophesy, but something in these four orations
tells us that future readers will honor them, and that a part of
Webster's work has won a secure place in American literature.

---

[1] Wendell, *A Literary History of America*, p. 253.

VI. MISCELLANEOUS WRITERS

The learned writers of this period are numerous and note-worthy enough to suggest that America was not, as Dickens and other foreign critics alleged, absorbed in politics and money-getting, but that, side by side with the litera-ture of power created by Bryant, Poe, Irving and Cooper, was an equally remarkable literature of knowledge. As in every period of our literature, the historians held a prominent place. Jared Sparks (1789–1866), by a lifetime of historical re-search and by his editorship of the *Library of American Biography*, has left all modern historians his debtors. Bancroft (1800–1891) after fifty-one years of labor produced his no-table *History of the United States*. Prescott (1796–1859), working in dark-ness, sent out into the light his *Ferdinand and Isabella* (1837) and two fascinating books, *The Conquest of Mexico* and *The Conquest of Peru*, which seem more like romances and adventure stories than like ordinary histories.

Historians

J. J. AUDUBON

More original and more remarkable than the historians are the great religious leaders, Bushnell and Channing, whose noble, inspiring message deeply affected the life of their age, and whose influence is still potent throughout the nation. We note also Audubon, with his wonderful bird book; and Schoolcraft, whose *Myth of Hiawatha* and *Indian Fairy Book* were as a literary storehouse to Longfellow, and whose *Algic Researches, Indian*

Tribes of the United States and *Personal Memoirs of Thirty Years among the Indian Tribes* form the basis of all subsequent ethnologic studies in America. We have by no means exhausted the list; these few names are given to suggest the broad, inviting fields which lie open to every reader.

There is another literary movement which appears in this age, and which, like the matter of amusement, deserves more thoughtful attention than we have thus far given it. We refer to the "juvenile" books which appeared suddenly and almost as numerously as a swarm of locusts. The Greeks to inspire their children gave them Homer. The American Colonists depended on the Bible and a few noble English classics for youthful reading. We have changed all that, we moderns. In the nineteenth century we gave our children the hundred milk-and-water volumes of Peter Parley (Samuel Goodrich) and the " Rollo and Lucy " books of Jacob Abbott. This unnatural, unwholesome stuff grows and multiplies like bacteria; every generation sees a new attack of " juveniles," milder or more malignant than the others; and the latest outbreak is the flaming, outrageous supplement to the Sunday newspaper. Our whole theory, or craze, of "books for the young " is based on the assumption that a book is like a Christmas toy, to amuse for an hour and then be flung aside and forgotten. It ignores these simple facts : that a good book is to be cherished next to a good friend ; that the best we have is none too good for the youngest reader ; and that girls and boys, if their taste be not poisoned, will instinctively choose the beautiful or heroic books that inspire the race of men from generation to generation.

Summary of the First National Period (1800–1840). The first half of the nineteenth century was, in general, a period of expansion, of extraordinarily rapid development of our territory, our resources and our institutions. Irving, who returned to America in 1832 after an absence of seventeen years, could hardly recognize his native town, and was filled with amazement at the changes which were transforming the face of the country. These changes are briefly summarized under four heads : (1) The intensive growth in nationality resulting from the success of the new government under the Constitution, from the War of 1812, and from bringing the states nearer together by means of roads, canals and railways. (2) The steadily advancing frontier; the acquisition of the vast Louisiana territory; the large increase of population; the new era of colonization, which made the Great West a part of the new nation. (3) The growth of the democratic spirit over the whole country, and the election of Andrew Jackson, the first man of the common people who ever held the office of President. (4) The industrial development of the East, and the agricultural development of the South and West; the appearance of a great merchant marine; the enormous increase in trade and wealth, resulting from new inventions, from the use of steam, and from uncovering the natural treasures of America that were hidden in her soil and forests, her mines and rivers.

During all these mighty changes the American states were united as they had never been before; yet the feeling of unity was so often disturbed by bitter political strife that a recent historian describes the famous "era of good feeling" as a calm between two storms. Towards the end of the period the unsettled questions of state rights and slavery were dangerously agitated, and the agitation increased in violence after 1840 until it led to civil war.

The literature of the period is especially worthy of study as a reflection of the new national consciousness. In the early part of the nineteenth century **Summary of Literature** the indifference of Europe to our literary products was expressed in the scornful question, " Who reads an American book ? " Our own critics were scarcely more appreciative, and many of our writers, in order to secure favorable attention, affected English ways or signed their books by English names. Before the end of this period Cooper's romances were published in thirty foreign cities, and were read throughout the civilized world; Irving was placed by English critics in the front rank of living writers; Bryant, Poe, and many lesser poets and story writers had produced works which the nation was proud to claim as its own. In a word, America had at last developed a national literature, which the Hartford Wits had dreamed of, and which Irving and his contemporaries made a reality that was honored at home and abroad.

There are at least four characteristics to be found in our first national literature : its individuality, its harmony with nature, its intense patriotism, and its emphasis on the moral and religious nature of man. In addition to these general qualities, we noted the beginnings of American literary criticism, of the short story, of the romance of the sea and wilderness, and of a recognized national poetry.

Of the major writers of the period, we studied the lives and analyzed the chief works of Irving, Bryant, Cooper, Poe and Simms. The typical orators were Clay, Calhoun, Everett and Webster. The so-called minor poets, such as Pinkney, Wilde, Pierpont, Brainard, Percival and Mrs. Brooks, or Maria del Occidente as she was called, introduced new and varied verse forms to American literature, but their works are nearly all forgotten. The most noteworthy of these minor bards were a group still known as the Knickerbocker School, of which Willis, Drake and Halleck were probably the most typical.

Among minor writers of fiction, whose works, in general, were characterized by patriotism and by historical interest, we noted especially Catharine Sedgwick, Herman Melville, John Pendleton Kennedy and Richard H. Dana, Jr. Among miscellaneous writers the most noted were the historians Bancroft and Prescott, and the great religious leaders Channing and Bushnell.

Selections for Reading. *Irving:* Sketch Book, edited for class use, in Standard English Classics (Ginn and Company); the same work appears in various other school series (see Texts, in General Bibliography); Alhambra, in Pocket Classics, etc.; selections from Bracebridge Hall, in Riverside Literature Series.

Bryant: Well-chosen selections in Pocket Classics, and in Riverside Literature; in the latter series also parts of Bryant's Iliad.

Cooper: Last of the Mohicans, in Standard English Classics, etc.; The Pilot, in Eclectic English Classics; The Red Rover and The Spy may be had in various inexpensive editions; the five Leatherstocking tales, in Everyman's Library.

Poe: Select Poems and Tales, in Standard English Classics, in Silver Classics, Johnson's English Classics, etc.

Webster: First Bunker Hill Oration in Standard English Classics, Riverside Literature, etc. Noted speeches of Webster, Clay, Calhoun (one volume) in American History in Literature Series (Moffat).

Selections from all poets mentioned in the text in Bronson, American Poems; in Lounsbury, American Poems, etc.; selections from prose writers in Stedman and Hutchinson, Griswold, etc. (See "Selections" in General Bibliography.)

For Simms's Revolutionary romances, The Partisan, etc., and for Kennedy's Horse-Shoe Robinson the public library must be searched. Selections from Simms, Kennedy and other Southern writers in Manly, Southern Literature; Trent, Southern Writers, etc. Simms's The Yemassee in Johnson's English Classics.

Bibliography. Textbooks of history, Montgomery, Muzzey, Channing; of literature, Richardson, Wendell, etc. The best works covering the whole subject of American history and literature are listed in General References at the beginning. The following works apply especially to the First National period.

History. Adams, History of the United States 1801–1817, 9 vols. (Scribner, 1891); Von Holst, Constitutional and Political History 1787–1861, 8 vols. (Chicago, 1892); Schouler, History of the United States under the Constitution 1789–1865, 6 vols. (Dodd); Hitchcock, The Louisiana Purchase (Ginn and Company); Sparks, Expansion of the American People; Lossing, Pictorial Field Book of the War of 1812; Mahan, Sea Power in its Relation to the War of 1812; Gordy, Political Parties in the United States; Katherine Coman, Industrial History of the United States; Low, The American People; Stanwood, History of Presidential Elections.

Biographical: Lives of Calhoun, Webster, Jackson, etc., in American Statesmen series (Houghton); Schouler's Jefferson, in Makers of America; Parton, Life of Jackson, of Jefferson, of Burr; Parton, Famous Americans; Trent, Southern Statesmen of the Old Régime; Hunt, American Merchants; Dolly Madison's Memoirs; Lyman Beecher's Autobiography; Horace Greeley's Recollections.

Supplementary: Expedition of Lewis and Clark, and Harmon's Voyages and Travels in the Interior of North America, in Original Narratives (Scribner); Dwight, Travels in New England and New York (New Haven, 1821); Page, The Old South; Lucy Larcom, A New England Girlhood; Griswold, Court of Washington; Benson, Thirty Years' View; Drake, Making of the West; McMaster, A Century of Social Betterment (in Atlantic, January, 1897); Lowell, Cambridge Thirty Years Ago, in Essays; Bushnell, The Age of Homespun, in Addresses.

Literature. There is no work devoted especially to the literature of this period. Good chapters may be found in Richardson, Trent, Moses, etc. (see General References); also in Stedman, Poets of America; Cairns, Development of American Literature 1815–1833 with Special References to Periodicals (University of Wisconsin, 1898); Loshe, Early American Novel; Link, Pioneers of Southern Literature. For special works on Irving, Poe, etc., see below.

Irving. Texts: Works, Crayon edition, 27 vols. (Putnam); many other editions by various publishers. Inexpensive editions of Sketch Book, etc., in Selections for Reading, above.

Biography and Criticism: Life and Letters, edited by Pierre M. Irving, 4 vols., in Crayon edition of Works; Life, by Warner, in American Men of Letters; by Hill, in American Authors; by Boynton (sketch), in Riverside Biographies, etc. Warner, The Work of Washington Irving, in Harper's Black and White series; Warner, Bryant and Putnam, Studies of Irving; Payne, Leading American Essayists; Brownell, American Prose Masters; Perry, Prose Fiction; Canby, The Short Story; Thackeray, Nil Nisi Bonum, in Roundabout Papers; Curtis, in Literary and Social Addresses; Howells, in My Literary Passions.

Bryant. Texts: Poetical Works, 2 vols., Prose Writings, 2 vols.; Poems, Roslyn edition, Household edition, etc. (Appleton); Translation of Homer, 4 vols., or Student's edition, 2 vols. (Houghton).

Biography and Criticism: Life, by Godwin, 2 vols.; by Bigelow, in American Men of Letters; by Bradley, in English Men of Letters; by Curtis. Wilson, Bryant and his Friends; Bryant's Seventy-fifth Birthday Festival, with poems, addresses, etc., Century Association (New York, 1865); Alden, Studies in Bryant (elementary school text). Essays: Collins, in Poetry and Poets of America; Stedman, in Poets of America; Curtis, in Orations and Addresses; Whipple, in Literature and Life; Burton, in Literary Leaders; Mitchell, in American Lands and Letters; Whitman, in Specimen Days.

Cooper. Texts: Works, Household edition, with Introduction by Susan Cooper, 32 vols. (Houghton); many other editions of works by various publishers.

Biography and Criticism : Life, by Lounsbury, in American Men of Letters ; by Clymer (brief), in Beacon Biographies. Brownell, in American Prose Masters ; Erskine, in Leading American Novelists ; Bryant's Oration on Cooper, in Prose Works ; Parkman's essay (North American Review, Vol. LXXIV) ; Susan Cooper, A Glance Backwards (Atlantic, February, 1887) ; Matthews, in Gateways to Literature.

Poe. Text: Works, Virginia edition, edited by Harrison, 17 vols., including biography and letters (Crowell, 1902) ; Works, Knickerbocker edition, edited by Richardson, 10 vols. (Putnam, 1904) ; Works, edited by Stedman and Woodberry, 10 vols. (Chicago, 1894). Many other editions, all incomplete.

Biography and Criticism : Excellent biographical sketches and critical notes in the above editions of Poe's works. Life and Letters, by Harrison, 2 vols. ; the same in Vols. I and XVII of the Virginia edition ; Life, by Woodberry, in American Men of Letters ; by Trent, in English Men of Letters ; by Griswold (1850), by Gill (1877), by Ingram (1886), etc. Sarah H. Whitman, Poe and his Critics ; Stedman, Poets of America ; Burton, Literary Leaders ; Brownell, American Prose Masters ; Higginson, Short Studies of American Authors.

Essays : Robertson, in Essays toward a Critical Method ; Matthews, The Short Story, in Pen and Ink ; Andrew Lang, in Letters to Dead Authors ; Gosse, Has America Produced a Poet? in Questions at Issue ; Gates, in Studies and Appreciations.

Bibliography : in Stedman and Woodberry edition of Works, Vol. X ; in Page, Chief American Poets (selections), pp. 636–638.

Simms. Texts: Novels, 10 vols. (Armstrong) ; Poems, 2 vols. (Redfield).

Biography and Criticism : Life, by Trent, in American Men of Letters. Brief studies, in Moses, Literature of the South ; in Baskerville, Southern Writers ; in Link, Pioneers of Southern Literature, etc. See also Tuckerman's John Pendleton Kennedy (New York, 1871).

The Short Story : Smith, The American Short Story (Ginn and Company, 1912) ; Matthews, Philosophy of the Short Story, and The Short Story : Specimens Illustrating its Development ; Dawson, Great English Short-Story Writers, 2 vols. ; Canby, The Short Story in English ; Evelyn Albright, The Short Story ; Higginson, The Local Short Story (in The Independent, March 11, 1892).

The Knickerbocker School : Hueston, The Knickerbocker Gallery (New York, 1855) ; Poe, The Literati ; Wilson, Bryant and his Friends ; Stoddard, Recollections Personal and Literary.

Willis : Works, 13 vols. (Scribner, 1849–1859) ; Works, 1 vol. (Redfield, 1846) ; Life, by Beers, in American Men of Letters.

Halleck : Poetical Writings (Appleton, 1869) ; Life and Letters, by Wilson.

Webster : Works, 6 vols. (Boston, 1851) ; Great Speeches and Orations, edited by Whipple (Boston, 1879). Life, by Curtis, 2 vols. ; by Lodge, in American Statesmen ; by Van Tyne, in American Crisis Biographies.

Historical Fiction. *Older Romances :* Brown, Arthur Mervyn ; Judd, Margaret ; Kennedy, Swallow Barn ; Paulding, Westward Ho !

Later Romances : Mrs. Stowe, Minister's Wooing; Hale, Man Without a Country; Cooke, Leather Stocking and Silk; Eggleston, Roxy, Hoosier Schoolmaster; Winthrop, John Brent.

Books for Young People. Brigham, From Trail to Railway (Ginn and Company); Bruce, Daniel Boone and the Wilderness Road; Paxson, The Last American Frontier; McMurray, Pioneers of the Mississippi Valley, Pioneers of the Rocky Mountains (Macmillan); Florence Bass, Stories of Pioneer Life (Heath).

Suggestive Questions. (For the general aim of these questions, see explanation on page 83. Specific questions on Irving, Cooper, etc., should be based on works of these authors that have been read by the students.)

1. Why is the half century following 1775 often called the Age of Revolution? What important literary movement accompanied the political revolution? Can you see any relation of cause and effect between the two movements?

2. What was the political significance of Jackson's election? Explain the statement that the aristocratic type of president went out of favor in 1829.

3. What are the prominent characteristics of our first national literature? Illustrate each by some well-known writers. What is meant by romanticism, and in what way is it illustrated in the works of Irving, Cooper and Bryant?

4. How do you account for the fact that early in this period our writers were timidly copying English manners and ways, and a little later were independent and confident? What writers, and what works, first brought foreign recognition?

5. Our first national writers laid emphasis on beauty for its own sake; can you explain why beauty was neglected by earlier writers, and why it was emphasized by Irving and his contemporaries? Apply the same question to the romantic treatment of nature.

6. Boston, Philadelphia, Charleston and New York have at different times been "literary centers"; how do you account for the fact that Washington, unlike the capitals of other countries, has never won literary recognition? What effect did the opening of the Great West have upon our literature? (Illustrate by works of Irving and Cooper.) What is meant by the romance of the West? Why did the West at first produce no literature? Compare the West in this respect with the early colonies.

7. *Irving.* (*a*) Name three notable achievements of Irving. What new types did he add to our literature? Why is he called "the father of American letters," and why "the American Addison"?

(*b*) Explain Thackeray's statement that Irving was the first ambassador from the New World of letters to the Old. Did the title have any connection with the fact that Irving was our minister to Spain? What American literary men may be called Irving's successors in this respect?

(*c*) Give a brief sketch of Irving's life, noting especially his youth, his home, his different kinds of work, his honors, and the personal elements that are reflected in his writings. In this sketch explain, if you can, why Irving and Scott were attracted to each other.

(d) Classify Irving's chief works according to type (essays, stories, etc.); according to theme (English, Spanish, American) ; according to periods (early, middle, later). What qualities of style are shown in all these works? Is there any significance in the name Jonathan Oldstyle, with which Irving signed some of his productions?

(e) Describe the general character of the *Sketch Book*, *Alhambra* and any other works of Irving that you have read. What two classes or types of literature are illustrated in each of these works? Why is the *Alhambra* called "the beautiful Spanish Sketch Book"? What is meant by the Knickerbocker History? Illustrate from passages in Irving, Franklin, etc. the difference between humor and wit. Compare Irving's earlier and later humor with the humor of Mark Twain.

(f) Give in your own words Irving's message, and tell what influence he has exerted on American life and literature.

8. *Bryant.* (a) Explain these three titles given to Bryant: the high priest of nature; the American Wordsworth; the Puritan poet. Which of these titles seems to you best in view of Bryant's work?

(b) Give a brief sketch of Bryant's life, noting especially his youth, his experience with law and journalism, the high position which he won, and the effect of each on his poetry. In this sketch account for his commanding position, and for the fact that his earliest verse was his best.

(c) Give the chief classes or divisions of his poetry, and account for each on personal grounds, and by the literary tastes of his age. How does his view of nature compare with that of earlier (Anglo-Saxon) and of later English poets, Tennyson for example? What points of resemblance and of difference do you find in Bryant and Wordsworth? How do his poems on death compare with those of Poe?

(d) What is the meaning of "Thanatopsis," and what is the general character of the poem? Why did Bryant add introductory and closing lines to the original poem? Note any lines in the poem which reflect Bryant's interest in the Greek classics, and other lines which suggest the influence of Wordsworth. What other poems of Bryant on the subject of death have you read, and how do they compare with "Thanatopsis"?

(e) Read "To a Waterfowl" (we suggest that you learn by heart the stanzas that appeal to you) and reproduce in your own words the different pictures which it calls up. Why should the last stanza be called Bryant's signature? Comment on Hartley Coleridge's criticism that this is the best short poem in the English language.

(f) Read the "Forest Hymn," and using the poem as a basis illustrate Bryant's style, his view of nature, his strength, and his limitations as a poet. It is said that "Thanatopsis" might have been written anywhere but the "Forest Hymn" could come only from America; criticize the statement. Read "The Poet," and determine whether the poem is merely a flight of fancy, or whether it is consistent with Bryant's theory and practice of verse.

(g) In what respect is Bryant "the New England poet"? How does he justify Emerson's criticism that he is the poet of America?

9. *Cooper.* (*a*) Why was Cooper called the American Scott? What resemblances and differences do you find in the two writers? In what ways did Cooper display marked originality?

(*b*) Name four elements of Cooper's power as a writer. Explain the interest aroused by his work in America and in Europe. How do you account for the fact that he was, and is, more widely known than any other American author?

(*c*) Give a brief sketch of Cooper's life, noting especially: personal elements or incidents that are reflected in his romances; the occasion and the result of his first literary venture; his success as a novelist; his journey abroad and its consequences.

(*d*) Classify his romances in three divisions, and name the important works in each. Which of these works seems to you the strongest, the best written, the truest to nature? Illustrate from one work the character of a romance, and the difference between a romance and a novel.

(*e*) *The Spy* was our first notable historical romance, and America's first contribution to international fiction; give the theme of the story; explain its hold on American and foreign readers. What qualities of strength and what limitations are suggested by the book? What is meant by Cooper's moralizing and what is its effect on the reader?

(*f*) Aside from its intrinsic value, why is *The Pilot* remarkable? Who are its typical heroes? What two qualities of Cooper give power and interest to all his sea stories?

(*g*) Name the five books of the Leatherstocking drama in their natural order. In what respect is *The Pioneers* better than the others? What is the chief interest of *The Last of the Mohicans?* What are the essential differences between the latter story and a dime novel of Indian adventure? How far does Natty Bumppo seem to you a true type of the American woodsman, and Chingachgook of the Indian? What are the strong and what are the weak elements in the portrayal of these characters?

(*h*) How do you account for the fact that Cooper's ladies and gentlemen are invariably weak and tiresome, while his common men are generally strong and interesting? What general literary tendencies and fashions are suggested by his feminine characters? Compare him in this respect with Brown or Scott. From the works you have read, make a list of Cooper's characters that you remember vividly. Which of these characters will probably appeal to readers in the future?

10. *Poe.* (*a*) In what respect is Poe different from all other prominent American writers? What notable contributions did he make to American literature? How do you account for the fact that he has been so long a subject of controversy?

(*b*) Give a brief sketch of Poe's life, noting especially his early years, his school life, his wanderings. Note the personal qualities that are reflected in his work; and explain, if you can, why his experience as a soldier, as a West Point cadet, as a journalist, etc., are never reflected in his writings.

(*c*) Group his works in three main divisions, and illustrate each. It is said that, whatever his subject, Poe always wrote about himself; criticize the statement.

(*d*) Divide his prose tales into three or four classes, and illustrate each. Is Poe the inventor or only the first notable manipulator of the short story? What is meant by the statement that Poe aimed chiefly at " effect"? What is meant by " Tales of the Grotesque and Arabesque"? What is the general character of Poe's stories?

(*e*) Which one of Poe's personages deserves to be called a character, and how does he reappear in later literature? In what story does Poe use the double personality as a motive? What later writers make use of the same motive? Describe Poe's characters in general. How do you account for the fact that there is very little conversation or dialogue and no natural landscape in his stories?

(*f*) What service did Poe render to literary criticism? Criticize (if you have read) his theory of poetry and of composition. How many of the authors whom he praised highly in *The Literati* are now remembered?

(*g*) How do Poe's poems illustrate his own idea of poetry in general? What is the chief quality of his poems? In what especially are they lacking? Illustrate Poe's use of the refrain, and name any other American poems in which refrains are used in the same manner.

(*h*) Can you explain on personal or literary grounds the contrast between Poe's definite, positive style or method and his vague, shadowy material? Poe's works are, comparatively, little read, yet he is given a very high rank by foreign critics; explain the discrepancy.

11. *Miscellaneous.* (*a*) What common characteristics have the fiction writers of this period? Name any of their works that are still read. If you have read any of the books of Melville, Dana, Judd, etc., describe their general qualities.

(*b*) Give an outline of Simms's work for American literature. What are his chief romances? How do they compare with those of Cooper?

(*c*) What are the chief works of Kennedy? Which of them suggests Cooper and Simms, and which is influenced by Irving? Describe Kennedy's relation to Poe and to Thackeray.

(*d*) What service was rendered by the minor poets of this period? In contrast with the Colonial and Revolutionary period, Richardson calls this period " the dawn of imagination"; explain the title.

(*e*) What is meant by the Knickerbocker school? Who were its writers (exclusive of Irving, Cooper, Bryant) and for what were they noted? Do you know of any of their works that are still read? Explain the joyous, buoyant spirit of Knickerbocker writings, and show how they were characteristic of the country.

(*f*) Who were the chief orators of this period? In what respect do they differ from Revolutionary orators? What were the questions at issue in most of their debates? What service did Everett render to American culture? Compare a speech of Calhoun with a speech of Webster, having in mind the personality of the speakers, their different points of view, their methods of appeal.

(Note: For questions on Webster's First Bunker Hill Address, Washington's Farewell Address, etc., the student is referred to Trent's *English Classics* (Ginn and Company), a little book devoted to the works required for college entrance English.)

Subjects for Research and Essays. Some novels that were popular one hundred years ago. Our first historical romances. The American short story. Old American chronicle plays. Catherine Sedgwick and the novel of manners. Robert Montgomery Bird and the modern dime novel. Poe's amateur detective in modern fiction. Willis as a type of popular author. A forgotten poet (James Gates Percival). The Charleston and the Knickerbocker schools. Influence of the Western Expansion on American literature (note the influence of English exploration and discovery on Elizabethan literature). English names for American authors (the American Scott, the American Wordsworth, etc.). American literary men who were also foreign consuls, ministers, ambassadors. Rip van Winkle before Irving discovered him. Bryant and modern journalism. Influence of journalism on literature (illustrate by American authors). The Homer of Bryant and Pope. Cooper's Indians. Leatherstocking as a race hero. Cooperstown then and now. The Bread and Cheese Lunch Club. What Cooper owed to Charles Brockden Brown. The Southern Literary Messenger. The North American Review. The "annual" and the modern magazine. The romance of the West: its discovery and exploitation. Juveniles old and new.

CHAPTER IV

THE SECOND NATIONAL OR CREATIVE PERIOD (1840-1876) [1]

Thou too sail on, O Ship of State!
Sail on, O Union, strong and great!
Humanity with all its fears,
With all the hopes of future years,
Is hanging breathless on thy fate!
We know what Master laid thy keel,
What Workmen wrought thy ribs of steel,
Who made each mast, and sail, and rope,
What anvils rang, what hammers beat,
In what a forge and what a heat
Were shaped the anchors of thy hope!
Fear not each sudden sound and shock,
'T is of the wave and not the rock;
'T is but the flapping of the sail,
And not a rent made by the gale!
In spite of rock and tempest's roar,
In spite of false lights on the shore,
Sail on, nor fear to breast the sea!
Our hearts, our hopes, are all with thee!
Our hearts, our hopes, our prayers, our tears,
Our faith triumphant o'er our fears,
Are all with thee, — are all with thee!

Longfellow, "The Building of the Ship"

I. HISTORY OF THE PERIOD

General Outline. As one who intends to travel a densely forested region should ascertain, if possible, the general trend of its mountains and watercourses, so one who enters upon the study of this tumultuous

---

[1] For the beginning of this period we have chosen the Harrison-Tyler administration (1841–1845). Then began the violent agitation of the slave question, over the annexation of Texas, which roused sectional feeling and brought on the Civil War. The period may well end with the administration of Grant (1869–1877), which witnessed the complete restoration of the Union, the spread of new states from the Atlantic to the Pacific, and the significant Centennial Exposition of 1876. By the latter date all the great writers of this period had practically finished their work.

ABRAHAM LINCOLN

"IT IS RATHER FOR US TO BE HERE DEDICATED TO THE GREAT TASK
REMAINING BEFORE US—THAT FROM THESE HONORED DEAD WE TAKE
INCREASED DEVOTION TO THAT CAUSE FOR WHICH THEY GAVE THE
LAST FULL MEASURE OF DEVOTION; THAT WE HERE HIGHLY RESOLVE
THAT THESE DEAD SHALL NOT HAVE DIED IN VAIN; THAT THIS NATION,
UNDER GOD, SHALL HAVE A NEW BIRTH OF FREEDOM; AND THAT THE
GOVERNMENT OF THE PEOPLE, BY THE PEOPLE, FOR THE PEOPLE, SHALL
NOT PERISH FROM THE EARTH"

period should keep in mind some guiding outline of its historic events. Such an outline would be something like the following:

1. The rapid westward expansion of the nation; the formation of new states and territories; the enormous increase in material prosperity, with its stimulus and its danger. With the admission of new states arose the question of the so-called balance of power between the South and the North.[1] We are concerned here, not with the question itself, but rather with its sad, disturbing implication, namely, that a great nation with the hope and expectation of mankind in its keeping had begun to split into two sections, divergent in their aims and antagonistic in their interests.

2. The sudden acquisition of a vast territory in connection with the annexation of Texas, the Oregon Treaty, and the war with Mexico. With this new territory plainly appeared two mutually hostile elements. The first was the apparent economic necessity of extending the area of slave labor to meet the increased demand for cotton in America and in Europe. The second was the growing conviction and determination that slavery must not spread to new territory but be confined to states where it already existed.

3. The years of political storm and stress, of struggle and compromise, which followed the attempt to reconcile the above irreconcilable factors. At the root of every struggle was the agitation of the slave question; at the heart of every compromise was the hope of preserving the Union. The various political organizations which appeared during this period may be grouped in three main classes:

a. The extreme proslavery party. This was composed of a relatively small but influential body of men, who held that slavery was an economic necessity; that it was justified by the laws of property and by the Constitution of the United States; that under slavery the negroes were happier and better protected than they could possibly be under any other system of labor; and that the slave system was, therefore, not only legally right but morally justifiable. The aim of this party was to extend slavery widely in the new territories.

[1] In the early period of our constitutional history, the southern and northern states had practically equal representation in both houses of Congress. The North gained more rapidly in population and, as the number of representatives increases with the number of people, soon had a majority in the lower house. To offset this advantage, the South strove to maintain in the upper house an equal representation. Hence the new states, each of which elected two senators, were for a long time admitted in pairs, or alternately, one from the South and another from the North, thus preserving, in the Senate at least, the old balance of political power.

b. The abolitionists and other extreme antislavery men, who re
garded the slave system as a moral evil which could no longer be
tolerated. They took no account of the difficulties and dangers involved in emancipation; they had small regard for economics, or
even for the Constitution when it appeared to stand in their way.
That the slave must be, and instantly, a free man was their only
issue. This party was small and persecuted at first, but it made up in
zeal and determination what it lacked in numbers.

c. The great body of moderate people, south and north, who regarded slavery as a "domestic institution," subject to state law and
not to the national government, as Congress had repeatedly declared.
The general method of this party was to compromise in view of the
rights of others; its ideal was to hold all the states together in a
harmonious development of the whole country; its immediate aim
was to take the slave question out of national politics, where it was
a perpetual source of discord and danger. Despite the earnest,
patriotic efforts of this moderate party, the extremists on both sides
made slavery the dominant national issue. It was violently agitated,
in season and out of season, until it became, as the aged Jefferson
had feared, like the wild ringing of a fire bell at night, and men rose
in alarm to meet the crisis.

4. Secession; the terrible last resort to arms; the destruction of
slavery; the reëstablishment of the Union on its old, unshaken
foundations; the perils and hardships of reconstruction.

5. The astonishing recovery of the nation after the fearful loss
and suffering of the war, and the orderly progress of Union and
Democracy.

It needs only a glance to suggest that the history included in such
a rugged outline cannot possibly be compressed into a few pages.
We shall not, therefore, attempt to review the war, with its long chain
of causes and consequences. Our interest in national literature leads
us rather to examine the years of controversy which divided the
country long before the call to arms had sounded. If we can enter
for a moment into the excitement of this period, we may understand
two classes of writing which appear in every time of turmoil: the
minor literature, voicing the feeling of an hour or a party; and the
major literature, which steadily reflects the unchanging ideals of
the American nation.

The Age of Agitation. Our pride and faith in a united country
make it hard for us now to understand the sectional strife and

bitterness of the twenty years before 1861. It was a time of political upheaval, of violent debate ending in threats or compromises, of sudden storm followed by a calm as ominous as that in the center of a whirlwind. The Wilmot Proviso, the Fugitive Slave Law, the Kansas-Nebraska Bill, the Repeal of the Missouri Compromise, the Dred Scott Decision, the Compromise of 1850, the Great Debate — we have to search memory or a textbook now to learn what such things mean; but at that time they kept millions of our countrymen in a state of intense excitement. On every one of these burning questions men, and women too, had to take a definite stand, and instantly defend it; and every person who wrote or spoke his conviction became a storm-center of controversy.

Those were tumultuous times in which our greatest writers were growing up. Some of our poets, notably Whittier and Lowell, threw themselves into the strife of tongues; and in consequence a portion of their work is so partisan in spirit that it cannot be classed with national literature. Other young poets of brilliant talents turned from poetry to politics, as Trumbull and Freneau had turned aside in '76, and never fulfilled their early promise to our literature.

The two fundamental questions involved in all this strife concerned the matters of state rights and slavery. Both questions had been **Fundamental** debated for the greater part of a century without ever **Questions** furnishing an occasion for war; and they might still have found just and peaceable solution had not the country been inflamed by other matters: by the passionate, uncompromising methods of the abolitionists; by the zeal, no less passionate, of a few large slaveowners who were determined to extend their system in face of the growing moral conviction that slavery must be restricted; by the legal or personal encounters that followed the escape of slaves into free territory; and by a general newspaper campaign of misunderstanding and recrimination.

All these irritating matters complicated the main issue between the South and the North, and swept the country from calm deliberation **Political** into a heated controversy, which rapidly broke up the **Factions** great moderate party into discordant fragments. In a single generation there appeared in the South eight or ten political organizations, most of which were divided into two factions, one advocating compromise and the other force in the pursuit of its immediate object. Meanwhile in the North there were Old Whigs and New Whigs, Republicans and " Black " Republicans, Democrats and Union Democrats, Free-soilers, Libertyites, Know-nothings, Abolitionists. And as the last-named reformers met to listen to the fiery denunciations of their orators, and to demand the immediate freedom of the slaves at any cost, presently a riotous mob would burst in upon them to smash the furniture, burn the building, and carry off the leader with a warning halter round his neck. With such conditions existing in the older, more conservative parts of the country, it seems only a natural consequence to find politics taking the form of anarchy and mob rule in the frontier settlements of "bleeding" Kansas.

Only as we remember this political babel, with its attendant emotional disturbance, can we understand the general uproar occasioned by the fanatic raid of John Brown, or the mighty wave of indignation which followed the melodramatic story of *Uncle Tom's Cabin*. It was as if a patient, suffering from fever, had suddenly developed a new symptom which alarmed the watchers beyond all reason, but which would hardly have produced a tremor if its psychological causes had been understood.

The general fever of the age, its political tumult, its moral unrest, its ceaseless agitation, are all clearly reflected in the minor and **Minor Writings** popular literature of the period — in its editorials, essays, tracts, pamphlets and newspaper verses. Generalization is difficult, but many of the writers who influenced public opinion after 1840 seem to display three characteristics: a zeal for some cause or reform; a sincerity arising from moral conviction; and, generally, a profound misunderstanding of other writers who were upholding opposite views with the same sincerity and the same passionate intensity.

Most of the minor works of the period have long since been forgotten; but one who reads them now begins to understand how armed conflict arose, not from inevitable necessity but from misunderstanding, between those who were born under the same flag, who worshiped the same God, and who honored the same virtues in man or woman. It was an age of agitation; the country was swept by wave after wave of emotional excitement; the voice of deliberation was lost in the louder cry of passion. The tumult reached its climax during the feeble administration of Buchanan, at a time when, if ever in its history, the ship of state needed a strong man at the helm; and then America, the peace-loving, was suddenly confronted by a terrible war which no sane person had ever desired or expected.

That war is still too near, too overwhelming in its impression of mingled horror and heroism, for us to treat it altogether dispassion-

The War   ately. The records of the period are all more or less partisan, reflecting a southern or a northern " view," because human judgment is easily affected by sympathy, and because our analysis of impersonal cause and effect is inevitably mingled with tender and sacred memories of the brave sires who died, of the gentle mothers who suffered in silence for the cause they loved. That the war revealed the indomitable will and the appalling fighting power of aroused America is now a matter of history. That it was all unnecessary may sometime be generally conceded. That it was fought on both sides by men who believed in the justice of their aims, who held honor dearer than life, and who heard above the shrilling of bugles and the roar of cannon the old Puritan battle-cry of "God for the right!" can no longer be doubted.

II. LITERARY AND SOCIAL MOVEMENTS

National and Sectional Literature. As one reviews the literature of this stormy period, two facts stand out prominently : first, that the turmoil of reform was reflected in prose and poetry ; second, that the enduring literary works were seldom influenced by the problems that kept men's minds in continual agitation. A third fact, which reflection renders more significant, is that the great writers of the period traced their ancestry back to the founders of America, and that the remembrance of their ancestors, who had worked and fought together to establish this nation, held them steadfast in the national spirit.

Of the minor writings we may say, in general, that they dealt with the surface of things, and that they seem now of little consequence. The major writings, undisturbed by temporary affairs, dealt with the moral and spiritual ideals which America has followed from the beginning ; and these writings gain steadily in interest as the years go by. So the literature of the period may be likened to a great river ; its surface is broken by waves or lashed by tempests, but just beneath the turmoil the water moves quietly, steadily onward to the sea.

To illustrate the matter : the antislavery movement, which at one time monopolized public attention, had its poet in Whittier and its novelist in Mrs. Stowe ; but the present reader is more interested in works of these writers which had nothing to do with slavery or political issues. Occasionally Lowell, as in his " Commemoration Ode," rises to national heights and sees the eternal ideal hidden in the passing event ; but the bulk of his work inspired by the reform movement has lost its power with the present generation. Longfellow's verses on slavery are of so little moment that they are often omitted from collections of his works. Whittier's are vigorous and sincere, but they are partisan and cannot endure. He himself lived to regret some of them. In numerous collections of the southern poetry of the period one finds here and there an exquisite reflection of our common joy or sorrow, and these are permanent ; but a large part of the verse is doomed, simply because it appeals to a sectional rather than to a general interest. Lanier, greatest of southern poets, is a splendid exception. Unlike Whittier, who in his early days fought valiantly with the pen, Lanier did all his fighting with the sword ; his pen was sacred to poetry and to humanity. In consequence he never strikes a false or partisan note, and his poetry grows steadily more precious to the entire nation.

Mental Unrest. Closely associated with the political was a profound mental or spiritual agitation, which the historian notes with interest because of its influence on all subsequent American literature. It showed itself, first, in a religious awakening under the leadership of Channing and Bushnell. Next it appeared in philanthropic guise : in the antislavery campaign, in the temperance reform, in the universal peace movement led by Elihu Burritt, and in the many other plans for the regeneration of human society which are suggested by Emerson's " New England Reformers." Then was the heyday of the lyceum and the lecturer ; every cause had its enthusiastic following, every town its lecture course ; and in a thousand halls

(margin note: Partisan Prose and Poetry)

throughout the country audiences gathered eagerly to hear the latest poet, prophet, or preacher of new gospels.

As a result of all this agitation, many believed that the old order was about to change; and in anticipation of the millennium there appeared numerous communistic societies, that is, companies of persons who sought either to reform the world or to escape its evils by living and working together in a kind of brotherhood.

The most famous of these phalanxes or phalansteries, as they were called, was Brook Farm, which was organized (1841) by **Brook Farm** George Ripley, and which numbered Hawthorne, Curtis and Dana among its hundred and fifty members. Emerson, Thoreau, Margaret Fuller, Channing, Greeley and many other notable persons were interested in the community, and sent frequent contributions to *The Dial*, which was the famous literary organ of the Brook Farmers. The members worked intermittently on their large farm in Roxbury (now a part of Boston) and their object was, in their own words, "to live in all the faculties of the soul." More specifically, they aimed to live close to nature, to dignify manual labor, to cultivate the spiritual side of life, and to help every member to be free, fearless, upright — an individual in the best sense of the word. Incidentally they hoped to give practical demonstration of the fact that brotherly coöperation is vastly better than our present competitive system of industry. Their aim was high, their effort sincere; but alas! they failed, partly for lack of capital, and partly because the support of such a community and the education of its children called for more manual labor than untrained muscles could endure. One of the first to be discouraged was Hawthorne, who writes in his *Notes*, after ten hours of unaccustomed toil, "It is my opinion that a man's soul may be buried in a furrow of the field just as well as under a pile of money."

A fire which consumed the main buildings in 1846 practically ended the community, but not until it had made a deep impression on American life and thought. Thousands of visitors came every year to visit Brook Farm; unnumbered references to it are found in the annals of the period; and a considerable body of literature has since appeared in memory of the heroic experiment.[1]

Besides Brook Farm, more than thirty other communities were established, some of which are still in existence.[2] In his **Failure of Communism** essay on Thoreau (1865) Lowell ridicules the whole movement, and though his criticism is superficial, it contains a grain of truth. The aim of all these communities, to coöperate and to know the joy and freedom of labor, has inspired men for ages, and will continue to inspire them until the aim is achieved. But unfortunately the age was too much influenced by agitators, and these communities soon attracted a host of zealots who made havoc of the enterprise. They had plenty of enthusiasm, but they lacked humor, balance, practical sense, and their vagaries brought ridicule upon an experiment which had originated in a noble ideal. Like the reformers in other fields during this period, they insisted upon an immediate transformation of human society; and their effort to hurry the world on its slow, upward way reminds us of Dr. Johnson's famous parody:

> Who drives fat oxen should himself be fat.

Transcendentalism. The unrest of the age, its passion for reform, its determination to win complete spiritual freedom, are all epitomized in the philosophic movement known as transcendentalism. There is a large literature on the subject, and we

---

[1] See, for instance, Swift's *Brook Farm* and Codman's *Brook Farm Memories*. Hawthorne's *Blithedale Romance* was occasioned by his experience as a member of the community. He was not sympathetic, however, and his motive in joining was personal rather than philanthropic. His book should be read simply as a romance, and not as a portrayal of Brook Farm.

[2] See the records of the Oneida and the Amana communities, for instance. The idea of such societies dates as far back, at least, as More's *Utopia*. In the eighteenth century there were several socialistic communities in Europe; and at least one, the Shakers, appeared in America before the Revolution. The sudden increase in the number here was due largely to the fact that the socialistic philosophy of Fourier was advocated by Greeley, Dana and many other Americans of influence. "Fourierism" was the name commonly used to designate the movement.

cannot here go deeply into it. We shall note only two facts: that transcendentalism exercised a strong, elevating influence on American life and letters; and that it was not a New England product, as is commonly alleged, but was simply the westward extension of a general European movement.

At the root of transcendentalism, as it appeared here in 1836, were three elements: the first, political or democratic; the second, literary or romantic; and the third, ideal or philosophic. The movement began, undoubtedly, at the time when the whole civilized world was shaken by the American and French Revolutions. For a full half century following these historic earthquakes European countries were in a state of political upheaval, and the object of every agitation was to secure greater liberty for the masses of common men. This democratic movement in politics was immediately followed by the romantic awakening in literature (which glorified and idealized plain humanity) and by a new philosophy of idealism which sought to free man's mind from error, as the French Revolution had freed his body from tyranny.[1] Goethe reflects the unrest of the whole civilized world at the beginning of the nineteenth century in the character of Faust, who longs for the "Beyond," that is, to escape from the slavery of the material world and to merge his life in the unseen, eternal forces that rule the universe.

All these mighty, earlier movements entered into what is known, inaccurately, as New England transcendentalism. The **Meaning of Transcendental** last word has never been defined, but we shall understand it readily if we recall the system of thought which it supplanted. The philosophy of the eighteenth century was, as a rule, skeptical and materialistic; it was concerned with this world chiefly; it was doubtful of God and even of the human soul; it alleged that all knowledge and all

[1] As a suggestion of the scope of the movement, we note the following: in this country, Bushnell and Channing succeeded in emancipating many of our people from the terrors of Calvinism; in France, Fourier advocated a new social order of coöperation, which had large influence throughout the world; in Switzerland, Pestalozzi reformed the world's common-school system and laid the foundation for all modern education; in Germany, Kant, Fichte, Schelling and Hegel established the philosophy of idealism.

ideas depend solely upon matter and sense, upon what we can see and touch. In this it followed out the theory of the English philosopher Locke, who taught that the mind is essentially a *tabula rasa*, a blank sheet, on which knowledge is inscribed only by experience. The idealists of the nineteenth century were radically opposed to such a view of man and of the universe. They taught that the human mind has a knowledge of its own, independent of the senses or of the material world ; that certain ideas — of right and wrong, for instance, of good and evil, of God, duty, freedom, immortality — are innate in the soul, a part of its very being ; and that such ideas transcend or go beyond experience. It was because Emerson and his followers exalted this innate knowledge, this " wisdom from within and from above," that they were called transcendentalists.[1]

This new philosophy (which was new only in name) took root at first in New England ; and from there it spread west-ward and southward till it influenced a large part of the country, partly by means of literature, partly through the lyceum, which was then, like the present Woman's Club, a center of culture in almost every large town. The first transcendental club, or " Symposium," was formed in Boston (1836) and numbered among its members Emerson, Thoreau, Hawthorne, Channing, James Freeman Clarke, Margaret Fuller, Jones Very the mystic poet, Orestes Brownson the theologian, Bancroft the historian, Theodore Parker the radical preacher, Cranch the artist, Ripley the founder of Brook Farm, Convers Francis the biographer, — we might continue the list indefinitely, if necessary, to show the varied types of men and the tremendous intellectual power behind a movement which is generally treated with scant courtesy.

Influence of Transcendentalism

[1] See Emerson's " The Transcendentalist." This essay, however, should be read with caution, as it is incomplete from the viewpoint of either history or philosophy. Tran-scendentalism came to this country by various channels : by the works of Coleridge and Carlyle ; and by numerous translations of European and especially of oriental literature. The last named, which were widely read here, emphasized an ideal view of the world. They taught that matter has no more reality than has a reflection in a mirror, and their teachings were largely accepted by Emerson and the transcendentalists.

Like the earlier idealism of the Puritan, transcendentalism aimed first to make man upright, and then to make him free in mind as well as in body. Whenever it appeared in literature it had two subjects, nature and man ; the one being regarded as an open book of the Lord ; the other, not as a poor creature of the senses, but as an immortal being and child of the Most High. These two fundamental conceptions — that the individual soul is of supreme importance, and that nature is but the symbol, the garment, the changing expression of one changeless spiritual force — colored with something of the hues of heaven the whole romantic movement in American literature.

So far transcendentalism was excellent, and America gave it hearty welcome. Unfortunately it had another and weaker side, **Its Fantastic** and by this the whole movement is often judged. **Side** Two elements contributed to bring it into disrepute. The first, which was inherent in transcendentalism as a system of thought, related to the doctrine of innate ideas. Because a man may have knowledge which transcends experience, shallow minds jumped to the conclusion that experience was unnecessary. Because an individual may be in touch with the divine source of knowledge, enthusiasts felt free to disregard the saints and sages. Because the Present offers its inspiration with its duty, even Emerson felt free to ignore the Past, where " dwells that silent majority whose experience guides our action and whose wisdom shapes our thought in spite of ourselves." It was inevitable, therefore, that this doctrine, like every other which fails to give due weight to the treasured wisdom and experience of the race, should tend to extremes and vagaries.

The second disruptive element was the same spirit of agitation that troubled our politics. Just as state problems of the hour were used by extremists to keep the country in a turmoil, so the new philosophy was demoralized by zealots. Every unbalanced enthusiast took it up ; visionaries snatched leadership away from the wise and prudent, and calling themselves " Apostles of Newness " went forth to preach the gospel of individualism, proclaiming that every man was his own and only source of wisdom and authority :

> I am the owner of the sphere,
> Of the seven stars and the solar year,
> Of Cæsar's hand and Plato's brain,
> Of Lord Christ's heart and Shakespeare's strain.[1]

Emerson describes one of their conventions as made up of " madmen, mad women, men with beards, Dunkers, Muggletonians, Come-outers, Groaners, Agrarians, Abolitionists . . . and philosophers." The classification is vague, but the impression is distinct that no order will proceed from such chaos. By such men was transcendentalism judged, though in truth the new philosophy was not responsible for them. They were a product of the age ; they belonged to the army of reformers that then had a mission, as Lowell said, " to attend to everybody else's business," and they seized upon transcendentalism as a new means of agitation.

The folly of such reformers, the impractical character of their communistic societies, the eccentricities of Alcott [2] and other **Its Ideal** enthusiasts,—all these furnished a tempting mark for **Truth** the fun-makers of the country, who fell upon the movement and smothered it in ridicule. It has been a fashion ever since to decry it, just as it was the thoughtless fashion long after *Hudibras* to jeer at Puritanism. The points worthy of remembrance are : that transcendentalism was an earnest reaffirmation of ideal truth, sublime and authoritative ; that it valued the individual soul above all institutions ; that it sought in nature a divine presence, and in religion a divine companionship ; that, in an age of material interests, it emphasized the life of the spirit ; that, when America was given to boasting of its size and prosperity, it insisted on culture, reverence, virtue and simplicity,

---

[1] From Emerson, " The Informing Spirit," an introduction to the essay on History.
[2] The career of Amos Bronson Alcott (1799–1888) should be read as a commentary on the transcendental movement. He is now remembered chiefly through his daughter, Louisa M. Alcott, whose *Little Women* and other " juveniles " have been widely read, and are still deservedly popular.

as more worthy of American manhood. Its influence on all subsequent thought and literature in this country is beyond measure.

General Characteristics. We have noted the significant fact
that, while minor writers of this period were absorbed in questions of the hour, the major writers stood apart, like Moses on
the hill of Rephidim, upholding the ideals which America has
followed since the days of Pilgrim and Cavalier, and which seem
to grow younger and ever more lovely with the passing centuries. Another fact worthy of attention is that our literary
field was immensely broadened after 1840 by the exploration of
oriental and European libraries. The old mystic books of India,
the imaginative splendor of Persian poetry, the primal vigor of
Scandinavian epics, the romance and sentiment of German,
French, Spanish and Italian literatures, — all these, in the form
of numerous translations, suddenly appeared to our writers,
enlarging their horizon till it included not only America but all
humanity.

Viewed as a national product, the major literature of the age
shows four common characteristics : (1) The harmony with
nature, which appeared in our first national poetry, is here
deepened and spiritualized. It becomes mystic also, especially
in the verse of Emerson and Whitman, showing the influence
of oriental literature. (2) The national spirit and an intense
loyalty to the nation's flag are everywhere in evidence, strengthened by the war ; and though historians still separate our writers
into eastern and southern and western "schools," the simple
fact is that the only books worth considering are those which
ignore such divisions and appeal to the whole American people.
(3) A strong moral tendency, which manifested itself in our
first Colonial writers, here reaches a climax. Almost every important book of this period, whether a novel of Hawthorne or
an idyl of Longfellow, aimed not simply to give pleasure but to
bring a message to men ; and the interest of story or poem
generally centered about a moral problem and its solution. With
the exception of Whitman, the major poets of this period were,

like the Victorian poets in England, essentially teachers of the nation, and the moral purity of their lives emphasized their doctrine. The moral aim and endeavor of practically all our American writers may be epitomized in two lines of Chaucer's Country Parson :

> Christës lore and his apostles twelvë
> He taughte, but first he folwed it himselvë.

(4) In contrast with preceding periods and with the age in which we live, the middle of the nineteenth century belongs emphatically to the poets ; and this is more remarkable in view of the fact that the genius of America had, up to that time, appeared practical and prosaic. Longfellow, Emerson, Whittier, Lowell, Holmes, Lanier, Whitman, — it needs only a partial list of names to suggest how far the poets exceeded the permanent achievement of the prose writers. We may begin our special study with more interest and gratitude, therefore, if we remember that it is our only opportunity in the long history of America to consider an age of poetry.

III. THE GREATER POETS AND ESSAYISTS[1]

HENRY WADSWORTH LONGFELLOW (1807–1882)

There are many reasons for beginning our study of this notable literary period with Longfellow, " our household poet." He is, first of all, the poet of the whole people, the most widely known and loved of all American authors. While he was still living among us our children began to celebrate his birthday,

---

[1] It is unusually difficult to group or classify the major writers of this period. Emerson and Lowell were both poets ; but their present fame seems to rest largely on their essays. Longfellow and Lanier had a reputation as prose writers ; and Holmes was either a poet who wrote fiction, or an essayist who wrote verse. As a writer's true place is not where he wrote but where he is read, we see no reason for grouping writers of the nation into "Cambridge" or other "schools." Various other classifications, such as "Transcendental" and "Antislavery" writers, are misleading in view of the fact that the chief works of such writers (Thoreau and Whittier, for instance) have nothing to do with either transcendentalism or slavery. Purely geographical divisions, into New England or western or southern writers, are out of place in a study of national literature.

HENRY WADSWORTH LONGFELLOW
From an engraving after the portrait by Lawrence

and the custom spread through the country until there were few schools that allowed February 27 to pass without some recognition of the poet's life and service. This exquisite tribute, which any author might desire, was not offered simply because Longfellow was the children's friend and wrote the pretty sentiment:

> Ye are better than all the ballads
> That ever were sung or said;
> For ye are living poems,
> And all the rest are dead.

It rested upon the solid fact that whoever is known and read of children has a secure place in the hearts of fathers and mothers the world over.[1]

Another reason for our choice of Longfellow to head the list of our poets is that he reflects not the surface but the deep undercurrent of American life, which is seen at its best in peace, and which flows on serenely, cherishing the love of home and homely virtues, under all the bubbles and froth of political excitement. His first book of poems, *Voices of the Night* (1839), came at the beginning of the turmoil which led to the Civil War; his last volume, *In the Harbor* (1882), appeared when the wounds of that frightful conflict were almost healed; and between these two came a score of other books, — cheery, patient, hopeful books, all loyal to American traditions. In the midst of political strife which divided our people, he sang the legends that united them in pride of a common country. In an age of intellectual agitation, which bubbled like a pot over Fourierism, transcendentalism and various other *isms*, he began to preach his little homilies: "Resignation," "Hymn to the Night," "A Psalm of Life," "The Ladder of Saint Augustine," "Excelsior," — we know them all by heart because they come

---

[1] This popular judgment is reflected abroad. Go into a foreign school, wherever English is studied, and you are almost certain to hear our household poet quoted. A prominent Scottish educator, familiar with schools in England and on the Continent, recently declared that Longfellow had led more people to love poetry than any other author of the nineteenth century.

straight from the heart, reflecting its unchanging faith and courage. Wearied by controversy, men listened with delight to this new preacher of peace and good will, forgetting their superficial differences, rejoicing together in the knowledge that whenever the heart of America is touched it is always found steadfast and true to its old ideals.

Not content with reminding us of our own legends and beliefs, Longfellow appropriated the literary treasures of Europe; he gathered a poem here, a story there, as one would cull flowers from an old-fashioned garden, and brought them all back to America, saying, " Your children are gathered from many lands: here are their native songs, their romance, their heroism, for these also are your heritage." To this new note, strange yet familiar, our people again listened with joy and wonder, as one listens to the first mocking bird. After the coldness of Bryant, the morbidness of Poe, this sweet, sympathetic singer of new-world hope and old-world memories went straight to their hearts. He sang for them, not as a great artist who prepares a concert for the few who can appreciate or pay for it, but as one who freely gives what music is in him to make life a little brighter and happier. Perhaps he was not a great, not an original poet; but he glorified the commonplace life which most men live by showing its essential beauty and truth; and America loved him for it, and gave him a place which no other poet has ever occupied. The witness of this is the volume of Longfellow's poems which is found not in the bookcase but on the table of so many households.

Life. It was Milton the Puritan poet who wrote, " He that would hope to write well . . . ought himself to be a true poem, that is, a composition and pattern of the best and most honorable things." Two centuries later Longfellow, a descendant of the Puritans, exemplified the doctrine finely. We are glad to remember that such a man lived and worked among us; but his life offers a hard task to the biographer, who can only state the simple facts, leaving the reader to discern the spirit, which is the only thing of consequence.

He was born in Falmouth (now Portland), Maine, in 1807. Like Bryant, he was descended from John and Priscilla Alden, of *May-*
Early Years *flower* renown, and like him he grew up in an atmosphere of plain living and high thinking. Bryant's first volume of poems appeared (1821) shortly before Longfellow began to write; and it was due partly to the fame of this little book, partly to sentimental reasons arising from a distant relationship, that Longfellow chose Bryant as his first master in poetry.[1]

In the public schools and in Bowdoin College, where Hawthorne was his classmate, Longfellow began his education. At his graduation,
Facing the in 1825, the question of what to do for a living was im-
World mediately forced upon him. Like Bryant, he had written youthful verses and had determined to be a poet; but his father pointed out the visionary character of his ambition, saying, "A literary calling, to one who has the means of support, must be very pleasant; but there is not enough wealth in this country to offer encouragement and patronage to merely literary men."[2] With a sorrowful farewell to poetry Longfellow had begun to study law in his father's office, when Bowdoin offered to establish for him a professorship in modern languages if he would prepare himself for the work. His answer was prompt and joyous; his destiny as a literary man was determined when he sailed (1826) for a long period of foreign study and travel. In those days few Americans went abroad; Europe seemed a world of romance, and Longfellow copied Irving in observing it through a rose-colored pair of spectacles. The result of this romantic pilgrimage appeared in his first book, *Outre Mer* (1835), a series of youthful essays modeled after Irving's *Sketch Book.*

For the next five years Longfellow taught at Bowdoin, preparing his own textbooks, and finding his work so exacting that he had small leisure for writing. Then he was offered the professorship of "Belles-Lettres" at Harvard, with the suggestion that he enlarge his knowledge of German. Another year or more was spent abroad, but the whole trip was saddened by the death of his wife in Holland. To understand Longfellow at this period one should read *Hyperion*, a romance which reflects his own state of mind as he wandered up and

[1] This is shown clearly in the "Earlier Poems" of Longfellow's *Voices of the Night.* Compare, for instance, Longfellow's "Spirit of Poetry" with Bryant's "Forest Hymn."
[2] This significant comment suggests the low state of literature here in 1825. Even in England few authors before this date had been able to earn a living by their pens. Most of them depended on private patrons or on a government pension.

down the Rhine, or lingered by the old castle of Heidelberg, steeping himself in the sentimentality of German romantic literature.

On his return, in the autumn of 1836, he began teaching at Harvard; and there for eighteen years he gave himself to his noble **Life as a** profession. He was again happily married (to the heroine **Teacher** of *Hyperion*); his home was blessed with children; and his work, though arduous, left him considerable time for writing. He lived in an old Tory mansion known as Craigie House, once the

headquarters of Washington, which had come into his possession after his marriage; his poems made him known to the whole country; he was surrounded by a rare circle of friends who encouraged him to his best efforts.[1] The spirit of this whole period is expressed in the last entry of his journal for the year 1845:

"Peace to the embers of burnt-out things; fears, anxieties, doubts, all gone! I see them now as a thin blue smoke, hanging in the bright heaven of the past year, vanishing away into utter nothingness. Not many hopes deceived, not many illusions scattered, not many anticipations disappointed; but love fulfilled, the heart comforted, the soul enriched with affection!"

THE FRONT HALL, LONGFELLOW'S
HOME, CAMBRIDGE

Such a life seems to us idyllic, leaving nothing to be desired; yet Longfellow was always haunted by the delusion of leisure. His professorship, which brought him useful work, an honored position, and

---

[1] The sonnets "Three Friends of Mine" should be read here. An excellent picture of life in Cambridge at that time is drawn by Howells in *Literary Friends and Acquaintance*. Longfellow, Hawthorne, Emerson, Thoreau, Lowell, Holmes, Sumner, Felton, Agassiz, Norton, Parkman, Prescott, Motley, Higginson, Dana, Channing, — here within a circle of a few miles was gathered the most remarkable body of literary men that this country has ever known.

a living, was regarded by him as a burden; and he resigned it gladly (1854) with the thought that now would the expectation of years be realized and leisure inspire him to write his masterpiece. The hope was vain; for his best work — with the possible exception of *Hiawatha* (1855), which was written in a joyous vacation spirit — had been done while he was a teacher, and not until comparatively late in life did his verse show any noticeable gain in quality. In his later work we shall often find a more finished expression or a greater depth of feeling, but his masterpiece (unless he regarded the *Tales of a Wayside Inn* in that light) was never written.

For seven happy years Longfellow gave himself up to leisure, his poetry meanwhile, though written in the prime of life, showing a **Leisure and** steady decline in creative vigor.. Then a frightful accident **Tragedy** occurred; his wife's dress caught fire, and she was burned to death even while he made frantic efforts to extinguish the flames. His ideal happiness, the blessing of years, was suddenly gone, blown out like a candle; but the tragedy which came with anguish in one hand carried in the other a boundless sympathy. The world, which had known Longfellow only as a poet, now learned to know him as a man, — one who shared its grief, who bore affliction in silence, and who worked on steadily with the determination of keeping himself from unmanly brooding and melancholy.[1] People came from far and near to speak their appreciation of his life and work; his house, like that of Tennyson, became the object of thousands of pilgrimages from all parts of Europe and America. Unlike the English poet, he received all visitors kindly, and seemed to rejoice in the thought that he had entered so helpfully into the life of men. The most welcome guests of all, however, were the children, who came in ever-increasing numbers to make a festival of the poet's birthday.

The influence of these two types of visitors is reflected in many of Longfellow's later poems, which are youthful, almost childlike in spirit, but which have a depth and tenderness of sympathy that come only from knowing both the joy and the sorrow of humanity. He passed away (1882) soon after his seventy-fifth birthday had been celebrated by many little friends in his home, and by the schools throughout the country, the spirit of the festival being enshrined in Whittier's tribute, "The Poet and the Children." The closing stanza of "The Bells of

[1] See the first sonnet on "The Divine Comedy," and "The Cross of Snow." The latter poem seemed to Longfellow too sacred for publication. It was found after his death among his private papers.

San Blas," composed soon after this last birthday, is noteworthy here in view of the fact that it was Longfellow's last written word:

> O bells of San Blas, in vain
> Ye call back the Past again!
>   The Past is deaf to your prayer;
> Out of the shadows of night
> The world rolls into light;
>   It is daybreak everywhere.

Earlier Works. The first or experimental period [1] of Longfellow's work began with the " Earlier Poems " of the little volume called *Voices of the Night* (1839), and ended with *The Waif, A Collection of Poems* (1845). During these early years two significant traits appear. First, Longfellow gave serious thought to his work as an educator, not simply of college boys but of the whole American people. To this end he made numerous translations of the best poems of other lands, and laboriously edited *The Poets and Poetry of Europe* (1845). It is easy for a modern scholar to criticize this work as superficial; the point to remember is that, when it appeared, very little was known here of foreign languages or letters, and that Longfellow was a pioneer in the unexplored field of Italian, French, Spanish, German and Scandinavian literatures.

A second trait of this early period was Longfellow's native power to reach the heart or conscience of his countrymen, in such **Quality of** artless poems as "The Village Blacksmith," "The **Early Poems** Old Clock on the Stairs," "Excelsior," and many others, each containing a moral or an allegory. It is the prerogative of critics to show that these poems are imitative, that their imagery is faulty and their moralizing too pronounced. Such criticism, though true enough, is unimportant. The significant

---

[1] We shall classify Longfellow's works according to periods, leaving the student to group his favorite poems according to type. We suggest the following, simply as a model for such classification: (1) Lyrics, such as " A Psalm of Life," " Resignation," etc.; (2) Ballads and Short Narrative Poems, such as " A Skeleton in Armor " and " Paul Revere's Ride "; (3) Long Narrative Poems, such as *Evangeline* and *Hiawatha*, the latter being a kind of epic narrative; (4) Dramatic works, such as *The Spanish Student*: and (5) Translations.

things are : that these poems of simple and genuine feeling found a welcome in thousands of homes where poetry was needed ; that in emphasizing the ethical element Longfellow was a true reflection of his age and of the sentiment of people trained in the Puritan school ; and that his verse always moved in the deep undercurrent of American life. Thus when "A Psalm of Life" appeared anonymously in the *Knickerbocker Magazine* (1838) it became almost immediately a national poem ; its unknown author was praised from one end of the country to the other for expressing the spirit of his age, " the very heartbeat of the American conscience." [1] That was nearly three quarters of a century ago, and America still reads many of the early poems, and responds as of old to their elemental sincerity.

Other popular works of Longfellow's early period, his attempts at dramatic poetry, at prose sketches and fiction — - for he was **Experimental Works** constantly experimenting — are now seldom read ; yet they well repay the examination of one who would appreciate the poet's strength and his limitation. The *Poems on Slavery* (1842) were a reflection of Longfellow's view of a matter which then kept North and South in a turmoil. Unfortunately he dealt with his subject, as he dealt with old German legends, in a sentimental way; and at that time the country was in no mood for a legendary treatment of slavery. *The Spanish Student* (1843), a long dramatic poem, reads fairly well and furnishes an occasional line or little song to remember ; but the work as a whole is lacking in action, in character drawing and in dramatic interest. Longfellow's first volume, *Outre Mer* (1835), is a series of sketches of travel, and suffers by comparison with the *Sketch Book*, on which it was evidently modeled. *Hyperion* (1839) is an inartistic but mildly interesting combination of guidebook and sentimental romance, the story serving as a thread on which

[1] Many enthusiastic references to " A Psalm of Life " are found in the magazines and newspapers of the period. Whittier wrote, " We know not who the author may be, but he or she is no common man or woman. These nine, simple verses are worth more than all the dreams of Shelley and Keats and Wordsworth. They are alive and vigorous with the spirit of the day in which we live, — the moral steam-enginery of an age of action."

to hang various local legends and description of scenery. It was once very popular, and is still occasionally read by those who would attain a romantic state of mind when traveling on the Rhine.[1]

Middle Period. All these experimental works may be regarded as a prelude to the harmony of Longfellow's middle period, which includes the fifteen years from 1845 to 1860. During this time he wrote some of his best poems of childhood ; in *The Seaside and the Fireside* (1849) he strengthened his hold upon the heart of the nation ; he made one magnificent appeal to American patriotism in " The Building of the Ship " ; and in such poems as " The Fire of Driftwood " and " The Lighthouse " he gave us some of our best lyrics of the sea. He wrote also *Evangeline, The Courtship of Miles Standish, Hiawatha*, and a part of the *Tales of a Wayside Inn*, — which are all of such importance that we must examine them more closely to find the secret of their popularity.

In the opinion of many readers, Longfellow reached the climax of his power in *Evangeline, A Tale of Acadie* (1847).[2] When **Evangeline** the poem first appeared Poe and the critics fell upon it savagely, while a multitude of uncritical people welcomed it with enthusiasm. After more than half a century we still read it with undiminished pleasure, and the reasons for our enjoyment are not far to seek. It is, first of all, a charming story,[3] unlike anything else in our literature ; and its ideals of faith, love and heroism are such as must always make a deep impression upon all normal hearts. Again, Longfellow told his

[1] Ten years later Longfellow wrote another romance, laying the scene in his own country. This was *Kavanagh* (1849), a "novel of character and manners." It was better than *Hyperion*, and was praised by Emerson and Hawthorne ; but it was soon forgotten.

[2] For the historical matter of the poem, relating to the expulsion of the Acadians, we must refer the reader to the American histories. Longfellow owes his story to the generosity of Hawthorne, who had intended to use it as the basis of a romance. See Samuel Longfellow's *Life of Longfellow* (II, 70) and Hawthorne's *American Note Book* (I, 203). There is a large literature on the subject ; but the student, after reading the poem itself, may be satisfied with Porter's *Evangeline : the Place, the Story and the Poem* (1882).

[3] Some readers may object to the occasional sentimentality of *Evangeline*. As there are several points of resemblance between this work and Goethe's *Hermann und Dorothea*, it is probable that Longfellow was influenced by the sentimentality of the German poet.

THE PARISH PRIEST

From "Evangeline," edition of 1882. Engraved by F. O. C. Darley; courtesy of Houghton Mifflin Company

story in a sympathetic way, and gave added pleasure by using a new meter, the dactylic hexameter.[1] On this score also the critics were emphatic, declaring that Longfellow did not and could not use classic hexameters ; but most readers found these " brimming, slow-moving, soul-satisfying lines " very pleasant, and well adapted to the kind of tale that the poet was telling. The characters of the poem are, on the whole, the best that Longfellow has portrayed. Evangeline, Gabriel, Benedict, stout Basil the blacksmith, gentle Father Felician, — here are men and women such as we find, not in the street, to be sure, but in some old romance, or in the dear memories of childhood. Altogether *Evangeline* is a delicate and childlike idyl, and again the American people showed good literary taste in claiming it for their own.

In *The Courtship of Miles Standish* (1858) Longfellow produced another American idyl, and repeated, in the fainter tones **Miles** of an echo, his popular success. He repeated also **Standish** his hexameters ; but of these we must confess that they are far below the standard set in *Evangeline*, and often go halt or lame in measures that are neither prose nor poetry. The whole story hangs on two remarks of Colonial characters which are fairly well authenticated.[2] The first is from the lips of Miles Standish, who declares :

That 's what I always say ; if you want a thing to be well done
You must do it yourself, you must not leave it to others.

[1] By " hexameter " is meant that each line has six feet or measures. A dactyl is a measure having one long and two short syllables, the first being accented. The student will appreciate the meter by reading the opening passage of *Evangeline*, strongly emphasizing the beat or accent, and using this exercise as a preparation for the musical reading of Virgil's *Æneid*. Many critics are doubtful whether this meter can be successfully used in English. It is seen at its best in the flexible Greek language ; and those who object to its present use do so on the ground that it cannot be copied in any language having the fixed accents of English. For a discussion of the measure in general, see Matthew Arnold's essay " On Translating Homer." For Longfellow's use of the measure, see Stedman's *Poets of America*, pp. 195–201.

[2] For his scant knowledge of Colonial life Longfellow seems to have depended upon Elliott's *History of New England*. For his local scenes he depended, as in *Evangeline*, upon his own imagination. Plymouth was at his door, and Acadia at the end of a pleasant journey ; yet Longfellow did not take the trouble to become acquainted with either place before writing his poems.

Then he shows his masculine consistency by sending another (John Alden) on the very important errand of asking the most beautiful of Pilgrim maidens to become his wife. The second remark comes roguishly from Priscilla herself :

> But as he warmed and glowed, in his simple and eloquent language,
> Quite forgetful of self, and full of the praise of his rival,
> Archly the maiden smiled, and, with eyes overrunning with laughter,
> Said, in a tremulous voice, " Why don't you speak for yourself. John ? "

About these two remarks, and the story which they suggest, Longfellow gathers a series of pictures of the Pilgrims, all colored by his own humor and sympathy. The poem is far from being a correct or adequate portrayal of pioneer life ; but it is wholesome and interesting, and has probably led more people to Plymouth Rock than have all the histories of the period.

In *The Song of Hiawatha* (1855) our poet made an entirely new departure, and the joyous spirit of it may be inferred from his journal.[1] Never was a poet more occupied and delighted with his own measures ; never did critics pounce more hawklike upon a work to rend it ; and never did a whole people more gladly accept and welcome a literary gift in the same childlike spirit in which it was offered. As *Hiawatha*, with its simple rhythm and endless repetitions, is a poem which any child can enjoy and which few men like to analyze, we leave it with the reader, repeating only the invitation :

Hiawatha

> Ye who, love a nation's legends,
> Love the ballads of a people,
> That like voices from afar off
> Call to us to pause and listen,
> Speak in tones so plain and childlike,
> Scarcely can the ear distinguish
> Whether they are sung or spoken, —
> Listen to this Indian Legend,
> To this Song of Hiawatha!

[1] " Hiawatha occupies and delights me," he writes enthusiastically. " Have I no misgivings about it ? Yes, sometimes. Then the theme seizes me and hurries me away, and they vanish." (See the *Journal*, October 19, 1854 ; or Samuel Longfellow's *Life of Longfellow*, II, 277.)

We must note, however, this paradox in passing : that *Hiawatha* was a strikingly original poem, by an author who showed little or no originality in either the form or content of his verse. The central figure, Hiawatha, for instance, had been known for years as a primitive folk-hero, a kind of Prometheus, Beowulf, Faust and Menabozo all in one. He was the teacher and defender of his people ; he had human and superhuman attributes ; he knew medicine, magic, and all the secrets of nature ; and he talked with all the birds as with his friends. Around this picturesque hero had gathered a host of legends and traditions, the material for a splendid epic ; yet all this poetic material lay neglected, waiting for some man to open his eyes and see it. Longfellow's originality consists, therefore, like that of most geniuses, in picking up what others had passed by, — much as Malory collected the *Morte D'Arthur*, and Sturluson the wonderful Scandinavian *Edda*. The material for *Hiawatha* came largely from Schoolcraft's records of the Ojibway Indians, and the form was copied from the Finnish epic of the *Kalevala*.[1]

As the latter poem suggested the rhythm, and possibly also some minor details, of *Hiawatha*, we submit a selection describing the singing of the hero Lemminkainen :

> Then began the reckless minstrel
> To intone his wizard sayings ;
> Sang he alders to the waysides,
> Sang he oaks upon the mountains,
> On the oak trees sang he branches,
> On each branch he sang an acorn,
> On the acorns golden rollers,
> On each roller sang a cuckoo ;
> Then began the cuckoos calling,
> Gold from every throat came streaming ;
> Copper fell from every feather,

---

[1] The *Kalevala* — meaning, like the Norse *Valhalla* "the abode of heroes" — is the national epic of Finland, and is among the five or six great epics of the world. It consists of over twenty thousand verses, in fifty runes or books. It owes its preservation and present form largely to the labors of Elias Loennrott (1802–1884). The selection which we quote for comparison is taken from Crawford's translation.

And each wing emitted silver,
Filled the isle with precious metals.

Sang again young Lemminkainen,
Conjured on, and sang and chanted,
Sang to precious stones the seasands,
Sang the stones to pearls resplendent,
Robed the groves in iridescence,
Sang the island full of flowers,
Many colored as the rainbow.

Sang again the magic minstrel,
In the court a well he conjured,
On the well a golden cover,
On the lid a silver dipper,
That the boys might drink the water,
That the maids might lave their eyelids.
On the plains he conjured lakelets,
Sang the duck upon the waters,
Golden-cheeked and silver-headed,
Sang the feet from shining copper.
And the island maidens wondered,
Stood entranced at Ahti's wisdom,
At the songs of Lemminkainen,
At the hero's magic power.

And here, for comparison, is a passage from *Hiawatha*, which
portrays Chibiabos the musician:

From the hollow reeds he fashioned
Flutes so musical and mellow,
That the brook, the Sebowisha,
Ceased to murmur in the woodland,
That the wood-birds ceased from singing,
And the squirrel, Adjidaumo,
Ceased his chatter in the oak-tree,
And the rabbit, the Wabasso,
Sat upright to look and listen.
Yes, the brook, the Sebowisha,
Pausing, said, " O Chibiabos,
Teach my waves to flow in music,
Softly as your words in singing ! " . . .
Yes, the robin, the Opechee,
Joyous, said, " O Chibiabos,

> Teach me tones as sweet and tender,
> Teach me songs as full of sadness ! " . . .
>   All the many sounds of nature
> Borrowed sweetness from his singing;
> All the hearts of men were softened
> By the pathos of his music ;
> For he sang of peace and freedom,
> Sang of beauty, love, and longing;
> Sang of death, and life undying
> In the Islands of the Blessed,
> In the kingdom of Ponemah,
> In the land of the Hereafter.

Later Period. The third period of Longfellow's work is included between the tragic loss of his wife (1861) and his death in 1882. All the work of this period speaks of growth, of broadened sympathy, of deeper feeling, of more artistic expression. In the earlier work one is sometimes repelled by the sentimental imagery (in such poems as " The Reaper and the Flowers," for instance) and is often wearied by the diffuse expression, the needless repetition of his narrative poems. In his later work, especially in his sonnets, one is rarely disappointed. The feeling is deep and true, the expression condensed, the imagery appropriate ; and we finish the reading of " Nature," " Milton," "Three Friends," "Divina Commedia "and "Giotto's Tower," with the thought that these are among the best sonnets in our language.

Another interesting characteristic of Longfellow's later work is that he returns to his early experiments. He writes new sonnets, lyrics, ballads, dramas ; he makes a famous translation of one of the great books of the world, the *Divine Comedy* of Dante ; when an " occasional " poem is called for, he answers with " The Hanging of the Crane " or " Morituri Salutamus ; [1]

---

[1] "The Hanging of the Crane " (1867) was written for the poet T. B. Aldrich. It celebrates an old Colonial custom, which led neighbors to hang a crane over the fireplace of a young married couple who were setting up housekeeping. " Morituri Salutamus " (1874), celebrating the fiftieth anniversary of Longfellow's class at Bowdoin, is a noble piece of work, on the whole the best occasional poem that Longfellow wrote. The theme was suggested by Gérôme's painting of gladiators, under which was written " Ave Caesar . . . morituri te salutant."

and in the *Tales of a Wayside Inn* and *Christus, A Mystery*, he attempts two ambitious flights which are plainly beyond his powers. By all this varied work he kept his heart young and responsive; up to his last lyric, "The Bells of San Blas," he retained, like Tennyson, the ability to surprise and delight his readers.

In the first of his sonnets on the "Divina Commedia," Longfellow reveals his reason for spending years on the trans-**The Divine** lation of Dante's work. It was, in a word, to occupy **Comedy** his mind; to keep him from brooding over the tragedy of his wife's death. To say that this translation is an accurate and praiseworthy work is to do it scant justice. It was Longfellow's custom to invite friends to dinner once a week, and in the evening to read his translation line by line, giving close heed to the comments of Lowell, Norton, and any other scholars who gathered about his table.[1] The finished translation represents, therefore, not simply the work of a poet but also, in some degree, the judgment of men who had made a life study of Dante. To those who can appreciate the beauty of the *Divine Comedy* in the original, Longfellow's work will probably be disappointing. It is too literal for poetry, and it lacks the satisfying simplicity of Norton's prose translation. It seems to us, nevertheless, the best metrical version of Dante which has appeared in our language, and students will cherish it as an excellent introduction to the mind and work of the Italian master.

The general plan of the *Tales of a Wayside Inn* (1863–1873) is a very old one, and the work suffers by comparison with the **The Way-** *Canterbury Tales* of Chaucer, or with *The Earthly* **side Inn** *Paradise* of William Morris. Longfellow gathers his characters, who are his friends thinly disguised,[2] into the Red Horse Inn, at Sudbury; there before the open fire they

---

[1] A pleasant description of these gatherings is found in Howells's *Literary Friends and Acquaintance*.

[2] The poet of the *Wayside Inn* was T. W. Parsons; the student, Henry Wales; the theologian, Professor Treadwell; the musician, Ole Bull; the Spanish Jew, Israel Edrehi; the Sicilian, Professor Monti, — all of whom were well known in Cambridge.

tell their favorite stories, and the poet binds the tales together with preludes and interludes, in the manner of Chaucer. For his material Longfellow goes to many sources, to the Talmud, to medieval legends, to modern history; but in "The Birds of Killingworth" he shows originality by creating a poetic American legend. The most vigorous of the tales are included in the "Saga of King Olaf," a series of narratives borrowed from the *Heimskringla*,[1] reflecting the adventurous spirit of the Vikings. Among the best of the twenty-one other tales, which make up the three books of the *Wayside Inn*, are "Paul Revere's Ride," "The Bell of Atri," "The Legend Beautiful" and "King Robert of Sicily."

The most ambitious, and perhaps the least successful, of Longfellow's works was the dramatic poem *Christus, A Mystery*,

Christus over which he labored many years, publishing parts of the work at intervals, and giving it final form in 1872. The aim of this modern attempt at a mystery play was, in Longfellow's words, "to present the various aspects of Christendom in the Apostolic, Middle and Modern ages." The book is in three parts: first, "The Divine Tragedy," which is Longfellow's metrical version of the Gospel story; second, "The Golden Legend," in which he retells a medieval story that he found in Hartmann's *Der Arme Heinrich;* and third, "New England Tragedies," which are gloomy narratives adapted from Winthrop's *Journal* and other Colonial records. It is perhaps sufficient criticism to say that Longfellow was not at his best in dramatic poetry, and that "The Golden Legend," which has been widely translated into foreign languages, is the only part of *Christus* which repays the reading.

General Characteristics. We have already called attention to some of Longfellow's qualities; we have noted his elemental appeal to the heart and conscience, his understanding of the

---

[1] The *Heimskringla* (world's circle) is a history of Norse kings, some mythical, some real, written by the Icelander Snorri Sturluson (1178–1241). It is the most important prose work in old Norse literature.

American home, his service in broadening our literary culture. We have suggested also his habit of borrowing from other writers, — a weakness which will probably exclude him from ever being considered among the world's original poets.[1] As we review now his entire work, several qualities stand out prominently. The first of his literary virtues is that, like Chaucer, he knows how to tell a tale in an interesting way ; and the writer who can tell a tale or a ballad as Longfellow told the " Legend Beautiful " or " Paul Revere's Ride " is forever sure of an audience. Most long poems have short lives, as a rule, but *Hiawatha* and *Evangeline* show no signs of age after half a century. That they are still widely and eagerly read is an indication of Longfellow's remarkable narrative power. These long poems have rendered a triple service : they have given pleasure to millions of readers ; they have added to the store of the world's good poetry ; and by showing the poetic side of American history they have opened a mine of literary material, out of which future poets will surely bring other and greater treasures.

The second quality of Longfellow is his remarkable simplicity. Deep and true feeling is always simply expressed, and Longfellow is the poet of feeling rather than of thought,
Simplicity of sentiment rather than of reason. Unlike his contemporaries Emerson and Lowell, he seldom attempts profound or brilliant themes ; if he touches a great subject he does it in such a simple manner that a child can usually understand him. His sympathy also makes him wise in the ways of the human heart ; he understands its joy and sorrow, its elemental faith, its love of sentiment, its satisfaction in a tale or poem that ends in harmony with the moral nature of man. With the great problems or tragedies of humanity Longfellow has little or

[1] Longfellow's imagination was not vigorous ; he depended on books for his inspiration, and in consequence there is a second-hand quality in many of his works. Thus, *Hiawatha* followed Schoolcraft and the *Kalevala* too closely ; *Evangeline* was influenced by Goethe's *Hermann und Dorothea ; Tales of a Wayside Inn* by the *Canterbury Tales ;* " The Belfry of Bruges " by Tennyson's " Locksley Hall " ; " The Building of the Ship " by Schiller's " Song of the Bell " ; *The Spanish Student* by *La Gitanilla* of Cervantes, etc.

nothing to do; he keeps close to common experience, and is well content with the place he holds as the laureate of the home and of all homely virtues. This simplicity, which appeals to the masses of men, is the more remarkable in view of his scholarly interests and associates, and of his long training as a teacher of literature.

A third quality of Longfellow is suggested by the frequent, and sometimes disparaging, criticism that he is "the poet of the commonplace." The title seems to us self-contradictory, for wherever the poet comes the commonplace vanishes away. It is his glorious function to give "beauty for ashes, the oil of joy for mourning, the garment of praise for the spirit of heaviness." Most of our poets have felt this strongly at times, and are all, in varying degrees, transformers of the commonplace. Bryant and Emerson ennoble it; Lanier reveals its music, and Whittier its spiritual meaning; Longfellow makes it always radiant and beautiful. From the homely material of common life he produced the glamor of poetry. Out of a few homespun threads he wove his cloth of gold, and used it not for the adornment of princes but for the common table, around which the American family gathers when the day's work is done. We honor him, therefore, as "our household poet," and of all the gifts which fortune brought him we cherish these two : that the children celebrate his birthday; and that his bust stands, where England honors her great dead, in the Poets' Corner of Westminster Abbey. The one symbolizes his hold on the human heart, the other his secure fame among all English-speaking people.

JOHN GREENLEAF WHITTIER (1807–1892)

If you would appreciate the homelike quality of Whittier's life and work, study a single scene in *Snow Bound*. The place is the solitary old farmhouse; the time, dusk of a winter evening. Outside, the night draws its shadowy curtain over a frozen landscape; within, safe from storm and cold in the shelter of the familiar kitchen, children and parents gather about the hearthstone to watch the fire lighted:

> Then, hovering near,
> We watched the first red blaze appear,
> Heard the sharp crackle, caught the gleam
> On whitewashed wall and sagging beam,
> Until the old, rude-furnished room
> Burst, flower-like, into rosy bloom.

That ruddy blaze, reflected from contented human faces, is symbolical of Whittier's poetry. There is always something warm, hearty, wholesome about it, which makes us echo Isaiah's rapturous exclamation, " Aha, I am warm, I have seen the fire ! "

The same scene lets us at once into the deepest yet simplest secret of human life. Viewed from without, the Whittier farmhouse seems a cheerless habitation; its inmates appear as an ordinary New England family of the period, slow of speech, reserved in manner, and of an appearance suggesting the stern discipline rather than the joy of living. When we study them within, however, by the light of the fire and the illumination of the poet's lines, we discover presently that these hard-working people are of noble breed; that they are wealthy also, having what St. John and St. Paul have named as the greatest of all possessions. It is love which holds them together, love which sends them out to toil, and "love's contentment more than wealth" which transfigures their plain faces in the firelight. And a life that is love-governed has already found its Paradise; it can never again seem poor or commonplace.

Another suggestion from the fire in *Snow Bound* is the broad humanity of Whittier's work. As all men, being at heart primitive, love an open fire and drop all false distinctions when they gather about it, so do they appreciate the plain manhood and womanhood which Whittier's fire reveals. He is called, and justly, the most intensely local of our poets. He lived and died in a corner of New England; it is her people, her virtues and traditions, her rivers and hills that are pictured in his poetry. But he who knows the heart of New England knows also the heart of Florida and California; and it is the fine heart-quality of Whittier that makes him universal.

How different he is from others of that group of writers who made his age the most splendid in our literary history! They

KITCHEN AND HEARTH IN WHITTIER'S HOUSE AT HAVERHILL

are men of culture, of travel, of the college and the great world of books; he is always the farmer's boy, the child of the soil, sharing the work and the reward of those who suffer and endure. He is different also from his people and ancestors. Some of them were Puritans; but he has the humor, the broad tolerance which the Puritans lacked. Others of his ancestors were Quakers; but while Quakers are proverbially prosperous, he must toil and save and deny himself. They are silent and peaceful; he appears in a crisis as spokesman for a militant party that set the whole country in a turmoil.

Compared
with Other
Poets

While he shows the fine spirit of his contemporaries, the rugged nobility of his ancestors, Whittier still differs from them all, not in kind but in degree ; he has more of our common humanity ; he lives nearer to the soil, nearer to the hearts of men. And for this reason we are inclined to regard him, as Scotchmen regard Burns, as the most typical of our national poets. Others undoubtedly wrote more finished poems, but none more finely revealed the rugged spirit of American manhood.

Life. In an old farmhouse in the Merrimac valley, where every east wind brought the sound and smell of the sea, our poet was born **The Old** in 1807. Biographers have called attention to the isola- **Homestead** tion of the Whittier farm in East Haverhill, to the hardship of the poet's early life and the barrenness of his education ; but there was one means of culture, one inspiration to poetry, which has been overlooked, and this is indicated by the old house itself. It was planned by one of Whittier's ancestors in 1688, when only a few settlers had gained foothold on the Atlantic coast, and when the great West was a silent wilderness. It was built, as houses were in those days, about a great square fireplace ; and before its open blaze, kindled like sacred vestal flames from older fires that were never suffered to die out, generations of American children had warmed themselves and listened in turn to the story of their country. The struggles of the pioneers, the expansion of the Colonies, the French and Indian wars, the coming of Washington, the heroism and sacrifice of the Revolution, the founding of the American nation, — all these were a part of family tradition in the days of few books, when young people learned history by their own firesides, in

> Old homesteads sacred to all that can
> Gladden or sadden the heart of man ;
> Over whose thresholds of oak and stone
> Life and Death have come and gone.[1]

In the Vedas, the old sacred books of India, the hearth is the symbol not only of family life but of nationality ; and in our own land practically all our national heroes learned to love their country before the open fires of home.

---

[1] From " The Prophecy of Samuel Sewall." In this poem, beginning at line 88, there is a fine description of the landscape which Whittier saw as a boy, a hint also of the strong love of home and country which inspires all his verse.

In such a homestead, ennobled by national tradition, made sacred by the mystery of life and death, Whittier passed all his formative **The Boy** years. During the " open " seasons he worked hard on **Whittier** the farm ; in the winter he trudged daily to the crude district school. So far he was like the great majority of American boys at that time, and he resembled them also in this, — that he had a boy's endless capacity for enjoyment, for getting fun out of work, for finding a romance on every path, an adventure on every highway. Thus his " Barefoot Boy," " In School Days," " My Playmate " and a score of similar poems reflect the glamor rather than the discomfort of old-time school life.[1] Writing of his boyhood he says :

" I found about equal satisfaction in an old rural home, with the shifting panorama of the seasons, in reading the few books within my reach, and dreaming of something wonderful and grand somewhere in the future. . . . I felt secure of my mother's love, and dreamed of losing nothing and gaining much."

Some biographers, viewing the poet's youth, note only its dreariness, its monotony, its grinding toil ; but in this picture of a boy " secure of his mother's love," and " dreaming of something wonderful and grand somewhere in the future," we see ourselves as we were in boyhood's golden days, and we understand Whittier's power to touch a man's heart by recalling the faith and the romance of his childhood.

A strong poetic talent which slumbered in Whittier was awakened when he first heard " Bonnie Doon " and " Highland Mary " sung **First Poems** by a wandering Scotchman. Later an itinerant schoolmaster — one Joshua Coffin, with the flavor of Nantucket in his name and ways — brought a copy of Burns to the house, and Whittier read it eagerly. He tells us later :

" This book was about the first poetry I had ever read — with the exception of that of the Bible, of which I had always been a close student — and it had a lasting influence upon me. I began to make rhymes myself. . . . I lived a sort of dual life, in a world of fancy as well as in the world of plain matter of fact."

Some of these " rhymes " were sent by Whittier's sister to the Newburyport *Free Press*, then edited by William Lloyd Garrison ;

---

[1] Glimpses of the same happy characteristics are found in Whittier's prose works. See, for instance, " Yankee Gypsies," " The Fish I Did n't Catch," " My Summer with Dr. Singletary," etc.

and presently this famous agitator rode over to see his new contributor. Finding not the mature poet he expected but a shy country lad, he stirred Whittier's ambition by praising his verses and urging an education. This was the beginning of a friendship that weathered all the storms of the abolition movement, in which these two men were leaders. From one of the farm hands Whittier learned to make slippers, and by this homely craft he supported himself for two terms in the Haverhill Academy. Then, at twenty-two, he went to Boston and found work on a weekly newspaper. His peaceful struggle with nature was ended; his grapple with the big world had begun.

During the next few years Whittier was plainly trying to find himself. He edited one newspaper after another, but in every case was obliged to give up the work because of illness, or because his labor was needed on the farm at home. Then he entered politics, won immediate favor with leaders and voters, and would probably have been elected to Congress had his age permitted. He also wrote much poetry; over a hundred of his effusions, as they were then called, were printed in the Haverhill *Gazette* alone. So he wavered from newspaper to farm, from politics to poetry, till the crisis came in 1833, when Garrison, who was stirring up a hornets' nest with his *Liberator*, urged Whittier to come out and join the abolitionists.

At that time Garrison and his followers were a small band of zealous reformers, whose radical principles and uncompromising **The Abolition** methods had aroused general fear and hostility. North **Movement** and South, Church, State and College were all against them, regarding them as dangerous fanatics; and for a man to join their ranks in those early days was to become an outcast. Whittier knew this perfectly, and through anxious days and sleepless nights counted the cost of his decision before he made it. Then, in June, 1833, he published his "Justice and Expediency." One who reads it even now finds something moving and heroic in this little pamphlet, which placed Whittier definitely with a despised minority.

The next thirty years carried Whittier through that terrible period of agitation and misunderstanding which culminated in the Civil War. **The Poet of** We have no mind to follow him; to see him mobbed **a Party** and stoned in cities bearing the lovely names of Concord and Philadelphia; to examine his ringing political verses, which reflect a sectional rather than a national interest, a fighting rather than a Quaker spirit. We note only two things: that his heroic decision destroyed both his political and his literary prospects, for no office was open to him and no magazine would publish his work; and that his devotion to what he believed to be right suggests the sacrifice of Milton when he abandoned his poetry to throw himself into the struggle for English liberty.[1] The magnificent "Laus Deo" (1865), a song of exultation following the Constitutional amendment prohibiting slavery, is a fitting close to this long period of storm and stress.

The last period of Whittier's life, from the close of the Civil War to his death in 1892, is one of unbroken calm. By his political verse he had roused a fighting spirit in the nation; but when the war came it saddened and sobered him. After the storm had passed he turned with relief to the quiet homes of the land, and to the eternal verities that are often forgotten in the time of turmoil:

> The roll of drums and the bugle's wailing
>   Vex the air of our vales no more;
> The spear is beaten to hooks of pruning,
>   The share is the sword the soldier wore!
>
> Sing soft, sing low, our lowland river,
>   Under thy banks of laurel bloom;
> Softly and sweet, as the hour beseemeth,
>   Sing us the songs of peace and home.[2]

In this new and chastened spirit Whittier wrote his *Snow Bound* (1866). This was his first notable success, after nearly fifty years of writing, and it brought two important results: it placed Whittier in the front rank of our national poets; and it brought enough financial reward to make an end of the poverty and anxiety which had been his portion for so many years. For the rest of his days he lived comfortably in a little white house at Amesbury,[3] presided over by his gentle niece, Elizabeth. Hitherto he had always written in a hurry; now he took leisure to improve and polish his verse, and his *Tent on the Beach* (1867), *Among the Hills* (1869), indeed all his works published after his threescore years, are incomparably better than those of his youth and vigorous manhood. In the early days he had been the voice of a small party; now he spoke for

The Poet of the People

---

[1] Lowell says of Whittier at this time, "He has Scaevola-like sacrificed on the altar of duty that right hand which might have made him acknowledged as the most passionate lyrist of his day." Whittier has described himself, and the loss of his cherished dreams, in the Prelude to *The Tent on the Beach*.

[2] From "Revisited," a song to the Merrimac (1865).

[3] The old Whittier farm, celebrated in *Snow Bound*, proved too much for the poet's strength, and was sold in 1836.

the whole American people, recalling to them with joy their love of home, their pride in a united country, their faith in a common Father. Criticism is silent before these calm, trustful expressions of an old man, whose life had been noble, whose heart was still the heart of a little child, and in whose presence men remembered the injunction:

"Whatsoever things are true, . . . whatsoever things are pure, whatsoever things are lovely . . . think on these things."

Whittier's Poetry. Whittier is often called the New England poet, but his work, like its symbol the hearthfire, belongs to no corner of the earth exclusively. As Washington is no longer "the Virginian," or Lincoln "the Kentuckian," so the poet who in *Snow Bound* reveals the warm heart of an American household, whose ballads recall the virtue and heroism of American pioneers, and whose religious lyrics express the faith and hope of American manhood, is no

JOHN GREENLEAF WHITTIER

longer a local but a national possession. Happily "The Barefoot Boy" is not confined to Haverhill, nor is "The Eternal Goodness" bounded on the north by Vermont and on the east by the Atlantic, as is a certain state described in the geographies. It broadens our critical horizon to read "Our Country," with its patriotic appeal that knows no sectional limits, or to sing the song of "The Kansas Emigrants,"

> We cross the prairie as of old
>   The Pilgrims crossed the sea,
> To make the West, as they the East,
>   The homestead of the free!

In a word, we shall never understand Whittier till we get rid of local pride and prejudice, and regard him steadily as the poet of the American people.

With the exception of certain immature works, such as *Mogg Megone*, in the field of Indian tradition, there is a remarkable unity in all of Whittier's poetry. The same spirit illumines it throughout, and Holmes was right when he declared that a single strain of a poem was enough to indicate whether or not Whittier had written it.[1] It is largely, therefore, for the sake of convenience that his works are grouped in classes called Reform Poems, Ballads and Legendary Pieces, and Lyrics of Home, Nature, and Religion. To these we add *Snow Bound* and *The Tent on the Beach*, which are individual enough to deserve separate classification.

Reform Poems. Of the reform poems, which Whittier gathered into a volume called *Voices of Freedom* (1846), perhaps the best that can be said is, "They had their day and ceased to be." They served for a time as battle cries[2] of the antislavery party, but that Whittier regretted them became increasingly evident in his later years. Even while writing them, amid the smoke and dust of conflict, he felt the sorrow of Milton at using, or misusing, his poetic talent to serve a political party.[3]

There are, however, a few of these reform poems that seem to us worthy of remembrance. One is the "Laus Deo," which we have mentioned; another is "Ichabod," that terrible rebuke administered to Webster after his Seventh of March speech, when many believed that he had been false to the people who had elected him. No other poem of our literature can approach

---

[1] See Holmes, "For Whittier's Seventieth Birthday," December 17, 1877.

[2] Though he was a Quaker, and opposed to war, the soldier blood of an unknown ancestor is evident in Whittier. He can hardly touch a subject of contention without showing the martial spirit, without suggesting in his ringing lines the waving of flags and the march of infantry. Note, for instance, "Faneuil Hall," "Song of the Free," "Texas" and "The Pine Tree" among the reform poems, and "Barclay of Ury" among the ballads.

[3] This appears in his letters, and an indication of it is found in the Prelude to *The Tent on the Beach*. See the part beginning, "And one there was, a dreamer born."

this in its powerful expression of the mingled scorn and grief of a people betrayed by its trusted leaders. In fairness we must add that this widely read poem, though of remarkable literary merit, was fundamentally unjust ; that Whittier sadly misjudged the spirit and purpose of Webster,[1] just as Browning in " The Lost Leader " misjudged the character and motive of Words-worth. " Ichabod " is valuable, therefore, only as we disassociate it from the man whom it condemns and from the event which gave it birth.

Ballads and Legendary Poems. As a ballad writer Whittier has no equal among American poets. One reason for his su-premacy in this field is that he evidently had a better knowledge of early American life than any other literary man of his age. As a child he listened eagerly to the legends and traditions of his country ; as a man he read and studied our earliest records, and so entered deeply into the spirit of the pioneers. Add to his knowledge and sympathy an intense feeling, an ability to grasp a dramatic situation, a rare gift of speaking in verse as spontaneously as a bird sings, and you have a list of the qualities that go to make an ideal ballad writer. Not only does Whittier tell his story rapidly, dramatically, as a ballad should be told ; he adds to the action the very life and feeling of an age long past.[2]

All the strange phases of that age are reproduced in Whittier's verse : its superstition in " The Garrison of Cape Ann " and " Cobbler Keezar's Vision " ; its view of witchcraft in " Mabel Martin " and " The Witch of Wenham " ; its antipathy to Quakers (a tender subject with Whittier) in " Cassandra South-wick " and " How the Women went from Dover " ; its border heroism in " The Ranger " and " Mary Garvin." There are

---

[1] In a later poem, "The Lost Occasion" (1880), Whittier attempted to do tardy justice to Webster. By that time he began to realize that Webster was probably right, and that his policy of compromise would have led eventually to peaceful emancipation. See Carpenter's *Whittier*, p. 221.

[2] This refers only to poems of his own people. His narrative poems on Indian sub-jects, " Pentucket," " The Funeral Tree," etc., are of inferior quality. In his first attempt in this field, the melodramatic " Bridal of Pennacook," Whittier was perhaps too much influenced by Scott's border ballads.

many others, grave or gay, treating of old Colonial life, such as "Amy Wentworth," "The Witch's Daughter," "Skipper Ireson's Ride," "The Prophecy of Samuel Sewall," "Nauhaught, the Deacon," and fine old "Abraham Davenport." These are but a suggestion of Whittier's variety, of his mastery of the ballad in his own familiar field ; and we must not forget "The Pipes at Lucknow," reflecting a dramatic incident in the Sepoy Rebellion, or "Barbara Frietchie," the best-known ballad of a mighty conflict.

Poems of Home, Nature, and Religion. In this large class of Whittier's works the first place must be given to certain idyls or pastorals, that is, simple descriptive poems treating of country scenes and the joys and sorrows of rural people. Here, for instance, is the well-known "Maud Muller," rather crudely done, to be sure, as if a schoolboy had written it, but very tender, very true in its feeling, and with a vague, immeasurable regret such as Lowell reflected in the lines :

> Old loves, old aspirations and old dreams,
> More beautiful for being old and gone.

In the same class, and more beautifully finished, are "The Barefoot Boy," "In School Days," "My Playmate," "Telling the Bees," and the love lyric, the sweetest that Whittier ever wrote, in the second part of "A Sea Dream." Such exquisite idyls are not to be analyzed like a botanical specimen ; they are to be known and cherished, as we cherish the first violets.

Though nature is always present and always inspiring in Whittier's verse, he seldom devoted a poem to any natural object, and the explanation is simple. Unlike Bryant, who loved nature for her own sake, and to whom a flower or a forest was an ample subject, Whittier regarded nature as a background for the more interesting drama of human life. He was a careful and accurate observer ; his descriptions of sea and shore, of storm and calm, of singing river and silent hills, are unsurpassed in our literature ; but these are always as the frame of a picture, emphasizing the

Nature in Whittier's Verse

central human figure and the play of human emotion. In the swinging lines of "Hampton Beach," for example, we are brought face to face with the open sea; we feel its salt wind in our faces, its tumult in our hearts; but our interest is strongly centered in the man whose eyes brighten and whose soul expands to the call of the deep:

> Good-by to Pain and Care! I take
> Mine ease to-day:
> Here where these sunny waters break,
> And ripples this keen breeze, I shake
> All burdens from the heart, all weary thoughts away.
>
> I draw a freer breath, I seem
> Like all I see —
> Waves in the sun, the white-winged gleam
> Of sea birds in the slanting beam,
> And far-off sails which flit before the south-wind free.
>
> So when Time's veil shall fall asunder,
> The soul may know
> No fearful change, nor sudden wonder,
> Nor sink the weight of mystery under,
> But with the upward rise, and with the vastness grow.

So also in the longer nature poems, "Among the Hills," "Summer by the Lakeside," "Last Walk in Autumn," and in such little gems as "The Trailing Arbutus" and "A Day," — in all these we are interested not so much in nature as in the human soul that discerns nature's spiritual meaning or feels her benediction. Occasionally, as in "A Mystery" and "The Vanishers," Whittier shows a touch of mysticism, a mingling of two worlds, seen and unseen, which brings a new and welcome element to our poetry of nature.

The simple religious faith of Whittier found expression in many exquisite lyrics. Unlike the stirring reform poems, which **Lyrics of Faith** roused the enthusiasm of one party and the hostility of another, these gentle, trustful hymns win all sorts and conditions of men by appealing to their deepest instincts. Their spirit is not that of the theologian who reasons, but rather of the child who prays. Among a score of such poems, all excellent, it is perhaps advisable to begin with "Questions of Life," which reflects many of the problems that a thoughtful man finds in his own heart. Then, in "The Eternal Goodness," "A Hymn," "My Psalm," "My Soul and I," "Trust," and "Our Master" we may read Whittier's faithful answer to the questions of here and hereafter.

Two of Whittier's longer poems deserve special mention. *The Tent on the Beach* (1867) is a collection of stories in verse, **The Tent on the Beach** which may have been suggested by Longfellow's *Tales of a Wayside Inn*. The plan of the poem, to bring a few congenial people together and let each tell a story, is almost as ancient as literature itself. Longfellow borrowed the idea from Chaucer, who borrowed it from Boccaccio, who borrowed it from the Greeks, who borrowed it from the orientals, who found it no one knows where. The only way to give variety to such a plan is to make new scenes and characters; and Whittier attempts this by setting up a tent by the seashore. In this tent three friends, a poet, a traveler, and a publisher,[1] camp together, and in idle moments the publisher furnishes entertainment by reading manuscripts from his portfolio. There are eleven stories in the collection, nine of them from American sources, and the criticism has been well made that the prevailing tone is too heavy and somber, especially for a camping party. Two of the most interesting tales are "The Wreck of Rivermouth" and "Abraham Davenport"; but some of the best lines of the book are found in the Prelude, in the poet's portrait of himself, and especially in the descriptive passages which reflect the changing lights and shadows of the sea.

Snow Bound. Whittier's most characteristic poem is *Snow Bound: A Winter Idyl* (1866). The student should by all means read this imperishable work before he reads anything about it, and then analyze it if he can. For, after a thousand criticisms, there is still something beautiful and intangible in

---

[1] The publisher is James T. Fields, the traveler Bayard Taylor, and the poet Whittier.

Whittier's poem which escapes, like a memory of childhood, even as we try to define it. Hear these two excellent appreciations, which do not, however, quite explain our love for *Snow Bound:*

" Home is narrow as the ancestral walls, but as broad as humanity ; and here is a work both local and general, — of the kind which tends to make the whole world kin. It is a little sphere seen through the transparent soul and style of the simple poet." [1]

" He, this old man who had been an East Haverhill boy, describes *his* homestead, *his* well-sweep, *his* brook, *his* family circle, *his* schoolmaster, apparently intent on naught but the complete accuracy of his narrative, and lo ! such is his art that he has drawn the one perfect, imperishable picture of that bright old winter life in that strange clime. Diaries, journals, histories, biographies and autobiographies, with the same aim in view, are not all together so typical as this unique poem of less than a thousand lines." [2]

Instead of attempting another analysis, therefore, we simply note these five points, which have impressed us in reading the poem : the fine descriptions of the winter landscape, which serve merely as a frame for a human picture ; the tenderly drawn portraits of an American family in their old homestead ; the sadness inevitably associated with all memories of the past, as if the golden age were indeed always behind us ; the inspiring religious faith of the poet, deep and silent for the most part, but occasionally expressing itself in a little sermon, without which no work of Whittier would be complete ; and the universal quality of *Snow Bound*, which makes it a reflection of the thought and feeling not only of Whittier but of every man and woman who has sat and mused alone before an open fire.

The poem which won instant recognition in 1866 still leaves its impression of truth and beauty upon countless readers, and The Charm of the secret of its power is revealed when we study Snow Bound its origin. For nearly half a century Whittier had tried many forms of prose and poetry, but had never won any marked success ; he had been known chiefly as " the trumpeter " of a reform. Then, at sixty years of age, when the ballads of

[1] Richardson, *American Literature*, II, 183.
[2] Carpenter, *John Greenleaf Whittier*, p. 271.

olden times had been written, when the political battle had been fought and won, Whittier found himself again by the old fire-place. He was thinking of life, of its changing and changeless elements, and of loved ones — long since gone — who used to sit beside him, sharing the light of fire, the divine peace of home. And in that hour of tender, sacred memories something whispered, " Look in thy heart and write." Following his inspiration he wrote *Snow Bound*, and this picture of his own home was welcomed in thousands of other homes from one end of America to the other. The old poet of New England had found that all hearts were essentially like his own, sorrowing or rejoicing in the same things, and that in the human heart alone is found the gold of all true literature.

Prose Works. To most readers Whittier is simply the poet; his prose works are unknown even by name; yet his vigorous style and his interesting Colonial subjects might have won him a place among our writers had he never written a poem. His first book, *Legends of New England* (1831), was in prose. Fourteen years later he published *The Stranger in Lowell*, a series of sketches of life in an American manufacturing town in the early days.[1] Then followed at short intervals *The Supernaturalism of New England, Leaves from Margaret Smith's Journal, Old Portraits and Modern Sketches*, and *Literary Recreations*. Though generally neglected, these works contain some of the best pictures of early American life to be found in our literature. In *Margaret Smith's Journal*, for instance, Whittier creates the fictitious character of a visiting English woman, who vividly portrays the life and the leaders of the Old Bay Colony in the days of Cotton Mather. The portrayal is generally too somber, and is at times misleading; but in criticizing it we must remember that Whittier had a wide knowledge of his subject, and that the incidents of this imaginary journal are nearly all based upon authentic records.

[1] To those interested in industrial matters *The Stranger* is well worth reading. It should be read in connection with certain chapters of Lucy Larcom's *New England Girlhood*, which describe mill life in the same city (Lowell) during the same period.

General Criticism. In many ways Whittier seems to us the most intensely American of all our poets. He smacks of the soil; he epitomizes the nobility of plain human nature. Though life has outwardly changed since Whittier's day, many of us still live close to the soil; we still honor common life by giving it opportunity and raising it to our highest offices; and we still earn our bread by rather too much work, just as the poet did. We sympathize, therefore, with the elemental virtues and ideals that find expression in Whittier's poetry. We understand him because he is like ourselves. As an extreme instance, take his antislavery verses,— which are meaningless unless we remember that the country was facing a crisis and calling on its sons South and North to show their colors. They not only speak of Whittier's loyalty to conviction; they are in many ways splendidly typical of a nation that rouses itself to meet a new crisis with every passing generation, and that has little respect for the man who dreams or idles or worships mammon while some great human problem clamors for solution. So, though we no longer read the reform poems, we honor the American author who loved humanity more than literature and who sacrificed his personal ambition upon the altar of duty.

Manly Quality of Whittier

Again, in his religious poems Whittier is typical of a nation that has no state church, and that has grown tolerant in welcoming the children of many different faiths. He sings of the common hope that inspires, of the charity that unites them all; he celebrates the peace of brethren who dwell together in unity, — a peace that had come after a long struggle in which Whittier and his forbears had borne manful parts. In many ways he remained as strongly Puritan as were any of his ancestors; he gloried in their sincerity, and in two lines he crystallized his opinion of their heroic effort to establish the democracy of justice:

Significance of his Religious Poems

> Praise and thanks for an honest man!
> Glory to God for the Puritan![1]

[1] From "The Prophecy of Samuel Sewall."

But some of the elder Whittiers had been Quakers, who had labored patiently to establish the democracy of love, to apply to problems of church and state the same charity that governs men in their family relations ; and from that greater ideal our poet never wavered. Here, in the mingling of Puritan and Friend, of justice and love, we have a suggestion of the American nation, which had passed through a somewhat similar development, — from the stern dogma of earlier days to the gentler conception of religion as consisting essentially of faith in God manifesting itself in all lovely ways of human service. It seems to us, therefore, that Whittier's poems, reflecting the mingled love of God and man, are not simply an expression of his own or of the Friends' belief ; they are symbols of the broadening faith of the whole American people during two centuries of effort to attain religious freedom.

Even in the qualities at which criticism looks askance Whittier seems to us to be typically American. His rimes are sometimes " loose " or faulty, showing the old-country speech of days gone by, when human nature was called " human nater." To nearly every poem he adds some moral or spiritual lesson ; and though many object to a moral as spoiling the artistic effect of a poem, we must note two significant facts. The first is that Whittier's moral lessons, in *Snow Bound* for instance, are so beautifully done that they are in themselves artistic :

> Yet Love will dream, and Faith will trust
> (Since He who knows our need is just)
> That somehow, somewhere, meet we must.
> Alas for him who never sees
> The stars shine through his cypress trees !
> Who, hopeless, lays his dead away,
> Nor looks to see the breaking day
> Across the mournful marbles play !
> Who hath not learned, in hours of faith,
>   The truth to flesh and sense unknown,
> That Life is ever lord of Death,
>   And Love can never lose its own !

The second fact is that Whittier's strongly ethical tendency appears in nearly all American poets from the earliest to the latest. In this, it may be, the poets are wiser than the critics ; for literature is a reflection of life, and the reflection is sadly incomplete, a thing of darkness and discord, unless it does justice to life's moral and spiritual instincts.

Finally, there is something broadly characteristic in Whittier's easy freedom of writing, and in the unstudied, spontaneous quality of his verse. " I never had any methods : when I felt like it, I wrote," he said. Such a free, joyous impulse might well have produced a work of art, a thing of pure beauty like a sonnet of Keats, but for two limitations : the first, that Whittier had always in view a definite object, to teach or to help others ; the second, that he had not the endless patience of genius to work over a poem till its form was so perfect that men must love it, as a flower, for its own sake. Therefore Whittier is not classed with the great poets or literary artists, since his eye is not so much on his work as on humanity. His spirit of service is reflected in a little poem of our own day, which is called " The House by the Side of the Road " :

> There are hermit souls that live withdrawn
> In the peace of their self-content ;
> There are souls like stars, that dwell apart
> In a fellowless firmament ;
> There are pioneer souls that blaze their paths
> Where highways never ran —
> But let me live by the side of the road
> And be a friend to man.

RALPH WALDO EMERSON (1803–1882)

> So nigh is grandeur to our dust,
> So near is God to man,
> When duty whispers low, *Thou must*,
> The youth replies, *I can*.

After reading the above lines from " Voluntaries," Holmes declared that they seemed to have been " carved on marble for

RALPH WALDO EMERSON

From an unfinished portrait by Furness

a thousand years." This is perhaps the best short criticism of Emerson that has yet been written. It indicates that quality of universality which attends such works as the *Republic* of Plato, the *Imitation* of Thomas à Kempis, the *Hamlet* of Shakespeare, — works that never grow old, and that belong to humanity rather than to any particular age or nation.

The difficulty of criticizing Emerson is suggested by the contradictory titles which his admirers have given him. To one he is "the western Buddha"; to another, "the winged Franklin"; to a third, "the Yankee Shelley"; and to a fourth, "the epitome of Puritan idealism and independence." After all such comparisons, the simple fact is that Emerson is an individual and defies classification. He illustrates his own saying that "he is great who is what he is from nature, and who never reminds us of others."

On two points, however, all the critics are agreed: that Emerson was always a moralist, a preacher of ethical ideals; and that the nobility of his life gave force to every word he uttered. Lowell wrote two brilliant essays in his praise, and a score of other leaders, as far apart as Tyndall and Carlyle, bore witness to the charm of Emerson's personality.[1] Wherever he went, to preach of beauty or heroism as reflections of the moral law, an audience gathered silently to hear him; and his presence was enough to convert a deal table into a pulpit, or a plain town hall into a house of God. When the lecture was changed to an essay or a poem, so much of Emerson the preacher went into it that it still seems to us a spoken rather than a written word; and behind the word we may feel the character of the man who gave it power. In an essay on Milton our poet-preacher says that it is the sure sign of a great man "to raise the idea of Man

[1] See Lowell's essay, "Emerson the Lecturer." Tyndall gives Emerson credit for shaping his life as a scientist. George Eliot speaks of him as "the first man I have ever seen." Carlyle, who had a strong tendency to faultfinding, writes after Emerson's visit, "I saw him go up the hill . . . and vanish like an angel." And Mrs. Carlyle records of the same visit that "it made one day look like enchantment, and left me weeping that it was only one day." Hawthorne's noble story "The Great Stone Face" is said to have been inspired by the character of Emerson.

in the minds of his contemporaries and of posterity," and to communicate to all his hearers "vibrations of hope, of self-reverence, of piety, of delight in beauty." Judged by this standard, which estimates a man's greatness by his power to inspire others, Emerson has hardly a peer in American literature. The "vibrations" which he set in motion sixty years ago are still potent, and we rise from reading his pages with a nobler idea of self and of all humanity. He belongs unquestionably in that small group of

> Olympian bards who sung
> Divine Ideas below,
> Which always find us young
> And always leave us so.

Life. At the beginning of a remarkable book stands this sentence: "There was a man in the land of Uz whose name was Job, and that man was perfect and upright, and one that feared God and eschewed evil." If we substitute for the distant Uz our familiar Concord, and for the Patriarch and his strange comforters a quiet American man among his neighbors, we shall have an excellent text for the life story of Emerson. The first and last impression which it produces is that of absolute integrity.[1]

He was born (1803) in Boston, and was the last of a long line of clergymen who had built their lives into the foundations of the American nation. They had helped clear the primeval forests, had planted towns as well as cornfields, had fought in the Revolution with their parishioners, and had been teachers of the first American citizens. They were ministers, Puritans, patriots, and their quality is reflected in the prose and poetry of the last and greatest of their line.

Emerson's father, who was pastor of the historic First Church, had died young, leaving a widow and six children. They were very poor, but they faced poverty with a heroism that is only faintly reflected in the poet's account of his own boyhood. In later years he named "the four angels" of his home, and they were Toil, Want, Truth and Mutual Faith. Under their inspiration four of the boys went to college; as soon as one graduated he taught school, and used the greater part of his salary for his next younger brother's education.

[1] This impression is general among biographers and critics. See, for instance, Brownell's *American Prose Masters*, p. 138.

At Harvard Emerson seemed very ordinary as a scholar but unusual in other ways. Perhaps his most notable trait was an indifference to **Formative Years** the traditions and societies which then, as now, held sway in the college world. He tells us that he was "a hopeless dunce in mathematics," and we learn from others that he had little care for science or philosophy. He was simply a reader of such books as he liked; and every book was as a mine out of which he gathered jewels, storing them in his notebook as illustrative material for his future lectures. Later he speaks as slightingly as did Cooper of academic methods, and declares that the best thing he found in college was a solitary chamber. After graduation he taught school for a time; then he read theology in a desultory way with a local minister and at the Harvard Divinity School, and at twenty-three he thought himself prepared to preach the Gospel.

The next six years may be regarded as Emerson's period of finding himself. He had his love story — a sweet story with a sad ending, for his young and beautiful wife died soon after their marriage — which is reflected in his poems "To Ellen." He was ordained minister of a church in Boston; he was honored in his large parish; and everything pointed to a successful career, when he suddenly resigned his position. He was not hostile but simply indifferent to the belief of his church, having already set up his own standard of faith. After a leisurely journey abroad [1] he settled in Concord, and from this village center proceeded to move the world to his way of thinking.

The essence of his thinking is distilled in the word "individualism," which furnished Emerson with a text for all his preaching. He had **His Individualism** gone to college, but felt no sympathy for either its discipline or its amusement. He entered the Church, but was never in harmony with her creeds, her ritual, her sacraments. He journeyed through Italy, France and England, but saw little to admire in the arts or institutions of those wonderful countries. Meanwhile, in long lonely walks, he had discovered himself, and he settled in Concord with the resolve "never to speak or write a word that is not entirely my own." The same resolve, the same disregard of tradition and outward authority, was later crystallized in the lines:

> Leave all thy pedant lore apart,
> God hid the whole world in thy heart.

[1] The most notable result of this journey was the friendship formed with Carlyle See Norton's *Correspondence of Carlyle and Emerson.*

His first book was *Nature*, a strange yet inspiring work, which regarded the visible world as a mere symbol of God, — a symbol to be interpreted not by science or theology but by individual men, each in his own way and place. In figurative language, nature was to him a looking-glass held up to the Lord, and man another looking-glass held up to nature. His second work was *The American Scholar*, a college address, in which he announced the intellectual independence of his country :

"We will walk on our own feet; we will work with our own hands; we will speak our own minds. . . . A nation of men will for the first time exist, because each believes himself inspired by the Divine Soul which also inspires all men."

These two works, the first fruits of Emerson's discovery of himself, are the most significant of all his writings. If we read them attentively, we shall find in them the germ of all his subsequent teaching.

For the details of Emerson's life at Concord we must refer readers to the abundant literature on the subject,[1] noting here only a few **Life in** significant features. First of all, though Emerson became **Concord** the acknowledged leader of transcendentalism, his sanity and humor preserved him from the vagaries of the movement; and though he became famous in the world, he never lost the character of the simple citizen, the good neighbor of a country village. The beauty he portrayed was such as he could see from his own kitchen door; the heroism and nobility he advocated were such as he discovered in plain farmers and townspeople. He found joy in the coming of the seasons; he shared the grief of humanity when he lost the little son whom he has immortalized in his " Threnody." He spent a large part of his time alone with nature, and his solitary communings furnished him with the material of all his poems :

> And when I am stretched beneath the pines,
> Where the evening star so holy shines,
> I laugh at the lore and the pride of man,
> At the sophist schools and the learned clan ;
> For what are they all, in their high conceit,
> When man in the bush with God may meet ?

[1] In addition to Cabot, *Memoir of Emerson* (the standard biography), see, for instance, E. W. Emerson, *Emerson in Concord;* Alcott, *Concord Days;* Curtis, *Homes of American Authors;* Stearns, *Sketches from Concord and Appledore;* Sanborn, *Emerson and his Friends in Concord;* Hawthorne, *Mosses from an Old Manse.*

From this idyllic retirement Emerson was presently called to address a national audience. We have spoken elsewhere of the growth of **As a** lyceums in this age of reform; and it is enough to add **Lecturer** that, of all the speakers who went up and down the land or overseas to England, this apostle of individualism was perhaps the most welcome and the most influential. It was not what he said — for the half of every address was unintelligible to his audience — but something noble and inspiring in the man himself that brought people to his lectures. As Lowell declared, they did not go to hear what Emerson said, but to hear Emerson. Soon a hundred reading desks

THE OLD MANSE, CONCORD

replaced the pulpit which he had abandoned, and the American people made amends for his lost congregation. The independence of his thought, the serenity of his spirit spreading through the world without conscious effort on his part, suggests his own " Woodnotes ":

> For Nature beats in perfect tune,
> And rounds with rhyme her every rune,
> Whether she work in land or sea,
> Or hide underground her alchemy.
> Thou canst not wave thy staff in air,
> Or dip thy paddle in the lake,
> But it carves the bow of beauty there,
> And the ripples in rhymes the oar forsake.

Another feature of his Concord life was a kind of grim joke which fate played, and which he had the humor to accept gracefully. To **Among Reformers** appreciate this we must remember that Emerson was by nature as retiring as a hermit thrush; that he was a mystic and dreamer, not a reformer; that he had an instinctive aversion to controversy and disorder of every kind; that though radical and positive in his thinking, he could not argue or proselyte, holding that truth must take its own quiet way to the hearts of men. And presently all the agitators, reformers and unbalanced enthusiasts of the country hailed him as comrade or leader. They wrote him endless letters; they waylaid him at his lectures; they entered his house to argue their theories, to expound their grievances, to make him join their propaganda. " Devastators of the day " he called them in helpless resignation; but because they had journeyed far to see him, they must all be welcomed and heard with patience. For this apostle of self, this believer in the divinity of his own nature, cherished for other men a respect bordering on reverence, which made those who met him think better of themselves forever afterwards. A knock at his door might herald a friend or a beggar, a great genius or a great bore; but each was a person, and personality was to Emerson sacred. Of the hundreds who sought him out and devastated his day, not one ever detected anything in his fine, mobile face but deference and perfect courtesy.

So for thirty years Emerson preached by word and deed the gospel of individualism. In 1866, after he had published a dozen small volumes of essays and poems, he knew that he had reached the limit of his power, and with the same faith that had inspired his youth and vigorous manhood he wrote his brave but pathetic " Terminus ":

> It is time to be old,
> To take in sail.

The rest of his life was like a summer day that grows more serene and beautiful as it fades into the twilight. He had almost reached his fourscore years when he died, in 1882. Our whole criticism of his life and work may be summed up in his own lines from " Threnody ":

> What is excellent,
> As God lives, is permanent;
> Hearts are dust, hearts' loves remain;
> Heart's love will meet thee again.

Emerson's Poetry. Whatever the form of his writing, Emerson's thought and expression are essentially poetic; and in reading him we appreciate Coleridge's contention that "poetry is not the proper antithesis to prose but to science." He speaks in symbols; he stirs the imagination; even his prose abounds in passages so rhythmic or beautiful that they can hardly be distinguished from his familiar runic verse. Indeed, a modern

EMERSON'S STUDY

critic has suggested that the chief difference between Emerson's poetry and prose is that in the one he talked with himself, and in the other he talked with the world.

The most obviously poetic works of Emerson fall naturally into two main classes: nature lyrics, and meditative verse. "I am by nature a poet," he said, "and therefore must live in the country"; and this expression suggests at once his power and his limitation. His power is to find beauty, order, symbolism in natural objects; his limitation is that he subordinates humanity, that he hardly seems conscious of the fact that, as a subject for poetry, human nature is more interesting than a bumblebee or a snowstorm. He creates no human characters; he reflects neither smiles nor tears; he is as impersonal as the face of the fields. He is almost alone among poets in never planning a drama, an epic, or a long poem of any kind. His range is therefore narrow, but within it he is a master. No other American poet, not even Bryant, has given us nature poems containing lines of such elemental power and suggestiveness.

The spirit of this poetry is reflected in a single short lyric, "The Apology," which should be read entire as an introduction

Nature Poems   to Emerson's nature verse. His conception of his own work is expressed in "Fragments on the Poet and the Poetic Gift," especially in the opening stanza:

> The gods talk in the breath of the woods,
> They talk in the shaken pine,
> And fill the long reach of the old seashore
> With dialogue divine;
> And the poet who overhears
> Some random word they say
> Is the fated man of men,
> Whom the ages must obey.

Other notable lyrics of this class are "The Humble Bee," "Rhodora," "Each and All," "Fable," "The Informing Spirit," "Waldeinsamkeit," "The Titmouse," "Forbearance," "Days," "The Snowstorm," "The Enchanter" and "Wood-notes." The reader may find others more to his liking, but in the above he will surely detect Emerson's chief characteristics as a nature poet: his recognition of the beauty and harmony of the world; his conception of nature as the garment or symbol of the invisible Spirit; and his runic style, crude but forceful, which is admirably suited to his thought and feeling.

We have spoken of these nature poems as an expression of Emerson's communing with himself, and the meaning of the criticism may be made clear by considering the history of a single lyric. One day, on the rocks of Cape Ann, Emerson listened to old ocean's message, and wrote it down in prose just as it came to him.[1] When he returned home he read to his family " what the sea said " to him, and with very slight changes the prose record fell naturally into blank verse. The result was " Seashore " (1857), which for power and sublimity has hardly a peer in all our nature poetry.

The calm, impersonal quality of these lyrics — a quality which suggests Emerson's absorption in nature — is reflected also in a few poems that have a more human interest. Perhaps the best of these poems is " Threnody," a noble elegy, which voices the poet's grief over the death of his little boy, and which is sometimes compared with Tennyson's " In Memoriam." Other typical poems with a strong human interest are " Good Bye," " To Ellen," " Give All to Love," and especially the Concord and Boston Hymns, which reflect the fine quality of Emerson's patriotism.

In his meditative verse Emerson is no longer simple and spontaneous. He is hampered by his philosophy; he is trying **Meditative** to develop a theory rather than to speak the feeling **Verse** of his own heart. "Astræa," "Bacchus," "To Rhea," — all such poems are attempts to crystallize certain doctrines which Emerson had expounded to better advantage in his essays. Here, for instance, is " Uriel," which makes scoffers of us, or else detectives intent on discovering a mystery:

> Line in nature is not found;
> Unit and universe are round;
> In vain produced, all rays return;
> Evil will bless, and ice will burn.

A solution of the enigma is outlined in the essay on " Circles," but not until we study the " Divinity School Address " do we learn what Emerson was trying to say : that evil is not real but only apparent or illusory; that it is temporary, not enduring,

---

[1] Emerson's Journal, July 23, 1857. Or see note to the poem " Seashore " in the Centenary edition of Emerson's works.

and is part of a general plan that results finally in goodness. Further analysis of the meditative verse may show that " The Problem " is simply a condensation of the essay on " Art " ; and that " Merlin " and " Saadi " are figurative expressions of Emerson's theory of poetry.

It is difficult to criticize such involved poems, which are often more cryptic than Browning at his worst, and which appeal in very different ways to different people. One reader finds them meaningless ; another discerns in them the thoughts of his own soul that he has tried in vain to express. One of the most typical is " Brahma," which condenses a well-known " Yoga " doctrine adopted by the transcendentalists, but which puzzled and mystified the whole country when it appeared in 1857.[1] Other characteristic poems of this class are " Voluntaries," " The Sphinx," and the two series of disjointed meditations called " Fragments."

Many people besides Holmes have poked fun at such poems for their vagueness, for their lack of rime and melody, but all such criticism is stilled by two suggestions : first, Emerson spoke modestly of himself as a forerunner, saying that he was " not a poet but a lover of poetry . . . merely serving as a writer in this empty America before the arrival of poets " ; and second, every one of these poems is worth reading, if only to discover some noble line or passage which it surely contains, and which we store away in the place where we keep things worthy of remembrance :

> The hand that rounded Peter's dome
> And groined the aisles of Christian Rome
> Wrought in a sad sincerity :
> Himself from God he could not free ;
> He builded better than he knew ; —
> The conscious stone to beauty grew.[2]

---

[1] An interesting reference to this poem and to its mystifying effect on readers is given in Scudder's *James Russell Lowell*. Whitman's chaotic poem " Chanting the Square Deific " attempts to express the same doctrine (see p. 379).

[2] These lines, from " The Problem," are an epitome of the essay on " Art," in which Emerson says, " Our arts are happy hits." See also the essay " Michael Angelo " and the poem " Each and All."

Prose Works.[1] We have already spoken of *Nature* as the most representative of all Emerson's works. It was the first notable expression of his thought, his belief, his gospel; and to read it now is to find the seed plot out of which sprang all his later volumes in prose and verse.

Representative Men is a series of seven lectures or essays, which we can hardly help comparing with Carlyle's *Heroes and Hero-Worship*, since the two books have much in common. The first essay is on the Uses of Great Men; the others treat of Plato the Philosopher, Swedenborg the Mystic, Montaigne the Skeptic, Shakespeare the Poet, Napoleon the Man of the World, and Goethe the Writer. Stimulating as they are, hardly one of these essays is an adequate or reliable portrayal of its subject; and all are perhaps more significant as a reflection of Emerson himself than of his strangely assorted heroes. If the reader must choose among them, let him begin with the essay on Plato; not because it is better than the others, but because Emerson was probably more influenced by the Greek philosopher than by any other writer.

English Traits, a series of personal impressions of the English people, is in marked contrast with most books of wholesale criticism. The impressions are fresh, vivid, original; the criticisms, though often too general to be trustworthy, are invariably suggestive; the style is delightfully frank and simple; and the whole is brightened by the play of a very delicate humor. This book, moreover, is unique among Emerson's works in that it has a plan, that is, a beginning, an end, and between these extremes some definite unity of structure. It is consistent, therefore, with his own theory that a book or any other work of art should be "organized like a flower." By this he meant not only that it should have unity and consistency, but also that it should be simple and natural, content with its own beauty or

---

[1] Practically all Emerson's prose is in the form of essays. Some of the titles of his books are *Nature* (1836), two series of *Essays* (1841, 1844), *Representative Men* (1850), *English Traits* (1856), *Conduct of Life* (1860), *Society and Solitude* (1870).

truth, like the exquisite " Rhodora," without attempting eithei
to explain itself or to influence the beholder.

As we have noted, the bulk of Emerson's prose is in the
form of essays, and these are of such number and variety that
they should be grouped in four or five classes. In
The Essays the first we place such essays as " Self-Reliance "
and " The American Scholar " ; in the second, " Heroism "
and " Behavior " ; in the third, " Fortune of the Republic " and
the " Historical Address " at Concord ; in the fourth, " The
Over Soul," " Spiritual Laws " and " Compensation." A dozen
other notable essays might be added, but these nine reflect
Emerson's conception of man in relation to his own soul, to
his neighbor, to his country, and to the Spirit of the universe.

The essay on " Art " is generally recommended, but though
it contains many excellent passages, some readers find it on the
Art, Love, whole like a misty morning, which obscures details
Friendship and makes common objects seem larger than they
are. Moreover, we are hardly inclined to trust the artistic judgment of one who could refer to the pictures of Europe as " crip-
ples and monsters," and who saw in sculpture chiefly " the toys
and trumpery of the theater." Two other essays, " Love "
and " Friendship," are commonly numbered among Emerson's
best works ; but after reading them one may question whether
the author had a true conception of either love or friendship, as
ordinary mortals understand these two dear gifts of God. He
listens too much to Plato, too little to his own heart ; and the
substance of his Platonic teaching is that we should cherish
love, not for individuals, but for beauty and truth ; that we
should entangle ourselves with persons no longer than is necessary to learn to live without them. Herein is suggested the
chief limitation of Emerson in all his work : he deals only with
the individual soul and with abstract ideas ; he cares little for
society ; he has small knowledge of man as a social being, who
does not live or die unto himself but enters into the joy and
grief, the struggle and the salvation of humanity.

Aside from the pithy style, which we shall examine later, there are certain remarkable qualities common to all of Emer-
Quality of son's essays, and perhaps the first is their wealth of
the Essays suggestion. They abound in memorable epigrams, in striking figures and symbols, in passages characterized by deep thought or rare beauty of expression. Yet to study any single essay critically is to discover that, notwithstanding its excellent details, the work as a whole is not consistently thought out from beginning to end; that it is evidently written without a plan; that it lacks unity of structure and definiteness of impression. In other words, it is often difficult to find any vital or logical connection between Emerson's thoughts, or to discover how they are related to his subject. Sometimes, indeed, it might puzzle us to tell what he is talking about so admirably. This lack of unity is due partly to his theory that a man should take thoughts as they come to him, without regard to whether or not they are consistent with other thoughts, and partly to his eclectic method of writing.[1]

A second characteristic of the essays is their ceaseless flow of apt quotations. " By necessity, by proclivity and by delight we all quote," he says, and illustrates that saying by filling his pages with an array so glittering that Holmes compared it with the miraculous draft of fishes. The same critic had the curiosity to examine all of Emerson's works, and discovered more than three thousand references to over eight hundred individuals.[2]

These excellent quotations, by the way, indicate a certain weakness in Emerson's most characteristic doctrine. If we understand him aright, he depends absolutely on his own intuitions; he regards his thoughts and ideas as so many direct inspirations from the Over Soul, which he accepts as true without

[1] Emerson kept many notebooks, carefully indexed, in which he recorded his own thoughts and any memorable passages that he found in his reading. When he composed a lecture or an essay he would collect from these notebooks everything that seemed related to his general subject. These went into his composition apparently without much arrangement. When he had enough to fill the required space he stopped.

[2] A summary of these references may be found in Holmes's *Emerson*, pp. 381–382.

doubt or gainsaying. He deplores, moreover, our common tendency to question our thoughts, to let our wills interfere with our impulses, since thought and impulse are to him as real, as dependable, as inexplicable as the phenomena of nature. Yet if we read one of his essays carefully, and then search out his references, we find that his originality often consists in stating in a modern way some bit of wisdom that was thoroughly questioned and proved before it was recorded by men of old ; and that some of the ideas which he regarded as intuitive were plainly borrowed from Epictetus, or from some other writer who may or may not be regarded as authoritative.[1]

A third remarkable quality of the essays, which we find hard to define, is their power to stimulate readers. There is hardly a page in Emerson's twelve volumes that does not contain at least one morning thought which awakens our dormant minds like a bird song, or else a bold, challenging summons to be up and doing. Strange to say, though Emerson is one of the most radical of thinkers, he seldom rouses our antagonism. We may deny the doctrine, but we do not oppose or fail to respect the man, since he invariably appeals to the noblest part of our nature. We cannot compare him with Bacon or Epictetus, or even with his great contemporaries Carlyle, Ruskin and Newman, simply because he is himself and unlike any other. It is perhaps enough to say that he measures up to the stature of these men, and that his best work, like theirs, can never grow old. We read his wonderful essays again and again ; each reading reveals a new depth of thought, a new beauty of expression, a new power to stimulate our thinking ; and we lay them aside with the conviction that they must be classed with the great prose works of modern literature.

Emerson's Philosophy. It is hard to systematize the thinking of one who confessed that he had no system, or even to

---

[1] For example, Epictetus taught that the highest wisdom is to desire nothing except freedom and contentment ; that evil is not real but only apparent ; that happiness depends wholly upon our will to be happy, etc. All this is restated by Emerson.

understand a philosopher who ignored the fundamental aim of all philosophies ; which is, in a word, to obtain a consistent, unifying world-view that shall explain man in his relation to the Infinite, to humanity, and to the world of nature. One must not be too confident, therefore, of explaining Emerson ; and a general criticism should be prefaced by the statement that any summary may unwittingly do injustice to his philosophy by emphasizing one doctrine which is plainly at variance with another. For Emerson was not a logical thinker, like Edwards, and took no care to make his teachings consistent. As he said :

" I seek no order or harmony or result. . . . I am not careful how they [his present thoughts] compare with other thoughts and other moods. I trust them for that."

So far as Emerson has a definite philosophy, it centers in the doctrine of individualism ; and this doctrine rests upon his theory of knowledge. In his view, knowledge is not a matter of effort or attainment, but rather of passiveness, of open-mindedness and receptivity. " I do not argue, I know," he tells us ; and again, " A thought is as natural, as true as a flower ; it does not need argument or explanation." We are reminded here of the word of the Lord to Jeremiah, saying, " I will put my law in their inward parts, and write it in their hearts." Emerson does not quote this, but his implicit faith in the doctrine appears in his frequent declaration that the Over Soul is for every man the immediate source of all authority and knowledge ; that it is not necessary to go back to the past or to consider the teaching of others, since every soul at every moment has free access to the original source of all wisdom. "If a single man plant himself indomitably upon his instincts and there abide, the huge world will come round to him." [1] This is the substance of his "American Scholar " and of his famous " Divinity School Address," which startled men by their fearless renunciation of tradition and all outward authority.

[1] In another place he says, " See that you hold fast by the intellect"; yet his teaching, as a whole, rests upon instinct or intuition rather than upon reason.

Of this radical teaching perhaps the first thing to note is that
it is simply a reflection of his own individualism, of the serene
Personal way in which he ignored his debt to the past and his
Element dependence on human institutions. Though he was
a clergyman, he thought it unnecessary to know church history
or theology; though a naturalist, he never studied science in
any form; though he wrote of art and literature and philosophy,
he was always lacking in scholarship, that is, in the mastery or
exact knowledge of any one subject. Viewed critically, therefore,
his system appears as a tree without much root. It is the measure of one man, not of humanity.

The next thing to note is that, to one of Emerson's training
and moral integrity, individualism may be a " safe and sane "
doctrine; but we need hardly point out that it has its dangers;
that, as a rule of life for all sorts of men, it must lead to all
manner of vagaries. A fanatic or an anarchist, no less than a
transcendentalist, may feel quite sure of himself; and the only
way to judge the quality of his intuitions is to compare them with
those of the race past and present. In other words, we must
know history and tradition, ethics and philosophy, all of which
Emerson was content to overlook.

To sum up the matter, Emerson's philosophy rests too much
on ecstasy and impulse, and too little on reason and will. It
glorifies the individual but ignores society, that is, man in his
relation to others, where he is always seen at his best. It is confident of the present moment without considering the wisdom
and experience of the past. We are to read it, therefore, as
Emerson read his favorite books, selecting the choice morsels
and neglecting the rest as of little consequence. In one matter
only he is always consistent, and that is the authority and the
loveliness of the moral law. Upon this subject he is the most
inspiring and energizing of all our literary masters.[1]

[1] This is perhaps the more remarkable in view of the fact that Emerson took the
moral law for granted because he found it in himself. Apparently he never sought for
the origin of the law; nor did he think it necessary to give any valid reason for its
authority.

General Characteristics. It is idle to analyze Emerson's style if we think of style as meaning order and arrangement; for his method of writing — by stringing together selections from his notebooks — made it impossible that his works should have any continuity of thought or unity of expression. But if we think of style simply as manner, as the reflection of personality, and then consider Emerson's most characteristic paragraphs, which suggest stars, flowers and glimmering crystals, then there is no style to compare with his in our literature. As Higginson says, our criticism is shamed into silence by finding frequent passages " so majestic in thought and rhythm, of a quality so rare and delicious, as to form a permanent addition to the highest literature of the human race."

The style of these single passages is better appreciated than described. The sentences are terse, vital, epigrammatic; yet they are always poetic rather than practical, and always **His Style** hint at much more than they express. Because he lives much out of doors and is intimate with earth, air and water, Emerson's figures have an elemental quality unlike those of any other writer. The dew and fragrance of the morning are in all his works. Because he has read widely, he gives an air of culture to the most homely matters by associating them with the great characters and the great books of the world. He has a large vocabulary at perfect command, but his instinct leads him to the simplest and most picturesque words. He chooses his expressions from the most unexpected places, here from the nursery, there from the Apocalypse or from the mystic books of the East; and not even Lowell approaches him in the ability to clothe his thought in a new dress, making it appear as fresh and original as if it had been spoken in Eden at the springtime of the world.

There is another element in Emerson's style, its eloquence, which is generally attributed to his public speaking, but which seems to be an expression of his own deepest nature or, it may be, of a tendency inherited from his ministerial ancestors.[1] Whatever the cause, Emerson is always striving after eloquence of expression, not to convince his hearers — such a per-

Eloquence

sonal motive would never occur to him — but simply because it is in his blood, because eloquence seems to him, as to the Indian, man's natural expression, his unconscious reflection of the harmony of the universe. "There are days which occur in this climate," he begins, and though his subject be the old, threadbare matter of the weather, Webster and Clay were never more eloquent over mighty problems of state. Again, in a lecture on "Behavior," he mentions the human eye ; it has nothing to do with his subject, but it inspires him and he cannot restrain himself. The passage that follows is of such beauty and eloquence that our best poets and orators have hardly rivaled it.

To Emerson's thoughts, and to his central doctrine of individualism, we have already called sufficient attention. The point to emphasize is, not its strangeness or danger, but rather its harmony with the spirit of America, which from the beginning has had to solve old problems in a new way, and which seems at times the most individual of nations. It was this harmony with the free spirit of its native land which led Holmes to call "The American Scholar" our intellectual declaration of independence. The individualist, as a rule, tends to extremes, to the vagaries and inconsistencies of transcendentalism ; but Emerson is a noble exception. He is invariably sane, wholesome, self-controlled, and typically American in his entire devotion to liberty. At his best he comes as near, perhaps, to representing the free modern man, the man who assumes the responsibility as well as the joy of his freedom, as any other writer at home or abroad.

If we examine Emerson's claim to greatness and permanence, it will be found to rest on three solid foundations. First, he treats of elemental things, of nature, love, friendship, heroism,

---

[1] As a young man, Emerson writes in his Journal that he " yearns after the power of Cicero." He tells us also that he has inherited from his ancestors "a passionate love for the strains of eloquence."

self-reliance, in which all men are forever interested. Second, he treats these themes in an independent way, speaking straight **Summary** from his own convictions, and always appealing to the nobility of our human nature. Third, his words seem as vital now as when they first came from his lips ; his readers, his fame and his inspiring influence increase with the passing years. Best of all, this fame remains unchanged in quality, and behind it stands a man in whom criticism finds nothing to pardon or regret. We think of him still as the men of Concord and America thought of him long ago : as holding aloft a spiritual ideal while they were busy with material things ; as proving the value of their individual and immortal souls while they were lost in a maze of business, politics and reforms. He was to them much as Galileo was to the people of Florence long ago ; while they ate and drank, he was thinking for them ; while they slept in forgetfulness, he was alone on his hilltop watching the eternal stars. In recording his personal impression Lowell has unconsciously expressed the feeling of all of Emerson's hearers :

". . . Emerson's oration was more disjointed than usual, even with *him*. It began nowhere and ended everywhere; and yet, as always with that divine man, it left you feeling that something beautiful had passed that way, — something more beautiful than anything else, like the rising and setting of stars. Every possible criticism might have been made on it but one, — that it was not noble. There was a tone in it that awakened all elevating associations. He boggled, he lost his place, he had to put on his glasses; but it was as if a creature from some fairer world had lost his way in our fogs and it was *our* fault, not his. It was chaotic, but it was all such stuff as stars are made of ; and you could n't help feeling that, if you waited awhile, all that was nebulous would be whirled into planets, and would assume the mathematical gravity of system. All through it I felt something in me that cried ' Ha, ha, to the sound of the trumpets ! ' " [1]

[1] From Norton, *Letters of James Russell Lowell*, I, 392. (Harpers' edition, 2 vols.) See also Lowell's essay on " Emerson the Lecturer."

James Russell Lowell (1819–1891)

There are two authors who have been regarded at home and abroad as representative of the best American life and letters. The first was Irving, who lived in an old world of romance, and who is associated in our thought with the pleasures of literature. The second was Lowell, who lived in a new world of practical achievement, and who stands for the power of literature to influence the thought and life of a nation. At home he used prose and poetry to help shape the destiny of his country; abroad he was the spokesman not only of American letters but also of American manhood, and of the steadfast ideals that guide and inspire the American people.

JAMES RUSSELL LOWELL

Life. "All the stars were propitious at his birth," writes a friend in beginning the story of Lowell's life. He was born (1819) in the old Lowell homestead "Elmwood," on the outskirts of the college town of Cambridge. On the side of his father, who was a minister, he was descended from Puritan ancestors who had made history in the Old Bay State. On his mother's side he traced his descent from some Gaelic forbears (of the Orkney Islands) among whom was a certain Sir Patrick Spens, the hero of a famous ballad. From his father he seems to have inherited strength and sanity of judgment; from his mother he may have received his lively, mercurial fancy; and these contradictory elements appear on almost every page of his writings.

Besides these native traits, two formative influences of his childhood should be noted: the first, that "Elmwood" was set in the midst of noble grounds, where nature looked in at every door and window; the second, that the library shelves were filled with the best books,

chosen and read by scholarly ancestors. Nature and books, the idealism of the Puritan and the wit of the Celt, — such are the influences
and elements that go to make up our Lowell.

Of his school life perhaps the best summary is his own remark,
that he read in Harvard everything except the textbooks prescribed

School Days by the faculty. He was always a great reader, like Mather,
whom he resembles in many ways; but Mather was in a
literary sense omnivorous, reading and mastering every known science,
while Lowell confined himself largely to what was then called belles-
lettres, or polite literature. In this he was influenced by the interest
in literary matters which then dominated our American colleges.[1] A
study of his early work shows that he took only a superficial interest
in matters which, to the nation at large, seemed of tremendous import.
America was then entering the whirlpool of intellectual and political
agitation to which we have referred; questions of slavery and states'
rights, of communism and transcendentalism, kept the country in
a turmoil; but Lowell saw in them only an occasion for sport. In his
class poem he made fun of reformers in general, and even sent a few
arrows of his wit at Emerson, whom he had met while "rusticated"
at Concord for disobeying the college regulations.

After his graduation (1838) Lowell studied law and opened an
office in Boston; but he had no clients, and spent his time largely, as
in college, in reading and writing poetry. We may judge the quality
of this work by his first volume of verse, *A Year's Life* (1841), and
by numerous love poems contributed to the magazines of the period.
If we seek the inspiration of these poems, such as "Irene," "My
Love," and the "Song" beginning, "O moonlight deep and tender,"
we shall find the woman who exercised the deepest influence on
Lowell's whole career.

With his marriage to Maria White (1844), a delicate, beautiful
woman with the faith of a saint and the zeal of a reformer, a marked

Finding change occurred in Lowell's life.[2] Hitherto he had been
Himself a mere dilettante; he had written a few poems and had
attempted a new magazine, *The Pioneer;* he had made a beginning
of criticism with his *Conversations on Some of the Old Poets;* and

[1] The first works of Irving, Cooper, Bryant, Longfellow, Poe and Hawthorne created
unbounded enthusiasm among college students. See Edward Everett Hale's *James
Russell Lowell and His Friends.*

[2] We refer here to the definite expression of Lowell's humanitarianism. The change
had probably begun before 1844. See Greenslet's *James Russell Lowell*, pp. 32, 44.

betimes he scoffed at the various reform movements and poked fun at transcendentalism. Gradually, as he came under his wife's influence, a definite purpose entered his life, and the most significant mark of it is that he joined the abolitionists, — who were then regarded with as much disfavor in New England as ever they were in the South. He became editor of the *Pennsylvania Freeman*, and contributed anti-slavery poems and articles to the few magazines that then dared print such dangerous matter. He worked hard for his daily bread, and was content with the small earnings which, even at that time, would hardly support a day laborer. He shared also the grief of humanity. In such poems as " The First Snowfall," " She Came and Went," " The Changeling," written after the death of his little girl, he touched the human heart as he had never done before.

The climax of this early period of hard, purposeful work came in 1848, when he published his best volume of *Poems*, and also *The Biglow Papers* (first series), *The Fable for Critics*, and *The Vision of Sir Launfal*. Then, largely in the hope of restoring his wife's health, he sold some of his land at " Elmwood " and traveled in Europe for a year. For Mrs. Lowell the journey was all in vain ; she failed steadily, and died soon after her return home. It was the darkest, saddest hour in Lowell's life ; but unless we search his letters we shall find hardly a trace of the grief which he bore in manly silence. On the morning that Mrs. Lowell died a daughter was born to Long-fellow, and the elder poet's sympathy for his friend and neighbor found expression in the little poem beginning,

> Two angels, one of Life and one of Death,
> Passed o'er our village as the morning broke.[1]

In the following year (1854) another change began in Lowell's life, and the change was made significant by the fact that he turned from **From Poetry** poetry to prose. At the Lowell Institute, in Boston, he **to Prose** gave a course of lectures on the subject, then popular, of English poetry, and the quality of his work was so unmistakable that he was speedily called to the professorship which Longfellow had resigned. With his work at Harvard (which began after a period of foreign study) began also his new editorial career. We can hardly overestimate his influence on our literature as the first editor (1857–1861) of the *Atlantic Monthly*, in which position he was continually

---

[1] From "The Two Angels." See Longfellow's letter, April 25, 1855, quoted in Samuel Longfellow's *Life of Longfellow*, II, 285.

on the watch to discover and encourage new writers of marked ability. His most notable works of this period, during which the country was in political upheaval, were the literary essays contributed to his magazine (afterwards collected in *Among My Books* and *My Study Windows*), *Fireside Travels* (1864), the " Commemoration Ode " (1865), and two little volumes of poetry, *Under the Willows* (1869) and *Three Memorial Poems* (1876). Much of his political prose produced during this period and his second series of *Biglow Papers* were too much influenced by the strife of the hour to be of permanent value ; but in his best poetry, and especially in his " Commemoration Ode," he rose above all sectional interests to speak nobly for the nation.

It was happily not a party recognition of his political services but rather a national acknowledgment of the honor due to literature which **Life in** led to the selection of Lowell as our minister to Spain **England** (1877) and to England (1880). Here we note a close parallel to the career of Irving ; but where Irving was essentially a learner, a discoverer of Old-World literary material, Lowell was emphatically a teacher, giving a splendid object lesson of the type of man and the type of democracy which the New World had developed. For Lowell was American to the root and fiber of his nature ; his patriotism was intense, his love of country pure and constant. He was always ready, moreover, to give a reason for the faith that was in him ; and his reason, backed by his fine literary culture, commanded instant respect. It is no small tribute to his personal charm and manliness that, though he was called " a typical Yankee," he became one of the most popular public men in London. Partly by his speeches, and partly by his firm yet courteous attitude in every diplomatic question that arose, he made England know and honor the ideals which America has cherished from the beginning, and he laid the foundation for a friendship based on sympathy between the two nations, which we trust will never again be broken.

The last period of his life began with his return home in 1885 :

> Home am I come : not, as I hoped might be,
> To the old haunts, too full of ghosts for me,
> But to the olden dreams that time endears,
> And to the loved books that younger grow with years ; . . .
> Little I ask of Fate, will she refuse
> Some days of reconcilement with the Muse ?
> I take my reed again and blow it free
> Of dusty silence, murmuring, Sing to me !

He resumed his professorship at Harvard, not because he ever liked it but because he was poor and must still earn his bread. He wrote poems, essays, political addresses, all in the old vein, but with something added of the wisdom of age and the tenderness that comes with a deeper knowledge of life. The end came (1891), while he still felt the joy of work and the sweetness of reward, in the same house in which he was born more than seventy years before.

LOWELL HOME, CAMBRIDGE

The Poetry of Lowell. A study of Lowell's works shows four chief interests: nature and patriotism, which he reflects in poetry; literature and democracy, which he reserves for prose.[1] Of these he always writes brilliantly, suggestively, and at times with deep feeling; but he gives the impression of being governed by taste or thought or sentiment rather than by a controlling passion, and of always trying to master his subject instead of letting his subject master him completely, as most other poets do. If we compare him with Whittier, for instance, we note that Whittier's love of nature is as spontaneous as a child's

---

[1] This generalization, like most others, is imperfect. It fails to include some of Lowell's best lyrics and sonnets on other subjects.

love for a brook, and that his lyrics are as unstudied as a child's singing; while Lowell has a well-cultivated taste for nature, and must bring his library even to the dandelion, saying,

> Thou art my tropics and mine Italy!

Again, both men are patriots who reflect their love of country in verse. Whittier is mastered by his love ; to him, as to Isaiah, the voice says, " Cry ! " and he must speak what is given him to speak ; his patriotism flames and flashes in lyrics that are flung off at white heat. Lowell thinks, plans, strives to master his subject, and invariably illustrates it from his wide reading. And the comparison might be carried further, to show that one man was a poet by inner compulsion, the other by careful training.

Among the most noteworthy of Lowell's nature poems are "To the Dandelion," " Indian-Summer Reverie," " The Foun-
Select Poems tain," " The Birch Tree," " Phœbe," " To a Pine Tree," and the opening stanzas of " Under the Willows." With these should be read a few simple lyrics of human love and grief, such as "My Love," " The Changeling," " She Came and Went," and " The First Snowfall " ; the exquisite sonnets, " For this true nobleness," " To the Spirit of Keats," " My Love I have no fear," " I ask not," and " Great Truths " ; and certain miscellaneous poems, such as " An Ember Picture," " Fountain of Youth," " An Incident," " Hebe," " The Shepherd of King Admetus," " Masaccio," " Aladdin," and " In the Twilight." [1]

There are other poems, longer and more ambitious, which many critics regard as more typical of Lowell's genius. Here, for instance, is " A Legend of Brittany," an early poem which Poe called the noblest ever written by an American. It has

---

[1] We have named the above poems as a guide to the beginner. For students who have Lowell's complete poetical works, it is a good plan to read four or five small volumes in the order of their production : *A Year's Life* (1841), *Poems*, first series of *Biglow Papers*, and *Sir Launfal* (1848). Then came an interval of twenty years, given largely to prose. The chief poetic works of Lowell's later life are *Under the Willows* (1869), *Three Memorial Poems* (1876), and *Heartsease and Rue* (1888).

many quotable lines, but as a whole it seems a little labored and artificial. Another ambitious poem which has received considerable praise is " The Cathedral " (1869), but many readers will sympathize with Emerson, who refused to criticize it. In a very different style and spirit is the poem " Agassiz," a noble tribute to a noble character, which is one of the finest of all Lowell's works in verse or prose.

Lowell's best-known work, *The Vision of Sir Launfal*, now stands apart from all the rest, — though it would probably have

Sir Launfal

found a place in *The Nooning* [1] if that lifelong dream had ever been realized. Our poet here follows Tennyson into the realm of Arthurian legend, and tells in his own way the old, beautiful story of the search for the Holy Grail. The result, however, is not very satisfactory. *Sir Launfal* has been widely read, and is still a favorite with many readers, but the poem is perhaps more admired for its moral lesson than for its artistic excellence. It shows that Lowell, like Matthew Arnold, though he knew all about the theory of verse, had not that instinctive sense of rhythm and melody which marks a great poet. In consequence he writes, " And the wanderer is welcome to the hall " and many other jarring lines which pound along, like raw recruits, without keeping step to the music. The materials which Lowell uses are scarcely more harmonious. The landscape with its flowers and birds is unmistakably American ; but the castle, the beggar, the knight and the story itself are all foreign to our life. The best parts of the poem are found in the preludes, especially the first, with its inspiring " And what is so rare as a day in June ? "

Sir Launfal is interesting in another way, as an epitome of Lowell's tendency to moralize overmuch, — a tendency which at that time (1848) was noticeable in all our poets with the exception of Poe. That Lowell was conscious of this failing is

---

[1] Like Longfellow and many other poets, Lowell planned a series of narrative poems in the manner of the *Canterbury Tales*. To these he gave the general title of *The Nooning*, but he completed only one narrative, " Fitz Adam's Story."

evident from his own description of himself in *A Fable for Critics*. He refers to it often in his letters, and enlightens us by saying, " I shall never be a poet till I get out of the pulpit. And New England was all meetinghouse when I was growing up." [1]

Of the patriotic poems, the most vigorous and spontaneous is " The Present Crisis," which was written (1844) in the midst **Poems of** of the political uproar occasioned by the annexation **Patriotism** of Texas. Never before did Lowell so surely " strike home " to the hearts of his readers. Instantly his poem became a battle cry, and for twenty years its ringing lines were applauded in hundreds of public assemblies. At the present time we are far removed from the bitter political issues that occasioned the poem, and we can all cherish the manly American spirit that finds expression in such passages as,

> Once to every man and nation comes the moment to decide,
> In the strife of Truth and Falsehood, for the good or evil side.

The " Commemoration Ode " (1865), written at the close of the Civil War as a tribute to the college students who had fallen in battle, is by many regarded as the noblest single poem occasioned by that mighty conflict. Here is no sectional pride or grief, but the very soul of a nation, honoring its noble dead, rejoicing in peace, and setting its face toward a glorious future. Though a little diffuse and labored, the poem is characterized by magnificent passages, such as the tribute to Lincoln, which will be read as long as the nation remembers its heroes. The *Three Memorial Poems* is in the same lofty strain, but here Lowell's genius fails to keep him on the heights ; he seems to be striving after something that he cannot quite reach. The same criticism applies to " A Glance behind the Curtain " and " Columbus." They all contain gold, but in scattered nuggets rather than in veins ; they are notable for occasional good lines or passages rather than for sustained excellence.

Satires in Verse. The literary satire called *A Fable for Critics* and the political satire of *The Biglow Papers* are by some historians counted among Lowell's masterpieces. The *Fable* (1848) is, as Lowell said, a mere *jeu d'esprit*. It consists of a tedious introduction, followed by a rambling commentary on the writers of the period, made up largely of quips, puns, jokes, tortured rimes and pedantic allusions. Regarded as literature, the wretched doggerel of this *Fable* is unworthy of serious consideration ; but if one has patience to read it, he may discover an occasional bit of criticism (on Cooper, for instance, or Poe, or Emerson, or Whittier, or Longfellow) which suggests that Lowell had a very shrewd critical sense, and that he anticipated the verdict which Time has since awarded to writers who were then as difficult to judge accurately, because of their nearness, as are the writers of the present day.

The Biglow Papers (1848, 1866) are two series of political tracts called forth by the Mexican War and the War for the Union. They are written in an alleged Yankee dialect, of tortured spelling and pronunciation, which serves to accentuate the individuality of the principal character, Hosea Biglow. This raw son of the soil treats us to an original discussion of the political matters that then disturbed and divided the country. In his speech one notes the mixture of native shrewdness and good sense, the deep love of the New England landscape and of New England traditions, and the keen, galling satire which, like satires in general, took no account of the ideals or even of the point of view of an opponent. The humor of the book is such as critics and literary persons appreciate, and these have given it a higher place in our literature than its local and temporary character would seem to warrant. The tedious prose effusions of Parson Wilbur, which make up a large part of *The Biglow Papers*, are now generally neglected.[1] Of the poetical selections there are three or four

---

[1] The only readable part of this prose padding is an excellent essay on the origin of certain provincial words and expressions.

which seem worthy of preservation. The first is "What Mr. Robinson Thinks," which will be applicable so long as we have politicians :

> But John P.
> Robinson he
> Sez this kind o' thing 's an exploded idee.

Others are "Suthin' in the Pastoral Line" and "The Courtin'," — two pretty little pastorals in the Yankee dialect which reveal Lowell's appreciation of nature and his insight into rustic character.

Prose Works. The best of Lowell's prose works, which deal in general with literature and democracy, are found in his *Democracy and Other Essays, Fireside Travels, Among My Books, My Study Windows,* and *Old English Dramatists.* A large portion of his political writing, though sparkling and suggestive, is plainly partisan in spirit; but in the first-named volume one may find essays, such as "Democracy" and "Our Literature," which are of national and permanent interest. Among the most notable of the miscellaneous essays are "Cambridge Thirty Years Ago," with its fine appreciation of the spirit of an old American town, "My Garden Acquaintance," "A Good Word for Winter," and "On a Certain Condescension in Foreigners." One who reads the last four works will find Lowell at his simplest, and perhaps his best, as a prose writer.

Of the numerous literary essays the reader should become acquainted with a chosen few (on Emerson, Chaucer, Walton, **Literary** Dante, and Milton) before considering the divergent **Essays** opinions of literary historians. Perhaps the first thing to record is, that Lowell's literary essays are, on the whole, the most brilliant that America has yet produced. They are interpretations of the best books by a man who is himself a poet and a scholar; who remembers that literature is but a reflection of human experience, colored by the author and by the age in which he lived; and who tries to show what life meant to an author who was like ourselves in all essentials, but who had the power to express what we can only think or feel. Moreover, as we read these essays, we are always in the company of Lowell; we share his literary culture, his love of poetry and life, his boyish enthusiasm and manly afterthoughts, his whims and prejudices, his wit and laughter; and this in itself is a very pleasant experience.

Our admiration for the personality revealed in such essays is generally accompanied by a regretful criticism; for Lowell's literary faults are almost as prominent as his virtues. Though his essays are packed with brilliant expressions and literary allusions, they are without unity or definite design; they suggest a cairn of quartz stones heaped over an author, rather than a carefully designed monument.

Last but not least among Lowell's prose works we place his *Letters*, which were collected and edited by his friend Charles

Letters Eliot Norton. Here are two large volumes of the most stimulating letters that have yet appeared from the American press. In their countless happy expressions they are, as a critic suggests, a storehouse of literary material, especially the kind of material known as "good things." The general reader, however, may find them disappointing; may even detect a certain reserve and self-consciousness, as if the author had thought of future publication, and could not indulge in that perfect freedom of intimacy which gives the finest flavor to a letter.[1] Though they cover the whole life of a notable personage, at a stirring period of American history, they tell us very little about Lowell himself, and throw absolutely no light on the literary or historical movements of the age. It is a marvel that such a man could write so much, and so well, and say so little of consequence. On the whole, these letters seem to us like a collection of bright beads which make neither a necklace nor a rosary, having no thread or chain of connected purpose.

---

[1] This may be due partly to the editor, who with excellent taste refused to publish many of Lowell's intimate letters.

General Characteristics. Lowell's style is something to enjoy even while we analyze it. Never was a better illustration of the aphorism that "style is the man." In the present case our man is witty and grave, serious and comical, manly and boyish, steady and flighty, — not in successive poems or essays, but often in the same stanza or paragraph. But style means also order, arrangement, continuity ; and judged by this standard Lowell can hardly be said to possess a definite style. He has extraordinary facility of expression ; he can indulge in any flight, and find felicitous words and figures wherewith to clothe his fancy ; but he seldom orders or arranges his thoughts. He lets every by-path lead him aside ; he hovers like a butterfly over every flower, and is satisfied with the thought, the mood, the expression of the moment, without regard to its appropriateness in view of his chosen subject. By long study of old authors he has a remarkable vocabulary ; he uses more rare words and idiomatic expressions than any other modern American writer ; yet every word, excepting only the wretched puns, is well chosen and well placed, and to read Lowell is to renew our conception of the wonderful flexibility of the English language.

To the matter of Lowell's poetry we have already called sufficient attention. As we think of his prose we are again reminded of Cotton Mather, and of the fact that Lowell is his only successor.[1] Both are learned and brilliant ; both are of the same "Brahmin caste" of intellectual aristocrats ; both are great readers and have remarkable memories ; both fill their pages with so many learned allusions that their subjects are often obscured ; both are a little fantastic at times, being fond of the odd, the whimsical, the unexpected. Only, as we have noted, Mather reads more widely and has as many storehouses as a squirrel, while Lowell has but one. Of history, science, philosophy, of any art except literature, he has comparatively little knowledge. Seldom does he enter the Bible or the religious

---

[1] Curiously enough, Lowell once spoke of Mather as "book-suffocated," — a criticism which applies in some degree to himself.

treasury of any people. His culture, being almost wholly literary, is deeply interesting to those who can appreciate its flavor, but seems restricted and a little " bookish " to the ordinary reader. He sees life as it has been reflected in poetry, rather than in history, or art, or religion, or in the daily struggle for daily bread. He is in sympathy only with the great masters of literature ; he writes for a small and select audience rather than for humanity. Here, in a word, is the secret of his strength and of his weakness.

In the foregoing pages a survey of Lowell's career has been attempted, but one is sadly conscious of having failed to grasp the fine spirit of it all. In this very failure may per-

Summary haps be found another suggestion of the poet, who tells us, in his " L'Envoi : To the Muse," that his life had been spent in following a genius which always eluded him :

> Whither ? Albeit I follow fast,
> In all life's circuit I but find,
> Not where thou art, but where thou wast,
> Sweet beckoner, more fleet than wind !
> I haunt the pine-dark solitudes,
> With soft brown silence carpeted,
> And plot to snare thee in the woods :
> Peace I o'ertake, but thou art fled !

Only to a few intimate friends did Lowell ever reveal himself freely. To us he appears, at times, aloof and superior, waiting for us to acknowledge his quality ;[1] and again the self-consciousness which he never quite overcame stands between us to prevent that personal allegiance which we cannot help giving to Lanier or Whittier. He seems to review his career in a single poem, " In the Twilight," which the student should read if he reads nothing else of Lowell. As we try to review it from the distance at which he keeps his readers, we are conscious of a scholarly and cultured gentleman who attained great honor at

---

[1] See Howells's impression of Lowell, in *Literary Friends and Acquaintance.*

nome and abroad, but who examined himself to find that his
deepest feeling was one of regret that he had never once attained
his ideal or done his best work. He might have been a great
poet, or a great critic, or a great teacher ; but he succeeded too
easily in many fields to win the highest success in one. The
most significant criticism of his work which we have heard was
uttered in conversation by his lifelong friend Norton, who said
in effect, " Only Lowell's friends could be disappointed in him,
because they alone knew how great were his unused powers,
how much better work he was capable of than he ever did."

OLIVER WENDELL HOLMES (1809–1894)

At the time when Holmes began to write, in 1830, humor was
not well recognized in American letters. Most of our writers
were sentimental ; a few were profound ; and the nation at large
began to be deeply agitated over social reforms and political
problems. The man who in such a period showed the possibilities of humor, and whose humor was invariably tempered by
culture and flavored with kindness, did a service to our literature
that can hardly be overestimated.

Life. There is so little of the unusual or dramatic in the life of
Holmes that the reader will do well to confine himself largely to the
author's works, in which he has reflected his own spirit more completely than any other American writer, not excepting even Franklin.
The latter name suggests, by contrast, a certain quality of distinction
that characterizes Holmes and other writers of the " Cambridge
school." In reading them we have always the impression of good
family and good breeding. We are, as Howells declares, in excellent
society, without a taint of bohemianism, when in their company.

Holmes belongs unmistakably to this class of literary aristocrats.
On his father's side his ancestors were all Puritans of the " Brahmin
The Brahmin caste," as he called them ; on his mother's side he was
Caste   related to the first governors of the Bay State, and to
Anne Bradstreet, our first Colonial poet. He was born in Cambridge ;
he graduated from Andover and from Harvard ; he lived practically

all his life in Boston; and his interest centers so completely in his college and in his city that many critics call him the most provincial of modern writers. Yet one who reads his Harvard lyrics finds them splendidly suggestive of that loyalty which binds every college man to his alma mater; and his city songs reflect the honest pride of an American in his home town, which has the priceless heritage of the faith and heroism of its founders.

After graduation Holmes studied law and medicine, completing the latter discipline in Paris. For a short time he was a teacher at Dartmouth; then for thirty-five years he held the chair of anatomy and physiology in the Harvard Medical School. Anatomy is said to be the driest, deadest subject in the whole range of human knowledge; but Holmes was one of the brightest, most alert men that ever taught any subject in an American college.

OLIVER WENDELL HOLMES

His literary career began in a striking way just as he reached his voting age. In **Literary Career** 1830 an order had been given to break up the old warship *Constitution*, which had played a heroic part in the naval war of 1812. Holmes saw a newspaper notice of the order, and instantly wrote " Old Ironsides," a poem which after eighty years still holds an honored place in our school readers. The ringing lines not only saved the glorious old ship; they roused the nation, and gave Holmes a place among its poets. For sixty years thereafter he wrote prose and poetry, and not once did he lose the firm hold on public attention which he had gained by his first effort.

His next notable literary achievement came when he was almost fifty years old. Meanwhile he had gained two reputations: as a scientist, by original contributions to medical lore, and as the brightest wit and talker of the Saturday Club, — a famous Boston society which included Longfellow, Agassiz, Hawthorne, Motley, Lowell and many others of almost equal mental caliber. When the *Atlantic Monthly* was started (1857), Lowell made it a condition of his taking the editorship that Holmes should be the chief contributor. The latter responded with *The Autocrat of the Breakfast Table*, which gave him a third reputation as a delightful prose writer. By that time the fame of Holmes as a witty talker had spread far and wide, and multitudes were eager to hear him. In *The Autocrat* their wish was gratified ; for these dramatic essays were simply the conversations of a bright and learned man transferred to paper. It was this combination, of a people eager to listen and a wit who had the rare gift of talking naturally in print, that made *The Autocrat* more successful and far more enduring than a popular novel.

The rest of the story is that of an acknowledged master in his own little field. Holmes was now the poet, not of a people like Longfellow, **The Poet** or of a party like Whittier, but of a city which he com- **of a City** placently regarded as the hub of the universe. Upon every important civic occasion he was called upon for a poem, and invariably responded in a way to delight his hearers and to increase his local reputation. He continued his work as professor ; he published every few years a slender volume of poems ; he transferred more table talk to the *Atlantic;* he made excursions into the realms of fiction and biographical writing. There is little else to record, except that his life was noble, and that love and sunshine were around him to the last. A thousand anecdotes are still told about him in Boston, all bearing witness to some fine personal trait of humor or kindness or sympathy.

There is another trait which his readers soon discover, namely, that he had always a boy's heart and a boy's delight in living. One by one his great contemporaries passed away, — an experience which saddens most men, but which gave Holmes a deeper interest in heaven while he still cherished the brightness and peace of this present earth. At eighty he published *Over the Teacups*, a book of tender reminiscences, in which we detect the first sign that the boy has become an old man ; but even here the spirit is still young, and the light is that of sunrise rather than of sunset.

Works of Holmes. One of the best commentaries on the poetry of Holmes is found in the title *Rhymes for an Hour*, which he gave to one of his collections. One half of his poetical work consists of occasional poems, that is, verses written for dinners, for class reunions, for welcome or farewell to an honored guest, and for various other " occasions " such as constantly occur in the life of a city. These all proceed not from inspiration but from good nature ; they are written, as he tells us :

> Not for glory, not for pelf,
> Not, be sure, to please myself,
> Not for any meaner ends, —
> Always " by request of friends."

The other half of his poetical work consists largely of mere *jeux d'esprit* and of poems called, for lack of a better name,

GREAT PINE ON WENDELL FARM, PITTS-
FIELD, OF WHICH DR. HOLMES
WAS VERY FOND

" society verse." Holmes was a master of such poetry, which at best is not of a very high order. He rejoiced like a child in the unmeasured praise which it brought him ; but he knew well that a poet cannot eat his cake and have it too, and that immediate praise rather than enduring fame was his literary portion. He is seen at his best, probably, in the class poems which he contributed regularly for forty years. The tender, whimsical spirit of all these reunions of men who were rapidly growing old is reflected in a single poem to which he gave the significant title of " The Boys."

At the beginning of his career, Holmes published two or three small volumes containing such poems as " The Height of the Ridiculous," " Daily Trials," " The Comet," " The Music Grinders " and " The Last Leaf." These five may be taken as the measure of his talent in humorous verse ; for he never wrote anything better. Like Bryant's, his first work was his best ; what **Typical Poems** he produced later was an addition but hardly an improvement. Lincoln's favorite, " The Last Leaf," with its blending of humor and pathos, is especially significant. The author outlived all his friends and literary contemporaries, and at eighty-five he must often have seriously recalled what he had written in jest at twenty-three :

> And if I should live to be
> The last leaf upon the tree,
>   In the spring,
> Let them smile, as I do now,
> At the old forsaken bough
>   Where I cling.

Occasionally Holmes attempted more ambitious works, such as " Poetry " and "A Rhymed Lesson," but a very few pages of either are enough to indicate that he was incapable of sustained poetic effort. Much more interesting are his short serious poems, such as " Nearing the Snow Line," " Contentment," " Grandmother's Story," " The Living Temple," " A Sun-day Hymn " and " The Voiceless." In *The Autocrat* will be found two poems of his later period, which are typical of the author's fine sentiment and humor. The first is " The Chambered Nautilus," an excellent little allegory, which has won a place in American poetry as secure and almost as high as Bryant's " To a Waterfowl." The second is " The Deacon's Masterpiece," which is one of our widely known humorous poems. Readers of this " Masterpiece " should note the satire involved in the subtitle, " A Logical Story." Logic is like a chain in being no stronger than its weakest link : if one premise or argument is false, the whole conclusion goes to pieces. " The Deacon's Masterpiece " was intended to symbolize logical arguments in general and Calvinism in particular, against which Holmes had a lifelong prejudice. The " shay " which went to pieces all at once is meant, of course, to satirize the deacon's theology.

The Autocrat of the Breakfast Table, our author's most original work, begins with the characteristic expression, " I was
The going to say, when I was interrupted." The alleged
Autocrat interruption occurred some twenty-five years earlier, when Holmes had contributed two forgotten essays in the same vein, and bearing the same title, to the *New England Magazine.* With this introduction he proceeds to talk of life in a half-whimsical, half-profound way, touching a dozen matters lightly but surely in each essay, and passing from one to another like a brilliant talker who introduces a new subject before his hearers lose interest in the old. In writing these dramatic essays, or monologues, Holmes reminds us of the memorable advice of Tony Weller, of *Pickwick Papers,* in regard to letter writing ; he knows the art of leaving off just at the point where we most wish him to continue. The scene is placed in a Boston boarding house ; the characters are the landlady, her son B. F., the old gentleman opposite, the young fellow by the name of John, the divinity student, the schoolmistress, and a few others, — all shadowy creatures, serving merely as a background for the Autocrat, who does most of the talking. Running through the series is a more or less continued story, which probably interested Holmes more than anybody else, and which undoubtedly led him at last to express his views of life in a novel rather than in a dramatic essay.

Three other books, with a slight thread of connection, belong in the same series with *The Autocrat.* These are *The Professor at the Breakfast Table* (1860), *The Poet at the Breakfast Table* (1872), and *Over the Teacups* (1890). Holmes also wrote three works of fiction, *Elsie Venner, The Guardian Angel* and *A Mortal Antipathy.* These were promptly labeled " medicated novels," to the wrath of the author, and the title with its implied criticism still clings to them. They are less typical of the life which Holmes attempts to describe than of the author himself, with his professional theories, his humor and sentiment, his whims and prejudices, his scientific interest in heredity. Of the three works *The Guardian Angel* is perhaps the most typical and the most interesting to the general reader. The list of prose works includes also two biographies (of Motley and of Emerson) and a series of bright sketches called *Our Hundred Days in Europe*, the last being a charming record of Holmes's final journey abroad, which from beginning to end was a kind of triumphal procession.

General Characteristics. We have already spoken of the importance of Holmes's work as a humorist, at a time when humor was hardly considered worthy of our national literature. We might suggest also that in Holmes we have, possibly, the true type of American humor, — a humor that depends not simply upon a droll imagination, but that is always associated with knowledge, kindness and human sympathy. We may appreciate this better if we contrast the delicate, playful, friendly humor of Holmes with the boisterousness of Irving's *Knickerbocker History*, or with the crude and often sensational chapters of Mark Twain in *Tom Sawyer* or in *Innocents Abroad*. Humor is always a personal rather than a national quality; but if there be such a thing as American humor, perhaps Holmes, who was American to the core and who represents our culture as well as our mirth, comes nearer to expressing it than any other writer. For humor is only wisdom smiling, and it is incomplete if it lack either the smile or the wisdom.

Aside from the question of humor, the chief characteristic of Holmes's work is its intensely personal quality. No matter what **Personal Quality** his subject, Holmes talks rather than writes, and talks invariably about himself, — about his thought and sentiment, his scientific and social theories, his pets and his prejudices, his whims, hobbies and convictions. In consequence, his collected writings are, with the exception of Sewall's *Diary*, probably the most complete reflection of a human mind in our literature. In another writer, like Whitman, this personal quality would be termed " egoism," but the word is altogether too harsh to apply to so lovable a character as Holmes. He had a theory that the only knowledge a man can have at first hand is of himself; all other knowledge is a matter of deduction or inference. Therefore did he begin with himself, as the one known quantity which might help to solve the $x + y$ of humanity. In his kindness and sympathy for all men (except, perhaps, reformers, homeopathists and strict Calvinists) he never doubted that they would be as interested as he was in his little self-revelations, which he hoped might be as sunbeams shining on human joy and sorrow. As he says, after assuring us that he is a person of no special gifts:

" This one thing I know, that I am like so many others of my fellow creatures that when I smile, I feel as if they must; when I cry, I think their eyes fill; and it always seems to me that when I am most truly my-self, I come closest to them, and am surest of being listened to by the brothers and sisters of the larger family into which I was born so long ago."

Sidney Lanier (1842–1881)

We measure some poets by their gifts to men, others by our sense of loss in their untimely death. Lanier belongs to the latter class. We think of his short, heroic life; we read the few poems that he wrote in moments snatched from weariness or pain, as a bird sings in the lulls of a tempest; and deep within us is the conviction that, had this man lived, he would have put a new song on our lips:

> To those who 've failed, in aspiration vast, . . .
> I 'd rear a laurel-cover'd monument,
> High, high above the rest — To all cut off before their time,
> Possess'd by some strange spirit of fire,
> Quench'd by an early death.[1]

We may estimate Lanier, however, by his deed alone, without weighing the difficulties he overcame in doing it. He has left us as a heritage a few of our most haunting lyrics; in the " Psalm of the West" he gave us a patriotic poem of broader sweep and more sustained beauty than anything that even

[1] From Whitman, " To Those Who 've Failed."

Lowell attempted ; in " Sunrise " and " The Marshes of Glynn "
he produced two wonderful poems that seem to be the working
out of a musical *motif* rather than the expression of thought ;
and in all his work he appears
as our foremost interpreter of
the changing melody of nature.[1]
As the elder Greeks, looking
at a fountain which leaped from
shadow into light, asked themselves if the water were not
thinking and what its thoughts
might be, so Lanier, hearing the
river murmuring to its banks,
the leaves rustling, the marsh
grass whispering to the wind,
was wont to ask what they were
all singing. His verse is but an
interpretation of their song in
English words. Because his
own soul was filled with melody,

SIDNEY LANIER

he heard an echo of its music everywhere ; or was he not
himself rather an echo of the wind and the leaves and the sea ?
We think of him sometimes as he thought of his own flute :

> I am not overbold :
>   I hold
> Full powers from Nature manifold.
> I speak for each no-tonguéd tree
> That, spring by spring, doth nobler be,
> And dumbly and most wistfully
> His mighty prayerful arms outspreads
> Above men's oft-unheeding heads,
> And his big blessing downward sheds.
> I speak for all-shaped blooms and leaves,
> Lichens on stones and moss on eaves,
> Grasses and grains in ranks and sheaves ; . . .

[1] See comparison between Bryant and Lanier, p. 205.

All tree-sounds, rustlings of pine-cones,
Wind-sighings, doves' melodious moans,
And night's unearthly under-tones;
All placid lakes and waveless deeps,
All cool reposing mountain-steeps,
Vale-calms and tranquil lotos-sleeps; —
Yea, all fair forms, and sounds, and lights,
And warmths, and mysteries, and mights,
Of Nature's utmost depths and heights,
— These doth my timid tongue present,
Their mouthpiece and leal instrument
And servant, all love-eloquent.[1]

Life. To record a life of high motive and heroic endeavor, unshaken by poverty or pain or death — this is no easy task. Indeed, the biographer has not yet appeared to do justice to Lanier, who combined the gentleness of a woman with the indomitable courage of a Norse hero. He lived like the simplest of men; but when the last stern call came he answered like Gunnar of old, who when bound and cast over a precipice flung a laugh to his enemies, a hail to death, swept the cords of his harp with his free foot, and went singing "home to his ancestors."

Those old ancestors of Lanier, by the way, are responsible for the music that was his lifelong passion. One of them, a Huguenot refugee, was musical composer at the court of Elizabeth; others were directors of painting and music for King James and King Charles. The first American Lanier came to Richmond in 1716, and from there the family migrated to other states. Our poet's father was a country lawyer of Georgia, his mother a Virginia woman of Scotch-Irish descent. He represents, therefore, the Celtic rather than the Saxon element in our life and literature.

He was born at Macon, Georgia, in 1842. One marked characteristic of his childhood was his delight in music, his ability to learn without instruction the use of any musical instrument. This **Love of Music** love of music went through life, lightening his college tasks, inspiring him and his fellow soldiers to a rarer courage and devotion, cheering his desperate struggle for health, till he could speak of it, in the way that Coleridge spoke of poetry, as soothing his afflictions, multiplying and refining his enjoyments, endearing his solitude, helping him to discover the good and the beautiful in all whom he met.

---

[1] From Lanier, the flute note, in "The Symphony."

At fourteen he entered Oglethorpe University at Midway, one of the small country colleges which made a brave beginning only to perish when the South was devastated by the war. A study of the boy here, as he reveals himself in his notebook and letters, shows that he combined with a musical and romantic temperament the instinct of a scholar, and withal a spiritual ideal so fine that he left upon all who met him an impression of almost feminine purity.

At his graduation Lanier was called to be tutor in his college; but the next year came another call, the clamor of drum and bugle, to **The Call to Arms** which every young southerner responded. The war came, and Lanier at nineteen went out to meet it with the first volunteers. All was enthusiasm in those early days of fighting; but as the war dragged out its horrible length, he saw in it the expression of all that is brutal and evil in humanity. He saw plenty of hard fighting, and for his courage and ability was thrice offered promotion, which he refused because his younger brother was in the ranks beside him. He would fight with the common soldier, he would watch over the brother who had been intrusted to his care, leaving the vain glory of chevrons or epaulets to others. In this quiet, unselfish heroism we see a picture of thousands of educated gentlemen who fought in the ranks and who made the regiments a wonder to all who beheld them, whether in camp or on the battlefield.

Lanier and his brother were transferred to the signal service, and were presently sent out as officers on the blockade runners. On one of these dangerous expeditions, Lanier was captured with his ship, and was imprisoned at Point Lookout. His flute, the old, loved companion of march and bivouac, was hidden in his ragged sleeve, and in its music prisoner and jailer found themselves brothers at heart, and wondered why they had been fighting each other. When the war ended and the prison door opened at last, Lanier started on foot for his home, five hundred miles away.

That was a sad home-coming, and it was typical of many others. For him there were no cheering crowds, no triumphal marches, no **The Home-coming** banners streaming in the wind. The banner he had fought for was furled forever. He returned solitary and silent, in the grim heroism of defeat. He was broken in health, weary in body and soul from marching without food and sleeping in the snow and the rain. Yet almost the first problem that confronted him was to earn his bread in a country devastated by the fire and scourge of war. As soon as he could stand — for his imprisonment followed by the weary march homeward brought on a fever of exhaustion — he went to work, taking the first job that offered. He was clerk in a hotel; he taught school, studied law, and wrote prose and verse which he tried, sometimes in vain, to sell. His *Tiger Lilies* (1867), a crude novel of army life and experience, was written in a few weeks. After an effort to be interested in the courts while his spirit called him to other fields, he abandoned the law and traveled northward, taking his beloved flute with him.

At Baltimore he was engaged to play in the Peabody orchestra, and for the first time in his life found himself in a congenial atmosphere of books and music. He began to work and study with splendid enthusiasm, but with the first effort he knew that he must pay for every smallest success with his life blood. He had consumption, and the disease had gained a terrible foothold in his army life of exposure and hardship. Then, knowing his power and that he had but a few years to live, he made a resolve which is best expressed in a paragraph from one of his letters:

" . . . My dear father, think how, for twenty years, through poverty, through pain, through weariness, through sickness, through the uncongenial atmosphere of a farcical college and of a bare army and then of an exacting business life, through all the discouragement of being wholly unacquainted with literary people and literary ways — I say think how, in spite of all these depressing circumstances, and of a thousand more which I could enumerate, these two figures of music and of poetry have steadily kept in my heart so that I could not banish them. Does it not seem to you, as to me, that I begin to have the right to enroll myself among the devotees of these two sublime arts, after having followed them so long and so humbly, and through so much bitterness? "

With his life in Baltimore (1873) began, says a biographer, "as brave and sad a struggle as the history of genius records." So far as Life in Baltimore we can separate them, Lanier's heroic struggle had four objects. The first and most immediate was to earn a living for his wife and children. The second was to write the poetry which he felt surging within him, like waves that beat upon the shore in ceaseless iteration. He writes to his wife, a noble and most helpful woman:

" . . . All day my soul hath been cutting swiftly into the great space of the subtle, unspeakable deep, driven by wind after wind of heavenly melody. The very inner spirit and essence of all wind-songs, bird-songs, . . . , soul-songs and body-songs hath blown upon me in quick gusts like the breath of passion, and sailed me into a sea of vast dreams, whereof each wave is at once a vision and a melody."

The third object was to gain the wider knowledge that his soul had always craved during a life which he describes as " intellectual drought and famine." It is not enough for Lanier to feel deeply and to write as he feels, —

> To range, deep-wrapt, along a heavenly height,
> O'erseeing all that man but undersees;
> To loiter down lone alleys of delight,
> And hear the beating of the hearts of trees,
> And think the thoughts that lilies speak in white
> By greenwood pools and pleasant passages.[1]

Other poets have been content to sing and to let others find, if they can, the laws of their singing; but Lanier has the instincts of a scholar. He must first learn, must study his art from the foundation; for he will not be like Poe, whose great fault, he said, was that he did not know enough. With books and a university at hand, he begins with Anglo-Saxon and makes a thorough study of English poetry; and because he thinks no art is of value unless used to ennoble human life, he shares the results of his solitary study by giving courses of lectures. Then in the midst of his happy study he is sternly interrupted by the first object of his struggle; he must leave his work to write a song, a booklet for a railroad company, a tale for *St. Nicholas,* — anything that will bring him a little money to meet the first duty of a gentleman, which is honorably to support those who love and depend upon him.

The last object of the struggle was for life itself. Everything else he could attain; but here he failed, and failed just when his ability **The Spirit** had secured for him a lectureship with an assured in- **of Lanier** come at Johns Hopkins University. We have no heart to enter into this last struggle, to follow him from Baltimore to Florida, to Texas, to Pennsylvania, to Carolina, in search of a climate where he could breathe deep without pain, and perchance gather a bit of strength, only to spend it freely upon his music and poetry. We only note, as suggestive of the man's brave, cheery spirit, that the wonderful poem " Sunrise " was written by a hand that had not strength to

---

[1] From " To Bayard Taylor." The whole poem is a tribute to one of Lanier's loyal and helpful friends.

raise a cup of water to the poet's lips ; that the inspiring lectures in Johns Hopkins were many of them delivered from an invalid's chair, in a voice scarcely above a whisper :

" . . . For, indeed we may say that he who has not yet perceived how artistic beauty and moral beauty are convergent lines which run back into a common ideal origin, and who therefore is not afire with moral beauty just as with artistic beauty — that he, in short, who has not come to that stage of quiet and eternal frenzy in which the beauty of holiness and the holiness of beauty mean one thing, burn as one fire, shine as one light within him ; he is not yet the great artist. . . . So far from dreading that your moral purpose will interfere with your beautiful creation, go forward in the clear conviction that unless you are suffused — soul and body, one might say — with that moral purpose which finds its largest expression in love, that is, the love of all things in their proper relation ; unless you are suffused with this love, do not dare to meddle with beauty ; unless you are suffused with truth, do not dare to meddle with goodness ; in a word, unless you are suffused with truth, wisdom, goodness and love, abandon the hope that the ages will accept you as an artist."

That is a lofty ideal, and our poet, like Chaucer's parson, lived it before he preached it. To be noble himself, then to kindle from his own fire the love of nobility in other men, was with Lanier a passion deeper even than his love of music and poetry. And he would not be conquered. In the face of poverty, pain and death he wrote his poetry. He did his work in the spirit of the young Athenian who went out to receive a message from an overwhelming army. Said the envoy from the hosts of Persia, " Our arrows will darken the sun." Quietly, steadily came the answer, " Then we Greeks will fight in the shade."

Such was Lanier, hiding the bravest of hearts under the gentlest exterior. When he died (1881) in a little tent in the Carolina hills, he had hardly reached the maturity of his power. He had never once been permitted to do his best ; but he left one volume whose excellence will sooner or later place him among our elder poets, and he had made upon all who knew him the impression that

> His song was only living aloud,
> His work, a singing with his hand.[1]

Works of Lanier. A single small volume of poems represents Lanier's permanent contribution to our national literature. Before we study this we note certain prose works, which a few

[1] From Lanier, " Life and Song."

students may be glad to read. First are the *Boy's Froissart* and three other volumes, the *King Arthur*, *Mabinogion* and *Percy*, — popular editions of these old favorites, written for younger readers who cannot perhaps appreciate the originals. Next in importance are *The English Novel and the Principles of its Development* and *The Science of English Verse*, two critical works which are largely composed of Lanier's lectures on English literature. The latter book, whether or not we agree with its fundamental theory, is our most original work on the subject of versification. It proceeds on the assumption that poetry is an art which is founded on exact knowledge, and that it is possible to formulate laws of poetry as definite as those of any other science.

Of this proposition we can only say that the great poets of the world have not so believed or so worked. Their best poems seem to be spontaneous, to be the natural expression of a genius that does not and cannot work by rule. Only second-rate poets found a "school"; the greatest have never been able to teach or even to explain their art to others.

Two other theories of this *Science of English Verse* must be noted, since they exercised a dominant influence on Lanier's **Poetry and** work. The first is that poetry and music are closely **Music** related and follow the same general laws. Perhaps because of his adherence to this theory, Lanier's verse is, with the possible exception of Poe's, the most musical in our literature; it is so pervaded by the spirit of music that it seems at times more like a rhapsody or improvisation than a poem. The second theory is that poetry appeals chiefly to our emotional nature, and that the effect of a poem depends more upon the sound than upon the sense. Here Lanier shows himself in some degree a follower of Poe, who had advanced and practised the same questionable theory.

Once he had developed his principle, that poetry in its "tone color," its rime, rhythm, alliteration and phrasing, follows the rules of musical composition, Lanier held to it steadily. He was severely criticized, of course,[1] but he was not disturbed. He declared with quiet, steadfast sincerity :

" My experience in the varying judgments given about poetry has all converged upon one solitary principle, and the experience of the artist in all ages is reported by history to be of precisely the same direction. That principle is, that the artist shall put forth, humbly and lovingly, and without bitterness against opposition, the very best and highest that is within him, utterly regardless of contemporary criticism."

With this introduction, which attempts to sum up Lanier's aim and motive, we leave the reader to his book of poems. Here

Typical Poems are lyrics not quite like any others of our acquaintance : " Evening Song," " Stirrup Cup," " Mocking Bird," " Tampa Robins," " Song of the Chattahoochee," and the two exquisite love songs, "My Springs" and "In Absence." Here are " The Revenge of Hamish," a terrible border story, vividly and powerfully told, and the exquisite " Ballad of Trees and the Master," which expresses many things besides the harmony of a great soul with nature. There are a score more of short poems, all worthy of remembrance, and those named are intended merely as a guide to the beginner.

The longer poems are of uneven merit. Of the " Psalm of the West," a patriotic poem of elevated and sustained beauty, the noble opening, the sonnets on Columbus, and the parable of the conflict between heart and head should be read by every student. " The Symphony " is regarded by some as an expression of the relation of poetry to music, and by others as a protest against the barbarism of trade and the general materialism of modern life ; but a few readers may find in it an entirely different meaning. The key is discovered in the last four lines :

> And yet shall Love himself be heard,
> Though long deferred, though long deferred.
> O'er the modern waste a dove hath whirred :
> Music is Love in search of a word.

[1] This was especially true when he wrote the Cantata for the Centennial Exposition of 1876, — a work which it is idle to criticize unless we consider it as part of the music, which was written by Dudley Buck.

With this key we may unlock the whole poem, and find that Lanier, like Tennyson, is teaching that divine love offers the only explanation of life, and that in human love may be found the solution of all earthly problems. In this connection the student should read also that strange poem " How Love looked for Hell," which teaches the same lesson. The meaning of the latter poem is, simply, that Love cannot possibly find hell, because where Love is no hell can be. It is like a sunbeam trying to find a shadow, and wherever the sunbeam goes the shadows flee away.

Of "Sunrise" and "The Marshes of Glynn" we have already spoken. They are not popular poems; they never will be; but to those who have ears to hear they are filled with melody and immortal aspiration. They are both characterized by many musical lines like the following which rouse the inexpressible emotions of a man who looks upon marsh and sea lying vast, silent, motionless under the setting sun:

And the sea lends large, as the marsh: lo, out of his plenty the sea
Pours fast: full soon the time of the flood-tide must be:
Look how the grace of the sea doth go
About and about through the intricate channels that flow
　　Here and there,
　　　　　Everywhere,
Till his waters have flooded the uttermost creeks and the low-lying lanes,
And the marsh is meshed with a million veins,
That like as with rosy and silvery essences flow
　　In the rose-and-silver evening glow.
　　　Farewell, my lord Sun!
The creeks overflow: a thousand rivulets run
'Twixt the roots of the sod; the blades of the marsh-grass stir;
Passeth a hurrying sound of wings that westward whirr;
Passeth, and all is still; and the currents cease to run;
And the sea and the marsh are one.

How still the plains of the waters be!
The tide is in his ecstasy.
The tide is at his highest height:
　　　And it is night.

And now from the Vast of the Lord will the waters of sleep
Roll in on the souls of men,
But who will reveal to our waking ken
The forms that swim and the shapes that creep
            Under the waters of sleep?
And I would I could know what swimmeth below when the tide comes in
On the length and the breadth of the marvellous marshes of Glynn.

General Characteristics. Aside from noting his choice of
melodious words and the rare musical quality of all his verse,
one seldom tries to analyze Lanier's style, simply because one
knows without trying that it cannot be done. Here, for instance,
in the first four stanzas of "The Marshes of Glynn," we have
a single sentence running through fifty lines. It begins in the
midst of an emotion; when it ends there is no pause in our
thought or imagination. Now the words rush on with the tide;
now they halt and quiver, like a sea gull poised over the deep;
and again they reveal without defining the feeling that stirs
deeply in one who looks out upon a tranquil landscape. Lanier
tries simply to be in harmony with his scene, and to analyze his
style is to describe the method of a musician who touches the
chords of an organ and then drifts away on the wave of his own
emotions.

The same poem serves to illustrate the quality of Lanier's
thought which most appeals to us, and that is a certain indefi-
Musical niteness. This is not due to any failure on the part
Quality of the poet to think or to speak clearly; it is rather
the recognition of the fact that some things, like the sunset, are
unbounded, and that certain human emotions have no adequate
expression. There comes a time when words fail, when we must
leave poetry and take up music, if we are to express what is in
us. So in most of Lanier's verse there is a sense of failure, of
incompleteness. He takes us as far as he can go and says, Your
own heart must finish the poem. Some have said that Lanier
failed because he followed rules or a mistaken theory of poetry,
and at times one might wish that he had never heard of the
"science" of verse; for his theory often interfered with his

spontaneity, — which is the first grace of a bird song or a poem. Then all such criticism is hushed by the reflection that music also is incomplete ; that the best music invariably leaves us unsatisfied or sad, and that Lanier's art may be more perfect than even his admirers have supposed. It is possible that he intended his verse to have the haunting, saddening quality of a symphony; that he deliberately left it incomplete in order to make it harmonize, not with his own theory, but with the known facts of human experience.

There is another characteristic of Lanier's work which the historian who remembers the terrible War of the States is glad **Universal** to emphasize, and that is its absolutely impersonal **Standards** quality, its devotion to universal standards. One who has been reading the passionate appeals and war lyrics of the period will turn with relief to this poet, who could fight with the bravest when the call came, but who never once lowered his verse to personal or sectional ends. For him there was no North or South, but only America and humanity. He had been through fire and flood ; he had languished in prison and slept among the dead upon the battlefield ; he had witnessed the suffering and injustice of "reconstruction"; but in his poetry there is nothing of the din and conflict of life, nothing of the smoke and cinders of civilization. Fighting and party politics are but transient, barbarous phases of existence ; love only is eternal and worthy of a poet's devotion.

A single great purpose dominated Lanier, and that was to present beauty and truth in such lovely guise that men everywhere must recognize and revere them. The shock of battle, the desperate struggle with poverty and death, the carping of ungenerous critics, — none of these bitter experiences ever disturbed Lanier's faith in God or man, or ever drew his steadfast gaze from the universal and eternal elements in human life. " The artist's market is the heart of men," he says. So long as the heart loves beauty and delights in harmony, this artist will be sure of his market.

WALT WHITMAN (1819–1892)

Out in the field yonder stands a wild apple tree that has never known the virtue of a pruning knife. Its trunk is hollow, its limbs sprawling, its top a wilderness of dead wood and unthrifty ramage ; but there is one great branch, vigorous and full of sap, stretching southward to the sun. In springtime the branch shows a splendor of pink blossoms ; in autumn it bears apples of strange shape and savor. And this uncultivated tree, with its one branch of bloom and fruit, may serve as a symbol of Whitman's poetry, the bulk of which is almost worthless, but a small part of which reveals the vigor and vitality of genius.

WALT WHITMAN

The majority of readers, seeing only the crudity of Whitman's work, reject and ridicule it. Meanwhile a small but enthusiastic band of worshipers insist that Whitman is America's greatest poet, the true bard of Democracy, and that he must and shall be recognized. So a critical controversy has arisen, into which we do not care to enter. We note only that poetry is one of the things that cannot be advertised. As the bee needs no bell to call him where the clover blooms, so man seems to have an instinct for good poetry, as for beauty and truth ; and one must trust this quiet instinct, rather than controversial opinions, in the difficult task of estimating the poet's life and work.

It should be clearly understood, however, that there are objections to Whitman, and that the objection applies occasionally to the matter as well as to the form of his verse. Some of his effusions indicate a lack of the fine moral sense that distinguishes nearly all American poets, and a few others are unpardonable. A small book of selections from Whitman is therefore desirable. Good taste need not and will not read what only bad taste could have written or published.

Life. The life of Whitman is almost exactly contemporaneous with that of Lowell. He was born (1819) and spent his early childhood on a little farm on Long Island, which he always called by its Indian name Paumanok. Presently the family moved to Brooklyn, and the boy grew up to love the noise and the crowd of the city streets even more than he loved the sea and the open country.

In the city Whitman received a little education, of the common-school kind; then he was by turns office boy, printer, teacher of a district school, carpenter, idler, reporter, and editor of small newspapers. By inclination he was something of a vagabond, not keeping any job longer than it pleased him, nor recognizing any social ties which interfered with what he considered his personal freedom. He made one leisurely journey down the Ohio to New Orleans, returning on foot by way of the Great Lakes and Canada, seeing practically the whole of our country as it then was, and making comrades of all classes of our laboring people. He came back to Brooklyn, worked at various jobs, wrote newspaper sketches and poems of a very ordinary kind, lived with his mother, and " paid his board when he had the money." At thirty-six years of age he published his first small volume, *Leaves of Grass* (1855), making a radical departure from all his previous methods of writing; and from that time on he followed an entirely new trail in literature.

The pleasantest part of the biographer's task, in dealing with a life which leaves much to be desired,[1] is to record Whitman's hospital **Hospital** service, — a tender, helpful service, without pay and **Service** above reward. His soldier brother was wounded, in 1862, and Whitman hurried to the front to take care of him. From the camp he followed some of the stricken soldiers to Washington, and found that city a huge hospital, its surgeons and nurses overworked in caring for fifty thousand sick and wounded, while thousands

---

[1] Because of the controversy over Whitman, accounts of his life generally take the form of attack or defense, and most of them are one-sided and misleading. A mild attempt to show Whitman as he was is made in Perry's *Walt Whitman* (1906).

more came pouring in, a ghastly flood, after every battle. The pity of it all touched Whitman deeply, and securing a small position in a government office, he gave all his spare time to the hospitals, making himself useful in every possible way to the suffering soldiers. In his *Drum Taps* he had caught the popular view of war, — the brass bands, the flags, the thrill of bugles and the long roll of the drums ; but now he sees, as he says, " the real war, which will never get into books " :

> Aroused and angry,
> I thought to beat the alarum, and urge relentless war ;
> But soon my fingers fail'd me, my face dropp'd, and I resigned myself
> To sit by the wounded and soothe them, or silently watch the dead.[1]

When that generous service was ended, Whitman's health was broken ; but he had gained a strength of spirit unknown to him before. His later poetry is still crude and often spoiled by egotism, but a deeper rhythm, like the beating of a heart, creeps into it ; and the coarseness vanishes, together with the animal pleasure of mere physical sensations. He has learned that man has a soul also, and at times the soul appears to him as of more consequence than the body. For some ten years he was a government clerk in Washington, and for the remainder of his life he resided in Camden, New Jersey. His *Leaves of Grass*, which he republished ten times with additions and corrections, brought him a very small income, and in the later years of his life he was largely dependent on friends, who gave freely because of his service and his genius.

These later years, though troubled by pain and poverty, were not without their triumph. Though the public would not read his verses, **Life in** a few good critics acknowledged his power, and his little **Camden** house became the object of pilgrimages from all parts of America and England. With all his comradeship and love of crowds, Whitman was always secretive about himself, and, as he has the habit of posing in his poetry, the biographer is often baffled in his search for truth. Toward the end of his life, however, we have the testimony of many who visited Whitman, and almost without exception these speak of him as one who had learned the discipline of living, who met suffering with patient heroism, and who left upon all his friends the impression of gentleness and sincerity.

---

[1] From *Drum Taps*. Those who would see the real war, and understand the better side of Whitman, should read his prose *Specimen Days*, and *The Wound Dresser*. The latter is made up of letters to his mother.

The Quality of Whitman's Verse. All of Whitman's poems
are now printed in a single volume, *Leaves of Grass*, the title of
which was meant to suggest that the work sprang from the poet
as naturally as vegetation grows from the bosom of mother earth.
The title would perhaps have been more descriptive if "weeds"
had been added to grass, for a large part of the verse is rank and
riotous. Witness this selection (which omits numerous chaotic
lines) from the opening and the close of the "Song of Myself."

I celebrate myself and sing myself,
And what I assume you shall assume,
For every atom belonging to me as good belongs to you.
I loafe and invite my Soul;
I lean and loafe at my ease, observing a spear of summer grass.
A child said, What is the grass? fetching it to me with full hands;
How could I answer the child? I do not know what it is any more than he.
I guess it must be the flag of my disposition, out of hopeful green stuff
    woven;
Or I guess it is the handkerchief of the Lord,
A scented gift and remembrancer, designedly dropt,
Bearing the owner's name someway in the corners, that we may see and
    remark, and say, *Whose?*
Or I guess the grass is itself a child, the produced babe of the vegetation.
Or I guess it is a uniform hieroglyphic,
And it means, Sprouting alike in broad zones and narrow zones,
Growing among black folks as among white;
Kanuck, Tuckahoe, Congressman, Cuff, I give them the same, I receive
    them the same.
And now it seems to me the beautiful uncut hair of graves.

Man or woman! I might tell how I like you, but cannot;
And might tell what it is in me, and what it is in you, but cannot.
I know perfectly well my own egotism;
I know my omnivorous lines, and will not write any less;
And would fetch you, whoever you are, flush with myself.
Do I contradict myself?
Very well, then, I contradict myself;
(I am large — I contain multitudes.)
The spotted hawk swoops by and accuses me — he complains of my gab
    and my loitering.
I too am not a bit tamed — I too am untranslatable;
I sound my barbaric yawp over the roofs of the world.

Between these two sections are thirteen hundred other lines, a few of them strongly poetic, the rest suggesting the word of a critic, that the art of writing consists largely in knowing what to leave in the inkpot. One moment the author is shouting, uttering what he calls "prophetical screams"; then he grows quiet, and his lines fall into a swinging rhythm as he contemplates the beauty of earth and sea. He interjects an irrelevant story which he has just read in the newspaper. He addresses himself, "What seest thou, Walt Whitman?" and for answer makes a catalogue of plants, towns, occupations, — everything that comes into his head. His admirers assure us that all this contains the elements of true poetry, and they may be right; a woodpile contains all the elements of a forest, though the two things are somewhat different. Whitman insisted on the poetic quality of his work, refusing to alter even the crudest lines, and defended himself in a striking bit of verse written after a visit to a canyon in Colorado, where he wrote in his notebook, "I have found the law of my own poems":

Spirit that form'd this scene,
These tumbled rock-piles grim and red,
These reckless, heaven-ambitious peaks,
These gorges, turbulent-clear streams, this naked freshness,
These formless wild arrays, for reasons of their own, . . .
Was 't charged against my chants they had forgotten art?
To fuse within themselves its rules precise and delicatesse?
The lyrist's measur'd beat, the wrought-out temple's grace — column and
    polish'd arch forgot?
But thou that revelest here — spirit that form'd this scene,
They have remember'd thee.

Forgetting the affectation of that word "delicatesse," most readers will welcome this verse for its own sake; but few will accept the implied argument, that the rugged canyons of the Lord and the crude verses of a poet are alike admirable. The chief difficulty in the appreciation of Whitman is that few readers have the patience to strip off the husk of crudity, exaggeration and bad taste which hides the kernel of his poetry.

Not until we have a sternly abridged edition of Whitman will his undoubted power and originality be generally understood.

Whitman's Better Poetry. As an introduction to the better part of Whitman's work, we quote the opening lines of a characteristic poem :

Night on the prairies,
The supper is over, the fire on the ground burns low,
The wearied emigrants sleep, wrapt in their blankets ;
I walk by myself — I stand and look at the stars, which I think now I never
    realized before.
Now I absorb immortality and peace,
I admire death and test propositions.
How plenteous ! how spiritual ! how résumé !
The same old man and soul — the same old aspirations, and the same content.

Here is one of the elemental scenes in which Whitman is at his best : the dusk-shrouded prairie, the low-burning fire, the blanketed forms, stars, silence, immensity of night. The poetry of the scene appeals to us strongly till our feelings are jarred by the poet himself, by his " résumé " [1] and his absurd testing of " propositions." This obtruding of himself in the vast landscape of earth and sky affects us like the clamor of house sparrows in the solemn splendor of twilight ; but he cannot help his egoism, and we must take him as he is, overlooking his faults in our search for his virtues.

If we read Whitman in this spirit, we shall find certain of his works as tonic as a sea wind. Though the best of them are crudely formed, though they violate all rules in the matter of rime and melody, we have only to read them carefully to discover at times a deep rhythm sounding through the verse, as in this stirring chant to the ocean :

With husky-haughty lips, O sea !
Where day and night I wend thy surf-beat shore,
Imaging to my sense thy varied strange suggestions, . . .
Thy troops of white-maned racers racing to the goal,

[1] Whitman uses many such expressions affectedly, because they sound fine to him, without any definite idea of their meaning.

> Thy ample, smiling face, dash'd with the sparkling dimples of the sun,
> Thy brooding scowl and murk — thy unloos'd hurricanes, . . .
> Some vast heart, like a planet's, chain'd and chafing in those breakers,
> By lengthen'd swell, and spasm, and panting breath,
> And rhythmic rasping of thy sands and waves,
> And serpent hiss, and savage peals of laughter,
> And undertones of distant lion roar, . . .
> The first and last confession of the globe.

The beginner, accustomed to regular verse forms, may well make the acqaintance of Whitman in " O Captain, My Captain," which is one of his splendid tributes to Lincoln. The swinging " Pioneers " may come next; and then, as the measure of Whitman's lyric quality, the song of the bird to its mate, in " Out of the Cradle Endlessly Rocking ":

> Shine! shine! shine!
> Pour down your warmth, great sun!
> While we bask — we two together.
>
> Two together!
> Winds blow south, or winds blow north,
> Day come white, or night come black,
> Home, or rivers and mountains from home,
> Singing all time, minding no time,
> While we two keep together.

Of the short poems in Whitman's peculiar rhythm, one of the most notable is " Come up from the fields," a finely

Selected Poems   drawn picture of an old father and mother who come trembling from their work to hear news of their boy, who is far away on the battle line. It is a picture of ten thousand fathers and mothers, in as many villages of the North and South, and it may appeal to some readers as the most exquisite and human of all Whitman's works. In strong contrast with this silent sorrow and heroism of mothers and fathers who sacrificed their sons in the great conflict is the " Beat, beat, drums," which reflects the stir and clamor of the first call to arms. Other significant short works are " A Clear Midnight," " Night on the Prairies," " On the Beach at Midnight," " The Mystic

Trumpeter," "Aboard at a Ship's Helm," "The First Dandelion," "Prayer of Columbus" and "The Ox Tamer." With
these should be read a few of Whitman's haunting poems on
the beauty of death, such as "Whispers of Heavenly Death,"
"Darest Thou Now, O Soul," "Assurances," "Joy, Shipmate,
Joy!" "A Noiseless Patient Spider," "Death's Valley," "Passage to India" and "Good-bye, My Fancy."

Of the longer poems, perhaps the finest is "When lilacs last
in the door-yard bloom'd," a beautiful threnody, in which the
flower, the star and the hermit thrush serve, like *motifs* in
music, to suggest the grief and hope of the nation at the death
of Lincoln. Especially beautiful is the thrush song, the carol to
death, "Dark Mother, always gliding near with soft feet":

Over the tree-tops I float thee a song,
Over the rising and sinking waves — over the myriad fields, and the
    prairies wide;
Over the dense-pack'd cities all, and the teeming wharves and ways,
I float this carol with joy, with joy to thee, O Death!

Of the many poems of patriotism, we indicate only "Thou
mother with thy equal brood," which some critics place beside
the "Commemoration Ode" of Lowell. It began originally in
a magnificent way, and was for years known by its opening lines:

As a strong bird on pinions free,
Joyous, the amplest spaces heavenward cleaving,
Such be the thought I'd think of thee, America,
Such be the recitative I'd bring for thee.

The theme of nearly all Whitman's verse is found in this
"Inscription" which, after many changes, he placed at the
beginning of his works:

One's Self I sing — a simple, separate Person;
Yet utter the word Democratic, the word *En-masse*.
Of physiology from top to toe I sing, . . .
Of Life immense in passion, pulse and power,
Cheerful — for freest action form'd under the laws divine,
The Modern Man I sing.

In these two words, "self" and "democracy," is found the explanation of Whitman's work, so far as it has any evident purpose or consistency. Of democracy, as related to law, government, society, he had no conception ; his verse is largely a glorification of men's bodies rather than of their minds or institutions. As Lanier said, Whitman's democracy was, in effect, "the worst kind of an aristocracy, being an aristocracy of nature's favorites in the matter of muscle." This purely physical note is dominant in Whitman's chant of democracy ; it is subdued a little in "As a Strong Bird" ; and it sinks to an undertone in the fine poems on death, which suggest that man may be essentially an immortal spirit rather than a body with appetites.

Whitman's Orientalism. In his glorification of self, Whitman seems an offshoot of transcendentalism, though we are still uncertain how far he developed his doctrine independently, and how far he was influenced by Emerson, Thoreau, Alcott, Margaret Fuller, and others who then made a cult of individualism.[1] To the indirect influence of Emerson he probably owes the characteristic which distinguishes him from all other American poets, namely, his orientalism, which is so pronounced at times that he seems almost like a dervish, chanting of ancient fate and pantheism in the midst of modern business and politics. Until he was thirty-six years old Whitman wrote only commonplace things, and there is little in his style to distinguish him from any other country editor.[2] Then suddenly he published *Leaves of Grass*, a work utterly unlike anything that had ever appeared in America ; and the question naturally arises, Where did Whitman get this new rhapsodical style and this rather startling material ?

A suggestion, at least, of an answer may be found in these considerations : that transcendentalism was most influential here

[1] *The Dial*, containing the works of all these writers, was published 1840–1844. Emerson and Thoreau both published their most characteristic works shortly before Whitman produced his *Leaves of Grass* (1855).

[2] Whitman destroyed nearly all his early work, but enough survives to judge it accurately.

at the time when Whitman wrote his chief work ; that it contained elements of mysticism and occult philosophy borrowed

Influence of Transcendentalism from oriental poets ; that several English translations of Sanskrit and Persian poetry appeared before 1855 ; that Emerson read them and advised others to read them, especially the *Bhagavadgita*[1]; and that a worn copy of the latter poem was found among Whitman's possessions. In this remarkable *Bhagavadgita* the god Krishna appears as the light and life of all things ; he is the beginning and the end, the cause and the effect, the mystery of birth and of death, and much more to the same effect. Many oriental poets have since expressed the same doctrine in exquisite verse ; one of them has written, " I was the sin that from Myself rebelled " ; and Emerson's " Brahma " is a new reflection of the old teaching :

> They reckon ill who leave me out;
> When me they fly, I am the wings;
> I am the doubter and the doubt,
> And I the hymn the Brahmin sings.

Emerson is here speaking for Brahma, of course ; but Whitman misunderstood the doctrine, or else was incredibly egotistic, when he applied it not to the gods but to himself :

. . . From this side Jehovah am I,
Old Brahma I, and I Saturnius am;
No time affects me — I am Time, old modern as any.
Consolator most mild, the promis'd one advancing,
With gentle hand extended — the mightier God am I,
Foretold by prophets and poets, in their most rapt prophecies and poems,
No time nor change shall ever change me or my words.
Life of the great round world, the sun and stars, and of man — I, the
    general Soul,
Here the square finishing, the solid, I the most solid,
Breathe my breath also through these songs.[2]

---

[1] The Sanskrit *Bhagavadgita* or *Bhagavat Gita* (meaning the song of the Adorable One) is a long dramatic poem, written by an unknown author, probably just before the Christian era. It contains the mystic teaching of earlier and later Hindu philosophy, expressed in noble poetic language.

[2] Abridged from " Chanting the Square Deific." The same doctrine is proclaimed in " We Two " and other chants of Whitman.

The one thing certain about such verse is that it was not and could not be inspired by our modern American life. Whitman appears here as the last, the most extreme of the transcendentalists, chanting an oriental philosophy of which he has only a superficial understanding.

Whitman's orientalism is shown in many other ways. His " Song of the Open Road," for instance, instantly suggests that other road or way which runs through oriental litera-
Oriental Elements
ture, and which is everywhere a symbol of human life. We must perforce think, not of the old country turnpike, but of that older caravan route when Whitman assures us that the universe is but " a road for traveling souls " :

Allons! we must not stop here!
However sweet these laid-up stores — however convenient this dwelling, we cannot remain here ;
However shelter'd this port, and however calm these waters, we must not anchor here ;
However welcome the hospitality that surrounds us, we are permitted to receive it but a little while.

All this, and more of his " Open Road," was expressed with much finer art by Hafiz, the Persian poet, in the fourteenth century :

'T is strange, at every stage along the road,
As soon as I have eased me of my load,
I hear the jangling camel bell's refrain,
Bidding me bind my burden on again.[1]

Again, in Whitman's *Calamus*, a book of verses celebrating manly friendships, his men kiss each other and sentimentalize in a way that reflects oriental poetry but that has no suggestion of American manhood. Some of his lines are vulgar or in bad taste, and here he copies the matter of Eastern poets without their style or unconsciousness. He is a fatalist; he allies himself with both good and evil; he cries out to earth and

[1] Quoted by Elsa Barker, in " What Whitman Learned from the East" (*Canada Monthly*, October, 1911).

heaven, — all in oriental fashion. Sometimes his verse has the warm sensuousness that characterizes the poetry of the East :

> Smile, O voluptuous cool-breath'd earth !
> Smile, for your lover comes !

More often he forgets the true poet's attitude toward nature, a reverent attitude born of mystery and beauty, and his lines seem like a crude parody of some Eastern singer :

> Earth, you seem to look for something at my hands;
> Say, old Top-not ! what do you want ? [1]

So also when Whitman ejaculates, calls himself by name, celebrates himself ; when he becomes, in a word, the dervish instead of the democrat, — in all this he has adopted the methods common to oriental poets. What in them is entirely natural seems in him an artificial posing ; and what we should expect in Persia or Arabia seems as out of place in America as camels or caravans would be, or the Muezzin's call to prayer.

In the above explanation of Whitman's method there is merely opened, not explored, an interesting field of study. We do not mean to imply that he deliberately copied oriental poets ; he was too independent, for one thing ; and he had neither the learning nor the patience to appreciate their peculiar art. Their philosophy seemed in harmony with his exaggerated notion of self ; and he claimed the same right as Emerson to express old oriental ideas in a new occidental way. A part of his material and his general rhapsodical method came undoubtedly from the East ; his vigor and originality no less than his oddity and extravagance are all his own.

At Home and Abroad. It appears strange at first that many foreign critics should acclaim Whitman, the least typical of American writers, as our most representative poet ; but the explanation of their choice is simple. To foreigners America has always appeared as an extraordinary country. Democracy,

[1] From " Song of Myself," ll. 986–987

freedom, the winning of a wilderness and the appropriation of its vast treasures, — all this, which to us is the most natural thing in the world, seems to them marvelous. In consequence of this mental attitude, they have expected that the literature which reflects our life should be entirely different from their own. To meet their expectation an American poem should have in it something strange and uncouth, some suggestion at least of a buffalo or a cyclone. Franklin and Irving tried in vain to disabuse them of this notion. Longfellow was and still is widely read and appreciated abroad ; but because he had culture and literary art, because he was essentially like their own poets, foreign critics did not consider him typical of America. Poe had appealed to their artistic sense, Cooper to their adventurous spirit, but not till Whitman appeared was their prejudice satisfied. His crudity and extravagance corresponded to their peculiar ideas of the New World, and because he was strange they called him representative. Meanwhile this very quality of strangeness must here prevent him from being considered a typical poet, though a part of his work, original and vigorous, will surely find a permanent place in the literature of the nation.

THE MINOR POETS

The historian must hesitate as he faces the abundant minor verse of this golden age of American poetry. Here, for example, are two goodly volumes containing the memorable lyrics of the great war, such as " Little Giffen," " The Confederate Flag," " Stonewall Jackson's Way," " Sheridan's Ride," " The Black Regiment," " All Quiet along the Potomac," " The Blue and the Gray," " High Tide at Gettysburg," and at least two ringing war songs : " Maryland, my Maryland," by James Ryder Randall, and the " Battle Hymn of the Republic," by Julia Ward Howe. The last-named lyrics, aside from their clear reflection of the martial spirit of the age, have an added value, tender and forever sacred,

Lyrics of War and Peace

from the fact that they were sung in trench or camp by thousands of brave men whose lips were silenced on the next day's battle field. In marked contrast with these stirring songs are the lyrics of peace, such, for instance, as Stephen Collins Foster's " Old Folks at Home " and " My Old Kentucky Home," which reflect the simplest and dearest of human emotions. There are literally scores of such poems, which have endeared themselves to countless Americans, and which suggest that the authors are worthy of our grateful remembrance. For he who creates even one true song or poem has added another Bill of Rights to the possessions of humanity.

Over the minor poets of the age, who produced each his book of verse, one must hesitate even longer, for two reasons : first, because it is often impossible to draw the line between major and minor writers ; and second, because our literary histories have recorded more than fifty " local " poets between 1840 and 1876, and to treat them adequately and impartially would in itself require a volume. In the history of an earlier period such poets would have received large space; but we must judge each age in turn by the best that it produced, and in the works of our so-called elder poets, from Longfellow to Lanier, we have already considered the poetry which seems most typical, not of North or South or West, but of the American people.

Southern Singers. Two of the most brilliant of the Southern poets of the period, Henry Timrod (1829–1867) and Paul Hamilton Hayne (1831–1886), are generally mentioned in the same sentence. They were both born in Charleston, and were members of the promising literary " school " which gathered around the poet-novelist Simms.[1] Both had published poetry before 1861, and both gave up their cherished literary dreams to serve their state at the first call to arms. Both were broken in health and fortune by the war, and thereafter waged a brave, lonely struggle against poverty and sickness. Finally, the works of each poet may be divided into two main classes : war lyrics,

[1] See p. 244.

reflecting the martial and sectional spirit of the moment, and a few simple poems that have enduring interest because they give beautiful expression to the permanent emotions of our human nature.

Timrod, who published a comparatively small amount of work, is perhaps the greater of the two poets. Among his best poems are his exquisite "Hymn: At Magnolia Cemetery," "The Lily Confidante," "Spring," "Katie," "Charleston," and "The Cotton Boll."

Of Hayne's war lyrics "The Battle of King's Mountain," which deals with a Revolutionary event, is the most widely known. Most readers, however, will be more interested in the poems which reflect the changing life of nature in the lonely pine barrens of the South, where the poet made his brave struggle after the war. As a reflection of the spirit of that sad struggle, the reader should know the poem called "A Little While." Other and better poems of Hayne are "Woodland Phases," "Mocking Birds," "The Pine's Mystery," "Vision at Twilight," "Pre-existence," "Above the Storm," and "Love's Autumn." The poet's laurel crown belongs unquestionably to these two men; and as one thoughtfully considers their work, one wonders, says a scholarly critic,[1] why they are not more generally known and appreciated.

Abram J. Ryan (1839–1886), who is more tenderly remembered as Father Ryan, is another gifted singer of war and peace **Father** in the South. There is a quality in his verse — brave, **Ryan** tender, sad, with here and there a touch of profound spiritual insight — which makes it different from all other works of the period, and which makes us regret that the author did not give more time to poetry. He tells us that his productions should be called "verses," not "poems," and that they were written at random, "off and on, here, there, anywhere, — just as the mood came, with little of study and less of art, and always in a hurry." At the outbreak of war he enlisted as chaplain in

1 Trent, *American Literature*, pp. 479–480.

the Confederate army, and his lyrics of the conflict, "The Death-less Dead," "The Sword of Lee," and especially "The Con-quered Banner," are among the finest that were written in the period of conflict. After the war he served as parish priest in various cities, and devoted his occasional verses to the ritual of his church and to the spiritual life.

In his own words, earthly existence was to Father Ryan "as the shadow of sadness," and only in the eternal life did he ex-pect to find the sunshine. Through all his verse one hears the subdued note of sorrow, which is saved from despair by reli-gious faith. For a reflection of this poet's quieter mood and style, one should read or study "Their Story Runneth Thus" —a beautiful little romance, in which the love, heroism and lifelong sorrow of two human hearts are all told, with rare art and perfect sympathy, in eleven short lines.

BAYARD TAYLOR

Bayard Taylor. James Bay-ard Taylor (1825–1878), who has left us more than thirty volumes of prose and verse, must be measured, like Simms, by the greatness of his literary aims and ideals. He was a critic, novelist, dramatist, journalist, translator, and always and every-where a troubadour possessed by the *Wanderlust*. One day might find him at his beautiful home "Cedarcroft" in Pennsyl-vania, occupied with vast farming or literary plans ; the next day would see his departure for Mexico, for Iceland, for the Orient, —wherever the mood or the magazine engagement called him. There are twelve volumes of travels, such as *Views Afoot* (1846), in which he has recorded his wanderings and impressions.

As one thinks of his work "there comes to mind," says Professor Richardson, "the memory of scattered successes and an irregular, conglomerate failure." This failure, if indeed it be such, may be laid to the fact that he attempted too much, that he explored too many fields to find the best treasures in any one. His conception of literature was as noble as any that our history has recorded; like Lanier he regarded poetry, the rhythmic creation of beauty, as the highest object of human effort; but he was perhaps too determined to win fame, and altogether too ready to furnish a story, an essay, a drama, a poem, a sketch of travel, or anything else that the omnivorous magazines demanded. Boker, his friend and fellow poet, said of him that " he toiled as few men have ever toiled at any profession, and wore himself out and perished prematurely of hard and sometimes bitter work." That he wrote for the present is perhaps the chief reason why the next generation, which had its own favorites, neglected his most ambitious works and remembered him as a symbol of heroic endeavor rather than of lasting achievement.

Perhaps the most notable thing to be recorded of this poet is that he had a remarkable talent, if not genius, for reflecting the **Taylor's Poems** very atmosphere of any place where he happened to find himself on his travels. It is this dash of local color and spirit which leads people to cherish, as the best of his works, certain unambitious little poems, the " Song of the Camp," " The Fight at Paso del Mar," " Bedouin Song," the song beginning " Daughter of Egypt," and a few tales in verse, such as " The Temptation of Hassan Ben Khaled," from his *Poems of the Orient*. The fine human sympathy of Taylor is reflected in such poems as " Euphorion," " Autumnal Dreams," and in " The Quaker Widow," which Stedman calls "that lovely ballad, unexcelled in truth and tenderness of feeling."

The longer poetical works of Taylor are of very uneven merit, and their labored passages, which obscure the finer or inspired stanzas, furnish some ground for Poe's contention that a true poem must be short. *The Poet's Journal* is interesting as a revelation of the author's heart and of his happiness at " Cedarcroft "; his patriotism is reflected in the " Gettysburg Ode " and the " Centennial Ode " (1876) ; and his conception of art is revealed in the poetic autobiography called *The Picture of St. John.* Of this last Lowell said that it was the most finished poem in our literature with the exception of *The Golden Legend.* Such contemporary criticism is doubtless extravagant and untrustworthy, but many readers consider this reflection of a poet's musings amidst the melancholy beauties of Italian scenery to be the most significant of all Taylor's works. It is less widely known, however, than is *Lars: A Pastoral of Norway* (1873), an interesting story in verse, in which the Norwegian fiords and mountains form the setting for a tragic romance. It had once many readers, but it failed to hold attention like *Evangeline,* on which it was probably modeled.

Among Taylor's dramatic works, written in his later years, the best are *The Masque of the Gods* and *Prince Deukalion,* **Dramas and** which are hardly fitted for the stage but which com- **Novels** pare favorably with the " closet dramas " of Longfellow or Tennyson. Among his best novels, which were once popular here and which were translated into several European languages, are *Hannah Thurston* (1863) and *The Story of Kennett* (1866). Both these novels deal with village life in America. The latter is the better piece of work and contains the best-drawn of Taylor's characters, but the former has a certain literary and historical interest in that it deals with the numerous strange reforms which characterized the age of transcendentalism.

More permanent than these novels, and most valuable of all Taylor's works to the student of general literature, is the translation of Goethe's *Faust* in the meter of the original. This notable work, which followed hard on Bryant's Homer and Longfellow's Dante, remains after half a century the standard translation of one of the famous books of the world.

Singers East and West. Two other poets, Boker and Stoddard, were closely associated with Taylor, and all three were by
their contemporaries ranked with the greater poets of America.
George H. Boker (1823–1890) was chiefly a dramatist, and has
the distinction, which is shared by very few American authors,
of having written a play, *Francesca da Rimini*, which can be
acted and which can also be seriously considered as a work of
literature. He published six volumes of dramas and poems, but
is now remembered by a few lyrics, such as his "Lancer's Song,"
"Dragoon's Song," "On Board the Cumberland," "Ballad of
Sir John Franklin," and especially by his fine "Dirge for a
Soldier" ("Close his eyes; his work is done!") and his "Dirge
for a Sailor," beginning

> Slow, slow, toll it low,
> As the sea waves break and flow.

There is a frequent suggestion of the powerful yet delicate
touch of Landor in the best work of Richard Henry Stoddard
(1825–1903). Like his friend Taylor, he attempted
Stoddard　too much and wrote at times too hurriedly for the
present market; but one who reads his volumes must often
wonder why he is not better known as a poet of the nation.
The good taste and the extraordinary knowledge of literature,
old and new, which appear in his critical work are reflected indirectly in his verse; and with them appear two other factors:
an imagination as wide ranging as that of any of our elder poets,
and a certain singing quality which led Stedman to speak of
his lyrics as "always on the wing and known at first sight, —
a skylark brood whose notes are rich with feeling." To understand this singer one should by all means read the entire poem
called "Hymn to the Beautiful," with its occasional imitation of
Shelley and Wordsworth:

> Spirit of Beauty! whatsoe'er thou art,
> I see thy skirt afar, and feel thy power;
> It is thy presence fills this charmèd hour,
> And fills my charmèd heart:

Nor mine alone, but myriads feel thee now,
That know not what they feel, nor why they bow.
    Thou canst not be forgot,
For all men worship thee, and know it not;
Nor men alone, but babes with wondrous eyes,
    New-comers from the skies.
We hold the keys of Heaven within our hands,
    The heirloom of a higher, happier state,
    And lie in infancy at Heaven's gate,
Transfigured in the light that streams along the lands.
Around our pillows golden ladders rise,
    And up and down the skies,
    With wingèd sandals shod,
The angels come and go, the Messengers of God!
Nor, though they fade from us, do they depart —
    It is the childly heart:
    We walk as heretofore,
Adown their shining ranks, but see them nevermore.
Heaven is not gone, but we are blind with tears,
Groping our way along the downward slope of years!

The student should also make acquaintance with Stoddard's "skylark brood" of lyrics in *Songs of Summer* (1856) and *The King's Bell* (1862). Of the longer poems a few of the best are: "Hymn to the Sea," "Abraham Lincoln," "The Fisher and Charon," the love story "Leonatus," and the tribute to Bryant in the noble blank verse of "The Dead Master."

Cincinnatus Heine Miller, or, as he preferred to call himself, Joaquin Miller (1841–1912), belongs so much to our own day **Joaquin Miller** that he is associated with the "rush to the Klondike," whither he followed his unquenchable pioneer spirit, his love of daring men and of untouched nature. His work, however, seems to belong to an earlier age than this, the age of Bret Harte and of the "roaring" mining camps, and his fame rests almost wholly on his earliest works: *Songs of the Sierras* (1871), *Songs of the Sunlands* (1873), and *The Ship in the Desert* (1875). The imaginative splendor of some of these poems, and their mighty background of burning desert or snowclad mountains, made an impression so strong that the author was hailed, in England especially, as one of the most promising of American poets. Though Miller never fulfilled that early promise, though his later verse still shows careless workmanship and too much dependence on the methods of Byron or Swinburne, his *Songs of the Sierras* are well worth reading, — for their own sake, and as an indication of the changing taste of an age which first welcomed the poem or story of strong "local" color and atmosphere. In this connection Miller's poems may well be read with the earlier works of Bret Harte and the *Pike County Ballads* of John Hay, which appeared in the same decade.

Other minor poets of the period who are more or less representative are : Jones Very, the mystic singer of transcendentalism ; Henry Howard Brownell, whose *War Lyrics and Other Poems* (1866) celebrated the battles, sieges, fortunes and misfortunes of the great conflict ; Thomas Buchanan Read, painter and poet, who wrote poetic sketches of emigrant life in *The New Pastoral* (1855) and a few widely known lyrics, such as " Drifting " and " Sheridan's Ride " ; and Josiah Gilbert Holland, a writer of prose and verse, as gifted and versatile as the once popular Willis. Holland's *Bitter Sweet* (1856), a long dramatic poem containing idyllic pictures of New England country life, was popular for a generation, but it seems now a little commonplace, and lacking in the artistic quality which makes a poem permanent. Some of his prose works, such as *Timothy Titcomb's Letters to Young People* and the romance *Sevenoaks*, are still occasionally read with pleasure, but it is probable that Holland will be remembered in the future chiefly by his " Gradatim," " Babyhood," and a few other minor works of a moralizing and sentimental nature, which find a place in representative collections of American poetry.[1]

---

[1] Doubtless some of these poets deserve more generous space than we have given them, and there are many more whose names and works are worthy of mention. Our object, however, is not an adequate study but rather a suggestion of the abundant minor poetry of the period. Certain other poets (Stedman, Aldrich, etc.), whose work began in this age, will be considered on pages 452–456.

IV. NOVELISTS AND STORY-TELLERS

NATHANIEL HAWTHORNE (1804–1864)

Ah! who shall lift that wand of magic power,
   And the lost clew regain?
The unfinished window in Aladdin's tower
   Unfinished must remain.[1]

The above lines, which are often quoted in connection with Hawthorne, reflect a general feeling of American readers that the Concord novelist has no successor. He is a man apart, a solitary genius, whose methods and materials are so exclusively his own that there is no other writer with whom we may even compare him. His style — a little old-fashioned but genuine and artistic, like Colonial furniture — is always in harmony with his sincerity of purpose. He does not tell an idle tale, but selects some law or impulse of the human heart and traces its course among men, showing due regard to the truth of his subject

NATHANIEL HAWTHORNE

and to the requirements of his own art. The scene of his story is set against a romantic background of history, and his characters are largely symbolical, — more like the shadowy creatures formed by our fancy to people the streets of an ancient

---

[1] From Longfellow, "To Hawthorne," a poem read at Hawthorne's funeral service (May 23, 1864). This stanza seemed especially significant in view of the unfinished manuscript which lay upon the coffin.

city than like men and women of the market place. Over them broods the melancholy twilight of days that are no more. Vague as these characters are, they are governed by the same moral law that prevails alike among their ancestors and their descendants ; and it is this steadfast law rather than the style or matter of the tale that rivets our attention.

Such are the qualities of Hawthorne, revealed in almost every chapter of his writing. The charm of reading him is akin to that of meeting an old friend who never surprises or disappoints us. Because of his high ideals and the artistic quality of his work, he has received more praise and less discriminating criticism than any other American writer. Lowell calls him the greatest imaginative genius since Shakespeare, and lesser critics have expressed a similar judgment in a different way. Many will feel that the praise is too extravagant, but few will question Hawthorne's power, or challenge his position as the supreme idealist in American fiction.

Life. Heredity plays a large part in the life and work of Hawthorne. He writes largely of the Puritans, from whom he was descended and whose moral quality he shares in large measure. He was born (1804) in the old seaport of Salem, where the first American Hathorne (as the name was spelled) had settled soon after his arrival with Governor Winthrop's colony. Some of his ancestors had been active in the witch trials ; one at least had been a gallant soldier, whose deeds inspired the Revolutionary ballad of " Bold Hathorne " ; the rest had followed the sea. When Hawthorne was but four years old his father, a sea captain, died of yellow fever in South America ; his mother isolated herself in her own room, where she seldom saw her own family, and the boy grew up with a shadow over him that was never quite dispelled. At the age of ten he went to live in Raymond, on the shore of beautiful Sebago Lake in Maine, and until he was twenty-one he spent a few weeks or months of each year in fishing, hunting and roaming the primeval solitudes.

For school life, for discipline of any kind except that which was self-imposed, Hawthorne had a strong aversion. Studying at odd hours and under private tutors he prepared for Bowdoin, where he met Longfellow and Pierce (afterwards President of the United States) as his college mates. He graduated in the famous class of 1825, and immediately disappeared from public view. He had debated with himself the question of a profession, and the result was announced in a characteristic letter to his mother:

" I do not want to be a doctor and live by men's diseases, nor a minister and live by their sins, nor a lawyer and live by their quarrels; so I don't see that there is anything left for me but to be an author."

Following this indefinite resolve he shut himself up in his own room, in a gray old house at Salem, and for twelve years lived in **Hermit** greater seclusion than Thoreau had ever known at Walden. **Life** Though living in the midst of a busy town, it was doubtful, he said, if a dozen persons knew of his existence. He brooded or wrote all day long; like his mother and sister he took his meals in his own room; in the evening he went out for a solitary walk on the seashore. He writes in his notebook:

" If ever I should have a biographer, he ought to make great mention of this chamber, because so much of my lonely youth was wasted here, and here my mind and character were formed; here I have been glad and hopeful, and here I have been despondent. And here I sat a long, long time, waiting patiently for the world to know me, and sometimes wondering why it did not know me sooner, or whether it would ever know me at all, — at least, till I were in my grave. And sometimes it seemed as if I were already in the grave, with only life enough to be chilled and benumbed. But oftener I was happy."

One result of this unnatural seclusion was that it gave him a style and a subject. Left so much to himself, brooding in his own room or by the lonely sea, he discovered certain laws and impulses of the human heart which he determined to use as the motive for his stories. And from this one subject, the law of the heart as seen against a background of Puritan history, he seldom departed. He acquired also the art of writing, burning much of his work and revising the rest, till he knew how to tell a tale with naturalness and simplicity. It is doubtful if any other American writer ever had twelve such years of discipline, solitary and self-imposed, in learning how to write.

He sent some of his stories to the magazines, and made vain efforts to find a publisher for the others. His first book, *Fanshawe* (1828) a crude romance of college days, was printed at his own expense, but he speedily tried to suppress it by destroying every copy he could find. In 1837 appeared *Twice-Told Tales*, which represented the best work of a dozen years, but which no one would publish until Hawthorne's friend [1] secretly agreed to assume the expense of a first edition. This

Literary Work book found a few readers, and was followed by *Grandfather's Chair* and three other volumes of children's stories, which brought little reward in either fame or money. While Willis and other writers of less ability were very popular, Hawthorne remained, as he said, " the obscurest writer in America." Poe writes of him in 1846, after he had published eight volumes, " It was never the fashion, till lately, to speak of him in any summary of our best authors."

Led by the necessity of earning a living, Hawthorne came out of his seclusion and found a subordinate place in the Boston customhouse. From this poor position he was discharged to make room for some politician who claimed the spoils of victory at the next election. Then he invested his small savings in Brook Farm,[2] hoping thus to secure a comfortable home for himself and for the woman whom he intended to marry ; but after a year of unwonted toil and transcendental talk, he knew that neither the comfort nor the home was possible in such a community of reformers. He had lost his savings, but he had gained some material for his *Blithedale Romance*, the only one of his stories which seems even remotely connected with his own experience.

Hawthorne's happy marriage (1842) marks the turning point of his life. He went to live in the " Old Manse " at Concord, which had

Life in the World been occupied by Emerson, and there, in the first sunshiny atmosphere he had ever known, he gave himself wholly to writing. His *Mosses from an Old Manse* (1846) was the result of four years' work in the midst of happiness so ideal that poverty could cast no shadow over it. In sore need of money he again entered the public service, as surveyor in the Salem customhouse,[3] only to repeat his previous experience by losing his place to another spoilsman. This discharge hurt and discouraged him, but his wife met him with the cheerful remark that now he could write his book. " His book " was *The Scarlet Letter* (1850), the most powerful and original of all his works, which gave him an instant reputation as the foremost of American novelists.

---

[1] This good friend was Horatio Bridge. See his *Personal Recollections of Nathaniel Hawthorne*.

[2] For a description of this community, see p. 277.

[3] Hawthorne's work here, and his unkind criticism of the people of Salem, is reflected in the introduction to *The Scarlet Letter*.

All his happiest works, *House of Seven Gables*, *Wonder Book*, *Snow Image*, *Blithedale Romance* and *Tanglewood Tales*, followed in the next few years; but again he turned aside from literature to enter a most uncertain public service. For the political campaign of 1852 he had written a life of his friend Franklin Pierce, and when the latter was elected president, Hawthorne was given the lucrative post of consul at Liverpool. He remained abroad seven years, four of which were spent in uncongenial office work, and three on a pleasant vacation, in Italy chiefly, where he gathered material for his *Marble Faun*.

THE WAYSIDE, CONCORD

In 1860 he returned to "Wayside," the house which he had purchased in Concord. There he was busy on a work which he intended to be his masterpiece when his strength deserted him. He died while on an invalid's journey to the White Mountains in 1864.

In addition to these salient facts, there are certain personal qualities which we must consider if we are to understand Hawthorne's **Personal** work. Prominent among these is his individualism, a **Quality** quality so pronounced that he seems, like Thoreau, to be entirely apart from his own age and nation. In his day America was buzzing with social theories and experiments; but after one experience at Brook Farm he would have nothing to do with reforms or re-formers. " The good of others, like our own happiness," he says in a letter, " is not to be attained by direct effort, but incidentally." He lived in a time of political agitation, when North and South were taking sides for a momentous conflict ; but his letters show that neither slavery nor states' rights troubled him ; that until the Civil War came he did not realize that he had a country ; that he did not even know what patriotism meant until he met an Englishman.[1]

His aloofness from his contemporaries is even more remarkable. He had no literary friendships, no marked sympathy with the poets and prose writers who made his age the most brilliant in American history. Unlike Longfellow, Lowell and many others who shared in a widespread intellectual movement, Hawthorne had little scholarship, and showed no interest in poetry or science, in history or philosophy. He went abroad, meeting the men and the institutions of England, France and Italy, but his letters and notebooks show not only a lack of enthusiasm but a strange lack of receptivity. He was satisfied, ap-parently, with the broodings of his own heart, which furnished him with the literary material that others seek in knowledge or culture or human society.

A second quality of Hawthorne is his apparent fatalism. In his twelve years of solitude he had discovered his subject and formed his **His Fatalism** style ; thereafter he made no effort to develop his knowl-edge or his native ability. His first romance, *The Scarlet Letter*, revealed a wonderful talent with a promise of sevenfold in-crease, but he would not cultivate it. Instead he wrote stories for children, sought a salary rather than a work at Liverpool ; and his later romances, though written in his prime of years, show a loss rather than a gain in constructive power. Continually he bewails his " lonely broodings," his " cursed habits of solitude " ; but such is his nature, and he will not try to change it. In a letter to Longfellow he says :

" By some witchcraft I have been carried apart from the main current of life. I have secluded myself from society. And yet I never meant any such thing."

In this confessed lack of effort, this drifting on the current of his own brooding, is an indication of the fatalism which dulled Hawthorne's

[1] See, especially, his letters quoted in Bridge, *Personal Recollections*, pp. 155, 169, 172, etc.

life, and which is reflected in the "hereditary curse" or some other imaginary doom of many of his stories.

The last suggestive quality of Hawthorne is the sense of mystery that forever surrounds him. Outside his own immediate family no one, not even his friends, ever really knew him ; and his expressed wish was that his biography should not be written.[1] That he had rare sweetness and purity of character is evident, but in a study of his life many questions arise which are not answered. For Hawthorne reveals little of himself in his writings. Indeed, one of the charms of his somber pages is the occasional glimpse which we have of the man who stands, quiet, smiling, uncommunicative, within the shadow which he has created.

Short Stories. The works of Hawthorne fall naturally into two classes, the first consisting of numerous tales or short stories, the second of his four romances.[2] Outside this classification are *Our Old Home* (1863), an interesting book of sketches of English life in the manner of Emerson's *English Traits*, and three volumes called *Passages* compiled by Hawthorne's family from his American and European notebooks.

From the short stories we first set aside four volumes intended for children, which have been probably more widely read than Juveniles   anything else that Hawthorne produced. The first is *Grandfather's Chair*, made up of stories from early New England history. Because he was dealing chiefly with the Puritans, Hawthorne called this book "an attempt to manufacture delicate playthings out of granite rocks," but few readers will consider the work in this hard way. The second is *True Stories from History and Biography*, in which many young readers have had their introduction to Franklin, Newton, Queen Christina and other heroes and heroines of history. The third

---

[1] Lowell and other worthy biographers were refused permission to use Hawthorne's letters, notebooks, and private papers. The biography prepared by his son, Julian Hawthorne, is rather gossipy and, though well written, too personal to be satisfactory.

[2] We have not included with the latter *The Dolliver Romance, The Ancestral Footstep, Septimius Felton*, and *Dr. Grimshawe's Secret*. These are but four variations of the same unfinished romance. They are less interesting to the general reader than to the student who would understand Hawthorne's methods of work.

and fourth are *A Wonder Book* and *Tanglewood Tales*, which are modern versions of the classic myths told by Greek mothers to the children of long ago. Hawthorne had a great respect for young people, and a great faith in their instincts for the best in life or literature. Those who would understand his method in preparing these juvenile works should read the preface to the *True Stories*.

The *Mosses from an Old Manse*, *Snow Image*, and *Twice-Told Tales* are the best of Hawthorne's volumes of tales for

Types of Stories grown people. The contents of these volumes may be loosely grouped in three classes : the first made up of sketches (or " pure essays," as Poe called them), the second of allegories, and the third of historical tales of early New England. The first chapter of *Mosses from an Old Manse* forms an excellent introduction to the sketches, which illustrate Hawthorne's habits of observation and of recording his impressions in his notebook. Other significant sketches are " A Rill from the Town Pump," " Sights from a Steeple," " Little Annie's Ramble," " Main Street," " Graves and Goblins," " Buds and Bird Voices " and " The Intelligence Office." Some of these sketches deal with human nature in some extraordinary manifestation. Thus, " Ethan Brand," which Hawthorne wrote as the last chapter of a romance, and which a modern critic considers the most typical of his tales,[1] seems to be neither romance nor story but a series of sketches, all leading to an analysis of a human heart which had hardened under selfish impulses till it turned to stone.

The allegorical tales, which are the most characteristic of Hawthorne's works, are seldom allegories in the true sense, yet

Symbol and Allegory they all reveal the author's strong tendency toward symbolism, that is, the use or description of some outward object (such as the falling rose petal in " The Maypole ") in such a way that we shall detect in it some hidden or prophetic

[1] See Richardson, *American Literature*, II, 346–351. Hawthorne characterized this sketch as " a chapter from an abortive romance."

meaning. His method is to make each tale revolve about one significant object, such as a veil, a cross, a footprint, which becomes the type or symbol of some moral quality or defect in his characters. Dealing thus with symbols rather than with nature, with abstract vices or virtues rather than with men and women, there is a general impression of unreality in Hawthorne's stories. As he says in his preface to *Twice-Told Tales*:

" They have the pale tint of flowers that blossomed in too retired a shade. Instead of passion there is sentiment; and even in what purports to be pictures of actual life, we have allegory, not always so warmly dressed in its habiliments of flesh and blood as to be taken into the reader's mind without a shiver. The book, if you would see anything in it, requires to be read in the twilight atmosphere in which it was written."

THE GREAT STONE FACE

One of the finest and most wholesome of these tales is " The Great Stone Face," which was suggested, it is said, by the character of Emerson. Other notable allegorical tales are " Lady Eleanore's Mantle " (in " Legends of the Province House "), " The Artist of the Beautiful," " The Birthmark," " Young Goodman Brown," " The Great Carbuncle," " Feathertop," " The Celestial Railroad," " The Ambitious Guest," " David Swan " and " Dr. Heidegger's Experiment." Scattered among these impressive stories we occasionally find one so thinly allegorical that it is almost lifeless, and another, such as " The Christmas Banquet," so morbid that we are instantly reminded of Poe. Reading them we find frequent indications of Hawthorne's boyhood, when his three favorite books were *Pilgrim's Progress*, *The Faery Queene* and *The Newgate Calendar*. The first two are famous allegories ; the last is a record of the most notorious criminals of Newgate prison. Allegory and sin, — here in two words we have an epitome of the greater part of Hawthorne's work.

The legendary tales — of which the " Legends of the Province House," "The Gray Champion," "The Gentle Boy," **Legend and** " Endicott and the Red Cross ", and " The Maypole **Tradition** on Merry Mount " may serve as examples — are all founded on New England traditions. In such stories Hawthorne first gave the American Puritan to literature, and his method was at once romantic and psychological. He was romantic in that he emphasized the idealism of Puritan life, its great principles applied to small duties, its superb faith glowing amidst prosaic details like wild flowers in a burned field. He was psychological in that he took up the problem of sin and judgment, with which the Puritan had struggled mightily, and showed the torturing effect of sin in the mind itself rather than in outward punishment. At times, in dealing with the Puritans, he seems a little harsh or gloomy ; and again his spirit is like that of Angelo, who could see in a rough block of marble the outlines of a sleeping angel. He has been called the historian of primitive New England ; but the title is misleading, for his historical knowledge was neither ample nor accurate. He was, in a word, an artist, not a historian ; he used New England merely as a romantic background, as Cooper used the wilderness, and Irving the Dutch settlements on the Hudson.

The Four Romances. Hawthorne's four great romances are chiefly studies of sin and its expiation. Most readers make acquaintance with the novelist in *The Scarlet Letter*, but a better book to begin with is *The House of the Seven Gables* (1851), which is less gloomy, has more human and lovable characters, and is better constructed with regard to the old unities of time, place and action. The theme is the terrible consequences of sin to the innocent rather than to the guilty ; when the curtain rises on the drama we see gentle characters still bearing the heavy burden of offenses committed long years before they were born. "The sins of the fathers shall be visited upon the children" seems to be Hawthorne's text;[1] but in his tenderness for poor old Hepzibah and for Phœbe Pyncheon, the most lovable of all his characters, he puts a little more sunshine than usual into his narrative, and contrives an ending more in accord with our expectation and our sense of justice.

The Blithedale Romance (1852) was undoubtedly suggested by Hawthorne's experience at Brook Farm, and is the only one
Blithedale   of his American romances to have a modern setting. Perhaps for this reason the heroine, Zenobia, is much less symbolical and more real, or human, than most of the author's creations.[2] The story centers in the desperate struggle of this lonely, passionate woman against fate and environment; and the lesson is, in Hawthorne's words, that the whole universe is set "against the woman who swerves one hair's breadth out of the beaten track." Though *Blithedale* is considered weaker than the other romances dealing with the same theme, many readers are fascinated by it as an indication of the author's power, and of his limitations, when he left the region of symbols to deal with plain men and women. Another feature of this interesting romance is that the author appears, more or less disguised, in the character of Coverdale, and that his distrust of all reformers is shown in the person of Hollingsworth the egotist.

The Marble Faun (1860) is the most popular of all Hawthorne's works at home and abroad. This may possibly be due
Marble Faun   to the fact that the scene is laid in Rome and that thousands of travelers have used the romance as a pleasant supplement to their guide books. Donatello, a happy young Italian who looks like the marble faun,[3] is the hero of the

---

[1] It is said that Hawthorne had in mind an incident in his own family history. One of the witches, condemned by an early Hathorne, left a curse upon his house. This alleged incident is suggested in the opening chapter.

[2] Critics have detected in the character of Zenobia some suggestions of Margaret Fuller, of Brook Farm and *The Dial*. In his preface Hawthorne admits that he had Brook Farm "in his mind" when he wrote *The Blithedale Romance*, but denies all intention of making his book a study of the place or of its characters.

[3] This refers to a famous antique statue of a satyr, in the Roman capitol.

story, which centers in his sudden impulsive sin and the consequent knowledge of evil that it brought into his joyous nature.
The story is so unusual, and is such a favorite with readers, that
to criticize it as a work of art becomes a thankless task. Viewed
frankly, in comparison with the best work of other novelists, it
will probably be seen that *The Marble Faun* is merely fanciful
rather than imaginative ; that it is marred by moralizing, descriptions, and guide-book matters ; that its characters are unreal, and
fade at last like shadows ; and that Hilda, the paragon of
feminine virtue, is interesting only when she stays in her high
tower with the doves. Such a criticism is largely personal, and
therefore of small consequence. The point is that the student
should look at *The Marble Faun* with his own eyes rather than
through the rosy spectacles of enthusiastic admirers.

The Scarlet Letter (1850) was the first and, in the general
opinion of critics, the most powerful and original of Hawthorne's
romances.[1] The theme is again the wages of sin, and
the moral lesson is powerfully impressed by the two
central characters, Hester and Dimmesdale, one of whom has
confessed the sin and who grows steadily in strength and purity
of character, while the other lives as a hypocrite and is tortured
daily until the tragic climax. Beside the central characters there
are two others : little Pearl the elf child, the most airy and
fanciful of Hawthorne's creations ; and Chillingworth, who has
been called " the Mephistopheles of this Puritan *Faust*." The
reader will appreciate this characterization after viewing that
scene (in the chapter entitled " The Leech and his Patient ")
where Chillingworth bends over the sleeping minister, opens
his gown, discovers the secret letter, and turns away :

> " But with what a wild look of wonder, joy and horror ! With what
> a ghastly rapture, as it were, too mighty to be expressed only by the eye
> and features, and therefore bursting forth through the whole ugliness of
> his figure, and making itself even riotously manifest by the extravagant

*Scarlet
Letter*

[1] The introductory chapter, dealing with the customhouse and harshly criticizing
certain people of Salem, is unnecessary and out of place. The reader will do well to skip
this chapter and begin with the story.

gestures with which he threw up his arms toward the ceiling, and stamped his foot upon the floor! Had a man seen old Roger Chillingworth at that moment of his ecstasy, he would have had no need to ask how Satan comports himself when a precious human soul is lost to heaven and won into his kingdom.

"But what distinguished the physician's ecstasy from Satan's was the trait of wonder in it!"

It is impossible to do justice to the power of this book in a short criticism. We note here only the originality of Hawthorne's genius, as shown in his new way of handling an old theme. He says, in connection with another story, "The mere facts of guilt are of little value except to the gossip and the tipstaff; but how the wounded and wounding soul bear themselves after the crime, that is one of the needful lessons of life." Following his theory he begins this story at the point where another writer would think of ending it; *The Scarlet Letter* is, therefore, not so much a romance in the ordinary sense as a tragic account of what follows the last chapter.

Though *The Scarlet Letter* is often ranked as the best work of American fiction, it is not so well known to foreign readers as are many other of our romances which have less power and originality. The theme is of universal interest, and is handled in a way that might well appeal to readers of any age or nation; but unfortunately, like most of Hawthorne's work, the story has the defect of unreality. The characters are not quite human; they are not so much men and women as well-constructed figures to illustrate a moral law, which Hawthorne sums up at the end:

"Be true! Be true! Be true! Show freely to the world, if not your worst, yet some trait whereby the worst may be inferred!"

Some may question the theory that to be true is to show the worst side of our natures; others may wonder what kind of social revolution would follow its general adoption; but the point is that great romances are not usually built on theories or laws, however excellent, but on men and women, however imperfect. Hawthorne's genius has produced in *The Scarlet Letter* a remarkable book, unlike any other of our acquaintance ; but it has not made a universal appeal, for the reason, probably, that its characters lack the final touch of reality and humanity.

General Characteristics. The manner of Hawthorne, always a pleasure to his readers, is one of those subtle things that defy description. In an effort to explain his own style he once said, " It is the result of a great deal of practice. It is a desire to tell the simple truth as honestly and vividly as one can." [1] Simple it always is, and quiet and deliberate, but the quality of vividness is hardly noticeable. Hawthorne uses few figures, holds to a high but uniform level, never hurries his narrative, and makes no attempt at rhetorical effect. At rare intervals he displays a touch of humor, but of a somber kind in view of the seriousness of his subject. He often reminds us of a man telling a story in the twilight, who unconsciously lowers his voice, who avoids gestures and all extravagance of speech, in order to be in harmony with the stillness, the solemn splendor, the fading light and deepening shadows of the exquisite hour.

In his matter, as in his manner, our novelist is so individual that critics have invented the word " Hawthornesque " to describe him. One very noticeable characteristic is his tendency toward allegory and symbolism, to which we have already referred.[2] Another is his fondness for dealing in mysterious terrors and omens ; and here he is, like Poe, a successor of Charles Brockden Brown. The latter, following the fashion of his age, invented some dread psychological mysteries ; Poe had a morbid interest in spectral horrors ; Hawthorne brooded over the terrors of sin and judgment in the manner of his Puritan ancestors. Lowell compares Hawthorne with Shakespeare ; Richardson likens him to Dante ; other critics find in him some resemblance to Spenser ; but to a few, who know our

---

[1] Quoted by Richardson, *American Literature*, II, 388.

[2] See p. 398. In the preface to " The Threefold Destiny " the author says : " Rather than a story of events claiming to be real, it may be considered as an allegory . . . to which I have endeavored to give a lifelike warmth." The criticism might well be applied to the greater part of Hawthorne's work.

Colonial literature, he may seem more akin to Wigglesworth than to any other writer. He has the same poetic soul, the same theme, the same interest in the doom of sin ; but he is more artistic in his method, and he makes man his own judge, punishing himself in this life instead of awaiting sentence at the final judgment. Wigglesworth and Hawthorne, the Colonial poet and the modern novelist, both dwell in the same gloomy shadow ; but where one sees only the hopelessness and terror of doom, the other discerns the bow in the cloud, and his work reflects a promise or a hope of better things to come.

A third characteristic is the strongly moral quality of Hawthorne and of his works. In this he is in accord with practically **Moral** all his American predecessors, and with the general **Quality** moral earnestness of English literature from Cædmon to George Eliot. His constant purpose is to show the austere beauty of the moral law, and at times he impresses us as one of the few writers who combine successfully a strong moral purpose with a strong artistic sense. At other times we question whether Hawthorne is not more concerned for the moral than for the story. Thus, he writes in his notebook concerning the search for buried treasure : " On this theme methinks I could frame a tale with a deep moral." Another writer would frame the tale to be true to life, and let the moral take care of itself. In many of the tales, such as " The Threefold Destiny," the moral is too prominent ; and throughout *The Marble Faun* the author's moralizing detracts from the artistic effect of his work, — which ends in a vague, unsatisfactory way, because Hawthorne was not certain what course the moral law would finally take with Donatello and Miriam.

A curious personal quality is indicated by this moralizing, namely, Hawthorne's struggle with himself when the Puritan in him rebelled at the story-teller. In his notebook he records :

" ' What is he ? ' murmurs one gray shadow of my forefathers to the other. ' A writer of story-books ! What kind of a business in life — what mode of glorifying God, or being serviceable to mankind in his day and generation — may that be? Why, the degenerate fellow might as well have been a fiddler!' Such are the compliments bandied between my great-grandsires and myself, across the gulf of time!"

Fanciful as the record is, it suggests Hawthorne's frequent attitude toward his own art. In his prefaces he is prone to apologize,[1] and he often halts his story to explain his motive, or to tell us, for example, that he does not know Miriam's secret because he overheard only a few fragments of her conversation. In a word, the Puritan in him constantly objects to the romancer, as if story-telling were a thing to despise. To please the Puritan he emphasizes the moral, and to please his conscience he explains to the reader that his attitude is only that of a child who says, "Let's pretend."

A fourth characteristic implied in the word "Hawthornesque" is the mental gloom, the clouded or defective vision which re-
Gloom of Hawthorne sulted from dwelling in the shadow, from brooding too much over sin, from neglecting the elemental soundness and hopefulness of human nature. As Emerson said, he "rode his dark horse of the night" too exclusively. Into hearts that feared or wept, into souls that bent and groaned under the doom of sin, he had a deep insight; but of hearts that were joyous, of manly souls that marched breast forward, "forgetting those things which are behind, and reaching forth unto those things which are before," he had too little knowledge. The chief fault in his romances is the lack of happiness; and as the instinct for happiness is one of man's greatest and most significant possessions, we conclude that Hawthorne did not see or record the whole of life. He saw the darker side steadily enough, but the light and hope in which we mostly live, or hope to live, is not reflected in his pages.[2]

Remembering this lack of the happy quality of romance which humanity desires, the question will be asked, Why then

---

[1] See, especially, the preface to *Twice-Told Tales*.

[2] That Hawthorne felt the need of a brighter view of life is frequently indicated. Once he wrote to Elizabeth Peabody: "When I write anything that I know or suspect is morbid, I feel as if I had told a lie."

does Hawthorne retain his place as the foremost of American romancers ? The answer is, probably, that he knew one feature of the human heart, and dealt with it faithfully. In a paragraph of one of his tales he reveals unconsciously the secret of all his work :

" The heart, the heart, — there was the little yet boundless sphere wherein existed the original wrong of which the crime and misery of this outward world were merely types. Purify that inward sphere, and the many shapes of evil which haunt the outward, and which now seem almost our only realities, will turn to shadowy phantoms and vanish of their own accord. But if we go no deeper than the intellect, and strive with merely that feeble instrument to discern and rectify what is wrong, our whole accomplishment will be a dream." [1]

This was the burden of Hawthorne, inherited from his ancestors, — the struggle of the human heart against inherited or acquired evil influences. The nobility of his theme and his sincerity in dealing with it will be more evident if we compare him with certain modern romancers, who go to the ends of the earth, to society or the slums, to the northern forests or the southern deserts, for their literary material. Hawthorne proved once again that the human heart is the only mine of romance, and that he who explores it faithfully will find it rich and exhaustless as ever.

SECONDARY WRITERS OF FICTION

In comparison with the poetry of the age the fiction is generally of secondary importance. Hawthorne is the only novelist of unquestionably first rank ; the work of the others suffers from two causes : from the war, which discouraged by its terrible reality the production of fiction ; and from the changing taste of the age, which seems to have wearied of the old-fashioned romances of Cooper and Simms, and to have welcomed stories of another kind — stories of the " Poker Flat " and " Innocents Abroad " variety — not because they were better, but largely because they were different. Up to about the year 1865, one could

---

[1] " Earth's Holocaust," in *Mosses from an Old Manse.*

easily predict the type of novel that would interest the public : it would have a background of Colonial or Revolutionary history, a leisurely, rambling style, and an abundance of romantic senti ment. Then appeared the story of local color and atmosphere, the mining-camp stories of Bret Harte, the crudely humorous works of Mark Twain, and the realistic school of fiction.

John Esten Cooke. Among those whom we may call the old-fashioned romancers John Esten Cooke (1830–1886) holds an honored place. If it be true, as an enthusiastic critic declares, that Cooke " aimed to do for Virginia what Simms had done for South Carolina, Cooper for the Indian and frontier life, Irving for the quaint old Knickerbocker times, and Hawthorne for the weird Puritan life of New England," [1] then we must acknowledge that he succeeded admirably in his own field, and that his success, though of a less degree, is of the same kind as that of his more famous rivals. The courtly cavalier society of the South, the brave pageants, the romance and sentiment that our imagination associates with the old régime, — all these are better reflected in Cooke's pages than in any other novels of the period.

The Virginia Comedians (1854), a highly colored romance of the Old Dominion in the days before the Revolution, is prob-

Cooke's Romances

ably the best of Cooke's works. In the same year in which it appeared he published two other romances, *Leather Stocking and Silk*, a story of pioneer life in the valley of the Shenandoah, and *The Youth of Jefferson*, a story of college life in Williamsburg, — romances which, if they revealed Simms's faults of hasty workmanship, have still the power to conjure up the romance and heroism of days gone by. These three novels, the work of a young man of twenty-three, gave splendid promise ; but presently the war came, and Cooke's energies were wholly and gallantly devoted to the service of his native state. When the war ended he took up his pen again, but one who reads his numerous later romances must miss something of the joyous vigor of his first work. Among his later

[1] Quoted in Richardson, *American Literature*, II, 402.

stories, dealing mostly with the war, the most notable is *Surrey of Eagle's Nest* (1886), a stirring historical romance introducing the events in which he had taken a personal part and the heroes with whom he had served in the field.

Two other works of Cooke, in which he carries out his first purpose, are *My Lady Pokahontas* and *Stories of the Old Dominion*, — a series of semihistorical and wholly romantic sketches of Colonial life in Virginia. In their pictures of early American society and manners these sketches compare favorably with Kennedy's *Swallow Barn*, with Simms's *Katherine Walton*, and with Cooper's *Satanstoe ;* but unfortunately Cooke had too little skill in constructing a plot or in the portrayal of character. His typical romance is a series of historical or social pictures bound together by a slender thread of narrative. One must miss in his work the absorbing plot and rugged characters which lend interest to the best works of Cooper, and which make us over-look his weakness of style in the vigor of his story. After reading *The Virginia Comedians* and *Surrey of Eagle's Nest* the student may prefer to postpone Cooke's other romances in order to make acquaintance with his more serious works. Among the latter are the lives of Lee and of " Stonewall " Jackson, two biographies filled with vivid details from the author's personal experiences ; and *Virginia : A History of the People*, an excel-lent narrative with an atmosphere of romance, which is one of the best thus far contributed to the " Commonwealths " series of American histories.

Harriet Beecher Stowe. To those who have read *Uncle Tom's Cabin* and who think of its gifted author, Harriet Beecher Stowe (1811–1896), as a woman of one book, it is surprising to learn that she was a diligent writer of fiction for the better part of half a century. In the standard edition of her works there are sixteen volumes, and among them one finds three or four, now almost forgotten, which seem from a literary viewpoint decidedly superior to the book that the world has hailed as a masterpiece. For instance, *Oldtown Folks* (1869), a study of Yankee life and character at the beginning of the nineteenth century, is certainly more artistic, and perhaps (one might say it confidently if the facts were not apparently against him) of more enduring interest than is the famous story of slavery. Among other notable works of Mrs. Stowe we should at least mention the *Minister's Wooing* (1859), *Pearl of Orr's Island* (1862), and especially the *Fireside Stories* (1871) as told by the inimitable Sam Lawson.

HARRIET BEECHER STOWE

All these works, though well written and displaying something akin to the genius of a novelist, seem almost insignificant in view of the popular triumph of *Uncle Tom's Cabin* (1852), a triumph which began soon after the story appeared in an obscure antislavery newspaper, and which continued with little sign of abatement for more than fifty years. In a keen search for the underlying cause of its hold upon the popular imagination a modern critic writes :

" When *Uncle Tom's Cabin* first appeared it was believed to be a campaign document which would not survive the circumstances that called it forth. A little later its popularity was explained as due to its historical importance. The dramatization was taken still less seriously. Professor Wendell wrote in his *Literary History of America :* ' To this day dramatized versions of it are said to be popular in this country.' If the current story is true, the week in which his book appeared saw the bill-boards nearest Harvard College Yard covered with announcements of the despised play. A year or two later a traveller whose attention had been quickened by this incident saw similar posters opposite the Martyrs' Monument at Oxford, and found, on his first stroll in Rome, the familiar faces of Uncle Tom and little Eva looking down at him from a bill-board near the Coliseum. Surely,

the Englishman and Italian who in the twentieth century attend perform-
ances of " Uncle Tom's Cabin " do not do so on account of any interest in
American social history. The play is of course the most intense melodrama,
and the tale on which it is founded is melodramatic. But melodramas ordinarily come and go, and the melodrama that holds its own in divers parts
of the world for sixty years can hardly be ignored in the literary history of
the country that produced it."[1]

In view of all that has been written upon the subject of *Uncle
Tom's Cabin* the historian can only advise the student to read
Appeal of Uncle Tom's Cabin the book, and then to explain, if he can, its almost
universal appeal. Regarded as a piece of artistic lit-
erature, it is faulty to a degree. The style is often
crude, and at times commonplace; the plot suggests accident
rather than design; the pathos is a little forced; the dialogue
and humor are of the conventional kind. It is probable also that
Mrs. Stowe knew little of slavery as it actually existed in the
South, and that her general picture of the system is sensational
and misleading; but all that is now of little consequence. The
world, which has well-nigh forgotten slavery, still reads the book
with pleasure, and probably would so read it if it pictured a suffering Turk or Eskimo instead of a negro slave. For it is essentially
a human book, dealing with elemental human nature. Though
it began as an antislavery tract, it differed from a thousand
others of its kind in that it created live characters, that it possessed dramatic intensity, moral earnestness, intense emotional-
ism and, above all, human interest.

A critical reader, meeting *Uncle Tom's Cabin* for the first
time and knowing nothing of its history, might confidently say
that it was not a great book; but we are dealing with facts, not
theories, and among the noteworthy facts concerning the book
are these: that it stirred a great nation to its depths and hurried
on a great war; that it made an imperative moral problem of a
matter that had long been considered in its political or economic
aspects; that it has been translated into some forty languages,

---

[1] Professor William B. Cairns, " Uncle Tom's Cabin and its Author," in *The Dial*, 1911

and has been read and enjoyed the world over; that, after
reading it, many American mothers offered their sons as a sacrifice in the fearful conflict that followed, while other mothers, as
far off as distant Siam, freed their slaves and began a campaign
of emancipation. In short, *Uncle Tom's Cabin* touched the heart
of the whole world, which has ever since felt more compassion
for suffering humanity. And a book which after more than half
a century retains, with all its original faults, its original power
to touch the human heart is one that the world must reckon
among its literary treasures.

Bret Harte. If Cooke be, as is often alleged, the last romancer
of the old school, Francis Bret Harte (1839–1902) is undoubtedly the originator of the new.[1] When his " Luck of Roaring
Camp " and other stories of the California gold fields appeared
(1868) in *The Overland Monthly*, he was immediately acclaimed,
at home and abroad, as the foremost American novelist, as the
founder of a new school which should reflect American life as
it is, rather than as it has been represented to be in the pages
of the old romance. That was long ago, when the East knew
even less of the real West than it now knows of the real Alaska,
— which is at present so thoroughly and turgidly misrepresented
in the pages of alleged realistic novels. People who knew the
real California immediately protested against Harte's stories as
sensational, but all such protests were unavailing. California
was then a new land, an Eldorado, and in such a place, if only
it be far enough away, all things are possible to the romancer
and to his delighted readers. Harte's first stories were as new
as the land, and different from anything that had ever appeared
in fiction ; they were also vigorous and interesting, and the surprised young author became the hero of a new type of fiction,
— the short story of local color and atmosphere, which has
ever since retained an immense popularity.

---

[1] The larger part of Harte's work belongs chronologically to the present age. His
most characteristic work appeared, however, before 1876. Since then his work has been
of the same kind as his first stories, and generally of inferior quality.

Harte's life story affords an interesting commentary upon his literary work. As a boy, poor and unknown, he had followed **Harte's** the Argonauts to California, soon after the discovery **Discovery** of gold in '49. There he tried all kinds of jobs, as express messenger, teacher, prospector, journalist, editor. Whatever his work, he was always surrounded by picturesque characters, by red-shirted miners, buckskin-clad scouts, Chinamen, Mexicans, Indians, nameless outcasts and adventurers, all excited by the prospect of sudden wealth, and all struggling like ants against a mighty background of canyon and mountain, of rushing river and silent forest. Suddenly it occurred to him to transfer this picturesque life to literature, and with his first attempt fame and fortune came to him as instantly as ever it came to a miner who "struck it rich" in vein or pocket of virgin gold. Excited by his great discovery he came East in a kind of triumphal procession ; he lectured and wrote of literary matters with an amateur's confidence and enthusiasm ; he rejected flattering offers of permanent positions with the magazines, and finally accepted the political office of American consul. Then he hurried abroad, where he was received as a literary lion, and where he spent the last fifteen years of his life. He wrote meanwhile without ceasing ; but the farther he removed from California the dimmer became his impressions, and his later work is as an echo, growing fainter and fainter, of his first overwhelming success.

There are thirty volumes of Harte's prose and a single volume of his verses. Of the latter, the humor and sentiment of a few **His Poems** poems, such as "Plain Language from Truthful **and Stories** James" ("The Heathen Chinee"), "Dickens in Camp" and "Society upon the Stanislaus" are still deservedly popular. Of all his prose works, probably the best are his first three stories, "The Luck of Roaring Camp," "The Outcasts of Poker Flat," and "Tennessee's Partner." If we add to this short list "Miggles" and "How Santa Claus came to Simpson's Bar," we shall have the full measure of Harte's talent ; for practically all his stories repeat the same scenes, the same characters, and the same picturesque surroundings. His aim was to picture the crude life of the mining camp ; his hero was generally a rough character, often an outcast ; his evident motive was to prove the " soul of goodness in things evil," to show that virtue is often concealed under the most unpromising exterior, and that even the abandoned or vicious character needs only the right opportunity to show his manhood. In his mingling of pathos, humor and sentimentality, and in his hovering on the borderland of the grotesque, Harte has frequent suggestions of Dickens, who was probably his literary master ; but his genius is, on the whole, strongly original, and even in his most exaggerated characters one recognizes elements that square with human nature and with the facts of human experience.

The fame of Bret Harte has waned almost as rapidly as it grew ; but though his work is almost neglected by the present **His Place in Fiction** generation, he has yet an important place in the history of American fiction. One should note, first, his artistic aim : to portray men and the scenes of a primitive country as he saw them ; to make his picture (however highly colored it might be) impersonal and impartial, letting whatever moral might attach to the matter speak for itself. His characters, whether good or bad, never pose, and there is a certain epic strength even in his sorriest heroes. Again, Harte is one of the most notable forerunners of the modern short story. That story had been developed by Irving, Poe and Hawthorne ; but Irving's story has a more or less legendary element, Poe's are morbidly unreal, and Hawthorne's largely symbolical, while Harte's have always a touch of present reality. Taken all together, his stories are not a profound study of life but rather a series of photographs, or flashlights, which might have been taken to illustrate certain dramatic situations in human experience.

Finally, Harte's place in fiction depends largely upon the fact that, like Irving, he was a discoverer of literary material in unexpected places. He discovered, or rather rediscovered, the humor which seems inseparable from American life whenever two grades of society, the primitive and the cultured, meet on the advancing American frontier.[1] He rediscovered also, in a new field, the fascinating literary material of pioneer life which inspired *The Oregon Trail* and the splendid histories of Parkman no less than the Leatherstocking stories of Cooper, and which makes the romance of the West as interesting as was ever the romance of the Scottish border.

Typical Story-Tellers. During this period there were several other writers of popular fiction ; such, for instance, as Theodore Winthrop, with his *John Brent* (1862), an interesting Western romance interwoven with personal experiences of a time when the West was still an unknown region ; Edward Eggleston, whose *Hoosier Schoolmaster, Roxy,* and other tales of pioneer experiences are of permanent value and interest ; Fitz-James O'Brien, whose brilliant short stories are strongly suggestive of Poe ; Marion Harland, with her well-written historical tales of Southern life ; John T. Trowbridge, the prolific writer of wholesome stories for boys ;[2] and Louisa M. Alcott, whose *Little Women, Jo's Boys, An Old-Fashioned Girl,* and other tales, are among the best stories for young people that America has yet produced. Nor must we forget such popular favorites as Edward P. Roe, who produced some sentimental romances before 1876, and who instantly secured a hold on the reading public which is comparable to that of Crawford and other romancers of our own day. Some of these writers may possibly deserve, or attain, a larger fame than certain others to whom we have given larger space, but of that only the future can speak. We have attempted here, not a survey of all the minor novelists of the

[1] This rough humor appears, not simply in Mark Twain's stories, but in the romances of Simms and Cooper, in Longstreet's *Georgia Scenes* (1836), in Baldwin's *Flush Times of Alabama* (1853), and in practically all stories of life " Beyond the Mississippi." See Smith, *The American Short Story* (1912), p. 32.

[2] Trowbridge is generally known by his *Cudjo's Cave*, the *Jack Hazard* series, the *Start in Life* series, etc. An interesting work for the student of literature is *My Own Story* (1903), which contains some valuable material on American life and letters in the middle of the past century.

age, but rather a sketch of certain tendencies and types at a time when the popularity of the old-fashioned romance was threatened by the first appearance of realism in American fiction.

V. THE PROSE (NONFICTION) WRITERS

HENRY DAVID THOREAU (1817–1862)

Thoreau is one of the writers who have been made obscure rather than familiar by what has been written about them. The memoirs of Emerson or Channing, for example, lay too much emphasis on Thoreau's peculiarities; Lowell's brilliant essay is lacking in sympathy and, consequently, in understanding; and Sanborn's official biography of Thoreau tends to distract attention from the man to the village of Concord or to the affairs of the transcendentalists.

All these records seem of small account in comparison with the remarkable self-revelation which Thoreau has left us in his own writings. Therefore read first Thoreau; live with him in *Walden;* go afield with him in the *Excursions;* leave behind you the cumbersome baggage of civilization and view humanity, as he viewed it, in its elemental simplicity. Then you may discover that Thoreau was a man, original and sincere, and that his life was as one of those hidden, spring-fed " logans " or rivulets that never seem to join but rather to retreat to unknown distances from the hurrying river of our national existence. In such a logan, deep and still, where the trout hide and the deer come to drink, the canoe-man floats at ease in quiet water, forgetting the rush of the outer current, and repeating softly to himself :

> Lean on your oars and rest awhile —
> This is the sweetest part of the stream ;
> Shadowy branches over the aisle
> Lure us to linger, list and dream.[1]

---

[1] Charles H. Crandall, " Lean on your Oars," in *Songs from Sky Meadows* (1909).

Thoreau is generally studied as part of the transcendental movement and as a follower of Emerson, but one may doubt the value of such classification. He had little to do with the transcendentalists and held aloof from all the societies which tried to reform America in the middle of the past century. Though he was influenced in his early years by Emerson, he soon abandoned all tutelage to blaze his own trail through life, ignoring the standards which contented other men and seeking for himself a larger independence or a more ample horizon. As Emerson says :

" He has muscles, and ventures on and performs feats which I am forced to decline. . . . I find [in Thoreau] the same thoughts, the same spirit that is in me, but he takes a step beyond, and illustrates by excellent images that which I should have conveyed in sleepy generalizations."

In comparing him with other individualists of his age, we may find that he was always practical where they were busy with theories, and steadily consistent where they were blown about by the winds of every new doctrine. In short, Thoreau's oddity has received perhaps too much attention, to the neglect of his better qualities, and for this reason the suggestion is made to the beginner to make the acquaintance of the man himself rather than of his critics or biographers.

Life. It is a modest task to record the few significant facts of Thoreau's simple life. He was born (1817) in Concord, Mass., and spent practically his entire life in the same village. He was educated at the local academy and at Harvard, from which he graduated with a good reading knowledge of the classics; but even in these early years he was strongly disinclined to learn from either books or men, declaring that they had only scraps of second-hand knowledge to offer him. He seemed to be always thirsty for first-hand experiences, and during his school days found more satisfaction in roaming over the face of the country than in the discipline of the classroom. Later he became in turn teacher, lecturer, surveyor, carpenter, tutor for Emerson's children, and pencil-maker, following in the last-named occupation the trade of his father.

Whatever task Thoreau attempted was always well done, but he refused to continue in any work after he had mastered the way of it. **Theory of Life** In this he was consistent with his own theory that a man should not repeat himself; that repetition was dwarfing and unnecessary in a world of infinite possibilities. He was determined to live simply, to avoid luxury and extravagance, which he called "the beginnings of evil"; and finding that the wages gained by six weeks of manual labor would support him for a year, he spent the greater part of his time in reading, writing, and in the observation of nature. His extraordinary way of living was made easier by the fact that his taste was ascetic, and that he had no wife or family dependent upon him. Though he lived much alone, he was by no means a misanthrope; and he was kept from the "queering" effect of too much solitude by having a home, in which he was always the dutiful son and brother. Though Thoreau is often represented as morose and unsocial, all those who knew him well bear witness to the unvarying sympathy and loyalty of his friendship.

In 1854 Thoreau made the experiment by which he is now generally remembered. He built a little hut in the woods by Walden **Imprison-ment** Pond and camped there close to nature for more than two years, doing all his own work and living in the utmost simplicity and cheerfulness. To the same period belongs another notable experience, his imprisonment in Concord jail for defying the majesty of government in the form of a tax bill. His town tax he paid willingly, since it was used to build roads and maintain schools; but the poll tax he rejected on the ground that it supported a government which was then waging an unjust war against Mexico in the interest of slavery. We cannot here examine the queer quality of such patriotism as is involved in Thoreau's remark (which is commended by Tolstoy) that "in a government which supports injustice the proper place for a just man is in jail." We note only the peculiar point of view in Thoreau's account of his imprisonment:

" . . . As I stood considering the walls of solid stone, two or three feet thick, the door of wood and iron, a foot thick, and the iron grating which strained the light, I could not help being struck with the foolishness of that institution which treated me as if I were mere flesh and blood and bones, to be locked up. I wondered that it should have concluded at length that this was the best use to put me to, and had never thought to avail itself of my services in any way. I saw that if there was a stone wall between me and my townsmen, there was a still more difficult one to climb or break

through before they could get to be as free as I was. I did not for a moment feel confined, and the walls seemed a great waste of stone and mor-
tar. I felt as if I alone of all my townsmen had paid my tax. They plainly
did not know how to treat me, but behaved like persons who are under-
bred. In every threat and in every compliment there was a blunder, for
they thought that my chief desire was to stand on the other side of that
stone wall. I could not but smile to see how industriously they locked the
door on my meditations, which followed them out again without let or hin-
drance, and *they* were really all that was dangerous. As they could not
reach me, they had resolved to punish my body; just as boys, if they cannot come at any person at whom they have a grudge, will abuse his dog."

Evidently there is something of both Cavalier and Puritan in Thoreau.
He reminds us here not only of Bunyan, writing an immortal work
in Bedford jail, but of that very different genius, Lovelace, who wrote:

> Stone walls do not a prison make,
>   Nor iron bars a cage;
> Minds innocent and quiet take
>   That for a hermitage.

It was during his hermitage in the woods that Thoreau observed
nature most closely, and prepared the only two books which were
published during his lifetime. He had gone to Walden to face the
fundamental facts of life; when he had learned all he could from
such an experiment, he came cheerfully back to civilization. His constant exposure to the weather at all seasons developed in him the
latent seeds of consumption, and he died after a heroic struggle in
1862, being then only forty-four years old.

Running through Thoreau's entire life there is a strain of elemental wildness, which most biographers note as his most characteristic
Love of quality. He was of mixed French and New England de-
the Wild scent, and the same love of the wild which sent so many
French voyageurs through the unmapped wastes of the North reas-
serted itself in this scholarly recluse. As he said himself, there was
" a yearning towards all wildness " in his nature. It was this wildness which led him to live alone, to be abroad at all hours making intimate acquaintance with every bird and beast and plant in the woods
about Walden Pond. For Indians he had always a strange sympathy.
The very thought of these rovers of the wilderness filled him with
rapture, or with envy at their superior knowledge; and it was largely
his desire to know how primitive men lived that led him three times

to the Maine woods. Like most lovers of the wild, Thoreau was on an endless quest, searching for what he could not even name.

Once, deep in the wilderness, we met an old man who had spent his life beyond the frontier and who was always " moving on." When he left an ideal spot, abandoning his camp and his trap lines, we asked him, " Why do you move? What better thing than you have are you looking for?" And with eyes fixed on the dying embers of his last camp fire, the old man answered, " I am looking for the boy I lost somewhere, long ago." He was looking for himself, as Thoreau always was, and the trails of both men had no ending.[1]

If Thoreau was half Indian, as his biographers declare, the other half of his nature points to the ancient Greek. Side by side with his **Indian or Greek?** notes on arrowheads or woodchucks are rare passages of literary criticism or appreciation, which speak unmistakably of the classical scholar. That he loved to roam by night, or spend hours with turtles or kittens, is more or less characteristic of all simple men of the woods; but that he also loved Greek is a thing to make us wonder. Emerson, who knew Thoreau's ability and deplored his lack of ambition, declared that he might be " an engineer for the nation instead of captain of a huckleberry party."

In the same regretful spirit that inspired Emerson's criticism many of Thoreau's readers, meeting a penetrating criticism of life or literature, have exclaimed, " What a pity that such powers should be wasted, that such a life should end in failure!"[2] Yet it is seldom given a man to know, as surely as Thoreau did, his errand in life; and failure and success cannot outwardly be measured. There is a vital quality in Thoreau which suggests the grain of wheat, of which it is written, that except it die it abideth alone, but if it die it bringeth forth much fruit. The works that were ignored in Thoreau's lifetime are now a source of inspiration to men and women whose numbers increase steadily, while books and authors that were then famous have long since been forgotten. For the rest, we record Thoreau's own view of the matter:

" If the day and the night are such that you greet them with joy, and life emits a fragrance, like flowers and sweet-scented herbs, — is more elastic, starry and immortal, — that is your success."

---

[1] Thoreau evidently recognized the sweet hopelessness of his wanderings and made a parable of it. See his story of the horse and the turtledove, in *Walden*.

[2] Our most original author was little known to his own generation. His first book, *A Week on the Concord and Merrimac Rivers*, could not be sold, and nearly the entire edition was stored in the garret. His second book, *Walden*, found only a few readers.

Thoreau's Works. The basis of all Thoreau's published works is the Journal which he kept for more than twenty-five years, and many readers find this unstudied record more interesting than any of the books which have been compiled from its pages. Thoreau had this Journal before him when he prepared *A Week on the Concord and Merrimac Rivers* (1849) and *Walden* (1854); and from its thirty closely written volumes Emerson and other editors produced *Excursions, The Maine Woods, Cape Cod, A Yankee in Canada, Early Spring in Massachusetts, Summer, Winter, Autumn,* and *Miscellanies.*

To the general reader the most interesting of these works is *Walden,* which records the thought and observation of Thoreau

Walden during the first year of his hermitage. Before reading this book it might be well to banish the prevalent opinion that the author hated society, that he withdrew to Walden Pond with the idea of escaping humanity and all human institutions. He was living in an age of political and social agitation, when a score of zealous societies were bent on reforming the world. He maintained that each of these societies, however small, contained all the discordant elements of society in general; that the only way to reform the world was to begin with the individual; and he had enough of the Puritan in him to maintain that the first individual to be reformed was Henry Thoreau. Aside from his love of the wild, his motive in withdrawing from the world may best be stated in his own words:

" I went to the woods because I wished to live deliberately, to front only the essential facts of life, and see if I could not learn what it had to teach, and not, when I came to die, discover that I had not lived. I did not wish to live what was not life, living is so dear; nor did I wish to practise resignation unless it was quite necessary. I wanted to live deep and suck out all the marrow of life; to live so sturdily and Spartan-like as to put to rout all that was not life; to cut a broad swath and shave close; to drive life into a corner and reduce it to its lowest terms, and if it proved to be mean, why then to get the whole and genuine meanness of it, and publish its meanness to the world; or if it were sublime, to know it by experience and be able to give a true account of it in my next excursion."

With this explanation of Thoreau's motive, we leave the reader with *Walden*, — which seems to us one of the few books in American literature that repay reading over and over again with the passing years. It has many faults, but chiefly these two : that its lack of sympathy leads to misunderstanding of both the joy and the sorrow of society ; and that its criticisms are generally destructive rather than helpful. These faults are soon forgiven, however, by one who discovers the large virtues of *Walden*, — its originality and independence, its forceful English, its thought-provoking epigrams, its rare sympathy with the innocent life of the fields, its illuminating and hopeful discovery that "to maintain one's self on this earth is not a hardship but a pastime, if one will live simply and wisely."

THOREAU'S HUT AND FURNITURE ON THE SHORE OF WALDEN POND

The reader's enjoyment of other works of Thoreau will depend entirely on his own literary taste. There are some very suggestive essays in the *Excursions*, and a lover of the open will delight in *Early Spring* and the other seasons in their succession. For those who would know the author more intimately, Thoreau's Journal and Letters are recommended ; but those who read *Letters to Various Persons* (1865), a book which seems unwisely edited, should read also the *Familiar Letters* (1894), which show a more human and lovable side of the author's nature.

The Quality of Thoreau. The style of Thoreau is so stimulating to one reader and so irritating to another that one should be wary of giving it either praise or blame. We can dwell on the author's moralizing, his occasional attempts at fine writing, his tendency to nurse his whims and to intrude himself in the landscape ; or we can forget all this in the vigor, the freshness, the epigrammatic quality which makes Thoreau the most quotable of American writers. On one page he charms us with an exquisite appreciation of nature ; on the next he takes some common work of man, lets his imagination play with it, and makes beautiful that which we had always thought commonplace and uninteresting. He walks under a telegraph line, and lo ! that useful but ugly thing becomes a wind harp, and the humming wood is " preserved in music," like the shell of a violin ; or he looks at a bean patch, and that which suggests to the ordinary observer a haunting memory of hoe and backache becomes instantly a field of poetry.

Another quality of Thoreau's style is its unexpectedness. To go with him is to be surprised at every turn, here by a startling paradox, there by a topsy-turvy humor, which generally consists of turning some old word of wisdom inside out for our inspection. All this, though written with painstaking care, seems to be done without effort. Thoreau always puts life before literature (which is only life reflected at second hand) and maintains that the simpler a man is in his thought the stronger will be his unconscious expression :

" As for style of writing, if one has anything to say, it drops from him simply and directly, as a stone falls to the ground. There are no two ways about it, but down it comes, and he may stick in the points and stops wherever he can get a chance. New ideas come into this world somewhat like falling meteors, with a flash and an explosion, and perhaps somebody's castle roof perforated. To try to polish the stone in its descent, to give it a peculiar turn and make it whistle a tune perchance, would be of no use, if it were possible. Your polished stuff turns out not to be meteoric, but of this earth."

The center of Thoreau's teaching (if indeed it have any center or circumference) is found in the word "individualism." **Individualism**   "Any man more right than his neighbors constitutes a majority of one already ; he who wants help wants everything,"—in these and a hundred other terse, self-centered expressions we recognize the man who declared that, after keeping his ears open for thirty years, he had yet to hear the first word of valuable advice from his elders. So far he is like Emerson and others of the transcendental school; but unlike them, he has no theory or system; he preaches no new gospel; he recognizes no literary or intellectual masters:

" The wisest man preaches no doctrines; he has no scheme; he sees no rafter, not even a cobweb against the heavens, — it is clear sky."

His habit is to look at church and state, at labor and society with frank, unbelieving eyes; to deny their authority or question their usefulness; to commend occasionally what good he finds in them, but more frequently to show how vain are most of our social customs in view of the fundamental realities of God and the individual soul. Living in an age of political and social reforms, he asserts calmly:

" The fate of the country does not depend on what kind of paper you drop into the ballot box once a year, but on what kind of man you drop from your chamber into the street every morning."

If we compare the individualism of Thoreau with that of Emerson, we shall find more of contrast than of resemblance Thoreau and in the two men. Thoreau lives the doctrine which Emerson Emerson preaches in " The American Scholar." His thought is more vigorous, more original, more practical than that of " the sage of Concord," though the latter is incomparably the greater writer. Emerson, as we have noted, is forever quoting and is largely influenced by ancient writers; Thoreau, though he has a better knowledge of the classics and is more widely read in oriental literature than is Emerson, uses comparatively few quotations, and we are seldom able to trace his ideas to any ancient source. He thinks his own thoughts, looks at the world from his own eyes, and wakes every morning open-minded for a new experience.

Again, in their reflections of the outdoor world the difference between the two men is striking. Emerson is the poet, the rhapsodist of nature; but he has little definite knowledge of his subject. Thoreau is at times quite as poetical as Emerson, but his knowledge of nature is immense and accurate. Indeed, it is as a nature writer, who sees clearly and who gives us the *anima* of an animal rather than its skin and bones, that Thoreau will be longest remembered.[1] He is first a naturalist, who becomes poetical in expressing the truth which he discovers in nature, while Emerson looks at nature with dreamy eyes because he is first a poet. In a word, Thoreau has his feet solidly on the earth, while Emerson is gloriously afloat in the ether. He has a definite, a practical quality which Emerson lacks ; he furnishes a foundation for what in Emerson is ideal or merely theoretical. As he says of castles in the air, " That is where they should be ; now put foundations under them."

That two such radically different men, each positive and uncompromising, should have been lifelong friends, without a shadow of misunderstanding between them, is one of the happy incidents of our literary history. It was Emerson who wrote this generous appreciation of Thoreau's life and work :

" A truth-speaker he, capable of the most deep and strict conversation ; a physician to the wounds of any soul ; a friend, knowing not only the secret of friendship, but almost worshipped by those few persons who resorted to him as their confessor and prophet, and knew the deep value of his mind and great heart. His soul was made for the noblest society ; he had in a short life exhausted the capabilities of this world ; wherever there is knowledge, wherever there is virtue, wherever there is beauty, he will find a home."

THE HISTORIANS MOTLEY AND PARKMAN

Closely associated in our minds with Bancroft and Prescott, whom we have considered all too briefly in the preceding chapter, are two other historians who have won a secure place in the

---

[1] Thoreau says, " I think the most important requisite in describing an animal is to be sure that you give its character and spirit, for in that you have, without error, the sum and effect of all its parts known and unknown. You must tell what it is to man. Surely the most important part of an animal is its *anima*, its vital spirit, on which is based its character and all the particulars by which it most concerns us. Yet most scientific books which treat of animals leave this out altogether, and what they describe are, as it were, phenomena of dead matter."

history of American literature. These are Motley and Parkman, whose works are read not simply for instruction but more largely for enjoyment,—to share in Motley's vivid pages the epic struggle of a nation, or to follow with Parkman the trail of Indian or voyageur in preparation for that mighty conflict which secured an empire to England and the great West to our own country. Each writer tells a splendid story and tells it in a splendid way; but Parkman is, to American readers at least, of more personal and enduring interest.

John Lothrop Motley (1814–1877). This historian began his literary career with two novels, one of which, *Merry Mount* (1849), a romance of Colonial life in Massachusetts, showed considerable promise. It revealed also that power of realistic description and that fondness for historical detail which later characterized his masterpiece. In the following year he became absorbed in the story of the Dutch struggle for liberty, and from that time on he was a devoted man. He did not have to select a subject, he tells us;[1] his subject selected him, forced itself upon him in an overwhelming impulse, and banished from his mind all inclination to consider any other. Then followed his plan, and a preparation such as is rarely given to any but the greatest of histories.

The breadth of Motley's plan is indicated by the fact that his field covered a large part of Europe at a time of tremen-
His Plan and dous political and religious agitation, and by his
Preparation general title, which was "The Eighty Years' War for Liberty." The work was to begin at a time (1555) when Charles V, weary of perpetual wars in a dozen of his realms, resigned Spain and the Netherlands to his son Philip; it was to trace the epic struggle of Holland, the history of the United Netherlands, and bring something like historic order out of that chaos of fighting states and nations known as the Thirty Years' War, which ended with the peace of Westphalia in 1648. In preparation for this mighty work Motley spent long years in a

[1] See his letter, quoted in Holmes, *Memoir of Motley*, pp. 63–65.

patient search of European archives, and as his work was largely a history of England, Spain and the German states, as well as of Holland, he employed expert copyists in all these countries for the purpose of obtaining duplicates of all important state papers. As a result of all this scholarly preparation there is an impression of exactness, almost of finality, in a large part of his work. Though his record be, as a learned critic says,[1] " as interesting as fiction, as eloquent as the best oratory," it is nevertheless a faithful record of men and events, as accurate in the main as the industry and scholarship of one man could possibly make it.

The first fruits of Motley's genius appeared in three stirring volumes called *The Rise of the Dutch Republic* (1856). With **Motley's** the exception of Prescott's fascinating work (which **Works** has hardly the same scholarly rank)[2] no such glowing historical record had ever graced our American letters, and it is doubtful if its superior can be found in any language. After an interval of several years appeared four more volumes, *The History of the United Netherlands* (1860–1868), in which the gallant story was continued in a way to delight Motley's readers at home and abroad. This part of the work was on a vast scale ; for, as the author wrote, he was dealing with a world-wide conflict which followed the death of William the Silent, and in which England and the leading continental states were all more or less involved. His record is, therefore, as a panorama of European history during the glorious Elizabethan age.

Another period of six years passed, years of enormous labor, before Motley's story was continued in the *Life and Death of John of Barneveld* (1874). This work, which, in addition to the dramatic career of a famous personage, sketches the underlying causes of one of the world's greatest wars, was well characterized by Holmes as the interlude between the second and third

[1] Richardson, *American Literature*, I, 506.

[2] In Prescott's wonderful stories of the conquest of Mexico and Peru, and even in his history of Philip the Second, one finds a frequent note of romance and of unreality. As John Fiske has pointed out, this is due largely to the fact that Prescott was obliged to depend on Spanish authorities, who leave much to be desired in the way of accuracy.

acts of a stupendous drama. For the author intended to close his record with a history of the Thirty Years' War; but death intervened, and the story as planned by Motley's genius must forever remain unfinished.

The Quality of Motley. To many readers, who go to Motley as to a historical romance, one of the charms of his work is that he throws himself heart and soul into his narrative; that he is not a dispassionate observer of men and events, but one whose sympathies are all on the side of the small hero struggling in the grasp of a despot. One cannot expect in such a writer the judicial attitude, the calmness of speech and reasoning which characterize the professional historian, — who must not take sides; who must explain every character, whether hero or tyrant, by the inner motive or purpose which actuated him; and who must depict a Philip or a despotic Duke of Alva with the same fidelity, the same impersonal judgment, that he uses in his picture of an Elizabeth or of a William the Silent.

Motley was not that kind of writer. He was intensely American in his love of freedom, in his sympathy for a nation struggling against odds for its precious liberty; at times he was intensely puritanic, and the American and the Puritan appear frequently in his narrative. He is plainly too generous to his Netherlanders and too severe with their Spanish oppressors; the bright colors in which he paints the one are in too brilliant contrast to the hues of darkness which suffice him for the other. Also he seems unable, whether from temperament or from religious training, to understand either the Dutch Calvinist or the Spanish Catholic. To the facts and the documents he is always faithful; but he uses the facts freely to plead the cause of liberty and to establish his main thesis, — which is, that freedom of speech and thought and worship is the greatest of national blessings; and that the smallest nation, intent as the Dutch were on this one blessing, is invincible against the hosts of the Philistines.

It is this personal attitude and motive (manly in itself, but dangerous in the historian) which sometimes carries Motley beyond strictly historical bounds, especially in his terrible delineation of religious persecution, and which leaves him open to the charge of partisanship.

Aside from this blemish, or notwithstanding it, Motley's *Rise of the Dutch Republic* and his *United Netherlands* must be classed with the great historical books of the world.

His Scenes and Characters A host of characters — kings, queens, statesmen, generals, noblemen, soldiers and sailors, all magnificently drawn — throng his pages, and among them moves the epic figure of William the Silent, a masterpiece of historical delineation. His pictures of court and camp, of secret intrigue and desperate action, are even more vivid and thrilling than his portrayal of historical personages. The fundamental greed and selfishness of war; its glittering pageants, disguising as with a mask its hellish countenance; its glorification of the few at the price of tears and suffering for the many; its brazen show to make savages rejoice, and its horror to make angels weep, — every phase of armed conflict, from chivalrous encounter to unspeakable barbarity, is here presented with vividness and power. And if Motley lingers too long over battles and sieges by land or sea, if we lose the thread of connected history in gorgeously picturesque details of the voyage of the Spanish Armada, of the relentless siege of Haarlem or the heroic defense of Leyden, one forgives the fault, if fault it be, and finishes the reading with a more vivid realization of the fearful part which war has played in the sad but stirring drama of human history.

Francis Parkman (1823–1893). In his New World theme, with its spacious background of the wilderness, and in his masterful way of handling it, Parkman will seem to many readers the most notable of all our historians. To Prescott and Motley, as to Irving, the material of American history was not sufficiently remote or picturesque to furnish a subject of universal interest; they found what they sought in the chaotic records of that decaying empire which had first explored the western continent. To Parkman's deep and patriotic insight the neglected records of his own land furnished a theme of world-wide significance; and never was that insight more clearly shown than when, as a college boy, he selected his subject and his life's work. His twelve volumes, filled to overflowing with action and heroism, constitute but a single chapter in our history; but that chapter is the most dramatic, the most fateful of all that intervened between the landing of the Pilgrims and the Revolution.

Before Parkman's day the Old French Wars, as they were called, were generally regarded as a mere Colonial episode, not **Parkman's** as a chapter in universal history. When his first **Theme** historical volume, *The Conspiracy of Pontiac*, was published in 1851, even our historians failed to see its significance. As Fiske says:

" I had once taken it down from its shelf just to quiet a lazy doubt as to whether Pontiac might be the name of a place or a man. Had that conspiracy been an event in Merovingian Gaul or in Borgia's Italy, I should have felt a twinge of conscience at not knowing about it; but the deeds of feathered and painted red men on the Great Lakes and the Alleghanies, only a century old, seemed remote and trivial." [1]

To the general reader, who was soon lost on the endless trails of marauding savages, Pontiac's conspiracy differed from a score of other desperate intrigues only in this: that its hero, treacherous and terrible as he was, had the redeeming trait of unselfishness; that he sought no glory or power for himself, but only to save his race from being crushed between two powerful nations that pressed in on either side with the relentlessness of fate. That the book failed in epic interest is due largely to the fact that the author failed to follow his hero with sympathy, and to keep him always in the center of the stage. [2] To Parkman, however, the Indian was simply a minor character, one who played

1 Introduction to Parkman's Works, Frontenac Edition, Vol. I, p. xii.
2 *The Conspiracy of Pontiac* was written first, probably because the materials for it were nearest to Parkman's hand. Its place is at the end of the series, for its action follows the fall of Quebec, which closed the long struggle between France and England.

a sinister but subordinate part in a stirring drama; and not until several more volumes had appeared, like successive scenes or acts, did his purpose become evident. It was, in a word, to interpret destiny by writing the history of the inevitable struggle between two types of civilization, as represented by France and England, for the possession and use of the North American continent. "Here," says Parkman, "the forest drama was more stirring and the forest stage more thronged with appropriate actors than in any other passage of our history."

FRANCIS PARKMAN

The issues of that titanic struggle were not of local but of universal significance. The long wars which ended in an English victory on the Plains of Abraham made possible the free expansion of the future American nation; in a larger sense they determined the essential character of that band of colonies which soon circled the globe, bringing with them not the feudal and military system, benevolent but despotic, which had long prevailed in Quebec and Acadia, but the liberty and democracy of the Anglo-Saxon. The theme which Parkman chose, and which he was the first to appreciate justly, is one which concerns not only America but humanity.

Parkman's Preparation. His preparation for his task and his Spartan heroism in overcoming obstacles challenge our admiration. The writer who would reproduce a great historical drama must keep in mind three elements: the scene, the characters, the action ; and for each of these Parkman had the eye and the patience of genius. His scene covers the wilderness, stretching in unbroken solitude from the St. Lawrence to the Florida Everglades, and Parkman learned to know and to love that wilderness in a way that no other American writer has ever rivaled. Hundreds of camps and marches, of raids and battles fill his pages ; he visited the place of each in turn, made himself familiar with its striking features, until, beneath the bandages that covered his eyes as he wrote, the wild scene spread before him in all its primal loneliness and beauty.

Across this vast stage moved a strange variety of characters : half-naked savages skulking through the woods or shooting **His Char-** down the white rapids in their bark canoes, keen-eyed **acters** Colonial rangers, clumsy soldiers of the Continent, silent half-breeds, garrulous voyageurs, intrepid priests in their black cassocks, scarlet-coated English generals, nobles of France in the gorgeous raiment of the court of Versailles, — a motley, picturesque assembly such as never before was gathered together to play its part in a single drama. With every typical character Parkman made himself acquainted, at first hand wherever possible, camping with the rangers and voyageurs, living with the monks in an Italian convent, visiting the remnants of Indian tribes in the East, and spending one summer in the lodges of a wandering band of Sioux among the Black Hills.

For the action of his drama, for the details of every incident that influenced the final outcome, Parkman's preparation was **Sources of** scholarly to the last degree. He read every history **his Material** of the period ; he made several voyages to France, where he ransacked the archives and employed copyists to translate every contemporary record ; he collected letters, journals, Indian treaties and state papers from local sources ; [1] he explored the closely written volumes of the Jesuit *Relations*, — that mine of unused literary material in which these devoted men

[1] In the library of the Massachusetts Historical Society there are nearly two hundred manuscript volumes containing Parkman's copies of original documents.

had left the records of their missionary journeys. Some of these records are pale, almost illegible : they were written in smoky wigwams, or beside winter fires in the forest, with an ink composed of gunpowder and water ; on some of them are faded brown stains, the blood of the martyrs who wrote with hands still mangled by savage torture ; nearly all contained some simple record of fortitude and sublime courage that makes the story of knight or Norseman seem tame by comparison. With such records to draw from, it was inevitable that a large part of Parkman's work should read like a romance of adventure.

As a result of his careful preparation, there is an impression of absolute reality in all Parkman's work ; of finality also, for so thoroughly did he explore his ground that there is very little left for later historians to discover.

The silent heroism of all this preparation is indicated by the fact that it was continued for over forty years, and that during a **The Personal** large part of the time Parkman was ill, suffering, and **Element** threatened with blindness. All his documents must be read to him ; as he listened he made notes, which were read to him in turn, and from which he dictated his absorbing story of France and England in the New World, — blazing, as it were, a straight road through a veritable wilderness of facts. At times, so severe was his illness, he was allowed only five minutes for work each day ; but still he worked, and discovered that by using one minute and resting the next he could prolong the five to ten, and then the ten to twenty.

During all these weary years Parkman's iron will, which is so often unconsciously exhibited in the pages of *The Oregon Trail*, kept not only his work but himself and his quivering nerves under perfect control. No wonder his pages glow with suppressed fire when he writes of Brébeuf, — that Jesuit of adamant purpose, whom no perils could daunt, from whose lips no savage torture could wring a word of complaint, and whose heart the Iroquois ate that they might perchance share his indomitable spirit. One feels, in reading the vivid paragraphs which portray

Brébeuf's life and death, that Parkman had recognized his equal; that the New England Puritan and the French Jesuit were two men whom nature had cast in the same heroic mold.

Works of Parkman. The scope of Parkman's work will be evident from the titles of his volumes, which are given here in the order of their historical sequence. The first, called *Pioneers of France in the New World*, is in two parts, one relating the story of the ill-fated Huguenot settlements in Florida, the other largely devoted to the adventurous career of Champlain, who first opened a way for all French settlements in the North. *The Jesuits in North America* tells, in three stirring volumes, the tragic story of French missions and settlements among the Indians. These were followed by *La Salle and the Discovery of the Great West*, one of the most absorbing volumes of exploration and adventure that have ever been written. The general policy of the French in contrast with the English settlements is revealed with keen insight and with a wealth of picturesque detail in the next two works of the series : *The Old Régime in Canada*, and *Count Frontenac or New France under Louis XIV*. Then follows *A Half Century of Conflict*, telling the story of the inevitable struggle between the French and English forces, each with its skirmish line of terrible Indian allies. There is almost a monotony of adventure in this book, for the Old French Wars which it portrays were a succession of barbarous raids, each with its accompaniment of perils and escapes, of fire and pillage, of battle, murder and sudden death. The series ends with *Montcalm and Wolfe*, the best planned and the most artistically written of Parkman's works, portraying the final struggle for the possession of a continent and the triumph of the English in the capture of Quebec.

The Conspiracy of Pontiac, a vivid account of the Indian wars which followed the destruction of the French power in America, must be regarded as an epilogue rather than as a part of the drama. The desperate character of Pontiac's uprising, his power to inflame the fickle tribes scattered over thousands of square

miles of forest, his sudden, appalling appearances, his mysterious retreats, the trail of blood and fire which he left behind,—
Conspiracy   all these made a deep impression on the American
of Pontiac   colonies. Hardly was the savage chieftain dead when
the melodrama of *Ponteach* [1] appeared on the stage to keep alive
his fearful memory. Then the Revolution came on, and the
story was forgotten till Parkman revived it nearly a century
later and made it immortal.

Parkman was but twenty-six when he wrote *The Conspiracy
of Pontiac*, and the spirit of a youth who loves the free adventurous life of the wilderness appears in every chapter. Though
the author failed, as we have noted, to follow his hero, and
though the epic element of the story is lost in a thousand unnecessary details of savage border wars, his book is a fascinating
record of picturesque characters, of stirring adventures, and of
the changing lights and colors of the wilderness in which the
scene is almost wholly laid. Another charm of the book is its
delineation of the Indian character, as seen not from within
but from without. Says Parkman :

" The stern, unchanging features of his mind excite our admiration from
their very immutability ; and we look with deep interest on the fate of this
irreclaimable son of the wilderness, the child who will not be weaned from
the breast of his rugged mother. And our interest increases when we discern in the unhappy wanderer, mingled among his vices, the germs of
heroic virtues, — a hand bountiful to bestow, as it is rapacious to seize, and
even in extremest famine imparting its last morsel to a fellow sufferer;
a heart which, strong in friendship as in hate, thinks it not too much to lay
down life for its chosen comrade ; a soul true to its own idea of honor, and
burning with an unquenchable thirst for greatness and renown."

This strange, savage compound of virtue and evil passion had
welcomed the Europeans not simply as friends but as superior
beings. When Ribault and his followers first landed on the coast
of Florida, their reception was such as must have touched any

---

[1] This play was called *Ponteach, or the Savages of America; a Tragedy*. It was
written, probably, by Robert Rogers, an American officer who had fought in the Indian
wars, and was published in London in 1766.

heart not hardened to insensibility. The Indians gathered without fear or suspicion, and ran into the water to ease the first
boats ashore. They stood in awed silence as the white men
knelt and took possession of the Indians' land ; they led the
strangers to their wigwams, brought them food and gifts, and
supported them all winter. When Ribault sailed away, he left
at the mouth of the River of May a stone column, graved with
the king's arms, to indicate French possession of the country ;
when Laudonnière returned to the spot, two years later, he found
the stone crowned with evergreen, and at its foot were offerings
of fruit and grain. For the Indians not only regarded the white
man, but — a marvelous thing in that age of religious controversy — they had respect also for his religion and for his God.

Then came the awakening, the fearful change of attitude,
when the Indian's keen eye detected in his fortune-hunting
visitor, not the virtue and justice of a celestial being, but greed,
selfishness, — all the vices of civilization. This change from
awe to contempt, from generous hospitality to ferocious hatred,
furnishes a psychological motive for many of the wars which
are portrayed in *The Conspiracy of Pontiac*, and which are
commonly attributed to Indian treachery.

Another of Parkman's books, which is outside his great historical series, is *The California and Oregon Trail* (1849). This
The Oregon is a vivid account of a journey through the then un-
Trail known Northwest, which Parkman undertook partly
to gratify his love of adventure, but largely to obtain a better
knowledge of pioneer and Indian life in preparation for his
historical work. It is perhaps the most notable, certainly the
most entertainingly written, of that long series of journals of
exploration and adventure that have appeared in American literature, and that are read as eagerly as were the records of early
sea voyages collected by Hakluyt. One reads it now for entertainment chiefly, as one reads any other record of adventure ;
but as a historical document its significance can hardly be over-
estimated. In its realistic pictures of mountain and forest and

virgin prairies, of winding pack trains and frontier outposts, of motley Indian tribes shifting their picturesque camps to be in range of the wandering buffalo herds, — in all this it is a veritable re-creation of life in the West, as it was before the tide of settlers rolled over the Mississippi. That life, the stirring adventurous life which we associate with the great West, has vanished forever. As Parkman writes regretfully :

" The wild cavalcade that defiled with me down the gorges of the Black Hills, with its paint and war plumes, fluttering trophies and savage embroidery, bows, arrows, lances and shields, will never be seen again."

It is fortunate, therefore, for the historian as well as for the general reader, that a true picture of that vanished life is preserved forever in Parkman's pages.

The Quality of Parkman. " My theme fascinated me," says Parkman, " and I was haunted with wilderness images day and night." How he visited all the scenes of his drama, and transferred them with all their glowing color to his record, has already been suggested. His story begins when the first French colonists, after a lonely voyage across the Atlantic, " saw the long, low line where the wilderness of waves meets the wilderness of woods." From that moment on, whether he follows the Frenchmen through the almost tropical forests of the South, where earth, air and water teem with abundant life, or whether he camps with Le Jeune and his Indians in the silent, snow-laden forests of the North, his scene is always minutely true to life. No other American writer, not even Cooper, has approached him in his realistic descriptions of the wilderness. His portrayal of individuals, especially of heroic individuals, is equally remarkable. There are literally scores of characters in his drama ; each appears, not as a shadow on a screen, as in most historical narratives, but as a living man whom we recognize and whom we remember. This fine reproduction of scene and character, together with Parkman's absolute fidelity to the facts as recorded in original sources, gives an impression of intense reality to a narrative which in other hands might appear as a work of the romantic imagination.

In one thing only Parkman seems lacking, namely, in spiritual perception. His own nature, reserved and a little skeptical, made **Portrayal of** it difficult for him to appreciate the spiritual ideals **Character** of other men. In his experience with Sioux Indians, for example, as described in *The Oregon Trail*, his attitude was always watchful and suspicious ; and such an observer sees only the outer shell of savagery, the custom not the philosophy, the religious rite not the belief which lies beneath it. As studies of the Indian, therefore, Parkman's works are not to be compared with those of later writers, such as Schultz and especially Dr. Eastman, who have revealed to us not the body but the soul of an Indian.

The same lack of sympathetic understanding appears also in Parkman's narrative of the Jesuit missionaries. Being brave himself, he admires and makes us admire the courage and fortitude of these men, but the spiritual ideal which animated them is not so clearly shown ; their motive never appears large enough to explain their colossal undertaking. In a word, Parkman gives us a series of photographs of men in action ; he seldom paints a portrait that makes us understand either the Indian's shadow dance or the Jesuit's self-sacrifice. He tells his story, and leaves the reader to draw his own conclusion from a document, a treaty, or perchance the fragment of a bloodstained letter :

" Do not imagine that the rage of the Iroquois and the loss of many Christians can bring to naught the mystery of the cross of Christ. We shall die ; we shall be captured, burned, butchered ; be it so. Those who die in their beds do not always die the best death. I see none of our company cast down. On the contrary, they ask leave to go up to the Hurons ; and some of them protest that the fires of the Iroquois are one of the motives for the journey." [1]

Parkman's style is admirably suited to his subject and to his purpose, which was, in his own words, " to imbue himself with

[1] From Lalemant's *Relation ;* quoted in *The Jesuits in North America*, II, 136.

the life and spirit of the time," and then, "while scrupulously adhering to the truth of facts, to animate them with the life **Parkman's** of the past." Though his notes and introductions **Style** reveal a fine critical insight, Parkman's work is not a critical or philosophical history, but rather a stirring narrative of human struggle and achievement. His style is the perfection of the narrator's art, — clear, forceful, unconscious, abounding in life and color, moving slowly or rapidly with the action, and so vividly realistic at times that one receives the strange impression that Parkman must have been an eye-witness of the event which he describes.

Thanks to this attractive style and to his immense knowledge of his subject, Parkman has created a work of literature as well as of history. He has, in truth, re-created the life of the past, as he aimed to do, and showed that the reality of the past may be as absorbing as its romance. He has given us a wonder book of American history, and not the least interesting thing about his wonders is that they are all true.

Summary of the Second National Period. The central historical event of the period is the Civil War. This was preceded by an intensely partisan controversy over the questions of slavery and state rights, and was followed by the bitter years of reconstruction. The war, therefore, with its long chain of causes and consequences, filled practically the entire period from 1840 to 1876. The country was divided into two antagonistic sections; parties were numerous and constantly changing, and the general spirit of the age was one of political excitement and agitation.

The turmoil of politics was accompanied by a profound mental and spiritual agitation which expressed itself in many ways : in moral and social reforms, in numerous communistic societies such as Brook Farm, in the eager study of foreign literatures, in the establishment of lyceums and lecture courses, and in the philosophic movement known as transcendentalism.

The literature of the period divides itself naturally into two classes : the minor writings, voicing the turmoil of politics or the appeal of temporary interests, which are more or less sectional or partisan in character; and the major writings, which reflect the permanent thought and feeling, the ideas, emotions, traditions and beliefs of the American people without regard to political or geographical divisions. During this entire period the American mind was stirred and quickened by the various reform movements, by the rapid broadening of our intellectual culture following study of European and oriental literatures, by the pressure of great public questions, and by all the heroism and sacrifice of the war which revealed to us the preciousness of nationality. Under this mental and spiritual stimulus literature flourished as never before, and the major writings of the period are the noblest that our country has yet produced. The age is especially distinguished by its poets and by the generally fine quality of its poetry.

In our study we have considered in detail the lives and the works of: (1) The greater poets and essayists, Longfellow, Whittier, Emerson, Lowell, Holmes, Lanier, and Whitman. To this was added a study of the chief works of Timrod, Hayne, Ryan, Taylor, Boker, Stoddard, and a brief survey of the minor poetry of the period. (2) The fiction writers, Hawthorne, Cooke, Mrs. Stowe, Bret Harte, and a few others less widely known who are generally classed with the secondary novelists. (3) The individualist Thoreau and the historians Motley and Parkman.

Selections for Reading. Selections from all authors named in the text may be found in the numerous collections listed in General References, at the beginning of this book. The best single volume of selections from our nine elder poets is Page, Chief American Poets (1905). All anthologies are unsatisfactory, and for a study of our chief writers the inexpensive editions named below are desirable.

Longfellow: Evangeline, parts of Hiawatha, Tales of a Wayside Inn, and selected short poems. These may all be found in the Riverside Literature series and in various other texts published for class use. The best of Longfellow's narrative poems are published in a single volume of the Lake English Classics.

Whittier: Snow Bound, and selected ballads and lyrics, in Maynard's Classics, Riverside Literature, and in other series.

Emerson: Representative Men, and selected essays, in Pocket Classics, Everyman's Library, etc.; selected poems, in Riverside Literature.

Lowell: Vision of Sir Launfal, selected poems, and selected essays, all in Riverside Literature.

Holmes: Poems, in Maynard's English Classics, etc.; The Autocrat, in Everyman's Library; selected prose and verse, in Holmes Leaflets, Riverside Literature.

Lanier: Selections from Lanier, Timrod, and Hayne, in one volume of Maynard's English Classics; the same in Pocket Classics.

Whitman: Selected poems in Maynard's English Classics. The best book for the general reader is Triggs, Selections from the Prose and Poetry of Walt Whitman.

Hawthorne: House of Seven Gables, and selected short stories, in Everyman's Library, Pocket Classics, etc.

Harriet Beecher Stowe: Uncle Tom's Cabin, in various school series; selections from Oldtown Folks, in Riverside Literature.

Thoreau: Walden, in Everyman's Library; selections from prose works, in Riverside Literature. Selections should include a few essays from *Excursions* and, if possible, a few passages from Thoreau's Journal.

Parkman : Oregon Trail, in Standard English Classics. Other works of Parkman are not yet published for class use. A good single volume is Edgar, The Struggle for a Continent, edited from Parkman's histories (Little, Brown).

Bibliography. Textbooks of history, Montgomery, Elson; of literature, Richardson, etc. See General References for works covering the entire subject of American history and literature. The following works are recommended for a special study of the Second National Period.

History. Rhodes, History of the United States, 1850–1877, 7 vols.; Schouler, History of the United States under the Constitution, 1789–1865, 6 vols. (new edition, 1899); Wilson, Division and Reunion; Schwab, The Confederate States of America (financial and industrial history); Davis, Rise and Fall of the Confederate Government, 2 vols., or Stephens, War between the States; Dodge, A Bird's-Eye View of our Civil War (a brief military history); Paxson, The Civil War; Rhodes, Lectures on the American Civil War; Macy, American Political Parties, 1845–1860; Stanwood, History of the Presidency; Coman, Industrial History of the United States. A supplementary book for younger readers is Hart, Romance of the Civil War (1903).

Biographical and Autobiographical: Lives of important historical personages in the American Statesmen and in the Great Commanders series. R. M. Johnston, Leading American Soldiers; Life of Lincoln, by Morse, by Schurz; for younger readers, Morgan, Abraham Lincoln, the Boy and the Man; Grant, Personal Memoirs; Gordon, Reminiscences of the Civil War; Recollections of Alexander Stephens; Carl Schurz, Autobiography; Greeley, Recollections; Blaine, Twenty Years in Congress; Hoar, Autobiography; Booker Washington, Up from Slavery.

Literature. There is unfortunately no work devoted to the literature of this great period. Incomplete chapters may be found in Richardson, Wendell, Trent, etc. (see General References), and brief treatment of a few leading writers in Stedman, Poets of America; Lawton, New England Poets; Erskine, Leading American Novelists; Vincent, American Literary Masters; Brownell, American Prose Masters; Burton, Literary Leaders of America.

Transcendentalism. Frothingham, Transcendentalism in New England; Swift, Brook Farm; Higginson, Old Cambridge; Cooke, The Poets of Transcendentalism (anthology); Emerson's Essays, The Transcendentalist, and New England Reformers; Louisa Alcott, Transcendental Wild Oats, in Silver Pitchers; Dowden's essay, in Studies in Literature. See also the biographies of Margaret Fuller, by Higginson; George Ripley, by Frothingham; Amos Bronson Alcott, by Sanborn and Harris.

Longfellow. Texts: Riverside edition, poetry and prose, 11 vols.; Poems, Handy Volume edition, 5 vols.; Cambridge edition, 1 vol., etc. (Houghton).

Biography: The standard Life of Longfellow, with extracts from his journal and correspondence, is by S. Longfellow (3 vols., 1891). Life, by Higginson, in American Men of Letters; by Carpenter, in Beacon Biographies; by Robertson, in Great Writers series; by Underwood, by Austin, etc.

Reminiscence and Criticism: Mrs. Fields, Authors and Friends; Curtis, Homes of American Authors; Higginson, Old Cambridge; Massachusetts

Historical Society, Tributes to Longfellow and Emerson; Stoddard, Homes and Haunts of our Elder Poets; Howells, Literary Friends and Acquaintance; Stedman, Poets of America; Lawton, New England Poets.

Essays: Curtis, in Literary and Social Essays; Hale, in Fireside Travels; Whitman, in Specimen Days; Fiske, Longfellow's Dante, in The Unseen World and Other Essays; Bent, The Wayside Inn; Porter, Evangeline. On Hiawatha, see S. Longfellow's Life of Longfellow, II, 272–311; Schoolcraft, The Myth of Hiawatha.

Whittier. Texts: Poems, Riverside edition, 4 vols., Prose, 3 vols.; Standard Library edition, complete works including life, 9 vols; Poems, Cambridge edition, 1 vol., etc. (Houghton).

Biography: The standard is Pickard's Life and Letters of Whittier, 2 vols. Life, by Carpenter, in American Men of Letters; by Burton, in Beacon Biographies; by Higginson, in English Men of Letters; by Underwood, etc.

Reminiscence and Criticism: Mrs. Fields, Whittier; Mrs. Claflin, Personal Recollections of Whittier; Higginson, Contemporaries; Pickard, Whittier Land; Trowbridge, My Own Story; Stearns, Sketches from Concord and Appledore; Stedman, Poets of America; Lawton, New England Poets; Hawkins, The Mind of Whittier; Mitchell, American Lands and Letters; Fowler, Whittier: Prophet, Seer and Man.

Essays: Wendell, in Stelligeri; Hazeltine, in Chats about Books; Bayard Taylor, in Critical Essays; Whipple, in American Literature; Woodberry, in Makers of Literature.

Emerson. Texts: Centenary edition, complete works, 12 vols.; Poems, 1 vol., Riverside edition, etc. (Houghton). Various editions of the Essays. Correspondence of Carlyle and Emerson, edited by Norton, 2 vols.

Biography: Cabot's Memoir of Emerson, 2 vols., and E. W. Emerson's Emerson in Concord together form a fairly complete record. Life, by Woodberry, by Holmes, by Garnett, by Sanborn, etc.

Reminiscence and Criticism: Alcott, Emerson, and Concord Days; Conway, Emerson at Home and Abroad; Mrs. Fields, Authors and Friends; Sanborn, Emerson and his Friends at Concord, and The Personality of Emerson; Stearns, Sketches from Concord and Appledore; Whipple, Recollections of Eminent Men; Woodbury, Talks with Emerson; Stedman, Poets of America.

Essays: Lowell, in Literary Essays; Hawthorne, in Mosses from an Old Manse; Matthew Arnold, in Discourses in America; Whitman, in Specimen Days; Everett, in Essays Theological and Literary; Beers, in Points at Issue; Chapman, in Emerson and Other Essays; Stearns, in the Real and Ideal in Literature.

Lowell. Texts: Elmwood edition, complete works including letters, and life by Scudder, 16 vols.; Riverside edition, 11 vols.; Poems, 1 vol., Cambridge edition, Household edition, etc. (Houghton); Letters, edited by Norton, 2 vols. (Harper); the same, 3 vols., in the Elmwood edition.

Biography: Scudder's James Russell Lowell, 2 vols., is the standard. Life, by Greenslet (a good critical and biographical study); by E. E. Hale, Jr., in Beacon Biographies; by Underwood, etc.

Reminiscence and Criticism : Hale, James Russell Lowell and his Friends; Howells, Literary Friends and Acquaintance ; Higginson, Old Cambridge, and Cheerful Yesterdays ; Underwood, The Poet and the Man : Recollections of J. R. L.; Briggs, Homes of American Authors ; Stedman, Poets of America.

Essays : Woodberry, in Makers of Literature ; Wendell, in Stelligeri ; Curtis, in Orations and Addresses ; Henry James, in Essays in London and Elsewhere.

Holmes. Texts : Complete works, Riverside edition, 14 vols.; Standard Library edition, 15 vols., including life by Morse ; Poems, Cambridge edition, 1 vol., etc. (Houghton).

Biography and Criticism : Life and Letters, by Morse, 2 vols.; Life, by Crothers. Stedman, Poets of America ; L. Stephen, Studies of a Biographer; Howells, Literary Friends and Acquaintance ; Haweis, American Humorists ; Kennedy, Oliver Wendell Holmes ; Ball, Dr. Holmes and his Works ; Lang, Adventures among my Books ; Noble, Impressions and Memories ; Stearns, Cambridge Sketches.

Lanier. Texts : Poems (edited by Mrs. Lanier), The English Novel, Science of English Verse, Music and Poetry, Letters, Select Poems (Scribner).

Biography and Criticism : Life, by Mims ; by Baskerville, in Southern Writers ; Memoir, by W. H. Ward, in Poems of Lanier ; West, Life and Writings of Lanier. Gilman, in South Atlantic Quarterly, 1905 ; Northrup, in Lippincott's Magazine, 1905 ; Ward, in the Century Magazine, 1888 ; Higginson, Contemporaries ; Kent, A Study of Lanier's Poems, in Publications of the Modern Language Association, Vol. VII.

Whitman. Texts : Works, Camden edition, 10 vols. (Putnam) ; Triggs, Selections from the Prose and Poetry of Walt Whitman.

Biography and Criticism : Life, by Perry ; by Platt, in Beacon Biographies; by Carpenter, in English Men of Letters ; by Bucke, etc. In re Walt Whitman (various papers and tributes published by Whitman's literary executors, 1893) ; Stedman, Poets of America ; Kennedy, Reminiscences of Walt Whitman ; Symonds, Walt Whitman : A Study ; Trowbridge, My Own Story ; Stevenson, Familiar Studies of Men and Books ; Swinburne, Studies in Prose and Poetry ; Dowden, Studies in Literature ; Gosse, Critical Kit-Kats ; Noel, Essays on Poetry and Poets ; Santayana, The Poetry of Barbarism, in Interpretations of Poetry and Religion.

Hawthorne. Texts : Works, Riverside edition, 12 vols. (Houghton) ; numerous editions of tales and novels, by various publishers.

Biography and Criticism : Life, by Woodberry, in American Men of Letters ; by Annie Fields, in Beacon Biographies ; by Henry James, in English Men of Letters ; by Conway, in Great Writers. An intimate biography is Julian Hawthorne's Nathaniel Hawthorne and his Wife, 2 vols. Lathrop, A Study of Hawthorne ; Rose Hawthorne Lathrop, Memories of Hawthorne ; Bridge, Personal Recollections of Hawthorne ; Perry, A Study of Prose Fiction ; Gates, Studies and Appreciations ; L. Stephen, Hours in a Library ; Higginson, Short Studies of American Authors ; Curtis, Literary and Social Essays; Fields, Yesterdays with Authors ; Hutton, Essays Theological and Literary.

Thoreau. Texts: Works, and Familiar Letters, 11 vols., Riverside edition (Houghton); numerous editions of Walden.

Biography and Criticism: Life, by Sanborn, in American Men of Letters; by Salt, in Great Writers. Page, Thoreau, his Life and Aims; Marble, Thoreau, his Home, Friends, and Books; Channing, Thoreau, the Poet-Naturalist; Emerson, in Biographical Sketches; Stevenson, in Familiar Studies of Men and Books; Lowell, in Among my Books; Higginson, in Short Studies of American Authors.

Motley and Parkman : Life of Motley, by Holmes; Correspondence, edited by G. W. Curtis, 2 vols. Life of Parkman, by Farnham, by Fiske, by Sedgwick. Jameson, History of Historical Writing in America; Whipple, Recollections of Eminent Men; Fiske, Introduction to Parkman's complete works, Frontenac edition (Little, Brown); Fiske, A Century of Science and Other Essays; Vedder, American Writers of To-day.

Suggestive Questions For the aim of the following general questions (which are not intended as an examination) see page 83. Specific questions on the works of Longfellow and other authors should be based largely on the student's own reading. It is hardly necessary to add that the chief object of all questioning is to bring out what little the pupil knows rather than to reveal the wide extent of his ignorance.

1. Give a brief outline of historic events from 1840 to 1876. Why are the twenty years before 1861 called the age of agitation? What effect did the political agitation have upon our national literature?

2. What marked difference has been noted between the major and the minor writers of this period? How do you account for the fact that the chief works of the greater writers do not reflect the political or social reforms that occupied the attention of the country?

3. Describe and illustrate the difference between sectional and national literature. Why should one be forgotten and the other remembered?

4. Name some of the common characteristics of the major works of the period. How do you account for the strong moral tendency in nearly all American writers? What effect did the study of European and oriental literature have upon Longfellow and other poets of the period? What is meant by the transcendental movement? Who were its leaders and its chief writers? What were some of its effects on American life and literature?

5. *Longfellow.* Why is Longfellow called our household poet? What poems of his do you like best? Give an outline of his life, and name his chief works. What is the general plan of *Hiawatha*, of *Evangeline*, of *Tales of a Wayside Inn*? Do you know of any works in other literatures having a similar plan? Comment on the statement that Longfellow is the poet of the commonplace.

6. *Whittier.* Make a brief comparison between Whittier and Longfellow, having in mind the training of the two men, their subjects, and the quality of their work. (For purposes of comparison the ballads of each may be taken, or Whittier's *Tent on the Beach* and Longfellow's *Tales of a Wayside Inn*.)

Read Whittier's " Proem " to *Voices of Freedom,* and tell in your own words his theory of poetry. Explain Whittier as a New England and as a national poet. What is the marked difference between his earlier and later works? between his reform poems and his lyrics of home and nature? Give the plan of *Snow Bound,* and your own estimate of the poem. Which of Whittier's ballads or short narrative poems do you like best, and why?

7. *Emerson.* What is meant by Emerson's individualism? by his mysticism? Illustrate the two qualities from his life and writings. What are the two main divisions of his poetry? Name some of the best poems in each class. Compare (if you have read the works) Emerson's *Representative Men* and Carlyle's *Heroes and Hero Worship.* Name some of Emerson's best essays, and explain their general style and matter. How do you account for his liberal use of quotations? Which essay do you like best? What is meant by the stimulating quality of Emerson's works?

8. *Lowell.* What practical use did Lowell make of his literary art? Compare him in this respect with Irving. Name some of his best poems of nature and of patriotism. What is the general plan and purpose of the " Commemoration Ode "? Name Lowell's two chief satires and describe each briefly. What are the two chief subjects of his essays? What are the strong and the weak qualities of his literary criticisms? Give the outline of *Sir Launfal,* your own criticism of the poem, and compare Lowell's story with that of older writers on the same subject.

9. *Holmes.* Describe the quality of Holmes's humor. Compare it with the humor of Mark Twain. What are the chief works of Holmes in prose and verse? Give the general plan and character of *The Autocrat.* Select two poems, one humorous and the other serious, that you consider to be the best that Holmes wrote (omitting the general favorites, " The Deacon's Masterpiece " and " The Chambered Nautilus "). What is meant by the statement that the chief characteristic of Holmes's work is its intensely personal quality?

10. *Lanier.* Give the story of Lanier's life, and name his chief works. Which of his short poems do you consider best, and why? In what respect did Lanier's theory of poetry differ from that of other American poets? Account on two grounds for the musical quality of his verse. Select one of Lanier's sonnets on Columbus (in the *Psalm of the West*) and one stanza from Lowell's " Columbus "; compare the work of the two poets. Read " The Marshes of Glynn," and explain what Lanier attempted to do in the poem. What is meant by the universal quality of Lanier's poems?

11. *Whitman.* How does Whitman's poetry differ from that of other American poets? What are his elements of strength and of weakness? What views of nature and of death are reflected in his verse? Why is he called by some the poet of democracy and by others the poet of barbarism? How do you account for the fact that he is considered abroad to be one of our most representative poets?

12. *Hawthorne.* Why is Hawthorne called the novelist of Puritanism? Comment on the statement that his works are all based on the Ten Commandments. What marked difference is noted between him and other great writers

of the period, Lowell for example? Name his chief romances and his best collections of tales. Which do you consider the best in each class? What is meant by Hawthorne's tendency to symbolism and allegory? (Illustrate and explain the matter by two or three of his short stories.) What effect did this tendency have on his portrayal of character? Which of Hawthorne's characters do you remember most vividly? Note some resemblances and differences in the tales of Poe and Hawthorne.

13. *Thoreau.* Tell briefly the story of Thoreau's career, and show how it differs from that of other American authors. Name his chief works, and explain their general character. Give quotations from Thoreau to illustrate his individualism and originality. Compare him in this respect with Emerson. Thoreau's observations of nature around Concord are sympathetic and unusually accurate; his observations recorded in *The Maine Woods* are frequently careless and unsympathetic; how do you account for the difference? Comment on the statement that *Walden* is one of the few books in American literature that repay frequent readings.

14. *Parkman.* Describe Parkman's general theme, and explain its importance. What preparation did he make for his work? Name the chief works in his great historical series. What is the general character of *The Oregon Trail?* of *The Conspiracy of Pontiac?* What are the notable qualities of Parkman as a historian? Explain the peculiar charm of his work to American readers.

15. Name some of the secondary writers of the period. Describe any works of these authors that you have read. What is the general character of Cooke's romances? What important work did Bret Harte do for American fiction?

Subjects for Research and Essays. Brook Farm. Communistic societies in America (note the Pilgrims' experiment, as recorded in Bradford's *Of Plimoth Plantation*). Transcendentalism at home and abroad. Songs and ballads of the Civil War. The moral tendency of American literature. Longfellow and Tennyson. Emerson and Carlyle. Norton and Ruskin. Whittier and Burns (use " Snow Bound " and " The Cotter's Saturday Night "). The Hiawatha legend. Lowell's Americanism. Lanier's theory and practice of poetry. Holmes as a humorist. School life in Whittier's works. A comparison of Timrod and Hayne. Famous collections of stories in prose or verse (like Longfellow's " Tales of a Wayside Inn "). The Cambridge group. The Concord group. The Charleston group. Class poems of Holmes. Nature in the poetry of Bryant, Emerson, and Whittier (use " A Winter Piece," " The Snow Storm," and the first part of " Snow Bound " for purposes of comparison). Hawthorne's use of allegory. Terror and mystery in the stories of Brown, Poe, and Hawthorne. Bret Harte and the local short story. Realism and romance illustrated from American literature (see the following chapter). Why *Uncle Tom's Cabin* continues to be popular. The Indian in American literature. The romance of the West. Thoreau: Indian or Greek? The stage and the actors in Parkman's drama. A comparison of Hawthorne's *Grandfather's Chair* and Scott's *Tales of a Grandfather*. Historical writing in America. My favorite American poet. My favorite American story-teller.

CHAPTER V

SOME TENDENCIES IN OUR RECENT LITERATURE

> Our slender life runs rippling by, and glides
>   Into the silent hollow of the past;
> What is there that abides
>   To make the next age better for the last?
>   Lowell, " Commemoration Ode "

There was once a wise man named Archimedes who said that he could move the world if he had a lever long enough and a place to stand on. The mention of the latter condition, of that unattainable place to stand on, indicates at once his wisdom and his human limitations. So the historian might with confidence speak of his own age if he could remove himself to the distant future and view the present event in its historical perspective, that is, in its relation to other events past and to come.

The same limitation is upon the contemporary critic or literary historian. Since 1876 nearly two hundred good writers and perhaps a thousand good volumes have appeared, and they are still too near to be viewed in their relation to the literary works of the past or to the world of men. These recent books have two ultimate judges, time and humanity, and no one has ever yet discovered the law by which time reaches its verdict. The poet Spenser spoke of his own age as barren, almost hopeless, — that same Elizabethan age which now appears as the most glorious in English letters. In our own country Poe, who was in many ways an excellent critic, wrote his *Literati* (1850) predicting fame for some thirty of his contemporaries. The world straightway neglected or forgot them all, and cherished the work of three or four whom he omitted from his study.

One might multiply similar striking examples : of keen critics who failed in their judgment of their own age ; of books once famous but now forgotten because they appealed to the mood or taste of the hour ; of other books that appeared unheralded and unpraised, and that abide because they satisfy the permanent emotions of humanity. In a word, a trustworthy history of present literature is humanly impossible. We shall not attempt it, therefore, but simply call attention to a few apparent tendencies in our recent prose and poetry.

Reminiscent Literature. Joining the present to the golden age of American letters which has just passed, and belonging as much to the one as to the other, is a varied group of writers — including Edward Everett Hale, George William Curtis, Thomas Wentworth Higginson, Donald Grant Mitchell, and many others — who have each produced some original work, but who are at their best when they write in a reminiscent mood of the elder poets and novelists. Edward Everett Hale, for example, found time in the midst of his busy, beautiful life to write of many subjects. He produced a number of clever short stories, such as " My Double and How He Undid Me " ; some widely read religious juveniles, such as *In His Name* and *Ten Times One is Ten ;* and one classic (perhaps we should say the classic) of American patriotism, *The Man Without a Country*, which has been called the best sermon on love of one's native land that has ever been written. The last-named work is undoubtedly permanent. We know not how long the others may endure, but we do know that in such works as *James Russell Lowell and His Friends*, *For Fifty Years*, and *A New England Boyhood*, this gentle, friendly writer has given added dignity and significance to the study of American life and letters.

It is so with the other writers of this remarkable group. Among Higginson's numerous volumes of stories, novels, essays, histories, biographies and translations, we are at present most inclined to cherish his reminiscent *Old Cambridge*, *Contemporaries*, *Cheerful Yesterdays*, and *Short Studies of American Authors*. The fanciful novel of *Prue and I* and the miscellaneous works that fill the dozen published volumes of Curtis are

THE LIBRARY OF CONGRESS, WASHINGTON, D.C.

succeeded, and perhaps superseded, by some of the *Easy Chair* papers and other literary appreciations. The pleasantly sentimental memories of Mitchell's (Ik Marvel's) *Dream Life* and *The Reveries of a Bachelor*, which once pleased a large company of readers, are followed by the more specific and perhaps more enduring reminiscences of his *American Lands and Letters.*

We have named but a few of the recent writers who are inspired by the literature of the past, but the few are enough to **Discovery of** indicate a decided and important tendency. Until **American** recently American critics, like Poe, were forced to **Literature** deal with the present or to anticipate the future; there was no body of American literature in the past that seemed worthy of their study. Since 1876, however, more than fifty good volumes of literary reminiscences have appeared. They indicate clearly that America has now a golden age of letters as well as of history, and that our literature is worthy of our grateful consideration. It is precious, not because it compares with the great literature of other lands, but because it is our own, — a true reflection of the American spirit, which attempted in a new land a new and heroic experiment in human living. Such is the good message of our reminiscent writers, a message which Stedman set to music after listening to the song of one of our native birds :

> And as my home-bred chorister outvied
> The nightingale, old England's lark beside,
> I thought — What need to borrow? Lustier clime
> Than ours Earth has not, nor her scroll a time
> Ampler of human glory and desire
> To touch the plume, the brush, the lips, with fire;
> No sunrise chant on ancient shore and sea,
> Since sang the morning stars, more worth shall be
> Than ours, once uttered from the very heart
> Of the glad race that here shall act its part:
> Blithe prodigal, the rhythm free and strong
> Of thy brave voice forecasts our poet's song![1]

---

[1] From Stedman, " Music at Home."

Recent Poetry

Ever since Whitman's day it has been said that American verse tends to become realistic, like American fiction ; but the word "realism," vague and undefined, is not one that should be applied to poetry, which may be described as imagination writing to melody. At the bottom of every true poem one finds some heartfelt emotion which gives the verse character and human meaning ; and if we study this emotional element in our recent singers we shall probably note a very significant tendency.

At the beginning of our national literature, that is, in the first half of the nineteenth century, the feeling expressed in hundreds of our poems, as collected in the various "Annuals" and "Tokens," ran largely to sentimentality. In this our minor singers, like our earliest novelists, were influenced by the romantic writers in Germany and England, who, as we have noted, made almost a fetish of "sensibility." [1] In reaction from this sentimentality some of our elder poets, notably Bryant and Emerson, went almost to the opposite extreme. To most readers Bryant appears cold and reserved, and Emerson's poetry is an expression of his thought rather than of his feeling. Other of our elder poets, Longfellow, Lanier, Whittier, and Lowell, are characterized by deep feeling, but a large part of their verse is a portrayal of the feeling not of present men and women but of past times and past heroes.[2] Whittier may serve as an excellent example. In his *Songs of Labor* and in his antislavery verses he tried to voice the feeling of the present, but these were of little moment in comparison with his *Snow Bound* or with his stirring ballads, in which he reflected the emotion of days gone by.

---

[1] See p. 159.

[2] This is a generalization, and therefore dangerous. There are abundant exceptions, but the generalization expresses at least a tendency of English and American poets in the past. Lyrics are of course excepted, because a lyric is the expression of the poet's own feeling.

The Poetry of the Present. In contrast with the work of our elder poets a considerable part of our recent verse reflects the feeling not of past heroes but of present men and women in field and factory, or even in the crowded city streets, where poetry seems as remote as a bird song. One recalls here the work of Eugene Field (1850–1895), of whom one must write with love. Nothing could be more prosaic than his work on a Chicago newspaper ; nothing more significant than his brave, cheery attempt to reduce the city noise to harmony, to show the poetry that is hidden in work, in daily companionship, and especially in hearts of parents and children, — our own children, who grow wide-eyed over his "Wynken, Blynken, and Nod," and our own hearts, that weep again over his "Little Boy Blue." In his verse one finds nothing distant or foreign; all is present, real, familiar as our own fun or our own sorrow.

EUGENE FIELD

The same note of present emotion, of deep and tender feeling among plain men and women, is sounded by many other singers. Lucy Larcom (1826–1893) finds inspiration for poetry not in Arthurian legend or Colonial heroism but in a New England factory among the working girls. The feeling of her "Hannah Binding Shoes" is as finely true as any that Tennyson ever gave to his princesses, or Longfellow to his Evangeline, and it is closer to common life.

The work of three poets, whom we may group together as singers of a new type of American folk songs, is especially significant in this connection. Emma Lazarus (1849–1887), a gifted young Jewish girl, has preserved some of the finest

The New Folk Songs feeling of her race — a race set free from oppression in a new land — in her *Songs of a Semite* and other volumes. Paul Laurence Dunbar (1872–1906) has given expression to negro thought and feeling in *Lyrics of Lowly Life* and *Lyrics of the Hearthside.*

JAMES WHITCOMB RILEY

Meanwhile the hearts of all simple people, at work in "the old town" or on "the old farm," are reflected with insight and true feeling in the poems of James Whitcomb Riley, our present poet-laureate of democracy. The very titles of Riley's books — *The Old Swimmin'-Hole, Neighborly Poems, Green Fields and Running Brooks, Old-Fashioned Roses, Rhymes of Childhood Days, Afterwhiles,* and *Poems Here at Home*—are an invitation; and one who accepts it finds himself again amidst pleasant homely scenes, sharing the faith and hope, the humor and pathos, the sentiment and sentimentality of those whom we think of, tenderly, as "the old folks at home."

A little farther removed and holding, in the estimation of critics, a leading place among our minor poets are Stedman and

Stedman Aldrich, two writers of large and varied talents who began their work amidst the elder poets, and who have steadily upheld the best traditions of American letters. Edmund Clarence Stedman (1833–1908) has placed all students of our literature in his debt by his *Poets of America* (1885), a fine appreciation of our earlier and later singers, which is without a rival in the field of American criticism. As a poet he has left a half-dozen volumes, including *Alice of Monmouth* (1863), which he called "An Idyl of the Great War," and which is one of the few sustained attempts to reflect in verse the scenes and emotions of a mighty conflict. All his books are characterized by careful workmanship and by a high but clearly defined ideal of poetry. It is significant of the changed taste of the age, however, that his most ambitious and carefully finished works seem remote, and that they are neglected in favor of a few homely poems, such as "Pan in Wall Street," "Country Sleighing," "The Doorstep," "The Lord's Day Gale," "Laura," and "Wanted — A Man." Such poems, which are very different from his "Blameless Prince" with its atmosphere of medieval romance, may possibly indicate that the scholarly Stedman no less than the simple Riley was at his best in dealing with the poetry of common life.

Thomas Bailey Aldrich. In the exquisite finish of his verse Thomas Bailey Aldrich (1836–1907) is perhaps the most artistic of our recent poets. We refer simply to the outer form, not to the soul of his poetry. For beauty of form he had a very high regard, and seldom has a poet given more thought or care to make his work outwardly perfect. His verse is invariably well done, often beautifully done, and on this account alone it well repays the reading, — though at the end one may be left with the impression of dealing with pleasant matters of small consequence. For Aldrich is, as has often been pointed out, a younger Herrick, more subdued and more refined than the elder. The American reader especially will miss in him the compelling ideal and the enkindling purpose of our greater poets and artists.

Of Aldrich's prose works the most notable is a classic of American boyhood, *The Story of a Bad Boy* (1869), which has **His Prose and Verse** retained its popularity for full forty years. A few of his admirable tales, the famous "Marjorie Daw" for example, may have claims to permanence, but the rest have gone the inevitable way of short stories in general. His poems may be grouped in three or four classes. In the first are his ambitious works, *Windham Towers* and *Judith and Holofernes*, which have shared the sad fate of all recent poems of immoderate length. For the present busy age seems to have adopted Poe's dictum that a poem must be short. In the second group are the polished trifles called "society verse," which he arranged in the final edition of his poems under the heading "Bagatelles." They still serve their original purpose of brightening a dull or amusing an idle hour. In the third group are certain glowing poems of the East and a few good medieval ballads under the alluring titles, "Cloth of Gold" and "Friar Jerome's Beautiful Book." Some of these poems deserve to be more widely known, but because they seem remote from present life they fail to satisfy the changed taste of the age.

THOMAS BAILEY ALDRICH

In the fourth group — the most significant in our study of recent poetry — are the sonnets, the Decoration Day ode called "Spring in New England," and such lyrics as "Before the Rain," "Voice of the Sea," "A Touch of Nature," "At Two and Twenty," "Nameless Pain," "Night Wind," and "Forever and a Day." In these short, simple poems, which may prove most enduring, Aldrich leaves the Acadian dreams which have haunted all the poets since Spenser wrote his *Faery Queene* and Sidney his *Defense of Poesie* and comes closer to his own age and his own people.

Though Aldrich seldom touches the heights or the depths of life, and though a large part of his work speaks of delicacy **The Quality** rather than strength, this one thing should be recorded **of Aldrich** and remembered of him : that he selected the dainty, pleasant part of human experience for his subject and, like a painter of miniatures, worked with conscientious care until he made himself a master in his own small field. The spirit of his life and work is best expressed in his sonnet of the " Enamoured Architect " :

> Enamoured architect of airy rhyme,
> Build as thou wilt ; heed not what each man says.
> Good souls, but innocent of dreamers' ways,
> Will come and marvel why thou wastest time ;
> Others, beholding how thy turrets climb
> 'Twixt theirs and heaven, will hate thee all thy days ;
> But most beware of those who come to praise.
> O Wondersmith, O worker in sublime
> And heaven-sent dreams, let art be all in all ;
> Build as thou wilt, unspoiled by praise or blame,
> Build as thou wilt, and as thy light is given :
> Then, if at last the airy structure fall,
> Dissolve, and vanish — take thyself no shame.
> They fail, and they alone, who have not striven.

America Singing. We have mentioned but a few of our recent singers, and with the purpose, chiefly, of calling attention to the fact that, as Chaucer turned from ancient themes to the busy life around him, so these singers seek in a modest way to find and reflect the poetry of present life. The same significant trait is evident in many others : in the country ballads of Will Carleton and John Hay ; in the varied lyrics, grave or gay, of Father Tabb ; in the finely spiritual dreams of Edward Rowland Sill and in the poetic drama of William Vaughn Moody,— both poets, alas ! cut off in their prime of years with a glorious promise unfulfilled ; in the nature poetry of Edith Thomas and Celia Thaxter ; in the " hermit thrush " songs of Richard Hovey and the "mocking bird" songs of Madison Cawein ; in the exquisite poems of love and motherhood of Helen Hunt Jackson, and in the glittering fragments of poetry that strew the pages of Emily Dickinson. To complete the list, especially if we read the characteristic works of each poet, is to understand Whitman's exclamation :

> I hear America singing, the varied carols I hear !

Though the age is said to be prosaic, and though any publisher will tell you that " poetry does not pay," while fame and financial reward await the writer of ephemeral short stories, still the singers will not be silenced. From every part of the country, from farm and town, from north, south, and west, the song arises ; for there are no more local " schools," the American muse having long since declared that she is no respecter of cities. Among these many singers there is no " dominant " poet, — perhaps because the life of our age and nation is too great to be expressed by one man, — but in each is a promise as he tries to deal faithfully with the two themes of enduring poetic interest : nature with its beautiful reality, and the soul of man with its more beautiful dreams :

> When the full-grown poet came,
> Out spake pleased Nature, saying, *He is mine;*
> But out spake too the soul of man: *Nay, he is mine alone !*
> Then the full-grown poet stood between the two, and took each by the hand.

Our Recent Fiction

In the primitive villages of the Celts and Anglo-Saxons the most welcome of all visitors was the story-teller, or tale bringer as he was then called. Modern readers seem to have returned to the taste of their ancestors, for the most popular forms of literature are now the novel and the short story. These appeal to all classes of readers, and so rapidly have they multiplied that one often hears modern letters in general characterized as a flood of fiction. While we are in the midst of this flood it is obviously impossible to judge or criticize it accurately. Our present concern is to point out its general tendencies.

Romance and Realism. In contrast with our earlier novels, perhaps the first characteristic of modern fiction is its tendency to realism, that is, to portray the common life of the present. The term "realism," like the terms "classicism," "romanticism," and "idealism," [1] is hard to define, and the difficulty is increased by the fact that when we speak of a romanticist or a realist we have in mind an extreme type,— a romanticist who uses his imagination so freely that his work seems far removed from life, or a realist who uses only his eyes and who therefore fails to see the great soul of humanity. Nor are we much helped by the definition that "realism is the kind of fiction which does not shrink from the commonplace or from the unpleasant in its effort to depict things as they are, life as it is." That is largely negative, and by examining certain typical works we may obtain a more positive conception. Thus, our first writers of fiction, Brown, Irving, Cooper, Poe, and Hawthorne, were all of the romantic school, while many of our recent novelists, notably Howells and James, are classed with the realists.[2] What are the essential differences in motive and method between the two classes of writers?

The romanticist, as typified by Cooper for example, must have first of all a story to tell, and the plot, the adventure, the dramatic

The Romanticist

action of his story must be interesting enough to carry the reader on to the end. As the earliest tale bringer played upon the instinctive curiosity of his audience, so the modern romancer constructs a plot that shall make us eager to know what happened. His scene is generally laid in the past, so far removed from present reality that we shall not question the

---

[1] For a discussion of romanticism and classicism see p. 138 and note.

[2] It should be noted that, as our first novelists were influenced by the romanticism of Germany and England, so our later novelists have been strongly influenced by the realism of continental writers, by Tolstoy, Turgenev, and Zola. Ibsen is also generally classed as an influential realist; but his best work, *Peer Gynt* for example, seems to us as romantic as *A Midsummer Night's Dream*.

probability of his story. He chooses picturesque scenes and unusual characters, — heroes more courageous and villains more unscrupulous than those of our acquaintance. He aims to interest us, to give us pleasure in his narrative ; and his deeper purpose is generally to stir our emotions, to emphasize the spiritual quality of life, to rouse our better natures into life and action. He proceeds on the principle that humanity in its deeper moments is forever following the injunction, "Build thee more stately mansions, O my soul!" and he tries to make his story true to the inner world of imagination and aspiration.

The realist, as typified by Howells, has a different motive and works by a different method. He pays little attention to the plot or the story element. Often, indeed, he tells **The Realist** no particular tale, and his book ends much as an acquaintance says good-by, leaving the important matter unfinished, the important question unanswered, — just as they are in everyday experience. He tries to interest us, not by adventures or dramatic situations, but by portraying a little matter which we shall recognize as true to life. His scene is generally laid close at hand, in order that we may better compare it with reality, and his characters are such men and women as we may meet in the shop or street. He has no ideal aim, but is content to construct a world like the present world, and is satisfied if we can say of his work that it is steadily true to fact, to humanity and nature as they are, not as we imagine or hope for them to be.[1]

There is another way by which the difference between the two classes of writers may be suggested, as in a parable. The ancient story-teller was either a keeper of old legends or else a traveler who brought to a humdrum village tales of strange lands

[1] We have tried to suggest the general difference between the romanticist and the realist. The generalization is, of course, open to exceptions. Many romancers, Shakespeare for example, seem more true to life and nature than are the best realists. Again, Dickens was a romancer, Thackeray a realist. Some of Thackeray's characters are those of Dickens with the exaggeration rubbed off to make them more true to life. Yet Dickens's characters, with all their exaggeration, seem to many readers more vital and human than are the similar characters found in Thackeray's pages. It should be noted also that the finest romance and the finest realistic novel approach each other. Others fly off to opposite extremes, and most of our definitions are based upon the extreme type.

and peoples. The wide-ranging spirit of this old story-teller reappears in the modern romance. Your true romancer is as a
A Parable of traveler who goes out to see the world. He has per-
Romance haps had enough of the ordinary or commonplace at
home ; now his eyes are opened wide for the extraordinary.
Like every traveler, he notes chiefly the picturesque features of
the new landscape, — features which are hardly noticed by the
inhabitants, whose eyes are blinded by custom and familiarity.
Ordinary people are passed over by our traveler; he is looking
for unusual characters, in whom he may see humanity written
large or small ; his glance lights with pleasure upon nobles,
heroes, brigands, mountaineers with strange garments, market
women with strange songs, boatmen, goatherds, monks, military
officers in ridiculous little caps, and drivers of ridiculous little
donkeys. All these are in the world for those who have eyes
to see. The traveler sees them all ; he takes us into the new
world and makes us also see them, each with his peculiarity a
little exaggerated, as they first strike an observer.

The realist bides at home and studies his own little village
minutely, psychologically. He does not take us into a new
world, but points out the quality of those familiar characters
whose homes may be seen from our back door or from our
front window. One novelist tells a story of the beckoning life,
and measures man by his free spirit ; the other tells of a life
repressed by custom, and strikes a general average of humanity
from its ordinary activities.

To sum up the matter : romance deals largely with the ideal,
and realism with the actual life of men. Both classes of fiction
The Ideal   have their place and their great names ; both aim
and the   to limn a true picture of life ; but the realist often
Actual   gives us but a temporary and superficial view, and
sometimes confuses the real with the apparent, what is with
what seems to be. It was a great writer and critic who said
that only the ideal is actual, meaning that the ideals of men
are immortal and unchanging, while their seeming actual life is

forever transient and variable. So the distinction of a modern critic, that the realist is the only " veritist," the truth seeker, can hardly be allowed. The romanticist also seeks truth, and seeks it among ideals, which are the only permanent realities. It should be noted, also, that realism tends generally to pessimism, and romance to faith and gladness; that the great writers of the world have nearly all the romantic spirit; that humanity is not and never has been satisfied with the actual, but ever hungers for the ideal. The true romance tends in some degree to satisfy such hunger, and for this reason, probably, it endures better and has more readers than the realistic novel.

Representative Realists. Among recent novelists a prominent place is held by Henry James and by William Dean Howells. The former has spent most of his life abroad, and his chief novels are as a rule of the so-called international type. His hero or heroine (if the name be not too vital for such small characters as he gives us) is generally an American, whose crudities or peculiarities the novelist analyzes to better advantage against the background of a more settled European society. Howells portrays the American in his native environment; and his pictures, faithfully drawn from life, are by some critics classed among the most valuable of recent contributions to our literature.

At present Howells holds an honored and well-deserved position as dean of American letters. His first printed book

William Dean Howells

appeared in 1860, at a time when Longfellow, Hawthorne, and their great contemporaries were at the height of their influence; since then he has published some forty volumes: poems, essays, criticisms, delightful sketches of travel in *Venetian Life* and *Italian Journeys*, valuable reminiscent studies in *Literary Friends and Acquaintance* and *My Literary Passions*, delicate farces or parlor comedies such as *The Sleeping Car* and *The Mouse Trap*, and a score of novels from *Their Wedding Journey* in 1871 to *The Son of Royal Langbrith* in 1905. In short, Howells has been a part of our American life for over half a century, and many phases of that life are reflected in his works with the fidelity and conscientiousness of a good workman.

Though generally engaged, like Aldrich, in what is termed "miniature" work, Howells has kept before him a high ideal of art, and has been steadily faithful to the best literary traditions. For their style alone — a graceful, flexible style that is an incentive to better writing — all of Howells's works are well worth the reading; and we should know a few of his typical novels, such as *The Rise of Silas Lapham, A Modern Instance,* and *The Quality of Mercy,* in order to appreciate the American realistic novel, which differs in many important respects from the European product.

Concerning the value and enduring interest of these novels there are many opinions. To the lover of romance they have **Value of Howells's Work** many faults, chief of which is that they are not "good stories." They fail to do justice to the heroic side of life; their characters, so finely analyzed, are frequently tiresome or unlovely; and with few exceptions their shallow feminine characters seem quite as untrue to American womanhood as are the romantically insipid "females" of Cooper. On the other hand, they contain some of the best pictures of American society "in the making" that have ever appeared in literature, and their style and delicate humor have a charm which allures the reader even when the story lags and the characters are most uninteresting.

For Howells's theory of his art, and for his motive in portraying the petty details of life, one should read his *Criticism in Fiction,* which does not, however, tell us why the interesting, the original, the lovable people one meets in real life are not better represented in his realistic pages. An explanation of the matter, and an estimate of Howells's place in fiction, are given by a contemporary critic:

"He tells his methods very frankly, and his first literary principle has been to look away from great passions, and rather to elevate the commonplace by minute touches. Not only does he prefer this, but he does not hesitate to tell us sometimes, half jestingly, that it is the only thing to do. 'As in literature the true artist will shun the use even of real events if they are of an improbable character, so the sincere observer of man will not desire to look upon his heroic or occasional phases, but will seek him in his habitual moods of vacancy and tiresomeness.' [1] He may not mean to lay this down as a canon of universal authority, but he accepts it himself; and he accepts with it the risk involved of a too-limited and microscopic range. . . . He is really contributing important studies to the future organization of our society. How is it to be stratified? How much weight is to be given to intellect, to character, to wealth, to antecedents, to inheritance? Not only must a republican nation meet and solve these problems, but the solution is more assisted by the writers of romances than by the compiler of statistics. Fourth of July orators cannot even state the problem : it almost baffles the finest touch. As in England you may read everything ever written about the Established Church, and yet, after all, if you wish to know what a bishop or a curate is, you must go to Trollope's novels, so, to trace American ' society ' in its formative process, you must go to Howells; he alone shows you the essential forces in action." [2]

Modified Types of Realism and Romance. There are other interesting types and phases of modern realism, — the local short story, for instance, which has been so rapidly and well developed since Bret Harte discovered its possibilities that the American short story is now almost a symbol of literary interest and good workmanship. Then there are the " specialized " novels, each dealing with a particular type of life, in the mountains or fields or factories of this varied America, and the " prop- aganda " novels, which aim directly at some needed reform in politics or society. The most notable example of the latter type is the *Ramona* (1884) of Helen Hunt Jackson, which aimed to do for the Indian what *Uncle Tom's Cabin* had done for the negro, and which, in its combination of realism with romantic interest, is one of the most notable of American novels.

Each of these types has been represented by many good writers, and so well have they done their work that fiction readers for a generation past have wandered, thirsty and hungry, in a desert of realism, have felt the horror of the slums or the

---

[1] Quoted from Howells, *Their Wedding Journey.*
[2] Higginson, *Short Studies of American Authors*, pp. 34–36.

stockyards, the loneliness of isolated farms, the grinding curse of modern industrialism. From this flat, weary desert we escape gladly to the uplands of life, to feel the spell of ancient days in the *Ben Hur* or *The Fair God* of Lew Wallace, to share the stirring romance of Colonial life in the *To Have and to Hold* of Mary Johnston, or to sweeten our realistic pessimism by the breezy, cleansing laughter of Frank Stockton. Or, it may be, we pick up the popular, ephemeral novel, expecting nothing, and find something hearty, wholesome and typically American in the humor and philosophy of an *Eben Holden*.

One suggestive tendency should be noted in this connection, namely, that our best romancers and realists are wary of extremes.
The Modern Novel Each corrects his individual theory by looking at life from the other's viewpoint, and the result is a story which often combines the good elements of romanticism and realism. This is especially noticeable in the work of many of the " local " or " specialized " novelists. In the finely wrought sketches of Creole life by George Washington Cable ; in the pathos and tragedy of an almost primitive existence amid the grandeur of the Great Smoky Mountains as revealed by Mary Noailles Murfree (Charles Egbert Craddock) ; in the delicate yet powerful novels of the New England coast by Sarah Orne Jewett, — in all such works one feels the influence of both romance and reality. The same interesting combination appears in our writers of fiction who are generally classed as romancers pure and simple, in the works of Marion Crawford, Elizabeth Stuart Phelps, Margaret Deland, Thomas Nelson Page, and many others. The above lists should be increased fivefold if we are to include all our novelists of distinction ; we have selected a few names simply to illustrate the fact that modern fiction avoids the romantic unreality of Poe and Hawthorne without going to the extreme of realism. Our typical novelists try faithfully to reflect life as they see it and where they see it, not slighting either the soul or the body of humanity ; they remember also the first duty of a novelist, which is to tell a story.

Mark Twain. Among recent American writers the most picturesque figure is that of Samuel L. Clemens (1835–1910), who is known wherever English books are read by his pen-name of Mark Twain. One of the striking things in his career is that it covers the greatest period of American letters and is yet a part of our own age. Since his first book appeared, in 1867,[1] all our great poets and some of our greatest prose writers have come

SAMUEL CLEMENS (MARK TWAIN)

or gone ; a hundred minor literary reputations have waxed and waned ; and not once in all that time has Mark Twain lost his firm hold on his audience, — which is now composed of the children and grandchildren of those who first heard him. His leading position seems due, therefore, to real power, not to chance or to his unfortunate reputation as a humorist, which led the public to expect a laugh even when his purpose was most serious.

The wandering life of Mark Twain, which hovered for years on the borderland of adventure, and which touched many phases of American life between the miner's shack and the millionaire's drawing-room, can be better read in his own works than in any biography. He was educated not in schools but on a great river flowing for the most part through pioneer territory ; and his *Life on the Mississippi* (1883) is a reflection of that education. This book with its vivid pictures

His Life

---

1 *The Celebrated Jumping Frog and Other Sketches.* This was made up of stories that had appeared in various magazines and that had given Mark Twain his first reputation as a humorist.

of nature and men, and with its comparative freedom from the author's worst faults, may possibly prove to be his most enduring work. In it he tells us that he met on the Mississippi the duplicate of every important character in history, biography and fiction, and that his experience as pilot of a river steamer completed his education. But another chapter was waiting on the Western frontier, and Mark Twain's experiences here are vividly portrayed in *Roughing It* (1872), a book somewhat cruder than the other, which reflects largely the sensational elements of frontier life. The enlarging of his horizon came with his journeys in foreign lands, which he recorded in three books, *Innocents Abroad* (1869), *A Tramp Abroad* (1880), and *Following the Equator* (1897). A fourth chapter of his education includes his life in the East as a successful literary man, and the best reflection of this experience is found in his unfinished *Autobiography*.

The reputation of a humorist, which clung to Mark Twain all his life, was even more objectionable to him than to his friends, **His Satire** who knew his seriousness of purpose. In his earliest **and Ridicule** sketches, which are broadly comic, he displayed that "genius for the incongruous" which is at the root of humor, and which some critics consider to be Mark Twain's most prominent quality. In his later works humor is an entirely subordinate element. Indeed, most of the works that readers welcomed as humorous are not given to humor, but to satire and ridicule, which are entirely different matters and pledged to a different object. *Innocents Abroad*, for example, which first made Mark Twain widely famous as a humorist, is almost wholly devoted to ridiculing travelers who see and record the romantic side of Old World history and institutions. It is the work of an iconoclast, crude, self-confident, without traditions and, therefore, without reverence or even respect for the past, who makes a joke of what other and wiser men look upon with kindling vision. *A Connecticut Yankee at King Arthur's Court* (1889) is chiefly an attack on the past evils of feudalism, a bitter satire on chivalry and knighthood, a parody — always questionable and at times unpardonable — on Malory's exquisite *Morte d'Arthur*. And so with *The Man that corrupted Hadleyburg*, and many other alleged humorous works; they are not an expression of humor in any true sense, but rather of ridicule of human society past or present. For Mark Twain was at heart a reformer, vigorous and sincere. Next to his love of a practical joke, his most prominent characteristic was a hatred of shams, old and new; but the greater part of his literary work is of doubtful value simply because he was inclined to ridicule as a sham whatever he did not understand.

There are good critics who believe that Mark Twain's more dignified works, such as *The Prince and the Pauper* and *Personal Recollections of Joan of Arc* (which begins strongly as a historical novel and develops weakly into a plea for the Maid of Orleans), will be longest remembered. At present, however, his most widely read works are *Tom Sawyer* and *Huckleberry Finn*, the former of which is extravagantly lauded as a classic of American boyhood, and the latter as an epic, an Odyssey even, of the Mississippi River.

In *Tom Sawyer* (1876) the author follows Brown and Poe in using terror and mystery to give added interest to his story, **Tom Sawyer** but the terrors — the midnight murder in the graveyard, and the renegade with his terrible knife — are largely of the dime-novel kind. The hero is essentially a liar, one who makes a virtue of falsehood; and his adventures are of a kind to make the thoughtless laugh and the judicious grieve. Thus, when one sees the hero (who is supposed to be drowned) hide in the church in order to chuckle at his own funeral and make a mockery of human grief, one must deplore not only the author's taste but his limited conception of the American boy. The picture drawn in *Tom Sawyer* is one-sided in that it emphasizes the lawless, barbarous side of boy life to the almost total neglect of its better qualities, its self-assertion without its instinctive respect for authority, its vigor without its natural refinement. The book is brimful of crude fun and of crude human nature, but it may be questioned whether its good qualities are sufficient to outbalance its dime-novel sensationalism.

Huckleberry Finn (1885) is a larger and better book than the one just considered, and though not free from objectionable **Huckleberry** elements is, on the whole, in better taste. The hero **Finn** is again a liar and a vagabond, and his experiences are such that one might regard the book as a humorous version of the picaresque novel. With a runaway slave as a companion, Huck Finn floats down the mighty Mississippi on a raft, meeting adventures at every turn ; meeting also ignorant and superstitious natives, gullible fools, dishonest schemes, deadly feuds, quacks, charlatans, scoundrels, cheats and impostors of every kind. It is a medley, a melodrama of knavery, which ends not in a moral climax but in a tedious description of how Tom Sawyer, lately arrived on the scene, insists on rescuing the runaway slave (who is already a free man) by the most approved dime-novel methods. The portrayal of all these astonishing scenes is vivid and intensely dramatic ; one needs hardly to add that it is a portrayal, not of the great onward current of American life, but only of its flotsam and jetsam.

With all its faults of mockery and sensationalism *Huckleberry Finn* is a powerful book, and it may serve well to suggest its **Quality** author's claim to a permanent place in our literature. **of Mark** First of all, his characters are vital ; they may be **Twain's** **Work** good or bad, they may even be grotesque, but they are real men and women. Not only the heroes, Tom Sawyer and Huck Finn, but the minor characters, the negro Jim in his simple manliness, the Grangerfords with their insane feud, the old lady who unmasks a boy disguised in girl's clothes by getting him to throw a stone at a rat, the varied assortment of gulls and impostors, — every one of these characters is so clearly, sharply drawn that he stands before us as an individual. The action of the story, though always more or less melodramatic, is of absorbing interest. The descriptions of nature, of storm and calm, day and night, are extraordinarily vivid. Cooper hardly drew more beautiful pictures of the sea than Mark Twain draws of the changing lights and shadows of the great river. Finally, there is an intensity in his best work, a moral intensity (though he stoutly disclaimed a moral purpose) which compels attention. For, as we have noted, Mark Twain was at heart a reformer, a hater of shams, and in ridiculing some real or fancied wrong he manifested the same moral earnestness that characterized Mrs. Stowe and other writers of the "propaganda" novel. Perhaps the chief quality of his work is its dramatic vigor ; its chief defect is the lack of good taste and refinement.

Joel Chandler Harris (1848-1908). Of most of the books that go to make up the flood of modern fiction the historian is a little doubtful, but there is one which he may confidently criticize as having already secured for itself an enduring place in literature. For it creates a new character, in some respects the most natural and lovable character that has ever appeared in American fiction, — our old friend, Uncle Remus. One writes the name with a smile, in which amusement is mingled with tenderness and gratitude. It is like opening a door into a new world of folklore ; it recalls the open-eyed wonder with which we first heard the stories of Br'er Rabbit's frolicsome adventures, or the deeper pleasure with which we tell them to our own children.

The author of the book calls himself an uncultivated Georgia "cracker," but the world is glad to acknowledge both the originality of his genius and the thoroughness of his preparation for his work. Only a genius, a born story-teller, could have created Uncle Remus, with his inexhaustible fund of animal lore ; only one who had studied the negro faithfully till he knew not only his dialect but the subtle working of his primitive mind could have given him such natural and admirable expression. Harris's first collection of stories, *Uncle Remus*, appeared in 1880, and was followed by *Nights with Uncle Remus, Uncle Remus and his Friends,* and *Told by Uncle Remus.* In these four books, all in the same delightful vein, he has given the old plantation negro and his folklore to our literature.

The plan of the work is simplicity itself. The characters are Uncle Remus and the little girl and boy who come to beg for a **Plan of** story, with an occasional glimpse of " Miss Sallie " **Uncle Remus** or some other minor personage. The hero of most of the tales is Br'er Rabbit, not the timid rabbit of the fields who furnishes food to hungry prowlers, but a gay, impudent, versatile rabbit who talks " big " to Br'er Bear, or " sassy " to Br'er Wolf, and who relies upon quick wit or pure mischief to get him safely out of his encounters with larger creatures. Note this scene in which the hero is at last caught by the fox, who proposes to make a terrible end of Br'er Rabbit's fooling. Says the fox to his helpless victim :

" ' En dar you is, en dar you 'll stay twel I fixes up a bresh-pile and fires her up, kaze I'm gwineter bobbycue you dis day, sho,' sez Brer Fox, sezee.

" Den Brer Rabbit talk mighty 'umble.

" ' I don't keer w'at you do wid me, Brer Fox,' sezee, ' so you don't fling me in dat brier-patch. Roas' me, Brer Fox,' sezee, ' but don't fling me in dat brier-patch,' sezee.

" ' Hit 's so much trouble fer ter kindle a fier,' sez Brer Fox, sezee, ' dat I speck I 'll hatter hang you,' sezee.

" ' Hang me des ez high ez you please, Brer Fox,' sez Brer Rabbit, sezee, ' but do for de Lord's sake don't fling me in dat brier-patch,' sezee.

" ' I ain't got no string,' sez Brer Fox, sezee, ' en now I speck I 'll hatter drown you,' sezee.

" ' Drown me des ez deep ez you please, Brer Fox,' sez Brer Rabbit, sezee, ' but do don't fling me in dat brier-patch,' sezee.

" ' Dey ain't no water nigh,' sez Brer Fox, sezee, ' en now I speck I 'll hatter skin you,' sezee.

" ' Skin me, Brer Fox,' sez Brer Rabbit, sezee, ' snatch out my eyeballs, t'ar out my years by de roots, en cut off my legs,' sezee, ' but do please, Brer Fox, don't fling me in dat brier-patch,' sezee.

" Co'se Brer Fox wanter hurt Brer Rabbit bad ez he kin, so he cotch 'im by de behime legs en slung 'im right in de middle er de brier-patch. Dar wuz a considerbul flutter whar Brer Rabbit struck de bushes, en Brer Fox sorter hang 'roun' fer ter see w'at wuz gwineter happen. Bimeby he hear somebody call 'im, en way up de hill he see Brer Rabbit settin' cross-legged on a chinkapin log koamin' de pitch outen his har wid a chip. Den

Brer Fox know dat he bin swop off mighty bad. Brer Rabbit wuz bleedzed fer ter fling back some er his sass, en he holler out:

"'Bred en bawn in a brier-patch, Brer Fox — bred en bawn in a brier-patch!' en wid dat he skip out des ez lively ez a cricket in de embers." [1]

There are scores of such whimsical tales, the most famous being "The Wonderful Tar-Baby Story," which should be read entire, for it is too good to spoil by quotation. Some of them may have originated with Uncle Remus; others are hundreds, perhaps thousands, of years old, and are told in various forms by primitive tribes as far apart as Africa and South America. Their chief value, however, is not as a collection of folklore stories, great as that value is, but rather as a revelation of the American negro. In the gay adventures of Br'er Rabbit, who typifies the triumph of weakness or mischief over strength, one may see a mental reflection of a race that could laugh and be happy in a condition of helpless slavery. In the person of Uncle Remus one sees a real character, vital, human, lovable, who has endeared himself to millions of children past and present, and who will sit by the fire on winter nights, a welcome guest, and tell stories to children of the future. The creation of that one character seems to be one of the most notable achievements of American fiction.

Conclusion. It is often said that the golden age of American life and letters is in the past; that the present material age shows no great promise or achievement, and no single writer of commanding genius. The same was said when Edwards died, in 1758, yet half of a century later America felt the first real stir of national enthusiasm which was reflected in a national literature. Nearly another half century passed before America was again deeply stirred by the transcendental and reform movements, and contrary to all expectations the awakened national spirit expressed itself in a great outburst of poetry. The present is an age of comparative quiet; its agitations are mostly on

---

1 From "How Mr. Rabbit was too Sharp for Mr. Fox." This is really a conclusion of "The Wonderful Tar-Baby Story."

the surface ; yet one must believe, from all our past history, that whenever America is again stirred to the depths, whether it be to-day or to-morrow, our larger national life will again express itself in a greater literature. It is well to remember also that the flowering of literature, like that of any other art, cannot possibly be forecast, that it always appears suddenly and with a surprise. The beautiful thought of God, which expressed in prose or verse is literature, comes to any mind that is open enough to receive it. We awaken some morning, and lo ! from some unexpected source, from some shepherd on the hills, from some boy holding horses at the door of the theater, comes the poem, the story, the drama that reflects the fleeting life and the deathless yearnings of humanity. So whether one faces the present, which cannot yet be judged, or the future, which guards its own secret, still may one reasonably assume that hopeful attitude which the aged Longfellow expressed in his last sonnet :

> Where are the Poets, unto whom belong
>   The Olympian heights ; whose singing shafts were sent
>   Straight to the mark, and not from bows half bent,
>   But with the utmost tension of the thong?
> Where are the stately argosies of song,
>   Whose rushing keels made music as they went
>   Sailing in search of some new continent,
>   With all sail set, and steady winds and strong?
> Perhaps there lives some dreamy boy, untaught
>   In schools, some graduate of the field or street,
>   Who shall become a master of the art,
> An admiral sailing the high seas of thought,
>   Fearless and first, and steering with his fleet
>   For lands not yet laid down in any chart.

CHAPTER VI

BOOKS AND WRITERS OF THE PRESENT DAY

> I'm going out to fetch the little calf
> That's standing by the mother. It's so young,
> It totters when she licks it with her tongue.
> I sha'n't be gone long — You come too.
>
> Robert Frost, " The Pasture " [1]

In contrast with the literature of a past age, which is easily apprehended because generations of readers have sifted out for us the few works of enduring interest, the literature of the present offers a baffling problem. As we approach the subject, note well its outstanding characteristics.

The first is vastness, as of a moving flood. Between five and six thousand new books are now published in America every year, far more than one meets in a history covering all the centuries of English literature. Granting that half of this annual product may be dismissed as works of instruction, there remain between two and three thousand books and a corresponding multitude of authors, all at once demanding our attention. Before we could examine these, at the rate of two or three books each week, twenty years would come and go, leaving fifty thousand more books as a contribution to present-day literature.

The second characteristic, undefined but real as a fog, is a bewildering vagueness. This is so pronounced that one may question whether present literature be not as illusory as the present moment. We are told that, of all moments, the present only is ours ; but there is never a present moment. While we think of it, lo! our moment is passed and another is passing. So with the flood of books that go by us continually : we call

1 From Robert Frost's *North of Boston* (Henry Holt and Company).

them present-day literature, ignoring the fact that true literature has a timeless or permanent quality, meaning that it appears but does not pass, remaining with us forever.

For example, there came recently from our press, without any trumpet of announcement, a little novel by Louis Hémon, a French writer domiciled in Canada, and its name was *Maria Chapdelaine*. It portrayed the lives of village people in the province of Quebec, in our own day ; but it was a work of pure genius in that it reflected faithful-hearted people of any province of earth in any age since man became civilized. No sooner was it here than it seemed to have been always with us, so beautiful it was, and so natural, and so human. One followed the story as one might listen to a church organ softly playing, or as one might watch the twilight with a star hanging over it and a wood-thrush singing. Beyond question this unpretentious novel is literature with its eternal quality ; but if you ask, What recent American books should be so classed ? there is no man wise enough to give answer. Literature must be sifted by time and humanity before one can know what books are passing and what are permanent.

With this introduction, let it be specified that present-day books will here be regarded as those of the last fifteen or twenty years. During this period some two thousand writers have claimed a place in American literature. The difficulty of adjusting their claim is manifest in the work of historians who wrestle with the subject. Thus, in 1915 appeared a history of recent literature dealing with about three hundred " prominent " or " promising " authors, and omitting many more. Most of the three hundred are still writing ; yet in 1922 appeared another record of " prominent " or " promising " authors, and hardly a dozen of those emphasized in the first book are emphasized in the second, though both historians deal as faithfully as they can with the material at hand. Moreover, you might search both records without finding the writer that seems to you most finely representative of the present day.

Authors and Readers. In explanation of this phenomenon of criticism one needs but to recall the fact that a score or more of promising new writers appear every year. Occasionally the first book of such a writer is as good, apparently, as the best work of authors who have long been conspicuous on the literary stage, or it may be decidedly better. Very often the writer's first book is his best book. Indeed, it may be the only book of his that is worth reading; but he follows his market (for writers are human, like other folk) and continues to write long after he has anything to say. Meanwhile the older writers are all busy, each producing a book every year or two, though one who reads their later work must wonder how it was that many of them so easily won a reputation which they so hardly keep.

The answer is simple : every new author is like a pleasant new visitor in that he forms a circle of acquaintances who like him or believe in him. If the circle be large enough, his literary success is assured, because publishers will print any dull book he may write, trusting his circle of readers to accept the offering. This is true of nearly all writers who have recently been prominent, and who suggest a curious literary contrast between the present and an earlier age.

Old Writers and New. Our elder writers, from Poe to Longfellow and from Irving to Emerson, all followed practically the same literary course, which is the course still commonly followed by the best writers of European countries. They began modestly; they won a place with more or less difficulty; they steadily developed their talent; and by works of increasing power they widened their audience, their influence, their reputation. In the end they became national figures, each standing for some manifestation of the American spirit; and they have more readers now, both at home and abroad, than ever they had during their lifetime.

The story of our younger writers is different, especially the story of our favorites during the past forty years. As a rule, they begin boldly with an original or striking work; they win a large audience easily; but for some unexplained reason they seldom develop or fulfil their early promise. In consequence they fail to become national figures, as Longfellow and Emerson were national; nor have they won recognition abroad to compare with that of Poe or Cooper or Whitman. Nearly every one of to-day's prominent writers, after his first success, has produced much ordinary work; yet so widespread is the interest in new literature, and so vast our country, that an author who once wins recognition is upheld by his circle of readers so long as he continues to write. Outside that circle your well-known writer who appears prominently in the literary reviews is a mere name, and may rightly be regarded as inferior to a score of writers who are not well known.

In fine, the tendency of present-day writers as a class, and with few individual exceptions, is to be too much absorbed in the present; that is, they reflect a passing interest or humor or novelty rather than the enduring truths of nature or of human nature. Such a generalization is open to challenge, and doubtless has its proportion of error; but it suggests, at least, an explanation of the common literary phenomenon of a writer who is enormously successful to-day, only to be forgotten when to-morrow brings forth its new interests, with new writers to make the most of their opportunity. Wordsworth's sonnet beginning "The world is too much with us" may be an excellent summary of the matter.

Limitations of our Study. Facing such conditions, it would be vain to pretend that one can write a trustworthy history or criticism of present-day literature. Aside from the vastness and vagueness of the subject, fair history and fair criticism of the present are both impossible. The sole purpose of this or of any similar chapter is, happily, to serve as a temporary guide for those who are bewildered by too many books.

If you conclude, after reading, that the selection of authors and types is too much governed by personal taste, you are probably right. If you ask, Why are not such and such favorite authors included? the only answer is that "favorite" has a rather personal meaning, and that a hundred million Americans have more favorites than any one American can understand. At every point in the narrative, therefore, you may have reason to differ from the opinion expressed, and you certainly have the right to follow your own taste. Lest our pleasant study become "like sweet bells jangled, out of tune and harsh," let two harmonious principles be understood: first, that we must omit the so-called younger writers who are supposed to be blazing a new trail through the old field of literature, because such trails commonly peter out in a squirrel track and end in a tree; and second, that there is ample room here for every personal impression that is modestly so expressed, but no room whatever for dogmatic judgment.

THE NOVELISTS

Because the novel is the most impressive form of modern literature, some have used it as a practical instrument of progress or reform; hence the problem novel and the novel of set purpose. There are scores of such, each aiming at reform of business or religion or politics or society. A few are well done, and may be effective by calling attention to this or that need or cry; but they are excluded from this study, because the moment you devote a novel to any other than its sole or proper purpose it becomes, in our imagination at least, a kind of tract or propaganda, and should be so classed. The first and last purpose of fiction is to give pleasure, and the purpose is accomplished by portraying certain types of men and women or certain human experiences in a way which, however colored by imagination or humor or emotion, still gives the impression of truth, as if we were dealing with real men and real experiences.

One American Novel. For more than a century now — ever since the day of Charles Brockden Brown — our people have been talking about "the great American novel" and confidently expecting its appearance. Such an expectation might possibly be realized in England or France, each with its ancient folk-lore, its settled tradition, its native population ; but it is an idle dream in America, for the reason that our country is too vast, with too many and too varied races of men and types of character, for any one novel to reflect it with even a semblance of truth.

Meanwhile a multitude of novelists are portraying life in this or that section, under this or that urge or handicap ; and one of these furnishes an admirable start for our study of present-day fiction. This is *Vandemark's Folly* (1922), one of the best American novels of this or any other period. The scene is laid along the Erie Canal and on the lonely Iowa prairies, at a time when the canal was a pioneer highway over which passed all sorts and conditions of men, lured by the call of land in the West. Into that westward-moving multitude comes a boy, a waif, who is molded into manhood by two influences ; namely, responsiveness to the vigorous life about him, and loyalty to the memory of his mother. There is nothing strange or forced or foreign in the story ; the narrative develops as naturally as life itself and becomes intensely real, intensely American,— real in that it pictures life as it is, or was, and American in that the action might well have occurred in Iowa or Kansas or any one of a score of our states, but could not have occurred in any other land on earth.

The author of the novel, Herbert Quick, cannot have lived the life which he portrays ; but he certainly knows those who have lived it, or else he has a most excellent imagination. He enters with the understanding of sympathy into the rough but essentially healthy spirit of the frontier ; his portrayal of the moving throng that thins out as it moves westward, until only a solitary driver is seen rising in his " schooner " over the prairie swells, like a ship alone on a vast sea, is marvelous in its fidelity to pioneer experience. Into the story come good men and bad, fine women and foolish, all portrayed with truth,

with humor, with charity ; and through the story runs a little
romance, as naturally, as inevitably, as a brook winds its way
through shade and sunshine to the waiting sea.

In sum, here is, if not a great novel, at least a good human
and national novel, a type of what the American novel should
be but seldom is. Almost simultaneously appeared *The Covered
Wagon*, by Emerson Hough, a story of the Oregon Trail, having
the same pioneer theme as *Vandemark's Folly*, the same wide
horizon and the same epic quality. Both novels are uncommonly good reflections of our moving frontier, the most stirring
scene in the American national drama. Many more such are
waiting to be discovered by the Connecticut and the Ohio, by
the Cumberland Road and the Santa Fé Trail, by every one of
the pioneer highways over which a free people passed in their
conquest of a continent.

Novels of Society. Among many novelists who deal each
with a section of American society, North or South or East or
West, two are here selected, not because they are the best, for
that cannot justly be said, but because it is better to read two,
any two, than to regard a hundred without reading.

One such portrayer of the people of a section is Booth
Tarkington, who aims to reflect the Middle West, and whose
novels of young life and the "gawky" age, *Penrod, Gentle
Julia*, and *Seventeen*, have been widely welcomed. Of his more
ambitious works *The Magnificent Ambersons* (1918) is perhaps
the best. After reading these books one has an impression
that the author has lost the child's imaginative view of life and
has not yet attained the man's view. He has a clever knack of
writing ; but the knack has not developed since he published
Monsieur Beaucaire in 1900. Concerning the quality of his
work there are two opinions. His circle of readers and some
critics declare that he reflects youth truthfully, as he sees it ;
that he not only reveals youth to itself, but gives age more
sympathy in dealing with the folly of children who have too
little work and too much liberty for their own good. That is

surely one phase of American society, and as such, a novelist
must deal with it. Other critics think that Tarkington's idea
of youth appears to be a mannerless cub of a boy and an im-
pertinent girl, both badly brought up by stupid relatives in an
atmosphere of sham culture, and that by portraying such types
as representative he unconsciously gives a false impression of
a whole society. And such critics are disappointed that one
who can write well should be content with a superficial portrayal of silly experiences, without ever facing the big things
of life, or reflecting the indomitable will and mighty achievement of the Middle West, or thinking out a plot to its logical
conclusion, or following the development of a character as
molded by steadfast ideal and changing circumstance.

Mrs. Edith Wharton portrays a different section in a different
way. Her mind is mature ; her talent is carefully cultivated ;
she aims to reflect from a cosmopolitan viewpoint one phase
of that vast complexity which we call America. Her field is
small and, it must be confessed, a little snobbish : she deals
with " society," and confines herself to that corner of society
which complacently regards itself as the best. In consequence
there are no wide horizons in her books, which are distinctly of
the indoor variety. In her method she has been influenced by
Henry James, a novelist who has an impressive way of picking
at petty things as if he would conjure something important out
of a nut. So, though her work is carefully planned and more
carefully labored, her every novel is marred (or improved, as
some think) by analytical details that seldom repay a reader for
the lack of action. Her short stories, on the other hand, are
very finely done, are indeed models of the short-story art. *The
Age of Innocence* (1920) gives a good impression of this author's
style and quality ; but many think that *The House of Mirth* (1905)
is a better novel.

The Romance of History. Writers of historical romances are
numerous. When upon rare occasion one of them writes a story
that helps us to visualize our heroic past, the instant and hearty

response indicates that this type of novel is quite as popular as ever it was in the day of Scott or Cooper. For example, a writer whose name was recently a household word among literary folk is S. Weir Mitchell, who ended his labors in 1914. He has to his credit over thirty literary works; but his *Hugh Wynne, Free Quaker*, an excellent novel of the War of Independence, has probably more readers than all his other books combined and is now practically his only book that is widely known.

Mary Johnston, a Southern writer with a charmingly Southern attitude, has given us one stirring romance of Colonial days in *To Have and to Hold*, and another of our Civil War in *The Long Roll*. Her works are few; for which we may be grateful, since she cultivates her talent, apparently, and when her work finally appears it rewards us for the waiting. Among all our writers of historical romance there is none that tells a better tale or tells it in a more satisfactory way.

At the present time, probably the best known of our historical novelists is Winston Churchill, who for over twenty years has devoted himself to portraying the stirring periods of American history. His most popular and, as many think, his best novel is *Richard Carvel* (1899), a story of the War of Independence, with the naval hero John Paul Jones as one of the characters. His novel of Civil War days, *The Crisis*, might well be read with Miss Johnston's *The Long Roll*, since one portrays the romance of the war from the Union and the other from the Confederate side. Though these works appeared earlier than the period which we have specified as the present, they are here recommended for the reason that, like most American writers of the past half century, the novelist does not fulfil his splendid early promise by works of increased power. *The Inside of the Cup* (1913) is perhaps the best of his later romances.

Types of Character. A score of novelists are devoted to the portrayal of different types of American character, especially types that begin to appear now as survivals of a simpler and more heroic age.

To this kind of novel a mighty impetus was given by *David Harum,* written by Edward Noyes Westcott near the beginning of the present century. Aside from its human interest, which is large, or its literary value, which is debatable, this homely story furnishes a commentary on critical publishers and uncritical readers. Our publishers are keen men ; they are alert to discover new writers ; each employs trained readers and, occasionally, a famous critic to examine manuscripts with the one purpose of finding a work that is worth printing ; they make it their chief concern to know what the public wants, and to supply it as attractively and as cheaply as possible, for such is the *business* of publishing. Yet these experienced men were as blind as moles to the human appeal of *David Harum,* which went begging from one to another, while critics could see nothing in it that was worth the small risk of publication. Then one publisher "took a chance," as he supposed, after suggesting certain changes to which the author agreed ; and hardly was the book out when readers welcomed it by the hundred thousand. Its popular success was tremendous, and few critics would now deny that its success was deserved. The story smacked of the soil. There was humor and kindness and unchanging human nature in it. One or two of the characters were as real in a literary sense as if they had stepped out of the pages of Dickens, and as real in the American sense as if we had known them about the stove of a country grocery store. The writer died before his story was published, and he remains, perhaps fortunately, a man of one book.

Working in the same field, Irving Bacheller has given us one excellent type of countryman in *Eben Holden* (1900), a readable novel that well deserved the welcome with which readers received it. Since then he has written several more novels, which show a falling off rather than a development of literary power. Another worker in the field is Joseph Lincoln, who, lured by that undefinable call of the near-sea which draws visitors to Cape Cod, has reflected in a dozen novels his idea of old-time characters with the tang of the brine in them. Read *Mary-'Gusta* (1916), which is perhaps his best work, or *The Portygee* (1920) or *Fair Harbor* (1922), not because they are particularly good novels but because they exemplify a type in which readers are interested. It is a mistake to assume that the writers of this or of any other age make literature. Some do — working apart in solitude ; but the great majority merely supply a demand that is created by readers. Nor does this apply to minor literature only: Homer's poems and Shakespeare's plays were both alike the response to a popular demand.

A different type of character appears in the work of James Lane Allen, whose field is the Bluegrass region of Kentucky. A good novel in which to become acquainted with this writer's style and method is *The Mettle of the Pasture* (1903). If a later work is desired, because it is more of the present day, try *The Kentucky Warbler* (1918). In a neighboring field John Fox, Jr., portrays a unique type, the so-called Mountain White or American Highlander ; and it is an interesting study to compare his happy romances with those of the more studious-minded Allen. His reputation was made by *The Little Shepherd of Kingdom Come* (1903). A later and more popular romance is his *Trail of the Lonesome Pine* (1908). The falling off which is characteristic of most American novelists is evident in *Erskine Dale, Pioneer* (1920), which is readable enough, but which has little to distinguish it from the work of a hundred amateurs.

The great West offers many human types: the Friar, the Don, the Plainsman, the Indian, the Peon, the Rancher, and, " cutting circles " around them all, the Cowboy, who is our most picturesque character since Leatherstocking. Here on the last frontier is a splendid field for fiction ; but the field is not well cultivated for the reason that, by apparently irresistible attraction, writers of Western fiction produce not a novel of character but a yarn of adventure. *The Virginian* of Owen Wister is an attempt, and almost the sole recent attempt in this field, to combine the novel of character with the popular adventure story.

Gertrude Atherton is of the West by birth and training; but not content with this ample field, she goes from California to New York and overseas to England in her search for material, becoming a cosmopolitan in her journeying. Her work is less a study of types than of social or political conditions which are supposed to mold the type. Her fifteen novels are of very uneven merit, some being excellently done, while others are best characterized by "smartness." *The Splendid Idle Forties*, dealing with the West, and *The Conqueror*, reflecting the political turmoil that centered in Alexander Hamilton, are regarded as her best works. Her latest and most popular novel is *Black Oxen* (1923), in which the heroine is a woman, once a "reigning beauty" in New York society, who returns after thirty years and a surgical operation as young and bewitching as ever. As literature the book is rather trashy; but it is an excellent example of the writer's power to hold her circle of readers by a portrayal of novel incidents enlivened by a brilliant style and society manners.

Very different is Mary Austin, who lived for years on the edge of the Mohave Desert, — lived as an Indian woman lives, and so entered into the desert secrets. You will know whether or not you want to read more of this rare writer's works, as some do, if you begin with her fanciful tales for children in *The Basket Woman*. The most remarkable work that has ever been done in the Western field with the Indian as a character appears in the little books of J. Willard Schultz, who is ignored by literary critics because he writes only adventure stories for boys. Would that those who write for men and women had the secret of his method! The heroes of all his tales are a white boy, the son of a fur trader, and his "almost brother" Pitamakan, a young Blackfoot Indian. The adventures and escapes of these two are a marvelous reflection of the habits and beliefs of savage riders of the Plains in the days of the buffalo. Schultz's way of telling a story — simple, straightforward, with constant action and dramatic dialogue — is near perfection, and was evidently learned by listening to Indian tale-tellers while he was a member of the tribe. Of all our writers, early or late, he is the only one who comes near to knowing the soul of an Indian.

The Social Novel. An extreme type of modern fiction is the so-called social novel, meaning one in which the chief character is not so much an individual as a whole class of men and women who give (to the novelist) an impression of being governed by economic law or industrial habit rather than by free will. In dealing with this peculiar type one should note, first, that the writers who gave it impetus were all young journalists (Stephen Crane, Frank Norris, Harold Frederic) accustomed to continuous excitement, which is not wholesome, and to snap judgments of men or events, which are very seldom right; and second, that they all selected Zola for their model, with the result that their earliest fiction was characterized by frequent brutality or bad taste, which they imagined was realism.

The most striking novel of this type was written by Frank Norris after he was done with realism of the Zola kind. Then he planned a trilogy of novels of the wheat, each being an allegory of industrial America. Thus *The Octopus*, which was intended to make the locomotive symbolic of its hero or villain, portrays the grain-grower in a losing war against the transportation trust, with its power and greed and alleged selfishness. The whole story, and the author's peculiar notion of railroads, is condensed into the episode of an engine plowing at full speed through a flock of sheep. The second of the trilogy, *The Pit*, deals with the financial manipulation of grain, as reflected by a deal in the Chicago wheat pit; and the third, *The Wolf* (never written), was planned to follow our American grain in its last journey to a starving community in Europe. The first novel was undoubtedly strong and original, but showed the journalistic craving for excitement. The second was weaker, with excitement more artificial; and it may be as well that the third was not written. The writer's plan was greater than his power to accomplish.

Norris, though **outside** our specified limits, is nevertheless selected because he was the greatest of a modern group, and because later novelists who make an allegory of the farm or the factory or the stockyard or of industry itself have all alike failed to give their themes reality, and have either entered other fields (as Crane wrote his *Red Badge of Courage*) or else have resorted in their novels to " stunts " more characteristic of the sensation-loving journalist than of the balance and restraint of the true novelist. Apparently the social novel is too big and too impersonal for satisfactory treatment, or else the right man has not yet appeared, to master it. If you doubt the criticism, select any social novel of recent days and put it to the test. The only approach to artistic success in this field since Norris wrote *The Octopus* appears in a very different novel, *The Reign of Law*, by James Lane Allen, in which we are only half persuaded that the hemp fields of Kentucky may govern the life of a community.

The Novel of Adventure. While literary critics are busy with such writers as we have named, a multitude of readers blithely follow their own taste, which leads them to the novel of adventure, — now as in all times the most popular form of fiction. Rafael Sabatini writes his *Captain Blood*, for example, and readers care not a whit what reviewers say or think, because they are satisfied with a well-told story of buccaneers and treasure and love and brave adventure.

The North is a favorite scene of such fiction, and a score of writers since Jack London have exploited it ; but all follow the same false trail, striving for " brutal " characters or incidents and drawing a grossly perverted picture of both nature and human nature. Not one of them has his eye on the truth of life ; their work is, in consequence, of no interest save to the many who like dime novels. Stewart Edward White made a much better beginning with his *Blazed Trail, Conjuror's House,* and *Silent Places* ; but presently he rambled off into other fields of fiction, without once taking his work or his reader seriously.

The West has long been the favorite location for outdoor adventure, and for a simple reason : it was our last frontier. The type of Western story is ever the same. There must be a cowboy hero, a girl in danger or distress, a gunman or bad man, and a band of rustlers or outlaws, the whole scrambled together with plenty of shooting and such varied humor and adventure as the writer finds in his unfettered imagination. The only departure from type appears when a writer, striving for novelty, begins with a Western scene and then produces a " gold brick " by making a conventional detective story, to be solved by the clock, or by using as his heroes and villains a band of " movie " actors who go through the motions of wild-west adventure in their usual flashy way.

Numerous writers are busily producing the romance of Western adventure ; but it would be unfair to discriminate among them, since all are doing the same thing in about the same way. Zane Grey is for tne moment the most popular writer in this field, and occasionally he tells a very good tale, as in *The Man of the Forest* ; but he has no humor, and his work is very uneven, — extremely crude in stories of the Ohio frontier, or rather hysteric in *The Wanderer of the Wasteland,* or given over to wordy descriptions besprinkled with purple adjectives. If you must have a specific example of the " real thing " in Western fiction, try Mulford's *The Man from Bar-20* and White's *Lynch Lawyers,* with their zest and humor and riding and shooting, and no pretense whatever save of pleasing you with a good, impossible yarn.

Such adventure stories (which are scoffed at by literary critics) represent the oldest type of fiction. They have always appealed to the most readers, for the reason that every proper man longs to get out of the humdrum into the adventurous life ; and they still furnish entertainment to uncounted readers who ask only that a novel hold to its first purpose of giving wholesome pleasure.

THE SHORT STORY

The modern short story, which is very different from the ancient tale, is America's peculiar contribution to literary types. In its present form it originated here and, encouraged by our many magazines, rose swiftly to its present leading place. In its material it covers every type and character and incident of our enormously varied life ; in its method it is bound by cast-iron rules, and must meet rigid tests prescribed by magazine editors. That these artificial tests might be " more honored in the breach than in the observance " is aside from the question : we are dealing with the short story as it is, not as it might better be.

Qualifications. Among the many prescribed tests are : (1) Originality, or at least ingenuity. In this the short story differs from the novel, which may follow old ways or old plots that have been used for ages. (2) Unity, as distinct from complexity of theme or treatment. The story must deal with a single incident or situation ; it must plan the one impression which is to be made, and work steadily at that impression without halt or digression. (3) Something must happen ; in other words, there must be constant action, as in a dialogue or play. The writer must have a moving tale to tell, and his matter is of much more consequence than his style or manner. (4) The tale must be modern, up to date or up to the minute, and must conform to the rule for visitors written over the door of Cotton Mather's study, " Be short ! "

There are other qualifications of the short story, as magazines now demand it ; but these four — originality, unity, action and up-to-dateness — are the essentials. If it can be adorned by a brilliant style or enlivened by the play of humor, so much the better. In form and structure the story should be as compact as the steel frame of a skyscraper ; but this rule needs no emphasis. Nature has decreed that the skeleton of a thing is all-important, and that it should be concealed.

Short-Story Writers. The surprising thing is that scores of writers are producing as many varieties of this far-from-easy type of fiction every year. To discriminate among them, measuring their relative place or value, would be very difficult because they change constantly, new favorites appearing while the old turn away to other work. The latest to attain a leading position in the crowded field was " O. Henry " (William Sydney Porter), who finished his work in 1910. No other has taken his place in our magazines or in our journalistic periodicals that strive to increase their huge circulation by printing something amazing every week.

One's first impression of this writer, so enormously popular and so bepraised by critics, is that ordinarily he has little truth in his work or sincerity in his method. He tells a mere anecdote, as any drummer or after-dinner speaker might tell it, with no other plan or purpose than to produce a laugh or a shock at the end. In this last he is as ingeniously surprising as a mousetrap baited with toasted cheese. His " art " is that of the vaudeville stage ; he pleases his audience by pulling a rabbit or something more startling out of a hat. His stories fall into two main groups : one reflects his rambling among tramps, escaped convicts and other misunderstood folk ; the other, his literary acrobatics in a Sunday newspaper.

Standing apart from the bulk of " O. Henry's " work, as of better quality, are some of the earlier stories, such as are collected in *The Four Million*. They reveal the author not as a mere entertainer, but as viewing soberly the complex life of a modern city, detecting the gleams of truth or beauty above the passing show, and reflecting something of the eternally heroic adventure of humanity. A few of these stories will undoubtedly find a permanent place in our literature.

There are many short-story writers who regularly do better work than " O. Henry " ever did ; but none of them has won such a prominent place, perhaps because no one has his knack of surprising " Mr. Everybody," for whom, he said, he wrote.

Of late the short story, which began with Irving as a type of literature, tends to become more and more journalistic, with the result that our best writers drop it for the novel or the drama or some other work that is less mechanical and more artistic. To get acquainted with our short-story craftsmen read the annual *Best Short Stories* or some other of the collections named in the bibliography at the end of the chapter.

POETRY

A recent history (1923) deals with over a hundred poets who are called prominent, in comparison with a larger number who are hopeful of winning recognition. If you would begin well in such a multitude and have pleasure in the beginning, let Sara Teasdale be your introduction to present-day poetry. What her relative place may be is of no consequence : she writes good poetry, and that is enough to say of any modern singer. Moreover, if you are wont to compare to-day's verse with the little songs of yesterday that have a place in your memory, she is one of the few can stand the comparison. Her poems are practically all lyrics ; they have the long virtue of shortness ; there are no strange words or obscure references to distract attention ; the style is limpid, so clear that it suggests the figure of still water in which images are reflected ; almost without exception the lines have a musical or singing quality, which to old-fashioned folk marks the difference between real and imitation poetry. Read first the *Love Songs* (1917), which was not Miss Teasdale's first book but the first to arouse the hope that a poet had come. Then, for a reflection of more thoughtful moods, read *Flame and Shadow* (1920). Before you have finished either volume you will probably say, Here is one who can reflect the beauty, the wonder, the mystery and the reverence of life in poems that are short and simple and always finely done.

When you have estimated these poems it would be well, for

a pleasant comparison, to read *Factories and Other Poems* (1915) or *The Old Road to Paradise* (1918) or *Cross-Currents* (1921), which are little books of verse by Margaret Widdemer. The two singers won recognition at about the same time, and you will have more benefit from comparing their works for yourself than from reading the second-hand criticism of any historian.

Most critics, but not most readers, would probably place Edwin Arlington Robinson first among present-day poets. He has carefully kept out of the limelight and labored in scholarly fashion to reflect the truth of life as he sees it. To him life appears rather fearfully austere, and his first volume, *Children of the Night*, is as depressing as a down-east fog. That has beauty, if one cares to search it out ; but most readers prefer to come in by the fire. In later volumes he emerges from the gray ; yet still he does not sing the joy of life, only its stern truth or duty. His craftsmanship is excellent ; no slipshod or hasty work escapes from him ; he seems to think, with Chaucer,

> Ther n' is no werkman, whatsoever he be,
> That may both werkë wel et hastily.

The Town Down the River (1910) is a good volume in which to make this poet's acquaintance. *The Man Against the Sky* (1916) has some pages of better poetry, but more that are rather heavy reading. *Collected Poems* (1921) contains all of the poet's earlier or later work that he thinks worthy of preservation, and with this volume in hand the reader can take the best possible way with any new poet, — go " skipping through," with liberty to linger wherever one likes. Two different types of poem appear in the collection : those that reflect the author's observation of life, and those that echo his study of history or literature. For a beginning, if you have no other guide, try " The Poor Relative " or "Octaves " or "The Master " (a study of Lincoln) or "Ben Jonson Entertains a Man from Stratford." But don't look for joyous singing in Robinson's verse ; the best you can expect is the monotone of the sea.

A Modern Minstrel. In every way different from the poet last named is Vachel Lindsay, a carefree rambler through our West and Southwest, who recites his way along and makes a camp meeting of every assembly, waving his arms to his verse as if he were a drum major. He is what we never expected to see in America, a minstrel, a troubadour, born out of time, out of place. To understand his poetry one should first read his prose, especially *A Handy Guide for Beggars* and *Adventures While Preaching the Gospel of Beauty.*

There is something of the reformer in our minstrel, something also of the buffoon. He has one streak of pure poetry and another of freakishness; which of the two will appear is always uncertain. He has no poetic model or master, imitates nobody, and dares to be himself without affectation. His verse is sometimes crude and sometimes splendid. Typical of the latter is "Abraham Lincoln Walks," one of the finest poems written during the Great War. Another is "General Booth Enters Heaven," written on the death of the Salvation Army leader; but here we have a suggestion of tambourines and glory-hallelujah shouting, as if the old hero of the faith must take his familiar audience with him into heaven.

Typical of Lindsay's "jazz" style, with its freakishness and rollicking measure, is his "Song of the Congo," which should be chanted rather than read, with a camp-meeting tune for the Mumbo Jumbo refrain. The short poem "Niagara" will suggest others that show the poet in his rôle of reformer or prophet. Of poems that may be read with dramatic or ventriloquial accompaniment "Two Old Crows" and "The Potato Dance" are good examples. Of his several collected works try first *The Congo and Other Poems* (1914), then *The Chinese Nightingale and Other Poems* (1917) and *The Golden Whales of California* (1920).

The Classical School. Among our so-called poets of culture is Edith M. Thomas, who has for many years produced poetry of uniform and excellent quality. She is a dreamer and, at times, a thinker whose work would seem more appropriate to the clear classical age of Greece than to the smoky industrial age of America. Any one of her dozen books of poetry will serve as an introduction to one who is well worth knowing, the earlier *Lyrics and Sonnets*, for example, or the later *Cassia and Other Verse*.

George Edward Woodberry is another good example of the same classical school of American poetry. He has written many books of prose (essays, criticisms, literary appreciations) and a few books of poetry, all alike rather remote from life and all characterized by thought and scholarship rather than by emotion. *The Roamer and Other Poems* (1920) is one of his latest volumes.

Almost as well known to critics, and perhaps better known to ordinary readers, is Katharine Lee Bates, who gave excellent promise as a poet, but whose work as a college teacher has always prevented her, she says, from following her heart longer than for a brief poetic holiday. Her patriotic poems are uncommonly good (note that the best poems of the Great War were nearly all written by women), and one of her lyrics, " America the Beautiful," is already so widely accepted that it bids fair to take a permanent place with Julia Ward Howe's " Battle Hymn of the Republic " as a national song. It would be well to begin acquaintance with this poet in *Fairy Gold*, which was written, and very well written, for children ; then for work of increasing power read *America the Beautiful and Other Poems, The Retinue*, and *Yellow Clover*.

Poets of the War. Two poets of the Great War, who are read largely because of their death on the battlefield, are Alan Seeger and Joyce Kilmer. Both had made a beginning of poetry before the war ; but whether they showed a promise greater than that of many others is not yet known, for the reason that we refuse to judge. Their work is cherished, like that of the young English poet Rupert Brooke, because of their sacrifice. Seeger's one memorable poem is " I Have a Rendezvous with Death," which proved prophetic. Kilmer's best poem is that which gives title to his tiny volume *Trees and Other Poems* (1915). For further reading the best work is *Joyce Kilmer* (1918), a book of poems, essays and letters published after the author's death.

Outdoor Poets. Most critics would probably agree that one of the most notable of recent poets is Robert Frost, who finds his poetry out of doors, either in the face of the fields or the faces of men who are in daily contact with the elemental realities of earth and sky. There are no joyous lyrics in his work, but only narrative, meditative and descriptive verse. Of him more than of any other recent poet the word "realistic" may be used in its best sense. He describes a scene or an incident in a way that makes you see what he sees, — a thing that few descriptive writers ever accomplish. Read "The Birches," for example, and see the graceful trees bending under the weight of a winter storm. So in all his work, he invents nothing; he is rather sternly accurate in picturing things as they are; any book of his gives the total impression of a winter landscape, gaunt, bare, cheerless, with sharp outlines and chilly blue shadows. His style is casual, often conversational or dramatic, and always terse, — the repressed style of an outdoor man, accustomed to silence, who wastes never a word. With all this matter-of-factness our poet is still a poet, one who sees beauty where others see only wood or stubble.

Frost began his poetic career in England with *A Boy's Will* (1913), which Englishmen welcomed as the work of a "truly American" poet, meaning one totally different from their own. The next year he settled on a New Hampshire farm and proceeded to put the farm into poetry, much as Charles A. Stevens (a writer for young people) put a Maine farm into prose with his Old Squire stories. "The Woodpile," "Christmas Trees," "After Apple Picking," "Mending Wall," "Putting in the Seed," — such poems are crystallized bits of life; anyone who has worked on a northern farm will recognize them as such, with memories of a time when the woodpile meant a buck saw, a tired back, a cold bath in a cold room, — anything but poetry. Two small but excellent volumes for the beginner are *North of Boston* (1914) and *Mountain Interval* (1916).

An outdoor singer of contrasting type is Clinton Scollard, who has published more than thirty books of verse. That is too many, — at least, one fears so ; yet there is nothing hurried or careless in the poet's work, though his mood be that of a linnet. His verse is always graceful, often pleasing, and it has the singing quality. The future may know more about him than does the present. One of the earlier volumes, *With Reed and Lyre*, for example, or *Hills of Song*, may give a better first impression of Scollard's joyously lyrical quality than some of the volumes published in more recent years.

Free Verse. Any examination of present-day poetry must include free verse, or *vers libre* as the writers thereof call it for some odd reason, — perhaps to show that they have "taken" freshman French. They are the "imagists," the "colorists," the "futurists," the "revolutionaries" of literature, and they have ingenious explanations of themselves and their formless verse. One theory is that, being artists, they must have complete freedom from rules and conventions ; another, that the modern world needs a more adequate expression than old poets have ever given it. Therefore do they speak with images or symbols rather than with words, sending forth thoughts in the mass or ideas in the birth or figures dimly shaped, as it were, in the rough marble, leaving the reader to grasp the main idea and fill in all details for himself. Especially do these writers insist that the new voice must speak as freely as the new soul thinks or feels.

There are two opinions of such new souls and voices. One is that they are really doing something rare and making an important contribution to our literature, as they themselves think. The other is that they are victims of an old delusion, which appears as frequently as a new cure or a new religion ;

that their easy and childish verse forms are an excuse to escape from the patient labor which finished verse demands ; that they do not write poetry but a poor substitute, which they would have us believe is " just as good " or even better.

Such are the opposing criticisms, both strongly held. If you would decide for yourself which is more nearly right, try any volume written by a modern apostle of free verse, avoiding the extremists, who are merely clownish in their attempt to be more irregular than others. Amy Lowell is, for the time being, the chief exponent of the new poetry. She has written seven volumes of verse, and many essays in explanation thereof. *A Dome of Many-Coloured Glass* (1912) is the most readable of her works, not because it is good poetry but because it is at least rhythmical, and so spares the reader the jolting gait of her later volumes. Though all free-verse makers think that they follow Whitman, very few of them have noticed that he commonly uses a chanting, rhythmic prose that falls pleasantly on the ear. More characteristic of Miss Lowell's fixed style and method are her later volumes; such, for example, as *Pictures of the Floating World* (1919) or *Legends* (1921).

If, or when, you weary of such verse, you may find something that is perhaps better, certainly more vigorous and original, in Carl Sandburg's crude hunks of poetry. Try his *Slabs of the Sunburnt West* (1922) or his earlier *Chicago Poems*. There are several more who easily write free verse ; but two are enough for a beginning. Some may find them too much.

THE DRAMA

Three different varieties of drama now occupy our stage. The first is made exclusively for acting ; often it is made for some particular actress or actor ; always, for better effect, it is made over by producer or manager until the author hardly recognizes his original work, the prime object being to draw a crowd and leave money in the box office. This is the commercialized play, sometimes good, more often sensational or sentimental or verging on the brink of indecency. Whether good, bad or indifferent, literature has nothing to do with such plays, since one never thinks of reading them. They must be seen on the stage or they have no existence.

The second kind of play is the dramatization of a popular novel, one which has had so many readers that the alert dramatist's attention is called to it as a probable money-maker on the stage. This also is commercialized, and with it literature has nothing to do ; especially not since the dramatized story is commonly a *Pollyanna* or a *Lightnin'* or some other accident of popular taste that is hardly worth consideration either as play or novel.

The third kind of play is what is becoming known as the literary and artistic drama, which places the portrayal of truth or beauty above all other considerations. Literature is concerned with this form of drama because it can be read with pleasure, apart from the stage with its always distressful glitter and frequently distressful acting. It is noteworthy that Jacinto Benavente, who is at the head of his craft in Spain (a land of great dramatists) and whose plays have been acted over most of the civilized world, has recently announced (1923) that he has abandoned the theater and will henceforth write plays for the *reading* public. Among his reasons are that, what with salaries and costumes and scenery, the expense of producing a play is now enormous ; that for a play to fail on the stage, after such expense, may be disastrous ; that, in consequence, the playwright no less than the producer must forever keep his eye on his audience rather than on the truth of life ; that, finally, the actors of a play commonly give a totally different impression from what the maker of the play intended. And he adds, with the conviction of experience, that only one who reads a drama as the author wrote it can appreciate its true value as a reflection of life.

The Little Theater. Until recent years the artistic drama had small chance of being either staged or read in America.

Suddenly appeared the so-called Little Theater (1911), and the response showed that many had been waiting for better plays than producers had thus far given them. The first aim of the Little Theater was to free the drama from commercialism ; the second, to give any dramatist of ability an audience and a fair hearing. The new impulse spread rapidly, powerfully, until within the space of ten years the Provincetown Players, the Washington Square Players, the Wisconsin Players, and fifty other organized groups as far south as New Orleans and as far west as Los Angeles offer to our dramatists not only the chance but the encouragement to do original and artistic work.

It is not meant by the above that our " regular " theaters deliberately discourage good work ; on the contrary, they are mostly eager for original plays, taking the best they can get and making them over in face of the stern alternative of pleasing an audience or losing money. The fact is, according to a dramatic critic who has been acquainted with the New York theater for twenty-odd years, that most playwrights have been quite as commercial as producers or managers in that they copy any trashy or sentimental model with a hopeful eye on the financial returns. Then came the Little Theater, saying, " The play's the thing ! " and frankly inviting good work for the work's sake. Whether this is but another fad or whether it will bring the American stage nearer to the European stage, with its more artistic plays and better acting, remains for the future to say.

Typical Plays. As an introduction to the modern literary and poetic drama, read *The Piper* by Josephine Preston Peabody. This is one of the many prize plays of recent years; it had its successful day on the stage, and after the footlights are out it is still good reading. The story is the old legend of the Pied Piper of Hamelin, who piped the rats out of a city into the river, and then, when the city refused to pay, piped its children away by his music. If you read more plays by this author (*Marlowe* and *The Wolf of Gubbio*) or by others who attempt the artistic drama, you must notice this disappointing quality, that they commonly search other lands and distant times for a theme. This is plainly a weakness or blindness of our dramatists; for yesterday appeared an Englishman, named Drinkwater, and his impressive *Abraham Lincoln* showed the kind of dramatic material which our own writers have long neglected.

Between the older and the newer dramatists stand two whose work is well worth examining, especially by one who is interested in the technique of playwriting. These are David Belasco and Augustus Thomas, who have to their credit several works that are distinctly better than the ordinary commercialized drama. *The Return of Peter Grimm* by Belasco and *The Witching Hour* by Thomas are, on the whole, the best works of those now called the older dramatists because, so rapidly do we change favorites, they produced their chief works before 1912.

Most promising of present-day dramatists is Eugene O'Neill, one of the Provincetown Players, who is associated with the Little Theater movement. He has originality, force, imagination and, above all, sincerity. Recognition came quickly to him because of his striking plays of the sea; such, for example, as *Anna Christie* and *The Moon of the Caribbees*. The best of all his plays is *Beyond the Horizon* (1920). His astonishing variety appears in *The Emperor Jones,* which portrays a negro ex-convict who imposes on the credulity of some West Indian natives to make himself monarch of the tribe. When they discover the fraud, the " emperor " flees by night to the forest, where he is beset by ghosts, hoodoos, hobgoblins, all the hallucinations begotten of a superstitious mind and a misspent life. Such a night! To see it even in pantomime is to remember Clarence, in *King Richard the Third*:

> O, I have passed a miserable night,
> So full of ugly sights, of ghastly dreams,
> That, as I am a Christian faithful man,
> I would not spend another such a night,
> Though 'twere to buy a world of happy days,
> So full of dismal terror was the time!

Contrasting with the vigor and originality of O'Neill is Percy Mackaye, who has written a dozen conventional plays, seven masques or pageants and three operas. He stands for the civic theater to replace the commercialized stage; at times he writes with the hope of influencing a town to take part in a drama, thus going back to the community idea that produced the miracle plays of the Middle Ages. *Caliban*, written to celebrate the tercentenary of the death of Shakespeare, is his best masque; the *Canterbury Pilgrims* (note the foreign material) is his best comedy; *The Immigrants* (now printed as a "lyric drama" but originally written as an opera) is his only dramatic work that shows originality. All these were intended to be seen on the stage to the accompaniment of music, lights, pageantry, and they give an inadequate or disappointing impression in tne reading.

William Vaughn Moody is a more forceful dramatist, especially when he reflects the conflict of Puritan ideals with the growing freedom of the West, in which some of the Puritan's descendants now find themselves, — an American theme surely. His best play is *The Great Divide*. Booth Tarkington may well be selected as typical of the many authors who, having won success in other fields, are lured away by the theater. He has written several plays which, with one exception, give the same impression as his novels. The exception is *Clarence* (1919), his best drama and, as some judge, the finest of all his works. Edward Knoblauch writes for stage effects chiefly, and his work is characterized by novelty. Thus, in *My Lady's Dress*, while the heroine sleeps, five dreamlike scenes (plays within a play) portray the care of silkworms in Italy, the weaving of silk in France, the making of lace in Holland, the manufacture of artificial flowers in London, and the trapping of furs in Siberia. Here is a veritable "movie" drama. It is mentioned here as an excellent example of the feminine appeal which attracts the modern woman (who is in the majority in almost every audience) and of the novelty which lures the playgoing man, the American man especially, who is ready to be amused or surprised after his day's work, but does not want to think if he can avoid it.

We have considered only a few typical novelists, poets and dramatists, to the exclusion of our many essayists, humorists, critics, historians and nature writers. To name them all briefly would be to make a mere catalogue; to select those most worthy of remembrance is not yet possible. Undoubtedly, for every book or author here mentioned, ten or twenty that may be quite as good have been passed over in silence, the reason being that no historian could read enough of their collective work to make fair estimate of their relative values. The best that can be done within the limits of a chapter is to make, as it were, a short cut through the middle of present-day literature. To compass the whole field would mean a long life's lesson — and a chaotic big book at the end.

Bibliography. *General History.* Cambridge History of American Literature, Vols. III and IV (Putnam, 1917–1921); a good miscellany by many authors, each dealing with one phase or type of literature. Pattee, History of American Literature since 1870 (Century Co., 1915); an excellent summary and criticism of the period from 1870 to 1900; chief writers from 1900 to 1915 briefly mentioned. Manly and Rickert, Contemporary American Literature (Harcourt, Brace and Company, 1923); a very condensed account of about two hundred writers; less a history than a good catalogue; valuable for its bibliographies, including studies and reviews of various authors that have appeared in recent magazines.

General Criticism. Perry, The American Spirit in Literature (1918). Sherman, On Contemporary Literature (1917). Hackett (editor) On American Books (1920); personal impressions of recent literature by five critics. More, Shelburne Essays, 11 vols. (1904–1921). Canby, Benet and Loveman, Saturday Papers (1921). Brooks, Letters and Leadership (1918). Mencken, Book of Prefaces, 1 vol. (1917); Prejudices, 2 vols. (1919–1920). Eliot, The Sacred Wood: Essays on Poetry and Criticism (1920). Underwood, Literature and Insurgency (1914).

The Novel. Van Doren, The American Novel (1921). Overton, Women Who Make Our Novels (1918). Gordon, Men Who Make Our Novels (1919). Cooper, Some American Story Tellers (1911). Phelps, The Advance of the English Novel in the Twentieth Century (1916).

The Short Story. Pattee, The Development of the American Short Story (Harper, 1923); latest on the subject, scholarly and readable. Baker, The Contemporary Short Story (1916). Lieberman, The American Short Story (1912). Canby, The Short Story in English (1909). Smith, The American Short Story (1912). Cross, The Short Story (1914). Books dealing with technique, and aiming to tell the beginner how to write, are: Barrett, Short Story Writing (1898); Esenwein, Writing the Short Story (1909); Williams, Handbook on Story Writing (1917).

Poetry. Cook, Our Poets of To-day (1918; revised by additions, 1920). Wilkinson, New Voices (1919). Peckham, Present-Day American Poetry (1917). Untermeyer, The New Era in American Poetry (1919). Lowes, Convention and Revolt in Poetry (1919). Amy Lowell, Tendencies in Modern American Poetry (1917). Aiken, Skepticisms: Notes on Contemporary Poetry (1919).

The Drama. Matthews, A Book about the Theatre (1916). Clark, British and American Drama of Today (1921). Phelps, The Twentieth Century Theatre (1918); Essays on Modern Dramatists (1920). Moses, The American Dramatist (1917). Chandler, Aspects of Modern Drama (1914). Cheney, The New Movement in the Theatre (1914); The Art Theatre (1917); The Open Air Theatre (1918). Eaton, The American Stage of Today (1908); Plays and Players (1916). Burton, The New American Drama (1913). Andrews, The Drama Today (1913). Lewisohn, The Drama and the Stage (1922). Nathan, The Critic and the Drama (1922). Goldberg, The Drama of Transition (1922). Constance Mackay, The Little Theatre in the United States (1917). Percy Mackaye, The Civic Theatre (1912); The Community Drama (1917). Beegle and Crawford, Community Drama and Pageantry (1916). Baker, Technique of the Drama (1915). Lewis, Technique of the One-Act Play (1918). Hamilton, Studies in Stagecraft (1914); Problems of the Playwright (1917).

Collections of Short Stories. Best Short Stories, edited by O'Brien, 8 vols., each containing the alleged best stories published during a year (Small, Maynard, 1916–1922). Law, Modern Short Stories (Century Co., 1918). Laselle, Short Stories of the New America (Holt, 1919). Heydrick, Americans All (Harcourt, 1920). Williams, Our Short Story Writers (Moffatt, Yard, 1920).

Anthologies. Cooper, Poems of Today, prepared for high-school use (Ginn and Company, 1923). Braithwaite, Anthology of Magazine Verse and Yearbook of American Poetry, annual volumes; Golden Treasury of Magazine Verse (Small, Maynard). Untermeyer, Modern American Poetry (Harcourt, 1921). Le Gallienne, Modern Book of American Verse (Boni and Liveright, 1919). Miscellany of American Poetry (Harcourt, 1920). Monroe and Henderson, The New Poetry (Macmillan, 1920). Richards, High Tide; Melody of Earth; Star Points, 3 vols. (Houghton, 1920). Rittenhouse, Little Book of Modern Verse; Second Book of Modern Verse, 1913, 1919, 2 vols. (Houghton). Stork, Contemporary Verse Anthology, 1916–1920 (Dutton). Clarke, Treasury of War Poetry, 2 vols. (Houghton). From the Front (Appleton, 1918). Erskine, American Humor in Verse (Duffield, 1917). Some Imagist Poets, 3 vols. (Houghton, 1915–1917). Cronyn, The Path on the Rainbow, Indian songs (Boni and Liveright, 1918).

Collections of Plays. Mantle, Best Plays, annual volumes (1920–) (Small, Maynard). Moses, Representative Plays by American Dramatists, 1918–1921, 4 vols. (Dutton). Mayorga, Representative One-Act Plays by American Authors, 24 plays by as many authors (Little, Brown, 1919). Knickerbocker, Plays for Classroom Interpretation (Holt, 1921). Cohen, One Act Plays by Modern Authors, Mackaye, Peabody, Rogers, Tarkington, and Young (Harcourt, 1921). Baker, Modern American Plays, by Belasco, Sheldon, and Thomas (Harcourt, 1920). Quinn, Representative American Plays, by Crothers, Mackaye, Sheldon, and Thomas (Century Co., 1917). Cook and Shay, Provincetown Plays, 1916, 1921, 4 vols. (Stewart Kidd). Dickinson, Wisconsin Plays, 1914, 1918, 2 vols. (Huebsch). Washington Square Plays, Drama League Series (Doubleday, 1916). Baker, Harvard Plays, written by students : Plays of the 47 Workshop, 2 vols.; Plays of the Harvard Dramatic Club, 2 vols. (Brentano, 1918, 1920).

Collections of Essays. Atlantic Classics, 2 vols. (Atlantic Monthly Press). Kilmer, Literature in the Making (Harper, 1917). Morley, Modern Essays (Harcourt, 1920).

INDEX

Titles of books, poems, stories, and essays are all set in italic type. When several minor references are given, the use of italic indicates a detailed study of an author's life and work.

Abbott, Jacob, 260
Abolitionists, the, 272, 306
Abraham Lincoln, 498
Adams, Abigail, 147
Adams, John, 94, 112, 126
Adams, Samuel, 89, 113, 127
Adventures of Captain Bonneville, 183, 190
Adventures while Preaching the Gospel of Beauty, 491
Agassiz, To, 344
Age of Innocence, The, 479
Agitation, the age of, 272, 281
Alcott, Amos B., 282
Alcott, Louisa M., 282, 415
Alcuin, 156
Aldrich, Thomas B., 453
Alhambra, The, 183, 189
Alice of Monmouth, 453
Allegory, of Poe, 236; of Hawthorne, 398
Allen, James Lane, 482, 485
Almanacs, early, 105
Alsop, George, 41
America the Beautiful, 492
American Scholar, The, 213, 322, 333, 336
Ames, Nathaniel, 105
Among My Books, 341, 347
Angels, Emerson's four, 320
Anna Christie, 498
Annalists, Colonial, 11, 39
Annuals, 174
Anti-Federalists, the, 91, 94, 117, 119
Art, different conceptions of, 245; Emerson's, 329; Lanier's, 364, 366
Art, Emerson's essay, 328, 330
Art of living, explained by Franklin, 110
Artistic literature, beginning of, 56, 179

As a Strong Bird, 377
Astoria, 183, 190
Atherton, Gertrude, 483
Audubon, J. J., 259
Austin, Mary, 483
Autobiography, Franklin's, 107; Jefferson's, 127
Autocrat of the Breakfast Table, The, 353, 356

Bacheller, Irving, 481
Balance of power, political, 271
Ballad of Nathan Hale, 133
Ballad of Trees and the Master, 366
Ballads, of the Revolution, 133; of Whittier, 310
Bancroft, George, 259, 280
Barlow, Joel, 134, 135
Bartram, John, 147
Basket Woman, The, 483
Bates, Katharine Lee, 492
Battle Hymn of the Republic, 382
Bay Psalm Book, The, 44
Beginnings of American literature, 3
Belasco, David, 498
Belknap's History, 147
Benavente, Jacinto, 496
Beverly, Robert, 42
Beyond the Horizon, 498
Bhagavadgita, 379
Bibliographies, general, xviii; Colonial, 80; Revolutionary, 163; First National period, 262; Second National period, 441
Biglow Papers, The, 340, 346
Biographies, our first, 68
Birth of the nation, 92
Bitter Sweet, 390
Black Oxen, 483
Blazed Trail, The, 485
Blithedale Romance, The, 394, 401

Boanerges, 61
Boker, G. H., 386, 388
Bold Hathorne, 392
Bonifacius, 61
Books, earliest printed, 44
Boy's Will, A, 493
Bracebridge Hall, 79, 187, 188
Brackenridge, Hugh, 145
Bradford, William, 4, 6, *11*, 22, 88;
 life, 11 ; works, 12; as a historian,
 18; style, 6, 11, 19; library, 12;
 Journal, 18; manuscripts, 19
Bradstreet, Anne, 23, 46, *47;* life, 48;
 poems, 49
Brahma, 328, 379
"Brahmin caste," 349, 352
Brébeuf, Parkman's story of, 433
Brewster, Elder, 12, 17, 18
Brick, story of a, 10
Bridge, Horatio, 394
Brook Farm, 277, 394
Brown, Charles Brockden, 93, *154*,
 404; life, 155; works, 157 ; Brown,
 Shelley and Godwin, 156
Brownell, H. H., 390
Brownson, Orestes, 280
Bryant, William Cullen, 170, 175, 177,
 194, 287, 389, 450; life, 195; works,
 199; poems on death, 201 ; nature
 poems, 202; characteristics, 204;
 compared with Lanier, 205
Burk, John, 145
Burwell Papers, The, 41
Busybody Papers, The, 109
Byrd, William, 32; his Journals, 34;
 significance of his work, 38

Cable, G. W., 463
Calhoun, John C., 255
Caliban, 499
California and Oregon Trail, The, 39,
 436, 438
Calvinism, 53, 75
Cambridge, literary life in, 288, 298
Canterbury Pilgrims, The, 499
Captain Blood, 485
Captain, My Captain, 376
Carleton, Will, 455
Carver, Governor, 18
Carver, Jonathan, 147
Cassia and Other Verse, 492
Cathedral, The, 344
Cavalier, the, in American literature,
 33, 144, 145
Cawein, Madison, 455

Cedarcroft, 385
Centralizing tendency in government,
 117
Chambered Nautilus, The, 355
Channing, W. E., 77, 153, 259, 276,
 280
*Character of the Province of Maryland,
 A*, 41
Charlotte Temple, 154
Chicago Poems, 495
Children of the Night, 490
Chinese Nightingale, The, 491
Chingachgook, 217, 223
Chivers-Poe controversy, the, 241
Christus, A Mystery, 299
Chronological History of New England,
 42
Churchill, Winston, 480
Citizen literature, 97
Clarence, 499
Clarke, James F., 280
Classic, and Classicism, 138
Clay, Henry, 255
Clemens, S. L. *See* Mark Twain
College lyrics of Holmes, 352, 354
Colleges, first American, 79
Colonial Period of Literature, intro-
 duction to, 1 ; spirit of, 4 ; why
 study, 10; typical annalists, 11 ;
 various chronicles, 39; satire and
 criticism, 41 ; histories, 42 ; Indian
 narratives, 42 ; poets and poetry,
 44; theological writers, 57 ; char-
 acteristics of, 79, 92 ; summary of
 history, 78; summary of literature,
 79; selections for reading, and bib-
 liography, 80
Colonists, the, character of, 8, 62 ;
 why they wrote few books, 7 ; ideals
 of, 46; earlier and later, 171, 172
Columbiad, The, 135
Columbus, Irving's, 182, 183, 189;
 Lowell's, 347 ; Lanier's, 366; Whitman's, 377
Commemoration Ode, Lowell's, 341,
 345, 377
Committee of Correspondence, the,
 125
Commonplace, the, in poetry, 301
Common Sense, 148
Communistic societies, 277, 278. *See
 also* p. 16
Concord, Emerson's life in, 322
Congo, The, 491
Conjuror's House, 485

Conqueror, The, 483
Conquest of Canaan, The, 135
Conspiracy of Pontiac, The, 430, 434
Constitution, the, 91, 118, 121
Continental Congress, the first, 88
Cooke, John Esten, 408, 412
Cooper, James Fenimore, 91, 99, 175, 207 ; life, 200 ; compared with Scott, 213 ; historical romances, 213 ; Leatherstocking tales, 217 ; sea stories, 220 ; characteristics, 223 ; popularity abroad, 224
Count Frontenac, 434
Courtin', The, 347
Courtship of Miles Standish, The, 293
Covered Wagon, The, 478
Craigie House, 288
Crane, Stephen, 484, 485
Crèvecœur, 146
Crisis, The, Paine's, 149 ; Churchill's, 480
Criticism, beginning of, 178, 233, 234
Croakers, The, 252
Cross-Currents, 490
Cross of Snow, The, 289
Culprit Fay, The, 252
Culture, literature of, 7
Curtis, G. W., 184, 448

Dana, R. H., Jr., 247
David Harum, 481
Day of Doom, The, 47, 51, 95
Daye, Stephen, 44
Deacon's Masterpiece, The, 355
Death as a subject in early literature, 192, 200, 201
Declaration of Independence, 89
Declaration of Independence, The, 128
Deerslayer, The, 218
Democracy, two elements of, 91 ; in First National period, 172 ; Whitman's, 378
Democracy and Other Essays, 347
Description of New England, A, 5, 39
Detective stories, 235, 236
Determinism, doctrine of, 75
Dial, The, 277, 378
Diary, Sewall's, 28, 31
Dickinson, Emily, 456
Divine Comedy, The, Longfellow's translation, 298
Dome of Many-Coloured Glass, A, 495
Dorcasina Sheldon. See *Female Quixotism*
Drake, Joseph Rodman, 251

Drama, modern, 495
Druillette, journey of, 12
Drum Taps, 372
Dual personality as a motive, 236
Dunbar, P. L., 452
Dunlap, William, 93, 145
Dwight, Timothy, 134, 135

Easy Chair Papers, 184
Eben Holden, 481
Edgar Huntley, 157
Edwards, Jonathan, 70, 87, 93, 100, 255, 470 ; life, 70 ; character, 73, 76 ; works, 74, 76
Eggleston, Edward, 415
Eliot, John, 42 ; Mather's Life of, 67
Elmwood, 338
Elsie Venner, 356
Emerson, Ralph Waldo, 277, 280, 282, 318, 399, 417, 450 ; life, 320 ; poetry, 325 ; prose works, 329 ; philosophy, 332 ; characteristics, 335 ; claim to greatness, 336
Emperor Jones, The, 498
Enamoured Architect, The, 455
English Novel, The, 365
"Era of good feeling," the, 171
Erskine Dale, Pioneer, 482
Essays to Do Good, 61, 100
Ethan Brand, 398
Eureka, 237
Evangeline, 292, 300
Everett, Edward, 256
Excursions, 422
Expansion of the nation, 171

Fable for Critics, A, 346
Factories and Other Poems, 490
Fair Harbor, 482
Fairy Gold, 492
Faithful Narrative, A, 73
Fall of the House of Usher, The, 227, 238
Fannie, 253
Fanshawe, 393
Farewell Address, Washington's, 115
Farmer Refuted, The, 121
Fashions, literary, 94, 146
Father Abraham's Speech, 107
Fatherland, the, 66
Faust, Taylor's translation, 387
Federalist, The, 121
Federalist party, the, 91, 94, 117, 119
Female Quixotism, 154
Fiction, beginning of, 154

Field, Eugene, 451
First Encounter, the, 14
Fiske, John, 118, 122
Flame and Shadow, 489
Folklore literature, 7
Foreign notions of America, 211, 381, 382
Forest Hymn, A, 176, 194
Foster, S. C., 383
Four Million, The, 488
Fourierism, 278, 279
Fox, John, Jr., 482
Francesca da Rimini, 388
Francis, Convers, 280
Franklin, Benjamin, 70, 73, 93, 99; life, 100; works, 104; humor and philosophy, 110, 111
Franklin, Temple, 108
Free verse, 494
Freedom of the Will, 53, 73, 74
Freneau, Philip, 93, 120, 138; life, 138; works, 140; as a romantic poet, 142
Friendship, 330
Frost, Robert, 493
Fuller, Margaret, 280, 378, 401
Full Vindication of Congress, A, 121

Garrison, W. L., and Whittier, 305, 306
General History of New England, 42
General History of Virginia, 5, 39
Gentle Julia, 478
Gettysburg Oration of Everett and of Lincoln, 256
Godfrey, Thomas, 47, 53; life, 54; works, 55, 56
Gold Bug, The, 188, 235, 242
Golden Legend, The, 299, 387
Golden Whales of California, The, 491
Goldsmith, Life of, 184, 190
Good News from New England, 40
Good News from Virginia, 40
Goodrich, Samuel, 260
Gookin, Daniel, 42
Gotham and Gothamites, 186
Gothic romance, the, 160, 161, 163
Grandfather's Chair, 394, 397
Great Awakening, the, 73, 76
Great Divide, The, 499
Grey, Zane, 486
Guardian Angel, The, 356

Hale, E. E., 448
Half Century of Conflict, A, 434

Halleck, Fitz-Greene, 253
Hamilton, Alexander, 93, 94, 118; life, 119; works, 120
Hampton Beach, 313
Handy Guide for Beggars, A, 491
Hanging of the Crane, The, 297
Hannah Thurston, 387
Harland, Marion, 415
Harris, Joel C., 468
Harte, Francis Bret, 408, 412, 462; his career, 413; place in fiction, 414
Hartford Wits, the, 134
Harvey Birch, 207, 214
Hasty Pudding, 135
Hawthorne, Nathaniel, 280, 292, 391; life, 392; short stories, 397; four romances, 400; characteristics, 404; unfinished romance, 397
Hay, John, 390, 455
Hayne, Paul H., 383
Hearthfire, symbol of the, 66, 302, 304, 308
Hearts of Oak, 96
Heimskringla, 299
Helen, To, 239
Hémon, Louis, 473
Henry, Patrick, 88, 93, 97, 113, 121
Hexameters, 293
Hiawatha, 294; compared with the *Kalevala*, 295, 300
Higginson, T. W., 335, 448, 461
Hills of Song, 494
Historians. *See* Colonial, Motley, etc.
Historical Collections of the Indians, 43
Historical romances, early, 178; modern, 479
History of the Dividing Line, A, 34
History of New England, Winthrop's, 24
History of Virginia, Beverly's, 42
Holland, J. G., 390
Holmes, Oliver Wendell, 309, 318, 351; life, 351; poems, 353; prose works, 356; humor, 351, 357; characteristics, 357
Homestead, the Whittier, 304
Hoosier Schoolmaster, The, 415
Horror, as a motive, in Brown, 160; in Poe, 237; in Hawthorne, 404; in Mark Twain, 466
Horse-Shoe Robinson, 248
Hough, Emerson, 478
House of Mirth, The, 479

House of the Seven Gables, The, 400
Hovey, Richard, 455
How Love looked for Hell, 367
Howe, Julia Ward, 382
Howells, W. D., 457, *460*
Hubbard, William, 41
Huckleberry Finn, 466, 467
Hugh Wynne, Free Quaker, 480
Humor, of Franklin, 110; of Irving, 187, 191; of Holmes, 351, 357; of Bret Harte, 415; of Mark Twain, 465
Hunt, Helen. *See* Jackson
Hymn to the Beautiful, 388
Hyperion, 287, 291

Ichabod, 309
Idealism, 280, 281, 282, 459. *See also* Jefferson
Idyls of Whittier, 311
I Have a Rendezvous with Death, 492
Iliad, Bryant's translation, 197
Immigrants, The, 499
Indians, as portrayed by Smith and Bradford, 5, 6; attack on the Pilgrims, 14; Byrd's account of, 35; early narratives of, 42; as seen by Parkman, 435, 438
Individualism, of Emerson, 321, 323, 334, 336; of Whitman, 381; of Hawthorne, 395; of Thoreau, 417, 418, 423; cult of, 281, 378
Innocents Abroad, 465
Inside of the Cup, The, 480
In the Harbor, 285
In the Twilight, 350
Irving, Washington, 175, *179,* 338, 357; life, 180; early works, 184; middle period (English, Spanish, and American themes), 187; late period, 490; characteristics, 191; message, 192
Israfel, 227

Jackson, Helen Hunt, 455, 462
James, Henry, 457, 460
Jamestown, landing at, 8
Jay, John, 121
Jefferson, Thomas, 93, 94, *122,* 151, 272; idealism of, 123; life, 124; works, 126; the Declaration of Independence, 128
Jesuits, the, 12, 432
Jesuits in North America, The, 12, 434, 438

Jewett, Sarah Orne, 463
John of Barneveld, 427
John Brent, 415
Johnson, Edward, 40
Johnston, Mary, 463, 480
"Jonathan Oldstyle," 185, 191
Jones, Abel, 108
Josselyn, John, 30
Journal, Bradford's, 18; Winthrop's, 20; Byrd's, 34; Winslow's, 40; Washington's, 115; Woolman's, 151; Thoreau's, 421
Journal of Julius Rodman, Poe, 231
Journal of Margaret Smith, Whittier, 315
Journey to the Land of Eden, A, 37
Justice and Expediency, 306
Juvenile Poems, Godfrey, 54
Juveniles, 260

Kalevala, 295
Kavanagh, 292
Kennedy, John P., 230, 248
Kentucky Warbler, The, 482
Kilmer, Joyce, 492
Knickerbocker History, 182, 186
Knickerbocker School, the, 250
Knoblauch, Edward, 499
Knowledge, Emerson's theory of, 333

Lanier, Sidney, 205, *358,* 386; life, 360; prose works, 364; his theory of verse, 365; poems, 366; characteristics, 368
Larcom, Lucy, 315, 341
Lars, 387
La Salle and the Discovery of the Great West, 434
Last Leaf, The, 355
Last of the Mohicans, The, 209, 219, 222
Laus Deo, 307
Lazarus, Emma, 452
Leather Stocking and Silk, 408
Leatherstocking tales, 217
Leaves of Grass, 371, 372, 373, 378
Lee, Richard H., 121
Leeds, Titus, 106
Legend of Brittany, A, 343
Legendary and historical tales, early, 177; of Hawthorne, 400
Legends, 495
L'Envoi: To the Muse, 350
Letters, of Jefferson, 126; of Revolutionary women, 147; of Lowell, 348
Letters from an American Farmer, 146

Letters of a Federalist Farmer, 121
Liberty, Winthrop's definition of, 23, 116
Liberty or Death, speech of Henry, 114
Life and Voyages of Columbus, 182, 183, 189
Life on the Mississippi, 464
Lincoln, Abraham, 88, 270
Lincoln, Joseph C. 481
Lindsay, Vachel, 491
Lionel Lincoln, 216
Literary Friends and Acquaintance, 288, 350
Literati, The, 231, 447
Literature, definition of, 56; of folk lore, 7; of culture, 7, 8. *See* Colonial, Revolutionary, etc.
Little Shepherd of Kingdom Come, The, 482
Little Theater, the, 496
Livingston, William, 95
Local color, stories of, 408, 412
Long Tom Coffin, 207, 221, 223
Longfellow, Henry Wadsworth, *284*, 392, 396, 471; life, 286; earlier works, 290; middle period, 292; later works, 297; characteristics, 299
Long Roll, The, 480
Love, Emerson's essay, 330
Love Letters, some old, 25
Love Songs, Teasdale, 489
Lowell, Amy, 495
Lowell, James Russell, 92, 319, 323, 337, *338*, 387; life, 338; poetry, 342; essays, 347; letters, 348; characteristics, 349; review of his career, 350
Loyalist Poetry of the Revolution, 133
Loyalists, the, 90
Luck of Roaring Camp, The, 412, 413
Lyceums, 276, 280, 323
Lynch Lawyers, 486
Lyric poetry, definition of, 203
Lyrics and Sonnets, 492

McCloud, James, 144
M'Fingal, 137
Mackaye, Percy, 499
Madison, Dolly, 147
Madison, James, 121
Magazines, early, 54, 178
Magnalia, 63; motive of, 64; fantastic elements, 66; heroes of, 67
Magnificent Ambersons, The, 478
Man Against the Sky, The, 490

Man from Bar-20, The, 486
Man of the Forest, The, 486
Manuscript Found in a Bottle, 238
Marble Faun, The, 395, 401, 405
Marco Bozzaris, 253
Margaret Smith's Journal, 315
Maria Chapdelaine, 473
Marjorie Daw, 453
Mark Twain, 357, 408, 415, *464*; satire and ridicule, 465; works, 466; his quality, 467
Marshes of Glynn, The, 365, 368
Mary-'Gusta, 482
Maryland, My Maryland, 382
Mason, John, 43
Mather, Cotton, 12, 32, *57*, 100, 339, 349; life, 58; works, 61; *Magnalia*, 63; portrayal of life, 69
Mather Dynasty, the, 58
"Maximarchist" party, 117
Maypole at Merrymount, 17
Meditative verse of Emerson, 327
Melodramas, early, 177
Melville, Herman, 247
Memorable Providences, 62
Mercedes of Castile, 215
Merry Mount, Motley's, 426
Mettle of the Pasture, The, 482
Miller, Joaquin, 389
"Minimarchist" party, 117
Mitchell, Donald G., 448, 449
Mitchell, S. Weir, 480
"Mobocrats," 118
Model of Christian Charity, A, 20
"Monocrats," 118
Monsieur Beaucaire, 478
Montcalm and Wolfe, 437
Monticello, 125, 127
Moody, William V., 455, 499
Moon of the Caribbees, The, 498
Moral tendency in American literature, 283, 317, 318, 344, 364, 405
Morituri Salutamus, 297
Morris, Gouverneur, 91
Morton, Nathaniel, 19, 41
Morton of Merrymount, 17
Mosses from an Old Manse, 394, 398
Motley, John Lothrop, 426; works, 427; quality of, 428
Mountain Interval, 494
Mourt's Relation, 14, 18
Mulford, Clarence Edward, 486
Murfree, Mary N., 463
Music and poetry, 365, 368
My Lady's Dress, 499

My Study Windows, 341
Mystery in fiction, 159, 160, 235, 237

Nathan Hale, Ballad of, 133
National literature, 77; contrasted with sectional, 275, 276. *See also* Preface
National Period, First, history, 169; literature, 174; major writers, 179; minor fiction, 247; minor poetry, 249; orators, 254; historians and miscellaneous writers, 259; summary, 260; selections for reading, 262; bibliography, 263
National Period, Second, historical outline, 270; the age of agitation, 272; literary and social movements, 275; transcendentalism, 278; general characteristics of literature, 283; greater poets and essayists, 284; minor poetry, 382; novelists and story-tellers, 391; minor fiction, 407; prose (nonfiction) writers, 416; summary, 439; selections for reading, 440; bibliography, 441
National Road, the, 170
National songs of the Revolution, 96
Nationality, effect on literature, 9; in Bryant's verse, 206
Natty Bumppo, 207, 217, 223
Nature, in poetry of the First National period, 176; of Second National period, 283; in Whittier's verse, 311; in Emerson's verse, 326; harmony of, 205; in Frost's verse, 493
Nature, Emerson's essay, 322, 329
Navy, History of the, Cooper's, 211, 212
New England Primer, The, 51, 52
New England Reformers, 276
New England's Crisis, 46
New England's Memorial, 42
New England's Prospect, 40
New England's Rarities Discovered, 39
Newspapers, early, 93
Night on the Prairies, 375
Nooning, The, 344
Norris, Frank, 484
North of Boston, 494
Norton, Charles Eliot, 298, 348, 351
Notes on Virginia, 127
Notions of Americans, 211
Novelists, modern, 476
Novels, modern, 476; of the frontier, 477; of society, 478; historical,

479; of character, 480; social, 484; of adventure, 485
Noyes, Nicholas, 62

Oakes, Urian, 46
O'Brien, Fitz-James, 415
Occasional poems, 354
Octopus, The, 484
Odell, Jonathan, 93, 140, 149
Odyssey, Bryant's translation, 197
"O. Henry." *See* Porter, William Sydney
Old English Dramatists, 347
Old Ironsides, 352
Old Régime in Canada, The, 434
Old Road to Paradise, The, 490
Oldtown Folks, 409
O'Neill, Eugene, 498
Open Road, Song of the, 380
Oratory, 94; of the Revolution, 111; of First National period, 254
Oregon Trail, The, 39, 436, 438
Oriental literature, influence of, 280, 283, 379
Orientalism of Whitman, 378
Otis, James, 93, 112
Our Hundred Days in Europe, 357
Our Old Home, 397
Outcasts of Poker Flat, The, 412, 413
Outre Mer, 287, 291
Over the Teacups, 353

Paine, Thomas, 147; works, 148; last years, 151
Parentator, 61
Parker, Theodore, 280
Parkman, Francis, 429; his theme, 430; preparation, 431; works, 434; quality of, 437
Partisan, The, 91
Partisan prose and verse, 276
Pathfinder, The, 209, 219
Patriot party, the, 90
Patriotism, Mather's appeal to, 58, 66; in First National period, 177; Lowell's, 340
Paulding, James K., 250
Peabody, Josephine Preston, 497
Pelham, Peter, 31
Pencillings by the Way, 251
Penrod, 478
Peter Parley. *See* Goodrich
Philosophic Solitude, 95
Philosophy, aim of, 333; Franklin's, 106, 110; Emerson's, 332

Picture of St. John, The, 387
Pictures of the Floating World, 495
Pierpont, Sarah, 72
Pike County Ballads, 390
Pilgrims, the, departure for America, 13; arrival of, 2; policy of, 12; character of, 12, 14, 15; communistic experiment, 16
Pilot, The, 210, 221
Pioneer interest in literature, 208
Pioneers, O Pioneers, Whitman, 169, 376
Pioneers, The, Cooper, 207, 209, 218
Pioneers of France in the New World, Parkman, 434
Piper, The, 497
Pit, The, 484
Plimoth Plantation, Of, 12
Pocahontas, Smith's story of, 5
Poe, Edgar Allan, 175, *224,* 363, 365, 394, 404; the Poe controversy, 225; double nature of, 227; life, 228; critical work, 234; tales, 235; poems, 239; characteristics, 240
Poems of the Orient, 386
Poet and the Poetic Gift, The, 326
Poetry, Poe's theory of, 239; the antithesis to science, 325; Lanier's theory of, 365, 369; the instinct for, 370; recent, 450. *See also* Colonial, Revolutionary, lyric, romantic, etc.
Poet's Journal, The, 387
Poet's Vision, The, 246
Poets of America, The, 452
Pokahontas, My Lady, Cooke, 409
Political parties, permanent, 116
Ponteach, a Tragedy, 435
Pontiac, story of, 430, 434
Poor Richard's Almanac, 100, 105
Porter, William Sydney, 488
Portygee, The, 482
Powhattan, 5
Prairie, The, 219, 220
Preacher, The, 87
Precaution, 209
Predestination, doctrine of, 75
Prescott, William H., 259
Present Age, the. *See* Recent Literature
Present Crisis, The, 345
Present-Day Literature, introduction, 472; authors and readers, 474; novelists, 476; short stories, 487; poetry, 489; drama, 495; bibliography, 500

Prince, Thomas, 19, 41, 42
Prince of Parthia, The, 55
Progress of Dulness, The, 134
Progress to the Mines, A, 37
Prophecy of Samuel Sewall, The, 304
Psalm of Life, A, 291
Psalm of the West, A, 358, 366
Pseudoscientific tales, 236
Purchase, His Pilgrimes, 18
Puritans, the, 20, 25, 33, 68, 201, 206, 303, 316; as portrayed by Hawthorne, 400

Quick, Herbert, 477
Quotations, Emerson's use of, 331

Ramona, 462
Ramsay's histories, 147
Randall, J. R., 382
Read, T. B., 390
Readers, relation to modern authors, 474
Realism, 457
Realist, the, in fiction, 458, 459
Recent Literature, introduction, 447; reminiscent writers, 448; poetry, 450; fiction, 456; romance and realism, 457
Red Badge of Courage, The, 485
Redeemed Captive, The, 43
Red Rover, The, 221, 223
Reign of Law, The, 485
Relations, Jesuit, 12, 432
Religious Affections, The, 73
Religious poems of Whittier, 308, 312, 316
Reminiscent literature, 448
Reply to Hayne, Webster's, 258
Representative Men, 329
Retinue, The, 492
Return of Peter Grimm, The, 498
Revenge of Hamish, The, 366
Revolution, the American, 89
Revolutionary Period, the, history, 86; general literary tendencies, 92; poetry, 94; prose, 97; transition from colony to nation, *see* Franklin; orators and statesmen, 111; poets, 132; prose writers, 146; beginning of American fiction, 154; summary, 162; selections for reading, 163; bibliography, 164
Rich, Richard, 46
Richard Carvel, 480
Rights of Man, The, 151

Riley, J. W., 452
Ripley, George, 277, 280
Rise of the Dutch Republic, The, 427, 429
Roamer, The, 492
Robinson, Edwin Arlington, 490
Roe, E. P., 415
Romance, of the West, 184, 185; of the Revolution, 214
Romance and realism, 457, 459; modified types of, 462
Romantic poetry, beginning of, 142
Romanticism, 138, 174, 178
Rowlandson, Mary, 43
Rowson, Susanna, 154
Ryan, Abram J., 384

Sabatini, Rafael, 485
Saga of King Olaf, The, 299
Salmagundi, 180, 181, 185, 250
Salt maker of Plymouth, the, 17
Sandburg, Carl, 495
Sandys, George, 47
Satanstoe, 216
Satire, in the Revolution, 95, 110, 120, 140; of Franklin, 109, 110
Saturday Club, the, 352
Scarlet Letter, The, 394, 396, 402
Schoolcraft, H. R., 259
Schools of literature, 234, 245, 249, 250
Schultz, J. Willard, 483
Science of English Verse, The, 365
Scollard, Clinton, 494
Scyld, story of, 1
Sea stories, of Cooper, 220; of Melville, 247
Seabury. *See* Westchester Farmer
Sectional literature, 275, 276
Sedgwick, Catherine, 175, 247
Seeger, Alan, 492
Selling of Joseph, The, 28
Sensibility in fiction, 159
Sentimentality in early literature, 159, 174, 192, 213, 450
Seventeen, 478
Sewall, Samuel, 27; his Diary, 28
Ships, coming of the, 1
Short story, the, 179, 235, 414, 487. *See also* Irving, Poe, Harte, Porter, etc.
Silence Dogood Essays, 109
Silent Places, The, 485
Sill, E. R., 455
Simms, William Gilmore, 91, *243;*

life, 244; works, 245; quality of, 246
Simple Cobbler, The, 12, 41
Sketch Book, The, 175, 182, 187
Slabs of the Sunburnt West, 495
Slavery, the question of, 271, 272, 273; poems on, 291, 316
Smith, Captain John, 4, 18, 39
Snow Bound, 301, 307, 313, 317
Snow Image, The, 398
Social development in the Revolutionary period, 86
Song of Myself, 373, 374
Songs of the Revolution, 133
Songs of the Sierras, 389, 390
Sonnets of Longfellow, 297
Sovereignty and Goodness of God, The, 43
Sparks, Jared, 259
Splendid Idle Forties, The, 483
Spy, The, 91, 210, 213
Stamp Act, the, 87
Standish, Myles, 17
Statesmen of the Revolution, 114
Stedman, Edmund C., 388, 449, 452
Stiles, Ezra, 130
Stockton, Frank R., 463
Stoddard, Richard H., 388
Story of a Bad Boy, The, 453
Stowe, Harriet Beecher, 409
Style, of Emerson, 335; of Lowell, 349; of Parkman, 439
Summary View, A, 123, 128
Sunnyside, 184
Sunrise, 359, 363, 367
Surrey of Eagle's Nest, 409
Swallow Barn, 248
Symbolism of Hawthorne, 395
Symphony, The, 359-360, 366
"Symposium," the, 280

Tabb, J. B., 455
Tales of the Grotesque and Arabesque, 237
Tales of a Traveller, 187, 188
Tales of a Wayside Inn, 298, 313
Tamerlane, 229
Tarkington, Booth, 478, 499
Taylor, Bayard, 363, *385;* poems, 386; dramas and novels, 387
Teasdale, Sara, 489
Tenney, Tabitha, 154
Tent on the Beach, The, 313
Tenth Muse, the, 47
Thanatopsis, 196, 201, 202

Thaxter, Celia, 455
Thomas, Augustus, 498
Thomas, Edith, 455, 491
Thompson, Benjamin, 46
Thoreau, Henry D., 280, *416*; life, 417; works, 421; quality of, 422; individualism, 423; compared with Emerson, 424
Thou Mother with thy Equal Brood, 377
Three Memorial Poems, 343, 345
Threnody, 327
Tiger Lilies, 362
Timrod, Henry, 383
To Have and to Hold, 480
Tom Sawyer, 466
Tories in the Revolution, 90, 94
Tour of the Prairies, A, 183, 189
Town Down the River, The, 490
Trail of the Lonesome Pine, The, 482
Transcendentalism, 278, 379
Travels through North America, 147
Treaty of Paris, the, 87
Trees, 493
Trowbridge, J. T., 415
True Relation, A, 5, 39
True Stories, Hawthorne's, 397
Trumbull, John, 134, 136
Tucker, St. George, 144
Twice-Told Tales, 393, 398, 399
Two Angels, The, 340
Two Years before the Mast, 247
Tyler, Royall, 93, 145

Uncas, 219. See also *Last of the Mohicans*
Uncle Remus, 105, 468, 470
Uncle Tom's Cabin, 48, 410
Under the Willows, 341, 343
Union of the Colonies, 88. *See also* Constitution
United Colonies of New England, the, 20, 78
United Netherlands, History of the, 427, 429
Unity, national, 170
Universal standards of poetry, 369
Uriel, 327

Vandemark's Folly, 477
Very, Jones, 280, 390
Views Afoot, 385
Virginia Comedians, The, 408
Virginian, The, 482
Vision of Sir Launfal, The, 340, 344

Voices of Freedom, 309
Voices of the Night, 285, 290

Walden, 421
Wallace, Lew, 463
Wanderer of the Wasteland, The, 486
Ward, Nathaniel, 12, 41
Warren, Mercy, 145
Washington, George, 89, 114
Washington, Everett's oration on, 256
Washington, Life of, by Weems, 149, 90; by Irving, 184, 190
Waterfowl, To a, 203
Wayside, the, 395
Wayside Inn. See *Tales*
Way to Wealth, The, 107
Webster, Daniel, 120, 184, *256*, 309, 310; typical orations, 258
Week on the Concord, A, 420, 421
Wept of Wish-ton-Wish, The, 215
West, romance of the, 184, 185
Westchester Farmer, The, 121
Westcott, Edward Noyes, 481
Westover Manuscripts, the, 34
Wharton, Edith, 479
What Mr. Robinson Thinks, 347
Wheatley, Phillis, 145
When Lilacs last in the Door-yard Bloom'd, 377
Whigs in the Revolution, 90, 94
White, Maria (Mrs. Lowell), 339
White, Stewart Edward, 485
White, William Patterson, 486
Whitman, Walt, 357, *370*; life, 371; quality of his verse, 373; his better poetry, 375; orientalism of, 378; at home and abroad, 381
Whittaker, Alexander, 33, 40
Whittier, John Greenleaf, 70, 86, *301*, 450; compared with other poets, 303, 342; life, 304; poems, 308; prose works, 315; characteristics, 316
Widdemer, Margaret, 490
Wieland, 156, 158
Wigglesworth, Michael, *50*, 450; his *Day of Doom*, 51; Calvinistic quality of, 53
Wilkinson, Eliza, 147
William Wilson, 236
Williams, John, 43
Willis, N. P., 250
Wilson, Alexander, 147
Winslow, Edward, 40

Winthrop, John, 8, *19*; Journal of, 20, 24; his speech on Liberty, 23, 116, 117; love letters of, 25; Mather's story of, 69
Winthrop, Margaret, 26
Winthrop, Theodore, 415
Wister, Owen, 482
Witchcraft, the Salem, 30, 62
Witching Hour, The, 498
With Reed and Lyre, 494
Wolfert's Roost, 184, 190
Wonder Book, A, 398

Wonders of the Invisible World, The, 62, 67
Wonder-Working Providence, The, 40
Wood, William, 40
Woodberry, George Edward, 492
Woolman, John, 151; his Journal, 152; character of, 153
Work of Redemption, History of the, 76

Yellow Clover, 492

Zumarra, Juan de, 44